ENCYCLOPEDIA OF AMERICAN LITERATURE

VOLUME III

THE MODERN AND POSTMODERN PERIOD

FROM 1915

ENCYCLOPEDIA OF AMERICAN LITERATURE

VOLUME III
THE MODERN AND POSTMODERN PERIOD
FROM 1915

Carl Rollyson

Facts On File, Inc.

Encyclopedia of American Literature, Volume III: The Modern and Postmodern Period from 1915

Copyright © 2002 by Carl Rollyson

Facts On File, Inc.
132 West 31st Street
New York NY 10001

Library of Congress Cataloging-in-Publication Data

Encyclopedia of American literature.
    p. cm.
  Includes bibliographical references and indexes.
  Contents: v. 1. The colonial and revolutionary era / Carol Ruth Berkin — v. 2. The age of romanticism and realism / Lisa Paddock — v. 3. The modern and post-modern period / Carl Rollyson.
  ISBN 0-8160-4121-0 (set: acid-free paper)
  1. American literature—Encyclopedias. I. Berkin, Carol. II. Paddock, Lisa Olson. III. Rollyson, Carl E. (Carl Edmund) IV. Facts on File, Inc.

PS21 .F33 2002
810'.3—dc21   2001040900

Facts On File books are available at special discounts when purchased in bulk quantities for businesses, associations, institutions, or sales promotions. Please call our Special Sales Department in New York at (212) 967-8800 or (800) 322-8755.

You can find Facts On File on the World Wide Web at http://www.factsonfile.com

Text design by Rachel L. Berlin
Cover illustration by Smart Graphics
Cover design by Cathy Rincon

Printed in the United States of America

VB FOF 10 9 8 7 6 5 4 3 2 1

This book is printed on acid-free paper.

CONTENTS

INTRODUCTION

Exactly when 20th-century American literature begins is a question that students and scholars continue to debate. To set the date at 1900 is arbitrary, since some 19th-century works like Herman Melville's *The Confidence Man* (1857) seem distinctly modern and "20th century" in their subject matter and point of view. Indeed, Melville was rediscovered in the 1920s precisely because his work seemed so relevant to the modern age. Modern or 20th-century literature often questions traditional conceptions of reality and presents literature not only as a distinctive way of looking at the world but also as a world in itself. Thus Melville's character, a confidence man, creates his own reality and challenges the solidity and reliability of American values. Other writers born after Melville, such as Edith Wharton, write in a more conventional, realistic style associated with the 19th century novel of manners championed by William Dean Howells. Overlapping with Melville, Wharton, and Howells is Henry James, whose later novels—particularly *The Ambassadors* (1903) and *The Golden Bowl* (1904)—develop a psychological realism as subtle and as complex as any later work of 20th-century American fiction.

Broadly speaking, however, 20th-century literature has been associated with the advent of World War I. America's involvement in a war President Woodrow Wilson claimed would make the world "safe for democracy" had a profound impact on the American imagination. Wilson motivated Americans to engage in world affairs and to make the world more American, so to speak, by actively promulgating American values abroad. At the same time, the disillusionment attendant on the failure to reshape Europe in accordance with American ideals provoked a degree of bitterness and alienation that Gertrude Stein summed up with her reference to a "lost generation," referring to those young Americans who had served in the war or felt displaced by it. The record of this lost generation is documented in John Dos Passos's *U.S.A.* trilogy, and in the novels and stories of F. Scott Fitzgerald, Ernest Hemingway, and William Faulkner.

These great writers arose out of a context that includes many other writers, key works, important ideas, literary movements, characters in literary works, genres, periodicals, places, and events. For example, a writer like William Faulkner can be profitably studied by referring to entries in this encyclopedia on the South, the southern agrarians, regionalism, World War I, stream of consciousness, other writers such as Sherwood Anderson, and modernism and the modern novel. The beginning student of 20th-century American literature will find essential entries on the novel, the short story, drama, and poetry, as well as histories of African-American, Asian-American, Jewish-American, and Native American literature. Terms like proletarian literature, confessional poetry, and New Criticism are described. Influential publications such as *Partisan Review* and the *New York Review of Books* are identified. Plot summaries are provided for works such as Tennessee Williams's *The Glass Menagerie*, J. D. Salinger's *The Catcher in the Rye*, Ken Kesey's *One Flew Over the Cuckoo's Nest*, and Robert Frost's "Mending Wall," which have become parts of the literary canon and the school curriculum. Explanations of the Group Theatre and the Provincetown Players are included as part of the story of 20th-century American drama. Greenwich Village, Chicago, and San Francisco are described as examples of sites where literary movements and important writers developed. Significant political events such as the trial of Sacco and Vanzetti and the Scottsboro case are discussed because they contributed to the growth of protest literature.

Beginning in the 1920s, American literature probed the idealism, materialism, progress, excesses, and decadence in American society. Fitzgerald's *The Great Gatsby* perhaps best captures both the enthusiasm and the corruption inherent in the American dream. Jay Gatsby believes he has the freedom to remake himself into both a gentleman and a successful businessman. His pretensions are severely challenged, though, and his fortune is built on alliances with gangsters and unethical financiers. His dreams of success end in death, although the romantic power of his imagination lingers in the wistful words of the novel's narrator, Nick Carraway.

Gatsby is an American provincial who puts on "airs," but he is treated with considerable sympathy by Fitzgerald, a midwesterner who empathized with his character's craving for success. Sinclair Lewis, on the other hand, tended to satirize American exuberance and show how it merely masked a vast emptiness and longing for a more substantial existence. Thus his most famous character, Babbitt, daydreams of a romantic life that will wrest him away from his world of Rotary Club luncheons.

Far darker depictions of modern life, in America and Europe, are provided by expatriates such as Ernest Hemingway, T. S. Eliot, and Ezra Pound. They evoked the wasteland mentality of Stein's lost generation, a feeling that civilization had exhausted itself, but also manifested a command of literary language that few 19th-century American authors achieved. Their counterpart in the theater is Eugene O'Neill, the father of American drama, who contributed to 20th-century American literature a rich body of work and who broke new ground with plays such as *Anna Christie* and *The Emperor Jones*—which concern prostitution and race—and *Strange Interlude* and *The Great God Brown*—which experiment with point of view and stream-of-consciousness techniques.

The Great Depression in the 1930s developed an increasing interest in the life of the lower classes and the laboring poor—often captured in works of proletarian fiction and in the epic novels of John Dos Passos, James T. Farrell, and John Steinbeck. This group of socially engaged writers expanded to include African Americans such as Richard Wright and Zora Neale Hurston, who introduced a naturalistic and anthropological view of America's ethnic and racial heritage. Langston Hughes and other writers of the Harlem Renaissance added a lyrical evocation of African-American life and also introduced the rhythms of jazz that later infiltrated one of the great American novels of the century, Ralph Ellison's *Invisible Man.*

World War II produced great novels by such writers as Norman Mailer and James Jones that explored how the American character shaped the war and, in turn, became transformed by war. But the war also signaled an opening up of American literature to the writing of Jewish Americans, Asian Americans, and Native Americans. The war accelerated calls for the integration of society and for increasing access to higher education—both of which generated writers who recreated and reassessed American history and literature.

These postwar changes extended the range of writers who have been able to amalgamate the traditional themes of American literature—particularly the quest for success—with the themes of ethnic literature, which center on the individual's effort to achieve an independent, stable self. In *The Human Stain,* Philip Roth, a Jewish-American writer, explores one of the signature stories of African-American literature: an account of an African American who passes for white. Conversely, in *Flight to Canada,* Ishmael Reed, an African-American writer, satirizes American icons such as Abraham Lincoln and mixes together 19th- and 20th-century history in a hilarious farrago of myth and fact.

Twentieth-century American literature has also been enriched by the jazzlike rhythms of Beat poetry, the confessional poetry of Robert Lowell and Sylvia Plath, the feminist sensibility of writers such as Adrienne Rich, and the perspectives of a new generation of gay and lesbian writers such as Edmund White and Dorothy Allison. While these writers have become more personal or autobiographical in their writing, they have also carried on the modernist tradition of 20th-century American literature, which focuses on the tragic and absurd aspects of life and questions the meaning of literature and writing itself.

CHRONOLOGY
1915–2001

1915

Lusitania sunk by German U-boat
Woodrow Wilson maintains neutrality in World War I
Revival of Ku Klux Klan

Margaret Widdemer, *Factories*
Edgar Lee Masters, *Spoon River Anthology*
Theodore Dreiser, *The "Genius"*
Ernest Poole, *The Harbor*
John Neihardt, *Song of Hugh Glass*
Willa Cather, *Song of the Lark*
Provincetown and Washington Square Players founded
Saul Bellow (1915–   )
Alfred Kazin (1915–1998)

1916

American forces invade Mexico
Federal Farm Loan Act
San Francisco Preparedness Day bombing, conducted by labor radicals protesting preparations for war. Ten people are killed and forty injured

Robert Frost, *Mountain Interval*
Carl Sandburg, *Chicago Poems*
Samuel Clemens (Mark Twain), *The Mysterious Stranger*

Edwin Arlington Robinson, *Man Against the Sky*
Amy Lowell, *Men, Women, and Ghosts*
Eugene O'Neill, *Bound East For Cardiff*
John Dewey, *Democracy and Education*
Edith Wharton, *Xingu*
Ellen Glasgow, *Life and Gabriella*
Ring Lardner, *You Know Me, Al*
Seven Arts (1916–1917) founded
Theatre Arts Magazine (1916–1964) founded
Walker Percy (1916–1990)

1917

Germany resumes unrestricted submarine warfare
U.S. enters World War I
Lions Clubs established, the world's largest service organization, engages in charitable work and runs youth camps
John F. Kennedy (1917–1963)

T. S. Eliot, *The Love Song of J. Alfred Prufrock*
Hamlin Garland, *Son of the Middle Border*
Edwin Arlington Robinson, *Merlin*

James Branch Cabell, *Cream of the Jest*
Joseph Hergesheimer, *Three Black Pennys*
Pulitzer Prizes established
The Dial (1917–1929) founded
Gwendolyn Brooks (1917–2000)
Carson McCullers (1917–1967)
Robert Lowell (1917–1977)

1918

World War I
Battles of Belleau Wood and Château-Thierry
Argonne and St. Mihiel offensives
Second Battle of the Marne
Woodrow Wilson's "Fourteen Points" and peace conference in Paris

Carl Sandburg, *Cornhuskers*
Zona Gale, *Birth*
Edith Wharton, *The Marne*
Booth Tarkington, *The Magnificent Ambersons*
Eugene O'Neill, *The Moon of the Caribbees*
Edward Streeter, *Dear Mable!*
Willa Cather, *My Ántonia*
Bliss Perry, *The American Spirit in Literature*

Theatre Guild (1918–   ) founded
Carolina Playmakers (1918–   )
    founded

1919

Treaty of Versailles
Eighteenth Amendment prohibits
    sale of liquor
Nationwide steel strike (ends in
    January 1920)
American Legion founded
Communist Party founded

Sherwood Anderson, *Winesburg,
    Ohio*
H. L. Mencken, *The American
    Language*
Thorstein Veblen, *Higher Learning
    in America*
John Reed, *Ten Days That Shook the
    World*
Louis Untermeyer, *Modern Ameri-
    can Poetry*
James Branch Cabell, *Jurgen* and
    Beyond Life
Joseph Hergesheimer, *Linda
    Condon*
H. L. Mencken, *Prejudices*
    (1919–1927)

1920

19th Amendment grants woman
    suffrage
Transcontinental air mail estab-
    lished
First commercial radio broadcast-
    ing
Attorney General Palmer conducts
    raids on suspected Communists,
    arresting 4,000
U.S. Senate votes against joining
    League of Nations

T. S. Eliot, *Poems*
Sinclair Lewis, *Main Street*
Carl Sandburg, *Smoke and Steel*
Edith Wharton, *The Age of Inno-
    cence*
Edwin Arlington Robinson, *Lancelot*
Zona Gale, *Miss Lulu Bett*
Eugene O'Neill, *The Emperor Jones*
    and *Beyond the Horizon*
Sherwood Anderson, *Poor White*

Edna St. Vincent Millay, *A Few Figs
    from Thistles*
F. Scott Fitzgerald, *This Side of
    Paradise*

1921

Warren Harding administration
    (1921–1923) begins
Industrial depression
U.S. immigration quotas estab-
    lished
First Sacco-Vanzetti trial

John Dos Passos, *Three Soldiers*
Eugene O'Neill, *Anna Christie*
Edwin Arlington Robinson,
    Collected Poems
Booth Tarkington, *Alice Adams*
Sherwood Anderson, *Triumph of
    the Egg*
James Branch Cabell, *Figures of the
    Earth*
Elinor Wylie, *Nets to Catch the Wind*
George S. Kaufman and Marc
    Connelly, *Dulcy*
Carl Van Doren, *The American
    Novel*
Richard Wilbur (1921–   )

1922

Coal and railway strikes
First one-day coast-to-coast flight
Rebecca Latimer Felton
    (1835–1930) appointed first U.S.
    female senator (Georgia)

T. S. Eliot, *The Waste Land*
Sinclair Lewis, *Babbitt*
E. E. Cummings, *The Enormous
    Room*
George Santayana, *Soliloquies in
    England*
Eugene O'Neill, *The Hairy Ape*
The Fugitive (1922–1925) founded
Reader's Digest (1922–   ) founded
Kurt Vonnegut, Jr. (1922–   )

1923

Calvin Coolidge administration
    (1923–29) begins
Minimum wage law declared un-
    constitutional

Teapot Dome scandal (1923–1924)
Ku Klux Klan terrorism in
    Oklahoma

Edna St. Vincent Millay, *The Harp-
    Weaver*
Willa Cather, *A Lost Lady*
Elinor Wylie, *Black Armour* and
    Jennifer Lorn
Robert Frost, *New Hampshire*
Gertrude Atherton, *Black Oxen*
Elmer Rice, *The Adding Machine*
Wallace Stevens, *Harmonium*
George Santayana, *Realms of Being*
    (1923–1940)
Time magazine (1923–   ) founded
Norman Mailer (1923–   )

1924

Industrial depression
New immigration quotas established
Soldiers" Bonus Act

Robinson Jeffers, *Tamar*
Ring Lardner, *How To Write a Short
    Story*
Sherwood Anderson, *Story Teller's
    Story*
Emily Dickinson, *Complete Poems*
Samuel Clemens (Mark Twain),
    Autobiography
Eugene O'Neill, *All God's Chillun*
    and *Desire Under the Elms*
Maxwell Anderson, *What Price
    Glory?*
George S. Kaufman and Marc
    Connelly, *Beggar on Horseback*
Sidney Howard, *They Knew What
    They Wanted*
Herman Melville, *Billy Budd*
Louis Bromfield, *The Green Bay
    Tree*
Ernest Hemingway, *In Our Time*
Edith Wharton, *Old New York*
James Baldwin (1924–1987)

1925

Scopes "Monkey" trial, in which
    Clarence Darrow and William
    Jennings Bryan debated the
    theory of evolution
Trinity College (North Carolina) is
    renamed Duke University

Standard Oil initiates eight-hour
day
Nellie Ross (1856–1937) elected
first female governor
(Wyoming)
Brotherhood of Sleeping Car
Porters organized by A. Philip
Randolph
Ku Klux Klan marches in Washington, D.C.
Florida land boom

John Dos Passos, *Manhattan Transfer*
Sherwood Anderson, *Dark Laughter*
Theodore Dreiser, *An American Tragedy*
Sinclair Lewis, *Arrowsmith*
Willa Cather, *The Professor's House*
Ellen Glasgow, *Barren Ground*
H.D. (Hilda Doolittle), *Collected Poems*
F. Scott Fitzgerald, *The Great Gatsby*
Robinson Jeffers, *Roan Stallion*
John G. Neihardt, *The Song of the Indian Wars*
Anita Loos, *Gentlemen Prefer Blondes*
Paul Green, *In Abraham's Bosom*
Ezra Pound, *Cantos* (1925–70)
American Speech (1925–   ) founded
The New Yorker (1925–   ) founded
Guggenheim Fellowships (1925–   ) founded
Truman Capote (1925–1984)
William Styron (1925–   )
Gore Vidal (1925–   )

1926
Transatlantic wireless telephone
Admiral Richard Byrd flies over North Pole
Army Air Corps created
Civil Aviation Act

Ernest Hemingway, *The Sun Also Rises*
Carl Sandburg, *Abraham Lincoln: The Prairie Years*
Eugene O'Neill, *The Great God Brown*
Langston Hughes, *The Weary Blues*
Carl Van Vechten, *Nigger Heaven*

T. S. Stribling, *Teeftallow*
Elizabeth Madox Roberts, *The Time of Man*
James Branch Cabell, *The Silver Stallion*
Sidney Howard, *The Silver Cord*
Thomas Beer, *The Mauve Decade*
William Faulkner, *Soldiers' Pay*
Book-of-the-Month Club founded
Allen Ginsberg (1926–1997)

1927
Aviator Charles Lindbergh flies across the Atlantic Ocean from New York to Paris
Sacco and Vanzetti executed
U.S. Marines invade Nicaragua (1927–1933)

Edwin Arlington Robinson, *Tristram*
Upton Sinclair, *Oil!*
Willa Cather, *Death Comes for the Archbishop*
Conrad Aiken, *Blue Voyage*
Constance Rourke, *Trumpets of Jubilee*
Ole Rölvaag, *Giants in the Earth*
Carl Sandburg, *The American Songbag*
Vernon Parrington, *Main Currents in American Thought*
Thornton Wilder, *The Bridge of San Luis Rey*
Ernest Hemingway, *Men Without Women*
Eugene O'Neill, *Marco Millions*
Hound and Horn (1927–1934) founded
American Caravan (1927–1936) founded
transition (1927–1938) founded
Literary Guild founded
John Ashbery (1927–   )

1928
Kellogg Pact outlaws war
First Richard Byrd exploration of Antarctica
Talking pictures invented
First Mickey Mouse cartoon

Eugene O'Neill, *Strange Interlude*
Archibald MacLeish, *The Hamlet of A. MacLeish*

Stephen Vincent Benét, *John Brown's Body*
Carl Sandburg, *Good Morning, America*
Robert Frost, *West-Running Brook*
American Literature (1928–   ) founded
Edward Albee (1928–   )

1929
Herbert Hoover administration (1929–1933) begins
Stock market crash
Great Depression
Admiral Richard Byrd flies over South Pole
Museum of Modern Art founded
Martin Luther King Jr. (1929–1968)

Ernest Hemingway, *A Farewell to Arms*
Joseph Wood Krutch, *The Modern Temper*
Thomas Wolfe, *Look Homeward, Angel*
William Faulkner, *The Sound and the Fury*
Conrad Aiken, *Selected Poems*
Sinclair Lewis, *Dodsworth*
Ole Rölvaag, *Peder Victorious*
Elmer Rice, *Street Scene*
Oliver La Farge, *Laughing Boy*
Robert Lynd, *Middletown*
Walter Lippmann, *A Preface to Morals*
Ellen Glasgow, *They Stooped to Folly*
John Hollander (1929–   )

1930
First supermarket
Smoot-Hawley high tariff on imports to the U.S. worsens Great Depression
United Airlines employs first flight attendants (all female)
Veterans Administration established
Institute for Advanced Study, Princeton, created to further fundamental research and definitive scholarship in a wide range of fields.

T. S. Eliot, *Ash Wednesday*

Hart Crane, *The Bridge*
William Faulkner, *As I Lay Dying*
Archibald MacLeish, *New Found Land*
John Crowe Ransom, et al. *I'll Take My Stand*
Marc Connelly, *Green Pastures*
Michael Gold, *Jews Without Money*
Philip Barry, *Hotel Universe*
Susan Glaspell, *Alison's House*
John Dos Passos, *42nd Parallel*
Elizabeth Madox Roberts, *The Great Meadow*
Katherine Anne Porter, *Flowering Judas*
Kenneth Lewis Roberts, *Arundel*
Sinclair Lewis is first American to receive Nobel Prize in literature
Fortune (1930–   ) founded
John Barth (1930–   )
Gary Snyder (1930–   )

1931

First Scottsboro trial
Hoover Dam Construction begins (1931–1936)
Gangster Al Capone sentenced to 11 years in prison for tax evasion
Henry Ford produces his 20-millionth automobile

Eugene O'Neill, *Mourning Becomes Electra*
Lincoln Steffens, *Autobiography*
Willa Cather, *Shadows on the Rock*
Edmund Wilson, *Axel's Castle*
T. S. Stribling, *The Forge*
Conrad Aiken, *Preludes for Memnon*
Pearl Buck, *The Good Earth*
George S. Kaufman and Morrie Ryskind, *Of Thee I Sing*
William Faulkner, *Sanctuary*
Group Theatre (1931–1941) founded
Tom Wolfe (1931–   )

1932

Reconstruction Finance Corporation established to provide loans to failing banks
U.S. and Canada agree to construct St. Lawrence Seaway, connecting the North American lakes with the Atlantic Ocean

War veterans' bonus march on Washington, D.C.
Charles and Anne Morrow Lindbergh's son kidnapped and murdered

Erskine Caldwell, *Tobacco Road*
James T. Farrell, *Young Lonigan*
Ellen Glasgow, *A Sheltered Life*
John Dos Passos, *1919*
Charles Nordhoff and James Norman Hall, *Mutiny on the Bounty*
Robinson Jeffers, *Thurso's Landing*
William Faulkner, *Light in August*
John Updike (1932–   )
Robert Coover (1932–   )

1933

Franklin D. Roosevelt administration (1933–1945) begins
National Industrial Recovery Act
Civilian Conservation Corps established
Tennessee Valley Power Project, the first federal corporation to bring electric power to an American region
Home Owners' Loan Act
Agricultural Adjustment and Farm Credit acts
Banking and Gold Reserve acts
U.S. recognizes U.S.S.R.
Twenty-first Amendment repeals Prohibition
German refugees leave Adolf Hitler's Germany for U.S.

Gertrude Stein, *The Autobiography of Alice B. Toklas*
Erskine Caldwell, *God's Little Acre*
Eugene O'Neill, *Ah, Wilderness!*
Granville Hicks, *The Great Tradition*
Ernest Hemingway, *Winner Take Nothing*
Philip Roth (1933–   )
Susan Sontag (1933–   )
John Gardner (1933–1982)

1934

Securities Exchange Act establishes regulation of the stock market
National Housing Act

Federal Communications Commission established
Upton Sinclair campaigns for California governorship
Outlaw John Dillinger is shot by FBI agents in Chicago movie theater

William Saroyan, *The Daring Young Man on the Flying Trapeze*
F. Scott Fitzgerald, *Tender Is the Night*
Lillian Hellman, *The Children's Hour*
Robert Sherwood, *The Petrified Forest*
James T. Farrell, *The Young Manhood of Studs Lonigan*
Edna St. Vincent Millay, *Wine from These Grapes*
Stark Young, *So Red the Rose*
John A. Lomax, *American Ballads and Folk Songs*
Henry Miller, *Tropic of Cancer*
Partisan Review (1934–   ) founded
Joan Didion (1934–   )
N. Scott Momaday (1934–   )

1935

Works Progress Administration (WPA) founded
Social Security Act enacted
Agricultural Adjustment Act enacted
National Labor Relations Act enacted
Public Utility Holding Company Act enacted
Regular transpacific air service
Alcoholics Anonymous founded
Louisiana senator Huey Long (model for Robert Penn Warren's Willie Stark) is assassinated

Sinclair Lewis, *It Can't Happen Here*
Thomas Wolfe, *Of Time and the River*
Vincent Sheean, *Personal History*
John Steinbeck, *Tortilla Flat*
Clarence Day, *Life with Father*
Ellen Glasgow, *Vein of Iron*
Maxwell Anderson, *Winterset*
Clifford Odets, *Waiting for Lefty* and *Awake and Sing*

Robinson Jeffers, *Solstice and Other Poems*
Federal Writers' Project (1935–1939) founded
American Writers Congress
Southern Review (1935–1942) founded
Richard Brautigan (1935–1984)
Ken Kesey (1935–2001)

1936

Rural Electrification Act brings electricity to rural homes and communities
Supreme Court finds Agricultural Adjustment Act, which paid farmers not to produce certain crops, dairy products, and animals such as pigs and lambs, unconstitutional
CIO (Congress of Industrial Unions) expelled from AFL (American Federation of Labor)
Inter-American Peace Conference

Van Wyck Brooks, *The Flowering of New England*
John Dos Passos, *The Big Money*
George Santayana, *The Last Puritan*
William Faulkner, *Absalom, Absalom!*
Robert Frost, *A Further Range*
Archibald MacLeish, *Public Speech*
Carl Sandburg, *The People, Yes*
Margaret Mitchell, *Gone With the Wind*
John Steinbeck, *In Dubious Battle*
T. S. Eliot, *Collected Poems*
Robert Sherwood, *Idiot's Delight*
Irwin Shaw, *Bury the Dead*
Eugene O'Neill receives Nobel Prize in literature
Federal Theatre Project (1936–39)
New Directions (1936–   ) founded
Tom Robbins (1936–   )

1937

CIO organizes sit-down strikes in glass and automobile industries
President Roosevelt signs U.S. Neutrality Act

German airship *Hindenburg* crashes and burns in Lakehurst, New Jersey
New York permits women to serve as jurors
Aviator Amelia Earhart vanishes on a round-the-world air flight
U.S. and U.S.S.R. sign trade pact
U.S. Housing Authority established

Ernest Hemingway, *To Have and Have Not*
Kenneth Lewis Roberts, *Northwest Passage*
Archibald MacLeish, *The Fall of the City*
John P. Marquand, *The Late George Apley*
John Steinbeck, *Of Mice and Men* and *The Red Pony*
Thomas Pynchon (1937–   )

1938

Wages and Hours Law establishes a minimum hourly wage of 25 cents
Mexico expropriates foreign oil holdings
Howard Hughes flies around the world in 91 hours
Naval Expansion Act

Robert Sherwood, *Abe Lincoln in Illinois*
Thornton Wilder, *Our Town*
Carl Van Doren, *Benjamin Franklin*
Marjorie Kinnan Rawlings, *The Yearling*
Pearl Buck receives Nobel Prize in literature
Joyce Carol Oates (1938–   )

1939

Regular transatlantic air service
Hatch Act forbids political activity by government employees
Labor radical Tom Mooney pardoned
U.S. ambassador to Germany recalled
George VI and Queen Elizabeth first British monarchs to visit U.S.

John Steinbeck, *The Grapes of Wrath*
Nathanael West, *The Day of the Locust*
Robert Frost, *Collected Poems*
Dorothy Parker, *Here Lies*
Carl Sandburg, *Abraham Lincoln: The War Years*
William Saroyan, *The Time of Your Life*
Mark Van Doren, *Collected Poems*
Thomas Wolfe, *The Web and the Rock*
Stephen Vincent Benét, *The Devil and Daniel Webster*
Lillian Hellman, *The Little Foxes*
Kenyon Review (1939–   ) founded

1940

Peacetime conscription
Congress approves sales of military equipment to Great Britain

Van Wyck Brooks, *New England Indian Summer: 1865–1915*
Richard Wright, *Native Son*
Carson McCullers, *The Heart Is a Lonely Hunter*
Walter Van Tilburg Clark, *The Ox-Bow Incident*
Thomas Wolfe, *You Can't Go Home Again*
Ernest Hemingway, *For Whom the Bell Tolls*
William Faulkner, *The Hamlet*
Willa Cather, *Sapphira and the Slave Girl*
Kenneth Lewis Roberts, *Oliver Wiswell*
Glenway Wescott, *The Pilgrim Hawk*
PM (1940–1948) founded

1941

"Lend-Lease" bill authorizes Congress to ship material to Britain and other anti-Axis powers
U.S. becomes "arsenal of democracy"
Atlantic Charter issued by U.S. and Britain, specifying common principles, such as the right of peoples to choose their own

government and to have access
to the world's natural resources
President Roosevelt delivers "Four
Freedoms" speech
Japanese attack Pearl Harbor
U.S. declares war on Japan
Germany declares war on U.S.
U.S. declares war on Germany
National Gallery of Art opens

Ellen Glasgow, *In This Our Life*
John Marquand, *H.M. Pulham, Esq.*
Lillian Hellman, *Watch on the Rhine*
F. Scott Fitzgerald, *The Last Tycoon*
Edna St. Vincent Millay, *Collected
Sonnets*
Edmund Wilson, *The Wound and
the Bow*

1942

U.S. troops surrender after battles
of Bataan and Corregidor
General Doolittle's bombers attack
Tokyo
Battles of Coral Sea, Midway, Santa
Cruz, Guadalcanal
U.S. troops bomb Germany
American and British forces land in
North Africa
Office of War Information
established
Office of Civilian Defense established
Price controls and rationing are in-
stituted by U.S. government

William Faulkner, *Go Down, Moses*
Thornton Wilder, *The Skin of Our
Teeth*
E. B. White, *One Man's Meat*

1943

Allied forces invade Sicily
Japanese power destroyed in south-
west Pacific
Franklin Roosevelt and Winston
Churchill demand "uncondi-
tional surrender" of Axis powers
Roosevelt, Churchill, and Joseph
Stalin meet at Tehran

Howard Fast, *Citizen Tom Paine*
Richard Rodgers and Oscar
Hammerstein, *Oklahoma!*

George Santayana, *Persons and
Places*
Betty Smith, *A Tree Grows in Brook-
lyn*
James Thurber, *Men, Women, and
Dogs*
Wendell Willkie, *One World*
T. S. Eliot, *Four Quartets*
James Tate (1943–)

1944

U.S. forces return to Philippines
U.S. bombs Japan
D-Day Allied invasion of Western
Europe
Dumbarton Oaks Conferences plan
United Nations
Bretton Woods Conference plans
World Bank and International
Monetary Fund

John Hersey, *A Bell for Adano*
Charles Jackson, *The Lost Weekend*
Ernie Pyle, *Brave Men*
Karl Shapiro, *V-Letter*
Lillian Smith, *Strange Fruit*
Saul Bellow, *Dangling Man*

1945

Yalta Conference: Roosevelt,
Churchill, and Stalin meet to
plan shape of postwar world, the
division of Germany into three
zones, the punishment of war
criminals, and the establishment
of a United Nations.
President Franklin Roosevelt dies
Harry Truman administration
(1945–1953) begins
Germany is invaded and surrenders
U.S. drops two atomic bombs on
Japan
Japan surrenders

Robert Frost, *Masque of Reason*
H. L. Mencken, *The American
Language, Supplement I*
Arthur Schlesinger Jr., *The Age of
Jackson*
Karl Shapiro, *Essay on Rime*
Gertrude Stein, *Wars I Have Seen*
Tennessee Williams, *The Glass
Menagerie*

Richard Wright, *Black Boy*
Commentary (1945–) founded

1946

First meetings of United Nations
U.S. conducts atomic bomb tests in
the Pacific
U.S. Atomic Energy Commission
established
UN commission explores international supervision of atomic
energy

Theodore Dreiser, *The Bulwark*
John Hersey, *Hiroshima*
William Carlos Williams, *Paterson*
Carson McCullers, *The Member of
the Wedding*
Robert Penn Warren, *All the King's
Men*
Eudora Welty, *Delta Wedding*
Robert Lowell, *Lord Weary's Castle*
Gore Vidal, *Williwaw*

1947

Marshall Plan rebuilds Europe
Taft-Hartley Labor Relations Act

Benard DeVoto, *Across the Wide
Missouri*
Robert Frost, *Masque of Mercy*
James Michener, *Tales of the South
Pacific*
Tennessee Williams, *A Streetcar
Named Desire*
Ann Beattie (1947–)

1948

Berlin blockade and airlift
House Committee on Un-American Activities (HUAC) investigates alleged communists
Alger Hiss, former State Department employee, indicted for
perjury after denying his part in
a communist spy ring
Peacetime draft established
President Truman outlaws segregation in armed forces
Organization of American States
(OAS) founded

William Faulkner, *Intruder in the Dust*
Norman Mailer, *The Naked and the Dead*
James Gould Cozzens, *Guard of Honor*
Ezra Pound, *Pisan Cantos*
Truman Capote, *Other Voices, Other Rooms*
W. H. Auden, *The Age of Anxiety*
Carl Sandburg, *Remembrance Rock*
T. S. Eliot receives Nobel Prize in literature

1949
American Communist Party leaders convicted of conspiracy
U.S.S.R. explodes its first atomic bomb

Arthur Miller, *Death of a Salesman*
Paul Bowles, *The Sheltering Sky*

1950
South Korea invaded by the north with Chinese assistance
UN sends troops to defend South Korea
Alger Hiss is sentenced to five years in prison for perjury

T. S. Eliot, *The Cocktail Party*
Ernest Hemingway, *Across the River and into the Trees*
Budd Schulberg, *The Disenchanted*
William Faulkner receives Nobel Prize in literature
National Book Awards established

1951
Twenty-second Amendment limits presidential tenure to two terms
President Truman recalls General MacArthur from Korea
Julius and Ethel Rosenberg are found guilty of stealing U.S. atomic secrets for the U.S.S.R.

William Faulkner, *Requiem for a Nun*
James Jones, *From Here to Eternity*

Carson McCullers, *Ballad of the Sad Café*
Marianne Moore, *Collected Poems*
J. D. Salinger, *The Catcher in the Rye*
William Styron, *Lie Down in Darkness*
Herman Wouk, *The Caine Mutiny*
Norman Mailer, *Barbary Shore*

1952
House Committee on Un-American Activities increases its investigations of Communists
Truman administration enforces loyalty oaths for government employees

Ernest Hemingway, *The Old Man and the Sea*
Archibald MacLeish, *Collected Poems*
John Steinbeck, *East of Eden*

1953
Truce in Korea
Dwight D. Eisenhower administration (1953–1961) begins
President Eisenhower creates Health, Education, and Welfare cabinet post
Julius and Ethel Rosenberg executed
Senator Joseph McCarthy charges that U.S. State Department is filled with Communists

T. S. Eliot, *The Confidential Clerk*
Robert Penn Warren, *Brother to Dragons*
Theodore Roethke, *The Waking*
Saul Bellow, *The Adventures of Augie March*
Richard Wright, *The Outsider*

1954
Supreme Court rules racial segregation unconstitutional
Senator McCarthy censured by Senate
St. Lawrence Seaway construction begins

Eudora Welty, *The Ponder Heart*
Ben Hecht, *A Child of the Century*
John Steinbeck, *Sweet Thursday*
William Faulkner, *A Fable*
Ellen Glasgow, *The Woman Within*
Robinson Jeffers, *Hungerfield*
Wallace Stevens, *Collected Poems*
Ernest Hemingway receives Nobel Prize in literature

1955
AFL and CIO merge
Jonas Salk develops polio vaccine
Bus boycott in Montgomery, Alabama
President Eisenhower conducts first televised presidential press conference, which is broadcast later
President Eisenhower suffers heart attack

Elizabeth Bishop, *North & South*
William Inge, *Bus Stop*
Norman Mailer, *The Deer Park*
Arthur Miller, *A View from the Bridge*
John O'Hara, *Ten North Frederick*
Tennessee Williams, *Cat on a Hot Tin Roof*

1956
Highway Act initiates interstate highway system
Montgomery bus boycott ends after city agrees to integrate public transportation
First African-American student admitted to University of Alabama
Dalip Singh Saund (1899–1973) becomes first Asian-American elected to U.S. House of Representatives (California)

Nelson Algren, *A Walk on the Wild Side*
John Berryman, *Homage to Mistress Bradstreet*
Allen Ginsberg, *Howl*
John F. Kennedy, *Profiles in Courage*
Edwin O'Connor, *The Last Hurrah*

Eugene O'Neill, *Long Day's Journey into Night*
James Thurber, *Fables for Our Time*

1957

Arkansas governor Orval Faubus uses State National Guard to prevent integration at Little Rock's Central High School
President Eisenhower sends National Guard to Little Rock, Arkansas, because of tensions over school integration
Southern Christian Leadership Conference (SCLC) established by Martin Luther King Jr. to work for integration
U.S. Civil Rights Commission established

James Agee, *A Death in the Family*
John Cheever, *The Wapshot Chronicle*
James Gould Cozzens, *By Love Possessed*
William Faulkner, *The Town*
Jack Kerouac, *On the Road*
Bernard Malamud, *The Assistant*
Richard Wilbur, *Poems*

1958

Congress passes National Defense Act authorizing low-interest loans for college education
Martin Luther King Jr. stabbed by African-American woman in Harlem
U.S. and Canada establish a missile defense system, NORAD (North American Air Defense Command)
Alaska becomes 49th state
U.S. launches earth satellite
U.S. begins jet airline service

T. S. Eliot, *The Elder Statesman*
Archibald MacLeish, *J.B.*
Vladimir Nabokov, *Lolita*
Theodore Roethke, *Words for the Wind*
Tennessee Williams, *Suddenly Last Summer*

1959

Hawaii becomes 50th state
St. Lawrence Seaway opened
Antarctica declared a scientific preserve by international treaty

Saul Bellow, *Henderson the Rain King*
Lorraine Hansberry, *A Raisin in the Sun*
Robert Lowell, *Life Studies*
Philip Roth, *Goodbye, Columbus*
Norman Mailer, *Advertisements for Myself*
W. D. Snodgrass, *Heart's Needle*

1960

Lunch counter sit-ins in the South protest racial discrimination
Candidates Richard Nixon and John F. Kennedy hold first televised presidential debates

William Faulkner, *The Mansion*
Randall Jarrell, *The Woman at the Washington Zoo*
William Styron, *Set This House on Fire*
John Updike, *Rabbit, Run*

1961

John F. Kennedy administration (1961–1963) begins
Peace Corps created
U.S. severs relations with Cuba and supports failed Bays of Pigs invasion
First U.S. suborbital space flight
President Kennedy conducts first live televised presidential press conference
Freedom Rides begin in the South to protest segregation

James Baldwin, *Nobody Knows My Name*
Robert Heinlein, *Stranger in a Strange Land*
Joseph Heller, *Catch-22*
Carson McCullers, *Clock Without Hands*
J. D. Salinger, *Franny and Zooey*

John Steinbeck, *The Winter of Our Discontent*

1962

Two Americans and two Russians orbit the earth
U.S.S.R. introduces nuclear missiles into Cuba
Telstar, first private communications satellite, launched
James Meredith is first African-American student to attend University of Mississippi

Edward Albee, *Who's Afraid of Virginia Woolf?*
Tennessee Williams, *The Night of the Iguana*
William Faulkner, *The Reivers*
Vladimir Nabokov, *Pale Fire*
Katherine Anne Porter, *Ship of Fools*
Edmund Wilson, *Patriotic Gore*
John Steinbeck receives the Nobel Prize in literature

1963

President Kennedy assassinated
Lyndon Johnson becomes president (1963–1969)
President Johnson appoints Warren Commission to investigate assassination of President Kennedy
Nationwide civil rights demonstrations
Martin Luther King Jr. writes "Letter from the Birmingham Jail"
U.S. Air Force Academy graduates first four African-American cadets
Medgar Evers, field secretary for NAACP, murdered in Mississippi
James Meredith graduates from University of Mississippi, the first African-American student to do so
Martin Luther King Jr. gives "I Have a Dream" speech in Washington, D.C., at the Lincoln Memorial

Nuclear test ban treaty signed by
    U.S. and U.S.S.R.

Mary McCarthy, *The Group*
Bernard Malamud, *Idiots First*
Thomas Pynchon, *V*
John Updike, *The Centaur*
William Carlos Williams, *Pictures
    from Brueghel*
The New York Review of Books
    founded

1964
Congress passes "war on poverty"
    program and landmark civil
    rights legislation
Lyndon Johnson elected to four-
    year term (1965–1969)
Federal Trade Commission man-
    dates health warning on ciga-
    rette packaging
Warren Commission issues report
    stating Lee Harvey Oswald acted
    alone in assassinating President
    Kennedy

Saul Bellow, *Herzog*
John Berryman, *77 Dream Songs*
Ernest Hemingway, *A Moveable
    Feast*
Gore Vidal, *Julian*

1965
U.S. increases support for South
    Vietnam
U.S. intervenes in Dominican Re-
    public
Twenty-fifth Amendment stipulates
    the process of presidential suc-
    cession
President Johnson gives "Great
    Society" speech
Civil rights activist Malcolm X is
    assassinated at a rally in Harlem
Martin Luther King Jr. awarded
    Nobel Peace Prize
Race riots in Watts, a section of Los
    Angeles, California, kill 34 peo-
    ple, injure 800, and result in
    over $200 million in property
    damage

Edward Albee, *Tiny Alice*

A. R. Ammons, *Tape for the Turn of
    the Year*
Alex Haley, *The Autobiography of
    Malcolm X*
Norman Mailer, *The American
    Dream*
Thornton Wilder receives first Na-
    tional Medal for Literature

1966
Medicare program established
U.S. planes bomb North Vietnam
Anti–Vietnam War protests

William Alfred, *Hogan's Goat*
John Barth, *Giles Goat-Boy*
Truman Capote, *In Cold Blood*
Norman Mailer, *Cannibals and
    Christians*
Bernard Malamud, *The Fixer*
James Merrill, *Nights and Days*
Thomas Pynchon, *The Crying of
    Lot 49*

1967
More U.S. troops sent to Vietnam
    for a total of 475,000
Antiwar protests increase
Race riots occur in several U.S.
    cities; 40 killed in Detroit

Richard Brautigan, *Trout Fishing in
    America*
Norman Podhoretz, *Making It*
William Styron, *The Confessions of
    Nat Turner*
Thornton Wilder, *The Eighth Day*

1968
Martin Luther King Jr. assassinated
Senator Robert F. Kennedy assassi-
    nated
Antiwar protests disrupt Democra-
    tic Convention in Chicago
American astronauts orbit the moon
Tet offensive, a massive Vietcong
    attack in South Vietnam, inten-
    sifies protests against the Viet-
    nam War in U.S.
My Lai massacre in Vietnam; Amer-
    ican troops murder between 200
    and 500 unarmed villagers

Joan Didion, *Slouching Towards
    Bethlehem*
Norman Mailer, *The Armies of the
    Night*
Arthur Miller, *The Price*
John Updike, *Couples*
Gore Vidal, *Myra Breckenridge*

1969
Richard M. Nixon administration
    (1969–1973) begins
Huge antiwar demonstration
    (150,000) in Washington, D.C.
Peace talks with North Vietnam
    begin
U.S. astronauts land on the moon

Elizabeth Bishop, *Complete Poems*
Lillian Hellman, *An Unfinished
    Woman*
N. Scott Momaday, *House Made of
    Dawn*
Philip Roth, *Portnoy's Complaint*

1970
Four Kent State University students
    shot by National Guardsmen
    during campus antiwar demon-
    stration
Independent U.S. postal service
    established

James Dickey, *Deliverance*
Joan Didion, *Play It As It Lays*
Ernest Hemingway, *Islands in the
    Stream*
Ezra Pound, *Cantos* (collected)
Tom Wolfe, *Radical Chic and
    Mau-Mauing the Flak Catchers*

1971
Twenty-sixth Amendment lowers
    voting age to 18
Amtrak, a new national rail system,
    created
Attica prison riot in New York state
    kills 31 inmates and 9 hostages

A. R. Ammons, *Collected Poems*
Peter DeVries, *Into Your Tent I'll
    Creep*
E. L. Doctorow, *The Book of Daniel*

Ernest J. Gaines, *The Autobiography of Miss Jane Pittman*
Bernard Malamud, *The Tenants*
Wallace Stegner, *Angle of Repose*
Edmund Wilson, *Upstate*

1972
President Nixon visits China
U.S. troops leave Vietnam
Watergate burglary, which leads to President Nixon's resignation from office (1974)

John Barth, *Chimera*
Joyce Carol Oates, *Marriages and Infidelities*
James Purdy, *I Am Elijah Thrush*
Ishmael Reed, *Mumbo Jumbo*
Eudora Welty, *The Optimist's Daughter*

1973
Vietnam War ends
Military draft ends
Watergate scandal results in several resignations from President Nixon's administration
Vice President Spiro Agnew resigns after paying fine for evading taxes on undercover payments

Allen Ginsberg, *The Fall of America*
Lillian Hellman, *Pentimento*
Robert Lowell, *The Dolphin*
Thomas Pynchon, *Gravity's Rainbow*
Gore Vidal, *Burr*
Kurt Vonnegut, *Breakfast of Champions*
Thornton Wilder, *Theophilus North*

1974
Impeachment hearings of President Nixon, who is accused of covering up crimes related to the Watergate burglary (1972)
President Nixon resigns
Gerald R. Ford succeeds Richard Nixon
Ford administration (1974–1977) begins

Ford grants Richard Nixon a pardon for any crimes he may have committed
Alison Lurie, *The War Between the Tates*
Evan S. Connell, *The Connoisseur*
William Everson, *Man-Fate*
Gary Synder, *Turtle Island*

1975
James Hoffa, former head of Teamsters Union, disappears
President Ford survives two assassination attempts

Edward Albee, *Seascape*
John Ashbery, *Self-Portrait in a Convex Mirror*
Saul Bellow, *Humboldt's Gift*
E. L. Doctorow, *Ragtime*
Anne Sexton, *The Awful Rowing Toward God*

1976
U.S. celebrates Bicentennial
Viking II lands on Mars

William Gass, *On Being Blue*
Alex Haley, *Roots*
Lillian Hellman, *Scoundrel Time*
Christopher Isherwood, *Christopher and His Kind*
Wallace Stegner, *The Spectator Bird*
Saul Bellow awarded Nobel Prize in literature

1977
Jimmy Carter administration (1977–1981) begins
President Carter pardons Vietnam War draft evaders
First National Women's Conference drafts women's rights program
Convicted murderer Gary Gilmore executed by Utah firing squad at his urging; his story becomes a national phenomenon treated in Norman Mailer's *The Executioner's Song* (1979)

Robert Coover, *The Public Burning*

John Gregory Dunne, *True Confessions*
Walker Percy, *Lancelot*
S. J. Perelman, *Eastward Ha!*

1978
U.S. relinquishes Panama Canal to Panama
More than 900 members of People's Temple cult, Jonestown, Guyana, die in mass suicide
President Carter mediates peace agreement between Israel and Egypt

Malcolm Cowley, *And I Worked at the Writer's Trade*
John Gardner, *On Moral Fiction*
John Irving, *The World According to Garp*
Alfred Kazin, *New York Jew*
Barbara Tuchman, *A Distant Mirror*
Herman Wouk, *The Winds of War*
Isaac Bashevis Singer awarded Nobel Prize in literature

1979
Iran seizes American hostages at U.S. Embassy in Tehran
U.S. and China establish formal diplomatic relations
Accident in nuclear reactor at Three Mile Island, Pennsylvania, releases radioactive material
Large antinuclear demonstration in Washington, D.C.

John Barth, *Letters*
Joan Didion, *The White Album*
Donald Justice, *Selected Poems*
Norman Mailer, *The Executioner's Song*
Philip Roth, *The Ghost Writer*
William Styron, *Sophie's Choice*
Louis Zukofsky, *"A"*

1980
Miami race riots kill 17
U.S. banking industry deregulated
U.S. trucking industry deregulated

Herbert Gold, *He/She*

Galway Kinnell, *Mortal Acts, Mortal Words*
Wright Morris, *Plains Song*
Joyce Carol Oates, *Bellefleur*
Walker Percy, *The Second Coming*
Tom Robbins, *Still Life with Woodpecker*

1981
Ronald Reagan administration (1981–1989) begins
Iran releases American hostages
President Reagan shot and wounded
Congress passes largest tax cut in U.S. history
Sandra Day O'Connor becomes first female U.S. Supreme Court justice

John Ashbery, *Shadow Train*
Ernest Hemingway, *Letters*
Philip Roth, *Zuckerman Unbound*
Gore Vidal, *Creation*
Barbara Tuchman, *Practicing History*
John Updike, *Rabbit Is Rich*

1982
Economic recession
Civil wars in Central America
Equal Rights Amendment fails to achieve ratification

Saul Bellow, *The Dean's December*
John Gregory Dunne, *Dutch Shea, Jr.*
Wallace Stegner, *One Way to Spell Man*
The Library of America establishes the publication of classic American literature in uniform editions

1983
Terrorist blows up U.S. Marine Corps barracks at Beirut, killing 183
President Reagan proposes anti-missile defense system
Martin Luther King Jr. national holiday established

Harold W. Washington (1922–87) becomes first African-American mayor of Chicago

Norman Mailer, *Ancient Evenings*
Richard Rodriguez, *Hunger of Memory*
Sam Shepard, *Fool for Love*
Alice Walker, *The Color Purple*

1984
Jesse Jackson first African American to run a national campaign for a major party presidential nomination
Geraldine Ferraro (1935–   ) first woman to be nominated vice president on a major party ticket

Louise Erdrich, *Love Medicine*
David Mamet, *Glengarry Glen Ross*

1985
Deficit in national budget exceeds $200 billion
Mikhail Gorbachev becomes leader of U.S.S.R.
Corporate mergers in U.S. increase dramatically
U.S. poverty figures decline by 2 million

James Baldwin, *Evidence of Things Not Seen*
Carolyn Kizer, *Yin*
Studs Terkel, *The Good War*

1986
Space shuttle *Challenger* explodes, killing 7 astronauts
U.S. bombs Libya
President Reagan's anti-missile defense system funded

Don DeLillo, *White Noise*
Larry McMurtry, *Lonesome Dove*
Anne Tyler, *The Accidental Tourist*
James Welch, *Fools Crow*

1987
Dow Jones plunges 508 points in one day

50,000 cases of AIDS reported in U.S.
Iran-Contra affair, selling of U.S. arms for U.S. hostages in Iran
Reagan and Gorbachev sign missile treaty

T. Coraghessan Boyle, *World's End*
Rita Dove, *Thomas and Beulah*
August Wilson, *Fences*
Tom Wolfe, *The Bonfire of the Vanities*

1988
President Reagan signs bill offering apologies and reparation to Japanese Americans interned by the U.S. government during World War II

Toni Morrison, *Beloved*
Alfred Uhry, *Driving Miss Daisy*
Wendy Wasserstein, *The Heidi Chronicles*

1989
Pro-democracy student demonstrations crushed in China
U.S. Supreme Court partially restricts abortions
200,000 infected with HIV virus
Exxon-Valdez tanker causes major oil spill in Alaska
U.S. overthrows President Manuel Noriega's regime in Panama
George Bush administration (1989–1993) begins

Oscar Hijuelos, *The Mambo Kings Play Songs of Love*
Amy Tan, *Joy Luck Club*
Anne Tyler, *Breathing Lessons*

1990
Eastern Europe frees itself from Soviet control
Dr. Jack Kevorkian develops "suicide machine" and begins helping terminally ill patients to end their lives
President Bush signs Americans with Disabilities Act

Camille Paglia, *Sexual Personae*
E. L. Doctorow, *Billy Bathgate*
Charles Simic, *The World Doesn't End: Prose Poems*
John Updike, *Rabbit at Rest*
Mona Van Duyn, *Near Changes*
August Wilson, *The Piano Lesson*

1991

U.S.S.R. dissolves, the Soviet empire breaks up into separate countries (Russia, Ukraine, etc.)
Eastern Airlines, Pan Am go out of business; TWA declares bankruptcy
Clarence Thomas confirmed as Supreme Court justice in spite of charges of sexual harassment

Philip Roth, *Patrimony*
Amy Tan, *The Kitchen God's Wife*

1992

Serious economic recession
52 killed in Los Angeles race riot
U.S. Navy Tailhook scandal involving charges of sexual harassment

Harold Brodkey, *The Runaway Soul*
Susan Sontag, *The Volcano Lover*
Don DeLillo, *Mao II*
Philip Levine, *What Work Is*
Camille Paglia, *Sex, Art, and American Culture*

1993

National debt reaches $4 trillion
Bill Clinton administration (1993–2001) begins
President Clinton's national health plan fails to pass in Congress
President Clinton initiates new "don't ask, don't tell" policy regarding gays in the military

Elizabeth Bishop, *One Art: Selected Letters*
T. Coraghessan Boyle, *The Road to Wellville*
Robert Olen Butler, *A Good Scent from a Strange Mountain*
David Mamet, *Oleanna*

John Updike, *Collected Poems*
Toni Morrison awarded Nobel Prize in literature

1994

Republican landslide captures both houses of Congress
Former professional football player O. J. Simpson tried for double murder
Baseball players' strike leads to cancellation of World Series
Mexico verges on financial collapse
President and Mrs. Clinton and their associates investigated for improper financial transactions

Edward Albee, *Three Tall Women*
William Gaddis, *A Frolic of His Own*

1995

Bomb explodes Alfred P. Murrah Federal Building in Oklahoma City, killing 169 and injuring 400; Timothy McVeigh (1968–2001), a Gulf War veteran, is charged with the crime
U.S. and Vietnam open diplomatic relations
O. J. Simpson acquitted of murder
Government shuts down over impasse between Republican majority in Congress and President Clinton over funding of federal budget

Ann Beattie, *Another You*
William Gass, *The Tunnel*
William Maxwell, *All The Days and Nights: The Collected Stories*
Joyce Carol Oates, *Zombie*
Alfred Kazin, *Writing Was Everything*

1996

President Clinton and Congress reach budget agreement
U.S. agents apprehend Theodore Kaczynski (1942–   ), "Unabomber" mail-bombing suspect
President Clinton signs welfare reform legislation

Sherman Alexie, *Indian Killer*
Joan Didion, *The Last Thing He Wanted*
Bruce J. Friedman, *A Father's Kisses*
William Kennedy, *The Flaming Corsage*
Henry Roth, *From Bondage*
Robert Pinsky, *The Figured Wheel: New and Collected Poems 1966–1996*

1997

Civil jury finds O. J. Simpson liable in wrongful deaths of his former wife, Nicole, and her friend Ronald Goldman
Timothy McVeigh found guilty of Oklahoma City bombing in 1995
President Clinton signs balanced budget bill

Saul Bellow, *The Actual*
Joyce Carol Oates, *Man Crazy*
Paul Theroux, *Collected Stories*
Kurt Vonnegut, *Timequake*
Edmund White, *The Farewell Symphony*

1998

"Unabomber" suspect Theodore Kaczynski pleads guilty to sending letter bombs and is given four consecutive life sentences
President Clinton admits to having "inappropriate relationship" with White House intern Monica Lewinsky
President Clinton is impeached

Philip Roth, *I Married a Communist*
Robert Stone, *Damascus Gate*
Tom Wolfe, *A Man in Full*
W. S. Merwin, *The River Sound*

1999

President Clinton acquitted in Senate impeachment trial
John F. Kennedy Jr. dies in plane crash
Two students kill 13, wound 23, then kill themselves in gun

attack at Columbine High
School in Littleton, Colorado
Larry McMurtry, *Duane's Depressed*
Oscar Hijuelos, *Empress of the
Splendid Season*
Ralph Ellison, *Juneteenth*
T. Coraghessan Boyle, *Collected
Stories*
E. Annie Proulx, *Close Range:
Wyoming Stories*

2000
Vice President and presidential
candidate Al Gore contests results of the presidential election
in Florida, asking for a recount
Hilary Rodham Clinton becomes
first First Lady to be elected to
the U.S. Senate

U.S. Supreme Court reaches
decision on Florida election,
reaffirming victory of George
W. Bush

Alice Adams, *After the War*
Saul Bellow, *Ravelstein*
Joyce Carol Oates, *Blonde*
Philip Roth, *The Human Stain*
Susan Sontag, *In America*
John Updike, *Gertrude and Claudius*
Stanley Kunitz, *The Collected Poems*

2001
George W. Bush administration
(2001–   ) begins
Economic downturn
Timothy McVeigh executed
World Trade Center in New York
City is attacked and destroyed
by two jet airliners; approxi-
mately 3,000 people are killed in
worst terrorist attack on U.S.
homeland
Airliner hijacked by terrorists attacks Pentagon in Washington,
D.C., destroying part of the military complex and killing more
than 100 people
U.S. attacks and deposes government in Afghanistan in war on
terrorism

Saul Bellow, *Collected Stories*
Don DeLillo, *The Body Artist*
Joan Didion, *Political Fictions*
Susan Sontag, *Where The Stress Falls*
Amy Tan, *The Bonesetter's Daughter*

A

Abbey, Edward (1927–1989) *novelist, essayist*

Abbey was born and raised in the Allegheny Mountains of Pennsylvania. He was educated at the University of Mexico, worked as a park ranger, and wrote about life in the desert in *Desert Solitaire* (1968). His work is important for its evocation of how the modern mind responds to and manages the wilderness. His feeling for mountain life is reflected in *Appalachian Wilderness* (1970). He also wrote several nonfiction books, including *Skyrock: The Canyon Country of Southeast Utah* (1971), *Cactus Country* (1973), *The Journey Home* (1982), and *Down the River* (1982). His later essays are collected in *Beyond the Wall* (1984) and *One Life at a Time, Please* (1987). October

Sources

Cahalan, James M. *Edward Abbey: A Life.* Tucson: University of Arizona Press, 2001.

Ronald, Ann. *The New West of Edward Abbey.* Reno: University of Nevada Press, 2000.

Abish, Walter (1931–) *novelist, poet*

The Austrian-born Abish became a United States citizen in 1960. He taught English at Columbia University for 10 years. Often called a postmodernist (see POSTMODERNISM), Abish writes experimental novels. In *Alphabetical Africa* (1974), for example, every word of the first chapter begins with an A. *How German Is It* (1980), a novel about an American of German extraction who returns home to investigate his father's wartime death, won the PEN/Faulkner Award for fiction in 1981. He has also published poetry, *Duel Site,* and short story collections, *Minds Meet* (1975) and *Future Perfect* (1977).

Eclipse Fever (1993) is a novel about Mexico and other Third World countries.

Sources

Hagen, W. M. "Eclipse Fever." *World Literature Today* 69 (Winter 1995): 137. Available on-line. URL: http://library.northernlight.com/SL19970923020047213.html?cb=0&sc=0#doc. Downloaded on May 21, 2001.

Shatsky, Joel and Michael Taub, ed. *Contemporary Jewish-American Novelists: A Bio-Critical Sourcebook.* Westport, Conn.: Greenwood Press, 1997.

abstract expressionism

A movement in U.S. art begun in the 1940s by Jackson Pollock (1912–56), Arshile Gorky (1905–48), Franz Kline (1910–62), Willem de Kooning (1904–97), and Mark Rothko (1903–70), it favored the use of intense color and texture. Paint was applied to the canvas in dynamic slashes, stripes, and splotches that prompted art critic Harold Rosenberg to call it "action painting." The most memorable image of the abstract expressionist or action painter was that of Jackson Pollock heaving gobs of paint at a canvas. The result seemed spontaneous, yet the paintings often had an exquisite sense of composition, of a surface of intricate layers formed by countless decisions the painter had made in his "attack" on the canvas. To the eye tutored in representational painting and classical composition, abstract expressionist art seemed merely chaotic. In fact, it reflected an anarchic impulse, but one still governed by a sense of form and style.

In literature, writers such as William BURROUGHS and Allen GINSBERG and others of the "BEAT" generation used abstract expressionist techniques in that their work was composed of fragments, or disjointed and plotless narratives. Frank O'HARA and the NEW YORK SCHOOL OF POETS also borrowed from or were inspired by abstract expressionist painters.

Sources

Auping, Michael. *Abstract Expressionism: The Critical Developments.* New York: Abrams in association with Albright-Knox Art Gallery, 1987.

Hobbs, Robert Carleton, and Gail Levin. *Abstract Expressionism: The Formative Years.* Ithaca, N.Y.: Herbert F. Johnson Museum of Art, Cornell University, 1978.

Sandler, Irving. *The Triumph of American Painting: A History of Abstract Expressionism.* New York: Praeger Publishers, 1970.

Accent periodical

Published at the University of Illinois between 1940 and 1960, this LITTLE MAGAZINE published both new and established authors. An important literary quarterly, it featured the work of Irwin SHAW, Kay BOYLE, Katherine Anne PORTER, Wallace STEVENS, and E. E. CUMMINGS, as well as literary criticism by Kenneth BURKE and David Daiches. The *Accent Anthology* was published in 1946. *Accent* remains an important source for understanding the development of literary MODERNISM in America and of how influential critics began to analyze it.

Acker, Kathy (1948–1997) novelist

Born and raised in New York City, Acker studied under poet Jerome Rothenberg. Her first work was published by small, independent presses as she negotiated the literary milieu of New York City in the 1960s. Some critics view her as a feminist writer, but others have found her graphic treatment of sex and violence—quite aside from any moral or political agenda—her most notable and provocative contribution to contemporary literature. Critical opinion of her work is sharply divided between praise and blame. Her novels include *I Dreamt I Was a Nymphomaniac* (1974), *Blood and Guts in High School* (1984), *In Memoriam to Identity* (1990), and *Pussy, King of the Pirates* (1996). She has been compared with Henry MILLER and William S. BURROUGHS because of her pornographic and surrealistic subject matter and style. Acker described her style and methods as the creation of a world. "If political content comes through it's not because I sat down with a political agenda for this book. I don't write in order to say this is what should be . . . I just basically wanted to do a girl's version of *Treasure Island.* . . ."

Sources

"Kathy Acker in conversation with Beth Jackson," *Eyeline,* Autumn/Winter 1996. Available on-line. URL: http://acker.thehub.com.au/ackerjack.html. Downloaded May 21, 2001.

Dodge, Trevor. "I Lost My Soul In San Francisco: An Interview/Journal Entry Starring Kathy Acker, Portland, and *Pussy.*" *Carbon* 14 #8 (1996). Available on-line. URL: http://acker.thehub.com.au/portland.html. Downloaded May 21, 2001.

Friedman, Ellen G. "A Conversation with Kathy Acker." *Review of Contemporary Fiction* 9, no. 3 (Fall 1989). Available on-line. URL: http://www.centerforbookculture.org/interviews/index.html.

Juno, Andrea, and V. Vale. *Angry Women.* San Francisco: RE/Search, 1991.

Activists, The organization

A San Francisco writers' group established in 1936, devoted to studying the relationship between language and emotion in poetry. The group thrived under the inspiration of Professor Lawrence Hart, who edited and commented on a selection of their work in the May 1951 issue of POETRY.

Adams, Nick character

The protagonist of Ernest HEMINGWAY's groundbreaking collection of short stories, IN OUR TIME (1925). Many of the stories are set in the Michigan woods, where Nick grows up. Interspersed between the stories of his youth are vivid descriptions of his experience in WORLD WAR I. In "Indian Camp" Nick watches his father, a doctor, deliver a breech baby and witnesses the horrifying impact of the event on the Indian father. In the most famous story of the collection, "Big Two-Hearted River," Nick embarks on a solitary fishing trip. The story is a meticulous record of his camping even as he tries to suppress memories of a violent war and his wounding. Nick is one of the quintessential Hemingway heroes, stoically learning about the tragedy of life.

African-American literature

The beginnings of 20th-century African-American literature derive from the period just before the 1920s when African Americans were returning from World War I with a new sense of their capacities and a desire to be recognized as full citizens. At the same time, a great migration of African Americans from the South to the North in search of employment jettisoned the old plantation sharecropper roles that had dominated their rural lives. Under the Old South system, African Americans farmed crops on small parcels of land they did not own. Their earnings were so small it was impossible to accumulate savings, and thus their work amounted to another form of slavery.

A key figure in this transition period was James Weldon JOHNSON, a poet and novelist. His *Autobiography of an Ex-Colored Man* explored a theme of "passing" that would become central in 20th-century African-American literature.

The unnamed narrator of the novel discovers that he can "pass" for white. To do so means that he can fully integrate himself into American society. But it also means forsaking his identity as an African American; passing means giving up one's people and one's past. The very fact that the narrator poses the problem suggests that passing is inherently a problem of authenticity—one that most African-American writers would have to encounter sooner or later. That the issue troubled Johnson himself is clear because he first published the novel anonymously.

"Passing" was also a question of literary style; that is, should the African American write white, so to speak, or develop a style distinctively associated with his race? This much-debated issue also is connected to the question of whether African-American literature itself should be viewed separately or as part of the mainstream of American literature.

Johnson's sole published work was soon accompanied by a flood of poetry, fiction, plays, and work in the other arts by a group of writers who collectively became known as the HARLEM RENAISSANCE. Countee CULLEN and Claude MCKAY used the traditional verse forms of English literature to express the plight of African Americans—their frustration and rage over not being accorded their full civil rights and respect as American citizens. At the same time, both poets took pride in their people and the beauty of black life. Their celebration of African-American culture did not merely bolster a people; it also elicited enormous respect from white writers such as Carl VAN VECHTEN and Eugene O'NEILL . These and other white writers created works of literature exploring the nature of African-American life, dramatizing both its promise and its peril.

McKay's novel *Home to Harlem* also helped focus attention on the "black metropolis" as a literary and cultural capital, the place to be to hear the best jazz in the country and to meet thinkers like Alain LOCKE. His nonfiction book *The New Negro* suggested just how far African-American artists had come in defining their own history and culture. While demonstrating how much African Americans had contributed to world culture, his emphasis on the idea of the new Negro suggested, as well, certain virtues and talents in African Americans that created a kind of mystique, a glamour that attracted whites to Harlem's Cotton Club and the Savoy Ballroom. For Locke, what was new about the "new Negro" was precisely his boldness and creativity. He was breaking the stereotype of the passive "darky" that had become familiar to Americans in the post-Reconstruction period.

The greatest figure to emerge out of the Harlem Renaissance was Langston HUGHES. Poems like "The Negro Speaks of Rivers" instill a grandeur in African-American history, a sense of a people with a long lineage and a closeness to the sources of creation. The cadence of this poem, established by its long lines and vowel sounds, made the African-American heritage flow along like the mighty rivers Hughes names in the poem. Unlike McKay, Cullen, Locke, and Jean

TOOMER (who wrote the most innovative fiction of the Harlem Renaissance), Hughes continued to produce literature of a very high caliber throughout his career. He wrote some of his greatest poems, for example, in the 1950s, when he captured the pent-up rage of a people who felt their dream of freedom had been deferred much too long.

Hughes also tapped the folklore of his people, creating a kind of common man in Jesse B. Semple ("Simple"), the hero of a series of short stories. Some of these stories were transformed into plays—not so successful as the fiction or poetry, but nevertheless essential to the development of African-American literature. As an autobiographer and anthologist as well, Hughes did as much, if not more, than any other single figure to foster the development of African-American literature.

Hughes's legacy might be compared with that of W. E. B. DU BOIS, whose book *The Souls of Black Folk* (1903) ranks with Johnson's as a precursor of the Harlem Renaissance. Du Bois believed in the indigenous strength of African-American culture, and as historian, sociologist, novelist, editor, political agitator, and educator he did as much as Hughes to sustain and promote African-American literature. Du Bois was a strong supporter of Hughes, McKay, and others, and he published their work in the NAACP's magazine THE CRISIS. At the same time, however, Du Bois became more radical than Hughes. Hughes drifted away from an early interest in the Communist Party and in Marxism; Du Bois strengthened his ties to both. Hughes never relinquished his integrationist stance; Du Bois left America for Africa and took positions that were later embraced and extended by black militants in the 1960s and 1970s.

By 1940, when the Harlem Renaissance was over, new African-American writers such as Richard WRIGHT, Melvin TOLSON, and Gwendolyn BROOKS produced a stream of novels, short stories, and poetry that explored the joy and heartbreak of African-American life—but with little of the Renaissance's sense of campaigning for a "New Negro." Indeed, Wright in his highly acclaimed novel *Native Son* portrayed a brutal urban environment that emasculated African-American men. Brooks, on the other hand, while not ignoring the grimness of African-American lives, also evoked their energy, determination, and wit.

Wright's powerful indictment of America had been echoed by white writers such as Theodore DREISER and John DOS PASSOS, yet his successors—notably Ralph ELLISON and James BALDWIN—were uneasy about Wright's naturalistic style, for it seemed too deterministic. In other words, Wright was placing too much emphasis on the environmental conditions that shaped his characters; he was depriving them of the ability to assert control over their lives. This made African Americans seem victimized beyond redemption, and it made the writing of fiction too constricted. Ellison's *Invisible Man* certainly acknowledges the injustice that Wright so painfully and accurately portrayed, and yet Ellison's narrator—unnamed, like the narrator of Johnson's novel—is more playful, more re-sourceful, more the author of his own existence than Wright's naturalism can allow any African-American man to be. Similarly, James Baldwin, while giving Wright praise for brilliantly exposing the damage done by racism, sought in *Notes of a Native Son* for a more flexible, open-ended perspective on the possibilities of being his own man.

A good deal of African-American literature since the generation of Wright, Ellison, and Baldwin has explored the tensions between separateness and integration that Johnson first explored in *Autobiography of an Ex-Colored Man*. A new generation of African-American women writers such as Lorraine HANSBERRY, Paule MARSHALL, Margaret WALKER, Alice WALKER, Toni MORRISON, Toni Cade BAMBARA, Nikki GIOVANNI, Audre LORDE, and Rita DOVE have provided new perspectives on African-American life and culture, the role of slavery, and the vexed relationships between black men and black women. Their great precursor was Zora Neale HURSTON, also a product of the Harlem Renaissance, a novelist with an anthropologist's eye. These women writers have revised and sometimes come into conflict with the legacy of African-American male writers such as Eldridge CLEAVER and Ishmael REED, and Reed has not hesitated to respond with his own indictment of Walker's "womanist" ideology. Reed's novels represent the most extended satire on American and African-American history ever published. Recent contentious debates within the African-American literary community suggest a rich diversity of opinion and creativity, no matter how troubling the issues may seem to their debaters.

Regardless of political opinions, African-American literature is particularly strengthened by the long tradition of autobiography, begun with 19th-century slave narratives and continued in the 20th century with Wright's *Black Boy*, Baldwin's *Notes of a Native Son, The Autobiography of Malcolm X* (1965), Claude BROWN's *Manchild in the Promised Land* (1965), Maya ANGELOU's *I Know Why the Caged Bird Sings* (1970), and Eldridge Cleaver's *Soul on Ice* (1968).

The African-American achievement in the drama has also been notable—not only in the work of Lorraine Hansberry but also in the inventive plays of the prolific Ed BULLINS, in Amiri BARAKA's searing dramas, and in the historical and contemporary treatments of African-American life in the work of Charles FULLER and August WILSON. Wilson's work has displayed techniques and themes that rival those of the American master Eugene O'Neill.

Sources

Davis, Thadious, and Trudier Harris. *Dictionary of Literary Biography*. Vol. 38, *Afro-American Writers After 1955: Dramatists and Prose Writers*. Detroit: Gale Research, 1985.

De Weever, Jacqueline. *Mythmaking and Metaphor in Black Women's Fiction*. New York: St. Martin's Press, 1992.

Gibson, Donald B. *The Politics of Literary Expression: A Study of Major Black Writers*. Westport, Conn.: Greenwood Press, 1981.

Stepto, Robert. *From Behind the Veil: A Study of Afro-American Narrative*. Urbana: University of Illinois Press, 1991.

Agee, James (1909–1955) *novelist, poet, film critic*

Best known for his book about sharecroppers in the GREAT DEPRESSION, the classic *Let Us Now Praise Famous Men* (1941), illustrated with photographs by Walker Evans, Agee was born in Knoxville, Tennessee. From his father, who was raised on a farm, Agee took an abiding interest in the land and in rural values. From his mother, he absorbed an interest in the business world, in the arts, and religion. Educated in private schools (Saint Andrew's, Exeter, and Harvard), Agee spent seven years (1932–1939) at *FORTUNE,* a business magazine founded by *TIME* entrepreneur Henry Luce, who hired many fine writers like Dwight MACDONALD and Whittaker Chambers.

Agee's first book, *Permit Me Voyage* (1934), published in the YALE SERIES OF YOUNGER POETS, exemplified his intense and careful commitment to style. His legendary collaboration with Walker Evans grew out of a *Fortune* magazine assignment, which sent him south to Alabama to document the life of tenant farmer families. This book also reflects Agee's lyricism and profound sensitivity to the agrarian life.

In 1939, Agee began work as a book reviewer for *Time*. Beginning in 1941, he reviewed films, quickly establishing himself as one of the country's finest critics of film and simultaneously elevating both film and the reviewing of film to a higher level. His deep engagement with film is evident in reviews that appeared in *The Nation* (1942–1948). Agee's work also appeared in literary and film journals such as *PARTISAN REVIEW* and *Sight and Sound*. Extending his range, Agee also worked on film scripts, including an adaptation of Stephen Crane's classic short story, *The Bride Comes to Yellow Sky* (1948), and C. S. Forester's *The African Queen* (1951). He wrote for television as well, and in 1951 produced his first novel, *The Morning Watch*. But it is his second autobiographical novel, *A Death in the Family,* published after his death in 1957, that enhanced his reputation and won a Pulitzer Prize in 1958. Responding to his father's death, Agee writes of it as a family event, as a series of revelations told with exquisite sensitivity. Agee's versatility and prose style have earned him a permanent place in studies of 20th century American culture. His *Collected Poems* was published in 1968.

Sources

Bergreen, Laurence. *James Agee: A Life*. New York: E. P. Dutton, 1984.

Kramer, Victor. *James Agee*. Boston: Twayne, 1975.

Lofaro, Michael, ed. *James Agee: Reconsiderations*. Knoxville: University of Tennessee Press, 1992.

Madden, David, ed. *Remembering James Agee*. Baton Rouge: Louisiana State University Press, 1997.

Age of Innocence, The   Edith Wharton (1920) *novel*

An almost anthropological look at the moneyed class and of the elite that governed the social and political life of New York in the 1870s, this fictional treatment of the setting of Wharton's youth won a Pulitzer Prize.

Newland Archer, a sophisticated member of New York City's elite, notices Countess Ellen Olenska at the opera. Intrigued, he finds out that she has just left her Polish husband—scandalous behavior for a woman from a good New York family. Archer is engaged to May Welland, but it is Ellen who has captured his imagination. She seems to represent a larger, more complex world than that of the provincial New York that harbors and yet inhibits Archer.

Archer's feelings are complicated when a partner at his law firm directs him to handle Ellen Olenska's case—she wishes to divorce her husband. Archer is dedicated to talk her out of the legal action, since her family disapproves of such a public exposure of her failed marriage. Archer does his job, convincing Ellen that is better to remain married even if society's rules seem too narrow.

Aghast at his own advice, Archer evades any more contact with Ellen and presses May to marry him sooner than expected. Yet Archer cannot stay away from Ellen and tells her she is the woman he would have married if he and she had been free to do so. Ellen, clearly in love with Archer, nevertheless reminds him that his own actions have made it impossible for them to be together. Archer receives May's consent to an early wedding.

Archer does his duty and marries May. Yet he cannot forsake Ellen, and when he sees her again, he tries to arrange some sort of relationship. But Ellen is steadfast in her refusal to consider Newland's implied proposition that they become lovers. She returns to her husband.

Thirty years later, Archer is in Paris with his son, Dallas who has arranged for his father to meet Ellen. But Archer finds that once he is just outside her apartment he cannot enter. Dallas visits her instead. Newland learns that Dallas has known all about Ellen from May, who all along understood much more than Archer supposed. A stunned Archer stands staring at Ellen's balcony, concluding, "It's more real to me here than if I went up."

Sources

Wagner-Martin, Linda. *The Age of Innocence: A Novel of Ironic Nostalgia.* New York: Twayne, 1996.

Agrarians

A term for the southern writers who published *I'LL TAKE MY STAND* (1930), a collection of essays that argued for the superiority of southern agrarian life over the modern, urban culture. The group included Allen TATE, John Crowe RANSOM, Robert Penn WARREN, Donald DAVIDSON, John Gould Fletcher, Stark YOUNG, and Andrew LYTLE. Many of these writers had also been associated with a literary movement called THE FUGITIVES. In general, the group argued for the superiority of the rural or pastoral way of life. *I'll Take My Stand* was sharply critical of northern industrialism and capitalism and the exploitation of labor. The book argued that southern ways not only were more relaxed and humane, but also created conditions more propitious for the imagination. To maintain this argument, the Agrarians had to downplay or rationalize the legacy of slavery and of sharecropping. The South's bigoted history received little attention—a fact that later bothered Robert Penn Warren, one of the group's younger members. In his subsequent work, he repudiated some of the group's values, particularly its positions on race and other aspects of politics. The group was at its most cohesive from 1928 to 1935. Thereafter, many of its members, including Warren, Tate, and Ransom, found academic employment in the North. Davidson and others remained in the South and stuck by their early views.

Sources

Conkin, Paul K. *The Southern Agrarians.* Knoxville: University of Tennessee Press, 1988.

Duncan, Christopher M. *Fugitive Theory: Political Theory, The Southern Agrarians, and America.* Lanham, Md.: Lexington Books, 2000.

Aiken, Conrad Potter   (1889–1973) *poet, novelist*

Conrad Aiken was born in Savannah, Georgia, but at age 10 he was sent to live with relatives in New Bedford, Massachusetts, after his father shot and killed his mother and then committed suicide. Educated at Harvard, Aiken soon embarked on a career in literature, marrying in 1912 and moving to Europe—as did his Harvard friend, T. S. ELIOT. Later in the 1920s Aiken settled near Boston and spent time on Cape Cod. He absorbed a good deal from psychology, particularly the works of Freud and William James. He won the Pulitzer Prize for poetry in 1929 for his *Selected Poems.* His *Collected Poems 1916–1970* (1970) brings together work from more than 30 books. His style has been called urbane, fragmented, and erotic. His themes include his New England ancestry and his efforts to develop his own Freudian-based theory of consciousness.

Aiken distinguished himself in virtually every poetic form, writing both very long and short poems, exploring musical structures, myths, and the modern consciousness. In *Ushant* (1952) he produced a work that is part fiction, part autobiography. It is perhaps his finest achievement in prose, although he also published several novels: *Blue Voyage* (1927), *Great Circle* (1933), *King Coffin* (1935), and others. His *Collected Novels* appeared in 1964 and his *Collected Stories* in 1960. Like James AGEE, Aiken's versatility has made him an indispensable voice in 20th-century American literature, and yet his achievements have been overshadowed by contemporaries such as T. S. Eliot and William Carlos WILLIAMS, perhaps because their finest poems have made a greater impact on the readers of modernist literature (see MODERNISM).

Sources

Butscher, Edward. *Conrad Aiken: Poet of White Horse Vale.* Athens: University of Georgia Press, 1988.

Hoffman, Frederick. *Conrad Aiken.* Boston: Twayne, 1962.

Martin, Harry. *The Art of Knowing: The Poetry and Prose of Conrad Aiken.* Columbia: University of Missouri Press, 1988.

Siegal, Catharine. *The Fictive World of Conrad Aiken: A Celebration of Consciousness.* De Kalb: Northern Illinois University Press, 1993.

Albee, Edward Franklin (1928–   ) *playwright*

Born in Washington, D.C., Edward Albee was adopted by Reed Albee, a producer and theater owner. Edward Albee grew up in Manhattan and in Westchester County, New York, attending the Lawrenceville School in New Jersey and then graduating in 1946 from the Choate School in Connecticut. After an unsatisfactory year in college, he settled in Greenwich Village and worked at various jobs, including sales and advertising. He traveled in Europe and served in the U.S. Army. He wrote his first play, the brilliant one-act *The Zoo Story* (1959), in three weeks. It takes place on a bench in Manhattan's Central Park, where a complacent, middle-class man is accosted by an aggressive young man who ridicules and goads his bourgeois victim into stabbing him. The play is a tour de force both in its psychological probing of character and its exploration of class identity.

Although *The Zoo Story* is written in a naturalistic style, Albee experimented early with SURREALISM and other antirealistic devices in such plays as *The Sandbox* (1960) and *The American Dream* (1960), in which characters such as Mommy, Daddy, and Grandma parody American middle-class values and express a degree of unease with conventional life. This surrealistic strain culminated in Albee's brilliant but elusive play *Tiny Alice* (1964) and in the more accessible *Seascape* (1975), which won the Pulitzer Prize. Albee the psychological realist is best displayed in his masterpiece, *Who's Afraid of Virginia Woolf?* (1962), made into a memorable motion picture with Richard Burton and Elizabeth Taylor in 1966. This searing drama about a cynical college professor, George, his vituperative wife, Martha, and their ability to draw a young couple into their marital conflicts, reveals a typical Albee strategy: As in *The Zoo Story,* normal, apparently conventional characters are shown to harbor the same tensions as the more extreme characters they confront.

Albee has written several plays that probe American family life, including *A Delicate Balance* (1966), which also won a Pulitzer Prize, and *All Over* (1971). His concern with marginal characters reflects the influence of Tennessee WILLIAMS, and Albee's depiction of troubled families clearly owes a debt to Eugene O'NEILL. Indeed, Albee's strength has been his ability to integrate the naturalistic and romantic traditions of the American theater. His plays explore the nature of how society shapes the individual while also making the individual a vibrant, intensely realized character.

Albee's later plays, *The Lady from Dubuque* (1980), *The Man Who Had Three Arms* (1982), *Faustus in Hell* (1985), and *Marriage Play* (1986), have not received as much attention from critics and have failed at the box office. His play *Three Tall Women* (1992), however, was an enormous success in New York and was greeted as a comeback for the playwright. The play draws on Albee's family background and includes a riveting main character based on Albee's adoptive mother.

Albee has produced several plays that are adaptations of stories and novels by other writers, including *The Ballad of the Sad Cafe* (1963, from Carson MCCULLERS's story), *Malcolm* (1966, from James PURDY's novel), and *Lolita* (1981, from Vladimir NABOKOV's novel).

Sources

Bloom, Harold, ed. *Edward Albee.* New York: Chelsea House, 2000.

Gussow, Mel. *Edward Albee: A Singular Journey: A Biography.* New York: Simon & Schuster, 1999.

Kolin, Philip C., ed. *Conversations with Edward Albee.* Jackson: University Press of Mississippi, 1988.

Alexander, Meena (1951–   ) *poet, novelist, essayist, social activist, educator*

Alexander was born in Allahabad, India, but her family soon moved to Khartoum, Egypt. Educated in England at Nottingham University, she came to the United States as a professor of English and creative writing at Hunter College and at the Graduate Center of the City University of New York. Both her poetry, *The Bird's Bright Ring* (1976), and her novel, *Nampally Road* (1971), reflect her sensitivity to the way women have been violated and hurt. *The Storm* (1989) is a memoir that evokes Alexander's feeling for her grandmother—as does another memoir, *House of a Thousand Doors* (1988). Although much of her work is set in India, Alexander clearly has the modern world as a whole in mind as she raises important questions about culture, politics, and the status of women and families. These themes coalesce in *Fault Lines: A Memoir* (1993), which is her most careful exploration of what it means to be a woman.

Sources

Alexander, Meena. "Observing Ourselves among Others: Interview with Meena Alexander." *Between the Lines: South Asians and Post Coloniality.* Edited by Deepika Bahri and Mary Vasudeva. Philadelphia: Temple University Press, 1996, 35–53.

Young, Jeffrey. "Creating a Life Through Education." *Chronicle of Higher Education* 43: 27 (March 14, 1997): B8–B9.

Alexie, Sherman (1966–   ) *poet, novelist, short story writer*

Alexie grew up on the Spokane/Coeur d'Alene reservation 50 miles northwest of Spokane, Washington. At the age of six months Alexie had an operation for water on the brain. His parents, both American Indians, were told that his chances of survival were slim and that mental retardation was likely. Alexie did suffer seizures, but he was not mentally incapacitated. Indeed, he learned to read at the age of three. One of his early major influences was John STEINBECK's *The Grapes of Wrath* (1939). Alexie pursued his high school education away from the reservation and later graduated from Washington State University, where he wrote poetry under the guidance of writing teacher Alex Kuo. Alexie's first book, *The Business of Fancydancing* (1991), earned him early recognition and support from the National Endowment for the Humanities and the Washington State Arts Commission. He quickly published five collections of poetry—*First Indian on the Moon* (1993), *Old Shirts and New Skins* (1993), *I Would Steal Horses* (1993), *Water Flowing* Home (1995), The *Summer of Black Widows* (1996), and *The Man Who Loves Salmon* (1998)—and a short story collection, *The Lone Ranger and Tonto Fistfight in Heaven* (1993).

Reservation Blues (1995) and *Indian Killer* (1996) earned Alexie more critical praise in mainstream newspapers and magazines such as the *New York Times* and the NEW YORKER. A screenplay, *Smoke Signals* (1998), was well received at the Sundance Film Festival.

Already a prolific author, in 2000 Alexie published *The Toughest Indian in the World*, a collection of stories, and *One Stick Song*, a collection of poetry.

Alexie has been praised and attacked for his wicked, irreverent humor. He dislikes the term *Native American,* calls himself an Indian, and is unsparing in his critical look at all parts of American culture, including that of reservation life.

Sources

Brill de Ramirex, Susan Berry. *Contemporary American Indian Literatures & the Oral Tradition.* Tucson: University of Arizona Press, 1999.

Egan, Timothy. "An Indian Without Reservations." *New York Times Magazine,* January 18, 1998. Available on-line. URL: http://archives.nytimes.com/archives/.

Gillian, Jennifer. "Reservation Home Movies: Sherman Alexie's Poetry." *American Literature* 68 (1996): 91–110.

The Official Sherman Alexie Site. Available on-line. URL: http://www.fallsapart.com.

Algonquin Round Table *organization*

A group of writers (Alexander WOOLLCOTT, Dorothy PARKER, and Robert Benchley, among others) who met regularly at the Algonquin Hotel in New York City and traded barbs, quips, and jokes. These writers were associated with the NEW YORKER and did much to earn that magazine its fame for wit and humor. They exemplified the boisterous, cynical temperament of New York City in the 1920s, and furthered the tendency to regard writers as public personalities. Benchley went on to have a career in Hollywood movies, Woollcott became an influential radio personality, and Parker went to Hollywood to write film scripts.

Sources

Bryan, III, J. *Merry Gentlemen (And One Lady).* New York: Atheneum, 1985.

Drennan, Robert E., ed. *The Algonquin Wits.* New York: Citadel Press, 1968.

Algren, Nelson (1909–1981) *novelist*

Although Algren was born in Detroit, Chicago became his turf. He wrote about characters that were American "outcasts," down-and-out urban denizens of the west side slums. His first novel, *Boots* (1935), evoked the bitterness of Depression-era youth. *Never Come Morning* (1942) explored immigrant Polish life in the city. The ethnic and naturalistic aspect of Algren's work earned him frequent comparisons with another Chicago author, James T. FARRELL. Algren's most important work is *The Man with the Golden Arm* (1949). The novel won a National Book Award and became a movie starring Frank Sinatra, whose performance captured Algren's searing depiction of Frankie Machine, a morphine addict. Algren's short stories are collected in *The Neon Wilderness* (1951) and *A Walk on the Wide Side* (1956).

Sources

Cox, Martha Heasley and Wayne Chatterton. *Nelson Algren.* Boston: Twayne, 1975.

Drew, Bettina. *Nelson Algren: A Life on the Wild Side.* New York: Putnam, 1989.

Allen, Paula Gunn (1939–   ) *poet, fiction writer, literary scholar*

Allen was born in Albuquerque, New Mexico, to a family of Laguna Pueblo, Sioux, and Lebanese heritage. She grew up among the Laguna and Aroma Pueblo communities in Dauber, New Mexico. She earned a Ph.D. in American studies from the University of New Mexico and has taught at San Francisco State University, the University of New Mexico, the University of California, and other schools. She has won several fellowships and prizes, including a National Endowment for the Arts Fellowship for Writing in 1978 and the Native American Prize for Literature in 1990. Among American literary influences she lists Gertrude STEIN, the BEATS, Adrienne RICH, Audre LORDE, and Denise LEVERTOV. She studied writing with Robert CREELEY. She came out as a lesbian in her Introduction to *The Sacred Hoop: Recovering the Feminine in American Indian Traditions* (1986). Her poetry collections include *Shadow Country* (1982), *Wyrds* (1987), and *Skin and Bones* (1988). *The Woman Who Owned the Shadows* (1983) focuses on Ephanie, a woman of mixed race who also has to come to terms with her lesbianism. In *Grandmothers of the Light* (1991), Allen draws on myths and stories that form a woman's "spiritual tradition." Allen also has edited anthologies: *Studies in American Indian Literature: Critical Essays and Course Designs* (1983) and *Spider Woman's Granddaughters* (1989), short stories by Native American women, which won an American Book Award in 1990. Allen has campaigned actively as a feminist and speaker for gay and lesbian rights.

Sources

Bruchac, Joseph. *Survival This Way: Interviews with American Indian Poets.* Tucson: University of Arizona Press, 1987.

Ruoff, A. LaVonne Brown. *American Indian Literatures.* New York: Modern Language Association, 1990.

Allen, Woody (Allen Stewart Konigsberg)
  (1935–) *writer, filmmaker*

Born and raised in New York, Allen got his start as stand-up comic and a writer for television comedy shows. He writes in the comic tradition of THE NEW YORKER, creating maladroit, hilarious characters like those of James THURBER who reveal the contradictions of marriage and other modern institutions. Allen has collected his stories and sketches in *Getting Even* (1971), *Without Feathers* (1975), and *Side Effects* (1980).

Sources

Meade, Marion. *The Unruly Life of Woody Allen.* New York: Scribner, 2000.

Allison, Dorothy (1949–) *novelist, short story*
  writer, poet, essayist

Born in Greenville, North Carolina, Allison has described her early life as mean and violent and terrifying. Self-identified as a lesbian novelist, Allison won critical acclaim for her novel *Bastard Out of Carolina* (1992), the story of a young girl in rural North Carolina, which was a National Book Award finalist. She attracted early attention for her poetry, including *The Women Who Hate Me* (1983) and for her first collection of short stories, *Trash* (1988). *Skin: Talking about Sex, Class, and Culture* (1994) is a collection of essays. Her other novels include *Cavedweller* (1998). *Two or Three Things I Know For Sure* (1995) is a memoir of her harsh North Carolina upbringing. Allison has been praised for the strong first-person voice of her narratives. She has also affirmed that being "queer" is an integral part of her identity as a writer.

Sources

Barbarism. "Dorothy Allison: Difficult Seductress," *Fat Girl.* Available on-line. URL: http://www.fatso.com/fatgirl/dorothy.html. Posted May 1995.

Drabelle, Dennis. "No Friends of Dorothy." *The Advocate* (March 9, 1993): 66–67.

Miller, Laura. "The Salon Interview: Dorothy Allison," *Salon.* Available on-line. URL: http://www.salonmag.com/books/int/1998/03/cov_si_31intb.html. Posted on March 31, 1998.

All the King's Men *Robert Penn Warren* (1946) *novel*

Warren's classic novel about Willie STARK is narrated by Jack Burden, who meditates about the meaning of history. Stark is modeled after Huey Long, the Louisiana senator who became a great popular figure and published *Every Man a King* to promote his populist credo of power and prosperity for all the people.

Jack Burden has abandoned his Ph.D. thesis, a biography of Civil War figure Cass Mastern, to work for Governor Willie Stark, a poor boy who has made good and vows to help the downtrodden. But Jack observes Willie make compromise after compromise to attain and to stay in power. Jack himself is compromised in the eyes of Judge Irwin, his mentor, for taking a job with Stark. Jack has forsaken his own ambition in order to keep state legislators in line for the governor. When Willie asks Jack to dig up dirt on Judge Stanton, who has become Stark's political opponent, Jack discovers that Stanton—until then a paragon of integrity—did in fact accept bribes when he was the state's attorney general.

When Jack tells Stanton's son Adam, a highly respected physician, about the judge's crime, Adam, who has refused Stark's offer to run the state hospital, accepts the governor's patronage. The judge's daughter, Anne, also disillusioned by Jack's revelation, becomes Stark's mistress.

When Stark threatens to make the judge's crime public, Stanton commits suicide, and Jack's mother reveals that the judge was, in fact, his father. When Adam is persuaded that Stark appointed him only because Anne is Stark's mistress, Adam assassinates Stark. Stark dies, saying it could all have been different.

Jack marries Anne (with whom he had had an affair as a young man), and begins to come to terms with Stark's legacy. Jack also finishes his thesis on Cass Mastern. Jack now understands and accepts Mastern's sense of doom and moral responsibility. Burden has faced similar conflicts, and like Mastern, recognizes how he has failed himself and others.

Warren's novel is one of the great works of political fiction in the 20th century. Stark thinks he can use any means to achieve his ends (improving the welfare of his people), yet the means corrupt the ends. If Stark errs in becoming mired in too many political compromises, Adam Stanton errs in his failure to accept that peoples' motivations are mixed and that the world is an unredeemable mixture of good and evil. Jack Burden, a disappointed idealist, takes refuge in cynicism until he realizes, after Stark's death, that the practical side of governing is useless without at least the effort to preserve the principles that should guide practice.

Sources

Beebe, Maurice and Leslie A. Field, ed. *Robert Penn Warren's All the King's Men: A Critical Handbook.* Belmont, Calif.: Wadsworth, 1966.

Chambers, Robert H., ed. *Twentieth Century Interpretations of All the King's Men: A Collection of Critical Essays.* Englewood Cliffs, N.J.: Prentice Hall, 1977.

Sochatoff, A. Fred. *All The King's Men, A Symposium.* Pittsburgh, Carnegie Institute of Technology, 1957.

American Academy of Arts and Letters
organization

Founded in 1898 as part of the National Institute of Arts and Letters, the Academy promotes the best in literature. Based in New York City, it began with just seven writers, including William Dean Howells and Mark Twain, and is now composed of 50 members. The Academy's annual prizes include the Brunner Memorial Award in Architecture and the Gold Medal for excellence in the arts. The Howells Medal, given every five years, honors a work of American fiction. The Award of Merit Medal is given in five categories of the arts to a person not affiliated with the Academy. The Academy maintains a museum and a library (23,000 volumes) in New York City. Three exhibitions a year showcase the Academy's permanent collection of memorabilia and works by members. Works under consideration for awards and works by newly elected members and award winners are also displayed.

American Caravan periodical

Published between 1927 and 1936, this annual volume edited by writers such as Van Wyck Brooks, Lewis MUMFORD and others, included contributions by Ernest HEMINGWAY, Gertrude STEIN, and John DOS PASSOS. Its main mission was to promote and encourage great contemporary literature.

American Heritage periodical

This historical magazine was first published in 1949. It began as a modest publication of the American Association for State and Local History, but in the 1950s, under the editorship of the popular Civil War historian Bruce Catton, the magazine expanded its focus and attracted a large audience. The magazine is distinguished for its well-illustrated and elegantly written articles on all aspects of American history and culture.

American Literary Scholarship periodical

Published by Duke University since 1964, this annual volume contains commentary on the year's scholarly publications on major American authors. Scholarly articles and books are annotated in bibliographical essays, emphasizing the most important research and literary criticism.

American Literature periodical

Founded in 1929, this academic journal of literary criticism is published by Duke University Press. It is an indispensable guide for scholars and students of American literature. In addition to lengthy articles on major American authors and literary movements, the journal contains reviews of important new books on American literature and maintains an up-to-date bibliography of current research.

American Mercury periodical

A magazine founded in 1924 by H. L. MENCKEN. The editor's wide-ranging interests led to the publication of articles on American culture in all its manifestations by major writers such as Margaret Mead and Lewis MUMFORD. Even more important, Mencken published major fiction by William FAULKNER and Sinclair LEWIS, and poetry by Carl SANDBURG and James Weldon JOHNSON. When Mencken retired in 1933, the magazine ceased to have an impact on American literature.

American Scholar periodical

Published by the honor society Phi Beta Kappa since 1932, this magazine appeals to a broad-based audience of intellectuals. Articles on social, literary, and historical matters are written in a style suited to nonspecialists. The magazine became known for its cultivation of the literate, elegant essay form.

American Spectator periodical

Published from 1932 to 1937, this monthly literary magazine was founded by the drama critic George Jean NATHAN and thrived due to his superb taste in literature. In its prime it published the best of contemporary American writers, including Eugene O'NEILL, James Branch CABELL, Theodore DREISER, and Sherwood ANDERSON. When the magazine was sold in 1935, it became a bimonthly, and the spirit that animated the magazine disappeared.

American Tragedy, An Theodore Dreiser (1926)
novel

Dreiser's great naturalistic novel, based on a real murder case, has often been cited as a precursor of what Truman

CAPOTE later called the nonfiction novel, because Dreiser blends the narrative skills of a novelist with the documentary record of a crime.

Clyde Griffiths is a teenager in Kansas City, Missouri, who accompanies his parents on their outings to evangelize on the street and sing hymns. Hoping to better himself and leave behind his shabby family, he secures a job at a soda fountain in the Green-Davidson Hotel. There he befriends the bellboys and meets promiscuous girls, but this part of his life ends suddenly when he is involved in a car accident that kills a little girl.

Clyde runs away and takes various jobs in different cities. At the Union League Club in Chicago he learns that his rich uncle, Samuel Griffiths, is in town. Clyde introduces himself, and his uncle offers him a job in his shirt and collar factory in Lycurgus, New York.

The socially inferior Clyde is rarely invited to his rich relative's home. Feeling isolated and alone, he meets and falls in love with Roberta Alden, one of the workers he supervises. Then he meets Sondra Finchley, the daughter of a wealthy Lycurgus manufacturer. Obsessed with Sondra, Clyde now desperately seeks some way to separate from Roberta. When he discovers that she is pregnant, he believes that to marry her would end his dreams of social and economic success.

Frenzied with worry, Clyde invites Roberta on an excursion at a remote lake. Clyde knows that she cannot swim. Although he has planned to kill Roberta and make her death look like an accident, on the lake he is suddenly overcome by anxiety. Roberta, sensing his distress, moves toward him. He suddenly strikes at her and swims away when she topples into the water.

Not having thought out how he would evade capture, Clyde is arrested and convicted of murder. In the novel's last pages—a harrowing account of his life inside prison—Clyde tries to find peace and to come to terms with what he has done, but he is overwhelmed by the forces of society and his own conflicting feelings.

Sources

Bloom, Harold, ed. *Theodore Dreiser's An American Tragedy.* New York: Chelsea House, 1988.
Orlov, Paul A. *An American Tragedy: Perils of the Self Seeking "Success."* Lewisburg, Penn.: Bucknell University Press, 1998.

Anaya, Rudolfo (1937–) *novelist*

Anaya was born in Pastura, New Mexico, of Mexican-American parents and educated at the University of New Mexico. His first novel, *Bless Me Ultima* (1972), made his reputation. It deals with the social implications of the atomic blast at White Sands, New Mexico. His later work, including *Heart of Aztlan* (1976) and *Tortuga* (1979) has been associated with the school of magical realism, a term often used for fiction that is set in a realistic locale—sometimes described in meticulous historical terms—and yet is full of characters and incidents that defy cause-and-effect explanations. His work deeply probes the past of the Southwest, which becomes at once a mythical and physical reality. Anaya has been active in promoting Chicano literature, and published *Cuentos Chicanos: A Short Story Anthology* in 1984. His other novels include *Albuquerque* (1992), *Zia Summer* (1995), *Jalamanta* (1996), and *Rio Grande Fall* (1996). His short stories have been collected in *The Silence of the Llano* (1982).

Sources

Dick, Bruce, and Silvio Sirias, eds. *Conversations with Rudolfo Anaya.* Jackson: University Press of Mississippi, 1998.
Vasallo, Paul, ed. *The Magic of Words: Rudolfo Anaya and His Writings.* Albuquerque: University of New Mexico Press, 1982.

Anderson, Margaret (1886–1973) *editor*

Anderson was the founder and editor of THE LITTLE REVIEW, one of the most significant of the literary LITTLE MAGAZINES. She ran the magazine from 1914 to 1929 in an uncompromising fashion, interested only in great literature, which she took to be one of the supreme reasons for living. She published Sherwood ANDERSON, Vachel LINDSAY, William Carlos WILLIAMS, and other important artists and critics, and is remembered for publishing excerpts from James Joyce's *Ulysses.* The U.S. Postal Service confiscated and burned four issues of her magazine because it was deemed pornographic. She tells her story in her memoir, *My Thirty Years War* (1930).

Anderson, Maxwell (1888–1959) *playwright, poet*

A winner of the Pulitzer Prize for *Both Your Houses* (1933), a political satire about a young congressman who is defeated by a corrupt system, Anderson was born in Atlantic, Pennsylvania, and attended the University of North Dakota and Stanford University. His most famous work, in collaboration with Laurence STALLINGS, is *What Price Glory* (1924), which probed WORLD WAR I combat with considerable realism, and his verse dramas *Elizabeth the Queen* (1930) and *Mary of Scotland* (1933). But his best work may be *Winterset,* based on the famous SACCO-VANZETTI CASE, because it probes the immigrant milieu with such psychological penetration and compassion.

Sources

Shivers, Alfred S. *The Life of Maxwell Anderson.* New York: Stein and Day, 1983.
———. *Maxwell Anderson: An Annotated Bibliography of Primary and Secondary Works.* Metuchen, N.J.: Scarecrow Press, 1985.

Anderson, Robert (1917–) *playwright*

A New York City native who studied at Harvard, Anderson served in the navy in World War II and turned his experience into an award-winning play, *Come Marching Home* (1945). His two most important and best-known plays are *Tea and Sympathy* (1953), a moving depiction of a young boy accused of homosexuality, and *I Never Sang for My Father* (1968), a melancholy drama of a father-son conflict.

Sources

Adler, Thomas P. *Robert Anderson.* Boston: Twayne, 1978.

Anderson, Sherwood (1876–1941) *novelist, short story writer, autobiographer*

Anderson was born in Camden, Ohio, and his family moved to Clyde, Ohio, when he was eight. This small Ohio town became the inspiration for much of his greatest fiction, which emphasizes an era of innocence and a preindustrial world where town and village values prevailed.

Anderson's family was extremely poor, a fact reflected in his many compassionate stories and novels about the underprivileged. But Anderson also believed in the American dream, and as a boy he read the Horatio Alger novels about the way to succeed. He worked in a paint factory, married, and lived a conventional life in Elyria, Ohio, until 1911, when the restless Anderson walked away from his dreams of business success and moved to Chicago. There he wrote autobiographical fiction, beginning with *Windy McPherson's Son* (1916), which contains an excoriating portrait of his alcoholic father.

Anderson's first great literary achievement came with the publication of *Winesburg, Ohio* (1919), a collection of stories so closely interrelated that it can be read as a novel. It concentrates on George Willard, a young man who gradually loses his innocence and develops a vision of the world that outstrips the provincial milieu of his small town. At the same time, that small town is rendered in accurate, loving detail. *Winesburg, Ohio* and the stories Anderson collected in *The Triumph of the Egg* (1921) greatly influenced William FAULKNER, who wrote a tribute to Anderson and credited him with showing how Faulkner's own "little postage stamp" of soil merited fictional treatment. Anderson had a similar influence on Ernest HEMINGWAY, although Hemingway's early novel, *Torrents of Spring*, satirizes Anderson's sentimental side.

Anderson's other long fiction was not as successful as *Winesburg, Ohio*, although such novels as *Poor White* (1920) and *Dark Laughter* (1925) contain powerful scenes and memorable portraits of the poor and of African Americans.

Aside from his short stories, Anderson's most important work was done in autobiography. *A Story Teller's Story* (1924) and *Tar: A Midwest Childhood* (1926) are brilliant confections of fact and fiction. *Sherwood Anderson's Memoirs* (1942) was published the year after he died.

Anderson's other important books include *Horses and Men* (1923), a collection of short stories, and *Death in the Wood and Other Stories* (1947). *The Letters of Sherwood Anderson* was published in 1953.

Sources

Anderson, David D., ed. *Sherwood Anderson: Dimension of His Literary Art.* East Lansing: Michigan State University Press, 1976.

Papinchak, Robert Allan. *Sherwood Anderson: A Study of the Short Fiction.* New York: Twayne, 1992.

White, Ray Lewis, ed. *The Achievement of Sherwood Anderson: Essays in Criticism.* Chapel Hill: University of North Carolina Press, 1966.

Angelou, Maya (Marguerite Johnson) (1928–) *autobiographer, poet, educator*

Angelou was born in St. Louis, Missouri. Her parents divorced when she was three, and she was brought up by relatives in Stamps, Arkansas. She was not reunited with her mother until her high school years in San Francisco. Her wayward existence led to a teenage pregnancy and the birth of a child, although she still managed to graduate from high school at 16. Before finding her vocation as a writer, Angelou worked as a cook, maid, prostitute, dancer, actress, singer, songwriter, and social activist on behalf of Martin Luther King Jr. She also joined the Harlem Writers Guild, in which she met James BALDWIN and Paule MARSHALL. She was encouraged to tell her life story by the wife of cartoonist Jules FEIFFER. Judy Feiffer put a Random House editor in touch with Angelou, who produced her first and most famous autobiography, *I Know Why the Caged Bird Sings* (1970), which won the National Book Award and has become a classic of American literature for its lyrical style, its candor about a woman's life, and its grappling with issues of African-American identity. Angelou has published several more volumes of distinguished autobiography: *Gather Together in My Name* (1974), *Singin' and Swingin' and Gettin' Merry Like Christmas* (1976), *The Heart of a Woman* (1981), and *All God's Children Need Traveling Shoes* (1986). She has also published poetry: *Just Give Me a Cool Drink 'fore I Diiie* (1971), *Oh Pray My Wings Are Gonna Fit Me Well* (1975), *And Still I Rise* (1978), *Shaker, Why Don't You Sing?* (1983), and *I Shall Not Be Moved* (1990). In 1977, she received an Emmy nomination for her role in the television dramatization of Alex HALEY's *Roots.* President Clinton commissioned her to write "On the Pulse of Morning," which she read at his 1992 inauguration.

Sources

Bloom, Harold, ed. *Maya Angelou.* Philadelphia: Chelsea House Publishers, 1998.

Elliott, Jeffrey M., ed. *Conversations with Maya Angelou.* Jackson: University Press of Mississippi, 1989.

Lupton, Mary Jane. *Maya Angelou: A Critical Companion*. Westport, Conn.: Greenwood Press, 1998.

Angstrom, Harry "Rabbit" character

The main character in John UPDIKE's tetralogy: *Rabbit Run* (1960), *Rabbit Redux* (1971), *Rabbit is Rich* (1981), and *Rabbit at Rest* (1990). Each novel charts Rabbit's sojourn in a different decade of American culture. In the 1950s he is the frustrated American male, a high school basketball hero but a failure as an adult, fleeing his wife and family responsibilities. In the 1960s and 1970s he settles down, working with his father at a printing company, but is bedeviled by his wife's errant behavior, which includes an affair. In the 1980s Rabbit becomes a prosperous car salesman, now worried about his son, a college dropout. In the 1990s he is retired, has a mistress, and is worried about his heart. But he continues to live recklessly, eating bad food and conducting an affair. He is near the end of his saga. A massive heart attack sends him to the hospital, where he may die.

Arendt, Hannah (1906–1975) essayist, political philosopher

Born and educated in Germany, Arendt fled from the Nazis and immigrated to the United States in 1941. Steeped in German philosophy, a student and lover of the philosopher Martin Heidegger, Arendt was peculiarly sensitive to the complexities of the modern world, and she became one of a forceful group of European thinkers who found refuge in America, especially in New York and Los Angeles. Arendt found it difficult to write in English and relied on editing from American friends and associates, but she threw herself into American life with vigor and sensitivity. She was befriended by the NEW YORK INTELLECTUALS, especially Alfred KAZIN, whose work was influenced by hers, and by Mary MCCARTHY, who became Arendt's confidant and promoter. Arendt wrote on the nature of totalitarianism for periodicals such as *Partisan Review* and in her books *Origins of Totalitarianism* (1951), *The Human Condition* (1958), and *Eichmann in Jerusalem* (1963), which grew out of a series of reports for the *NEW YORKER*. Her work sparked enormous controversy and debate after she coined the phrase "banality of evil" to characterize the Nazi official Adolf Eichmann's rather bland and seemingly matter-of-fact defense of his crimes that he was merely carrying out orders from his superiors. She also became a center of controversy for suggesting that the Jews of Europe did not do enough to forestall the Holocaust. She wrote one more book before she died, *On Violence* (1970).

Sources

Hinchman, Lewis P. and Sandra K. Hinchman, eds. *Hannah Arendt: Critical Essays*. Albany: State University of New York Press, 1994.

Young-Bruehl, Elisabeth. *Hannah Arendt: For Love of the World*. New Haven, Conn.: Yale University Press, 1982.

Arnow, Harriet (1908–1986) novelist

Born in Wayne County, Kentucky, Arnow went to Berea College to become a teacher, but she soon yearned to write. She wrote a series of novels about her native region, the most famous of which is *The Dollmaker* (1954). The novel describes an Appalachian woman and her family, whose lives embody the pain and confusion that occurred during the mass migration of more than seven million people from rural Appalachia to northern cities in the 1940s to seek employment. Arnow herself experienced this migration as she moved from Louisville to Cincinnati to Detroit.

Sources

Chung, Haeja K., ed. *Harriet Simpson Arnow: Critical Essays on Her Work*. East Lansing: Michigan State University Press, 1995.

Ashbery, John Lawrence (1927–   ) poet

Born in Rochester, New York, John Ashbery studied at the Deerfield Academy, Harvard, and Columbia University. W. H. AUDEN and Wallace STEVENS have been the greatest influences on his poetry. He is often associated with the NEW YORK SCHOOL OF POETS, which also included Kenneth KOCH and Frank O'HARA. Like them, he has been influenced by modern art, especially ABSTRACT EXPRESSIONISM. He is considered a difficult, elusive poet because of the complexity of his metaphors, yet he achieved critical renown relatively early in his poetic career. He won the National Book Award, National Book Critics Circle Award, and Pulitzer Prize in 1975 for *Self-Portrait in a Convex Mirror*. He has a devoted following among academics who are attached to his experiments in form and his highly developed aesthetic sense, although some critics find his work too abstruse. His other collections of poetry include *Some Trees* (1956), *The Tennis Court Oath* (1962), *Selected Poems* (1967), *The Double Dream of Spring* (1970), *The Vermont Notebook* (1975), *Houseboat Days* (1977), *As We Know* (1979), *Selected Poems* (1985), *Three Books* (1993), and *And the Stars Were Shining* (1994).

Sources

Bloom, Harold, ed. *John Ashbery*. New York: Chelsea House, 1985.

Schultz, Susan M. *The Tribe of John: Ashbery and Contemporary Poetry*. Tuscaloosa: University of Alabama Press, 1995.

Asian-American literature

Early 20th-century Asian-American literature focused on autobiographies that told the story of immigration to the

United States and of memories of the homeland. Younghill KANG's *Grass Roof* (1931) and *East Goes West* (1937) are the best examples of the genre. Toshio Mori was one of the first Asian Americans to write fiction about Japanese-American life. His collection of short stories, *Yokohama, California,* appeared in 1949. In *America Is in the Heart* (1943), an autobiographical novel, Carlos BULOSAN depicted the struggle of Filipino immigrants who worked as farm laborers and experienced harsh discrimination.

Beginning in the late 1940s, a steady succession of novels addressed Asian-American family life and community concerns: Lin Yutang, *A Chinatown Family* (1948); C. Y. Lee *Flower Drum Song* (1957); Louis Chu, *Eat a Bowl of Tea* (1961); Virginia Lee, *The House that Tai Ming Built* (1963); and Chuang Hua, *Crossings* (1968). These portrayals of Chinese-American life were not matched by Japanese-American writers, many of whom wanted to forget the bombing of Pearl Harbor and their families' dreadful experiences in American detention camps. With the exception of John Okada's *No-No Boy* (1957), it was not until the 1970s that Japanese-American novelists began to address the experience of World War II and contemporary life in America. The civil rights movement and the increasing interest in ethnic literature encouraged Asian Americans not only to write about their experiences but also to see their writing as a contribution to American literature and to popular culture.

The prominence and value of Asian-American literature became evident in the work of two best-selling authors, Maxine Hong KINGSTON and Amy TAN. Kingston's *The Woman Warrior* (1976), *China Men* (1980), and *Tripmaster Monkey* (1989) combined autobiography, fiction, and feminist concerns in a style that attracted a national audience, best-seller status, and critical praise. Similarly, Amy Tan's *The Joy Luck Club* (1989), *The Kitchen God's Wife* (1991), and *The Hundred Secret Senses* (1995) appealed to a broad range of readers who became interested not merely in her ethnic background but also in the relationships she portrayed between women, their families, and their communities.

Also important has been Asian-American drama. R. A. Shiomi's *Yellow Fever* (1982), Philip Gotanda's *Fish Head Soup* (1986), David HWANG's *FOB* (1979), and Wakako Yamauchi's *And the Soul Shall Dance* (1982) reveal the humiliation Asian Americans have suffered in mainstream American culture but also celebrate the strengths of Asian-American families and communities. Hwang has attracted a large audience with his dramas that probe the nature of identity—sexual as well as ethnic—in his immensely successful play and movie *M Butterfly* (1989).

Beginning in the late 1970s Asian-American poets began to publish books that captured memories of Asia and the manners and customs of Asian-American communities. Some of the more noteworthy works are Eric Chock's *Ten Thousand Wishes* (1978), Fay Chiang's *In the City of Contra-dictions* (1979), Ronald Tanaka's *Shino Suite* (1981), Chungmi Kim's *Selected Poems* (1982), Amy Ling's *Chinamerica Reflections* (1984), and David MURA's *After We Lost Our Way* (1989).

Important anthologies of Asian-American literature include *Aiiieeeee! An Anthology of Asian-American Writers* (1974); *The Big Aiieeeee! An Anthology of Asian-American Writers* (1990); and *Making More Waves: New Writing by Asian-American Women* (1997).

Sources

Bloom, Harold, ed. *Asian-American Writers.* New York: Chelsea House, 1999.

Cho, Song. *Rice: Explorations into Gay Asian Culture & Politics.* Toronto: Queer Press, 1998.

Trudeau, Lawrence, ed. *Asian American Literature: Reviews and Criticism of Works by American Writers of Asian Descent.* Detroit: Gale Research, 1999.

Wu, Jean Yu-wen Shen and Min Song, eds. *Asian American Studies: A Reader.* New Brunswick, N.J.: Rutgers University Press, 2000.

As I Lay Dying *William Faulkner* (1930) *novel*
Faulkner's experimental, tragicomic novel about the Bundren family's journey to bury their mother is composed of a sequence of interior monologues. Addie Bundren speaks from beyond the grave, commenting on her life as a woman and mother. Anse, her slow-witted but dogged husband, takes the family on their improbable journey to Jefferson, Mississippi, to bury Addie where she was born. Anse persists in the journey through flood and fire, even after the body begins to decompose. Darl, one of the sons, is the most sensitive member of the family and is so disturbed by the events of the journey that he ends up in a mental institution. Dewey Dell, Addie's 17-year-old daughter, is pregnant, and searches on the trip for a way to get an abortion. Like the other characters, she speaks in a language that is not so much the way she would actually talk as a reflection of her intense feelings: "I feel like a hot seed in the wet blind earth," she says to herself. Jewel, the illegitimate son of Addie and the Reverend Whitfield, does not know that he is his mother's love child. Jewel and his half brother Cash are the most levelheaded members of the family, while Vardaman, the youngest child, hardly knows what is happening.

No description of the plot or the characters of the novel can do justice to its beautifully crafted language and structure. Faulkner uses an intense and elevated style to explore the uniqueness of each character. But he is also keenly observant of the way in which the Bundrens—for all their differences—act together as a family unit. Only Darl cannot reconcile himself to family or society. The novel captures both the heroism and the absurdity of the trip, which is Faulkner's supreme achievement in the tragicomic mode.

As I Lay Dying is often paired with THE SOUND AND THE FURY as Faulkner's two most important works of experimental fiction.

Sources
Cox, Dianne L., ed. *William Faulkner's As I Lay Dying: A Critical Casebook.* New York: Garland, 1985.

Asimov, Isaac (1920–1992) *novelist*
Asimov moved with his family to the United States from Russia when he was three. In New York, his parents opened a candy store. He went to high school in Brooklyn and studied chemistry at Columbia University, earning a B.A. in 1939 and an M.A. in 1941. He worked as a chemist in the navy during World War II and taught afterwards at Boston University's School of Medicine, where he became an associate professor in 1955.

He began writing science fiction in the late 1930s. *Pebble in the Sky* (1950) was his first science fiction novel. By 1958, he was writing full time. An extraordinarily prolific writer, he produced well over 400 books, including nonfiction titles such as the *New Intelligent Man's Guide to Science.* But he is best known for his science fiction Foundation Trilogy, loosely based on the history of the Roman Empire.

Like many genre writers, Asimov constructed intricate, well-made plots but rarely explored human character or psychology to any great degree. His work emphasizes how worlds are constructed, maintained, and destroyed. Among his noteworthy books are *Foundation* (1951), *Foundation and Empire* (1952), *Second Foundation* (1953), *The Martian Way and Other Stories* (1955), *Fantastic Voyage* (1966), *Buy Jupiter and Other Stories* (1975), *The Bicentennial Man and Other Stories* (1976), *Foundation's Edge* (1982), *Foundation and Earth* (1986), *Prelude to Foundation* (1988), and *Robot Visions* (1990). Asimov greatly expanded the range of subjects for science fiction, grounding it in his superb grasp of modern science. He also wrote several children's books: *Space Ranger* (1952), *The Rings of Saturn* (1974), and *Limericks for Children* (1981).

Sources
Gunn, James. *Isaac Asimov: The Foundations of Science Fiction.* Metuchen, N.J.: Scarecrow Press, 1996.

Touponce, William F. *Isaac Asimov.* Boston: Twayne, 1991.

White, Michael. *Asimov: The Unauthorised Life.* London: Millennium, 1994.

Atherton, Gertrude (1857–1948) *novelist, short story writer, biographer*
Born in San Francisco, Atherton wrote novels, short fiction, biographies, and histories. Her first important work was *The Californians* (1898), which announced her basic interest in California—its people and geography, past and present. She also published *California: An Intimate History* (1914). Some critics have called her work uneven, but Atherton was a wide-ranging writer who wrote on many different themes with original results. *The Conqueror* (1902) is a fictional biography of Alexander Hamilton that has been praised for its innovative form. Her novel, *Black Oxen* (1923), with its emphasis on the sexual nature of life, became popular and controversial; critics compared it to HEMINGWAY's THE SUN ALSO RISES and James Branch CABELL's *Jurgen*. She deals with her own work in *Adventures of a Novelist* (1932), which has been praised for its remarkable candor. Her female characters tend to be restless and unconventional, perhaps reflecting her own 11 years of an unhappy marriage, which ended when her husband died and she could pursue a full-time writing career in New York City. Her last two novels, *The House of Lee* (1940) and *The Horn of Life* (1942), address the changes in women's lives following World War II. Atherton also produced *My San Francisco* (1947), which is both a memoir and a history of the California that formed her.

Sources
Leider, Emily Wortis. *California's Daughter: Gertrude Atherton and Her Times.* Stanford, Calif.: Stanford University Press, 1991.

McClure, Charlotte S. *Gertrude Atherton.* Boston: Twayne, 1979.

Atlantic Monthly *periodical*
Founded in 1857, this magazine of literary and current events magazine initially published notable New England writers such as Ralph Waldo Emerson and Harriet Beecher Stowe. In the 20th century it has broadened both its range of writers and readers. Under the editorship of Edward Weeks (1938–1966), the magazine introduced regular discussions of international events. It also continued to publish distinguished short fiction by important writers such as Bernard MALAMUD, Raymond CARVER, and Louise ERDRICH.

Auchincloss, Louis Stanton (1917–) *novelist*
A lawyer who has written numerous books on high society, especially as seen from the 1880s to World War I, Louis Auchincloss was born in Lawrence, New York, and educated at private schools, including Yale. He served in the navy during World War II, but otherwise has spent his entire life in New York City. Auchincloss writes about the descendants of the New World aristocrats that Edith WHARTON and Henry James portrayed in their fiction. He regards himself as an observer, eschewing labels such as satirist or social critic. Like Wharton, he has an almost anthropological interest in peoples' manners and their codes of behavior. Like Wharton, he is not as fastidious as James in probing human psychology, preferring to focus on the story instead of the consciousness

of its narrator. Auchincloss has been praised for his elegant, concise prose. He is a prolific writer of fiction and nonfiction. Among his more important novels are *The Romantic Egoists* (1954), *The Rector of Justin* (1965), *Diary of a Yuppie* (1986), and *Three Lives* (1993). He has written well about other writers in *Edith Wharton* (1961), *Ellen Glasgow* (1964), *Pioneers and Caretakers: A Study of Nine American Women Novelists* (1965), *Edith Wharton: A Woman of Her Time* (1971), and *Reading Henry James* (1975). Of his own work he writes perspicaciously in *A Writer's Capital* (1974). His handling of dual careers in the law and literature is canvassed in *Life, Law, and Letters: Essays and Sketches* (1979). He has also edited several books, including *An Edith Wharton Reader* (1965) and *Diaries of Old Manhattan* (1989). In 2000, he published a biography, *Woodrow Wilson*.

Sources

Gelderman, Carol. *Louis Auchincloss: A Writer's Life.* New York: Crown, 1993.
Parsell, David B. *Louis Auchincloss.* Boston: Twayne, 1988.

Auden, Wynstan Hugh (1907–1973) *poet, dramatist, critic*

Although W. H. Auden was born in England and is considered an English poet, he immigrated to the United States in 1939 and became an American citizen in 1946. Educated at Oxford, he became for the Left in England and the United States the example of a great poet who was also a progressive in political matters—opposing Yeats, T. S. ELIOT, and POUND, whose fascist tendencies embarrassed many advocates of MODERNISM. Auden published in American periodicals such as the NEW YORKER and the NEW YORK REVIEW OF BOOKS and served as a consultant to the YALE SERIES OF YOUNGER POETS, which became a means of recognizing and furthering the careers of several generations of American poets. He also edited the influential anthology *The Faber Book of Modern American Verse* (1956). He was a part of the New York literary scene and taught and gave readings at many American universities and colleges. *The Age of Anxiety* (1947), a collection of essays, won a Pulitzer Prize. His *Collected Poems* appeared in 1976.

A brilliant essayist as well, Auden helped to define the modern age for the Anglo-American community, emphasizing both the social and political commitment of the writer as well as his dedication to the highest literary standards. His most notable nonfiction includes *The Enchafed Flood* (1950), *The Dyer's Hand and Other Essays* (1962), *Selected Essays* (1964), *Forewords and Afterwords* (1973).

Auden's most noteworthy plays are *The Dog Beneath the Skin* (1935) and *The Ascent of F6*—both written with Christopher ISHERWOOD, who accompanied Auden on his journey to America, becoming part of the flourishing expatriate community in southern California during World War II.

Sources

McDiarmid, Lucy. *Auden's Apologies for Poetry.* Princeton, N.J.: Princeton University Press, 1990.
Mendelson, Edward. *Later Auden.* London: Faber & Faber, 1999.

Auster, Paul (1947–) *novelist, short story writer*

Auster, a New Jersey native, is best known for his New York trilogy (1986), three mystery stories (*City of Glass, Ghosts,* and *The Locked Room*) that have been widely praised as metaphysical thrillers because his characters probe the mysteries of identity without necessarily finding solutions to their problems and cases. His fiction is distinguished by his subtle use of language to explore obsessive states of mind. His later work includes *Leviathan* (1992), *Mr. Vertigo* (1994), and *Timbuktu* (1999).

Sources

Barone, Dennis, ed. *Beyond The Red Notebook: Essays on Paul Auster.* Philadelphia: University of Pennsylvania Press, 1995.

Authors League of America *organization*

Founded in 1911, the Authors League, which includes the Authors' Guild and the Dramatists' Guild, is dedicated to protecting the rights of authors. The League is active in examining issues related to authors' copyright, publishers' contracts, the development of the literary marketplace, innovations in electronic publishing, and other legal and societal developments that have an impact on the livelihood and integrity of the writing profession.

Autobiography of an Ex-Colored Man, The James Weldon Johnson (1912) *novel*

James Weldon Johnson's provocative account of an African-American man who tries to "pass" as white is one of the formative novels of the African-American experience. The work was first published anonymously, which enhanced its appeal as a story from a person who had been compelled to live in disguise, hiding his origins and identity. The novel's theme of a dual or double consciousness, and the narrator's statement that he is much more keenly aware of what white people think than white people are of African Americans, introduces themes that would resound in later classics of African-American literature such as Ralph ELLISON's INVISIBLE MAN.

The novel's narrator is the child of a white southerner and a light-skinned African-American woman. He grows up in a small Connecticut town, where he early on exhibits great talent as a pianist. Discovering that he is black, the narrator resolves to attend a Negro college. After his money is stolen, however, he is forced to take a job in a cigar factory among African Americans of varying backgrounds, beliefs, and shades of color. When the factory closes, the narrator heads for New York City and a bohemian life. He finds a job as a ragtime musician, is adopted by a white patron, tours Europe, and decides to adapt his knowledge of African-American music into traditional European art forms. A trip south, where he witnesses a lynching, drives him to repudiate his artistic commitment and to return to New York City. There he passes for white, determined never to suffer the outrages against blacks that he has witnessed. On the white side of the color line he raises a family in the full knowledge that he has repudiated his ancestry.

Johnson did not acknowledge authorship of the novel until 1927. It is not only a remarkable work of literature, narrated with poetic economy, but also a work prophetic of the struggle of many African-American authors, such as James BALDWIN, to maintain some balance between their commitment to art and their rage at social and racial injustice.

Sources

Sundquist, Eric. *The Hammers of Creation: Folk Culture in Modern African-American Fiction.* Athens: University of Georgia Press, 1992.

Autobiography of Malcolm X, The Malcolm X with Alex Haley (1965) autobiography

The account of the rise of a black militant leader, his role in the Black Muslim movement, and his breakaway to become an independent spokesman for African-American freedom has become a staple of the American canon. It was written by Alex Haley, who interviewed Malcolm X and shaped his words into a well-edited narrative. The book appeared after Malcolm X's assassination in 1965, and it did much not only to make him a legend but also to fuel the Black Power Movement. The autobiography is the riveting story of an African American who grows up as "Red" in East Lansing, Michigan. He becomes a street hustler, a convict, a Nation of Islam (Black Muslim) minister, and a black nationalist. Haley gives Malcolm X's story a fablelike quality, and Malcolm X himself proves to be a keen observer. The men who run the numbers racket on the street, for example, are shown to be of considerable intelligence and shrewdness, choosing an illegal occupation because it is lucrative and suits their status as part of a race marginalized by a dominant white society. Malcolm X also dramatizes his own changing racial perspective—from narrow-minded dedication to hatred of whites fomented by the Nation of Islam to his own more tolerant and sophisticated views that developed out of his world tour of Islamic societies.

Clearly, Malcolm's X's thinking was still evolving when Haley interviewed him for the book. It has been said there are "many Malcolms" in the book. The protean nature of its protagonist, his evolving identity, makes *The Autobiography of Malcolm X* not only a classic of African-American literature but also an indispensable text for the study of American literature whose great works have continued to question the nature of the American character.

Sources

Andrews, William L., ed. *African American Autobiography: A Collection of Critical Essays.* Englewood Cliffs, N.J.: Prentice Hall, 1993.

Wood, Joe, ed. *Malcolm X: In Our Own Image.* New York: St. Martin's Press, 1992.

Babbitt *Sinclair Lewis* (1922) *novel*

Sinclair Lewis's satirical portrait of an American business-man and of middle-class midwestern life in the 1920s centers on George Follansbee Babbitt, a successful realtor. Babbitt thinks of himself as an average American. He lives in Zenith, a typical small town. He is a faithful, if not romantic husband. He has three children, a nice home, and all the modern conveniences. He believes in progress, and that society is gradually reforming itself. Yet he feels frustrated, imagining he has never done a daring thing in his life. He has a fantasy that he is visited by a "fairy child," a young, desirable woman who appreciates the dashing true self hidden behind Babbitt's dull exterior.

After his closest friend, Paul Riesling, one of Zenith's leading citizens, shoots his wife and is sent to prison, Babbitt abandons propriety and begins to have affairs. He tries to reform himself but realizes he cannot go back to the status quo. The prospect of a new, truly risky career disturbs him. When his wife has an attack of appendicitis, he recovers his affection for her and reconciles himself to his middle-class life. He realizes, however, that something is missing, and he urges his son to pursue a less conventional course. "Do not be bound by Zenith," he tells Ted, "tell 'em to go to the Devil!"

So effective was Lewis's portrayal of Babbitt as a type that the name became synonymous with a type of American boosterism that touted material well-being over any sort of spiritual, intellectual, or sensual satisfaction. Certainly Lewis satirizes American complacency, but his vivid characterization of Babbitt makes the character a whole human being, not simply the target of social criticism.

Sources

Grebstein, Sheldon. *Sinclair Lewis.* New York: Twayne, 1962.

Lingeman, Richard. *Sinclair Lewis: Rebel from Main Street.* New York: Random House, 2002.

Schorer, Mark, ed. *Sinclair Lewis: A Collection of Critical Essays.* Englewood Cliffs, N.J.: Prentice Hall, 1962.

Babbitt, Irving (1865–1933) *critic*

Born in Ohio, Babbitt graduated from Harvard and was a professor at Williams College, then at Harvard University, from 1894 to 1933. An outstanding scholar, he promulgated the idea of a "New Humanism," which rejected the romanticism of the 19th century and argued for a return to more classical values such as an appreciation of literary form. His most important work is *Rousseau and Romanticism* (1919), which presents his most effective argument against relying on intense emotion and personal feeling rather than on tradition. T. S. ELIOT studied under Babbitt and was influenced by him, although the poet ultimately rejected the idea of the New Humanism in favor of a more traditional allegiance to orthodox Christianity.

Sources

Panichas, George. *The Critical Legacy of Irving Babbitt: An Appreciation.* Wilmington, Del.: ISI Books, 1999.

Baldwin, James (1924–1987) *novelist, essayist*

Baldwin was born and grew up in Harlem, the son of a preacher, whom Baldwin was to write about in his first remarkable novel, *Go Tell It on the Mountain* (1953). From his early saturation in the black church, Baldwin moved to an immersion in literature, especially in novels like *Uncle Tom's Cabin* and the works of Charles Dickens. One of the turning points in Baldwin's life came when he took classes from the HARLEM RENAISSANCE poet Countee CULLEN.

By the mid-1940s Baldwin was living in Greenwich Village, where he met the great African-American novelist Richard WRIGHT. By 1946 Baldwin was writing essays for national magazines. In 1948, he moved to Paris, looking—as did his mentor, Wright—for an environment in which to write and to be free from racism. But Baldwin's removal to Paris was also a declaration of independence from his literary influences, including Wright, whose novel, *Native Son,* Baldwin criticized in *Notes of a Native Son* (1955). Baldwin rejected Wright's NATURALISM for a more supple form of literary narrative often associated with the stylistic and psychological complexities of Henry James.

Baldwin returned to the United States in 1957 to report on the civil rights movement. His essays, collected in *Nobody Knows My Name: More Notes of a Native Son* (1961) and *The Fire Next Time* (1963), transformed Baldwin into a national spokesman on matters of race. At the same time, the essays were so eloquent and polished that they enhanced Baldwin's literary reputation. He wrote with enormous authority, melding his experience with the history of African Americans, while engaging other writers—white and black—in a national dialogue.

None of Baldwin's later work in fiction and nonfiction quite matched the brilliance of his writing in the 1950s and 1960s, when he achieved notable success with a novel, *Another Country* (1962), and a play, *Blues for Mister Charlie* (1964).

Baldwin's other novels include *Giovanni's Room* (1956), *Tell Me How Long the Train's Been Gone* (1968), *If Beale Street Could Talk* (1974), and *Just Above My Head* (1979). He collected his later essays in *No Name in the Street* (1971), *The Devil Finds Work* (1976), *The Evidence of Things Not Seen* (1985), and *The Price of the Ticket* (1985).

Sources

Campbell, James. *Talking at the Gates: A Life of James Baldwin.* New York: Viking, 1991.

Standley, Fred L. and Nancy V. Burt, eds. *Critical Essays on James Baldwin.* Boston: G. K. Hall, 1988.

Standley, Fred L. and Louis H. Pratt, eds. *Conversations with James Baldwin.* Jackson: University Press of Mississippi, 1989.

Bambara, Toni Cade (1939–1995) *novelist, short story writer, essayist, filmmaker, lecturer, educator*

Bambara's various careers were all infused with a sense of social mission and political activism. She was born in New York City and grew up in New Jersey and the South. With her father, she attended shows at the Apollo Theater in Harlem in the 1940s. Her mother inspired much of her early efforts to write—as did Bambara's friend, Toni MORRISON. After studying at Queens College and working in New York's City's welfare department, Bambara taught at City College while publishing stories and articles in such magazines as *Essence, Redbook, Negro Digest, Prairie Schooner, Phylon, Ms., Black World,* and *Liberator.* She held a number of visiting appointments at colleges and universities. In 1970 she published *The Black Woman,* an anthology that included the work of Alice WALKER, Paule MARSHALL, Nikki GIOVANNI, and other prominent African-American women as well as work by her students. A second anthology, *Tales and Stories for Black Folks,* was aimed specifically at high school and college students. It included stories by Langston HUGHES and Ernest J. GAINES, with more student contributions. She published two well-received collection of stories, *Gorilla, My Love* (1972) and *The Sea Birds Are Still Alive* (1977). Her first novel, *The Salt Eaters* (1981), won the American Book Award and brought together a lifetime of experience as a black woman, educator, and activist.

Bambara is one of the great stylists in the contemporary American short story, bringing to the form an exquisite feel for urban life and a mastery of colloquial language that is reminiscent of Mark Twain. When she died, she had almost completed a new novel, *These Bones Are Not My Child,* which deals with the Atlanta child murders in the early 1980s. Toni Morrison edited the 1,800-page manuscript and had it published in 1999.

Sources

Butler-Evans, Elliott. *Race, Gender, and Desire: Narrative Strategies in the Fiction of Toni Cade Bambara, Toni Morrison, and Alice Walker.* Philadelphia: Temple University Press, 1989.

Tate, Claudia, ed. *Black Woman Writers at Work.* New York: Continuum, 1983.

Banks, Russell (1940–) *novelist, publisher, editor*

Banks was educated at Colgate University in Hamilton, New York, and at the University of North Carolina. He formed the Lillabulero Press, which he ran from 1966 to 1975, and which published his first novel, *Waiting to Freeze* (1967). His other early work includes *Snow* (1975) and *Family Life* (1975). The novel *Hamilton Stark* (1978) is set in the rugged environment of New Hampshire, as is his collection of short stories, *Trailerpark* (1981). *The Relation of My Imprisonment* (1974) is a historical novel set in 17th-century New England. Three of Banks's later novels, *Continental Drift* (1985), *Affliction* (1989), and *The Sweet Hereafter* (1991), have been made into movies. They deal with working and middle-class characters—a school bus driver, an oil-burner repairman—and explore the nature of friendship and family conflicts. *The Book of Jamaica* (1980) is partly based on Banks's own experiences in the Caribbean. All of his work explores the internal lives of characters who come into conflict with social and economic forces. His most recent novels include *Rule of the Bone* (1995) and *Cloudsplitter* (1998), a novel about the 19th-century radical abolitionist John Brown.

Sources

Niemi, Robert. *Russell Banks*. New York: Twayne, 1997.

Baraka, Amiri (LeRoy Jones) (1934–) *poet, essayist, music critic, novelist, short story writer, playwright*

Born Everett LeRoy (later changed to LeRoi) Jones in Newark, New Jersey, Baraka attended public schools and then Rutgers and Howard universities. After a period of enlistment in the air force he settled in New York City, where he studied comparative literature at Columbia University and befriended many avant-garde artists on the LOWER EAST SIDE. Early on he was influenced by the BEATS. His first collection of poems, *Preface to a Twenty-Volume Suicide Note* (1964), and two absurdist plays, *The Baptism* and *The Toilet,* performed in 1961 and 1964 but published together in 1967, earned him early fame. Soon Baraka felt uncomfortable with the apolitical Beats, and he sought a way to wed the innovative forms of avant-garde art with a deep engagement with social issues.

In 1965 he published his only novel, *The System of Dante's Hell*, but he had already solidified his reputation with two provocative plays, *Dutchman* and *The Slave* (1964), and a collection of poems, *The Dead Lecturer* (1964). These works took on racial themes directly and were products of what came to be called the "BLACK AESTHETIC." In these works Baraka wrestles with the problem of being both an artist and a political activist, an African American engaged with his peoples' struggle and with his art. By the mid-1960s Baraka had committed himself to the Black Arts Repertory Theater/School, signaling his move away from his Greenwich Village roots. A few years later, Baraka moved back to Newark, established his own theater company, changed his name from Leroi Jones to Amiri Baraka, and became a militant Black Nationalist. In *Black Magic: Collected Poetry 1961–1967* (1969), *It's Nation Time* (1970), and *In Our Terribleness* (1970), Baraka takes on a prophetic role aimed at attacking white majority culture and radicalizing African-American readers. Baraka did not forsake his commitment to art and experiment, however, particularly in *Four Revolutionary Plays* (1969), which are in the tradition of modernist literature.

Throughout this period Baraka remained a political organizer at the Pan African Congress of African Peoples in Atlanta (1972) and the National Black Political Convention in Gary, Indiana (1974). He declared himself a Marxist-Leninist and published works that incorporated his support of Mao Zedong, Fidel Castro, and other Communist leaders.

Hard Facts (1975), *Poetry for the Advanced* (1979), and *Daggers and Javelins* (1984) reflect this mixture of Marxism and Black Nationalism, which received harsh treatment from certain critics. Baraka's role as an enabler of African-American culture—sponsoring artists and artistic movements—is impressive, although the extent to which his own work will provide an enduring legacy remains an open question.

Sources

Benston, Kimberly W. *Baraka: The Renegade and the Mask.* New Haven, Conn.: Yale University Press, 1976.

Harris, William J. *The Poetry and Poetics of Amiri Baraka: The Jazz Aesthetic.* Columbia: University of Missouri Press, 1985.

Barkley, Catherine *character*

Frederic Henry's tragic beloved in Ernest HEMINGWAY's romantic World War I novel, *A Farewell to Arms* (1929), she is an English nurse serving in Italy and has lost her sweetheart in the war. When she meets Henry, an American volunteer in the Italian army's ambulance corps, she is attracted to him, but he resists falling in love. After taking care of his wounded knee, Catherine becomes involved in his life, and soon they fall in love and plan to marry. She has a premonition that one or both of them will die. Henry returns to the front, but in disgust he deserts and reunites with Catherine in Milan. They hope to find a haven in Switzerland, where they spent the winter months of Catherine's pregnancy. After a difficult childbirth Catherine dies as an inconsolable Henry watches the rain, the very same rain that appeared in Catherine's premonition of death. The bleakness of the ending emphasizes the inevitability of human suffering and death, of which the war is merely one manifestation, and which Catherine has been conscious of much more than her lover.

Barnes, Djuna (1892–1982) *novelist, essayist, poet, playwright*

Barnes is best known for her classic novel, NIGHTWOOD (1936). She was born in Cornwall-on-Hudson, New York. She grew up in a household permeated with sexual tension (her father included in his household both his wife and mistress). She was educated at home by her father and mother and was heavily influenced by her grandmother's feminism and mysticism. In 1912, three years after an arranged marriage, she escaped to New York City. There she published her first book of poems, *The Book of Repulsive Women* (1915). The PROVINCETOWN PLAYERS also performed several of her early plays. But it was not until publication of *A Book* (1923) that she became widely known in avant-garde circles and among critics. In the 1920s she settled in Europe, where she wrote *Nightwood* (published by T. S. ELIOT) and *Ryder,* two novels that explore the elastic nature of human sexuality and identity. Barnes tended to write about lesbians and sexually ambiguous characters. Her prose is often as elusive as some poetry. She returned to Greenwich Village in the 1930s but produced little work and lived as a recluse, although her verse play *The Antiphon* (1958) is considered a major work that deals with the family in a tragic context. Barnes's standing remains high as an experimental artist and provocative thinker.

Sources

Barry, Alyce, ed. *Interviews: Djuna Barnes.* Washington, D.C.: Sun & Moon Press, 1985.
Broe, Mary Lynn, ed. *Silence and Power: A Reevaluation of Djuna Barnes.* Carbondale: Southern Illinois University Press, 1991.

Barth, John Simmons (1930–) *novelist*

A Maryland native, John Barth has had dual careers as a university professor and creative writer. His work is experimental and learned in its use of fictional models and elaborate narrative strategies. In *The Sot-Weed Factor,* for example, he creates a fictitious 18th-century narrative, including a journal by the intrepid English explorer, Captain John Smith, purportedly an account of Smith's sexual adventures with Pocahontas. GORE VIDAL and other critics have accused him of writing novels for the sole purpose of being studied in the academy, yet Barth's playful sense of humor and wonderful transformations of literary tradition make him attractive to educated, though not necessarily academic, readers. His novels tend to be long and intricate. His major works include *The Floating Opera* (1956), The *Sot-Weed Factor* (1960), *Giles Goat-Boy* (1966), *Lost in the Funhouse* (1968), *Chimera* (1972), *Letters* (1979), *Sabbatical* (1982), *The Tidewater Tales* (1988), *The Last Voyage of Somebody the Sailor* (1991), and *Coming Soon!!!* (2001).

Sources

Bowen, Zack R. *A Reader's Guide to John Barth.* Westport, Conn.: Greenwood Press, 1994.
Waldemeir, Joseph J., ed. *Critical Essays on John Barth.* Boston: G. K. Hall, 1980.

Barthelme, Donald (1931–1989) *short story writer, novelist*

Barthelme is one of the most widely admired writers in contemporary American literature. He was born in Philadelphia and grew up in Houston, Texas. After graduating from the University of Houston, he became a reporter at the *Houston Post,* then served in the army during the KOREAN WAR. By the 1960s he lived in New York City, where he began publishing fiction in the *NEW YORKER* and taught at City College. He has described his technique as that of collage, an intricate juxtaposing of characters and incidents, often with a surrealistic or fairy-tale quality—as in *Snow White* (1967), an episodic novel that rearranges the events and fragments the narrative of the traditional story. He achieved his greatest influence through several short story collections: *Come Back, Dr. Caligari* (1964), *Unspeakable Practices, Unspeakable Acts* (1968), *City Life* (1970), *Sadness* (1972), *Guilty Pleasures* (1974), *Great Days* (1979), *The Emerald* (1980), *Sixty Stories* (1981), *Overnight to Many Distant Cities* (1984), *Forty Stories* (1989). His other important novel is *The Dead Father* (1976), a rather gruesome but haunting evocation of a family that hauls its father cross-country to his death.

Sources

Patteson, Richard F., ed. *Critical Essays on Donald Barthelme.* New York: G. K. Hall, 1992.
Trachtenberg, Stanley. *Understanding Donald Barthelme.* Columbia: University of South Carolina Press, 1990.

Beach, Sylvia (1887–1962) *bookseller, publisher*

Beach opened her famous bookshop, Shakespeare & Co., patronized by such important literary figures as James Joyce and Ernest HEMINGWAY, in 1919. At No. 12 Rue de L'Odeon in Paris, she stocked the work of the great modernist writers (see MODERNISM) and welcomed the visits of young new writers in the 1920s. She published James Joyce's *Ulysses* in 1922 at a time when publication in the United States was blocked (the book was deemed pornographic) and when the book confronted other legal challenges in Europe. She published a memoir, *Shakespeare & Co.,* in 1959.

Sources

Fitch, Noel Riley. *Sylvia Beach and the Lost Generation: A History of Literary Paris in the Twenties and Thirties.* New York: W. W. Norton, 1983.

Beats, the

Also known as the Beat Generation, this community of artists, primarily writers, included Jack KEROUAC, Allen GINSBERG, Lawrence FERLINGHETTI, and Gregory CORSO—with other writers such as William BURROUGHS and Gary SNYDER also associated with the group. The key texts are Ginsberg's "HOWL," Ferlinghetti's *A Coney Island of the Mind,* and Kerouac's *ON THE ROAD.* In an earlier generation, the Beats would have been called bohemians, artists who frequented GREENWICH VILLAGE in New York City, and were associated with various avant-garde movements. In the 1950s, the Beats (the term combines the desire to beatify the artist and acknowledge his sense of disgust with conventional society), inspired by improvisational jazz and filled with scorn for the conformism of mainstream society, sought an alternative way of life in the Village and in the North Beach section of San Francisco, where Ferlinghetti owned a bookstore, City Lights, that also published Ginsberg and other writers of the

Beat movement and what was sometimes called the SAN FRANCISCO RENAISSANCE.

The Beats were not so much social rebels in the 1960s sense as they were disaffected and disaffiliated. They were, in a sense, loners who formed their own club. They were anarchists and radical individualists who found company and stimulation in literature and music. They were "hipsters," as Ginsberg calls them in "Howl." They were literally "beat" in the sense of having been worn out by conventional society. They were also, again in Ginsberg's language, "angelheaded": Their attraction to drugs and to Eastern philosophy represented a search for transcendental values and expressed their rejection of commercial culture.

Unlike the proletarian writers of the 1930s or the activist writers of the 1960s, the Beats turned inward. They wanted to transform themselves, not society, although Ginsberg, one of the most talented and flamboyant of the group, sought public attention and promoted Beat ideas in numerous public events and on television.

As writers, the Beats were experimental. Ferlinghetti used the rhythms of jazz in his poetry and sometimes gave public readings accompanied by jazz musicians. Ginsberg revived Walt Whitman's experimentation with the poetic line and with an expansive poetic voice that Ginsberg used to express a kind of eccentric populism. In *On the Road*, Kerouac captured the restless, troubadour quality of the Beats, the spontaneous, episodic quality of their lives and of their art.

Other Beats pursued a consistent exploration of Buddhism and Asian philosophy as well as an attachment to the natural world that was reminiscent of earlier writers such as Ralph Waldo Emerson and Henry David Thoreau. Beat poets like Gary Snyder were rigorous and disciplined craftsmen. William Burroughs, particularly in his novel *Naked Lunch*, explored the psychedelic and surrealistic consciousness that verged on nihilism—one of the extreme options available to a Beat writer.

Sources

Foster, Edward Halsey. *Understanding the Beats*. Columbia: University of South Carolina Press, 1992.
Lee, A. Robert, ed. *The Beat Generation Writers*. London: Pluto Press, 1996.
Tytell, John. *Naked Angels: The Lives & Literature of the Beat Generation*. New York: McGraw-Hill, 1976.

Beattie, Ann (1947–) *novelist*

Born in Washington, D.C., Beattie earned a B.A. degree from American University in 1969 and an M.A. degree from the University of Connecticut in 1970. Her stories began to appear in the NEW YORKER in 1973. She gained a significant reputation with the publication of her first novel, *Chilly Scenes of Winter* (1976), the story of a young man's frustrated search for love and fulfillment, which was made into a movie. Other novels such as *Falling in Place* (1980) and *Love Always* (1985) have received less critical approval, and some of her later stories have been dismissed as superficial. She writes about her generation, focusing on upper-middle-class characters. Yet she has been compared to John UPDIKE in her mastery of her characters' traits and manners and to Donald BARTHELME and Raymond CARVER as a stylist in the tradition of minimalism. Her later novels have struck other readers as her best, especially *Picturing Will* (1990), *Another You* (1995), and *My Life, Starring Dara Falcon* (1997). She has published four short story collections: *Where You'll Find Me and Other Stories* (1986), *What Was Mine* (1991), *Park City: New and Selected Stories* (1998), and *Perfect Recall: New Stories* (2001).

Sources

Montresor, Jay Berman, ed. *The Critical Response to Ann Beattie*. Westport, Conn.: Greenwood Press, 1993.
Murphy, Christina. *Ann Beattie*. Boston: Twayne, 1986.

Bellow, Saul (1915–) *novelist, short story writer, essayist*

Although born in Lachine, Quebec, Bellow, the son of Russian Jewish parents, grew up in Chicago, which is featured in many of his stories and novels.

Bellow earned a B.A. degree from Northwestern University, briefly attended the University of Wisconsin as a graduate student, and worked for the Works Project Administration during the DEPRESSION. He served in the merchant marine during World War II, and his first novel, *Dangling Man* (1944), centers on a young man agonizing over his wait to be drafted into the army. The novel shows the influence of Dostoevsky and other European writers, as do Bellow's later novels, which combine a wonderful comic sense of character with a philosophical sensibility and an intelligence based on a fervid reading of the Western classics.

The Adventures of Augie March (1953), often called a picaresque novel, established Bellow's reputation as one of the great contemporary novelists and the key member of the Jewish-American renaissance in the 1950s. Its hero, Augie, is as exuberant as his creator's language. Bellow creates a Jewish character who fits into the mainstream of modern American life, and invents a racy yet sophisticated language for the novel, which was recognized with a National Book Award for fiction.

Bellow's next work was a novella, *Seize The Day* (1956), notable for its exquisitely controlled prose and vivid depiction of its main character, Tommy Wilhelm, who gets caught up in the corruption of a society fixated on money. *Seize the Day* is the somber but riveting counterpart to the comedy of *Augie March*.

Bellow followed his bleak novella with another comic masterpiece, *Henderson the Rain King* (1959), justly praised for its daring scenes set in Africa (which Bellow had never visited). Like *Augie March, Henderson* can be called a picaresque novel, although this time Bellow combines elements of the fable and of realistic fiction in creating another memorable character.

Surprisingly, Bellow's most difficult novel, *Herzog* (1964), proved to be his most popular. This story of a middle-aged professor meditating on his unfortunate past struck a lyrical note of sardonic humor.

Beginning with *Mr. Sammler's Planet* (1970), set in New York City, Bellow began to earn a reputation as a conservative. Reviews of the novel were mixed; some criticized Bellow's handling of contemporary race relations, but acknowledged the author's gift for populating a novel of ideas with striking characters.

Bellow was awarded the Nobel Prize in literature in 1976. He published several novels in the 1980s to mixed critical response: *The Dean's December* (1982), *More Die of Heartbreak* (1987), *A Theft* (1989), *The Bellarosa Connection* (1989), and *The Actual* (1997).

Ravelstein (2000), a novel based on the life of his friend and colleague Allan Bloom, the best-selling author of *The Closing of the American Mind* and a fellow member of the Committee on Social Thought at the University of Chicago, has been widely praised as Bellow's best novel in two decades because of its vivid portrait of an intellectual and sense of humor reminiscent of *Humboldt's Gift* (1975), his fictional portrait of Delmore SCHWARTZ, which won a Pulitzer Prize.

Bellow has also written distinguished short fiction, collected in *Mosby's Memoirs and Other Stories* (1968), *Him with His Foot in His Mouth and Other Stories* (1984), *Something to Remember Me By: Three Tales* (1991), and *Collected Stories* (2001).

To Jerusalem and Back: A Personal Account (1976) is Bellow's best piece of nonfiction prose. It explores his deep attachment to Israel and reveals much about his complex creative sensibility.

Sources

Atlas, James. *Bellow: A Biography.* New York: Random House, 2000.

Bach, Gerhard, ed. *The Critical Response to Saul Bellow.* Westport, Conn.: Greenwood Press, 1995.

Cronin, Gloria L. and Ben Siegel. *Conversations with Saul Bellow.* Jackson: University Press of Mississippi, 1994.

Trachtenberg, Stanley, ed. *Critical Essays on Saul Bellow.* Boston: G. K. Hall, 1979.

Beloved Toni Morrison (1998) *novel*

Toni MORRISON's novel about social injustice and the supernatural tells a traumatic story of slavery and postwar America. Sethe, a slave, is haunted by her dead child, Beloved, whom Sethe has killed rather than see her fall into the hands of a slavemaster. Beloved, a restless spirit, haunts the house

Sethe has set up after the Civil War and her release from prison. Then a young woman shows up who announces she is Beloved. She looks to be about 19, but she has the soft skin of a baby, and she sleeps and wets the bed like a baby. Beloved latches onto Sethe and listens to her stories. In return, Beloved reminisces about her time among the dead. Paul D., Sethe's lover, is alarmed at Beloved's presence. Later Beloved visits him in his shed and forces herself upon him. When the townspeople, aroused by reports of Beloved, appear to exorcize her from Sethe's household, Beloved suddenly disappears.

Sources

Connor, Marc C., ed. *The Aesthetics of Toni Morrison: Speaking the Unspeakable.* Jackson: University Press of Mississippi, 2000.

David, Ron. *Toni Morrison Explained: A Reader's Road Map to the Novels.* New York: Random House, 2000.

Duvall, John M. *The Identifying Fictions of Toni Morrison: Modernist Authenticity and Postmodern Blackness.* New York: Palgrave, 2000.

Gutmann, Katharina. *Celebrating the Senses: An Analysis of the Sensual in Toni Morrison's Fiction.* Tübingen, Germany: Francke Verlag, 2000.

Benét, Stephen Vincent (1898–1943) *poet*

Benét is best known for his poetry, particularly *John Brown's Body*, which won the Pulitzer Prize in 1928 and is distinguished for its sympathetic and realistic treatment of the Civil War, and of John Brown, the militant abolitionist who attacked Harpers Ferry and hoped to instigate a slave rebellion. The work was dramatized in New York City in 1953. Benét also wrote several novels. The most memorable is *The Devil and Daniel Webster* (1937) because of Benét's vivid portrait of Webster, one of America's greatest political orators and stout defenders of the Union.

Sources

Fenton, Charles A. *Stephen Vincent Benét; The Life and Times of an American Man of Letters, 1898–1943.* New Haven, Conn.: Yale University Press, 1958.

Berger, Thomas (1924–) *novelist*

Berger was born and grew up in Cincinnati, Ohio. His novels focus on the dark comedy and absurdity of life. *Little Big Man* (1964), an irreverent fictional account of Custer's Last Stand, remains Berger's best-known work, but he has published many other novels. *Crazy in Berlin* (1958) began his Reinhart series—about an American GI who has picaresque adventures abroad and at home in the Midwest—which continued in *Reinhart in Love* (1962) and *Vital Parts* (1970). Berger's other novels include *Arthur Rex* (1978),

Orrie's Story (1990), *Meeting Evil* (1992), *Robert Crews* (1995), *Suspects* (1996), and *The Return of Little Big Man* (1999). He is known for parodying literary genres, including the western (*Little Big Man*, 1964), the hardboiled detective novel (*Suspects*, 1996), the true crime documentary (*Killing Time*, 1967), Arthurian romance (*Arthur Rex*, 1978), and the spy story (*Nowhere*, 1985).

Sources

Landon, Brooks. *Thomas Berger*. Boston: Twayne, 1989.
Madden, David W., ed. *Critical Essays on Thomas Berger*. New York: G. K. Hall, 1995.

Berry, Wendell (1934–) *novelist, poet, essayist*

Berry's family farmed for five generations in Henry County, Kentucky, where he was born. After studying under Wallace STEGNER at Stanford University and teaching briefly at New York University, Berry returned to Kentucky and made his region as much a part of his writing as did William FAULKNER of the Deep South. Berry has been particularly concerned with exploring environmental and ecological themes. His work is filled with detailed descriptions of the flora and fauna of rural life. His books include *Remembering* (1988), a novel; *The Discovery of Kentucky* (1991), a collection of poetry; and *Standing on Earth* (1991), selected essays.

Sources

Angyal, Andrew J. *Wendell Berry*. New York: Twayne, 1995.
Merchant, Paul, ed. *Wendell Berry*. Lewiston, Idaho: Confluence Press, 1991.

Berryman, John (1914–1972) *poet*

An Oklahoma native, John Berryman was born John Smith, but took the Berryman name from his stepfather after his father committed suicide. (Berryman himself would later die by jumping from a bridge in Minneapolis.) A professor at the University of Minnesota, he was part of a postwar generation of poets, including Robert LOWELL and Randall JARRELL, who were highly competitive and keen for fame. Berryman's early poetry is traditional, but like both Lowell and Jarrell he later moved toward a more informal, CONFESSIONAL style. His work has an elegance and polish that has been compared to Robert Lowell's, but Berryman uses elements of African-American speech patterns and is even more intense than Lowell in evoking the feelings of doom that would lead to his suicide. His first important collection was *Homage to Mistress Bradstreet*, poems addressed to Anne Bradstreet, the 17th-century Puritan poet. Berryman's later poetry centers on Henry, the poet's surrogate, and his "dream songs." Berryman won the Pulitzer Prize for *77 Dream Songs* (1964). *Collected Poems, 1937–1972* was published in 1990. His autobiographical novel, *Recovery* (1973), deals with his lifelong battle with alcoholism. Berryman also wrote a well-received biography, *Stephen Crane* (1950), notable for his psychoanalytical probing of the writer's life and work.

Sources

Bloom, Harold, ed. *John Berryman*. New York: Chelsea House, 1989.
Kelly, Richard J. and Alan K. Lathrop. *Recovering Berryman: Essays on a Poet*. Ann Arbor: University of Michigan Press, 1993.
Mariani, Paul. *Dreamsong: The Life of John Berryman*. New York: Morrow, 1990.

Bishop, Elizabeth (1911–1979) *poet*

Born in Worcester, Massachusetts, Bishop lost her parents at an early age: Her father died shortly after her birth, and a few years later her distraught mother was committed to a mental institution. Bishop was cared for at first by maternal aunts in Great Village, Nova Scotia, a setting that would figure in some of her finest poems and prose pieces. At age seven she was brought back to Worcester to be cared for by paternal grandparents, and never saw her mother again. These disruptions may have contributed to the onset of Bishop's asthma, which restricted her activity well into her school years. Asthma, depression, and later alcoholism would result in significant periods of disability. But at age 16, Bishop had the good fortune to meet the poet Marianne MOORE, who became the mentor the shy Bishop badly needed.

Overcoming her early illnesses, Bishop traveled extensively after her graduation from Vassar College. She lived in Key West, Florida, from 1939 to 1949. *North and South* (1946), her first published book of poetry, contains several poems that have been anthologized, including "Roosters" and "The Fish." The latter recounts her catching a large trout and then releasing it to admire its huge burst of color. The poem demonstrates the poet's precise use of description and of minute details to build up to an explosion of feeling. This kind of devotion to particulars has been compared to Marianne Moore's intricate interest in the physical aspects of life as a way of expressing emotion. Bishop's second collection, *A Cold Spring* (1955), won the Pulitzer Prize. Bishop was much admired by the poet Robert LOWELL, who helped to advance her career. He liked her keen eye and humor, and they maintained a lifelong friendship.

In the early 1950s Bishop fell in love with Maria Carlota Costellat de Macedo Soares, with whom the poet established a household in Brazil, where they were to live for more than a decade, and where Bishop produced some of her finest poetry, including *Questions of Travel* (1965). After this relationship foundered and Soares committed suicide, Bishop returned to the United States, settling in Massachusetts and teaching at Harvard.

Bishop's poetry has been praised for its informal yet polished style, and its combination of spontaneity and careful composition. She won the National Book Award for *Collected Poems* (1970). Although recognized as a fine poet in her lifetime, Bishop's reputation since her death has grown even greater. She aimed at a universality that made her reject such designations as "woman poet." She objected, in fact, to the inclusion of her work in anthologies of women's poetry. Her *Complete Poems 1927–1979* was published in 1983 and *Collected Prose* in 1984. Her correspondence, *One Art: Selected Letters*, was published in 1993.

Sources

Bloom, Harold, ed. *Elizabeth Bishop.* New York: Chelsea House, 1985.

Miller, Brett C. *Elizabeth Bishop: Life and the Memory of It.* Berkeley: University of California Press, 1993.

black aesthetic

The term derives from the 1960s, a period when some African-American literary and art critics called for a vision of art and artists contingent on black experience. The precursors of the black aesthetic can be traced to such writers as W. E. B. DU BOIS and his classic text, *The Souls of Black Folk,* which explores the unique characteristics of African-American culture, especially the development of the spiritual as a musical form. During the HARLEM RENAISSANCE, Claude MCKAY introduced a militant cry of resistance that became associated with the artist's search for a revolutionary or protest art. In the poem "If I must Die," for example, McKay urges blacks threatened with annihilation to fight back like men, not docile beasts. In the 1930s Richard WRIGHT and other radical African-American writers depicted the isolation of African Americans and advocated the revival of folk traditions and programs of international solidarity among African Americans. In the 1950s, African-American writers such as Lorraine HANSBERRY and Ralph ELLISON took a much more integrationist view of the African-American experience. These writers reacted against the evils of segregation and hoped to bring African Americans into the mainstream of the arts in America. Radicals of the 1960s, in turn, rejected Ellison's universalist bias, believing it had deprived African Americans of the unique features of their culture. Writers such as Amiri BARAKA advocated an aesthetic based on a militant sense of the uniqueness of the black experience and thus on the separateness of black literature. The aesthetic is expressed in *William Styron's Nat Turner: Ten Black Writers Respond* (1967).

Sources

Gayle, Addison. *The Black Aesthetic.* Garden City, N.Y.: Doubleday, 1971.

Martin, Reginald. *Ishmael Reed and the New Black Aesthetic Critics.* Basingstoke, England: Macmillan, 1988.

Black Arts movement

This term is associated with the BLACK AESTHETIC. The poet and playwright Amiri BARAKA, poet and publisher Dudley RANDALL, and literary critic Addison Gayle, among others, argued for a view of African-American art that was uncontaminated by white prejudices. To the movers of the Black Arts movement, art became an act of self-defense against an oppressive white establishment which used "universal" as a code word for white art. By the 1970s, writers such as Ishmael REED attacked the Black Arts movement as too restrictive, but maintained a consciousness of the ways in which white culture tended to usurp African-American cultural forms. African-American writers of the 1980s and 1990s, including Toni MORRISON and Alice WALKER, have sought to create a balance between their desire to inspire the African-American community and to write literature that speaks to people of all races. It is significant, for example, that Walker worked closely with the Jewish director Steven Spielberg on the filming of her novel *The Color Purple,* whereas a generation earlier the African-American actor James Earl Jones had to withdraw from taking the role of Nat Turner in the proposed filming of William STYRON's controversial novel *The Confessions of Nat Turner,* which had provoked the ire of several African-American writers. The proposed film, to be directed by a white man, Norman Jewison, was deemed contrary to the black aesthetic by certain black critics.

Sources

Jones, LeRoi and Larry Neal, ed. *Black Fire: An Anthology of Afro-American Writing.* New York: Morrow, 1968.

Black Boy Richard Wright (1945) autobiography

Richard WRIGHT's autobiography provides a searing description of the first 19 years of his life. Born in Jackson, Mississippi, he experienced the degradation of poverty and racism. He describes periods of hunger so great that he would turn on a garden hose full blast and try to fill his stomach. Life within his family is harsh. He is severely beaten after he accidentally burns down the family home. His mother beats him again when he comes home bloodied from a fight with whites. Her severity, however, indicates how much she fears that her son will not conform to a white world.

Wright clearly meant his own story to represent the oppression suffered by millions of other African Americans, yet his own story of growth and his journey to the North, where he begins his career at 19 in Chicago, is also a tribute to the tenacity and ingenuity of the human spirit. *Black Boy,* originally titled *American Hunger,* represents only the first part of Wright's autobiography; the second section was not published until 1977. It had been suppressed when the Book-of-the-Month Club stipulated that it would not publish the entire book, particularly its indictment of northern racism. The entire autobiography, as Wright intended it to be published, appeared in 1992.

Sources
Felgar, Robert. *Understanding Richard Wright's Black Boy: A Student Casebook to Issues, Sources, and Historical Documents.* Westport, Conn.: Greenwood Press, 1998.

Rampersad, Arnold, ed. *Richard Wright: A Collection of Critical Essays.* Englewood Cliffs, N.J.: Prentice Hall, 1995.

Black Mountain Poets

In this group of poets led by Charles OLSON at Black Mountain College in North Carolina, Olson propounded free verse forms, what he called "open" or "projective" poetry. The poem, according to Olson, should be organized and live and breathe like a body. The poets that clustered around Olson and the North Carolina college's journal, *The Black Mountain Review,* began to receive significant attention in the 1960s. These poets included Robert CREELEY, Robert DUNCAN, Denise LEVERTOV, Paul Blackburn, Larry Eigner, and Paul Carroll. Although they took their inspiration from Olson, members of this group often disagreed with one another. They represented not so much a united movement in the arts as a collective dedicated to exploring various new forms of contemporary poetry. Later poets associated with the Black Mountain canon include Ed DORN, Joel Oppenheimer, Jonathan Williams, and John Weiners—all of whom studied under Olson. Black Mountain College itself proved hospitable to many different kinds of writers, including critics and cultural commentators who visited the college to discern how Olson and others were creating their art. These poets extended the works of predecessors such as William Carlos WILLIAMS who helped to make American poetry more visual, informal, and close to everyday American speech.

Sources
Duberman, Martin. *Black Mountain: An Exploration in Community.* New York: Dutton, 1972.

Blackmur, Richard Palmer (1904–1965) *editor, critic, poet*

The influential editor of the literary magazine *Hound and Horn,* R. P. Blackmur is best known for his incisive literary criticism, one of the first examples of the NEW CRITICISM, in such books as *The Double Agent* (1935), *Language as Gesture* (1952), and *Value in Modern Poetry* (1957). He was also a respected poet. His best-known book of poems is *From Jordan's Delight* (1937).

Sources
Fraser, Russell A. *A Mingled Yarn: The Life of R. P. Blackmur.* New York: Harcourt Brace Jovanovich, 1981.

Pannick, Gerald J. *Richard Palmer Blackmur.* Boston: Twayne, 1981.

Bly, Robert Elwood (1926–) *poet*

Robert Bly grew up on a farm in Madison, Minnesota. After serving in World War II and studying literature at St. Olaf College in Northfield, Minnesota, he went to Harvard, where he met fellow writers John ASHBERY and John HAWKES. A prolific poet, he won the National Book Award for *The Light Around the Body* (1967). His *Selected Poems* appeared in 1986. His poetry has been described as spare and stark because of his vivid imagery. His work has also explored political issues, especially his fierce opposition to the Vietnam War. He achieved popular success with *Iron John: A Book About Men* (1991), in which he explores the myths of masculinity.

Sources
Davis, William V., ed. *Critical Essays on Robert Bly.* New York: G. K. Hall, 1992.

———. *Understanding Robert Bly.* Columbia: University of South Carolina Press, 1988.

Bogan, Louise (1897–1970) *poet*

Bogan was born in Livermore Falls, Maine, to an Irish-American family. She left Boston University in 1916 to marry, and followed her husband during World War I to Panama, where they had a daughter. After her husband died of pneumonia in 1920 Bogan settled in New York City and began for the first time to associate with groups of writers. She had studied poetry seriously at the age of 14, but she did not publish her first book of poetry, *Body of This Death,* until 1923. After publishing another volume of poetry, *Dark Summer* (1929), she became poetry critic for the NEW YORKER, a position she held from 1931 to 1969. Throughout this period she published several more volumes of poetry and of poetry criticism. Her work is notable for its epigrammatic quality: She tends to favor compact forms in which she explores the ambiguity of human psychology. Like Elizabeth BISHOP, Bogan disliked identification as a woman poet, yet she is said to have influenced such poets as May SARTON and Sylvia PLATH. The most complete collection of her poems is *The Blue Estuaries: Poems 1923–1968.*

Sources
Collins, Martha, ed. *Critical Essays on Louise Bogan.* Boston: G. K. Hall, 1984.

Bontemps, Arna Wendell (1902–1973) *novelist, writer of children's literature, critic, anthologist*

Arna Bontemps was born in Louisiana and was educated at the University of Chicago. He was part of the HARLEM REN-AISSANCE. His most important novel is *Black Thunder* (1936), a riveting account of a slave revolt. His most important nonfiction is *The Story of the Negro* (1948). *Sam Patch* (1951) is his best children's book. *The Arna Bontemps-Langston Hughes Letters, 1925–1967* appeared in 1980.

Bontemps's style is direct and descriptive. He avoids psychologizing his characters, as in *Black Thunder, Drums at Dusk* (1939), his account of a slave revolt and the liberation of blacks, which emphasizes the power of a people to help themselves. His work as critic and anthologist helped to establish the canon of African-American literature. His important collections include *The Book of Negro Folklore* (1959) and *American Negro Poetry* (1963). In 1972, he published *The Harlem Renaissance Remembered*.

Sources

Jones, Kirkland C. *Renaissance Man from Louisiana: A Biography of Arna Wendell Bontemps.* Westport, Conn.: Greenwood Press, 1992.

book clubs

The modern American book club began in 1926 with the founding of the Book-of-the-Month Club. The founder, Harry Scherman, thought American readers would enjoy receiving books at home that were chosen by a board of distinguished literary judges. The club began with 4,750 members and had more than a million subscribers by the end of the 1920s. Other book clubs like the Literary Guild proliferated—some created by publishers such as Doubleday—despite publishers' initial objections that book clubs posed unfair competition. By the 1950s book club sales may have accounted for close to one-third of all book sales in the United States. Book clubs continue to thrive, but they have to contend with much competition from Internet booksellers and superstore chains. Niche or speciality book clubs—such as the Mystery Book Club and the History Book Club—have found new ways to attract readers with well-defined interests, although these clubs are owned by parent clubs such as Book-of-the-Month.

Book-of-the-Month Club

See BOOK CLUBS.

Bookman, The periodical

First published in 1895, this magazine became a forum for the new humanism. It was primarily a journal of criticism and literature that invited lively debates between English and American authors—publishing, for example, Rebecca West and Hugh Walpole, English authors who took issue with H. L. MENCKEN's view of American culture at home and abroad.

Boothe, Clare (1903–1987) *playwright*

Born in New York City, Boothe worked at *VOGUE* and *VANITY FAIR* in jobs that contributed to her exquisite sense of style—a combination of a sharp wit and acute observation of social manners. Her play, *The Women* (1936), became a successful motion picture and a landmark of the period because it was so outspoken about the ambitions of women and the rivalries among them. Her other plays include *Kiss the Boys Goodbye* (1938) and *Margin for Error* (1939). She was married twice, the second time to Henry Luce, founder of *TIME* magazine. This marriage enhanced her public visibility and power. She had a second career as a conservative politician. She was elected to Congress twice (1943–47) and served as ambassador to Italy (1953–1956).

Sources

Fearnow, Mark. *Clare Boothe Luce: A Research and Production Sourcebook.* Westport, Conn.: Greenwood Press, 1995.

Morris, Sylvia Jukes. *Rage for Fame: The Ascent of Clare Boothe Luce.* New York: Random House, 1997.

Boston, Massachusetts

The city was most famous as a literary capital in the 18th and 19th centuries, when New England authors dominated the national literature, but it became a focal point in the 1920s during the SACCO-VANZETTI TRIAL. Harvard University in nearby Cambridge has educated some of America's finest contemporary writers, including Norman MAILER and Susan SONTAG. Amy LOWELL and Robert LOWELL, descendants of the Lowells who distinguished American letters in the 19th century, added luster to the name in the 20th. Except as a setting for novels by such authors as J. P. MARQUAND and Edwin O'CONNOR, however, the city is no longer a literary capital, although the publishers Houghton Mifflin, Little Brown, and Beacon Press continue to operate offices there.

Bourjaily, Vance Nye (1922–) *novelist*

The Ohio-born Bourjaily was one of a generation of novelists to come of age during WORLD WAR II. *The End of My Life* (1947) is an account of a young man's breakdown during the war. *Confessions of a Spent Youth* (1960) focuses on the romantic adventures of a young man during and after the war. *Brill Among the Ruins* (1970) is his well-received novel about the turmoil of the 1960s and its impact on a middle-aged man. Bourjaily has also published two nonfiction books about life in the country: *The Unnatural Enemy* (1963) and *Country Matters* (1973).

Sources

Aldridge, John W. *The Devil in the Fire: Retrospective Essays on American Literature and Culture, 1951–1971.* New York: Harper's Magazine Press, 1972.

Bowles, Jane Auer (1917–1973) *short story writer, novelist, playwright*

Bowles was born in New York City and was sent to Switzerland at 15 for treatment of tuberculosis. On her way home she met the French novelist Louis Ferdinand Celine, whose work she was then reading. Their meeting confirmed her desire to become a writer. She took up residence in New York and pursued the literary life in GREENWICH VILLAGE. She met artists of all kinds and in 1938, when she had just turned 21, she married the composer and writer Paul BOWLES. The couple traveled in Central and South America and Mexico, where she wrote her first novel, *Two Serious Ladies* (1943). The novel has been cited for its evocation of a "woman's sensibility." Although Bowles remained married, she pursued many lesbian relationships. She also influenced several male writers, including John ASHBERY, Tennessee WILLIAMS, and Truman CAPOTE. Her most notable play is *In the Summer House* (1948), a penetrating study of two women. Between the late 1940s and 1960s the Bowleses lived in Morocco, each pursuing their writing and engaging in affairs with others. During the latter part of this period Jane Bowles's health began to fail as a series of strokes left her partly immobilized and blind. She also suffered writer's block. In 1966, with the help of her husband, she was able to publish *Plain Pleasures,* a collection of short stories. At the same time her *Collected Works* was published in the United States. The last five years of her life were spent in a clinic in Spain. *My Sister's Hand in Mine* (1978) is an expanded edition of her collected works.

Sources

Dillon, Millicent. *A Little Original Sin: The Life and Work of Jane Bowles.* New York: Holt, Rinehart, and Winston, 1981.
Skerl, Jennie, ed. *A Tawdry Place of Salvation: The Art of Jane Bowles.* Carbondale: Southern Illinois University Press, 1997.

Bowles, Paul (1910–1999) *novelist*

Paul Bowles was born in Jamaica, New York. Sent to the University of Virginia, Bowles twice fled to Paris, where Gertrude STEIN mentored him. In his early career as a composer, he wrote scores for ballets, chamber groups and orchestras, movies, and plays. In 1931, he studied music in Europe with the American composer Aaron Copland. In Berlin he befriended Christopher ISHERWOOD, who used his new friend's last name for his character Sally Bowles in *The Berlin Stories* (1945). But it was his wife's novel, *Two Serious Ladies,* that inspired Paul Bowles to pursue a literary career. He had married Jane Auer (BOWLES) in 1938, and although they suffered periods of estrangement, they maintained their sense of collaboration and mutual support. Something of their relationship is captured in Bowles's most famous work, *The Sheltering Sky* (1946), which was made into a motion picture in 1990. Bowles, whose work has sometimes been called existential, settled in Morocco in the 1940s and became the center of a network of artists who lived in or visited the country in the decades that followed. He explored isolated individuals—Europeans and Americans in a Moroccan setting—who are bereft of love and feel isolated and alienated. His *Collected Stories 1939–1976* appeared in 1979, his *Collected Poems 1926–1977* in 1981. Bowles was also a distinguished translator. His translation of Jean Paul Sartre's play *No Exit* was a Broadway success in 1946. His interest in Moroccan literature is evident in *Five Eyes: Short Stories by Five Moroccans* (1979) and in *Two Years Beside the Strait: Tangier Journal 1987–1989* (1990).

Sources

Dillon, Millicent. *You Are Not I: A Portrait of Paul Bowles.* Berkeley: University of California Press, 1998.
Miller, Jeffrey. *Paul Bowles: A Descriptive Bibliography.* Santa Barbara, Calif.: Black Sparrow Press, 1986.
Pulsifer, Gary, ed. *Paul Bowles by His Friends.* London: Peter Owen, 1992.

Boyle, Kay (1903–1992) *novelist, short story writer, poet, memoirist*

The product of a well-read mother and a wayward father, Boyle spent much of her youth traveling around the United States and Europe. She had little formal schooling, although she did study music and architecture in Cincinnati. Without a degree, she got a job in 1922 as assistant to the Australian poet Lola Ridge, the New York editor of *Broom* magazine, which published Boyle's early poetry. Boyle married in 1923, and she and her husband, Richard Brault, a Frenchman, moved to Paris, where she had an affair with Ernest Walsh, editor of *This Quarter.* She had a daughter with Walsh and published poetry in his journal as well as in the avant-garde magazine *transition. Wedding Day and Other Stories* appeared in 1930 and her first novel, *Plagued by the Nightingale,* in 1931. After Boyle separated from Brault and Walsh died, Boyle made a home for herself among the expatriate Parisian community. In 1931, she married the writer Laurence Vaill, with whom she had three children. The family stayed in France until 1941, when Boyle divorced Vaill and married Joseph von Frankenstein, an Austrian baron. After World War II, he worked in Germany and Boyle became a correspondent for the NEW YORKER. They had two children, and he died in 1963. Boyle then spent several years in the United States actively protesting the Vietnam War. By 1979, she had retired to San Francisco.

Her work developed no signature style, yet her integral place among the American writers of her time and her often autobiographical work has proven its worth over many decades. Her novels have been called experimental and lyrical, placing her within the modernist (see MODERNISM) camp of American authors. Her work is also marked by a strong feminist point of view. She explores the world of expatriates and artists, the institution of marriage, and such issues as nationalism and international politics. She published several short story collections, including *Fifty Stories* (1980) and *The Crazy Hunter* (1993). *Words That Must Somehow Be Said: Selected Essays 1927–1984* appeared in 1985. Her volumes of poetry include *Collected Poems* (1962), *Testament for My Students and Other Poems* (1970), and *This Is Not a Letter and Other Poems* (1985). For children she wrote *The Youngest Camel* (1939), *Pinky, the Cat Who Liked to Sleep* (1966), and *Pinky in Persia* (1968).

Sources

Elkins, Marilyn, ed. *Critical Essays on Kay Boyle.* New York: G. K. Hall, 1997.

Mellen, Joan. *Kay Boyle: Author of Herself.* New York: Farrar, Straus & Giroux, 1994.

Boyle, Thomas Coraghessan (1948–) *novelist, short story writer*

T. C. Boyle grew up in Peekskill, New York, the son of Irish immigrant parents. With an early interest in music, he did not consider literature seriously until he was out of his teens, when he read Thomas PYNCHON and John BARTH. By 1972, Boyle had enrolled in the famous IOWA WRITERS' WORKSHOP, where he studied with Vance BOURJAILY and John IRVING. He earned a Ph.D. with a collection of stories, and in 1979 published his first collection, *Descent of Man,* which won the St. Lawrence Award for Short Fiction. Since his first breakthrough collection he has published several novels: *Water Music* (1982), *Building Prospects* (1984), *World's End* (1988), *East is East* (1990), *The Road to Wellville* (1993), *The Tortilla Curtain* (1995), *Riven Rock* (1998), and the following short fiction collections: *Greasy Lake and Other Stories* (1985), *If the River was Whiskey* (1989), *Without a Hero* (1994), *The Collected Stories of T. Coraghessan Boyle* (1998). He has taught writing at the University of Southern California.

Boyle is a superb stylist and prober of cultural development. Various terms have been used to describe his work, including black humor and satire. It is also called flashy and some critics are wary of his "pyrotechnical" tendencies.

Sources

Adams, Michael. "T. Coraghessan Boyle." *DLB Yearbook 1986*: 281–286.

Utley, Sandye. "All About T. Coraghessan Boyle Resource Center." Available on-line. URL: http://www.tcboyle.net/criticism.html. Updated on July 7, 2001.

Bradbury, Ray Douglas (1920–) *novelist, short story writer*

Perhaps America's best-known science fiction writer, Bradbury grew up in Waukegan, Illinois. This region remains a defining place in his work, even in stories and novels that seem far removed from the Midwest. Bradbury began his career by publishing in the PULPS. His breakthrough came when he urged Christopher ISHERWOOD to read *The Martian Chronicles* (1950). No devotee of science fiction, Isherwood nevertheless found the book so compelling that he reviewed it and helped spark interest in an author ignored by the mainstream media. Isherwood sensed what has remained Bradbury's signature style: downplaying the plots and fascination with machinery and inventions that mark much science fiction in favor of expressive themes of "alienation and separation," as one commentary on his work put it.

Bradbury's work expresses interest in an extraordinary range of intellectual, social, and cultural issues. He combines social criticism and science fiction. He is skeptical of technocratic societies and employs what has been called a romantic conception of the human imagination. His style is often praised for its lyricism and poetic quality. Like modernist writers (see MODERNISM), his theme is often the alienation of the individual from his or her community, family, or society. Because of his Midwest settings, he has also been called a regionalist (see REGIONALISM) writer.

Two of Bradbury's novels, *The Illustrated Man* (1951) and *Fahrenheit 451* (1953), have been made into major motion pictures. The former presents a horrifying picture of a future totalitarian state in which people are not allowed to own books and state-controlled television is the only source of information. The latter—linking several stories together by the tattoos on his character's body—is partly set on Mars and reflects his blending of the science fiction and fantasy genres. His other novels include *Dandelion Wine* (1957), *Something Wicked This Way Comes* (1963), *Death is a Lonely Business* (1985), *A Graveyard for Lunatics* (1990), and *Green Shadows, White Whale* (1992). A prolific writer of short stories, his collections include *The Golden Apples of the Sun* (1953), *The October Country* (1956), *The Day It Rained Forever* (1959), *A Medicine for Melancholy* (1959), *The Machineries of Joy* (1964), *The Autumn People* (1965), *The Vintage Bradbury* (1965), *Tomorrow Midnight* (1966), *Long After Midnight* (1976), *To Sing Strange Songs* (1979), *The Last Circus and the Electrocution* (1980), *Dinosaur Tales* (1983), *A Memory of Murder* (1984), and *The Toynbee Convector* (1989).

Bradbury has also written plays, including an adaptation of *Moby Dick* in 1956 and of *Dandelion Wine* (1980). He began publishing poetry in the 1970s with *Old Ahab's Friend and Friend to Noah, Speaks His Piece* (1971). Other volumes of poetry include *That Son of Richard III* (1974), *Where Robot Mice and Robot Men Run Round in Robot Towns* (1977), *The Haunted Computer and the Android Pope* (1981), and *The Complete Poems of Ray Bradbury* (1982). For children he has written *Switch on the Night* (1955), *R is for Rocket* (1962); *S is for Space* (1966), *The Ghost of Forever* (1981), and *The Million Year Picnic and Other Stories* (1986). His most notable nonfiction volume is *Zen and the Art of Writing and The Joy of Writing* (1973).

Sources

Greenberg, Martin Henry and Joseph D. Olander, eds. *Ray Bradbury.* New York: Taplinger, 1980.
Mogen, David. *Ray Bradbury.* Boston: Twayne, 1986.
Touponce, William F. *Naming the Unnameable: Ray Bradbury and the Fantastic After Freud.* Mercer Island, Wash.: Starmont House, 1997.

Brautigan, Richard (1935–1984) *novelist, short story writer, poet*

Brautigan grew up in Washington state and spent much of his childhood fishing. Both the act of fishing and the relaxed rhythms of angling inform much of his best fiction. Brautigan launched his career in San Francisco, where he photocopied his poems and handed them out on the street. He frequented the sites where the BEATS held court, and pursued his ambition with a gentle humor and quirkiness that charmed people. His work reflects a bemused view of life as a bizarre and entertaining enterprise. In a short piece like "Complicated Banking Problems" he could evoke standing in line at a bank as a boring yet funny experience. Brautigan's characters and his writer's persona epitomized the anarchic side of the 1960s, but he also was a dedicated writer who became depressed when the vogue for his writing faded. After a period of drinking heavily in isolation, he committed suicide.

Brautigan began his career with the whimsical novels *A Confederate General from Big Sur* (1964) and *The Abortion* (1966). *Trout Fishing in America* (1967) is his masterpiece, although subsequent novels, *In Watermelon Sugar* (1968) and *The Revenge of the Lawn: Stories 1962–1970* (1971) show no diminution of his talent. The later novels strain somewhat to retain his sixties style, although they all have moments of brilliance: *The Hawkline Monster* (1974), *Willard and His Bowling Trophies* (1974), *Dreaming of Babylon* (1976), *Sombrero Fallout* (1976), *The Tokyo-Montana Express* (1980), and *So the Wind Won't Blow it Away* (1982). Brautigan also wrote several volumes of poetry: *The Galilee Hitch-Hiker* (1958), *Lay the Marble Tea* (1959), *The Octopus Frontier* (1960), *All Watched Over by Machines of Loving Grace* (1967), *The Pill Versus the Springhill Mining Disaster* (1968), *Please Plant This Book* (1968), *Rommel Drives Deep into Egypt* (1970), *Loading Mercury with a Pitchfork* (1976), and *June 30th – June 30th* (1978).

Sources

Chenetier, Marc. *Richard Brautigan.* London: Methuen, 1983.

Broadside Press *publisher*

Founded in 1963 by the African-American poet Dudley RANDALL, this small press was instrumental in disseminating the early work of many distinguished African-American writers, including Gwendolyn BROOKS, Nikki GIOVANNI, and Sterling BROWN. In Detroit, Randall began publishing his own poetry on loose sheets of paper called broadsides, a form of publication dating back several hundred years. Between 1965 and 1977, Broadside published nearly 60 books of poetry, which became the most concerted effort to sustain the life of poetry, especially among the African-American literary community. Unlike larger publishers, Broadside's sole mission was to keep poets in print and encourage young poets to publish. In later years, Randall fought illness and found it difficult to continue as a publisher. In 1985, new owners took over Broadside and established it as a nonprofit press.

Brodkey, Harold (Aaron Roy Weintraub) (1930–1996) *novelist, short story writer*

Born Aaron Roy Weintraub, Brodkey was adopted by his father's second cousin and renamed. Brodkey's mother died when he was two, and his distraught father became withdrawn and mute. Harold would often write about this childhood trauma. He moved from Illinois to New York in 1953 to become a writer. He married, divorced, and then remarried novelist Ellen Schwamm. His short stories began appearing in the NEW YORKER and were collected in *First Love and Other Sorrows* (1957). An elegant stylist of the urban milieu, Brodkey published no more books of fiction for nearly 30 years and built up a mystique about a long-awaited novel in progress. He encouraged his image as a Great American Novelist—indeed his work and career are, in essence, about the pursuit of greatness. His avid literary politicking in New York City literary circles burnished his reputation. When his novel *Runaway Soul* (1991) was published, it received only a mixed reception, and critics suggested that Brodkey, while a noteworthy writer, had not fulfilled his promise. He published *Stories in An Almost Classical Mode* in 1988. Before Brodkey died of AIDS, he wrote a compelling memoir of his illness, *The Wild Darkness: The Story of My Death* (1996).

Sources

Elgrably, Jordan. "Breaking the Language Barrier: A Conversation with Harold Brodkey." *Blue Penny Quarterly* (Summer 1996). Available on-line. URL: http://ebbs.english.vt.edu/olp/bpq/8/front8.html.

Brooklyn, New York

Brooklyn was an independent city until 1898, when it became a borough of New York City. Its fame in 20th-century literature has largely been a product of the writing about Jewish immigrants. Alfred KAZIN describes his upbringing in the

Brownsville section of the borough in *A Walker in the City* (1951). The Brooklyn Bridge has long inspired the work of artists and writers, including Hart CRANE in *The Bridge* (1930). Arthur MILLER, who grew up in Brooklyn, set his play *A View From the Bridge* (1956) in the borough. Norman MAILER, who also grew up in Brooklyn, describes it memorably in *Barbary Shore* (1951). Among the other writers who have set their novels, stories, and poems in Brooklyn are Thomas WOLFE, Daniel Fuchs, Joseph HELLER, David IGNATOW, Bernard MALAMUD, Norman PODHORETZ, Hubert SELBY, Gilbert SORRENTINO, and Ronald SUKENICK.

Brooks, Gwendolyn (1917–2000) *poet*

The first African-American woman to win a Pulitzer Prize (1950), Brooks published more than 25 books of frequently anthologized poetry and fiction. Born in Topeka, Kansas, Brooks grew up in and was very much defined by Chicago. Although she traveled widely, she always returned to the South Side of the city. She received all her schooling in Chicago, and her early experiences inform her rendering of black speech patterns and urban life.

Brooks met Langston HUGHES and James Weldon JOHNSON in the early 1930s just after she began to write poetry. Hughes encouraged her to read the great modernist (see MODERNISM) poets, including Ezra POUND, T. S. ELIOT, and E. E. CUMMINGS. Following Hughes's advice, she wrote as much as she could and established a poetry column in the African-American newspaper *CHICAGO DEFENDER*.

Her career advanced when she became associated with Harriet MONROE's magazine *POETRY*. In 1945 she published her first book, *A Street in Bronzeville*. Her second volume, *Annie Allen* (1949), won an award from *Poetry* magazine, and the following year Brooks received the Pulitzer Prize. Many awards, prizes, honors, and prestigious teaching positions followed, culminating in her selection as the 1994 Jefferson Lecturer by the National Endowment for the Humanities. Brooks taught at several universities, including Columbia and University of Wisconsin. By the 1960s she had become deeply involved in the BLACK ARTS MOVEMENT.

Brooks experimented with virtually every poetic form, although she never left her roots in the African-American community or her interest in the impact of urban life on the imagination and language of its inhabitants. Poems such as "We Real Cool" and "The Blackstone Rangers" reflect Brooks's sure grasp of contemporary idioms and social issues. Although published successfully by Harper & Row, she turned to Dudley RANDALL's BROADSIDE PRESS in Detroit to publish several volumes of poetry: *Riot* (1969), *Family Pictures* (1970), *Aloneness* (1971), and *Aurora* (1972). She also published *Report from Part One* (1972), an autobiography. Her *Selected Poems* appeared in 1963. Her novel, *Maud Martha*, is about an African-American woman who asserts herself in a confrontation with a racist society.

Sources

Kent, George E. *A Life of Gwendolyn Brooks.* Lexington: University Press of Kentucky, 1990.
Wright, Stephen Cadwell, ed. *On Gwendolyn Brooks: Reliant Contemplation.* Ann Arbor: University of Michigan Press, 1996.

Brown, Claude (1937–2002) *autobiographer*

Author of the renowned *Manchild in the Promised Land* (1965), Brown made his life a book, vividly describing his early years in Harlem and the trouble his parents—migrants from South Carolina—had adjusting to city ways. Brown became part of a street gang and at age 11 was sent to a reformatory, the Wiltwyck School for Delinquent Boys. As he explains in his autobiography, this institution instilled in him a sense of morality and discipline—although it would be many years before he could bring himself to the task of building a reasoned, adult life. His autobiography was published the year he graduated from Howard University, and he was hailed as the next James BALDWIN. Other favorable comparisons to Ralph ELLISON and Richard WRIGHT emphasized Brown's vivid realism and gift for the comic. A second book, *The Children of Ham* (1976), which details the plight of Harlem residents, was greeted with far less enthusiasm, perhaps because Brown seemed unable to capture the brio of his riveting autobiography.

Sources

Locher, Frances Carol, ed. "Claude Brown." *Contemporary Authors* 73–76 (1978): 88–189.

Brown, Rita Mae (1944–) *poet, novelist*

Brown grew up in York, Pennsylvania, and Fort Lauderdale, Florida. Her family was poor, but she was encouraged to write from an early age. Educated at the University of Florida, she moved to New York City in 1964, attended New York University, and became involved in the theater, civil rights activism, feminism, and gay and lesbian liberation movements. Her first book, *The Hand That Cradles the Rock* (1971), was a collection of poetry. *Rubyfruit Jungle* (1973), her first novel, was a critical and popular success. Translated into several languages and a standard text in courses on lesbian literature, it tells with considerable energy and wit the coming-of-age story of a lesbian. Brown's work has been taught in women's studies courses as an example of a new generation of writer not bound by the taboos that writers of earlier times, such as Amy LOWELL had to observe when talking about the intimate sex lives of women. In other words, Brown has been much more explicit in her descriptions of lesbian sexuality and its place in the lives of her characters.

Brown published a second novel, *In Her Day* (1974), and wrote for screen and television. Ten more novels followed, many of them whimsical mysteries: *Six of One* (1978), *South-*

ern Discomfort (1982), Sudden Death (1983), High Hearts (1986), Rest in Pieces (1992), Venus Envy (1993), Dolley: A Novel of Dolley Madison in Love and War (1994), Riding Shotgun (1996), Loose Lips (1999), and Outfoxed (2000). Songs to a Handsome Woman (1973) is a collection of poetry. Plain Brown Wrapper (1976) collects her essays. She is also the author of Starting From Scratch: A Different Kind of Writer's Manual (1988), in which she discusses her views of language, plot construction, dialogue, and the economics of surviving as a writer. Rita Will: Autobiography of a Literary Rabble-Rouser was published in 1997.

Sources

Ward, Carol Marie. Rita Mae Brown. New York: Twayne, 1993.

Brown, Sterling Allan (1901–1989) poet, critic, anthologist

Sterling Brown was born into the African-American middle class of Washington, D.C. His father was a distinguished pastor and theologian. Educated at the Dunbar High School, Brown went on to Williams College, where he made Phi Beta Kappa and graduated cum laude. He earned an M.A. degree in English at Harvard. His discovery of Louis UNTERMEYER's anthology, Modern American Poetry (1921), made him aware of poetry as an exemplar of democratic values and demotic speech. In a series of appointments at Negro colleges in the 1920s (Virginia Seminary and College, Lincoln University, and Fisk) Brown explored the origins and development of African-American folklore, which culminated in his most striking poetry collection, Southern Road (1932), and in three anthologies: The Negro in American Fiction (1937), Negro Poetry and Drama (1937), and The Negro Caravan (1941), the most complete collection of literary work up to that time. Brown's later poetry failed to find a publisher for many years until Dudley RANDALL's BROADSIDE PRESS published The Last Ride of Wild Bill (1975). Brown's Collected Poems were published in 1980.

Sources

Gabbin, Joanne V. Sterling Brown: Building the Black Aesthetic Tradition. Westport, Conn.: Greenwood Press, 1985.
Sanders, Mark A. Afro-Modernist Aesthetics and The Poetry of Sterling A. Brown. Athens: University of Georgia Press, 1999.

Buck, Pearl Sydenstricker (1892–1973) novelist

The first American woman to win the Nobel Prize in literature (1938), Pearl S. Buck also won the Pulitzer Prize for The Good Earth (1931). She was born in West Virginia, but her missionary parents took her to China when she was five months old. She attended Randolph-Macon College and Cornell University, and taught in Nanking from 1921 to 1931. Many of her books have a Chinese setting and portray the East in a sympathetic and dramatic light. While her work sold well and her efforts to promote world understanding were admired, literary critics and, more important, the literary establishment scoffed at her as a serious writer and questioned the appropriateness of awarding her a Nobel Prize. Her many books include The First Wife and Other Stories (1933), Dragon Seed (1942), What American Means to Me (1943), Pavilion of Women (1946), My Several Worlds: A Personal Record (1954), Letter from Peking (1957), Stories of China (1964), and The Good Dead and Other Stories of Asia (1969). She wrote portraits of her mother and father in The Exile and Fighting Angel (1936). She published more than 100 books, including plays and books for children.

Sources

Conn, Peter. Pearl S. Buck: A Cultural Biography. New York: Cambridge University Press, 1996.
Doyle, Paul A. Pearl S. Buck. Boston: Twayne, 1980.

Bukowski, Charles Henry (1920–1994) poet, novelist

Born in Andernach, Germany, where his father had met and married a German woman, Charles Bukowski moved with his family to Los Angeles in 1923. Bukowski wrote about his traumatic childhood (he was often beaten by his father) in his autobiographical novel, Ham on Rye (1982).

In and out of college in the 1940s and leading a rough life that included heavy drinking in bars, Bukowski also began writing stories, although his reputation as a poet was not established until the 1960s, with works such as Flower, Fist and Bestial Wall (1960), Long Shot Poems for Broke Players (1962), and Cold Dogs in the Courtyard (1965). As his titles suggest, his writing is earthy, pungent, and verging on the pornographic, while at the same time revealing considerable humor in prose pieces such as All the Assholes in the World and Mine (1966), which is, among other things, an account of "one man's hemorrhoid operation." His other collections of poetry include The Days Run Away Like Wild Horses Over the Hills (1969), Love Is a Dog from Hell (1977), Alone in a Time of Armies (1985), and Supposedly Famous (1992).

Bukowski is just as well known for his fiction, especially Confessions of a Man Insane Enough to Live with Beasts (1965), which introduced Bukowski's alter ego, Henry Chinaski, who appears as well in the novels Post Office (1971) and Factotum (1975). Bukowski's work and life reflected an outspoken, ornery, and raunchy sensibility that mixed provocatively with his vigorous, eloquent style. His other novels include The Most Beautiful Woman in Town (1986) and Hollywood (1989).

Bukowski wrote the screenplay for the film Barfly (1987). Run with the Hunted: A Charles Bukowski Reader was a published in 1993, The Bukowski-Purdy Letters, 1965–1974 in 1983, and Beerspit Night and Cursing: The Correspondence of Charles Bukowski and Sheri Martinelli, 1960–1967 in 2001.

Sources

Brewer, Gay. *Charles Bukowski.* New York: Twayne, 1997.
Cherkovski, Neeli. *Hank: The Life of Charles Bukowski.* New York: Random House, 1991.
Harrison, Russell, ed. *Against the American Grain: Essays on Charles Bukowski.* Santa Rosa, Calif.: Black Sparrow Press, 1994.

Bullins, Ed (1935–) *playwright*

Bullins achieved his greatest renown during the 1960s and 1970s as one of the principal playwrights in a dynamic BLACK ARTS MOVEMENT. His work grows out of his early years in North Philadelphia, where he experienced street life and gang violence. A high school dropout, Bullins almost lost his life in a stabbing incident. He decided to leave home, deliberately choosing the other end of the American continent, where he took classes at Los Angeles City College and began to write in 1961. Although he sympathized with revolutionary movements such as the Black Panthers, Bullins was devoted to playwriting as an art. Bullins projected a cycle of 20 plays about African-American life, beginning with *In the Wine Time* (1968), and including *The Duplex* (1970), *The Fabulous Miss Marie* (1971), and *Home Boy* (1976). In *The Taking of Miss Janie* (1975) he produced one of his most sensitive plays about interracial relationships. Bullins has cited Amiri BARAKA, as well as Eugene O'NEILL and Chester HIMES, as early influences on his work. His later plays, *A Teacup Full of Roses* (1989) and *Dr. Geechee and the Blood Junkies* (1991), include attacks on the drug culture. *Salaam, Huey Newton, Salaam* (1990) explores the life of the famous Blank Panther leader. Bullins's plays possess "raw power," and critics have been divided in their reactions to his uneven output of well over 50 plays.

Sources

Hay, Samuel A. *Ed Bullins: A Literary Biography.* Detroit: Wayne State University Press, 1997.

Bulosan, Carlos (1913–1956) *poet, autobiographer*

A Filipino-American, Bulosan was once a migrant laborer. He educated himself and in 1946 published his autobiography, *America Is in the Heart,* based on his experiences in the canneries and in the fields of the American West in the 1920s and 1930s. He compared the ideal United States, which he had learned about in school, to the harsh United States he found when he immigrated.

Sources

Lee, Rachel C. *The Americas of Asian American Literature: Gendered Fictions of Nation and Transnation.* Princeton, N.J.: Princeton University Press, 1999.

Burroughs, Edgar Rice (1875–1950) *short story writer, novelist*

The creator of Tarzan and author of *Tarzan of the Apes* (1914), Burroughs was born in Chicago and educated at Phillips Academy. He served in the U.S. Cavalry, and after working at many different occupations he decided to try writing. He had read the PULPS and believed that he could write at least as well (or as badly) as other popular authors. He began with science fiction: "Under the Moons of Mars" was serialized in *All-Story Magazine* in 1912. He wrote more than 70 books and reportedly was grateful for his popularity but did not take his work too seriously. He tried to write more realistic fiction, but it proved less successful than his Tarzan series. His books have been translated into at least 30 languages, selling upward of 36 million copies.

Sources

Holtsmark, Erling B. *Edgar Rice Burroughs.* Boston: Twayne, 1986.
Taliaferro, John. *Tarzan Forever: The Life of Edgar Rice Burroughs, Creator of Tarzan.* New York: Scribner, 1999.

Burroughs, William Seward (1914–1997) *novelist*

Burroughs grew up in a socially prominent family in St. Louis, Missouri. He was educated at Harvard and then served in the army during World War II until he was released on psychiatric grounds. Burroughs had trouble holding a job, and was a drug addict from 1944 to 1957. His first book, *Junkie: Confessions of an Underground Drug Addict* (1953), had an enormous impact on BEAT writers such as Jack KEROUAC and Allen GINSBERG. Burroughs was remarkably unapologetic about drugs and presented a view of the addict's life without sentimentality or moralizing. His novel *Naked Lunch* (1959) made him both a celebrated and a cult figure. The novel was banned in the United States until 1962, and such writers as Norman MAILER had to go to court to defend Burroughs's surrealistic book as literature. What impressed Mailer and others was Burroughs's gift for language, which at its best was both hallucinatory and captivating. Burroughs seemed to be the harbinger of the liberated 1960s. Burroughs continued in the same vein with *The Soft Machine* (1961), *The Ticket that Exploded* (1962), *Nova Express* (1964), *Wild Boys: A Book of the Dead* (1971), *Port of Saints* (1973), and *Exterminator!* (1974). After living in Paris and Tangier for many years, Burroughs returned to the United States, living in New York, California, and finally in Kansas, where he died. His books after 1974 were less avant-garde, although hardly realistic. In *Cities of the Red Night* (1981), *The Place of the Dead Roads* (1984), and *The Western Lands* (1985) he explored telepathy, cosmic struggle, time and space travel, and ancient Egypt. He wrote two noteworthy movie scripts: *The Last Words of Dutch Shultz* (1970) and *Blade Runner* (1979).

Sources

Caveny, Graham. *Gentleman Junkie: The Life and Legacy of William S. Burroughs.* Boston: Little, Brown, 1998.
Skerl, Jennie. *William S. Burroughs.* Boston: Twayne, 1985.

Busch, Frederick (1941–) *novelist*

Born in Brooklyn, New York, Busch received a degree from Columbia University in 1967. His theory of fiction is expressed in his critical study, *John Hawkes* (1973), in which Busch favors innovative, experimental prose. Busch's novels concern familial and parental relationships in *Manual Labor* (1974), *Domestic Particulars* (1976), *Take this Man* (1984), and *Long Way from Home* (1993). His nonfiction includes *A Dangerous Profession: A Book About the Writing Life* (2000).

Butler, Octavia (1947–) *novelist*

Butler was born in Pasadena, California, and educated in Los Angeles. She is one of the few African-American women to write science fiction. Her protagonists are often African-American women and her subjects include space travel, telepathy, aliens mating with survivors of a nuclear holocaust on earth, and other questions about human identity and the survival of the species. Her novels include *Patternmaster* (1976), *Mind of My Mind* (1977), *Survivor* (1978), *Wild Seed* (1978), *Dawn* (1987), *Adulthood Rites* (1988), *Imago* (1989), and a novel set in California in 2024, *Parable of the Sower* (1993). *Goodchild, and Other Stories* appeared in 1995 and another novel, *Parable of the Talents,* in 1998.

Sources

Barr, Marleen S., ed. *Suzy McKee Charnas / Marleen S. Barr. Octavia E. Butler / Ruth Salvaggio. Joan D. Vinge / Richard Law.* Mercer Island, Wash.: Starmont House, 1986.

Butler, Robert Olen (1945–) *novelist, short story writer*

Butler was born in Granite City, Illinois. He developed an early interest in drama and majored in the subject at Northwestern University. He then earned an M.F.A. degree in playwriting from the University of Iowa. In 1971 he enlisted in the army and learned Vietnamese so that he could serve as a language expert and understand the country's culture. He remained in Vietnam until 1975 and then returned to the United States, working in New York and writing his first novels. His novels are distinguished by their sense of authenticity—his meticulous attention to the details of the physical, social, and political environment—and his concern with both the American reaction to the Vietnamese and the response of the Vietnamese to Americans. His work is the fullest fictional treatment of what it was like to live in Vietnam during the war and of what happened when Vietnam veterans returned home and tried to resume normal lives. His novels include *The Alleys of Eden* (1981), *On Distant Ground* (1985), and *They Whisper* (1994). He won a Pulitzer Prize for his short story collection *A Good Scent from a Strange Mountain* (1992). *Tabloid Dreams: Stories* appeared in 1996. Since 1985, Butler has taught fiction writing at McNeese State University in Lake Charles, Louisiana.

Sources

Weich, David. "Robert Olen Butler Plays with Voices," Powells.com Interviews. Available on-line. URL: http://www.powells.com/authors/butler.html

Cabell, James Branch (1879–1958) *novelist, essayist, poet, historian*

Cabell belonged to one of Virginia's founding families and was educated at the College of William and Mary. His romance and fantasy novels were extremely popular, particularly *Jurgen* (1919), which is said to have influenced William FAULKNER. Cabell tended to set his stories in the medieval past. His heroes' sexual involvements led some critics to accuse the author of immorality, but the controversy primarily increased Cabell's sales. He had an elaborate interest in genealogy, and his novels trace the intricate story of the character Dom Manuel and his descendants, a story that can be read in chronological order, which is not the order in which the novels were written and published. In order of the sequence of events, his important books follow this order: *Beyond Life* (1919), *Domei* (1920, first published as *The Soul of Melicent* in 1913), *Chivalry* (1909), *Jurgen, The Line of Love* (1905), *Gallantry* (1907), *The Certain Hour* (1916), *The Cords of Vanity* (1909), *The Rivet in Grandfather's Neck* (1915), *The Eagle's Shadow* (1904), *The Cream of the Jest* (1917), *Figures of Earth* (1921), *The High Place* (1923), *The Silver Stallion* (1926), and *Something about Eve* (1927). Much admired in his day, Cabell was less popular with later generations of readers and critics put off by Cabell's complex use of artifice.

Sources

Inge, M. Thomas and Edgar E. MacDonald, eds. *James Branch Cabell: Centennial Essays.* Baton Rouge: Louisiana State University Press, 1983.

MacDonald Edgar. *James Branch Cabell and Richmond-in-Virginia.* Jackson: University Press of Mississippi, 1983.

Cahan, Abraham (1860–1951) *journalist, novelist*

In 1897, Cahan founded the *Jewish Daily Forward,* and under his editorship, the newspaper climbed in circulation to nearly a quarter of a million readers. His most important work of fiction is *The Rise of David Levinsky* (1917), a groundbreaking novel that dealt with the immigrant dream of success in America. Cahan was born in Russia and came to the United States in 1882. A fervent socialist, he saw early that the Soviet government was a tyranny. His other books include *The Imported Bridegroom and Other Stories of the New York Ghetto* (1898) and *Yekl, a Tale of the New York Ghetto* (1896). See also JEWISH-AMERICAN LITERATURE.

Sources

Marovitz, Sanford E. *Abraham Cahan.* New York: Twayne, 1996.

Cain, James Mallahan (1892–1977) *journalist, novelist, short story writer*

Born in Annapolis and educated at Washington College in Maryland, James M. Cain began his writing career at the *Baltimore Sun* and later worked for the *New York World.* After writing freelance magazine pieces, he published his first novel, *The Postman Always Rings Twice* (1934). His terse, hard-boiled style was compared to Ernest HEMINGWAY's, but Cain is closer to PULP novelists in his ability to unfold a story swiftly and often violently. Widely admired by the public and his fellow writers, Cain produced a string of successful novels, many of them made into movies. His novels include *Serenade* (1937), *Mildred Pierce* (1941), *Love's Lovely Counterfeit* (1942), *Three of a Kind* (1943), *Double In-*

demnity (1944), *Past All Dishonor* (1946), *The Butterfly* (1947), *The Moth* (1948), *Galatea* (1953), *Mignon* (1962), *The Magician's Wife* (1965), *Rainbow's End* (1975), and *The Institute* (1976). His stories are collected in *The Baby in the Icebox* (1981).

Sources
Hoopes, Ray. *Cain*. New York: Holt, Rinehart and Winston, 1982.
Madden, David. *James M. Cain*. New York: Twayne, 1970.

Caldwell, Erskine Preston (1903–1987) *novelist, short story writer*

Born in Moreland, Georgia, Erskine Caldwell attended several colleges, including the University of Virginia and the University of Pennsylvania, but his milieu was always the South. He worked as a reporter on the *Atlanta Journal* (1925) and as a screenwriter in Hollywood in the late 1930s. However, with the publication of his novels *Tobacco Road* (1932) and *God's Little Acre* (1933), he achieved pre-eminence among southern writers who focused on poor whites. *Tobacco Road* became a hugely successful play that ran for seven years on Broadway. Caldwell's ribald humor and gritty realism were immensely appealing. His lean, economical prose was also admired by his contemporaries, particularly William FAULKNER, who ranked Caldwell among the five best contemporary American writers. His later novels failed to capture the critics' attention, although he continued to fare well with the public and his work sold in the tens of millions. Caldwell deals with southern racism in *Trouble in July* (1940) and the South during World War II in *Tragic Ground* (1944). *A Place Called Estherville* (1949) explores relationships between African Americans and whites. Caldwell wrote about other subjects and places as well, including Maine and the Soviet Union, but he owed his popularity to his grasp of southern life.

Caldwell also was a superb short story writer. His short fiction is collected in *We Are the Living* (1933), *Kneel to the Rising Sun* (1935), *Jackpot* (1940), *Georgia Boy* (1943), *The Courting of Susie Brown* (1952), *Gulf Coast Stories* (1956), *When You Think of Me* (1959), and *Men and Women* (1961). His *Complete Stories* appeared in 1953.

Caldwell was married to the brilliant photographer Margaret Bourke-White, and their collaborations are noteworthy: *You Have Seen Their Faces* (1937), depicting southern sharecroppers; *North of the Danube* (1939), a portrait of Czechoslovakia on the eve of World War II; *Say! Is This the U.S.A.?* (1942), and *Russia at War* (1942). Caldwell also wrote several important books of nonfiction, including *Deep South* (1968) and *Call It Experience: The Years of Learning How to Write* (1965). *In Search of Bisco* (1965) recounts Caldwell's effort to find an African-American man who had been his boyhood friend.

Sources
Devlin, James. *Erskine Caldwell*. Boston: Twayne, 1984.
Klevar, Harvey L. *Erskine Caldwell: A Biography*. Knoxville: University of Tennessee Press, 1993.

Calisher, Hortense (1911–) *novelist*

Calisher grew up in Yorkville, a German-Jewish neighborhood in New York City. Educated at Hunter High School and Barnard College, she wrote about the lives of middle-class Manhattanites. Her career started slowly: She began writing at 36, and published her first volume of short stories, *In the Absence of Angels*, in 1951. Her *Collected Stories* was published in 1975. Her later novels include *The Bobby-Soxer* (1986) and *Age* (1987), but she may be most remembered for her memoir, *Herself* (1972).

Sources
Snodgrass, Kathleen. *The Fiction of Hortense Calisher*. Newark: University of Delaware Press, 1993.

Campbell, Joseph (1904–1987) *scholar, critic, editor*

A scholar of comparative myths, Campbell joined the faculty of Sarah Lawrence College in 1934, where he explored the recurrence of archetypes in world literature. His most important book is *The Hero With a Thousand Faces* (1949) a popular and critical success. Its wide-ranging exploration of myths in Indian, Greek, Christian, Eskimo, Tibetan, Chinese, Japanese, and Australian cultures has led to its adoption for classroom study. A combination of anthropology and literary criticism, the book has appealed to scholars in many different disciplines. Campbell also published a four-volume study, *Masks of God* (1959–1967). *Myths to Live By* (1972) and *The Mythic Image* (1974) did much to popularize Campbell's work—as did his appearances on a Bill Moyers television series about mythology, *Joseph Campbell and the Power of Myth* (1991). Campbell edited *The Portable Jung* (1971).

Interviews with Joseph Campbell have appeared in several publications: *An Open Life: Joseph Campbell in Conversation with Michael Toms* (1988); *The Hero's Journey: The World of Joseph Campbell: Joseph Campbell on His Life and Work* (1990); and *The Way of Myth: Talking with Joseph Campbell* (1994).

Sources
Ellwood, Robert S. *The Politics of Myth: A Study of C.G. Jung, Mircea Eliade, and Joseph Campbell*. Albany: State University of New York Press, 1999.
Segal, Robert A. *Joseph Campbell: An Introduction*. New York: Garland, 1987.

Capote, Truman (1924–1984) *novelist, short story writer*

Capote's early novels—*Other Voices, Other Rooms* (1948) and *The Grass Harp* (1951)—derived from his childhood spent among various relatives in the South. His parents divorced when he was four, and his mother moved to New York City. Capote went to live first in Monroeville, Alabama, and then, at age 10, in New Orleans. From the beginning, he wrote with an elegance that many writers achieve only after writing several books. Celebrated as a wunderkind, he became attracted to high society, celebrities, and fashionable subjects—reflected in *Breakfast at Tiffany's* (1958), his charming story of Holly Golightly, who tries to perfect her life so that it is like the jewelry at Tiffany's, and *Music for Chameleons* (1980), a collection of stories and memoirs that feature his experiences with stars such as Marilyn Monroe and his fascination with fashionable society. Although classified as a writer with a sensitive grasp of what it was like to grow up in the South, Capote expanded his scope and his audience when he published *In Cold Blood* in 1966. He called his account of the gruesome murder of a Kansas family, the Clutters, by Perry Smith and Dick Hickok a "nonfiction novel." Although the best-selling book was based on fact, Capote wrote a narrative of such power that it has been compared with such masterpieces of NATURALISM as Theodore DREISER's *An American Tragedy.* As Capote developed the scene of the crime he shifted points of view—entering, for example, the mind of Perry Smith. Instead of simply quoting from interviews with Smith and Hickok, Capote reassembled their stories in his own poetic prose.

Although Capote continued to write deft profiles of personalities and exquisite short stories after *In Cold Blood,* he found it impossible to produce another major work. Fragments of a novel, *Answered Prayers,* were published after his death in 1987. This work was intended to be his exposé of high society, and many of the characters were based on his close friends, who felt he had betrayed them by writing about them. A frequent guest on television interview programs, Capote became the embodiment of the celebrated writer. His other nonfiction includes *The Muses Are Heard* (1956) and *The Dogs Bark: Public People and Private Places* (1973).

Sources

Clarke, Gerald. *Capote: A Biography.* New York: Simon & Schuster, 1988.

Grobel, Lawrence, ed. *Conversations with Capote.* New York: New American Library, 1985.

Plimpton, George. *Truman Capote: In Which Various Friends, Enemies, Acquaintances, and Detractors Recall His Turbulent Career.* New York: Doubleday, 1997.

Carolina folk plays

In 1919 the Carolina Playmakers, a regional theater group associated with the University of North Carolina, began having notable playwrights such as Paul GREEN and Thomas WOLFE draw on regional materials and traditions. These "folk plays" marked a deliberate turning away from the conventions of the commercial theater as Green, in particular, had experienced them. He wanted a closer contact with local materials and communities. The plays avoid melodrama and tend to be much longer than the two- to three-hour plays produced on Broadway. Paul Green's *The Lost Colony* (1937), a dramatization of what happened to Virginia's first settlers, is a good example of the folk play's use of pageantry and tableau rather than the clear story lines and character conflicts associated with the commercial theater. Folk songs and historical chronicles are also featured in folk plays, which tend to include very large casts of characters.

Frederick Koch edited a quarterly selection of the plays, *The Carolina Play-Book,* beginning in March 1928. The plays were collected in a single volume in 1941.

Carraway, Nick *character*

The narrator of F. Scott FITZGERALD's THE GREAT GATSBY, Nick is a Wall Street bondsman from a wealthy midwestern family. Through Nick's sensitive perceptions, the novel examines the mysterious, mythic character of Jay Gatsby. Gatsby's lover, Daisy Buchanan, is Nick's distant cousin. Nick becomes seduced, in certain ways, by Gatsby's romantic pursuit of Daisy and the American dream, but Nick is also wary, realizing how blind Gatsby is to the realities of his situation. After Gatsby is shot, Nick pulls away from the rich, self-absorbed life that Daisy and her husband, Tom, represent.

Carruth, Hayden (1921–) *poet*

Born in Connecticut, Carruth writes hard-edged poetry that has been compared to the understated but sharply phrased work of Robert FROST and T. S. ELIOT. *The Selected Poetry of Hayden Carruth* was published in 1986. He is also the editor of the influential anthology, *The Voice That Is Great Within Us: American Poetry of the Twentieth Century* (1970), which often is used in the classroom because of its comprehensiveness. *Reluctantly,* a collection of autobiographical essays, was published in 1998.

Sources

New York State Writers Institute. "Talking to Hayden Carruth" [two interviews]. New York State Writers Institute—Writers Online, Vol. 1, No. 3 (spring 1997). Available on-line. URL: http://www.albany.edu/writers-inst/olv1n3.html#carruth. Downloaded May 25, 2001.

Carver, Raymond (1938–1988) *short story writer*

Carver was born in Clatskanie, Oregon, and educated at colleges in California and at the University of Iowa, where he earned an M.F.A. degree in 1966. Carver worked at various odd jobs (janitor, delivery man, salesman) until he began publishing stories in the 1970s, which led to a series of teaching assignments at prestigious universities. Carver has sometimes been compared to Ernest HEMINGWAY for his minimalist style, which relies more on description than on elaborate metaphors or on startling imagery. His first two story collections, *Put Yourself in My Shoes* (1974) and *Will You Please Be Quiet, Please?* (1976), emphasize character over plot and develop domestic situations in a style reminiscent of Chekhov's meticulous attention to everyday life. Carver is the master dramatist of ordinary people in fairly ordinary circumstances. Carver's later collections, *Cathedral* (1983) and *The Stories* (1985), reflect a somewhat more verbose style and signify a departure from his earlier, rather bleak vision of human character. What unites all of his work, however, is an exquisite sense of the short story's form and its unique capacity to explore scenes and people with meticulous, minute, and telling detail. Carver's *Where I'm Calling From: New and Selected Stories* was published in 1988. His poetry is less well known and has not been considered a major part of his work. *In a Marine Light: Selected Poems* was published in 1987.

Sources

Runyon, Randolph. *Reading Raymond Carver.* Syracuse, N.Y.: Syracuse University Press, 1992.
Stull, William L. and Maureen P. Carroll, eds. *Remembering Ray: A Composite Biography of Raymond Carver.* Santa Barbara, Calif.: Capra Press, 1993.

Cassill, Ronald Verlin (1919–) *novelist*

Born and raised in Iowa, R. V. Cassill was educated at the University of Iowa and teaches creative writing there. He has published provocative novels on a wide range of subjects, including *Eagle on the Coin* (1950), the story of an African American's effort to be elected to a local school board; *Clem Anderson* (1961), the tragedy of a young writer; *The President* (1964), about the career of an ambitious college president; *La Vie Passionee of Rodney Buckthorne* (1968), set in academia and Greenwich Village; *Dr. Cobb's Game* (1970), a spirited retelling of the 1963 John Profumo political and sexual scandal in Great Britain; *Flame* (1980), the life of a female film star; and *After Goliath* (1985), a fictional biography of King David. His short fiction is collected in *Three Stories* (1982). This highly versatile and accomplished author has been neglected by the critics.

Catch-22 Joseph Heller (1961) *novel*

Joseph Heller's black comedy about WORLD WAR II centers on John Yossarian, a bombardier who believes that everyone is conspiring to kill him. He tries every kind of ruse to get out of going on bombing missions and finally decides to fake his own crash landing. He sets off on a raft, in imitation (he believes) of a friend who was shot down over the Mediterranean and was later picked up.

The novel is a devastating attack on the absurdity of war, the callousness of the officers who send men to their deaths, and the resulting paranoia among the men who actually have to fight. Heller's novel has been hailed as a work of fiction that ushered in the 1960s, a decade in which attacks on war, the tyranny of government, and the creative anarchism of individuals was celebrated.

Sources

Nagel, James, ed. *Critical Essays on Catch-22.* Encino, Calif.: Dickenson Pub. Co., 1974.
Woodson, Jon. *A Study of Joseph Heller's Catch-22: Going Around Twice.* New York: Peter Lang, 2001.

Catcher in the Rye, The J. D. Salinger (1951) *novel*

Holden CAULFIELD, the hero of J. D. SALINGER's classic novel, has to negotiate his way through a world of "phonies." He flunks out of prep school and is estranged from his parents. He goes to New York City and has a demoralizing encounter with a prostitute, then with an old girlfriend who rejects his proposal that they live together. Yet Caulfield persists in thinking of himself as a "catcher in the rye"—one who stands near a cliff and makes sure that playing children do not fall off the edge. A former teacher seems to offer help, but when the teacher seems to make a physical advance Holden is horrified. His one confidant remains his 10-year-old sister, Phoebe. Having failed in his breakout from school, Holden is last seen in the hospital under the care of a psychoanalyst. The question of how Holden will be able to adjust when he returns to school remains unresolved, since he seems to long for another effort to define himself even at the risk of failing once again.

Salinger's novel has become a staple of the American canon as well as a cult novel for adolescents. Its strength derives from its meticulous portrait of an adolescent consciousness as well as its biting social criticism.

Sources

Salzberg, Joel, ed. *Critical Essays on The Catcher in the Rye.* Boston: G. K. Hall, 1990.
Salzman, Jack, ed. *New Essays on The Catcher in the Rye.* New York: Cambridge University Press, 1991.

Cather, Willa Sibert (1873–1947) *novelist, short story writer*

Willa Cather was born in Back Creek Valley, Virginia, to a father who sided with the Union in the Civil War and a strong mother who became the model for Rachel in Cather's last novel, *Sapphira and the Slave Girl* (1940).

When she was nine, Cather moved to Nebraska with her family. The Midwest sparked her imagination as she learned about the immigrants who had settled the prairie. At the same time, she found small-town life constricting, especially for a woman bent on having a career. In her third novel, *The Song of the Lark* (1915), Cather drew on these stimulating but also stifling adolescent years.

Cather went to the University of Nebraska in Lincoln and enjoyed meeting intellectuals and theater people. After her graduation in 1894, Cather wrote for local newspapers and by 1903 had earned her big break, writing for a national magazine, *McClure's*. She published her first novel, *Alexander's Bridge*, in 1912, but it was her second novel, *O Pioneers!* (1913), that established her reputation. It dramatized the lives of the immigrants with a lyricism and melodramatic verve that captured a broad audience of readers. Her heroine, Alexandra Bergson, is earthy but also romantically conceived.

My Ántonia (1918), regarded as Cather's masterpiece, is set in Black Hawk, Nebraska. Jim Burden and Ántonia Shimerda marry and become mired in an unproductive farm. After several humiliating experiences, including work as a maid and a failed marriage, Ántonia remarries, asserts her rugged pioneer strength, and becomes the core of a new family.

Cather wrote with an exceptional feeling for the American land and for the character of its stalwart women. As her work matured, she developed a powerful grasp of American history and of the tension between nature and civilization. Feminist critics have much to praise in Cather's work, but the scope of her writing transcends any easy categorization. Sinclair LEWIS is said to have acknowledged her as one of the great American writers when he said she deserved the Nobel Prize more than he did.

Cather's novel *One of Ours* (1922) won a Pulitzer Prize. Her other important novels include *A Lost Lady* (1923), *The Professor's House* (1925), *My Mortal Enemy* (1926), and *Death Comes for the Archbishop* (1927).

Cather's short fiction is collected in *The Troll Garden* (1905), *Youth and the Bright Medusa* (1920), *Obscure Destinies* (1932), and *Old Beauty and Others* (1948). Her *Collected Short Fiction: 1892–1912* was published in 1965 and *Collected Fiction, 1915–1929* in 1973.

Sources

Bloom, Harold, ed. *Modern Critical Views: Willa Cather.* New York: Chelsea House, 1985.

Gerber, Philip. *Willa Cather: Revised Edition.* New York: Twayne, 1995.

Woodress, James. *Willa Cather: A Literary Life.* Lincoln: University of Nebraska Press, 1987.

Caulfield, Holden   *character*

The protagonist of J. D. SALINGER's coming-of-age novel, *THE CATCHER IN THE RYE,* Holden tells his own rather bitter story,

his view of a society composed of "phonies." He is disenchanted with school, does poorly, and leaves for a spell in New York City. He checks into a hotel, has a brief, clumsy encounter with a prostitute, goes on a date with a girl he knows and tells her how "fed up" he is with everything. He gets drunk and calls his sister, Phoebe, telling her his dream about being a "catcher in the rye," someone who catches children at play who wander too near the edge of a cliff. Like Mark Twain's Huckleberry Finn, Holden dreams of moving west, but the novel ends with Holden in a hospital, telling his story to a psychiatrist.

Sources

Bloom, Harold, ed. *Holden Caulfield.* New York: Chelsea House, 1990.

Century Magazine   *periodical*

Founded in 1874, the magazine published important American writers such as Jack LONDON and Mark Twain. After 1913, it focused on journalism and its circulation (once as high as 200,000) declined. It then enjoyed an intense literary period (1921–1925) under the editorship of Glenn Frank, who once again published notable British and American fiction writers. The magazine merged with *The Forum* in 1930.

Chandler, Raymond Thornton   (1888–1959)
novelist, screenwriter

Raymond Chandler was born in Chicago. His parents were divorced when he was seven, and his mother moved with him to London. Chandler received a classical English education and began to write for magazines. He came to the United States in 1912, settling in southern California and working at a variety of jobs before serving in the U.S. Army during World War I.

Although he wrote short fiction after the war and immersed himself in the southern California environment that would figure so memorably in his fiction, Chandler went through many years of alcoholism and failure. His fortunes improved in 1933 when he published a detective story in *Black Mask,* a PULP magazine.

By the 1940s Chandler was writing for Hollywood studios, employment he earned from the success of his detective novels, *The Big Sleep* (1939) and *Farewell, My Lovely* (1940), which featured his brilliant creation of detective Philip Marlowe.

Chandler has been praised for bringing a highly polished literary style to the genre of the detective novel. His books contain allusions to other writers such as Ernest HEMINGWAY and T. S. ELIOT, reflecting Chandler's desire to fit the mystery story and detective novel into the context of MODERNIST literature. Los Angeles is evoked so vividly it has been called Chandler's greatest character. Like Dashiell HAMMETT, Chandler has his detective uncover the corruption of city and family life. Marlowe appears in all of Chandler's novels—most effectively in *The Long Goodbye* (1953).

Both *The Big Sleep* and *Farewell, My Lovely* have been filmed several times—evidence of Chandler's enduring hold on the popular as well as the literary imagination.

Chandler's short fiction has been collected in *Five Murderers* (1944), *Five Sinister Characters* (1945), *Finger Man and Other Stories* (1946), *Red Wind* (1946), *Spanish Blood* (1946), *Trouble Is My Business* (1950), *The Simple Art of Murder* (1950), *Pick-up on Noon Street* (1952), *Smart-Aleck Kill* (1953), *Pearls Are a Nuisance* (1958), *Killer in the Rain* (1964), *The Smell of Fear* (1965), and *The Midnight Raymond Chandler* (1971).

Chandler was an eloquent commentator on writing, and some of his commentary is included in *Raymond Chandler Speaking* (1962).

Sources

Hiney, Tom. *Raymond Chandler: A Biography.* New York: Atlantic Monthly Press, 1997.

MacShane, Frank. *The Life of Raymond Chandler.* New York: Dutton, 1976.

Chang, Diana (1934–) *poet, novelist*

Chang was born in New York City but grew up in China. She returned to the United States after World War II to attend high school. She majored in English at Barnard College, publishing her early poetry in the literary journals PO-ETRY and *Voices*. She completed her first novel, *Frontiers of Love*, in 1956, and it immediately established her reputation as a promising writer. She published five more novels: *A Woman of Thirty* (1959), *A Passion for Life* (1961), *The Only Game in Town* (1963), *Eye to Eye* (1974), and *A Perfect Love* (1978). She also published three volumes of poetry: *The Horizon Is Definitely Speaking* (1962), *What Matisse Is After* (1984), and *Earth Water Light* (1991). Chang explores Chinese-American life from the perspective of a writer thoroughly grounded in the Western tradition. She has been called an existential (see EXISTENTIALISM) writer because she focuses so much on questions of identity formation and consciousness of self. She is one of the first Asian-American women authors to attain a major reputation.

Sources

"Diana M. P. Chang," The International Poetry Hall of Fame. Available on-line. URL: http://poets.com/DianaChang.html. Downloaded May 25, 2001.

Hamalian, Leo. "A Melius Interview with Diana Chang." *Melius* 20 (Winter 1995): 29.

Chappell, Fred (1936–) *novelist, poet*

Born and raised in North Carolina, Chappell has taught at the University of North Carolina at Chapel Hill since 1964.

Much of his work might be termed regionalist (see REGIONALISM). His novels—*It is Time, Lord* (1963), *Dagon* (1968), *The Gaudy Place* (1973), *I Am One of You Forever* (1985), *Brighten the Corner Where You Are* (1989), *Farewell, I'm Bound to Leave You* (1996), *Look Back All the Green Valley* (1999)—include North Carolina settings and characters who explore the nature of family and community life, religion, sexuality, and education. An accomplished poet, Chappell has published several collections: *The World Between the Eyes* (1971), *River* (1975), *Bloodfire* (1978), *Wind Mountain* (1979), and *Earthsleep* (1980). Chappell is noted for his ability to combine humor and intensity. His later poetry includes *Source* (1985), *First and Last Words* (1989), and *Family Gathering* (2000).

Plow Naked: Selected Writings on Poetry appeared in 1993 and *A Way of Happening: Observations of Contemporary Poetry* in 1998.

Sources

Bizzaro, Patrick, ed. *Dream Garden: The Poetic Vision of Fred Chappell.* Baton Rouge: Louisiana State University Press, 1997.

Lang, John. *Understanding Fred Chappell.* Columbia: University of South Carolina Press, 2000.

Chase, Ilka (1905–1978) *novelist, memoirist*

Born in New York City, Chase grew up in New York high society and appeared by the age of 18 on radio programs and on the New York stage. An editor of *Vogue* and a popular novelist, she is best known for her memoir *Past Imperfect* (1942), one of the classic American autobiographies for its vivid portrayal of New York theater and society.

Chayefsky, Paddy (Sidney Chayefsky) (1923–1981) *playwright, screenwriter, novelist*

Born in New York City and a graduate of City College, Chayefsky turned to television writing after service in WORLD WAR II. His most famous work is *Marty*, a sensitive story about a Bronx butcher and his tentative courtship of a schoolteacher, first shown on television in 1953 and made into a successful film in 1955. Chayefsky's work is a blend of realism and sentimentality. He finds the good in common people. His great period of popularity was the 1950s—when he wrote *The Bachelor Party*, presented on television in 1954 and on film in 1957, and *The Catered Affair*, a 1955 television production and a 1956 film. Much later in his career he achieved success in two remarkable films, *Network* (1975), the story of a television anchorman, and *Altered States* (1978), a science fiction film based on his novel of the same title. Chayefsky also had moderate success as a playwright with *The Tenth Man* (1959), which focuses on Judaism, and *The Passion of Josef D* (1964), a treatment of Stalin, Trotsky, Lenin, and the

Russian revolution. He collected his work in *Television Plays* (1955). He is indeed one of the few writers for television who achieved both success and critical esteem and who is still studied for this grasp of the culture of the 1950s.

Sources
Considine, Shaun. *Mad as Hell: The Life and Work of Paddy Chayefsky.* New York: Random House, 1994.

Cheever, John (1912–1982) *short story writer, novelist*
Born in Quincy, Massachusetts, Cheever, a precocious writer, drew on his personal experience with his first short story, "Expelled," published in the NEW REPUBLIC on October 10, 1930, which is an account of his own expulsion from Thayer Academy. Other than a close relationship with an older brother, he grew up without a mentor—his father lost his job and his self-respect during the DEPRESSION, and his mother was preoccupied with the gift shop she opened to support her family.

By the mid-1930s Cheever was publishing in the NEW YORKER his elegantly written stories of American city and suburban life. His work centers on exploring how his characters react to their comfortable, privileged world. They may fail, but they also persevere. Existence can seem absurd, yet Cheever reports its ridiculousness with care, humor, satire, and irony that reflect serious moral concerns. Occasionally Cheever strives for surrealistic (see SURREALISM) effects, as in the title story of *The Enormous Radio and Other Stories* (1953). The whimsical cast of his fiction is reflected in the title *Some People, Places, and Things That Will Not Appear in My Next Novel* (1961). *The Stories of John Cheever* (1978) includes nearly all of his collected stories.

Cheever made his reputation as a novelist with *The Wapshot Chronicle* (1957) and *The Wapshot Scandal* (1964). These novels document the decline of a fictional New England town and the adventures of two boys who forsake their New England heritage for avid involvement in modern life, represented by New York City.

Bullet Park (1969) recovered some of Cheever's comic gifts, especially in his depiction of the novel's hero, Eliot Nailles, a rather naive and yet accomplished man attuned to the natural world and to working with his hands. The setting is the suburbs, which Cheever treats both affectionately and critically.

Falconer (1977), a model of narrative compression, enhanced Cheever's reputation not only because of its beautiful prose but also because of its riveting depiction of prison life. This novel is one of the finest examples of a contemporary novelist's ability to balance a view of society with the drama of his main character's disintegrating personality.

Oh What a Paradise It Seems (1982) is a slighter novel, but it retains Cheever's trademark satirical views of modern life and compassion for his characters.

The Letters of John Cheever was published in 1988 and *The Journals of John Cheever* in 1991.

Sources
Donaldson, Scott, ed. *Conversations with John Cheever.* Jackson: University Press of Mississippi, 1987.
———. *John Cheever: A Biography.* New York: Random House, 1988.
Meaner, Patrick. *John Cheever Revisited.* New York: Twayne, 1995.

Chicago, Illinois
After New York and San Francisco, Chicago has long been a literary center of American literature in the 20th century. At the turn of the century it inspired writers like Theodore DREISER, who developed his naturalistic view of life in the city. During World War I, Ben HECHT founded the *Chicago Literary Times* (1914–1918), which expressed the robust writing of the period and Hecht's own blend of journalism and fiction. The city also attracted Sherwood ANDERSON, who kept returning to it for inspiration. Carl SANDBURG called Chicago the "city of the big shoulders" and did much to further its image as a dynamic center of industry and the arts. Richard WRIGHT set his grim naturalistic novel, *Native Son* (1940), in Chicago, which also became the scene of Lorraine HANSBERRY's landmark play, *A Raisin in the Sun*. Saul BELLOW made the city the site of many of his stories and novels. David MAMET grew up in Chicago and tried out many of his early plays there.

Chicago critics
A group of academics centered at the University of Chicago in the 1940s and 1950s, it included R. S. Crane, Richard McKeon, Elder Olson, and W. R. Keast—all of whom practiced a critical method derived from Aristotle's *Poetics*. They subscribed to no single method of interpretation. Instead, they emulated Aristotle in their attempt to describe and analyze the constituent parts of a work of art (character, setting, action). The key question for them was how these parts came together to make a whole work of art that moved an audience or readers. Unlike the New Critics (see NEW CRITICISM), the Chicago critics did not focus exclusively on the elements of the work itself. They acknowledged that art can be examined in a larger context of culture and history and that questions about a work of art might lead to the examination of an author's life or body of work. This examination in turn might elicit new and different questions about a work of art than might arise from a consideration of the formal elements alone.

Sources
Mukherjee, Tutun. *The Chicago Critics: An Evaluation.* Delhi: Academic Foundation, 1991.

Chicago Defender periodical

Established in 1905 by Robert S. Abbott, this local newspaper commented on the state of affairs in African-American life. It reported instances of injustice and worse (lynchings in the South, for example) and on improvements in the social and political lives of African Americans. It gradually became an influential voice in both local and national affairs—particularly in the Middle West and the South. In 1917, the *Defender* began a campaign urging the migration of blacks to the North. It also featured the columns of Langston HUGHES, in which he created his memorable character, Jesse B. Semple ("Simple").

Christmas, Joe character

William FAULKNER's scapegoat hero in *LIGHT IN AUGUST,* Joe is an orphan suspected of having black blood. He engages in an affair with Joanna Burden, a white southern woman and a descendant of Northern abolitionists. Joe has been brought up by a white family, the McEacherns. His foster father is a religious fanatic who treats Joe harshly until Joe strikes back and apparently kills him. Joe escapes to Jefferson, Mississippi, where he lives quietly and takes odd jobs. His two-year affair with Joanna Burden ends violently, however, when he slits her throat, enraged by her effort to dominate him and in frustration over his own confused identity. He is then lynched by Percy Grimm, a virulent racist, who sees Joe as a black man who has defiled a white woman's bed.

Chu, Louis (1915–1970) novelist

Chu came to Newark, New Jersey, from his native Canton, China. He was educated at New York University and served in the army in World War II. He provides a vivid portrait of New York City's Chinatown in *Eat a Bowl of Tea* (1961), a novel notable for its grasp of everyday Chinese-American speech and social conflict.

Sources

Frank Chin, ed. *An Anthology of Asian American Writers.* New York: Meridian, 1997.

Ciardi, John (1916–1985) poet, editor

Ciardi was born in Boston and educated at Bates College in Maine and Tufts University in Massachusetts. He taught English at Harvard and Rutgers and was poetry editor of the *SATURDAY REVIEW* from 1956 to 1972. Ciardi had a wonderful feel for the way Americans spoke, and he was a stickler about the proper use of words, which he would discuss with charming pedantry in his radio talks on National Public Radio. He was a considerable poet, celebrated for his wit in volumes such as *Homeward to America* (1940), *Other Skies* (1947), *Live Another Day* (1949), *From Time to Times* (1951), *As If,*

Poems New and Selected (1955), and *I Marry You* (1958). His later work, *In Fact* (1963) and *Lives of X* (1971), dealt with his early years. *Fast and Slow* (1975) is a collection of essays.

Sources

Cifelli, Edward M. *John Ciardi: A Biography.* Fayetteville: University of Arkansas Press, 1997.

Cisneros, Sandra (1954–   ) novelist, short story writer, poet

Born in Chicago, Cisneros is the child of a Mexican-American mother and Mexican father. She grew up in Humboldt Park, Illinois, and graduated from Loyola University. She went to the University of Iowa to study writing, and she has taught at the University of Michigan and other colleges. She has published three collections of poetry: *Bad Boys* (1980), *My Wicked Wicked Ways* (1987), and *Loose Woman* (1994). Both *The House on Mango Street* (1984), a novel, and *Woman Hollering Creek and Other Stories* (1991), stories, deal with the Chicana experience in the United States. Cisneros explores the nexus between ideas of individuality and community. Her prose tends to be poetic, but it is also clear and concise. She has identified herself as a feminist and spoken strongly on the need for collective action by Chicana women.

Sources

Internet School Library Media Center. Sandra Cisneros: Teacher Resource File. Available on-line. URL: http://falcon.jmu.edu/~ramseyil/cisneros.htm. Updated on January 28, 2000.

Rodriguez Aranda, Pilar E. "On the Solitary Nature of Being Mexican, Female, Wicked and Thirty-Three: An Interview with Writer Sandra Cisneros." *Americas Review* 18:1 (Spring 1990): 64–80.

Voices from the Gaps: Women Writers of Color: Sandra Cisneros. Available on-line. URL: http://voices.cla.umn.edu/authors/SandraCisneros.html. Downloaded on July 25, 2001.

City Lights bookstore

Owned by the poet Lawrence FERLINGHETTI, this San Francisco, California, store became the focal point of a SAN FRANCISCO RENAISSANCE and a publishing venue for the BEATS, including Allen GINSBERG, William BURROUGHS, and Ferlinghetti himself. The store also published the work of the Beats in slim and compact paperback editions.

Clampitt, Amy (1920–1994) poet

Born in New Providence, Iowa, Clampitt was educated at Grinnell College, where she earned a B.A. degree in 1941. She then moved to New York City and worked in publishing as a researcher, editor, and librarian. She began publishing her poetry in 1978 in the *NEW YORKER*. Her first book of poems,

Kingfisher (1983), reflects her sensitivity to the natural world. She has also published *What the Light Was Like* (1985), which ranges in subject matter from her native Iowa to Mexico, and *Archaic Figures* (1987), in which she evokes various female figures such as Margaret Fuller, Dorothy Wordsworth, and George Eliot. The book's epigraph quotes Virginia Woolf on Eliot's heroines: "The ancient consciousness of women, charged with suffering and sensibility, and for so many ages dumb, seems, in them, to have brimmed and overflowed." Her *Collected Poems* appeared in 1997.

Sources

Jackson, Katharine. "In the Subtropics with Amy Clampitt: A Memoir," *Verse*. Winter 1993. Available on-line. URL: http://world.std.com/~jpwilson/kjmemoir.html.

Clark, Eleanor (1913–1996) *novelist*

Clark was born in Los Angeles but grew up in Connecticut. She earned a B.A. degree from Vassar College (1934), where she associated with Mary MCCARTHY and published in the school's literary magazine, *Con Spirito*. Her early work—short stories, essays, and reviews—appeared in PARTISAN REVIEW, KENYON REVIEW, and the NATION. Her first novel, *The Bitter Box* (1946), was well received. In 1952, she married Robert Penn WARREN and raised two children. During this period she wrote mainly nonfiction—*Rome and a Villa* (1952) and *The Oysters of Locmariaquer* (1964), which won a National Book Award. *Eyes, Etc.* (1977) is her memoir about going blind. Her second novel, *Baldur's Gate* (1970), centers on a woman, Eve, who confronts what a woman's role in society should be. *Camping Out* (1986) is the story of two writers, one a lesbian, and the other enmeshed in a problematic marriage. When the two women are attacked, they confront the issue of sexual violence in America. Clark's stories are collected in *Dr. Heart* (1974).

Clark, Walter Van Tilburg (1909–1971) *novelist*

Born in Maine, Clark was educated at the University of Nevada and the University of Vermont. He wrote poetry and short stories, but he is best known as the author of an American classic, THE OX-BOW INCIDENT (1940), made into a superb movie in 1942, a literary classic that probes the dangers of vigilante justice and mob violence.

Sources

Laird, Charlton, ed. *Walter Van Tilburg Clark: Critiques.* Reno: University of Nevada Press, 1983.

Cleaver, Eldridge (1935–1998) *autobiographer*

Cleaver's family moved from Arkansas, where he was born, to Los Angeles, in order to find better work and to escape southern racism. Cleaver became a teenage delinquent and in the 1950s served prison terms for rape and selling marijuana. The example of Malcolm X changed Cleaver, who became interested in politics and history and began work on his autobiography, *Soul on Ice,* a provocative, engaging, and candid account of his hatred of white people. A critical and popular success, the book made Cleaver a national celebrity as well as a prominent radical—Minister of Information for the Black Panther Party in 1967. In 1968, Cleaver fled the United States to evade arrest for violations of his parole. For the next seven years he was an exile in Cuba, Algeria, and other countries. By the time he returned to the United States in 1975 Cleaver had turned away from black militancy and from a radical view of the world. He had witnessed the corruption of Communist and Third World states and had come to appreciate American institutions. In *Soul on Fire* (1978), he explained his turn toward conservatism and his experience as a born-again Christian. Robert Scheer edited *Eldridge Cleaver: Post-Prison Writings and Speeches* (1969).

Sources

Rajiv, Sudhi. *Forms of Black Consciousness.* New York: Advent Books, 1992.
Rout, Kathleen. *Eldridge Cleaver.* Boston: Twayne, 1991.

cold war

A term given to the rivalry and state of tension between the United States and the Soviet Union that arose at the end of WORLD WAR II. The cold war began with conflicts over postwar plans for Central and Eastern Europe, most of which the Soviet Union occupied as a result of defeating Germany. The United States argued that these Soviet-occupied countries should be able to determine their own fate. But Stalin installed friendly governments composed of Communists, and the United States used economic aid (the Marshall Plan) to rebuild countries allied to it in Western Europe.

Certain key events define the nature of the cold war. In 1948–1949, the Soviets blockaded Berlin (divided after World War II into an eastern Soviet zone and Allied western zones), in an attempt to subdue the West Berliners and unify the city under Soviet control. The Allied response was to mount an unprecedented massive airlift of supplies to the West Berliners. Instead of confronting the Soviets militarily, the West used what came to be known as the "containment policy," a series of nonmilitary maneuvers designed to stop the spread of communism in Europe and in other parts of the world. The policy seemed to work; the Soviets eventually dropped their blockade and Germany remained divided.

The debate about the cold war in the United States has always been whether the Soviet Union was, in fact, an aggressive power intent on dominating the world or rather a defensive state attempting to create a buffer between itself and an aggressive Germany backed by the Western powers.

American historians called revisionists interpreted Soviet foreign policy as reactive—that is, the Soviets were always countering an aggressive American capitalism as it spread across the world.

The contest between the United States and the Soviet Union is vividly dramatized in such novels as Norman MAILER's epic *Harlot's Ghost* (1991), large parts of which are set in West Berlin and concern the machinations of both the Central Intelligence Agency (CIA) and the KGB (the CIA's Soviet counterpart). West Berlin, with its huge population of secret agents and informants, might be considered the capital of the cold war world. Symbolically it was also the center of the cold war because of the Berlin Wall, a graphic demonstration of the divide between East and West, the so-called Communist and free worlds. William Gass treats this aspect of the cold war in his novel *The Tunnel* (1995).

The cold war had its impact on American domestic life. Controversies arose over the extent to which Communists had infiltrated the American government, especially the State Department. It was alleged that the Soviet Union had been able to produce its atomic weapons so quickly after World War II because it had the help of American agents, including Julius and Ethel Rosenberg, a married couple executed in 1953 for conspiracy to commit espionage. Many Americans believed the Rosenbergs were the victims of paranoia about communism and scapegoats for Republican conservatives. The two best fictional accounts of the Rosenbergs and their significance in American culture are E. L. DOCTOROW's *The Book of Daniel* (1971) and Robert Coover's *The Public Burning* (1977). The latter deals not only with the Rosenbergs but also with the career of Richard Nixon (who narrates part of the novel). Both novels extend enormous sympathy to the Rosenbergs, although the preponderance of evidence (some of it available only after these novels were published) shows that the Rosenbergs were indeed guilty as charged.

Norman Mailer's *Barbary Shore* (1951) is among the best fictional evocations of the early cold war. Mailer conveys the allegorical feeling of cold war tensions, the conviction that the period was about a fight between forces of good and evil, in which even one's neighbor might be a spy, a Communist, or fellow traveler (a liberal inclined to support Communist policies).

Other key events of the cold war include the Korean War; the Hungarian uprising against the Communist government in 1956; the building of the Berlin Wall and the Cuban missile crisis in 1961; the U.S.-supported coups in Iran (1953) and Guatemala (1954) to forestall the possibility of Communist governments; the Soviet invasion of Czechoslovakia in 1969 when its Communist government became too liberal; the U.S. war in Vietnam (U.S. policy declared it was a war to stop Communist aggression); and the dramatic military arms buildup of the Reagan administration, a buildup that increased tensions between the United States and the Soviet Union but also led to Mikhail's Gorbachev's realization that

his country could not overcome the U.S. militarily or economically. The cold war is said to have ended in 1990, by which time Gorbachev no longer wished to exercise control over Eastern Europe and the Berlin Wall had been torn down.

Norman Mailer's *Harlot's Ghost* covers some of the events leading to the end of the cold war. Many of his essay collections and his memoir, *The Armies of the Night* (1968), along with Gore VIDAL's *United States: Essays* (1993) and his novels, especially *Washington, D.C.* (1967), also reflect the way the cold war was viewed in the American literary community. John F. Kennedy's assassination has been linked to cold war politics, which have received their most profound fictional treatment in Don DELILLO's *Libra* (1998). Ursula LE GUIN's novel *The Dispossessed* (1974) is a kind of cold war allegory in which competing powers are measured against an anarchist system of values.

Sources

Axelsson, Arne. *Restrained Response: American Novels of the Cold War and Korea, 1945–1962.* New York: Greenwood Press, 1990.

Brunner, Edward. *Cold War Poetry.* Urbana: University of Illinois Press, 2000.

Schaub, Thomas Hill. *American Fiction in the Cold War.* Madison: University of Wisconsin Press, 1991.

Seed, David. *American Science Fiction and the Cold War: Literature and Film.* Edinburgh: Edinburgh University Press, 1999.

Color Purple, The Alice Walker (1982) *novel*

Alice's Walker's brilliant and controversial novel won the Pulitzer Prize and the National Book Award and was made into a major motion picture by Steven Spielberg. Some African-American critics—especially men—took exception to Walker's depiction of how an African-American woman had been abused by black males. But Walker's novel also has been praised for asserting the power of female bonding and female love, including portrayals of lesbian and bisexual relationships.

Celie is Walker's protagonist, who is 14 when the novel opens. Celie has been so terrorized that she is silent, except for the letters she writes to God. She has been raped repeatedly by her stepfather, Alfonso, and has had two of his children, whom he gives away without consulting her. Later, she is coerced into an arranged marriage. Nettie, Celie's sister, is left behind with Alfonso, but Nettie eventually escapes to Africa and sends letters to Celie.

Celie's husband, Albert, beats her and is in love with another woman, Shug, whom Celie befriends. Shug helps Celie find the courage to leave Albert. The two women go to Memphis, and Celie starts a clothing business. After her stepfather dies, Celie returns home and is reunited with Nettie. She also reconciles with Albert.

Celie story's is clearly meant to express not only the suffering of African-American women but also their endurance and desire to prevail.

Sources

Allan, Tuzyline Jita. *Womanist and Feminist Aesthetics: A Comparative Review.* Athens: Ohio University Press, 1995.

Montelaro, Janet J. *Producing a Womanist Text: The Maternal as Signifier in Alice Walker's The Color Purple.* Victoria, B.C.: English Literary Studies, University of Victoria, 1996.

Commentary periodical

A monthly journal founded by the American Jewish Committee in 1945. Under the distinguished editorship of Elliot Cohen (1945–1959) and Norman PODHORETZ (1960–1995), such writers as Hannah ARENDT, Saul BELLOW, Paul GOODMAN, and Lionel TRILLING published some of their best work. Under Podhoretz, the magazine became more conservative in its treatment of both domestic and international issues.

Commonweal periodical

Founded in 1924 by Roman Catholic laymen, this biweekly journal has followed an independent line in reporting on current events and culture. The journal contains book reviews and editorials. Its circulation is smaller than the more political and polemical journals such as the NEW REPUBLIC and the *Nation.*

confessional poetry

Autobiographical verse prevalent in the late 1950s and 1960s, generally thought to have been given its impetus by Robert LOWELL's classic volume, *Life Studies* (1959).

The origins of American confessional poetry have been traced back to the English romantic poets, especially to William Wordsworth and Samuel Taylor Coleridge, because of their intimate explorations of their states of mind. But the confessional poets of the 1950s were much more revealing: their work often included personal details about their friendships, loves, and marriages. Some of the BEAT poets, particularly Allen GINSBERG, fostered the role of the bard who made a poetic example of his own life.

Later, in the 1970s, feminist poets such as Anne SEXTON dealt with their distraught states of mind and their personal lives. Sylvia PLATH, in such poems as "Daddy," wrote bitter, even savage accounts about themselves and their families. W. D. SNODGRASS—like Plath, one of Lowell's students—wrote in the acclaimed *Heart's Needle* (1963), an account of his relationship with his daughter after his divorce.

Although some confessional poetry seems undisciplined and lacking in structure, the best of the confessional poets, like Plath, Lowell, and John Berryman crafted poems of striking discipline and beauty. The poems reflected Wordsworth's definition of poetry as "emotion recollected in tranquillity." No matter how intense or spontaneous these poems seemed to be, they were worked over, revised and revised again, to achieve their perfect form.

Confessional poetry should also be seen in the context of its age. Many poets in America in the late 1950s and early 1960s were searching for freer, more open literary styles, reacting against what was viewed as the stifling conventionality and conformism of the 1950s. It is not an accident, for example, that both Lowell's *Life Studies* and Norman MAILER's *Advertisements for Myself* appeared in 1959. Both writers were searching for new forms of expression based on their own experience. Mailer acknowledged their affinity in a portrait of Lowell in *The Armies of the Night* (1968), which is itself a piece of confessional literature.

Sources

Phillips, Robert. *The Confessional Poets.* Carbondale: Southern Illinois University Press, 1973.

Connell, Evan Shelby (1924–) *novelist, historian, short story writer, poet*

Evan S. Connell was born in Kansas but has lived much of his life in California. He is best known for his novels *Mrs. Bridge* (1959) and *Mr. Bridge* (1969), works that evoke suburban life and marriage with considerable humor and irony. He has also published *Son of the Morning Star* (1984), an extraordinary nonfiction account of General George Armstrong Custer's last stand that sensitively portrays the man and the myth, as well as the Native American perspective on Custer. Connell has collected his short fiction in *The Anatomy Lesson* (1957), *At the Crossroads* (1965), and *St. Augustine's Pigeon* (1980). He has also published two long philosophical poems, *Notes from a Bottle Found on the Beach at Carmel* (1963) and *Points for a Compass Rose* (1973).

Sources

Bottoms, Greg. "Brilliant Careers: Evan S. Connell." Available on-line. URL: http://www.salon.com/people/bc/2000/07/connell/index.html.

Connelly, Marcus Cook (1890–1980) *playwright*

Born in Pennsylvania, Marc Connelly worked as a journalist before turning to playwriting. He worked with George S. Kaufman on a comedy, *Dulcy* (1921). Much of his work consisted of adaptations of novels for the stage and screen. His greatest success was his dramatic adaptation of Roark Bradford's stories about African-American tales based on the Bible: *The Green Pastures* (1930) won a Pulitzer Prize. Connelly published *Voices Offstage,* a memoir, in 1968.

Sources
Nolan, Paul T. *Marc Connelly.* New York: Twayne, 1969.

Conroy, Jack (1899–1980) novelist

Conroy grew up in Missouri and in the late 1930s became deeply involved in the PROLETARIAN LITERATURE movement. He wrote a classic of this genre, *The Disinherited* (1933), an account of the common laborer or "working stiff," full of detailed descriptions of working-class life and the arduous efforts of people to find and keep their jobs. His other work includes another novel, *A World to Win* (1935), and a study of African-American migration to the North, *They Seek a City* (1945)—later expanded as *Anyplace But Here* (1966), written in collaboration with Arna BONTEMPS. Conroy also edited a collection of proletarian writings from the late 1930s, *Writers in Revolt* (1973). *The Jack Conroy Reader* appeared in 1980.

Sources
Wixson, Douglas C. *Worker-writer in America: Jack Conroy and the Tradition of Midwestern Literary Radicalism, 1898–1990.* Urbana: University of Illinois Press, 1994.

Corso, Gregory Nunzio (1930–2001) poet

Born in New York City, Gregory Corso had a troubled childhood among foster parents and institutions. He spent three years in jail before he was 20. With Allen GINSBERG's encouragement he became a poet. He published many collections of humorous and sometimes bitter poetry, including *Gasoline* (1958) and *Elegiac Feelings American* (1970).

One of the original BEAT poets, Corso nevertheless disliked being considered part of the Beat movement or the voice of a generation. Some of his other poetry collections include *Bomb* (1958), *The Happy Birthday of Death* (1960), and *Minefield* (1989). He also wrote a play, *This Hung-Up Age* (1955); a novel, *The American Express* (1961); and an autobiography, *What I Feel Right Now* (1982).

Sources
Skau, Michael. *"A Clown in a Grave": Complexities and Tensions in the Works of Gregory Corso.* Carbondale: Southern Illinois University Press, 1999.

Crane, Harold Hart (1899–1932) poet

As a young man Hart Crane moved from Ohio to New York City, where he worked at odd jobs and wrote poetry. His first work appeared in POETRY and the LITTLE REVIEW. *White Buildings* (1926), his first collection of poetry, reflected the influence of the French symbolist poets, especially Arthur Rimbaud.

Crane's view of MODERNISM clashed with T. S. ELIOT's. While Eliot depicted the bleakness of contemporary culture, Crane, particularly in *The Bridge*, celebrated the American ideal, invoking such poets as Walt Whitman. In terms of style, however, Eliot was a major influence on Crane, whose verse was as allusive and complex as Eliot's.

More than Eliot, however, Crane drew on American sources and symbols, making symbolic use of figures such as Christopher Columbus and Pocahontas. For Crane, modern inventions such as the subway train and engineering feats such as the Brooklyn Bridge also are integrated in a style that fluctuates from the highly concrete to the mystical.

Crane had a difficult life. He confronted a father who disapproved of his writing. His personal relations with fellow poets were often tense. Sailing back from Mexico, where he had been on a Guggenheim Fellowship to support research for a poem on the Spanish conquest, Crane apparently committed suicide by jumping overboard. He seems to have been distraught over signs that his creativity was waning.

Crane's *Collected Verse* was published in 1933.

Sources
Bloom, Harold, ed. *Hart Crane.* New York: Chelsea House, 1986.

Unterecker, John. *Voyager: A Life of Hart Crane.* New York: Farrar, Straus and Giroux, 1969.

Creeley, Robert White (1926–) poet

Born in Arlington, Massachusetts, Robert Creeley was an ambulance driver during World War II. A Harvard dropout, he went to Europe to pursue a career as a poet, but found his metier when he returned to the United States and founded the *BLACK MOUNTAIN REVIEW* with Charles OLSON, Robert DUNCAN, and Edward DORN. Creeley also became closely associated with the BEATS, visiting Allen GINSBERG, Jack KEROUAC, and Gary SNYDER in SAN FRANCISCO. Creeley's work is in the tradition of Ezra POUND and T. S. ELIOT, although he favors simple verse forms and is notable for his use of short lines. His *Collected Poems, 1945–75* appeared in 1982 and a revised edition in 1984. Creeley is also the author of a novel, *The Island* (1963), and stories, *The Gold Diggers* (1954). He published his *Collected Essays* in 1989 and *Echoes*, a poetry collection, in 1994.

Sources
Foster, Edward Halsey. *Understanding the Black Mountain Poets.* Columbia: University of South Carolina Press, 1995.

Crisis, The periodical

This monthly magazine of the National Association for the Advancement of Colored People (NAACP), founded by W. E. B. DU BOIS in 1910, was the first to publish many of the writers of the HARLEM RENAISSANCE. The magazine included articles about lynchings, meetings of African Americans and Pan-Africans congresses, poetry, reviews, translations, and short stories. Langston HUGHES published one of his most important poems, "The Negro Speaks of Rivers," in *The Crisis*. The magazine continues to be a monthly publication of the NAACP, and publishes articles of general interest concerning African-American culture and politics.

criticism, American literary

The development of 20th-century American literary criticism and of criticism about American literature tend to merge. In other words, even as American literature as a subject of serious criticism was established, a new generation of American critics was achieving renown and developing distinctive ways of interpreting literature. In *Studies in Classic American Literature* (1923), the British novelist D. H. Lawrence wrote a highly opinionated and influential history of American literature, praising its distinctiveness as a time when American literature—other than a few 19th-century classics—was not taught in schools and was not taken seriously by Europeans. The first full-scale scholarly history of American literature is Vernon L. PARRINGTON's *Main Currents in American Thought* (three volumes, 1927–1930). Parrington's rather sociological and dry study was succeeded by Van Wyck Brooks's *The Flowering of New England 1815–1865* (1936), a more elegant and literary work for the general reader that attempted to define the Puritan roots of America's literary culture. Far different in tone and substance were H. L. MENCKEN's irreverent essays of the 1920s in magazines such as the *AMERICAN MERCURY*. Mencken ridiculed America's lack of culture, especially in the South, and denounced notions that America had come of age as a literary society. At the same time, Mencken hailed such writers as Theodore DREISER, whom Mencken believed were addressing the reality of American life from both literary and journalistic points of view. Writers like Dreiser, in Mencken's view, were finally destroying the genteel tradition.

The New Critics (see NEW CRITICISM) who emerged in the late 1920s and early 1930s brought an increasing sophistication to the study of literature, particularly in American colleges and universities. John Crowe RANSOM, Robert Penn WARREN, and Allen TATE, all poets as well as critics, developed a focus on the integrity of the work of art—insisting that literature was autonomous and not simply a comment on life—that was lacking in the earlier histories of American literature. In practice, this erudite New Criticism also meant that American authors such as Herman Melville and Walt Whitman, as well as contemporary writers such as Ernest HEMINGWAY and William FAULKNER, were appraised in terms of the structure, the imagery, and the symbolism of their work and not simply in terms of the content, or the themes, of their writing.

At the same time, Alfred KAZIN, Lionel TRILLING, and other New York writers outside of the New Criticism circle brought to bear a sense of history, society, and politics on the work of literature. Kazin treated literature as part of the evolving story of the writer and his culture, whereas Trilling borrowed from Freud in order to explore the psychological aspects of literary creation. *On Native Grounds* (1942), Kazin's brilliant survey of American literature from the 1880s to the 1940s, practiced a kind of criticism that was both politically astute and capable of evoking the literature on which it commented. His work galvanized students of literature and prepared the way for literary study in the postwar American universities, which began to offer courses in the history of American literature and on major American writers. Similarly, Lionel Trilling's classic text, *The Liberal Imagination* (1950), brought a searching moral vision and an impressive command of psychological theory to the study of literature.

Other independent critics—most notably Edmund WILSON—borrowed from many different schools of criticism to provide searching studies of European and American literature. In *Axel's Castle* (1931) Wilson provided some of the first important interpretations of 20th-century giants such as James Joyce and T. S. Eliot. In *The Wound and the Bow* (1941) he studied the lives of European and American authors for the sources of their creativity. Unlike the New Critics, Wilson did not restrict himself to just interpreting the work itself but rather the entire context in which it was created. This biographical criticism was also informed by a sensitivity to contemporary Marxist criticism and theories of history.

By the early 1970s the predominance of New Criticism waned in English departments, and it was replaced by intense interest in the work of French literary theorists such as Jacques Derrida. He attacked the idea of the autonomous work of art and of the independent author. Literary works became unstable constructs of words that required deconstructing, a process that proved the meanings of literary works were often conflicting and contradictory. The very idea that there could be an objective or stable interpretation of a work of literature was cast into doubt. Academic critics at Yale and Duke led this particular movement, which governed the study of English at the graduate level at many institutions.

Deconstruction and New Criticism both became popular approaches in interdisciplinary programs. In Women's studies and African-American studies in particular, works of literature were analyzed in connection with social, cultural, historical, and political issues, so that the author of a literary work was seen as expressing his or her place in a spectrum that came to be called cultural studies. In other words, both the idea of the author as an autonomous creator and the idea of the work of art as an expression of universal values gave way to an approach that defined the work by its historical period and the race or sex of the author.

In recent years many scholars and critics have reacted against what they see as the compartmentalizing of literature.

One of the most outspoken opponents of cultural studies has been Harold Bloom, a Yale University professor who has sought in books like *The Western Canon* (1994) to persuade both a general literary audience and his academic colleagues to re-establish the idea of an exclusive canon, a canon based on the universal validity of certain classic authors.

Sources

Leitch, Vincent B. *American Literary Criticism From the Thirties to the Eighties.* New York: Columbia University Press, 1988.

Lentricchia, Frank. *After the New Criticism.* Chicago: University of Chicago Press, 1980.

Murray, David, ed. *American Cultural Critics.* Exeter, England: University of Exeter Press, 1995.

Seaton, James. *Cultural Conservatism, Political Liberalism: From Criticism to Cultural Studies.* Ann Arbor: University of Michigan Press, 1996.

Spikes, Michael P. *Understanding Contemporary American Literary Theory.* Columbia: University of South Carolina Press, 1997.

Cullen, Countee (1903–1946) *poet, anthologist, novelist, translator, writer of children's literature, playwright*

Cullen remains something of an elusive figure in spite of his key role in the HARLEM RENAISSANCE. Even his birthplace has not been authenticated. Cullen said he was born in New York City, but on a college application he listed Louisville, Kentucky as his birthplace. He was an adopted child who perhaps felt free to create his own origins. Cullen's great intelligence first manifested itself at Dewitt Clinton High School in New York City. He became editor of the school newspaper and wrote poetry for its literary magazine. His sense of destiny is clearly marked out in an early poem, "I Have a Rendezvous with Life," which won an award in a citywide competition. During the Harlem Renaissance he published three brilliant books of poems: *Color* (1925), *Copper Sun* (1927), and *The Ballad of the Brown Girl* (1927). Although Cullen often took African-American life as his subject, he wrote in a traditional style associated with English romantic poets such as John Keats. Certain critics faulted him for not relying more on black rhythms and speech patterns. Compared to writers such as Langston HUGHES, Cullen seemed formal and aloof, although his best work certainly is informed by intense passions. A learned and traditional poet, Cullen's appeal crossed racial lines. His mainstream acceptance was heralded with the publication of "Shroud of Color" in H. L. MENCKEN's *AMERICAN MERCURY*. With his Phi Beta Kappa key from New York University and a master's degree from Harvard, Cullen cut a sophisticated figure in literary circles. By the end of the 1920s, however, Cullen's poetic drive seemed to diminish and *The Black Christ and Other Poems* (1929) received mixed reviews. He wrote less and took up teaching. His most famous student was James BALDWIN. Cullen's novel, *No Way to Heaven,* retains great value as retrospective on the Harlem Renaissance, and his books of children's verse, *The Lost Zoo* (1940) and *My Lives and How I Lost Them* (1942), remain charming. Cullen's own selection of his best poetry is *On These I Stand* (1947).

Sources

Shucard, Alan R. *Countee Cullen.* Boston: Twayne, 1984.

Cummings, Edward Estlin (1894–1962) *poet, critic, novelist*

E. E. Cummings was born in Cambridge, Massachusetts, and educated at Harvard. He attracted early recognition with a novel, *The Enormous Room,* based on his WORLD WAR I experiences. He also wrote *Him* (1927), an EXPRESSIONIST drama, and *Eimi,* his record of a trip to Russia.

But it is as a poet that Cummings made his mark. Idiosyncratic and eccentric, his verse experiments with typography, slang, dialect, jazz rhythms, and jagged lines that mimic the sound or movement of his subjects. The very shape of his poems emphasize the forms of human expression. A poem about spring, for example, will be written in jumpy, bursting accents that the season itself represents. No other American poet has celebrated love with such a lyrical free spirit, a spontaneity and joy. But Cummings could also be critical of society and of American culture. His frequently anthologized poems include "in Just" (an evocation of spring), "Buffalo Bill's defunct," and "next to of course god america i." *The Complete Poems of e.e. cummings 1913–1962* was published in 1972. His memoir *i, six nonlectures,* appeared in 1953.

Sources

Friedman, Norman, ed. *(Re)valuing Cummings: Further Essays on the Poet, 1962–1993.* Gainesville: University Press of Florida, 1996.

Kennedy, Richard S. *E. E. Cummings Revisited.* New York: Twayne, 1994.

Dahlberg, Edward (1900–1977) *novelist, autobiographer, critic*

Born in Boston, Dahlberg grew up in a Jewish orphan asylum in Cleveland, an experience he described in his autobiography, *I Was Flesh* (1964). He also wrote about this period of his life in a novel, *Bottom Dogs* (1929), a good example of proletarian fiction in which he writes about his experiences as a hobo and slum dweller. In another novel *Those Who Perish* (1934), he explores American Jews' attitudes toward Nazism. A vigorous critic of literature influenced by D. H. Lawrence, he published *Do These Bones Live?* (1941, revised in 1947 and 1960). *Flea of Sodom* (1950) is a good example of his parables, which flay modern civilization. His letters about modern literature sent to British critic Herbert Read are collected in *Truth is More Sacred* (1961). Additional letters are collected in *Epitaphs of Our Times* (1967). *Confessions* (1971) is a memoir.

Sources

DeFanti, Charles. *The Wages of Expectation: A Biography of Edward Dahlberg.* New York: New York University Press, 1978.

Davidson, Donald Grady (1893–1968) *poet, essayist*

Born in Tennessee and educated at Vanderbilt University, Donald Davidson was a great exponent of REGIONALISM and the most conservative member of the group known as the Nashville AGRARIANS. *The Attack on Leviathan* (1938) is a collection of essays expressing his hostility to a centralized and industrialized state. *Lee in the Mountains* (1938) is a series of short narrative poems about the central figures of the south-

ern past. *Still Rebels, Still Yankees* (1957) is his best known essay collection. *Poems,* a collected edition of his verse, appeared in 1966.

Sources

Winchell, Mark Royden. *Where No Flag Flies: Donald Davidson and the Southern Resistance.* Columbia: University of Missouri Press, 2000.

Death of a Salesman *Arthur Miller* (1949) *play*

Arthur's MILLER's greatest play is a staple of the American repertory and a canonical work of American literature. Willy LOMAN, a traveling salesman, has trouble concentrating on his job (he repeatedly has driven his car off the road). A failure, he invests his hope in his older son, Biff, a high school football hero who has wasted his opportunities. Willy's wife, Linda, stands by him but realizes that Willy is tired. At age 63 Willy loses his job, and Biff comes home for a visit. Father and son are estranged: Biff once saw his father in a hotel room with another woman, and this shattered his idealized image of his father. Happy, Willy's younger son, can do no more than play along and pretend to believe the family myth that Biff will be a success and that Happy is—as Willy likes to say—"well liked." Willy ultimately realizes that his life has been based on an illusion. He kills himself, hoping that his insurance policy will take care of his wife and give his sons a new start.

Arthur Miller argued in a famous essay, "Tragedy and the Common Man" (1949), that modern drama need not have a great hero for its tragic figure. Critics have argued whether Willy, who does not articulate his understanding of his failure, can merit the term "tragic." At any rate, Miller's careful crafting of character and his expert blending of realistic social drama with scenes that reflect Willy's confused and grandiose consciousness attracted the praise of critics and the support of theater audiences. The original production ran for 742 performances. It was made into a major motion picture, adapted for television, and has been revived as a play many times.

Sources

Bloom, Harold, ed. *Arthur Miller's Death of a Salesman*. Philadelphia: Chelsea House, 1998.

Weales, Gerald, ed. *Arthur Miller: Death of a Salesman, Text and Criticism*. New York: Penguin Books, 1977.

Delany, Samuel Ray (1942–) *novelist, short story writer, critic, autobiographer*

Born in Harlem to an upper-middle-class family, Samuel R. Delany was sent to the Dalton School in Manhattan. Dyslexic, he had difficulty with the progressive curriculum but began to write short stories and read science fiction. He graduated from the Bronx High School of Science and then attended City College in Manhattan for a year. Other attempts to gain a college degree stalled, but by the mid-1960s his writing had received critical and popular acclaim.

What distinguishes Delany's work is his ability to fuse storytelling with intellectual intensity. His science fiction has much in common with medieval allegories and other forms of fantasy literature that explore the roots and the results of civilization. Highly sensitive to language, Delany is powerfully aware of how words shape our vision of society and the myths we make of our lives. This is especially true in his series of novels: *Tales of Neveryon* (1979), *Neveryon: Or, The Tale of Sings and Cities* (1983), and *Flight from Neveryon* (1985).

Delany's novel *Dhalgren* (1975) has been compared to Vladimir NABOKOV's *Ada or Ardor* (1969) and Thomas PYNCHON's *Gravity's Rainbow* (1973). Like them, he combines family sagas—intricate plots with comic characters—with a sophisticated use of fantasy and literary allusion. Indeed, Delany's consciousness of literary tradition and of the major influences on his work is reflected in both his fiction and literary criticism. Another novel, *Triton* (1976), has been called an answer to Ursula LE GUIN's classic *The Dispossessed* (1974) because it attacks the idea of Utopia portrayed in her famous novel. His other important novels include *Babel-17* (1966), *Stars in My Pocket Like Grains of Sand* (1984), *They Fly at Ciron* (1993), and *The Mad Man* (1994), a probing exploration of biographers and biography.

Delany's short fiction has been collected in *Ten Tales of Speculative Fiction* (1971), *Distant Stars* (1981), and *Atlantis: Three Tales* (1995). His important nonfiction includes *The American Shore: Meditations on a Tale of Science Fiction by Thomas M. Disch* (1978); *Starboard Wine: More Notes on the Language of Science Fiction* (1984); and *Longer Views* (1996), a work that demonstrates how deeply Delany has read modern thinkers such as Walter Benjamin and Antonin Artaud.

Delany has written some of the most important volumes of autobiography in contemporary American literature, distinguished both for their style and for their commentary on the genre of autobiography. These works include *The Motion of Light in Water: Sex and Science-Fiction Writing in the East Village, 1957–1965* (1988); *Bread and Wine: An Erotic Tale of New York City, an Autobiographical Account* (1998); and *Times Square Red, Times Square Blue* (1999).

Sources

McEvoy, Seth. *Samuel R. Delany*. New York: Frederick Ungar, 1984.

Sallis, James, ed. *Ash of Stars: On the Writing of Samuel R. Delany*. Jackson: University Press of Mississippi, 1996.

DeLillo, Don (1936–) *novelist*

Born in New York City and educated at Fordham University, DeLillo has shied away from publicity while slowly building an audience of dedicated readers. His novels often challenge traditional methods of storytelling even as they take on popular American subjects. In his first novel, *Americana* (1971), a television network executive, David Bell, suffers an identity crisis. He proposes to heal himself by going on a cross-country tour, ostensibly to film a documentary about American life. Yet "reality" constantly upsets his expectations, and the images he produces do not reflect the history he wishes to capture. It is this elusive nature of reality and of the self to which DeLillo constantly returns.

End Zone (1972), DeLillo's second novel, focuses on an ex-football player whose obsession with the sport serves as a metaphor for war, a subject that constantly arises as he watches cadets practice their war games at a Texas college. He tries to see in women an escape from his preoccupation with nuclear war and death, but ultimately they cannot provide the security he seeks.

In *Great Jones Street* (1973) the protagonist is a rock star; in *Ratner's Star* (1976), the hero is a teenage genius in mathematics who wins the Nobel Prize. *The Names* (1982) and *White Noise* (1985) are formidable treatments of modern marriage, cult groups, and counterintelligence (CIA) agents. The themes of paranoia and conspiracy tempted DeLillo to explore the John F. Kennedy assassination in *Libra* (1988), which, like *Mao II* (1991), investigates terrorist groups and the making of fiction itself. *Underworld* (1997) is yet another effort to explore America's postwar world—this time through the metaphor of baseball and the 1951 World Series. The COLD WAR, including the Cuban missile crisis, becomes part of the shifting focus between the 1950s and the 1990s. As the novel's title implies, the country's surface reality—the subject DeLillo explored in his first novel—is constantly disrupted by an underworld of characters, conspiracies, and competing agendas.

In 2001 DeLillo published a novella, *The Body Artist,* an ambiguous ghost story and a meticulous presentation of a woman's life that has been compared to Henry James's classic tale *The Turn of the Screw.*

Sources

Civello, Paul. *American Literary Naturalism and Its Twentieth-Century Transformations: Frank Norris, Ernest Hemingway, Don DeLillo.* Athens: University of Georgia Press, 1994.

LeClair, Tom. *In the Loop: Do DeLillo and the Systems Novel.* Urbana: University of Illinois Press, 1987.

Depression

See GREAT DEPRESSION.

detective fiction

Twentieth-century American detective fiction encompasses many different varieties of the mystery story. Before WORLD WAR I, the genre was dominated by English novels and stories in the Sherlock Holmes tradition. S. S. Van Dine transformed the genre in America, creating the cosmopolitan detective Philo Vance. In such novels as *The Benson Murder Case* (1926), Van Dine created a suave American version of the British detective, a cerebral type much admired by William FAULKNER, who turned his southern lawyer Gavin Stevens into a detective in *Knight's Gambit* (1949).

Less polished but more popular were the Ellery Queen detective stories and novels, begun in 1929 with *The Roman Hat* and continuing in *The Dutch Shoe Mystery* (1931), *The Door Between: A Problem in Deduction* (1937), and more than 30 other titles. *Ellery Queen's Mystery Magazine* was established in 1941. Equally popular was Erle Stanley Gardner's lawyer-detective Perry Mason.

The stories and novels featuring Queen and Mason did little to advance the genre as literature, but Rex STOUT created a detective, Nero WOLFE, who was a fascinating character in his own right, a mysterious Montenegran who grew orchids. Wolfe's manner, his style of life, and his thoughts about crime extended and deepened aspects of the genre that Van Dine had adumbrated.

Dashiell HAMMETT and Raymond CHANDLER eliminated the last vestiges of the genteel British mystery in their creation of what came to be known as "hard-boiled" detective fiction. Hammett began his career by writing for *Black Mask,* one of the PULPS (magazines printed on cheap paper for a mass audience). Most stories in these magazines were melodramas with little character development and clichéd views of society. Hammett, however, a former Pinkerton detective, developed a fresh, understated style (influenced by

Ernest HEMINGWAY) and a dark, pessimistic view of human nature and society. In such novels as *Red Harvest* (1929) and *The Dain Curse* (1929), his detective, Sam SPADE, inevitably came to grips with corruption in business and government. The detective was a loner battling long odds, and the mysteries involved not only the murder of an individual but also the death of a just society. Compared to his early work, Hammett's later novels such as *The Maltese Falcon* (1930) and *The Thin Man* seem less bleak and more romantic.

Chandler, an Englishman who resettled in Los Angeles, evoked the seamy side of urban life with a stunning realism and lack of sentimentality. His detective, Philip Marlowe, like Sam Spade, confronts corporate corruption and forces that threaten to crush not only him but the very idea of individuality. *The Big Sleep* (1939), Chandler's masterpiece, combines a love story with crimes of incest and political machinations that delve into how Los Angeles itself was created and sustained.

Chester HIMES brought a racial twist to the detective novel in *Cotton Comes to Harlem* (1965) and *Run Man Run* (1966), which portrayed two Harlem policemen, Grave Digger Jones and Coffin Ed Johnson. These books have been praised for their sardonic humor in a vividly violent world.

Later novelists have imitated Hammett and Chandler, but none has equaled their exquisite use of language, plot, theme, and tone. John D. MACDONALD created a lively series based on the detective Travis McGee. For sheer, crude energy, no writer has rivaled the immensely popular Mickey SPILLANE. Ross MACDONALD is perhaps the finest heir to the tradition of Hammett and Chandler. His work, especially *The Underground Man* (1971), has been highly praised by such writers as Eudora WELTY, who have said that his understanding of human nature transcends the melodramatic conventions of the detective story genre.

The vitality of the detective fiction in mid-century America shifted from the private investigator to the police detective as the hero. Such writers as Ed McBain in his 87th Precinct novels and Joseph Wambaugh, who provides a complex and sympathetic, though realistic, treatment of the Los Angeles police department, focus on procedure—the process law enforcement has to go through in order to solve a crime. Such novels depend on their sense of authenticity, suggesting that the writer has inside knowledge of the way police departments and detectives actually work. Criminal psychology and forensic police work become acutely important.

In Patricia Cornwell's Kay Scarpetta series, Scarpetta is a coroner who works closely with police detectives. She is just one example of a flood of female detectives that began to transform the genre in the 1980s. Sue Grafton led the way with her female detective, Kinsey Millhone, who made her debut in *A is for Alibi* (1982), the first in a series of novels with titles that start with a letter of the alphabet. Sara Paretsky also created an appealing series of detective novels featuring V. I. (Victoria Iphigenia) Warshawski who debuted in *Indemnity Only* (1982), and Walter Mosley has created an African-American detective, Easy Rawlins: *Devil in a Blue Dress* (1990), *A Red Death* (1991), *White Butterfly* (1992), *Black Betty* (1994), and *A Little Yellow Dog* (1996).

Sources

Delamater, Jerome H. and Ruth Prigozy, ed. *The Detective in American Fiction, Film, and Television.* Westport, Conn.: Greenwood Press, 1998.

Docherty, Brian, ed. *American Crime Fiction.* New York: St. Martin's Press, 1988.

Klein, Kathleen. *The Woman Detective: Gender & Genre.* Urbana: University of Illinois Press, 1995.

Landrum, Larry. *American Mystery and Detective Novels: A Reference Guide.* Westport, Conn.: Greenwood Press, 1999.

Marling, William. *The American Roman Noir: Hammett, Cain, and Chandler.* Athens: University of Georgia Press, 1995.

DeVoto, Bernard Augustine (1897–1955)
educator, editor, novelist, historian

Bernard DeVotto was born in Utah, and this background in the West would lead to his most important work, *Across the Wide Missouri* (1947) a history of the Rocky Mountain fur trade, which won the Pulitzer Prize. After an early career as an English professor at Northwestern University and Harvard, DeVoto made his mark as the editor of the SATURDAY REVIEW OF LITERATURE (1936–1938) and of HARPER'S (1935–1955). A specialist in Mark Twain, he published the well-received *Mark Twain's America* (1932) and *Mark Twain at Work* (1942). His other important nonfiction books on America include *The Year of Decision: 1846* (1943) and *The Course of Empire* (1952). He collected his editor's columns in *The Easy Chair* (1955). He wrote several novels, none of which enhanced his literary reputation.

Sources

Stegner, Wallace. *The Uneasy Chair: A Biography of Bernard DeVoto.* Garden City, N.Y.: Doubleday, 1974.

Dewey, John (1859–1952) *philosopher, educator*

Born in Vermont, Dewey received his B.A. at the University of Vermont and his Ph.D. from Johns Hopkins University in 1884. He taught at several universities, including Minnesota, Michigan, Chicago, and Columbia. He is best known for theories of progressive education propounded in *Psychology* (1887), *The School and Society* (1899), *The Child and the Curriculum* (1902), *Moral Principles in Education* (1909), and *Interest and Effort in Education* (1913). These early works reflected Dewey's pragmatism, an approach to philosophy and education pioneered by William James. Dewey believed the modern education had to take into account a changing industrial society, the findings of science, and the tenets of

democracies. For Dewey, education had to infuse students with the practical applications of what it taught; thus education became not merely a way of acquiring wisdom but also of transforming the world.

Dewey developed his own concept of "instrumentalism," arguing that truth and knowledge grew out of a changing reality. Education therefore had to be dynamic and the curriculum subject to constant revision. Through constant observation, as in the natural sciences, a democratic society would prosper. Dewey expanded on this approach in *Studies in Logical Theory* (1903), *How We Think* (1909), *The Influence of Darwin on Philosophy* (1910), *Democracy and Education* (1916), *Reconstruction in Philosophy* (1920), *Experience and Nature* (1925), *Individualism, Old and New* (1930), *Art as Experience* (1934), *Liberalism and Social Action* (1935), and *Freedom and Culture* (1939).

Dewey's stature as a public intellectual was extraordinary. Although he was not a political activist, his work was certainly regarded as one of the pillars of liberal civilization and Dewey himself a man of outstanding integrity. When Stalin directed the purge trials of 1935, which led to executions of Bolsheviks who had waged the Russian Revolution, Dewey headed a commission to determine whether the defendants were receiving fair hearings. His findings that the trials were, in fact, bogus turned many liberal thinkers away from the notion that the Soviet Union could serve as a model of the socially responsible welfare state.

Dewey's philosophy and political stance were clarified in later works such as *The Public Schools and Spiritual Values* (1944) and *Problems of Men* (1946), a collection of essays.

Sources

Archambault, Reginald D., ed. *Dewey on Education: Appraisals.* New York: Random House, 1966.

Caspary, William R. *Dewey on Democracy.* Ithaca, N.Y.: Cornell University Press, 2000.

Haskins, Casey and David I. Seiple, ed. *Dewey Reconfigured: Essays on Deweyan Pragmatism.* Albany, N.Y.: State University of New York Press, 1999.

Ryan, Alan. *John Dewey and the High Tide of American Liberalism.* New York: W. W. Norton, 1995.

Shook, John R. *Dewey's Empirical Theory of Knowledge and Reality.* Nashville: Vanderbilt University Press, 2000.

Dial, The periodical

A monthly journal of literary criticism, *The Dial* was founded in Chicago in 1880 and moved to New York in 1918. In the 1920s the magazine broadened its focus to include the best of modernist literature (see MODERNISM). The distinguished poet Marianne MOORE became the publication's editor (1925–29) and welcomed the work of T. S. ELIOT, Gertrude STEIN, and Edwin Arlington ROBINSON, among many other important American writers. In 1959 a new *Dial* was published as a literary quarterly, featuring the work of writers like Herbert GOLD and Bernard Wolfe.

"Diamond As Big as the Ritz, The" *F. Scott Fitzgerald* (1922) *short story*

One of F. Scott FITZGERALD's classic evocations of the 1920s, this story begins when Percy Washington invites John T. Unger, a prep school classmate, to his home, telling him that his father owns a diamond as big as the Ritz Carlton Hotel. John is dazzled by the Washingtons' home, set on a mountaintop overlooking a beautiful isolated valley. Percy confides to John that his grandfather discovered the diamond mountain, which has been the source of the family's wealth—so far undiscovered by the government. Then John meets and falls in love with Kismine, Percy's sister, who tells him that no visitor has ever escaped from the estate. John's impulse is to flee, but his love for Kismine holds him there, even though he knows several aviators have been captured and have died in their attempts to discover the diamond mine. After the estate is attacked by airplanes, John and Kismine escape. She welcomes the chance to be "free and poor," but he insists she take the contents from her jewelry box. In a secluded spot in the woods, John watches Percy's father, Braddock, accompanied by two slaves, lift a huge diamond up to the sky, as if in propitiation to God. But the sky darkens, and then the mountain explodes. As Percy, John, and Kismine leave the estate, John discovers that Kismine has only brought rhinestones with her. She thinks the incident is all a dream, but a dejected John says youth is a dream. He wraps himself in a blanket and falls asleep.

Sources

Bryer, Jackson R., ed. *The Short Stories of F. Scott Fitzgerald: New Approaches in Criticism.* Madison: University of Wisconsin Press, 1982.

Kuehl, John. *F. Scott Fitzgerald: A Study of the Short Fiction.* Boston: Twayne, 1991.

Dick, Philip Kindred (1928–1982) *novelist*

This Chicago-born science fiction writer concentrates on characters who just barely manage to survive in environments that undermine their psychological equilibrium. Unlike the typical heroes of science fiction, Philip K. Dick's characters find existence itself is a dilemma. He was a prolific author of novels and short stories. His important works include *The Man in the High Castle* (1962), which won a Hugo award in 1963; *Do Androids Dream of Electric Sheep?* (1968); *Galactic Pot-Healer* (1969); and *A Scanner Darkly* (1977). *Blade Runner,* based on *Do Androids Dream of Electric Sheep?,* became an instant cult classic movie when it was released in 1982. Like much of his work, it explores the difficulty of discriminating between illusion and reality—exemplified in the movie by "skin jobs," artificially created creatures eventually indistinguishable from human beings.

Sources

Umland, Samuel J., ed. *Philip K. Dick: Contemporary Critical Interpretations.* Westport, Conn.: Greenwood Press, 1995.

Dickey, James Lafayette (1923–1997) *poet, novelist*

James Dickey was born and raised in Atlanta, Georgia. After serving in the Army Air Force in World War II, he attended Vanderbilt University and earned a B.A. and an M.A. in English. He taught at Rice University, served in the Korean War, and then taught at the University of Florida as well as at other colleges as a poet-in-residence. He won a National Book Award for his collection of poems, *Buckdancer's Choice* (1965). His novel *Deliverance* (1970), a grim, shocking story of men out in the wilds confronted by a vicious gang, was made into a major motion picture starring Jon Voight and Burt Reynolds. Dickey has a small part in the film and later said that he wrote the novel to explore what happened to civilized men who were suddenly confronted with a realm of violence entirely outside of their conventional experience. Another novel, *Alnilam* (1987), was a critical and popular failure.

Some of Dickey's most impressive poems are based on his war experiences, although biographical research has subsequently proven that he greatly exaggerated his firsthand experience of battle. Nevertheless, poems like "The Firebombing" have been praised for their directness and immediacy. Dickey's poetry sometimes draws on the South's agrarian past and the poet's desire to remain authentic and close to the land. Dickey generally favored free verse over rhyme, the rhythms of the line rather than conventional meter.

Dickey's other important collections of poetry are *Helmets* (1964), *Poems, 1957–1967* (1967), and *The Zodiac* (1976), a poem in 12 parts about an alcoholic. His *Collected Poems 1945–1992* was published in 1992.

Dickey published several volumes of nonfiction: *The Suspect in Poetry* (1964), *Spinning the Crystal Ball* (1967), *From Babel to Byzantium* (1968), *Metaphor as Pure Adventure* (1968), *Self-Interviews* (1970), *Sorties* (1971), *Night Hurdling* (1983), and *The Voice Connections of James Dickey* (1989).

Sources

Hart, Henry. *James Dickey: The World as a Lie.* New York: Picador, 2000.

Kirschten, Robert, ed. *"Struggling for Wings": The Art of James Dickey.* Columbia: University of South Carolina Press, 1997.

Didion, Joan (1934–   ) *novelist, journalist*

Born and raised in Sacramento, California, in a family that help settle the state, Didion grew up during World War II and went to public schools, receiving a B.A. degree in English from the University of California at Berkeley in 1956. An avid reader and writer at a young age, she won VOGUE magazine's Prix de Paris award, which brought her to New York City, where she worked on the magazine as a caption-writer, copy-writer, associate features editor, and then as a freelance writer. She describes this period in her much praised essay "Goodbye to All That," collected in *Slouching Toward Bethlehem* (1968), a book that made her reputation as one of the most incisive and shrewd journalists of her era.

Didion married the novelist and journalist John Gregory DUNNE in 1964. Their early married years were spent in California, where they worked together on screenplays such as *Panic in Needle Park* and *A Star Is Born*. The couple also jointly wrote columns for the *Saturday Evening Post* and *Life* magazine. They adopted a daughter in 1966.

Didion's essays have explored a range of issues in American life, from art to politics and social phenomena. *The White Album* (1979) explores the shocking story of Charles Manson and his "family," the Black Panthers, and the Hollywood milieu. *Salvador* (1983) is a searing, condemnatory account of the U.S. involvement in El Salvador's civil war. *Miami* (1987) is a measured, critical examination of the city and particularly of its Cuban exiles.

Didion's novels have enjoyed almost as high a reputation as her journalism. Her first novel, *Run River* (1963), draws heavily on her California background as it probes the disintegration of one of Sacramento's founding families. Didion's second novel, *Play It As It Lays* (1970), is considered her masterpiece. Its portrait of an actress suffering a mental breakdown in the corrupting decadent milieu of 1960s Hollywood is haunting and beautiful in spite of its despairing vision. Didion and Dunne wrote the screenplay for the successful film version, which starred Tuesday Weld.

With *A Book of Common Prayer* (1977), Didion began drawing on her knowledge of Central America to write fiction reminiscent of Joseph Conrad in its somber relentlessness. Two female outsiders dominate a vivid cast of characters in the imaginary country of Boca Grande, which like Joseph Conrad's imaginary Costaguana in *Nostromo* allows the author to probe the development of modern political history. Didion's novels *Democracy* (1984) and *The Last Thing He Wanted* (1996) continue her concerns with Central American and Latin politics.

Didion's other books include *After Henry* (1992), a collection of essays, *Telling Stories* (1978), which includes an essay by Didion on her short fiction as well as three short stories, and *Political Fictions* (2001), her essays on two decades of American politics.

Sources

Felton, Sharon, ed. *The Critical Response to Joan Didion.* Westport, Conn.: Greenwood Press, 1994.
Winchell, Mar\|- Royden. *Joan Didion.* Boston: Twayne, 1989.

Dillard, Annie (1945–) *essayist, novelist, poet*

Dillard won a Pulitzer Prize for *Pilgrim at Tinker Creek* (1974), a nonfiction work that evokes the wonder of nature and has been compared to Henry David Thoreau's *Walden*. Like Thoreau, Dillard is a keen observer of the seasons and natural cycles. Other titles that extend her view of nature and the act of writing about it are *Teaching a Stone to Talk* (1982), *Living by Fiction* (1982), and *Writing Life* (1989). In *An American Childhood* (1987) she describes her conventional childhood in middle-class urban America. Her novel, *The Living* (1992), has been compared to Wallace STEGNER's brooding, philosophical REGIONALISM. Like Stegner, she reveals a feeling for the way people interact with the land—in this case, loggers in the Pacific Northwest at the turn of the last century. She has also written two poetry collections, *Tickets for a Prayer Wheel* (1974) and *Mornings Like This* (1995). *Holy the Firm* (1977), another nature study, emphasizes the mystical, theological bent of Dillard's imagination.

Sources

Johnson, Sandra Humble. *The Space Between: Literary Epiphany in the Work of Annie Dillard.* Kent, Ohio: Kent State University Press, 1992.

Dobie, James Frank (1888–1964) *short story writer, historian*

Dobie is one of the key figures in the literature of the SOUTHWEST. A Texas native, he wrote about the life of a cattleman in *A Vaquero of the Brush Country* (1929), based on a true story. His other important books include *Guide to Life and Literature of the Southwest* (1943), *The Voice of the Coyote* (1949), *Tales of Old-Time Texas* (1955), and *Cow People* (1964). Dobie has been praised for his painstaking research, which has helped to establish an authentic view of the Southwest and to correct earlier accounts that were highly fictionalized and relied too much on legend.

Sources

Tinkle, Lon. *An American Original: The Life of J. Frank Dobie.* Austin: University of Texas Press, 1978.

Doctorow, Edgar Lawrence (1931–) *novelist*

A native of the Bronx, New York, E. L. Doctorow has centered much of his fiction on New York City. After graduating with a B.A. degree from Kenyon College, Doctorow worked as an editor in New York. In 1960 he published his first novel, *Welcome to Hard Times,* a parody of the myths that motivate the genre of the western. Unlike the conventional western, however, Doctorow's novel presents a grim view of America, where justice does not prevail and where heroes do not triumph. Much of Doctorow's fiction presents a subtle appreciation of American beliefs even as it severely challenges the country's faith that its ideals have been put into practice. Because Doctorow writes with great economy and elegance, his work avoids the didactic, overbearing quality of political novelists such as John Dos Passos and other writers of PROLETARIAN LITERATURE of the 1930s, although Doctorow is clearly in sympathy with their convictions.

In *The Book of Daniel* (1971), Doctorow delves directly into American political history, fashioning a mock-memoir of the anti-Communist cold war era: a narrative as told by Daniel, the son of a couple executed for treason. This thinly disguised retelling of the fate of Julius and Ethel Rosenberg, who were executed in 1953 for their roles in a spy ring that stole atomic secrets for the Soviet Union, also contrasts the Leftists of the 1950s with the radicals of the 1960s.

Doctorow achieved great critical and popular acclaim for *Ragtime* (1975), a superb re-creation of turn-of-the-20th-century America, in which historical figures such as Henry Ford and J. P. Morgan appear alongside fictional creations such as Coalhouse Walker. As in *Welcome to Hard Times*, Doctorow portrays the American past with great fondness while also exposing grievous faults like racism. His blending of fact and fiction enchanted some readers even as it disturbed others who resented the novelist's manipulation of the historical record. *Ragtime* won the National Book Critics Circle Award in 1976.

World's Fair (1985), a loving re-creation of New York in 1939 and of Doctorow's own family life, won the American Book Award in 1986. *Billy Bathgate*, a rollicking reenactment of the Prohibition era modeled after *Adventures of Huckleberry Finn*, won the 1990 National Book Critics Circle Award and the PEN/Faulkner Award. In later novels, *The Waterworks* (1994) and *City of God* (2000), Doctorow continues to shuttle back and forth between 19th- and 20th-century American history, demonstrating no diminishment in his power to both celebrate and criticize American culture.

Doctorow has also published *Lives of the Poets: Six Stories and a Novella* (1984); a play, *Drinks Before Dinner* (1978); and one book of cultural commentary and literary criticism, *Jack London, Hemingway, and the Constitution: Selected Essays, 1977–1992* (1993). *Conversations with E. L. Doctorow*, edited by Christopher D. Morris, was published in 1999.

Sources
Fowler, Douglas. *Understanding E. L. Doctorow.* Columbia: University of South Carolina Press, 1992.
Williams, John. *Fiction as False Document: The Reception of E. L. Doctorow in the Postmodern Age.* Columbia, S.C.: Camden House, 1996.

Donleavy, James Patrick (1926–) *novelist*
The Brooklyn-born author of *The Ginger Man* (1955), a novel about an American law student at Trinity College in Dublin, J. P. Donleavy writes with a ribald sensibility that has been compared to that of James Joyce. Like Joyce, he finds a good deal of comedy in the subject of sex. He has continued to write exuberant prose in *A Singular Man* (1963), *The Beastly Beatitudes of Balthazar B* (1968), *The Destinies of Darcy Dancer, Gentleman* (1977), *The Lady Who Liked Clean Rest Rooms: The Chronicle of One of the Strangest Stories Ever to Be Rumoured About Around New York* (1995), and *Wrong Information Is Being Given Out at Princeton* (1998). He also wrote his autobiography, *The History of the Ginger Man* (1994).

Sources
Masinton, Charles G. *J. P. Donleavy: The Style of His Sadness and Humor.* Bowling Green, Ohio: Popular Press, 1975.

Doolittle, Hilda (H. D.) (1886–1961) *poet, novelist*
Known as H. D., Doolittle was a pioneer of the IMAGISM movement in poetry, which focused on spare language and vivid pictures and discarded regular poetic rhythms in favor of musical ones. H. D. spent much of her life in Europe, befriending Ezra POUND and other important writers. Her *Collected Poems* appeared in 1925 and 1983. She also wrote several avant-garde novels, including *Palimpsest* (1926) and *Hedylus* (1928). Her titles indicate her fascination with classical antiquity.

Sources
Bloom, Harold, ed. *H. D.* New York: Chelsea House, 1989.
DuPlessis, Rachel Blau. *H. D., The Career of That Struggle.* Brighton, Sussex: Harvester Press, 1986.
Taylor, Georgina. *H. D. and the Public Sphere of Modernist Women Writers 1913–1946: Talking Women.* New York: Oxford University Press, 2001.

Dorn, Edward Merton (1929–1999) *poet*
Ed Dorn was born and raised in Villa Grove, Illinois, and attended the University of Illinois. From 1951 to 1954 he studied at Black Mountain College, where he came under the influence of Charles OLSON and the BLACK MOUNTAIN POETS. He wrote what Olson called "projective verse," a form of free verse suited to the way the individual poet actually spoke. Dorn's first published work was *What I See in the Maximus Poems* (1960), which discussed Olson's magnum opus.

Dorn's major subject was the American West. He is best known for his verse epic *Gunslinger*, published in four volumes (1968, 1969, 1972). Dorn's West is a mythic fantasy, with a dope-smoking talking horse named Claude Levi-Strauss; a cowboy demi-god (the Gunslinger); a brothel madam called Liz; Kool Everything, a hipster; and an academic, Dr. Flamboyant. Dorn's anticapitalist and anti-industrial themes show an affinity to the work of the BEATS.

Some critics have found Dorn's poetry too didactic; others, especially in England, have called him one of America's great political poets. (He taught for many years at the University of Essex.) Dorn was a great supporter of Native Americans and satirized business figures like Howard Hughes.

Dorn's other poetry collections include *Collected Poems 1956–1974* (1975), *Selected Poems* (1978), *Yellow Lola* (1981), *Captain Jack's Chaps* (1983), *Abhorrences* (1984), and *High West Rendezvous* (1997).

Dorn also published a history, *The Shoshoneans: The People of the Basin Plateau* (1966), and *The Poet, the People, the Spirit* (1976). His *Views, Interviews* was published in two volumes in 1980, and *Was West: Stories, Essays and Verse Accounts 1963–1993* in 1993.

Sources

Wesling, Donald, ed. *Internal Resistances: The Poetry of Edward Dorn.* Berkeley: University of California Press, 1985.

Dos Passos, John Roderigo (1896–1970) *novelist*

John Dos Passos, the illegitimate son of a prominent attorney, was born in Chicago but raised by his mother in Brussels, London, and in other parts of Europe. There were fitful periods of reunion with his father, who influenced his son's view of politics and literature. After his father's first wife died, his father married his mother. Dos Passos enrolled at Harvard, where he was greatly influenced by the work of radical journalist John REED, particularly the book *Insurgent Mexico* (1914).

After graduating from Harvard, Dos Passos studied architecture in Spain and traveled in the Near East. He also served as an ambulance worker during WORLD WAR I, out of which he produced his first important novel, *Three Soldiers* (1921). Like Stephen Crane's *The Red Badge of Courage,* it explores the experience of the common soldier and shows the brutality of war. Dos Passos portrays the disillusionment and dehumanization resulting from the war, but he also attempts to capture the regional differences among American soldiers from California, Indiana, and Virginia, creating characters from different parts of the country and recording their distinctive manners and styles. The vivid visual quality of the novel reflects Dos Passos's study of art, especially his radical juxtaposition of images in the "Camera Eye" sections, which has been compared to cubist paintings.

In the novel *Manhattan Transfer* (1925) Dos Passos shifts his attention from war to the city. New York looms over the characters with a dynamic and terrifying materiality. The novel is divided into sections titled "Ferryslip," "Tracks," "Rollercoaster," "Steamroller," "Revolving Doors," and "Skyscrapers," which emphasize how human lives are enveloped in an energy and power that threatens to overwhelm them. Again, Dos Passos employs a collage/cubist technique—fusing bits of dialogue, action, newspaper clippings, signs, and fragmented glimpses of the scenes of city life. Human experience is speeded up, and characters clash, rep-

resenting the forces of modern labor and business, the press and the world of entertainment.

Three Soldiers and *Manhattan Transfer* preceded Dos Passos's classic trilogy, *U.S.A.* (1937), which includes *The 42nd Parallel* (1930), *1919* (1932), and *The Big Money* (1936). In this great epic of American history, the novelist draws on newsreels, headlines, songs, letters, placards, slang, and mini-biographies of historical figures as he explores the lives of fictional characters and presenting through his "Camera Eye" section his own intensely personal and autobiographical reflections, drawing on memories of his childhood and early youth.

The 42nd Parallel focuses on Mac McCreary (Middletown, Connecticut), a printer who joins the revolutionary movement in Mexico; J. Ward Moorehouse (Massachusetts), a public relations man; Eleanor Stoddard (Chicago), an interior decorator; and Charley Anderson (Fargo, North Dakota), an airplane manufacturer. These characters represent not only different parts of the country but also the changing face of American culture and its economy. This sweeping novel presents the idea of having an image or public persona, the radical changes heralded by air travel, the notion that modern life will be dominated by professional tastemakers, and the rumbling underground efforts of radicals to protest these massive changes in American life.

Dos Passos juxtaposes his narratives of fictional characters with abrupt, succinct, and poetic capsule histories of such public figures as the socialist Eugene V. Debs; President Woodrow Wilson; three-time Democratic presidential nominee William Jennings Bryan; and the inventor Charles Proteus Stenmetz, whose mathematical calculations became the property of General Electric. In a Dos Passos novel, the fate of individuals becomes ensnared in the complex transformations of American commerce and politics. Indeed, the onslaught of change and its oppressive influence on people brings Dos Passos to the brink of determinism: His characters seem incapable of bucking these coercive trends. The most successful characters adapt to change, allowing their principles and temperaments to be guided by the fluctuations of fashion.

The great sweep of this novel also includes "Camera Eye" sections that trace the development of Dos Passos's own consciousness, from his early years in Europe to the advent of World War I and his intensifying political convictions. Indeed, it is the novelist's own consciousness that draws the novel to a close and anticipates the next phases of American life, as well as of his own biography.

1919 goes well beyond *Three Soldiers* in dramatizing the impact and the consequences of World War I. Fictional characters such as Dick Savage, a Harvard graduate, express Dos Passos's own literary sensibility and experience. Savage becomes enmeshed in the careers of J. Ward Moorehouse and Ben Compton, the son of a Jewish immigrant. Meanwhile, Eleanor Stoddard advances her career by having an affair with J. Ward Moorehouse. By contrast, John Reed, another Harvard man, is portrayed as keeping his faith that the world will be transformed by political revolution, not big business. Theodore Roosevelt is treated as perhaps the last of an era of genuine Americans who distrust the big-money world exemplified by Dos Passos's excoriating portrait of J. P. Morgan.

The "Camera Eye" sections in *1919* accentuate the grim horrors of war as Dos Passos experienced them in the ambulance service. The author contrasts the devastation of war with industrial unrest at home in America and the author's acute consciousness of the postwar industrial and commercial world.

The last novel of the trilogy is certainly the most pessimistic in its portrayal of Americans caught up in the cash nexus. Charley Anderson, for example, has been entirely undone by his capitalistic career. His drinking and womanizing end suddenly in a fatal car crash in Florida. Other characters seem to have turned themselves into products. Margo Dowling, the Hollywood starlet, is merely a commodity controlled by the powerful producer Sam Mongolies. Only Mary French continues the tradition of John Reed: she works for the Communist Party and protests the executions of SACCO AND VANZETTI. The novel celebrates heroes in mini-biographies of Isadora Duncan (dedicated to the art of dance) and the Wright brothers (although their invention of the airplane fuels the war and capital-producing machinery of the country).

The "Camera Eye" sections make the transition from the 1920s to the 1930s, emphasizing the bankruptcy of capitalism and the onset of the DEPRESSION. Even so, these sections retain a lingering faith in the common man and the possibilities of renewal.

Although *U.S.A.* and Dos Passos's other early novels branded him as a leftist, his concern was less with ideology than with the individual and the forces that hampered the development of individuality. The Communist Party and individual revolutionaries seemed to him to represent core American values that were under attack in corporate America. In the late 1930s Dos Passos's view of the threat to individuality shifted dramatically, however, with his reaction to the SPANISH CIVIL WAR in 1936. He witnessed firsthand the perfidy of Communists—particularly those working for Stalin, who assassinated those on the Left who did not hew to the Stalinist line. In other words, Dos Passos realized that individuals were no safer among radicals than they were among reactionaries.

Critics have debated whether Dos Passos's shift in political perspective harmed his art or whether the energy and brilliance of *U.S.A.* simply marked a peak of achievement that he could not equal in subsequent work. For whatever reason, later novels such as his trilogy *District of Columbia* (1952)—composed of *Adventures of a Young Man* (1939), *Number One* (1943), and *The Grand Design* (1949)—lacked the experimental verve of his greatest work.

Dos Passos wrote several historical narratives in his later years, including *The Ground We Stand On: Some Examples from the History of a Political Creed* (1941), *The Head and Heart of Thomas Jefferson* (1954), and *Mr. Wilson's War* (1962).

Sources

Becker, George. *John Dos Passos.* New York: Ungar, 1974.
Carr, Virginia Spencer. *Dos Passos: A Life.* Garden City, N.Y.: Doubleday, 1984.
Maine, Barry, ed. *Dos Passos: The Critical Heritage.* London: Routledge, 1988.
Nanney, Lisa. *John Dos Passos.* New York: Twayne, 1998.
Wagner, Linda W. *Dos Passos as American.* Austin: University of Texas Press, 1979.

Dove, Rita (1952–) *poet, novelist, short story writer, dramatist, essayist, educator*

Born in Akron, Ohio, Dove graduated summa cum laude in 1973 from Miami University in Ohio and then held a Fulbright scholarship at the University of Tübingen in West Germany. In 1977 she published *Ten Poems,* and in 1980 *The Only Dark Spot in the Sky* and *The Yellow House on the Corner.* Dove's highly structured and disciplined poetry has been compared to the work of Gwendolyn BROOKS. Although her work often deals with race and the history of slavery, it also addresses the fate of women and Dove's own family history. In 1987 she won the Pulitzer Prize for *Thomas and Beulah,* a poetry collection.

Dove published her first novel, *Through the Ivory Tower,* in 1992 and her first play, *The Darker Face of the Earth,* in 1994. She also published a collection of stories, *Fifth Sunday,* in 1985. Her novel concentrates on the life of an African-American woman, an artist-in-residence in Akron, Ohio, and it is clearly based on her own experience.

In 1993 Dove published her *Selected Poems* and became the first African-American woman to be named the U.S. poet laureate. *Mother's Love,* another collection of poetry, appeared in 1995; *On the Bus with Rosa Parks: Poems* in 1999; and *The Poet's World,* a collection of essays, in 1995.

Sources

Steffen, Therese. *Crossing Color: Transcultural Space and Place in Rita Dove's Poetry, Fiction, and Drama.* New York: Oxford University Press, 2001.
Vendler, Helen. *The Given and the Made: Strategies of Poetic Redefinition.* Cambridge, Mass.: Harvard University Press, 1995.

drama

Twentieth-century drama is commonly thought to have begun with the work of Eugene O'NEILL, whose work single-handedly transformed the American theater. O'Neill despised the 19th-century tradition of sentimental, genteel, and melodramatic plays. He aspired to create a dramatic literature that was the equal of American and European achievements in the novel and in poetry. He began his work with the PROVINCETOWN PLAYERS. His early plays of the sea draw on the work of Herman Melville and Joseph Conrad. Already O'Neill was developing a brooding sense of fate and family disorder that would mark his mature later plays. His style ranged from impressionistic dramas such as *The Hairy Ape* (1922) to studies of America myth in *The Fountain* (1925), based on the legend of Juan Ponce de León and the fountain of youth. O'Neill even used a novelistic STREAM-OF-CONSCIOUSNESS technique in plays like *The Great God Brown* (1926) and *Strange Interlude* (1928), and his use of masks in the former work is reminiscent of the ancient Greek theater. Indeed, O'Neill was simultaneously influenced by Freud and Sophocles, as he demonstrated again in his version of the Orestia trilogy, *Mourning Becomes Electra* (1931). Later in his career, plays such as *More Stately Mansions* (1964) reflected his interest in American history as a shaper of human character. In THE EMPEROR JONES (1920) and *All God's Chillun Got Wings* (1924) he took on controversial issues such as black power and miscegenation.

In O'Neill's last phase, his two masterpieces, *The Iceman Cometh* (1939) and LONG DAY'S JOURNEY INTO NIGHT (1956) exhibited a heightened REALISM that was just as intense as his earlier experimental plays.

Other playwrights followed O'Neill's example—experimenting boldly with theme and subject matter. Elmer RICE in *The Adding Machine* (1923) created an expressionistic (see EXPRESSIONISM) drama that criticized a civilization increasingly dominated by commercial considerations that turned people into numbers or adding machines. Playwright Paul GREEN, on the other hand, wrote searing realistic dramas about the plight of poor whites and blacks, providing a folk-based critique of the capitalistic system that would later result in spectacle-plays in which large casts dramatized the history of America.

In *Our Town* (1938) and *The Skin of Our Teeth* (1942), Thornton WILDER played with the concept of time and the use of stage space to create characters that were American originals often expressing small-town values and yet also world citizens, so to speak, responding to social, psychological, and economic changes occurring in the modern world.

Far more conventional plays, especially comedies, were also written during this period of experimentation. Playwrights such as George S. KAUFMAN, Moss HART, and William SAROYAN took a more lighthearted, if no less satirical, view of American culture, including politics and the cult of celebrity—especially in plays like Kaufman and Hart's *The Man Who Came To Dinner* (1939) and Philip Barry's *The Philadelphia Story* (1939).

An entirely different kind of drama was created by such playwrights as Sidney HOWARD, Clifford ODETS, and Lillian HELLMAN. Influenced by Marxist thought, which emphasized class differences and the exploitation of labor and the lower classes, these writers created rousing plays that were really melodramas about the need for social and political action. Howard dramatized slum life provocatively in his hit Broadway play *Dead End* (1935), which Hellman adapted for the movies. Hellman herself showed the crass and cruel nature of a competitive society in plays such as *The Little Foxes* (1939) and *Another View of the Forest* (1946). But Odets was the most rabble-rousing of all with plays such as *Waiting for Lefty*, about a crowd of strikers waiting for their leader, and *Golden Boy* (1937), which showed how the American dream was a sham.

After World War II, Arthur MILLER and Tennessee WILLIAMS dominated the American stage. Miller tended to use family dramas to explore political and social issues. Williams explored the psychology of his characters in a heightened realism. For all their differences, however, both playwrights saw the theater as a way to reveal characters in conflict with themselves. Willy Loman in Miller's DEATH OF A SALESMAN (1949) is a disappointment to himself; and the same can be said of BLANCHE DUBOIS in Williams's *A STREETCAR NAMED DESIRE* (1947). Although expressionist elements can be found in their work, Miller and Williams eschewed much of O'Neill's conspicuous experimentation—as O'Neill himself did in his later plays.

Edward ALBEE emerged in the 1960s not only as the innovative heir to O'Neill but also as the American playwright most influenced by the absurdist drama of European playwrights, especially Samuel Beckett. Albee's early play *The American Dream* (1960) is antirealistic, while *The Zoo Story* (1959) take a realistic setting and pushes it to an extreme conclusion. Even his most realistic play, WHO'S AFRAID OF VIRGINIA WOOLF ? (1962), contains expressionistic elements. Indeed, this play is Albee's masterpiece in part because it continues the tradition of the family drama of O'Neill, Miller, and Williams in such a seamless and riveting way.

Lanford WILSON, David MAMET, and Sam SHEPARD have been great innovators in American drama since the late 1960s. Their work, like Albee's, reflects a spectrum of styles—realism, EXPRESSIONISM, and NATURALISM—as does the work of other important contemporary playwrights. Ed BULLINS, Amiri BARAKA, and August WILSON, for example, have built on the legacy of O'Neill and of African-American playwrights such as Lorraine HANSBERRY to create an American theater that encompasses a diverse sense of American history. Marsha NORMAN, Beth HENLEY, and Wendy WASSERSTEIN present a woman's view of American culture and analyze the way in which men and women interact in the family and in society at large. Tony KUSHNER's epic series of plays, *Angels in America* (1991, 1993), portray American history through a gay perspective. While playwrights such as

Kushner and Wasserstein have clearly allied themselves with feminist and gay viewpoints, their work also reflects the contemporary American theater's desire to continue to reach mass audiences through comedy and a broad sense of familial and national issues.

Sources

Bryer, Jackson, R., ed. *The Playwright's Art: Conversations with Contemporary American Dramatists.* New Brunswick, N.J.: Rutgers University Press, 1995.

Engle, Ron and Tice L. Miller, ed. *The American Stage: Social and Economic Issues from the Colonial Period to the Present.* New York: Cambridge University Press, 1993.

Frankel, Aaron. *Writing the Broadway Musical.* Cambridge, Mass.: Da Capo, 2000.

Gassner, John, ed. *Best Plays of the Modern American Theatre.* New York: Crown, 1947.

———. *Theatre at the Crossroads: Plays and Playwrights of the Mid-century American Stage.* New York: Holt, Rinehart & Winston, 1960.

Dreiser, Theodore Herman Albert (1871–1945)
novelist

Theodore Dreiser was born in Terre Haute, Indiana, and spent much of his early life in that city and in other Indiana towns. His father was seriously injured in a mill accident and never recovered his health or his will to succeed. While his brother, Paul, succeeded as a songwriter, Theodore struggled at various menial jobs and quit Indiana University in Bloomington after a year of frustration. He moved to Chicago, where he wrote for newspapers. Other journalistic jobs took him to midwestern cities and then to New York, where Dreiser achieved some success as a magazine editor.

Sister Carrie (1899), Dreiser's first novel, established his prowess in the naturalistic school of American fiction. Dreiser stripped this story of a young woman of all of its sentimentality. He did not moralize; he also did not strive to achieve a happy ending. Consequently, his brutal vision of how a young woman could achieve success in turn-of-the-last-century America outraged the reading public and the publishing industry. Carrie crassly uses any man who comes to hand—the slick Drouet, the stylish Hurstwood. Her life is a triumph that flouts every genteel virtue that late 19th-century America professed to uphold. That she prevails by using her sexuality is a condemnation of society, not a judgment of her.

Dreiser's belief that human beings often acted on impulse and on a raw biological drive seemed to challenge the rules of society and mock conventional religious beliefs. At the same time, discerning readers were exhilarated with Dreiser's frankness about the role of sex in human relationships and the power a woman like Carrie could wield because of her physical appeal. Dreiser's own ambition made him sympathize with characters who broke the rules of society and faced the overwhelming forces of America's commercial culture and industrial might.

Jennie Gerhardt (1911) extends Dreiser's merciless analysis of a corrupt and grasping culture, but he also presents a heroine with a softer, more compassionate nature than Carrie's—although the women come from similar backgrounds. Jennie is a fallen woman, but her decision to live with a man who is not her husband proves to be an expression of her loyal and loving temperament, not a sign of her sinful nature. Dreiser treats the seduction of Jennie by Senator Brander Matthews with a sensitive, even loving attitude. Even when the senator dies, Jennie is not to be pitied, because her second lover, Lester Kane, cherishes Jennie and sets up a clandestine life with her. Although he ultimately proves to be less than a great man and exposes Jennie to much sorrow and hardship, she survives largely because of her own generous interpretation of human nature and society. The novel demonstrates how certain individuals can triumph even in a society that marks them for destruction.

Dreiser next embarked on a major exposé of American business culture in his trilogy, *The Financier* (1912), *The Titan* (1914), and *The Stoic* (1947). All three novels center on tycoon Frank Cowperwood, modeled after the Chicago businessman Charles T. Yerkes. Dreiser's exploration of the American economy as a for-profit culture that demeans individuals was heavily influenced by the works of Arthur Schopenhauer, Friedrich Nietzsche, Karl Marx, and Herbert Spencer. In this grim social Darwinist world there is still room for magnificent individuals like Frank Cowperwood, although even his character is in part driven by what Dreiser calls his "chemisms," the biological imperative that makes human society a contest, a survival of the fittest. None of these novels equals the raw power of *Sister Carrie*, but they advance Dreiser's uncompromising vision of the battle between individuals and a coercive society.

Dreiser surpassed the achievement of *Sister Carrie* in AN AMERICAN TRAGEDY (1925), a massive novel about the pursuit of the American dream of success. He based his work on the story of Chester Gillette, who murdered a young working-class girl when her pregnancy became an obstacle to his match with a society woman. The sensational trial that ensued became the basis not only for Dreiser's story but also for the meticulous documentary feel of the novel, especially the final pages, which are set on death row.

Dreiser's CLYDE GRIFFITHS is the quintessential American dreamer. Coming from a family of religious fanatics, he sets off on his own to seek his fortune. After a disappointing beginning, he finds a promising niche at a rich relative's factory. There he meets a working-class girl, Roberta Alden, with whom he falls in love and impregnates. Roberta becomes a burden when Clyde is introduced to Sondra Finchley, a beautiful society girl. The climactic scene of the novel takes place in a boat, with Clyde wavering between his compassion for Roberta and his determination to get rid of her. He knows she cannot swim, and he has already contrived a situation that ensures her drowning. But does he actually rock the boat? As she falls into the water, he remains seated, unable (apparently) to save her.

The focus in this novel is as much on Clyde's society as on Clyde himself. What kind of a world is it, Dreiser asks, in which success can seem so all-important that Clyde violates his own humanity by not coming to Roberta's rescue?

Although Dreiser has often been criticized for his clumsy style and crude philosophizing, his creation of vibrant characters and compelling dramatic scenes has ensured his place in the canon of American literature.

Dreiser wrote a great many works of journalism, philosophy, and autobiography, including *A Traveler at Forty* (1913), *A Hoosier Holiday* (1916), *Hey, Rub-a-Dub-Dub!* (1920), *A Book About Myself* (1922), The *Color of a Great City* (1923), and *Tragic America* (1931). The *Letters of Theodore Dreiser* was published in 1959; *American Diaries, 1902–1926* in 1982; and the *Selected Magazine Articles of Theodore Dreiser* in 1985. His short fiction is collected in *Free and Other Stories* (1918), *Chains: Lesser Novels and Stories* (1927), *Fine Furniture* (1930), and *The Best Stories of Theodore Dreiser* (1947). Dreiser wrote several plays, including *Plays of the Natural and Supernatural* (1916) and *The Hand of the Potter: A Tragedy in Four Acts* (1919). His poetry appears in *Moods: Cadenced and Declaimed* (1926), *The Aspirant* (1929), and *Epitaph: A Poem* (1929).

Sources

Gerber, Philip. *Theodore Dreiser Revisited.* New York: Twayne, 1992.
Lingemann, Richard. *Theodore Dreiser: At the Gates of the City 1871–1907.* New York: Putnam, 1986.
———. *Theodore Dreiser: An American Journey 1908–1945.* New York: Putnam's, 1990.
Orlov, Paul A. *An American Tragedy: Perils of the Self Seeking "Success."* Lewisburg, Pa.: Bucknell University Press, 1998.
Pizer, Donald. *Critical Essays on Theodore Dreiser.* Boston: G.K. Hall, 1981.

Drury, Allen Stuart (1918–1998) *novelist*

Allen Drury was born in Texas and graduated from Stanford University. He worked as a Washington correspondent for the *New York Times,* which gave him the background to write his Pulitzer Prize–winning novel, *Advise and Consent* (1959), which dramatized the political conniving involved in confirming a secretary of state. Drury's other fiction—including *Capable of Honor* (1966) and *Come Nineveh, Come Tyre: The Presidency of Edward M. Jason* (1973)—did not achieve the popular or critical success of his first novel.

Sources

Kemme, Tom. *Political Fiction, The Spirit of the Age, and Allen Drury.* Bowling Green, Ohio: Bowling Green State University Press, 1987.

DuBois, Blanche *character*

Tennessee Williams's tragic heroine in *A STREETCAR NAMED DESIRE* is an aging southern belle who has lost her plantation. When she visits her sister, Stella, in New Orleans, Blanche is desperate to start a new life even as she mourns the elegant, if decadent, past of the plantation. She is met by a skeptical Stanley Kowalski, Stella's husband, who has little patience for Blanche's airs of superiority. It is Blanche's fate to be attacked by Stanley, who sees her only as a hypocrite and exploiter of his wife's trust. A distraught Blanche is eventually taken away to a mental institution, speaking her famous line to the doctor who comes to get her: "I have always depended on the kindness of strangers." On the one hand, Blanche can be viewed as symbolic of a decadent and dying southern way of life. On the other, she represents another one of those sensitive souls in Williams's work that seem crushed by a crude culture.

Du Bois, William Edward Burghardt

(1868–1963) *historian, biographer, journalist, critic, editor, novelist*

Born in Great Barrington, Massachusetts, W. E. B. Du Bois grew up among a community of African Americans who had settled there during the American Revolution. Although his father deserted his mother after he was born, Du Bois experienced a traditional and conventional environment, which included members in the Congregational Church.

Du Bois showed early promise as a scholar, but his studies at Fisk University in Nashville, Tennessee, exposed him for the first time to the barbaric nature of what he later called the "color line," the absolute separation of whites and blacks. From Fisk, Du Bois went to Harvard to study history under such famous figures as William James and George SANTAYANA. He went on to the University of Berlin to study sociology. By 1894, he was back in "nigger-hating America," and found it difficult to get job in spite of holding a Ph.D. Eventually he found positions at Wilberforce University in Ohio and then at the University of Pennsylvania and Atlanta University. His dissertation, *The Suppression of the African Slave-Trade to the United States, 1638–1870,* was published in 1896. This brilliant work of history was followed by the groundbreaking sociological study *The Philadelphia Negro* (1899).

Du Bois's development as a writer took a great leap forward with his collection of essays, *The Souls of Black Folk* (1903), a powerful affirmation of African-American identity and an attack on Booker T. Washington's accommodationist position, which Du Bois believed deprived African Americans of their dignity and their own cultural heritage. His book remains a classic of American literature, and a source of inspiration to generations of African-American writers.

From 1905 to 1909, Du Bois suspended his work as a scholar to edit the general-circulation magazines *Moon* and *Horizon* in the belief that he had to reach a broader audience and advocate more radical positions than African-American leaders of the time were espousing. He also wrote a biography, *John Brown* (1909), emphasizing the virtues of extremism. In 1910 he resigned his professorship at Atlanta University and became the publicity director for the NAACP as well as the founder and editor of its magazine, THE CRISIS.

In these years, he forecast a resurgence of African-American creativity and published a novel, *The Quest of the Silver Fleece* (1911). Set in rural Alabama and concentrating on young African-American protagonists, Du Bois exposed the evils of the plantation system in a style that has been compared to naturalists such as Frank NORRIS and Upton SINCLAIR. At the same time, he believed that the plight of African Americans should be seen in a more global and specifically Pan-Africanist perspective, which he explored in his historical and sociological account *The Negro* (1915).

Although Du Bois welcomes a new generation of writers, especially the poets Langston HUGHES and Countee CULLEN, he attacked them in "The Negro in Art" (1926) for being insufficiently radical. His second novel, *The Dark Princess* (1928), is an explicitly propagandist work in which the darker nations rise up and rid themselves of white domination.

By 1934 Du Bois had so radicalized himself that he broke with the NAACP, which he considered too moderate. He resumed teaching at Atlanta University, publishing in 1935 *Black Reconstruction in America,* which took a Marxist view of the conditions that had led to strict segregation of blacks in American society. He explained the evolution of his own thinking in an autobiography, *Dusk of Dawn: An Essay Toward an Autobiography of a Race Concept* (1940).

Although Du Bois rejoined the NAACP in 1944, his tenure there was short, and he gravitated toward Communist affiliations and anticolonialist organizations. In 1950 he ran for the U.S. Senate as a member of the Labor Party. In 1951 he was indicted by the U.S. government as the agent of a foreign power, but a judge threw the case out of court and Du Bois published an account of the experience in *In Battle For Peace: The Story of My Eighty-Third Birthday* (1952).

By the 1950s Du Bois was largely ignored by both white and black readers, although he published *The Ordeal of Mansart* (1957), *Mansart Builds a School* (1959), and *Worlds of Color* (1961)—a trilogy of novels that presents his view of African-American and world history. In 1959 he moved to Ghana and began work on the *Encyclopedia Africana,* which he left uncompleted at the time of his death.

Du Bois is an inimitable figure in African-American history, the founder of the very idea of the black intellectual and the idea of a BLACK AESTHETIC. Unlike the trajectory of many American intellectuals, black or white, he grew more radical in his later years, sometimes preferring propaganda over art. He remains one of the few figures in American history able to be both activist and intellectual, artist and historian—combining roles, in other words, that have become separated in contemporary culture.

Sources

Andrews, William L., ed. *Critical Essays on W. E. B. Du Bois* Boston: G.K. Hall, 1985.

Lewis, David Levering. *W. E. B. Du Bois: Biography of a Race, 1868–1919.* New York: Holt, 1993.

———. *W. E. B. Du Bois: The Fight for Equality and the American Century 1919–1963.* New York: Henry Holt, 2000.

Rampersad, Arnold. *The Art and Imagination of W. E. B. Du Bois.* Cambridge, Mass.: Harvard University Press, 1976.

Duncan, Robert Edward (1919–1988) *poet*

Robert Duncan's mother died in childbirth, and his father gave him up for adoption. He studied at the University of California, Berkeley, from 1936 to 1938 and again from 1948 to 1950. Like fellow writer William S. BURROUGHS, Duncan was discharged from the army during World War II on psychological grounds. Duncan matured as a poet and teacher at Black Mountain College, where he worked closely with Charles OLSON and Robert CREELEY. Influenced by Ezra POUND, his poems have been praised for their exquisite musical quality. His work is also marked by his fascination with the occult—a subject his adoptive father introduced to him. Duncan made his homosexuality an important component of his work. His *Selected Poems 1942–1950* was published in 1959. But he wrote distinguished work beginning with his first collection, *Heavenly City, Earthly City* (1947) to his mid-career *Bending the Bow* (1968) to *Ground Work: Before the War* (1984). He also published nonfiction, including *As Testimony: the Poet and the Scene* (1964), *The Truth and Life of Myth* (1968), and *Fictive Certainties* (1979).

Sources

Johnson, Mark Andrew. *Robert Duncan.* Boston: Twayne, 1988.

Dunne, John Gregory (1932–) *journalist, novelist*

Dunne grew up in a large Irish family (which included his brother Dominick) in Hartford, Connecticut. He worked for several years in New York City on various magazines, including the *National Review,* where he met his wife, Joan DIDION. They left New York to pursue their careers as novelists, journalists, and screenwriters in California. Dunne made a stunning debut as a novelist with *True Confessions* (1977), the story of a hard-boiled police detective in the Raymond CHANDLER tradition, and the detective's brother, an ambitious priest. *The Red, White, and Blue* (1987) is an epic novel of U.S. politics loosely based on the lives of the Kennedys. In *Playland* (1994), he produced a novel about Hollywood reminiscent of F. Scott FITZGERALD's *The Last Tycoon*. Dunne's nonfiction is as good, if not better, than his fiction. *Delano* (1967) is about Cesar Chavez and his United Farmworkers union. In *The Studio* (1969) and *Monster* (1997) he has written amusingly and insightfully about the movie industry. *Quintana and Friends* (1978) is a collection of his essays. *Harp* (1989) is a candid, engaging memoir about himself, his family, his marriage, and his obsession with the Irish. Together with Didion he has written several movie scripts, including *Panic in Needle Park* (1971), *Play It as It Lays* (1972), *A Star Is Born* (1976), and *Up Close and Personal* (1996).

Sources

Rollyson, Carl. "John Gregory Dunne." *Critical Survey of Long Fiction.* Pasadena, Calif.: Salem Press, 2000.

Winchell, Mark Royden. *John Gregory Dunne.* Boise, Idaho: Boise State University, 1986.

Eastman, Max Forrester (1883–1969) *poet, editor, social critic, historian, autobiographer*

Max Eastman began his literary career as editor of the radical journals THE MASSES (1912–1917) and *The Liberator* (1918–1922). His first book of literary criticism, *Enjoyment of Poetry* (1913), was also his most successful. It foretold his interest in linking art to society, making art criticism and social criticism a single, radical way of both enjoying and assessing life itself. He collected his own poetry in *Poems of Five Decades* (1954). His other important books include *Marx, Lenin, and the Science of Revolution* (1926) and *The Literary Mind: Its Place in an Age of Science* (1931). Eastman opposed Stalinist communism and favored Trotsky's view; American Trotskyites supported an international Communist revolution, which they believed Stalin had repudiated by expelling Trotsky from the Communist Party and from the Soviet Union. Eastman translated Trotsky's *History of the Russian Revolution* in three volumes (1932–1933). His attack on Stalin appears in *Stalin's Russia* (1940). Like many radicals, Eastman became disenchanted with the collective state, and his growing conservatism is expressed in *Reflections on the Failure of Socialism* (1955). Active in both social and political circles, Eastman wrote about this aspect of his life in *Great Companions* (1959), which includes portraits of Ernest HEMINGWAY and Edna St. Vincent MILLAY. *Love and Revolution* (1965) is his autobiography.

Sources

Cantor, Milton. *Max Eastman.* New York: Twayne, 1970.

Aaron, Daniel. *Writers on the Left: Episodes in American Literary Communism.* New York: Harcourt, Brace, 1961.

Edel, Joseph Leon (1907–1997) *biographer, critic*

Leon Edel was born in Pittsburgh and educated at McGill University in Montreal and the University of Paris. He worked as a journalist in the 1930s and in 1950 began his academic career at New York University, where he established himself as an authority on Henry James. Edel edited editions of James's plays and tales, and then embarked on an ambitious, controversial biography of the novelist, a five-volume opus published between 1953 and 1972. Some critics praised Edel for changing the form of biography: He relied heavily on psychological analysis and the scene-setting techniques favored by novelists. Other critics argued that he manipulated the facts more than is justifiable in biography. Edel's example and influence on modern biography, however, are undeniable. The biography, published in a one-volume edition as *Henry James: A Life* (1985) won both a Pulitzer Prize and National Book Award. Edel's major work about the writing of biography is *Writing Lives: Principia Biographica* (1984), a revision of his book *Literary Biography,* published in 1957. He also published several notable books of literary criticism, including *The Modern Psychological Novel* (1955) and *Stuff of Sleep and Dreams: Experiments in Literary Psychology* (1982). He helped to found the Center for Biographical Research at the University of Hawaii, where he ended his teaching career.

Sources

Fromm, Gloria G., ed. *Essaying Biography: A Celebration for Leon Edel.* Honolulu: University of Hawaii Press, 1987.

Powers, Lyall H., ed. *Leon Edel and Literary Art.* Ann Arbor, Mich.: UMI Research Press, 1988.

Edmonds, Walter Dumaux (1903–1998) *novelist*

Born and raised in New York, Walter Edmonds graduated from Harvard University in 1926. In the tradition of James Fenimore Cooper, he wrote historical novels set in upstate New York. His most famous novel is *Drums Along the Mohawk* (1936), set during the American Revolution and made into a major motion picture. His other novels include *The Wedding Journey* (1947), set on the Erie Canal in 1855, and *The Boyds of Black River* (1953), the story of New York farmers in the early 1900s.

Sources

Wyld, Lionel D. *Walter D. Edmonds, Storyteller*. Syracuse, N.Y.: Syracuse University Press, 1982.

Eiseley, Loren Corey (1907–1977) *anthropologist, poet, autobiographer*

A professional anthropologist, Loren Eiseley attracted a broad, literary audience for his sensitive, eloquent, and autobiographical books, including *The Immense Journey* (1957), an account of how life established itself on earth, and *The Man Who Saw Through Mirrors* (1973), a biographical meditation on Francis Bacon, the 17th-century philosopher and scientist. Eiseley humanized science and wrote about his personal involvement with it. He wrote poetry as well, collected in *Notes of an Alchemist* (1972) and *Another Kind of Autumn* (1977). *All the Strange Hours* (1975) is a beautifully written autobiography.

Sources

Christianson, Gale E. *Fox at the Wood's Edge: A Biography of Loren Eiseley*. New York: Henry Holt, 1990.

Eliot, Thomas Stearns (1888–1965) *poet, playwright, critic*

Born in St. Louis, Missouri, T. S. Eliot came from a family with deep New England roots. In St. Louis, one of his grandfathers founded both a Unitarian Church and Washington University. Although Eliot's father was a businessman and did not pursue his family's involvement in cultural affairs, he nevertheless inherited the Eliot sense of dedication to ethical and moral values. Eliot's mother was a social reformer and amateur poet.

Eliot began his college education in 1906 at Harvard, which was dominated at the time by the humanism of Irving BABBITT. But Eliot gravitated toward the French symbolist poets, the harbingers of a MODERNISM that Eliot would promote and embody. To his literary interests Eliot added a profound interest in philosophy, which led to his work on the philosopher F. H. Bradley. Although Eliot finished his Ph.D. thesis, he never returned to Harvard to accept his degree. Instead, beginning in 1914 he pursued a literary career in London. There he came under the influence of a fellow American, Ezra POUND, who helped Eliot hone his classical yet modern style. Pound, an imagist (see IMAGISM) who ruthlessly cut verbiage from poems, helped Eliot to perfect an elliptical yet precise style. Eliot's first great poems were dramatic monologues such as "THE LOVE SONG OF J. ALFRED PRUFROCK" (1910–1911), written at a time when Eliot was traveling in Europe. Although the poem owed something to the 19th-century dramatic monologue as perfected by Robert Browning, Eliot infused the form with a STREAM-OF-CONSCIOUSNESS technique that opened up new possibilities for poetry. Browning's monologuists spoke in complete sentences as if delivering soliloquies or addressing another person. When Prufrock refers to "you and I," he could be speaking to someone else, to himself, or just thinking the words of the poem. The poem's many literary allusions to writers such as Shakespeare and Andrew Marvell and its abrupt, aborted scenes presage Eliot's more experimental works. *The Waste Land* (1922), "The Hollow Men" (1925), and *Ash Wednesday* (1930) are devastating explorations of modern alienation and anomie, which Eliot linked to the ancient ideas of a land blighted and bereft of meaning. These poems, written in the wake of WORLD WAR I, also expressed the disillusionment of a generation that had seen millions killed and the world no better for it—indeed, more corrupted by the mass violence.

Despite the modernist style of his work, Eliot tended to withdraw from the modern world. He became politically and religiously conservative. His literary criticism, especially volumes such as *After Strange Gods* (1934) and *Notes Toward the Definition of Culture* (1948) earned him a reputation for being a reactionary—even anti-Semitic, especially since certain poems like "Gerontion" (1920) contained rather gross descriptions of Jews. Eliot summed up his views in the famous phrase, "an Anglo-Catholic in religion, a classicist in literature, and a royalist in politics."

Nevertheless, Eliot retained enormous authority as critic and poet. His *Four Quartets* (1943) is a magnificent exploration of the meaning of history and of civilization. The long poem is written in a supple verse that is both objective and autobiographical as Eliot expresses his grasp of the temporal world and his yearning for a transcendental, religious one. Similarly, his critical essays on English literature have been standard texts taught in college classrooms and became touchstones for his fellow writers and critics. His enormous influence derived from his overwhelming command of the history of English and world literature and from his own achievement as a poet. It was this welding of theory and practice that made Eliot such a formidable figure. His essay "Tradition and the Individual Talent" defined the modernist view that the work of literature, not its creator, should be the focus of the reader and critic. Opposed to biographical interpretations of literature, Eliot portrayed the writer as a tool of literature, with each great work of art modifying the canon of great works that came before and after it. It was the history of literature, in other words, not the psychology of the author, that mattered—a view that would influence both the NEW CRITICISM and a later generation of commentators on literature such as Susan SONTAG.

Eliot's plays are another significant contribution to literature and culture. He worked diligently to bring the verse play back into fashion. His most notable success was his first play, *Murder in the Cathedral* (1930), a dramatization of the murder of St. Thomas à Becket, the archbishop of Canterbury, in December 1170. This martyr for a religious cause defined Eliot's reverence for the saint and the man of conviction. The play also evoked the tremendous temptations of a corrupt world, especially in the brilliant and cunning speeches delivered by Becket's assassins. Eliot's other plays, such as *The Family Reunion* (1939) and *The Cocktail Party* (1950), are clever comments on modern life, but they lack both the gravity and wit of the first play.

Eliot's more whimsical verse, *Old Possum's Book of Practical Cats* (1939), was the basis of the enormously successful musical *Cats. Poems Written in Early Youth* was published in 1967; *Complete Poems and Plays* appeared in 1969. Among Eliot's most important works of criticism are *The Sacred Wood* (1920), *Selected Essays* (1932), *The Use of Poetry and the Use of Criticism* (1933), *The Idea of a Christian Society* (1939), *Poetry and Drama* (1951), and *On Poetry and Poets* (1957).

The Letters of T. S. Eliot: Volume I, 1898–1922 appeared in 1988.

Sources
Ackroyd, Peter. *T. S. Eliot.* London: Hamish Hamilton, 1984.
Davidson, Harriet, ed. *T. S. Eliot.* New York: Longman, 1999.
Donoghue, Denis. *Words Alone: The Poet T. S. Eliot.* New Haven, Conn.: Yale University Press, 2000.
Gordon, Lyndall. *T. S. Eliot: An Imperfect Life.* New York: W. W. Norton, 1999.
Moody, A. David, ed. *The Cambridge Companion to T. S. Eliot.* Cambridge: Cambridge University Press, 1994.

Elkin, Stanley Lawrence (1930–1995) *novelist*

Stanley Elkin's work is often associated with the term black humor. The author takes a satirical, verging on sardonic, view of American life. His first novel, *Boswell* (1964), is a comic story about a young man who attaches himself to famous people. *The Dick Gibson Show* (1971) exploits what Elkin saw as the surrealistic nature of mass entertainment—in this case, radio and the life of a radio announcer. In a similar vein, *The Franchiser* (1976) explores the life of a man whose life is creating motels and restaurants. Elkin's later work includes *Pieces of Soap* (1992), a collection of essays; *Van Gogh's Room at Arles: Three Novellas* (1993); and *Mrs. Ted Bliss* (1995), a novel set in Florida. Elkin produced

several collections of his shorter pieces, including *Criers and Kibitzers, Kibitzers and Criers* (1966), *Searches and Seizures* (1973), *Stanley Elkin's Greatest Hits* (1980), and *Early Elkin* (1985).

Sources
Dougherty, David C. *Stanley Elkin.* Boston: Twayne, 1991.

Ellison, Ralph Waldo (1914–1994) *novelist, critic*

Ralph Ellison grew up in Oklahoma City, Oklahoma. In the frontierlike atmosphere of the Southwest, he interacted freely with whites and blacks, heavily influenced by his mother's socialist politics. By his teenage years, Ellison demonstrated a strong interest in music, which would figure in his fiction and his literary criticism. With training in both classical music and jazz, Ellison would develop into one of the most sensitive literary interpreters of the way music has forged the American identity. Ellison studied music and literature at the all-black Tuskegee Institute in Alabama before moving to New York City in 1936, where he would spend much of the rest of his life.

Although Ellison learned a great deal from his African-American contemporaries such as Richard WRIGHT and Langston HUGHES, he was influenced even more by such writers as T. S. ELIOT and James Joyce. While Ellison's themes grew out of African-American life, his devotion to style and point of view derived from his study of the greatest European and American writers.

In early short stories Ellison focused on the radical politics of the 1930s, but he gradually developed an ironic and to some extent conservative view of race relations and American society. His education and street experience in New York City culminated in the classic American novel *Invisible Man* (1952). Ellison's unnamed narrator is like Dostoevsky's underground man in *Notes from Underground:* an alienated individual who speaks for the disaffection of masses of people, black and white. The narrator/protagonist recounts his bitter experience at a repressive black college, his devastating and life-threatening experiences in the radical politics of Harlem, and his determination to take refuge underground and create a new identity for himself. This masterpiece brims with great characters and analyses of culture as Ellison portrays the realities of American life. The religion, politics, and music of the African-American community, and the obtuseness of whites (to whom the book suggests all African Americans are invisible), receive shrewd treatment. The mordant humor and literary sophistication of the novel brought African-American literature to a new peak. At the same time, *Invisible Man* is a modernist (see MODERNISM) achievement that explores the isolation of the individual in mass society. Not just African Americans, but all Americans are subject to exploitation by society's institutions.

Ellison struggled to write another novel that rivaled the comprehensiveness and sagacity of his first major work. The second novel proceeded slowly, until the manuscript was destroyed in a fire. Ellison rewrote the novel, and at his death a good deal of the manuscript had been reworked several times. *Juneteenth* (1999), a version of the novel edited after his death, concerns a black minister, Hickman, who raises a boy as African American even though the boy looks white. The title refers to June 19, 1865, the day the Union army announced the freeing of the slaves in Texas: The novel is about how human identity can be discovered and liberated. While critics have not ranked *Juneteenth* as the equal of *Invisible Man,* the second novel again demonstrates Ellison's impressive grasp of American society and his desire to integrate the experience of African Americans into the experience of the whole country.

Ellison's short fiction is collected in *Flying Home and Other Stories* (1996). He was a superb critic and commentator on writing, culture, and music. *The Collected Essays of Ralph Ellison* was published in 1995.

Sources

Bloom, Harold, ed. *Ralph Ellison.* New York: Chelsea House, 1986.

Busby, Mark. *Ralph Ellison.* Boston: Twayne, 1991.

Butler, Robert J., ed. *The Critical Response to Ralph Ellison.* Westport, Conn.: Greenwood Press, 2000.

Watts, Jerry Gafio. *Heroism and the Black Intellectual: Ralph Ellison, Politics, and Afro-American Life.* Chapel Hill: University of North Carolina Press, 1994.

Ellmann, Richard (1918–1987) *biographer, literary critic*

Ellmann was born in Highland Park, Michigan. Educated at Yale, he became a professor at Northwestern University and ended his career at Oxford University. His early critical and biographical studies in Irish literature, especially *Yeats: The Man and the Masks* (1948) and *The Identity of Yeats* (1951), led to his landmark biography, *James Joyce* (1959), revised in 1982. Ellmann and Leon EDEL are often cited as the two most important biographers in modern literary study. Some critics prefer Ellmann over Edel because Ellmann did not employ the psychological analysis and novelistic techniques that Edel exploited. Ellmann himself expressed certain reservations about Edel's approach in *Golden Codgers* even as he acknowledged the importance of psychology in modern biographies and predicted that its use would increase. Ellmann's monumental biography *Oscar Wilde* was published after his death. The biography was an immense popular success and won a Pulitzer Prize.

Sources

Dick, Susan, ed. *Essays for Richard Ellmann: Omnium Gatherum.* Kingston, Ontario: McGill-Queen's University Press, 1989.

Heaney, Seamus. *The Place of Writing.* Atlanta, Ga.: Scholars Press, 1989.

Emperor Jones, The Eugene O'Neill (1921) *play*

Eugene O'NEILL's play, which centers on an African-American hero, is one of the first major works of the 20th century to give serious treatment to African-American experience. Set on a West Indian island that resembles Haiti, Brutus Jones, a former Pullman porter, reigns. A fugitive from justice (there is a warrant for his arrest on charges of murder) he is a manipulative tyrant who claims to his superstitious subjects that only a silver bullet can kill him. The arrogant Jones fails to foresee the uprising that forces him to flee. The play centers on his bewildering journey in the jungle—a metaphor for his confused consciousness. In his delirium he relives scenes from his past life and is finally brought down with the very silver bullets of which he often spoke. Although Jones is hardly an exemplary hero, the power of his imagination and ambition reflect how artists—white as well as African American—were reconceiving the African-American experience, finding characters and themes that were an important part of the national experience. O'Neill's focus not only on Jones's biography but also on his psychological state make both the style and content of the play an extraordinary contribution both to the American theater and to American literature. The play was both a popular and critical success.

Sources

Houchin, John H. ed. *The Critical Response to Eugene O'Neill.* Westport, Conn.: Greenwood Press, 1993.

Manheim, Michael, ed. *The Cambridge Companion to Eugene O'Neill.* New York: Cambridge University Press, 1998.

Erdrich, Louise (Karen Louise Erdrich) (1954–　) *novelist, poet*

Louise Erdrich grew up in Wahpeton, a small town in North Dakota. Her grandfather was tribal chair of the Turtle Mountain Band of the Ojibwa Nation. Her father, Ralph Erdrich, was a German immigrant who taught at the American Indian boarding school in Wahpeton. Erdrich earned degrees in creative writing from Dartmouth (B.A., 1976) and Johns Hopkins (M.A., 1979). In 1981 she married Michael Dorris, a professor of anthropology and head of the Native American studies program at Dartmouth. The couple adopted three Lakota Sioux children and had three more children of their own. They also collaborated on several works, including *The Broken Cord* (1989), which deals with fetal alcohol syndrome, an issue the couple had to confront when they adopted the children of alcoholic mothers. But the marriage was troubled, and there were also problems with their children, one of whom was killed in 1991 in a car accident. Dorris committed suicide in 1997.

Erdrich's early work, including her first novel, *Love Medicine* (1984, revised in 1993), was heavily influenced by William FAULKNER. She was impressed with his handling of the broad spectrum of human experience, his family sagas, and his comic genius. Critics praised Erdrich's novel, an interweaving of 14 stories of mixed-blood and Chippewa families, for the poetic quality of the prose and the sense of humor. Erdrich's second novel, *The Beet Queen* (1986), explores the German immigrant side of her family background. Set in a town similar to Wahpeton, it is a family and historical saga covering the period from 1932 to 1972. *Tracks* (1988) and *The Bingo Palace* (1994) cover more concentrated periods of time but continue the stories of characters in the earlier novels. *The Antelope Wife* (1998) introduces a new set of characters but continues the author's major themes: the interrelatedness of American Indian and white characters, the connections between the past and the present, and the influence of the midwestern environment on the histories of families and individuals.

Erdrich has also published two volumes of poetry, *Jacklight* (1984) and *Baptism of Desire* (1989); two volumes of nonfiction, *The Blue Jay's Dance: A Birth Year* (1995), and a novel for children, *The Birchbark House* (1999). She continued her sequence of novels about Native American life in *The Last Report on the Miracles at Little No Horse* (2001).

Sources
Beidler, Peter G. and Gay Barton. *A Reader's Guide to the Novels of Louise Erdrich.* Columbia: University of Missouri Press, 1999.
Chavkin, Allan, ed. *The Chippewa Landscape of Louise Erdrich.* Tuscaloosa: University of Alabama Press, 1999.
Jacobs, Connie A. *The Novels of Louise Erdrich: Stories of Her People.* New York: Peter Lang, 2001.
Stookey, Lorena Laura. *Louise Erdrich: A Critical Companion.* Westport, Conn.: Greenwood Press, 1999.

Evergreen Review (1957–1973) *periodical*
This influential avant-garde magazine published the BEATS and promising writers of the 1960s. Barney Rossett, the founder and editor, became famous for assembling an impressive collection of work by such controversial writers as Susan SONTAG, Henry MILLER, and Jack KEROUAC. Unlike many other literary quarterlies, however, *Evergreen Review* also devoted itself to the graphic arts, music (especially jazz), and social issues. The magazine's stance exemplified what came to be called the "counterculture" in the 1960s.

Everson, William (1912–1994) *poet*
Reared in California as a Christian Scientist, Everson served as a conscientious objector in World War II. He is often grouped with the writers of the SAN FRANCISCO RENAISSANCE.

His poetry is antiwar and often religious, with an erotic emphasis. He has been compared to Robinson JEFFERS, who explores similar themes with great intensity. Everson's collections include *The Residual Years: Poems 1934–1948* (1968) and *The Masks of Drought: Poems 1972–1979* (1980).

Sources
Bartlett, Lee. *William Everson: The Life of Brother Antoninus.* New York: New Directions, 1988.

existentialism
A European philosophy championed in different ways by Jean Paul Sartre and Albert Camus. The existentialists believe they must create their own existence. There is no essence, no God, upon which to rely for values or standards of behavior. This strenuous code means that individuals must invent themselves, because the universe has no pre-established meaning—just the significance that humankind attributes to it and can enforce by their own actions. On the one hand, existentialism posits an isolated individual who often has an agonizing struggle to establish an identity. On the other hand, it is the very struggle to achieve an identity or selfhood that ennobles human beings, who often realize that their persistence is futile and yet they must continue to struggle, for it is the only source of dignity they can acquire and maintain. To some degree, Saul BELLOW, Paul BOWLES, Ralph ELLISON, William STYRON, and Richard WRIGHT have been influenced by existentialism, for they have created characters who exist on the margins of society, or who have been oppressed by society's institutions, and seek ways to master their own fate. Norman MAILER has perhaps more than any other American writer used the term to define his life and work. One of his collections of essays is entitled *Existential Errands* (1972).

Sources
Finkelstein, Sidney. *Existentialism and Alienation in American Literature.* New York: International Publishers, 1965.
Lehan, Richard. *A Dangerous Crossing: French Literary Existentialism and the Modern American Novel.* Carbondale: Southern Illinois University Press, 1973.

expressionism
In the American theater, expressionism is an aesthetic movement that emphasizes the way mood and attitude affect works of art. Some of the scenes in Arthur MILLER's *DEATH OF A SALESMAN*, for example, have been called expressionistic because they seem to be projections of Willy Loman's mind. Two of Eugene O'NEILL's early plays, *The Hairy Ape* and *THE EMPEROR JONES*, feature an expressionist style that creates the effect of the world closing in on characters whose freedom of action is slowly circumscribed.

Elmer RICE's *The Adding Machine* has often been cited as a good example of expressionist drama because it exaggerates and distorts scenes in order to express what is in the characters' minds.

Sources

Valgemae, Mardi. *Accelerated Grimace: Expressionism in the American Drama of the 1920s.* Carbondale: Southern Illinois University Press, 1972.

Farewell to Arms, A Ernest Hemingway (1929)
novel

HEMINGWAY's classic novel about WORLD WAR I focuses on Frederic Henry, a wounded American serving in the ambulance corps, who falls in love with his nurse, Catherine BARKLEY. The novel depicts their doomed romance: They believe they can escape the war, but Catherine dies in childbirth, leaving Henry bereft. The novel has often been called an example of postwar nihilism. Certainly Hemingway offers no comforting words in his portrayal of a world that shows no mercy for individuals—whether they are in the line of fire during a war or simply the victims of their biology and circumstances. Although the novel is not deterministic or naturalistic, *A Farewell to Arms* does convey a sense of despair and futility. Human beings continue to act against the odds, exhibiting a rare grace that Hemingway greatly admires, but courage and escapism cannot dilute for long the grim recognition of mortality. Hemingway's spare prose controls the novel's great weight of emotion. Although *A Farewell to Arms* has been filmed twice, in 1932 and 1958, no screen version has come close to Hemingway's complex vision—at once austere and romantic.

Sources
Donaldson, Scott, ed. *New Essays on A Farewell to Arms.* New York: Cambridge University Press, 1990.
Monteiro, George, ed. *Critical Essays on Ernest Hemingway's A Farewell to Arms.* New York: G. K. Hall, 1994.
Reynolds, Michael S. *Hemingway's First War: The Making of A Farewell to Arms.* Princeton, N.J.: Princeton University Press, 1976.

Farrell, James Thomas (1904–1979) *novelist,*
short story writer

A Chicago-born novelist in the naturalist (see NATURALISM) school, James T. Farrell grew up among Irish immigrant families who provided the substance of his fiction. He saw both poverty and affluence in the lives of his grandparents and parents, and he used his observations in works that explore the inequality of circumstances and upbringing in his characters' lives. Farrell went to Catholic schools in CHICAGO and attended night classes at De Paul University, where he absorbed the work of Herman Melville and other great writers. He visited New York in the late 1920s and then returned to Chicago, where he began to write fiction in 1929. Farrell wrote dozens of short stories, but his major work is the Studs Lonigan trilogy: *Young Lonigan: A Boyhood in Chicago Streets* (1932), *The Young Manhood of Studs Lonigan* (1934), and *Judgment Day* (1935). Farrell's great achievement was to combine the moving story of a young man's life with a portrait of an age (the GREAT DEPRESSION) and of a society, especially the Catholic Irish enclave in Chicago. Farrell dramatized the opportunities and the corruption of city life in a style reminiscent of Theodore DREISER, whom Farrell acknowledged as an influence. Farrell was acutely conscious of the social forces that affect a person's life, yet his evocative portrayal of his characters prevents them from becoming stereotypes. Farrell's ability to depict human character and its connection to society inspired Norman MAILER, whose war novel, THE NAKED AND THE DEAD, is clearly derived from Farrell's style and subject matter. Although Farrell was a prolific novelist, no other work attracted readers or the critical praise that has accorded the Studs Lonigan trilogy a place in the American canon.

Farrell also published the O'Neill-Flaherty series, *A World I Never Made* (1936), *No Star Is Lost* (1938), *Father and Son* (1940), *My Days of Anger* (1943), and *The Face of Time* (1953). His main character, Danny O'Neill, differs from Studs Lonigan in that Danny is able to cope with the forces that threaten to overwhelm him. In the Bernard Carr trilogy, *Bernard Clare* (1946), *The Road Between* (1949), and *Yet Other Waters* (1952), Farrell shifts his attention to struggling artists and radical political activists in Depression-era New York City, with flashbacks set in Chicago. (Farrell had to change the name of his title character from Clare to Carr after he was sued for libel by a man named Bernard Clare.)

The prolific Farrell published several other novels in his long career, including *The Silence of History* (1963), *Invisible Swords* (1971), and *The Death of Nora Ryan* (1978). He wrote several short story collections, including *The Short Stories of James T. Farrell* (1937), *An Omnibus of Short Stories* (1956), and *Judith and Other Stories* (1973). *The Collected Poems of James T. Farrell* was published in 1965. His nonfiction includes *A Note on Literary Criticism* (1936), *The Fate of Writing in America* (1946), *Reflections at Fifty and Other Essays* (1954), and *On Irish Themes* (1982).

Sources

Branch, Edgar M. *James T. Farrell*. New York: Twayne, 1971.
———. *Studs Lonigan's Neighborhood and the Making of James T. Farrell*. Newton, Mass.: Arts End Books, 1996.
Wald, Alan M. *James T. Farrell: The Revolutionary Socialist Years*. New York: New York University Press, 1978.

Fast, Howard Melvin (1914–) *novelist*

Howard Fast, who has lived in New York City for much of his career, has written in a range of genres but is best known for his historical fiction, especially *Citizen Tom Paine* (1943) and *Freedom Road* (1944), set during Reconstruction. His novel *Spartacus* (1951), the story of a Roman slave revolt was made into a major motion picture. Fast also worked as a screenwriter in Hollywood. A man of outspoken radical beliefs, he wrote about his membership in the Communist Party from 1943 to 1956 in *The Naked God* (1957). *Being Red* (1990) revisits that story, going into more detail about the development of his politics. His later fiction includes *Seven Days in June: A Novel of the American Revolution* (1994), *Redemption* (1999), and *Greenwich* (2000). *War and Peace: Observations on Our Times* (1993) is a collection of his essays.

Sources

Macdonald, Andrew. *Howard Fast: A Critical Companion*. Westport, Conn.: Greenwood Press, 1996.

Faulkner, William Cuthbert (1897–1962) *novelist, short story writer*

A native of New Albany, Mississippi, Faulkner lived most of his life in and around Oxford, Mississippi, where his father owned a business and where Faulkner attended public school and the University of Mississippi. Although he was a precocious child, he did not adapt well to formal learning and never received a high school or university degree. His mother, a painter, encouraged her son even in the face of his father's ridicule and his community's skepticism. Faulkner began to write early in life. His first love was poetry, but the stilted and derivative nature of his verse eventually convinced him that fiction was his forte. Faulkner's early verse is collected in *The Marble Faun* (1924), *A Green Bough* (1933), and *William Faulkner: Early Prose and Poetry* (1962).

The turning point for Faulkner came when he met Sherwood ANDERSON in New Orleans. In such works as *Winesburg, Ohio*, Anderson demonstrated that a fiction writer need not look to foreign sources to write inspired and innovative prose. As Faulkner put it, Anderson convinced him that writing about his "postage stamp of native soil" would yield literary treasure. After *Soldiers' Pay* (1926) and *Mosquitos* (1927), Faulkner began to hit his stride with his third novel, *Sartoris* (1929), a severely cut version of what was later published as *Flags in the Dust* (1973), the full text of the original novel. This novel reveals the author's great love of the southern environment. Set in the period just after World War I, this work explores the experiences of southerners disoriented by and still obsessed with the lost cause of the Civil War. With humor and romanticism, Faulkner evokes the characters of small-town life and their desperate search for meaning.

Faulkner's first indisputably great novel is THE SOUND AND THE FURY (1929). Obviously influenced by James Joyce's STREAM-OF-CONSCIOUSNESS technique, Faulkner explores the lives of one of his most important southern families, the Compsons. The first section of the novel is told through the eyes of Benjy, the family idiot, whose world of brute but also lyrical sensation results in a brilliant sort of poetry. From this concentration on the basic sensations Faulkner goes to the other extreme in the highly intellectual and abstruse internal monologue of Benjy's brother Quentin Compson, who finds it impossible to cope with his family's legacy of defeat. Quentin commits suicide even as his crass brother Jason, who has jettisoned the pretension of southern gentility and mocks his family's airs, strives for success in modern commercial culture. The final section of the novel is a magnificent, orderly, third-person narrative that puts into perspective the themes and characters of the novel, showing both reasons for hope and despair in a South that is slowly remaking itself in the wake of war.

Faulkner pursued the themes of southern life in a series of brilliant experimental novels—from *As I Lay Dying* (1930) to LIGHT IN AUGUST (1932) to *Absalom, Absalom!* (1936), which is arguably his greatest work. In telling of the story of

Thomas Sutpen, the West Virginia boy who becomes a West Indian grandee and then a southern planter, Faulkner re-creates on a grand historical scale both the doom of the South and ironies of the American quest for success. Each narrator of the novel—Rosa Caulfield, Mr. Compson, Quentin Compson, and his Harvard roommate Shreve McCannon, a Canadian, is designed to expand the novel's historical and geographical reach.

Nearly as great is *Go Down, Moses* (1942), a collection of connected stories that can be read as a novel of history. Isaac McCaslin, part of another great southern family in Faulkner's fiction, struggles with both his place in history and his attempts to transcend his connection to the degrading history of slavery that his own family has perpetuated in the segregated South.

Although Faulkner has been most highly praised for his novels of the late 1920s and 1930s, such works as *Sanctuary* (1931) and *The Wild Palms* (1939) deserve mention as well, for in these works he explored the perverse attraction of humanity to violence and the self-torturing aspects of romantic love.

Faulkner created another enduring vision of the American South in his Snopes trilogy: *The Hamlet* (1940), *The Town* (1957), and *The Mansion* (1959). Although the last two novels of the trilogy are generally regarded as inferior to his best work, they also represent his direct confrontation with the South's relationship to the rest of the country and to Europe. His concern shifts in these later novels from the psychological and moral damage of evil to a search for ethical standards by which to live a good life. Thus his attention is directed away from doomed characters such as Thomas Sutpen and Quentin Compson and to survivors such as V. K. Ratliff and Chick Mallison, who become the sensible narrators of *The Town* (1957).

Faulkner's work in the short story is as distinguished as his novels. Stories such as "A Rose for Emily," "Dry September," and "That Evening Sun" evince the same concern with the crushing tyranny of small-town life, but also with its comic aspects. Wild West humor enlivens such short story classics as "Spotted Horses." Even in his most serious work Faulkner is likely to inject considerable humor, for he was especially sensitive to the absurdities of human existence. *Collected Stories* (1950) is a highly integrated and carefully structured presentation of Faulkner's short fiction. The *Uncollected Stories of William Faulkner* was published in 1979.

Faulkner won the Nobel Prize in literature in 1950 and continued to produce first-rate fiction, including his last novel, *The Reivers* (1962), a nostalgic, comic return to the grim setting of *Sanctuary*. The wisdom of this final novel has been compared to Shakespeare's last play, *The Tempest*. Like that play, *The Reivers* is the product of a great creative imagination reconciled to the flawed nature of the world.

In recent years, considerable attention has also been paid to Faulkner's screenplays—particularly *To Have and Have Not* (1945) and *The Big Sleep* (1946). *Faulkner's MGM Screenplays* was published in 1982.

In the last stages of his career, Faulkner gave many important interviews, collected in *Conversations with William Faulkner* (1999). *William Faulkner: Essays, Speeches, and Public Letters* was published in 1965. His *Selected Letters* appeared in 1977.

Sources

Blotner, Joseph. *Faulkner: A Biography.* 2 vols. New York: Random House, 1974.

Brodhead, Richard H., ed. *Faulkner: New Perspectives.* Englewood Cliffs, N.J.: Prentice Hall, 1983.

Fargnoli, A. Nicholas, and Michael Golay. *William Faulkner A to Z.* New York: Facts On File, 2001.

Gray, Richard. *The Life of William Faulkner: A Critical Biography.* Oxford: Blackwell, 1994.

Hamblin, Robert W., and Charles A. Peete, eds. *A William Faulkner Encyclopedia.* Westport, Conn.: Greenwood, 1999.

Millgate, Michael. *The Achievement of William Faulkner.* Lincoln: University of Nebraska Press, 1978.

Paddock, Lisa. *Contrapuntal in Integration: A Study of Three Faulkner Short Story Volumes.* Lanham, Md.: International Scholars Publications, 2000.

Fauset, Jessie Redmon (1882–1961) *editor, writer, educator*

One of the figures of the HARLEM RENAISSANCE, Fauset was born in Camden County, New Jersey, and knew racism firsthand. She was denied admission to Bryn Mawr College because of her race and instead attended Cornell University, where she graduated Phi Beta Kappa in 1905. After teaching in Washington, D.C.'s public schools, she earned an M.A. degree from the University of Pennsylvania in 1919. She continued her studies at the Sorbonne. In New York Fauset stimulated a challenging intellectual atmosphere: As literary editor of THE CRISIS she fostered the talents of Countee CULLEN, Claude MCKAY, Jean TOOMER, and Langston HUGHES, who called her the "literary midwife" of the Harlem Renaissance. She cofounded a magazine for children, *Brownies' Book*, which featured articles about important African Americans such as Sojourner Truth and Denmark Vesey. She published poetry and essays, contributing to Countee's Cullen's poetry anthology *Caroling Dusk* (1927) and Alain LOCKE's history *New Negro* (1925). She also published four novels: *There is Confusion* (1924), *Plum Bun* (1929), *The Chinaberry Tree* (1931), and *Comedy: American Style* (1933). In fiction she presented African Americans, particularly in southern settings, as more than the stereotypes she saw in the works of white southerners. She returned to schoolteaching from 1927 to 1944 at DeWitt Clinton High School in New York City, where she taught French. She continued to write poetry, although she published no more books.

Sources

McLendon, Jacquelyn Y. *The Politics of Color in the Fiction of Jessie Fauset and Nella Larsen.* Charlottesville: University Press of Virginia, 1995.

Fearing, Kenneth (1902–1961) *poet, novelist*

Fearing was born in Chicago but spent his adult life in New York. He often wrote satirically about a degenerating society. His best novel, *The Big Clock* (1946), was made into a sinister movie starring Charles Laughton and Ray Milland. The film and novel reflect his concern about a society corrupted by capitalist competition. His *New and Selected Poems* appeared in 1956.

Sources

Barnard, Rita. *The Great Depression and the Culture of Abundance: Kenneth Fearing, Nathanael West, and Mass Culture in the 1930s.* New York: Cambridge University Press, 1995.

Federal Theater Project

Established in 1935 under the federal Works Progress Administration, a Roosevelt administration agency that employed artists and writers and funded arts programs, this project produced the "Living Newspaper," a dramatization of social and economic issues. The project also subsidized original, experimental theater, new playwrights, and lowered ticket prices to make the performances affordable for the poor. Notable productions by the project included Elmer RICE's *The Adding Machine,* Marlowe's *Dr. Faustus,* and Shakespeare's *Macbeth.* Congress eliminated funding for the project in 1939: Like other programs in the arts, the project was attacked by conservatives who rejected public subsidies for artists.

Sources

Flanagan, Hallie. *Arena: The Story of the Federal Theater.* New York: Duell, Sloan and Pearce, 1940.
Gagey, Edmond. *Revolution in American Drama.* New York: Columbia University Press, 1947.

Federal Writers' Project

Established in 1934 as part of the federal Works Progress Administration, the project produced the classic WPA Guides to the states, book-length histories of the people, places, culture, and geography of the individual states. Writers also worked on almanacs, historical pamphlets, collections of folklore, and other writing assignments concerned with local and national history and culture. Government employment of writers was a controversial policy attacked by conservatives and others who believed that the arts should not receive direct support from public funds. The Federal Writers' Project, like many other New Deal programs established during the GREAT DEPRESSION, ceased to operate by the beginning of World War II. Until its demise, the project employed in its local and state branches more than 6,000 writers, including Saul BELLOW, Erskine CALDWELL, John CHEEVER, Ralph ELLISON, Archibald MACLEISH, Edmund WILSON, Richard WRIGHT, and Frank YERBY.

Sources

Mangione, Jerre. *The Dream and the Deal: The Federal Writers' Project, 1935–1943.* Boston: Little, Brown, 1972.

feminist literary criticism

Feminist literary criticism grew out of the women's movement in the 1970s. If women were the victims of a patriarchal culture, it stood to reason that literature and what was considered a classic were male impositions. Thus feminist critics took their place beside African-American and other minority critics, including gay and lesbian writers (see GAY AND LESBIAN LITERATURE) who argued that white, male, heterosexual standards had also shut out certain minority writers from the canon. Feminist literary criticism—also inspired by deconstructionist criticism—questioned whether the masterpieces selected by white males truly represented universal values or only their own. At the very least, the feminist critics contended, the canon needed to be re-evaluated.

Feminist criticism has pursued three paths: investigating how the white male tradition has dominated the establishment of a literary canon; the pursuit of an alternative women's canon or the enhancement of the traditional canon to include works by women and minority groups; and a wide-ranging exploration of the impact of gender on the institution of literature. Within these broad categories there is an enormous diversity of opinion that makes it impossible to speak of feminist criticism as a monolithic methodology or theory.

Kate Millett's *Sexual Politics* (1969), one of the early key texts of feminist criticism, concentrated on the way such authors as Henry MILLER and Norman MAILER had created negative images of women. In *The Resisting Reader* (1977), Judith Fetterley argued that male authors tended to identify with male characters and to slight female characters or treat them in adversarial fashion. Elaine Showalter in *A Literature of Their Own* (1977) and Sandra Gilbert and Susan Gubar in *The Madwoman in the Attic* (1979) began the task of reconstructing the canon, searching out a tradition of women writers—a task that eventually led to Gilbert and Gubar's *The Norton Anthology of Literature by Women* (1985). Similarly, Bonnie Scott edited one of the defining collections of the feminist literary canon, *The Gender of Modernism: A Critical Anthology* (1990).

Feminist criticism has focused attention on a core of 20th-century women authors, especially Edith WHARTON, Gertrude STEIN, Zora Neale HURSTON, H.D. (Hilda DOOLITTLE), Marianne MOORE, Eudora WELTY, Gwendolyn BROOKS,

Adrienne RICH, Toni MORRISON, and Alice WALKER. These and other authors have become major sources of study in academic journals such as *Feminist Studies, Tulsa Studies in Women's Literature,* and *Genders.* A more broad-based publication aimed at reaching beyond an academic audience is the *Women's Review of Books.*

Challenging Boundaries: Gender and Periodization (2000), edited by Joyce W. Warren and Margaret Dickie, includes essays on the women of the HARLEM RENAISSANCE, Amy LOWELL, Gertrude Stein, Edith Wharton, and Adrienne Rich, as well as an exploration of American REALISM and the nature of women's masterpieces. Susan Gubar assesses the role of feminism in literary criticism in *Critical Condition: Feminism at the Turn of the Century* (2000).

Ferber, Edna (1887–1968) *short story writer, playwright, novelist*

Born in Michigan, Ferber lived in New York City most of her life. She was a member of the ALGONQUIN ROUND TABLE and first made her reputation with a series of short stories about a businesswoman named Emma McChesney. This early work was collected in *Roast Beef, Medium* (1913), *Personality Plus* (1914), and *Emma McChesney and Co.* (1915). But Ferber's reputation is founded on her novels, especially *Fanny Herself* (1917), the Pulitzer Prize–winning *So Big* (1924), *Showboat* (1926), *Cimarron* (1930), *Come and Get It* (1935), *Giant* (1950), and *Ice Palace* (1958). In her fiction the versatile Ferber portrayed career women, gamblers, the land rush in Oklahoma in the 1880s, the logging industry in Wisconsin, the oil industry in Texas, and modern Alaska. *Showboat* was made into a popular and often revived classic stage musical as well as two films, and *Cimarron, Come and Get It,* and *Giant* became major motion pictures.

Ferber also had considerable success as a playwright, especially with *The Royal Family* (1927), a satire about an acting family like the Barrymores; *Dinner at Eight* (1932), a light comedy about a fashionable dinner party, and *Stage Door* (1936), all successful movies as well.

Ferber published two autobiographies: *A Peculiar Treasure* (1939) and *A Kind of Magic* (1963).

Sources
Gilbert, Julie Goldsmith. *Edna Ferber: A Biography.* Garden City, N.Y.: Doubleday, 1978.
Shaugnessy, Mary Rose. *Women and Success in American Society in the Works of Edna Ferber.* New York: Gordon Press, 1977.

Ferlinghetti, Lawrence (1920–   ) *publisher, poet, novelist*

One of the founders of the San Francisco BEAT movement, Ferlinghetti was born in Yonkers, New York, and brought up by relatives when his father died and his mother suffered a nervous breakdown. He graduated from the University of North Carolina with a journalism degree and served in the U.S. Navy during World War II. He returned to New York and studied at Columbia University, then in Paris at the Sorbonne, where he completed a dissertation in French, "The City as a Symbol in Modern Poetry." In 1950 Ferlinghetti settled in San Francisco. He consorted with local artists and wrote reviews for the *San Francisco Chronicle* and the *Arts Review.* In 1953 he established the CITY LIGHTS BOOKSTORE and publishing house, which became especially notable for its pocket editions of poetry, one of the engines of the SAN FRANCISCO RENAISSANCE. He collected his own poems in *Pictures of the Gone World* (1955). He also initiated poetry readings. Allen Ginsberg read his acclaimed *HOWL,* at City Lights, and the poem was subsequently published in the pocket series. Ferlinghetti came into his own as a popular poet with the publication of *A Coney Island of the Mind* (1958). It remains his best-selling work, and is praised for its unpunctuated free form that seems inspired by jazz. *Open Eye, Open Heart* (1973) has also received considerable critical praise. In 1973 the poet sponsored a Poet's Theatre, a series of public poetry readings to benefit such causes and organizations as the United Farmworkers, Greenpeace, and antinuclear campaigns. Meanwhile his publishing house continued to make available the work of Paul BOWLES, William Carlos WILLIAMS, Kenneth PATCHEN, and many other writers. He published the *City Lights Anthology* in 1974.

Sources
Silesky, Barry. *Ferlinghetti, The Artist in His Time.* New York: Warner Books, 1990.
Smith, Larry. *Lawrence Ferlinghetti, Poet-At-Large.* Carbondale: Southern Illinois University Press, 1983.

Fiedler, Leslie Aaron (1917–   ) *critic, novelist*

Leslie Fiedler taught at several universities, including Montana State and the State University of New York at Buffalo. His most important work is a provocative literary study, *Love and Death in the American Novel* (1960). Along with *Waiting for the End* (1964), a collection of essays about American culture and society, Fiedler has written with a flair and iconoclasm rare among intellectuals in academia. He has challenged, for example, the idea of the literary canon and its exclusion of popular culture in *What Was Literature: Class Culture and Mass Society* (1982). His *Collected Essays* appeared in 1971; *Fiedler on the Roof: Essays on Literature and Jewish Identity* in 1991; and *A New Fiedler Reader* in 1999. His work as a short story writer and novelist is less well known. His short fiction appears in *The Last Jew in America* (1966) and *Nude Croquet* (1969). His novels include *Back to China* (1965) and *The Messengers Will Come No More* (1974).

Sources

Kellman, Steven G. and Irving Malin, ed. *Leslie Fiedler and American Culture.* Newark: University of Delaware Press, 1999.

Winchell, Mark Royden. *Leslie Fiedler.* Boston: Twayne, 1995.

Fierstein, Harvey (1954–) *playwright*

A Brooklyn native, Fierstein went to Brooklyn public schools and received a B.F.A. degree in art from Pratt Institute in 1973. In the early 1970s he began a career as a drag performer in New York City clubs and played a lesbian in Andy Warhol's only play, *Pork* (1971). Fierstein wrote a series of unpublished plays (*Freaky Pussy, Flatbush and Tosca,* and *Cannibals*). As an actor he appears in the films *Garbo Talks* (1984), *The Harvest* (1993), and *Mrs. Doubtfire* (1993) as well as in television shows. But he is best known for the Tony Award–winning *Torch Song Trilogy* (1982), which concerns the life of Arnold Beckoff, a professional female impersonator, followed by *Safe Sex* (1987). He has also had an OFF-BROADWAY production of *Spookhouse* (1984). He wrote the book for the Broadway musical *La Cage aux Folles* (1983), for which he won a Tony Award for distinguished achievement in theater. Fierstein writes candidly and eloquently about gay life and has managed dual careers in and out of the mainstream. Some critics find his work too conventional, but others cite his extraordinary ability to portray fully realized gay characters with a heightened realistic style.

Sources

"Harvey Fierstein." Available online. URL: http://www.bedford-stmartins.com/litlinks/drama/fierstein.htm

Fisher, Vardis Alvero (1895–1968) *novelist*

Fisher grew up in Idaho and set much of his fiction in the West. Novels like *Toilers of the Hills* (1928) and *Dark Bridwell* (1931) put him in the regionalist (see REGIONALISM) tradition. His subject is often the frontier and the hardships of living off the land. In 1939 he published *Children of God,* a historical novel about Joseph Smith and the Mormons. In the 1940s he published a series of 12 novels dealing with prehistoric man, including *Darkness and the Deep* (1943), *Golden Rooms* (1944), and *Intimations of Eve* (1946). Still later novels such as *Adam and the Serpent* (1947), *The Divine Passion* (1948), *The Valley of Vision* (1951), and *Jesus Came Again* (1956) explored biblical history and the origins of Christianity.

Fisher collected his essays in *The Neurotic Nightingale* (1935) and his stories in *Love and Death* (1959). He also wrote a memoir, *Thomas Wolfe as I Knew Him* (1973).

Sources

Chatterton, Wayne. *Vardis Fisher: The Frontier and Regional Works.* Boise, Idaho: Boise State College, 1972.

Flora, Joseph M. *Vardis Fisher.* New York: Twayne, 1965.

Fitzgerald, Francis Scott Key (1896–1941)

novelist, short story writer

Born in St. Paul, Minnesota, F. Scott Fitzgerald was educated at the Newman School near Hackensack, New Jersey, and then at Princeton University. He left college to enlist in the army in 1917. In 1918 he met Zelda Sayre, who would become his wife shortly before the publication of his first novel, *This Side of Paradise* (1920), often called a novel of the Jazz Age, that period of the 1920s that is associated with a boom period of unconventionality and dissipation. The couple lived among the wealthy in Europe and in America, and Fitzgerald's fascination with rich people would become one of the constant themes of his fiction. His heroes, from Amory Blaine in *This Side of Paradise* to Anthony Patch in *The Beautiful and Damned* (1922) to Dick Diver in *Tender Is the Night* (1934), become enmeshed in the lives of the rich and have their integrity undermined. In Fitzgerald's work wealth is not an evil in itself; quite the contrary, his characters are attracted to the glitter and the promise of enjoyment and success that money can afford them. But money corrupts because it deadens the desire to succeed. Unlimited resources lead Fitzgerald's attractive men to squander their opportunities.

Perhaps it is not accidental that Fitzgerald's two greatest novels, THE GREAT GATSBY (1925) and *The Last Tycoon* (1941), which remained incomplete at the time of his death, center on characters—Jay Gatsby and Monroe Starr—who are cut down even as they strive for greatness. Neither man reaches the summit of his desires. *Gatsby* is also enhanced by its narrator, Nick CARRAWAY, a figure like Joseph Conrad's narrators in that he is part of and yet somewhat removed from the main story. As participant-observer, Nick is able to witness Gatsby's hopeless attachment to Daisy Buchanan and his self-destructive pursuit of a woman who symbolizes the American dream for him.

Critics have often cited *Gatsby* as a perfectly written novel, a work exquisitely poised between the idealism fostered by the American dream and the corrupt reality of the compromises the characters must make to get ahead. Gatsby, like FAULKNER's Thomas Sutpen in *Absalom, Absalom!,* is a self-made man with the illusion that he can triumph entirely on his own terms.

Fitzgerald's own life followed the pattern of dissolution that entrapped his characters. He and Zelda (see below), the beautiful couple of the 1920s, were decimated by drink, marital tensions, and mental illness. Zelda was institutionalized, and by the mid-1930s Fitzgerald seemed to have lost the ability to concentrate on major work. Yet near the very end of his life, with the support of the gossip columnist Sheila Graham, Fitzgerald made one more supreme effort with *The Last Tycoon,* a magnificent study of the very capital of American dreams: Hollywood.

Fitzgerald's impact on American literature includes a considerable body of first-rate short fiction. His collections of stories virtually chart his career as both popular author and respected craftsman. Although Fitzgerald wrote many potboiler stories in order to support himself, his best work can be found in *Flappers and Philosophers* (1920), *Tales of the Jazz Age* (1922), *All the Sad Young Men* (1926), and *Taps at Reveille* (1935). *The Stories of F. Scott Fitzgerald* was published in 1951. *Afternoon of an Author: A Selection of Uncollected Stories and Essays* appeared in 1958 and *The Last Uncollected Stories of F. Scott Fitzgerald* in 1979.

Fitzgerald detailed his own decline as a writer in *The Crack-Up* (1945), a volume edited by his friend Edmund WILSON. Several volumes of Fitzgerald's letters have been published, including *The Letters of F. Scott Fitzgerald* (1963) and *Dear Scott/Dear Max: The Fitzgerald-Perkins Correspondence* (1972).

Sources

Bloom, Harold, ed. *F. Scott Fitzgerald.* New York: Chelsea House, 1985.

Gale, Robert L. *An F. Scott Fitzgerald Encyclopedia.* Westport, Conn.: Greenwood Press, 1998.

Gross, Dalton and MaryJean Gross. *Understanding "The Great Gatsby": A Student Casebook to Issues, Sources, and Historical Documents.* Westport, Conn.: Greenwood Press, 1998.

Kuehl, John F. *F. Scott Fitzgerald: A Study of the Short Fiction.* Boston: Twayne, 1991.

Meyers, Jeffrey. *Scott Fitzgerald: A Biography.* New York: HarperCollins, 1994.

Fitzgerald, Zelda Sayre (1899–1948) *novelist*

The wife of F. Scott FITZGERALD, she was her husband's inspiration, but she became unstable and was institutionalized. Her husband has been accused of stealing her material, or at least of using her for the purposes of his fiction. Zelda Fitzgerald chronicled her marriage in *Save Me the Waltz* (1932), her only sustained work of fiction, which has been credited as demonstrating her considerable powers as a novelist.

Sources

Milford, Nancy. *Zelda: A Biography.* New York: Harper & Row, 1970.

Taylor, Kendall. *Sometimes Madness is Wisdom: Zelda and Scott Fitzgerald: A Marriage.* New York: Ballantine, 2001.

Flanagan, Thomas (1923–) *novelist, educator*

Born in Connecticut, Flanagan has taught at the University of California, Berkeley, and the State University of New York at Stony Brook as a specialist in Irish literature. His first historical novel, *The Year of the French,* won a National Book Award and was highly praised for both its understanding of history and its style. The novel is set in 1798, the year of a failed Irish rebellion. *The Tenants of Time* (1988) begins with the Fenian movement in Ireland in 1867 and ends with the death of the great Irish politician Charles Stewart Parnell in 1891. *The End of the Hunt* (1955) continues the story of modern Ireland's history to the Easter Rising of 1916 and the its aftermath in the 1920s.

Sources

Skow, John. "Ballad's End: Thomas Flanagan Brings His Irish Trilogy to a Rueful End," *Time.* May 23, 1994, Vol. 143, No. 21. Available on-line. URL: http://www.time.com/time/magazine/archive/1994/940523/940523.books.flanagan.html.

Flanner, Janet (1892–1978) *journalist*

Born in Indiana, Flanner spent much of her life in Paris. She contributed as "Genet" to the NEW YORKER for decades as a foreign correspondent. She befriended many of the important writers of her time, including Lilliam Hellman and Rebecca West. She also wrote a novel, *The Cubical City* (1926), and *An American in Paris* (1940), a memoir. Three volumes of her *Paris Journal* appeared in 1965, 1971, and 1972. She is considered to be one of the finest American reporters of cultural life abroad.

Sources

Wineapple, Brenda. *Genet: A Biography of Janet Flanner.* New York: Ticknor & Fields, 1989.

Foote, Shelby (1916–) *novelist, historian*

Foote's writings often center on the descriptions and effects of the Civil War, including the novels *Follow Me Down* (1950) and *Shiloh* (1952). Foote was born in Mississippi and educated at the University of North Carolina. After World War II he began to write novels heavily influenced by William FAULKNER. His masterpiece is generally considered to be his three-volume history of the Civil War. The book's title is important: *The Civil War: A Narrative* brings to history all the skills of a novelist. Scrupulous as history, the trilogy nevertheless recreates scenes, such as John Wilkes Booth's assassination of Abraham Lincoln in Ford's Theater, and uses language at a level of eloquence rarely attained by professional historians. Foote is one of few 20th-century American writers to treat the writing of history as literature. His respect for the exact sequence of events is reflected in his titles: *Fort Sumter to Perryville* (1958), *Fredericksburg to Meridian* (1963), and *Red River to Appomattox* (1973). After 20 years of research and writing on the Civil War, Foote returned to fiction, producing the novel *September* (1978), the story of whites who kidnap an African-American boy. In 1981 he published *The Novelist's View of History.*

Sources
Phillips, Robert L., Jr. *Shelby Foote: Novelist and Historian.* Jackson: University Press of Mississippi, 1992.

Forché, Carolyn (1950–) *poet, essayist*
Born in Detroit into a Slovak family, Forché has written about her ethnic heritage and her Michigan childhood. Both come into play in her first book of poetry, *Gathering of the Tribes* (1976), which immediately established her importance as a contemporary poet. *The Country Between Us* (1982), which won the Lamont Prize, draws from the author's human rights work in El Salvador with Amnesty International. Allied to this work is her anthology *Against Forgetting: 20th Century Poetry of Witness* (1993), and another poetry collection, *The Angel of History* (1994).

Sources
Thompson, Jon. "A Turn Toward The Past" [Review of *The Angel of History*]. *Postmodern Culture* 5:2 (January 1995). Available on-line. URL: http://jefferson.village.virginia.edu/pmc/text-only/issue.195/review-6.195. Downloaded May 29, 2001.
Forché, Carolyn. Carolyn Forché's Home Page. Available online. URL: http://osf1.gmu.edu/~cforchem/index.html. Downloaded October 25, 2001.

Ford, Richard (1944–) *novelist*
Ford grew up in Jackson, Mississippi, and studied creative writing at the University of Michigan and Princeton University. His first novel, *A Piece of My Heart* (1976), is reminiscent of William FAULKNER in its evocation of a violent southern setting. It would be another decade before Ford found his own voice and gritty, realistic style. He first won acclaim with *The Sportswriter* (1986). He is also the author of *Wildlife* (1990) and *Independence Day* (1995), the latter recipient of a Pulitzer Prize. The novel returns to the story of the character introduced in *The Sportswriter*, Frank Bascomb, who is middle-aged, disaffected, and divorced and in this novel seeking to renew his life in a Fourth of July weekend with his son.

Sources
Lee, Don. "About Richard Ford." *Ploughshares* 22 (Fall 1996): 226–235.
"The Mississippi Writers Page": Richard Ford. Available on-line. URL: http://www.olemiss.edu/depts/english/ms-writers/dir/ford_richard/. Updated June 2, 2001.
Majeski, Sophie. "The Salon Interview: Richard Ford," *Salon*, 1999. Available on-line. URL: http://www.salonmagazine.com/weekly/interview960708.html. Downloaded May 29, 2001.

Fortune (1930–) *periodical*
A magazine about business established by Henry Luce, the founder of *TIME*. Although it has concentrated on the development of industry, finance, and technology, the magazine has also employed distinguished literary figures such as Archibald MACLEISH, James AGEE, Alfred KAZIN, and Dwight MACDONALD, who have brought a more liberal and cosmopolitan sensibility to the discussion of cultural issues in a capitalist society.

Frank, Waldo David (1889–1967) *novelist, critic*
Waldo Frank came from New Jersey and first established his reputation by founding *SEVEN ARTS*, a literary magazine. His early novels *The Dark Mother* (1920) and *Rahab* (1922) express a mystical and poetic sensibility. *Holiday* (1923) depicts racism in the South, and *The Bridegroom Cometh* (1939) embodies a Marxist mentality and a concern for social reform. Frank also published several works of nonfiction that probed the American past and present, the development of American industrialism, and the need for revolutionary change. Among his more noteworthy titles are *Our America* (1919), *The Re-Discovery of America* (1928), *In the American Jungle* (1937), and *Chart for Rough Water* (1940). His last works were *Bridgehead* (1957), about Israel, and *Cuba: Prophetic Island* (1961).

Sources
Carter, Paul J. *Waldo Frank.* New York: Twayne, 1967.

French, Marilyn (1929–) *novelist, nonfiction writer*
Born in New York City, French was educated at Hofstra University and later at Harvard, where she earned an M.A. and a Ph.D. She is a feminist author who studies the treatment of women throughout history. Her most influential work is *The Women's Room* (1977), a novel about the growth of a woman pursuing graduate studies at Harvard in the 1960s. French's other works include *Beyond Power: On Woman, Men, and Morals* (1985); a generational saga of mothers and daughters, *Her Mother's Daughter* (1987); and *A Season In Hell: A Memoir* (1998).

Sources
Pearlman, Mickey, ed. *Mother Puzzles: Daughters and Mothers in Contemporary American Literature.* New York: Greenwood Press, 1989.
Liukkonen, Petri. "Marilyn French." *Books and Writers 2000.* Available on-line. URL: http://kirjasto.sci.fi/mfrench.htm. Downloaded on May 29, 2001.

Friedan, Betty (1921–) *nonfiction writer*

Friedan was born in Peoria, Illinois, and graduated from Smith College with a degree in psychology. She was a promising graduate student at the University of California, Berkeley, before she left to marry Carl Friedan. She was actively involved in the labor movement in the 1940s, but it was her experience as a suburban housewife that stimulated her to write the groundbreaking feminist classic, *The Feminine Mystique* (1963). The book was an all-out assault on the identification of women with domestic work. Friedan was not hostile to family or home life, but she rebelled against the idea that women should be connected exclusively with those tasks, and she spoke for a generation of women restless with the inferior tasks given to them in post–World War II America after their contributions to the war effort in the 1940s. In 1966 Friedan cofounded the National Organization for Women (NOW), which campaigns for equal opportunities for women. Friedan's strength was as a journalist and polemicist, and she made enemies in the women's movement because she operated outside of organizational discipline. Her two other important books are *It Changed My Life: Writings on the Women's Movement* (1976) and *The Second Stage* (1981). This later work received a mixed reception: Supporters admired what Friedan called her "middle American pragmatism" and detractors felt she had lost her radical drive.

Sources

Hennessee, Judith. *Betty Friedan: Her Life.* New York: Random House, 1999.
Horowitz, Daniel. *Betty Friedan and The Making of The Feminine Mystique: The American Left, The Cold War, and Modern Feminism.* Amherst: University of Massachusetts Press, 1998.

Friedman, Bruce Jay (1930–) *novelist, short story writer, playwright*

Born and bred in New York City, Friedman most often writes about the neurotic Jewish male. *Stem* (1962), his first novel, signaled his penchant for black humor. *A Mother's Kisses* (1964) skewers the Jewish mother by dramatizing her negative influence on a neurotic son. *About Harry Towns* (1974), one of Friedman's best-known novels, is the story of a middle-aged screenwriter. Friedman's later fiction includes *The Slightly Older Guy* (1995) and *A Father's Kisses* (1996).

Friedman has also produced popular and critically acclaimed plays, including *Scuba Duba* (1968) and *Steambath* (1970). His stories are collected in *Far from the City of Class* (1963), *Black Angels* (1966), *Let's Hear It for a Beautiful Guy* (1984), and *Short Stories Selections* (1995). He tends to see contemporary life as rather ridiculous and comic. He has also published *The Lonely Guy's Book of Life,* a send-up of self-help manuals.

Even the Rhinos Were Nymphos: Best Nonfiction appeared in 2000.

Sources

Cole, Stephen. "An Interview with Bruce Jay Friedman," Broadway Theater Archive. Available on-line. URL: http://www.broadwayarchive/feature_steambath.asp. Downloaded on May 29, 2001.
Schulz, Max F. *Bruce Jay Friedman.* New York: Twayne, 1974.

From Here to Eternity James Jones (1951) *novel*

James JONES's classic war novel about the U.S. Army just before the Japanese attack on Pearl Harbor is set in Hawaii and is dominated by three characters. First Sergeant Milton Anthony Warden—nicknamed "the Warden"—has disciplined Company G into the best condition it has ever known. Warden is tough, but he commands his company's respect.

Warden seduces Karen, the wife of Captain Holmes, a conniving political animal. Warden begins the affair only with pleasure and vengeance—he hates commissioned officers—in mind, but he falls in love, smitten by Karen's strong personality. Because he wants to marry her, he agrees to Karen's plan that he apply for an officer's commission, which will protect him should the affair be discovered and will allow Karen to retain custody of her son. Yet when Warden receives his commission, the love affair wanes. Warden, in a drunken spree, tears up his papers because he knows he can only love Karen as long as he does not become like Holmes.

Angelo Maggio, a young soldier from Brooklyn, has joined the army only to escape his job as a shipping clerk. Even though he is a complainer, he has a cheerful personality and the men like him, especially Robert Prewitt, Maggio's drinking buddy. When Maggio misses curfew and refuses to sneak back to base, he is sentenced to six months of hard labor. Maggio is now so desperate to get out of the army that he conceives of committing an offense that will put him in solitary confinement and lead to his discharge from the army for insanity. Put in the gruesome "hole" for 24 days, Maggio survives beatings and interrogations and is discharged from the army, winning the admiration of the other men in the stockade.

Prewitt, Maggio's friend, comes from Harlan County, Kentucky, and has joined the army after several hard years on the road. At age 30 he is still a low-ranking enlisted man, but the army means everything to him. A fine boxer, "Prew" nevertheless refuses to join the company team, having vowed many years earlier to his mother never to fight with the intention of hurting anyone. Prew is given "the treatment"—harsh physical punishment, heavy surveillance, and hard labor—for his obstinacy. On furloughs in town he find solace with a prostitute, Lorene, with whom he falls in love. When he gets into a fight with another soldier, he is put in the stockade and subsequently murders the sadistic Staff Sergeant Judso. He deserts and feels bereft because he cannot join the action after the attack on Pearl Harbor. When a patrol spots him, he keeps on running and is shot to death.

This novel was an enormous success. It provided an inside view of the army with an authenticity that surpassed other fine war novels like Norman MAILER's THE NAKED AND THE DEAD and Irwin SHAW's *The Young Lions*. Jones's vivid, fluent writing established his reputation as a major American writer.

Sources

Carter, Steven R. *James Jones: An American Literary Orientalist Master.* Urbana: University of Illinois Press, 1998.

Giles, James R. *James Jones.* Boston: G. K. Hall, 1981.

Waldmeir, Joseph J. *American Novels of the Second World War.* The Hague: Mouton, 1969.

Frost, Robert Lee (1874–1963) *poet*

Although Robert Frost has always been associated with New England, he was born in San Francisco. When his father died and was buried in his native New Hampshire, Frost's widowed mother decided to stay, rather than embark on a trip west that she could ill afford. Frost was very much influenced by his mother's strict Scottish Presbyterianism, which saw in nature portents of the mystery of existence.

After graduating from high school in 1892, Frost, the class poet, married his co-valedictorian, Elinor Miriam White. Although his family wanted him to be a lawyer, he had already decided on poetry as a vocation. To make a living, he taught school (although he did not complete his education at Dartmouth), then tried journalism and other odd jobs. After another abortive try at college (he left Harvard after two years), he became a farmer and spent as much time as possible on his poetry, which by 1905 had yielded only a few modest publications and little attention. More teaching proved unsatisfactory, and in 1912 Frost moved his family to England, determined to establish his reputation as a poet. In an intense three-month period, he assembled a volume of verse, *A Boy's Will* (1913), which received mixed reviews. But his next book, *North of Boston* (1914), which contains some of his finest dramatic narratives, established his reputation. In his 40th year he finally achieved recognition as a major poet.

When Frost returned to the United States in 1915, *North of Boston* had become a best-seller. Frost settled on a farm in New Hampshire and began to give public readings of his poetry. He accepted positions as poet-in-residence at several colleges and universities, including Amherst College, the University of Michigan, Harvard, and Dartmouth College. In his public lectures and appearances, Frost burnished his reputation as a NEW ENGLAND poet-farmer in the tradition of the 19th-century nature poets such as Emerson and Thoreau. Although this suggested that he was not part of mainstream MODERNISM as exemplified by T. S. ELIOT and Ezra POUND, many of Frost's poems, such as "Design" or "Neither Far Out Nor in Deep," presented a very modern, inquiring, skeptical, and brooding sensibility. In "Provide," a poem that advocates self-reliance and the virtue of a certain hardcore prudence, he enunciated a skepticism verging on cynicism and was anything but the greeting-card poet that some of his lighter or deceptively simple poems seemed to represent.

In poems like "Design" and "MENDING WALL" Frost revealed a well-developed sense of irony in his work that was reminiscent of Emily Dickinson, whose 19th-century poetry represented a harbinger of modernism. Frost's later poems and the verse dramas *A Masque of Reason* (1945) and *A Masque of Mercy* (1947) developed a more philosophical mode, in which ideas about life are more explicitly addressed.

Frost's poems are so frequently anthologized that perhaps no other American poet has made as great a mark on the American consciousness. Whether it is "Stopping by Woods on a Snowy Evening," "Nothing Gold Can Stay," "MENDING WALL," or "Acquainted with the Night," Frost's informal yet strictly controlled verse transforms ordinary, everyday speech into profound commentary on the individual's effort to comprehend the meaning of existence.

In virtually all of his poetry Frost favored regular meters and rhymes. He wrote relatively few essays about poetry, but prose works such as "A Figure a Poem Makes" are classic formulations of the modern poet's theory and practice.

Frost won four Pulitzer Prizes and many other major literary awards. The Nobel Prize in literature eluded him, but his international stature has been recognized in *Homage to Frost* (1996), published by three Nobel laureates, Joseph Brodsky, Seamus Heaney, and Derek Walcott.

Collected editions of his poetry have been published in 1939, 1949, 1956, 1967, and 1995, *The Selected Letters of Robert Frost* in 1964, and his *Selected Prose* in 1966.

Sources

Bloom, Harold, ed. *Robert Frost.* New York: Chelsea House, 1986.

Cady, Edwin H. and Louis J. Budd, eds. *On Frost.* Durham, N.C.: Duke University Press, 1991.

Gerber, Philip, ed. *Critical Essays on Robert Frost.* Boston: G. K. Hall, 1982.

Meyers, Jeffrey. *Robert Frost: A Biography.* Boston: Houghton Mifflin, 1996.

Wilcox, Earl J. *His "Incalculable" Influence on Others: Essays on Robert Frost In Our Time.* Victoria, B.C.: English Literary Studies, University of Victoria, 1994.

Fugitives, the

This group of poets and critics centered in Nashville, Tennessee, and Vanderbilt University in the 1920s published a magazine, *The Fugitive* (1922–1925), and had a major impact on American literature. Members included John Crowe RANSOM, Allen TATE, Robert Penn WARREN, and Cleanth Brooks, among others. Brooks and Warren produced a major college text, *Understanding Poetry* (1938), and founded SOUTH-

ERN REVIEW (1935–1942). Ransom published *The New Criticism* in 1941, a book that underlined many of the principles that a whole generation of critics would practice. He also founded the influential literary quarterly *KENYON REVIEW*. As the group's name implies, the members initially thought of themselves as outside the literary mainstream, espousing principles that were in conflict with majority thinking, but by the end of the 1940s their way of approaching literature (through close readings of texts) had become the standard approach in the American classroom. The political and social aspects of the Fugitives thinking became manifest in their roles as AGRARIANS.

Sources

Bradbury, John M. *The Fugitives: A Critical Account.* Chapel Hill: University of North Carolina Press, 1958.

Cowan, Louise. *The Fugitive Group: A Literary History.* Baton Rouge: Louisiana State University Press, 1959.

Fuller, Charles (1939–   ) *playwright*

Fuller grew up in Philadelphia. As a child he became fascinated with his father's work in a printing plant. Theater seemed a natural choice for a young man entranced with how people in the African-American community spoke about their lives. He is best known for *A Soldier's Play* (1984) which was made into the motion picture *A Soldier's Story* and is only the second play by an African-American playwright to win a Pulitzer Prize. In this work, Fuller presents the riveting trial of a black soldier accused of murder.

Sources

Anadolu-Okur, Nilgun. *Contemporary African American Theater: Afrocentricity in the Works of Larry Neal, Amiri Baraka, and Charles Fuller.* New York: Garland, 1997.

Gaddis, William (1922–1998) *novelist*

Gaddis was born in New York City. He attended Harvard and published articles in its magazine *The Lampoon,* but he left before graduating. He worked as a fact checker at the NEW YORKER, traveled widely in Europe and Central America, and published his first novel, *The Recognitions,* in 1955. Although the novel was well received, its reputation took on a kind of mystique accorded only to a few authors such as Thomas PYNCHON. Gaddis seemed to have an encyclopedic knowledge of the world, with a Joycean penchant for recondite allusions. His second novel, *JR* (1975), was just as sophisticated: it contained not only penetrating observations on the contemporary world but also an exploration of the disinformation that confuses issues and daily life in the form of corporate life and shoddy business practices. *Carpenter's Gothic* (1985) seemed more accessible but no less concerned with a world that may be exhausting itself with information and pseudoinventiveness. Gaddis's work has been called entropic because like Henry Adams in his autobiography he explores the extent to which the modern world's energy is enervating as well as inspiring. His final novel, *A Frolic of His Own* (1994), explores the role of the law and litigiousness in American life. Like John BARTH and Don DE LILLO, Gaddis is particularly attuned to the uses of language, of how institutions and professions use language to obscure rather than to illuminate meaning. Although Gaddis avoided the limelight of literary life, he is the subject of a thriving academic industry with whole issues of journals devoted to his complex work. *JR* won a National Book Award in 1975.

Sources

Knight, Christopher J. *Hints and Guesses: William Gaddis's Fiction of Longing.* Madison: University of Wisconsin Press, 1997.

Moore, Steven. *William Gaddis.* Boston: Twayne, 1989.

Gaines, Ernest James (1933–) *novelist*

Ernest J. Gaines was born on a Louisiana plantation, and by the age of eight he was cutting sugar cane. His experience of racism informs all of his work. The works of William FAULKNER were a major influence as Gaines tried to come to terms with the sharecropping system in the South and the denigration of African Americans. Gaines sets all his fiction in Louisiana, developing a regional sensitivity that again derives, in part, from Faulkner. Gaines's first two novels, *Catherine Carmier* (1964) and *Of Love and Dust* (1967), explored the passions and the conflicts of white-black relationships. The second novel, told in the first person, has become a trademark approach for Gaines, leading to *Bloodline* (1968), a collection of first-person narratives, and to the celebrated *The Autobiography of Miss Jane Pittman* (1971). The strong sense of history and of an individual voice in the latter work brought Gaines a large audience of readers and viewers, who saw Cicely Tyson enact the title role in an impressive television movie. Gaines's later novels, *In My Father's House* (1978), *A Gathering of Old Men* (1983), and *A Lesson Before Dying* (1993) have not been as popular with the critics or with the public, but they still show his powerful skill at characterization and his profound grasp of southern manners and history.

Sources

Babb, Valerie Melissa. *Ernest Gaines.* Boston: Twayne, 1991.

Estes, David E., ed. *Critical Reflections on the Fiction of Ernest J. Gaines.* Athens, Ga.: University of Georgia Press, 1994.

Gale, Zona (1874–1938) *novelist, playwright, autobiographer*

Gale grew up in Wisconsin and set much of her fiction there. A midwestern REGIONALIST, she won a Pulitzer Prize for the dramatization of her novel, *Miss Lulu Bett* (1920), about a woman confronting a cheerless midwestern environment. *Birth* (1918), dramatized as *Mr. Pitt* (1924), put a male in a similar environment. Gale told the story of her own life in an evolving narrative: *When I Was a Little Girl* (1913), *Portage, Wisconsin* (1928), and *Still Small Voice* (1940).

Sources

Simonson, Harold Peter. *Zona Gale.* New York: Twayne, 1962.

Williams, Deborah Lindsay. *Not in Sisterhood: Edith Wharton, Willa Cather, Zona Gale, and the Politics of Female Authorship.* New York: Palgrave, 2001.

Gallant, Mavis (1922–   ) *novelist, short story writer*

Montreal-born Gallant was schooled in Canada and the United States. After publication in Canadian magazines, she attracted the attention of the NEW YORKER, where many of her most important stories have appeared. Her first collection, *The Other Paris* (1956), explores the differences between American and European sensibilities. So does her first novel, *Green Water, Green Sky* (1959). Her other collections include *My Heart Is Broken* (1964), *The Pegnitz Junction* (1973), *The End of the World and Other Stories* (1974), *From the Fifteenth District* (1979), *Home Truths* (1981), *Overhead in a Balloon* (1985), *In Transit: Twenty Stories* (1988), and *Across the Bridge* (1994). She has published one collection of nonfiction, *Paris Notebooks: Essays and Reviews* (1986) and one play, *What Is to Be Done?* (1983).

Sources

Smythe, Karen E. *Figuring Grief: Gallant, Munro and the Poetics of Elegy.* Montreal: McGill-Queen's University Press, 1992.

Gardner, Erle Stanley (1889–1970) *novelist*

Gardner, a lawyer himself, created the detective-fiction hero Perry Mason, an attorney who solves mysterious cases, beginning with *The Case of the Velvet Claws* (1933). Sales of Gardner's dozens of mysteries have exceeded 140 million copies. The Perry Mason character has appeared in several movies and a long-running television program starring Ray-

mond Burr. In the latter, Mason worked more as an attorney than as a detective.

Sources

Hughes, Dorothy B. *Erle Stanley Gardner: The Case of the Real Perry Mason.* New York: Morrow, 1978.

Gardner, John Champlin, Jr. (1933–1982) *novelist*

John Gardner, a highly regarded novelist, was born in Batavia, New York, where two of his novels, *The Resurrection* (1966) and *The Sunlight Dialogues* (1972), are set. His father was a farmer and his mother an English teacher. Gardner said he grew up saturated in literature. Even as a child he wrote poetry and fiction. He graduated from Washington University in 1955 and earned a Ph.D. in classical and medieval literature from Iowa State University in 1958. He then taught at several colleges, including Oberlin, San Francisco State, and the State University of New York at Binghamton. His interest in medievalism and earlier periods of English literature obviously informs novels such as *Grendel* (1971), a re-working of *Beowulf*. His philosophical temper has been compared to John BARTH's and William GASS's, because of his experiments with point of view. He wrote a controversial nonfiction book, *On Moral Fiction* (1978). It disturbed his fellow writers, who thought he was moralizing—that is, putting moral beliefs before the creation of literature, which should exist independent of belief systems, ethical considerations, and judgmental attitudes. Gardner's other novels include *The Wreckage of Agathon* (1970), *Nickel Mountain* (1973), *October Light* (1976), *Freddie's Book* (1980), and *Mickelsson's Ghosts* (1982). He wrote two short story collections: *The King's Indian* (1974) and *The Art of Living* (1981). He also wrote a controversial biography of Chaucer, *The Life and Times of Chaucer* (1977), which became the subject of charges of plagiarism. He wrote books for children: *Dragon, Dragon* (1975), *Gudekin the Thistle Girl* (1976), *A Child's Bestiary* (1977), and *In The Suicide Mountains* (1977). His death in a motorcycle accident raised questions about whether he took his own life.

Sources

Chavkin, Allan, ed. *Conversations with John Gardner.* Jackson: University Press of Mississippi, 1990.

McWilliams, Dean. *John Gardner.* Boston: Twayne, 1990.

Garrett, George Palmer (1929–   ) *poet, novelist, biographer, children's playwright*

George Garrett's novels *Do, Lord, Remember Me* (1965) and *Death of the Fox* (1971) are among his most popular works. The latter, which imagines the life of Sir Walter Raleigh, is part of a historical novel series that also includes *The Succes-*

sion: *A Novel of Elizabeth and James* (1983), which re-creates the lives of Elizabeth I and her successor James VI, and *Entered from the Sun* (1990), a fictional biography of Christopher Marlowe. Garrett was born in Florida and often sets his fiction there. *The Finished Man* (1959) is about Florida politics, and *Do, Lord, Remember Me* (1965) is about an evangelist's visit to a southern town. His *Collected Poems* appeared in 1984.

Garrett is an astute critic and commentator on American literary life. His biography of James JONES appeared in 1984. *My Silk Purse and Yours: The Publishing Scene and American Literary Art* and *The Sorrows Of Fat City: A Selection Of Literary Essays and Reviews* were published in 1992. *Understanding Mary Lee Settle* (1988) is a fine example of his literary criticism. Some of his early short fiction is collected in *A Wreath for Garibaldi, and Other Stories*. Garrett has continued to write vigorous, engaged, and comic fiction—as in *The Kingdom of Babylon Shall Not Come Against You* (1996), set in Florida. Formerly a distinguished teacher of writing at the University of Michigan and University of Virginia, Garrett recently retired to devote his full time to writing.

Sources

Dillard, R. H. W. *Understanding George Garrett.* Columbia: University of South Carolina Press, 1988.

Gass, William Howard (1924–) *novelist*

Born in Fargo, North Dakota, Gass knew at an early age that he would become a writer. He read omnivorously—French novels, detective and adventure fiction, whatever came to hand. He was educated at Kenyon College and Wesleyan University and stationed in China and Japan for three years in the navy. At Cornell he wrote a dissertation, "A Philosophical Investigation of Metaphor." There he also studied under the philosopher Wittgenstein, whose theories of language influenced Gass's own view of literature as a self-contained universe. Gass has been a professor at Washington University in St. Louis since 1969. His first novel, *Omensetter's Luck* (1966), established his reputation among his fellow writers and in literary circles. This story of a man who settles in an Ohio town demonstrates Gass's ability to weld literary and philosophical concerns. Gass's feel for words is remarkable, but the self-referential quality of his fiction has necessarily limited his audience, since he does not write the kind of REALISM that appeals to the general reader. Gass's fiction, as he himself argues, is more about language and style than about the world outside the work of fiction.

Gass is important because both his fiction and criticism have complemented the efforts of writers like John BARTH, Donald BARTHELME, and Thomas PYNCHON to see fiction as a verbal construct, a made thing, sufficient to itself and not a representation of the world. He has published only two more novels, *Willie Masters' Lonesome Wife* (1971), and the lengthy *The Tunnel* (1994), which received respectful yet mixed reviews for its probing of the post–cold war world. Gass has also written three short fiction collections: the highly regarded *In the Heart of the Heart of the Country and Other Stories* (1968) and *The First Winter of My Married Life* (1979), and *Cartesian Sonata and Other Novellas* (1998). His nonfiction has been influential and has won him awards. His most notable work is *Fiction and the Figures of Life* (1970), *On Being Blue: A Philosophical Inquiry* (1976), *The World Within the Word* (1978), *Habitations of the Word* (1985), and *Finding a Form: Essays* (1996).

Sources

Holloway, Watson L. *William Gass.* Boston: G. K. Hall, 1990.

Kellman, Steven G. and Irving Malin, eds. *Into the Tunnel.* Newark: University of Delaware Press, 1998.

gay and lesbian literature

It has only been since the late 1970s and early 1980s that gay and lesbian literature as a category of literary study has been recognized. Gay and lesbian writers have largely been responsible for this development in the academic study of literature and in the identity of writers. Some authors, like Edmund WHITE, openly embrace the designation of gay writer; others, like Gore VIDAL, who have been equally open about their homosexuality, reject the gay label as limiting or even insulting in much the same way as William FAULKNER did not like the designation "southern novelist" or "regionalist writer." Such terms, some writers believe, restrict the implication of their work and their effort to reach a broad audience, not just segments of the reading public.

The impetus for examining literature from a gay and lesbian perspective, and for identifying certain work as examples of a gay and lesbian aesthetic or sensibility, has come in part from autobiographical works such as Merle Miller's *On Being Different: What It Means to Be a Homosexual* (1971), Audre LORDE's *Zami, a New Spelling of My Name* (1982), Joan Nestle's *A Restricted Country* (1987), Paul Monette's *Becoming a Man: Half a Life Story* (1992), and James MERRILL's *A Different Person: A Memoir* (1993).

Certain historians—most notably Martin Duberman—have not only made gay and lesbian history and literature a primary focus, but also have been instrumental in establishing gay and lesbian studies as an academic field. The growth in this field of study has also prompted a debate about whether there is a "queer aesthetic," a defining theory about the nature of literature created by gays and lesbians. The issue is similar to the one debated among African-American writers about a "BLACK AESTHETIC." Are there particular standards especially suited to gay and lesbian works of literature, or should they be judged by the same standards applied to all of literature? This argument between gay and lesbian assimilationists and gay and lesbian militants is also reminiscent of the African-American debate about integration and separation, that is, these different camps debate the extent to which minority literature should emulate and be included in mainstream or majority literature and culture.

As with any other body of literature, gay and lesbian literature has its own canon of great and historically important works. Among the American works are Dorothy ALLISON's *Trash* (1988); James BALDWIN's *Giovanni's Room* (1956); Rita Mae BROWN's *Rubyfruit Jungle* (1973); Mart Crowley's *The Boys in the Band* (1968); Larry KRAMER's *The Normal Heart* (1985); Armistead Maupin's *Tales of the City* (1978); Paul Monette's *Taking Care of Mrs. Carroll* (1978); Dale Peck's *Martin and John* (1993); John Rechy's *City of Night* (1963); May SARTON's *The Education of Harriet Hatfield* (1989); Gore Vidal's *The City and the Pillar* (1948); Alice WALKER's *The Color Purple* (1982); Edmund White's *The Beautiful Room is Empty* (1988); and Tennessee WILLIAMS's *Collected Stories* (1985).

Sources

Bergman, David. *Gaiety Transfigured: Gay Self-Representation in American Literature.* Madison: University of Wisconsin Press, 1991.

Clum, John M. *Acting Gay: Male Homosexuality in Modern Drama.* New York: Columbia University Press, 1992.

Lilly, Mark, ed. *Lesbian and Gay Writing: An Anthology of Critical Essays.* Basingstoke, England: Macmillan, 1990.

Rule, Jane. *Lesbian Images.* London: Pluto Press, 1989.

Zimmerman, Bonnie. *The Safe Sea of Women: Lesbian Fiction, 1969–1989.* Boston: Beacon Press, 1990.

Gelber, Jack (1932–) *playwright*

A Chicago native educated at the University of Illinois, Gelber became a major factor in the OFF-BROADWAY movement of the 1960s. *The Connection* (1962) used improvisation, jazz, and other techniques to break down the distance between audience and actors in a play about heroin addiction. His other plays include *The Apple* (1961), *The Cuban Thing* (1968), *Sleep* (1972), and *Rehearsal* (1976).

Sources

Cutler, Bruce. *Two Plays of the Living Theatre: The Difficult Wisdom of Nothing.* Wichita, Kan.: Wichita State University, 1977.

Gellhorn, Martha Ellis (1908–1998) *journalist, novelist*

Martha Gellhorn was a war correspondent who covered most of the major world conflicts from the SPANISH CIVIL WAR to Nicaragua. She grew up in St. Louis in a progressive family and attended Bryn Mawr College for three years before striking out on her own to see and report on the world. Her first novel, *What Mad Pursuit* (1934), was an immature and hasty fictionalizing of her career as cub reporter for the *Albany Times-Union* and her adventures abroad. Much more substantial was her second book, *The Trouble I've Seen* (1936), a collection of stories based on her work for the Federal Emergency Relief Administration during the DEPRESSION. As a journalist, Gellhorn came into her own in Spain, reporting on the Spanish Civil War. As a correspondent for *Collier's* magazine she covered WORLD WAR II and other major world conflicts while continuing to write fiction—notably *A Stricken Field* (1940), based on her firsthand observations of Czechoslovakia on the eve of the German invasion. In Spain she met Ernest Hemingway, whom she married in 1940. It was a stormy marriage, during which Gellhorn was able to complete another novel, *Liana* (1944), set in the Caribbean, where she did much of her reporting during this period. Gellhorn left Hemingway (they were divorced in 1945) and her home in Cuba to cover the final phases of World War II, not only filing remarkable reports for *Collier's* but also writing one of the best novels of the war, *The Wine of Astonishment* (1948). Gellhorn first collected her war reports in 1959 under the title *The Face of War,* interspersing her articles with a running commentary on her life and career. She updated this key work several times. It reached its final form in 1986. A comparable collection of her peacetime writings, *A View From the Ground,* was published in 1988. Gellhorn was also an engaging and amusing travel writer. *Travels with Myself and Another* (1978) is a classic of the genre. She published several collections of short stories, but her metier was the novella, a fact recognized and celebrated in her definitive collection, *The Novellas of Martha Gellhorn* (1993).

Sources

Rollyson, Carl. *Beautiful Exile: The Life of Martha Gellhorn.* London: Aurum Press, 2001. Revised edition of *Nothing Ever Happens to the Brave: The Story of Martha Gellhorn.* New York: St. Martin's Press, 1990.

Gibson, William (1914–) *playwright*

Born in New York City, Gibson attended City College. He published a collection of poems, *Winter Crook* (1948), and a novel, *The Cobweb* (1954), but he achieved no acclaim until his play *Two for the Seesaw* (1959)—the comic story of a romance between a Bronx girl and a Nebraska lawyer—became a Broadway hit and popular film. *The Miracle Worker* (1960), based on the life of Helen Keller, was his major success. He also wrote *Dinny and the Witches,* a fantasy produced OFF BROADWAY in 1959, and *Golda* (1977), a play about Golda Meir. In 1965 he adapted *Golden Boy,* a play by Clifford ODETS, for the musical stage. *The Seesaw Log* (1959) details the life of Gibson's play on the road, and *A Mass for the Dead* (1968) is a memoir. His most recent published theatrical work is *Monday After The Miracle: A Play In Three Acts,* and the vocal score for *Nativity: O Star That Makes the Stable Bright* (1987). He also wrote a study of Shakespeare, *Shakespeare's Game* (1978).

Sources

Olsen, Lance. *William Gibson.* San Bernadino, Calif.: Borgo Press, 1992.

Gilchrist, Ellen (1935–) *short story writer, novelist*

Gilchrist was born in Vicksburg, Mississippi, and grew up at the Hopedale Plantation in Grace, Mississippi. She ran away from home at the age of 19, married, divorced, and married again—four marriages and divorces altogether. She earned a B.A. degree from Millsaps College in 1967, but she did not begin her professional career until she was 40, working then for the *Vieux Carre Courier* newspaper in New Orleans. After taking a creative writing class, Gilchrist published her first book, a collection of poetry called *The Land Surveyor's Daughter,* in 1979. But her metier proved to be the short story, in which she explored the often comic plight of privileged southern white women. Her breakout book was *In the Land of Dreamy Dreams* (1981), a popular and critical success, which she followed with a novel, *The Annunciation.* By the time she won the National Book Award for her story collection, *Victory over Japan* (1984), she was a popular writer noted for her droll delivery of stories on National Public Radio. Her collected stories, *Drunk with Love,* appeared in 1986 and another collected edition, *Light Can Be Both Wave and Particle* in 1989, and another *The Blue-Eyed Buddhist* in 1990. Three novellas are collected in *I Cannot Get You Close Enough* (1990). Her other novels include *The Anna Papers* (1988), *Net of Jewels* (1992), *Anabasis: A Journey To The Interior* (1994), *Starcarbon: A Meditation On Love: A Novel* (1994), and *Sarah Conley: A Novel* (1997). She has been compared to Carson MC-CULLERS, Eudora WELTY, and Flannery O'CONNOR for her brilliant ability to create characters. Like them, she combines humor with a taste for exotic characters and tragicomic domestic stories. Of her contemporaries, she has been compared to Lee Smith, Lee Zacharias, and Bobbie Ann MASON. Her most recent short fiction is collected in *The Age of Miracles: Stories* (1995), *The Courts of Love: Stories* (1996), and *Flights of Angels: Stories* (1998). She has also published *Falling Through Space: The Journals of Ellen Gilchrist* (1987).

Sources

Bauer, Margaret Donovan. *The Fiction of Ellen Gilchrist.* Gainesville: University Press of Florida, 1999.
McCay, Mary A. *Ellen Gilchrist.* New York: Twayne, 1997.

Ginsberg, Allen (1926–1997) *poet*

Born in Newark, New Jersey, Ginsberg attended public schools in Patterson, New Jersey, and went on to Columbia University, where he was expelled in 1943 for apparently writing an anti-Semitic obscenity on a classroom window and for criticizing the university president. He worked at odd jobs, then was readmitted to Columbia, graduating in 1948 but staying on to do graduate work there.

In the late 1940s, Ginsberg began to experience mystical visions of the poet William Blake, which seem to have contributed to his search for an alternative to conventional standards of behavior and belief. He began to travel to the West Coast and to Mexico, making friends with such writers as Lawrence FERLINGHETTI and becoming part of what came to be called the "beat generation" (see BEATS), a term applied to writers who were disenchanted with the conformity of 1950s America, critical of the status quo, and who prized the creativity of the societal dropout.

Ginsberg made his mark as a poet with "HOWL," a lament for a lost generation of the 1950s, a group of younger writers who did not fit conventional roles. Ginsberg was openly gay in a time before such a word and way of life came into common parlance. He used drugs, especially marijuana, and celebrated poets like William Carlos WILLIAMS and Walt Whitman, who embraced America in all of its diversity and creativity. Indeed many of Ginsberg's opinions, his style of dress, and political views were later seen as precursors of the 1960s counterculture.

Ginsberg favored Whitman's long, proselike poetic line and free verse. Although some of Ginsberg's poetry angrily protests American culture, much of his work is also playful and cheerful—as in his amusing fantasy that he spots Walt Whitman in "A Supermarket in California."

The titles of Ginsberg's poems can give the impression that he is a casual, offhand poet, and yet he was deeply read in world literature and wanted poetry to reflect not only this world consciousness but also poetry's connection to everyday life and to the language people actually speak. Among his important poetry collections are *Kaddish and Other Poems* (1960), innovative poems that draw on his Jewish heritage, *Reality Sandwiches* (1963), and *The Fall of America* (1973).

Unlike some of the poets of the beat generation, Ginsberg continued to write excellent poetry well beyond the 1950s. His *Collected Poems 1947–1980* was published in 1984. *Allen Verbatim, Lectures on Poetry, Politics, Consciousness* appeared in 1974.

Sources

Miles, Barry. *Ginsberg: A Biography.* New York: Simon & Schuster, 1989.
Morgan, Bill. *The Response to Allen Ginsberg, 1926–1994: A Bibliography of Secondary Sources.* Westport, Conn.: Greenwood Press, 1996.
Schumacher, Michael. *Dharma Lion: A Critical Biography of Allen Ginsberg.* New York: St. Martin's Press, 1992.
———. *Family Business: Selected Letters Between a Father and Son.* New York: Bloomsbury, 2001.

Giovanni, Nikki (Yolande Cornelia Giovanni) (1943–) poet

Giovanni grew up in Cincinnati, Ohio, but spent summers with her grandparents in Tennessee, where she was born. She graduated from Fisk University, where she took writing workshops directed by John Oliver KILLENS. Her first two volumes of poetry, *Black Feeling, Black Talk* (1968) and *Black Judgement* (1969), were originally self-published, and third, *Re: Creation* (1970) was brought out by BROADSIDE PRESS. But Giovanni quickly became a popular and critical success, furthered by her award-winning album, *Truth Is on Its Way* (1993), on which she performed some of her early work. Her early poetry reflects a good deal of anger at a white-controlled world, but her later work is less militant and explosive—as in the transitional *My House* (1972). Her style retains its hyperbolic tendencies,—she favors exaggeration and startling statements—but with a more introspective tone that marks *The Women and Men* (1975), *Cotton Candy on a Rainy Day* (1978), and *Those Who Ride the Night Winds* (1983). *The Selected Poems of Nikki Giovanni* (1996) brings together 150 poems that document the development of her career, which has been marked by a vigorous use of everyday speech filtered through her own autobiography and her conversations with African-American writers. Giovanni has engaged earlier generations of African-American writers, most notably in *A Dialogue: James BALDWIN and Nikki Giovanni* (1972), *A Poetic Equation: Conversations Between Nikki Giovanni and Margaret WALKER* (1974), and the HARLEM RENAISSANCE in *Shimmy Shimmy Like My Sister Kate* (1996). Her poetry for children is included in *Spin a Soft Black Song* (1971), *Ego Tripping and Other Poems for Young Readers* (1973), and *Vacation Time* (1979). *Love Poems* appeared in 1997 and *Blues: For All The Changes: New Poems* was published in 1999; *Conversations With Nikki Giovanni* in 1992. *Gemini: An Extended Autobiographical Statement On My First Twenty-Five Years Of Being A Black Poet* was published in 1972.

Sources

Fowler, Virginia C., ed. *Conversations with Nikki Giovanni.* Jackson: University Press of Mississippi, 1992.
———. *Nikki Giovanni.* New York: Twayne, 1992.

Glasgow, Ellen (1873–1945) novelist

Born in Richmond, Virginia, Glasgow grew up in a large family of 10 children. She avidly read Charles Dickens, Henry Fielding, and Jane Austen. She found her father's strict Puritanism stifling and gravitated more toward her sophisticated and sensitive mother. She also found conservative southern society a trial and rejected the cruelty she witnessed during the post–Civil War period. She began to write fiction in the late 1880s, publishing her first novel, *The Descendant,* in 1897. She traveled abroad and launched her prolific writing career. *Barren Ground* (1925), considered her masterpiece, focuses on Dorinda Oakley, who hopes to marry Dr. Jason Greylock and escape her poverty. But Jason succumbs to his father's wish that he marry another woman, and Dorinda, already pregnant, escapes to New York City. She loses her baby and has to return home. Further setbacks fail to crush her, however, and she manages not only to master her fate but also to become a successful landowner. For its breadth of social observations and psychological perception, as well as its presentation of a fully realized strong woman, *Barren Ground* is unequaled in Glasgow's body of work. Nearly as accomplished are *The Romantic Comedians* (1926) and *The Sheltered Life* (1932). These novels demonstrate Glasgow's gifts as a novelist of manners and her shrewd handling of point of view. She can also be read as an astute analyst of southern womanhood, creating such types as Eva Birdsong, whose aim is to create the perfect marriage.

Glasgow's other important novels include *Vein of Iron* (1935), set in rural Virginia and *In This Our Life* (1941), an account of a prominent but declining Virginia family, which won the Pulitzer Prize. Her revealing autobiography, *The Woman Within,* was published in 1954, *The Letters of Ellen Glasgow* in 1958, and *The Collected Stories of Ellen Glasgow* in 1963.

Sources

Goodman, Susan. *Ellen Glasgow: A Biography.* Baltimore: Johns Hopkins University Press, 1998.
Inge, M. Thomas, ed. *Ellen Glasgow: Centennial Essays.* Charlottesville: University Press of Virginia, 1976.
Matthews, Pamela R. *Ellen Glasgow and a Woman's Traditions.* Charlottesville: University Press of Virginia, 1994.
Scura, Dorothy M., ed. *Ellen Glasgow: New Perspectives.* Knoxville: University of Tennessee Press, 1995.

Glaspell, Susan (c. 1882–1948) playwright, novelist, biographer

Glaspell was born in Davenport, Iowa, and in 1899 graduated from Drake University with a degree in journalism. During work at Des Moines newspapers she wrote short stories and her first novel, *The Glory of the Conquered* (1909). In 1913 she married George Cram Cook, one of the founding members of the PROVINCETOWN PLAYERS, a group that would launch Glaspell's career as a dramatist as well that of Eugene O'NEILL and other important writers. The Players produced Glaspell's play *Suppressed Desires* in 1915. But it is her first play, *Trifles,* that has become a standard text in American literature anthologies and a classic of feminist literature. In this short drama, Glaspell probes the lives of women, using the dramatic form to explore male and female points of view and illuminate the arrest of a wife for her husband's murder. Her first three-act play, *Bernice,* was produced in 1919. Her next two plays, *Inheritors* (1921) and *The Verge* (1921), showed the influence of Henrik Ibsen and confirmed Glaspell's stature as an acute analyst of the female mind.

Glaspell's later plays have not received as much attention, although *Alison's House* (1930), based on the life of Emily Dickinson, won a Pulitzer Prize. Glaspell's later novels include *Brook Evans* (1928), *Fugitive's Return* (1929), *Ambrose Holt and Family* (1931), *The Morning Is Near Us* (1939), and *Judd Rankin's Daughter* (1945).

Glaspell published dozens of short stories and also wrote a biography of George Cram Cook, *The Road to the Temple* (1926).

Sources

Ben-Zvi, Linda, ed. *Susan Glaspell: Essays on Her Theater and Fiction.* Ann Arbor: University of Michigan Press, 1995.
Waterman, Arthur E. *Susan Glaspell.* New York: Twayne, 1966.

Glass Menagerie, The Tennessee Williams (1944)

Tennessee Williams's first success, which brought a new poetic vision to the American theater, *The Glass Menagerie* opened in Chicago in December 1944 and in New York in March 1945. Tom Wingfield, the play's narrator, reminisces about his mother and sister and their life of genteel poverty. The era is the GREAT DEPRESSION, and Tom is a dreamer who frequents movie houses and writes poetry. His mother, Amanda, is domineering, outspoken, and nostalgic about her southern past and her many gentlemen callers. The title refers to the collection of glass animals of Tom's sister, Laura, frail and shy. The collection is a metaphor for her delicate world, but also for the fragile hopes of all the Wingfields. Laura has only one gentleman caller, Jim O'Connor, who disappoints her. The sad ending to Laura's hopes is part of what drives Tom away from home. But he relates the Wingfield story with such sensitivity and eloquence that it becomes an evocation of the melancholy of human life itself, not merely the fate of one family. The play established Williams's reputation, and it quickly became a classic of the American theater, rivaled only by the sensational success of *A STREETCAR NAMED DESIRE*.

Sources

Parker, R. B., ed. *The Glass Menagerie: A Collection of Critical Essays.* Englewood Cliffs, N.J.: Prentice Hall, 1983.
Presley, Delma E. *The Glass Menagerie: An American Memory.* Boston: Twayne, 1990.
Siebold, Thomas, ed. *Readings on The Glass Menagerie.* San Diego, Calif.: Greenhaven Press, 1998.

Godwin, Gail (1937–) *novelist, short story writer*

Born in Birmingham, Alabama, Godwin was educated at Peace Junior College in Raleigh, North Carolina, and at the University of North Carolina. After obtaining her bachelor's degree in 1959, she worked at the *Miami Herald*, married in 1960, had two sons, divorced, worked in London, and then returned to the United States to obtain an M.A. and Ph.D. in English from the University of Iowa. Her early novels, *The Perfectionists* (1970), *Glass People* (1972), and *The Odd Woman* (1974), center on women who feel oppressed by husbands, and even her later fiction—notably *Violet Clay* (1978), *A Mother and Two Daughters* (1982), and *The Finishing School* (1985)—portray women who are determined to establish their autonomy. Godwin writes with perfect poise, creating enormous tensions between her characters' will (or lack thereof) and the conditions (the fate, the destiny) of their lives. Godwin is constantly questioning the extent to which women can liberate themselves—or even understand clearly what it is they want. Her later novels include *Father Melancholy's Daughter* (1991), *The Good Husband* (1994), and *Evensong* (1999). A bestselling author, Godwin has also won considerable critical acclaim for her work.

Godwin's short stories, frequently anthologized, have been collected in *Dream Children* (1977) and *Mr. Bedford and the Muses* (1983).

Sources

Hill, Jane. *Gail Godwin.* New York: Twayne, 1992.
Xie, Lihong. *The Evolving Self in the Novels of Gail Godwin.* Baton Rouge: Louisiana State University Press, 1995.

Gold, Herbert (1924–) *novelist, short story writer*

Born in Cleveland, Ohio, Gold was educated at Columbia University and the Sorbonne. After serving in the army, he taught at several colleges, including Wayne State University in Detroit and Baruch College in New York City. He is perhaps best known for *The Fathers: A Novel in the Form of a Memoir* (1967), which recounts his family life and presents a riveting portrait of his Russian-Jewish immigrant father. *Therefore Be Bold* (1960) draws on Gold's experience to tell the story of an Jewish adolescent in the Midwest. *Family* (1981) pursues the immigrant experience further. Gold's style is difficult to describe, since it changes often depending on his subject, but his most distinctive characteristic is his penchant for the witty turn of phrase. His first novel, *Birth of a Hero*, appeared in 1951. His other novels include *The Prospect Before Us* (1954), *The Man Who Was Not With It* (1956), *The Optimist* (1959), *Salt* (1963), *Swiftie the Magician* (1974), *Waiting for Cordelia* (1977), *He/She* (1980), *True Love* (1982), *Mister White Eyes* (1984), and *A Girl of Forty* (1986). He has published several collections of short stories: *Love and Like* (1960), *Stories of Misbegotten Love* (1985), and *Lovers and Cohorts* (1986). *The Magic Will* (1971) and *A Walk on the West Side: California on the Brink* (1981) contain stories and essays. *The Age of Happy Problems* (1962) is an essay collection. *My Last Two Thousand*

Years (1972) is an autobiography. Gold has traveled many times to Haiti and is the author of the acclaimed *The Best Nightmare on Earth: A Life in Haiti* (1991), *Travels in San Francisco* (1990), and *Bohemia: Where Art, Angst, Love, and Strong Coffee Meet* (1993).

Sources

Fiedler, Leslie. *Waiting for the End.* New York: Stein and Day, 1964.

Gold, Michael (Irwin Granich) (1894–1967)
novelist, editor, playwright, critic, editor

Gold grew up on New York City's Lower East Side, then a refuge but also a site of exploitation for the teeming immigrant masses looking for a better world. A prominent exponent of PROLETARIAN LITERATURE, Gold was influential as editor of the Communist journal, THE MASSES, later renamed *The New Masses.* Gold first coined the term *proletarian literature* in a magazine, THE LIBERATOR (February 1921), in an article, "Towards Proletarian Art." His novel, *Jews Without Money* (1930), is an earnest and sentimental celebration of the working masses. It became a model for other novelists claiming the mantle of the progressive writer who was on the side of the proletariat in a class-ridden society. Gold's early fiction is collected in *The Damned Agitator and Other Stories* (1926). His articles have been republished in *Change the World* (1937) and *The Hollow Men* (1941). Additional stories and articles appear in *The Mike Gold Reader* (1954), and *Mike Gold: A Literary Anthology* (1972). His plays include *Hoboken Blues* (1928) and *Battle Hymn* (1936), a play about the radical abolitionist John Brown.

Sources

Bloom, James D. *Left Letters: The Culture Wars of Mike Gold and Joseph Freeman.* New York: Columbia University Press, 1992.
Pyros, John. *Mike Gold: Dean of American Proletarian Writers.* New York: Dramatika Press, 1979.

Goodman, Paul (1911–1972) *social critic, psychoanalyst, novelist, playwright, poet*

Born in New York City, Goodman aspired at an early age to be a renaissance man. In 1947 he published *Communitas*, a book about city planning. In 1951 he published *Gestalt Therapy*, based on his own work as a psychoanalyst. A nontraditional thinker who often attacked conventional American institutions, Goodman won his greatest audience with a polemical book, *Growing Up Absurd* (1960), one of the key works of the 1960s, which argued for a complete reformation of the way American youth were educated and employed. He found the American workplace an inauthentic world cut off from nature. At the same time Goodman was publishing fiction like *The Empire City* (1959), an ambitious work that

charted the changes in American society from the 1930s to the 1950s. None of Goodman's creative work received the same degree of attention or praise as his nonfiction did. His other novels include *The Grand Piano* (1949), *The Dead of Spring* (1950), and *Making Do* (1963). His published plays include *The Young Disciple* (1955) and *The Theory of Comedy* (1960). His short stories were published in *The Break-Up of Our Camp* (1949). His *Collected Poems* was published in 1974.

Sources

Parisi, Peter, ed. *Artist of the Actual: Essays on Paul Goodman.* Metuchen, N.J.: Scarecrow Press, 1986.
Widmer, Kingsley. *Paul Goodman.* Boston: Twayne, 1980.

Go Tell It on the Mountain James Baldwin (1953)
novel

James BALDWIN's debut novel is considered his most intense and authentic vision of the African-American experience. The novel has been praised for its shapely construction and elegant style. Much of the content derives from Baldwin's own life. The story concerns John Grimes, a Harlem adolescent. He is 14 in March 1935. His quest for identity and love is set against the storefront church presided over by his stepfather, Gabriel Grimes. Each member of the Grimes family, including Gabriel's sister Florence and his second wife, Elizabeth, are portrayed against the arc of African-American experience from slavery to the years of migration to the North. Gabriel is like an Old Testament patriarch, arbitrary and authoritarian. He also abuses his wife and child, and has a strong sexual drive masked by his born-again preacher stance. The novel culminates in John's conversion experience and his movement toward self-definition.

Sources

Harris, Trudier, ed. *New Essays On Go Tell It on the Mountain.* New York: Cambridge University Press, 1996.

Gordon, Caroline (1895–1981) *novelist*

The Kentucky-born Gordon was given a complete education in the classics by her father, James Morris Gordon, a classics teacher. She graduated from Bethany College with a B.A. degree in 1916 and married the FUGITIVE poet Allen TATE in 1924. The couple divorced in 1959. Gordon began her literary career when as a secretary to the British novelist Ford Madox Ford he encouraged her to write her first novel, *Penhally* (1931). The novel embodies the author's concern with family history and classical values. Her next novel, *Alex Maury, Sportsman* (1934), the story of a sportsman and a scholar, brought her recognition for her superb handling of male dominance in an agrarian society. *None Shall Look Back* (1937) explored the Civil War and Gordon's southern roots even more intensely, while *The Garden of Adonis* (1937) and *Women on the Porch* (1944) were set in the contemporary South. After the author converted to Roman Catholicism in 1947, her novels *Strange Children* (1951) and *The Malefactors* (1957) focused on spiritual themes and the search for grace. Gordon was also a literary critic, publishing *House of Fiction* in 1950 and *How To Read a Novel* in 1957. She was a superb stylist who often taught writing courses. She had a close friendship with Flannery O'CONNOR, and is said to have influenced Walker PERCY.

Sources
Waldron, Ann. *Close Connections: Caroline Gordon and the Southern Renaissance.* New York: Putnam, 1987.

Gordon, Mary (1949–) *novelist*
Gordon grew up on Long Island, New York, the child of Catholic parents. Educated at Barnard College and Syracuse University, she has taught at several colleges and is a professor of English at Barnard. Her novels often feature religious and feminist themes. She is still perhaps best known for her novel, *Final Payments* (1978), which won the Kafka Prize. Her other noteworthy fiction includes *The Company of Women* (1981), *Men and Angels* (1985), and *The Other Side* (1989). She is also the author of *Good Boys and Dead Girls: And Other Essays* (1991); *The Shadow Man* (1996), a memoir of her father; and two collections of short fiction: *Temporary Shelter: Short Stories* (1987) and *Spending: A Utopian Divertimento* (1998).

Sources
Kessler-Harris, Alice and William McBrien, eds. *Faith of a Woman Writer.* New York: Greenwood Press, 1988.

gothicism
The gothic strain in American literature stems from the English gothic novel. It often featured an intense, romantic hero with a fatal flaw, a doomed family, or a haunted house, as in Edgar Allan Poe's tales and Nathaniel Hawthorne's novels and stories. A medieval atmosphere of evil and corruption or a haunting of some kind is in order. Shirley JACKSON's *The Haunting of Hill House* (1959) is one of the masterpieces of the genre. Gothic elements appear in many southern novels by William FAULKNER, Flannery O'CONNOR, and Carson MC-CULLERS. Faulkner's *Absalom, Absalom!,* for example, features a demonic hero, Thomas Sutpen, and a haunted house, Sutpen's Hundred. Gothicism suggests the idea of a curse, often a family crime, that must be expiated. Anne RICE's vampire series is also gothic in its exploration of the human desire to achieve immortality through power over other human beings—the vampire as gothic hero. Gothicism deals with the irrational and the grip of the past on the human psyche. It opposes the idea that human beings are rational and can control their appetites.

Sources
Fiedler, Leslie. *Love and Death in the American Novel.* [revised edition] New York: Anchor Books, 1992.
MacAndrew, Elizabeth. *The Gothic Tradition in Fiction.* New York: Columbia University Press, 1979.

Goyen, William (Charles William Goyen)
(1915–1983) *novelist, short story writer, playwright*
A Texas native, Goyen was educated at Rice University in Houston, Texas. His novel *The House of Breath* (1950) is an exuberant story of a boy growing up in a small Texas town. *Ghost and Flesh* (1952) contains stories with a Texas setting as well, and they reflect his distinctive blending of realism and fantasy. *Had I a Hundred Mouths* (1985) collects stories from throughout Goyen's career. His plays include *The House of Breath* (1956), *The Diamond Rattler* (1960), and *Christy* (1964). *William Goyen: Selected Letters from a Writer's Life* was published in 1995.

Sources
Horvath, Ruth, Irving Malin, and Paul Ruffin, eds. *A Goyen Companion: Appreciations of a Writer's Writer.* Austin: University of Texas Press, 1997.

Grapes of Wrath, The John Steinbeck (1939) *novel*
John STEINBECK's novel about the Dust Bowl farmers who were forced off their land (because it had quite literally turned into clouds of dust, making farming virtually impossible) and migrated to California is among the greatest American works about the GREAT DEPRESSION.

The novel centers on the Joad family and their long, arduous journey to the "promised land" in the West. Ma Joad holds the family together. Pa dies on the way. Rose of Sharon, the oldest daughter, is pregnant and has trouble finding enough food to keep her strength. Her husband, Connie, deserts her, and she eventually gives birth to a stillborn child. Tom Joad, her brother and the family's new leader after Pa dies, sees the family's simple quest for shelter and jobs met in California by hostile growers and police who regard the Okies as human refuse.

The family is accompanied by Jim Casey, a former preacher who has given up his ministry because of his tendency to seduce young women. But Casey remains religious in that he believes in transcendent values and in helping his fellow man. He and Tom become the moral focal points of the novel. Tom is forced to leave the family when he kills a man in a labor dispute: He has become an activist who realizes that his family will never be secure unless the structure of society itself is changed.

Steinbeck's novel can be regarded as an example of PRO-LETARIAN LITERATURE, since it ennobles the working people and sees the Depression-era country dividing more than ever into classes of haves and have-nots. But Steinbeck's vision is also naturalistic (see NATURALISM) in that his characters seem driven by social and economic forces that destroy their individuality. The biblical theme of a search for the promised land elevates the novel to a universal plane, suggesting that the Joad family drama is also the drama of the human family playing out over thousands of generations.

Sources

French, Warren, ed. *A Companion to The Grapes of Wrath*. New York: Penguin Books, 1989.

Heavilin, Barbara A. *The Critical Response to John Steinbeck's The Grapes of Wrath*. Westport, Conn.: Greenwood Press, 2000.

Grau, Shirley Ann (1929–) *novelist, short story writer*

Born in New Orleans and educated at Tulane University, Grau has been described as a regionalist (see REGIONALISM) concerned with racial issues. She won considerable praise for her first novel, *The Keepers of the House* (1964), which dealt with interracial marriage, politics, and the Ku Klux Klan. In *The Hard Blue Sky* (1960), *The House on Coliseum Street* (1961), *The Condor Passes* (1971), and *Evidence of Love* (1974), she has written novels that track the lives of generations of Louisianans in New Orleans and in its outlying areas and islands. Her short stories are collected in *The Black Prince* (1955), *The Wind Shifting West* (1973), and *Nine Women* (1986). In the novel *Roadwalkers* (1994) she portrays the lives of African-American women and the subject of homelessness.

Sources

Kissel, Susan S. *Moving On: The Heroines of Shirley Ann Grau, Anne Tyler, and Gail Godwin*. Bowling Green, Ohio: Bowling Green State University Popular Press, 1996.

Inge, Tonette Bond, ed. *Southern Women Writers: The New Generation*. Tuscaloosa: University of Alabama Press, 1990.

Schleuter, Paul. *Shirley Ann Grau*. Boston: Twayne, 1981.

Great Depression (1929–1941)

In its severity and its length, the Great Depression marks the worst period of economic, social, and political turmoil in the history of the United States. The Great Depression seems all the worse because it was preceded in the 1920s by one of the greatest economic booms in American history, a boom also marked by extravagant optimism and changes in social manners—perhaps best described in F. Scott FITZGERALD's stories and novels. Many new millionaires emerged from stock market speculation, from illicit trafficking in liquor during PROHIBITION, and from the increase in gangsterism that such illicit activity promoted.

The overheated economy resulted in the stock market crash of 1929. Initially, both the government and business regarded this event as no more than a recession: Stock would recover and industrial productivity would bring the nation out of its slump. But lessening demand and falling prices provoked further cuts in production. Banking panics eroded confidence that the capitalist system could protect people's money.

Although President Hoover made a belated effort to employ people and to aid business through government programs, his optimism at the time of the crash and his stubborn public speeches that the economy would correct itself seemed callous and out of date by the time he was defeated by Franklin D. Roosevelt in 1932.

President Roosevelt promised a "New Deal," the first phase of which started with the National Industrial Recovery Act (later declared unconstitutional), which aimed to stabilize prices and stimulate an industrial boom. In the short term, such policies resulted in a partial recovery and hope among Americans that the new administration cared about their plight and was willing to try different programs that would promote national recovery. Under Harry Hopkins, head of the Federal Emergency Relief Administration, for example, people on relief were put to work in building programs. The journalist Martha GELLHORN would write about the government efforts in *The Trouble I've Seen* (1935) and later in her collection of articles, *The View from the Ground* (1988). John STEINBECK provided a vivid picture of a government work camp in THE GRAPES OF WRATH (1939). Many other writers like John Dos PASSOS and James T. FARRELL wrote with great sympathy about the government effort to help the poor and the labor classes.

To conservatives, Roosevelt's policies seemed like socialism or—even worse—communism. Indeed, during some periods of his administration in the 1930s he drew considerable support from the American Communist Party, which formed a "Popular Front" with liberals to campaign on behalf of government programs that provided work and welfare, although Roosevelt did not seek Communist support.

By 1937, the economy faltered again badly, and it was only in the late 1930s and early 1940s, as the country began to gear up for war, that the nation experienced virtually full employment. Already in the late 1930s, Dos Passos and other writers were reevaluating their faith in government action and in liberalism. A reaction against the Roosevelt programs set in after WORLD WAR II, when the activities of Communists and certain liberals came under intense scrutiny in the COLD WAR period.

Lillian HELLMAN's play *Days to Come* (1935), John Steinbeck's novels *In Dubious Battle* (1936) and *The Grapes of Wrath*, and the proletarian novels of Michael GOLD and Daniel Fuchs give a vivid impression of life during the Depression and the feeling among many writers that the country might be headed for revolution.

Sources

Garraty, John A. *The Great Depression: An Inquiry into the Causes, Course, and Consequences of the Worldwide Depression of the Nineteen-Thirties, As Seen by Contemporaries and in the Light of History.* New York: Anchor Press/Doubleday, 1987.
Louis, L. J., ed. *The Depression of the 1930's.* Melbourne, Australia: Cassell, 1968.

Great Gatsby, The F. Scott Fitzgerald (1925) *novel*

Fitzgerald's greatest novel is a virtually perfect work of literature about American aspirations. Set in the society of the well-off in New York City and Long Island, the novel is filtered through the narrative voice of Nick CARRAWAY, an onlooker and friend to the characters. Jay Gatsby, a man of ambiguous social standing, pursues Daisy Buchanan, the girl he fell in love with before going off to war. However, Daisy is married to the thuggish Tom Buchanan, whose social status Gatsby can never attain. Yet Gatsby thinks that anything is possible—that he can overcome all obstacles and jettison his past. In the story of Gatsby's failure to win Daisy, of Daisy's failure to assert herself, of Nick's fascination with characters who are cynical and give the lie to Gatsby's romanticism, Fitzgerald presents a bleak yet compelling picture of the American dream.

Sources

Bloom, Harold, ed. *Gatsby.* New York: Chelsea House, 1991.
Bruccoli, Matthew J., ed. *F. Scott Fitzgerald's The Great Gatsby: A Documentary Volume.* Detroit: Gale, 2000.
Lockridge, Ernest H., ed. *Twentieth Century Interpretations of The Great Gatsby: A Collection of Critical Essays.* Englewood Cliffs, N.J.: Prentice Hall, 1968.

Green, Paul Eliot (1894–1981) *playwright*

A North Carolina native who taught at the University of North Carolina, Paul Green scored a Broadway success and won the Pulitzer Prize for *In Abraham's Bosom* (1927), a sympathetic exploration of black lives in the South. He wrote for Hollywood movies and devoted much of his life to folk plays produced by the North Carolina playmakers. He withdrew from the commercial theater, preferring to write "symphonic dramas" which included large casts and often group recitations of choruses set in his native region. He published several collections of plays, including *Lonesome Road: Six Plays for the Negro Theater* (1926) and *The House of Connelly and Other Plays* (1931). His later symphonic dramas include *The Lost Colony* (1947), *Wilderness Road* (1955), and *We the People* (1976).

Sources

Avery, Laurence G. *A Southern Life: Letters of Paul Green, 1916–1981.* Chapel Hill: University of North Carolina Press, 1994.
Kenny, Vincent S. *Paul Green.* New York: Twayne, 1971.

Greenwich Village, New York

A neighborhood in lower Manhattan, the Village became a kind of literary colony that by the 1920s had attracted E.E. CUMMINGS, Floyd Dell, Max EASTMAN, Edna St. Vincent MILLAY, Eugene O'NEILL, Carl VAN VECHTEN, and many other writers. The intimate and oddly angled small streets of this part of the city encouraged a sense of community and promoted eccentricity. Writers who could not afford the rent elsewhere, or who were alienated from the accelerated pace of the uptown business economy, found refuge in the Village. The PROVINCETOWN PLAYERS founded a theater there and premiered many of their innovative plays. Many literary magazines also found a home in the Village, including THE LITTLE REVIEW, SEVEN ARTS, and *Quill.*

In the 1950s and 1960s, the Village experienced a revival. Writers like Edward ALBEE and the BEAT poet Gregory CORSO settled there. Lanford WILSON and other OFF-BROADWAY playwrights premiered many of their experimental dramas in the Village. The neighborhood also became the site of many small movie theaters called revival houses, which showed older films that merited rediscovery or continued appreciation.

Sources

Broyard, Anatole. *Kafka Was the Rage: A Greenwich Village Memoir.* New York: Southern Books, 1993.
Churchill, Allen. *The Improper Bohemians: A Re-creation of Greenwich Village in its Heyday.* New York: Dutton, 1959.
Stansell, Christine. *American Moderns: Bohemian New York and the Creation of a New Century.* New York: Holt/Metropolitan Books, 2000.
Wakefield, Dan. *New York in the Fifties.* Boston: Houghton Mifflin, 1992.

Griffiths, Clyde *character*

Theodore DREISER's conflicted hero in the great naturalistic (see NATURALISM) novel *AN AMERICAN TRAGEDY* comes from a poor family and dreams of great success. He seems to find it when he is taken in by a rich uncle, but Clyde's relatives do not treat him as an equal, and he falls in love with Roberta Alden, a daughter of the poor farmers Clyde supervises for his uncle. Then he meets Sondra Finchley, a spoiled rich girl who rekindles his desire to be wealthy and admired. Meanwhile Roberta becomes pregnant. Seeing his plan to succeed threatened, Clyde takes her out on a lake, and when their boat tips over, he swims away from the screaming girl who cannot swim. Clyde is apprehended for the crime and is haunted by the fatality of his life as he spends his last days harrowed by his impending execution in the electric chair. For Dreiser, Clyde reflected the individual lost in the chaotic atmosphere of an America where the desire to succeed eclipsed all other considerations. Clyde is not condemned or judged in strict conventional moral terms but is seen instead as a victim of his own as well as his culture's craving for personal wealth and distinction. In other words, like Richard WRIGHT's Bigger Thomas and like other characters created by John STEINBECK and John DOS PASSOS, Clyde is viewed in the naturalistic tradition as a character shaped by powerful social forces he neither understands nor controls.

Sources

Orlov, Paul A. *An American Tragedy: Perils of the Self Seeking "Success."* Lewisburg, Pa.: Bucknell University Press, 1998.

Salzman, Jack, ed. *The Merrill Studies in An American Tragedy.* Columbus, Ohio: Merrill, 1971.

Group Theatre, The

Established in 1931 to present plays of social significance, The Group consisted of radical playwrights, actors, and producers. They produced a Broadway hit, Paul GREEN's *The House of Connelly* (1931), but their most notable production was Clifford ODETS's rousing proletarian play, *Waiting for Lefty* (1935). Other successful productions included Sidney KINGSLEY's *Men in White* (1933), Irwin SHAW's *The Gentle People* (1939), and William SAROYAN's *My Heart's in the Highlands* (1939). Many of the Group Theatre figures, including directors and teachers Lee Strasberg and Harold Clurman, would have a lasting impact on American drama. Others, such as actors John Garfield and Franchot Tone, would achieve success in Hollywood. Clurman described the Group's history in *The Fervent Years* (1945).

Sources

Clurman, Harold. *The Fervent Years: The Story of the Group Theatre and the Thirties.* London: Dobson, 1946.

Smith, Wendy. *Real Life Drama: The Group Theatre and America, 1931–1940.* New York: Alfred A. Knopf, 1990.

Guare, John (1938–) *playwright*

Guare was born in Queens, a borough of New York City. From an early age he amused himself by writing plays and going to the theater. Educated in Catholic schools, he graduated from Georgetown University with a B.A. degree in 1961. In 1963 he received an M.F.A. from Yale University. After a period in the air force reserve and travel in Europe, he returned to writing plays. *The Loveliest Afternoon of the Year* (1966) was his first play that would reflect his mature interest in isolated and lonely people. *Muzeeka* (1967), about a

Vietnam veteran upset over the superficiality of the media that trivialize the war, was an OFF-BROADWAY production and won an Obie award. *Cop-Out* (1968), another Obie award winner, was a play about police brutality written in an absurdist vein that Guare took up again in *The House of Blue Leaves* (1971), This play, winner of a New York Drama Critics Circle Award, explores Guare's conflicting feelings about Catholicism by centering on the pope's visit to New York and an attempt to assassinate him.

Guare wrote several other noteworthy plays, including *Lydie Breeze* (1982) and *Moon over Miami* (1988), but it was *Six Degrees of Separation* (1990), winner of an Obie and a New York Drama Critics Circle Award, that solidified his popular and critical success. Based on a true story, the play portrays a young black con man who masquerades as the son of the actor Sidney Poitier. In fact, this young man is working out not only his fantasies of associating with upper middle-class professionals but also their desire to be associated with the son of a celebrity. In other words, the young black man's ruse exposes a kind of inauthenticity in a society that is obsessed with brand names and famous figures. Like many of Guare's plays, *Six Degrees of Separation* is a kind of farce that shows society itself to be a farce.

Guare has written screenplays for the films *Taking Off* (1971), *Atlantic City* (1981), and *Six Degrees of Separation* (1993).

Sources

Kolin, Philip C., ed. *American Playwrights Since 1945: A Guide to Scholarship, Criticism, and Performance.* New York: Greenwood Press, 1989.

Gunther, John (1901–1970) *journalist*

Gunther made his reputation with his "Inside" travel books, well-informed accounts of life in Africa, Europe, South America, and other continents, and with a classic memoir, *Death Be Not Proud* (1949), about the death of his young son. Gunther began his career as a reporter in Chicago on the *Daily News* in 1922. There he met the visiting English writer Rebecca West, who encouraged him to expand his journalism to include reports from around the world. In his day, Gunther was one of the best-known journalists in the world, combining news reporting with travel and history writing. *A Fragment of Autobiography* was published in 1962.

Sources

Cuthbertson, Ken. *Inside: The Biography of John Gunther.* Chicago: Bonus Books, 1992.

Gurney, Albert Ramsdell (1930–) *playwright*

A graduate of Williams College and Yale, A. R. Gurney writes with sophisticated humor about urban characters in such plays such as *The Dining Room* (1981), *The Cocktail Hour* (1984), *Love Letters, and Two Other Plays: The Golden Age and What I Did Last Summer* (1990), and *Later Life* (1993). There is a sadness and almost a sense of futility in Gurney's characters, whose saving grace is an ability to find humor in their predicaments and to reach some understanding of their plight.

Sources

Colony Theatre Company. "A. R. Gurney," The Colony Theatre Company. Available on-line. URL: http://www.colonytheatre. org/bios/gurneyAR.html. Updated on February 2, 2001.

Dibactani, John L., ed. *A Search for a Postmodern Theatre: Interviews with Contemporary Playwrights.* New York: Greenwood Press, 1991.

Stage Door. "Playwright: A. R. Gurney," Stage Door: Southwestern Ontario Theatre Resource. Available on-line. URL: http://www.stage-door.org/authors/gurney.htm. Downloaded on May 29, 2001.

Guthrie, Alfred Bertram (1901–1991) *novelist, short story writer*

A. B. Guthrie was born in Indiana but grew up in Montana, becoming a regionalist (see REGIONALISM) writer whose territory encompassed a good part of the West. *The Big Sky* (1947), a novel set in the 1830s and 1840s about a mountain man from Kentucky who travels west and lives with the Indians, is perhaps his best-known work. Guthrie won a Pulitzer Prize for *The Way West* (1949), a novel about a pioneer trip from Missouri to Oregon in 1846. *The Big It* (1960) collects his stories. He also wrote an autobiography, *The Blue Hen's Chick* (1965), and the screenplay for one of Hollywood's most famous westerns, *Shane* (1953).

Sources

Ford, Thomas W. *A. B. Guthrie.* Austin, Tex.: Steck-Vaughn, 1968.

❧◎❧

Hagedorn, Jessica (1949–) *poet, playwright, novelist*

Hagedorn came to the United States from the Philippines when she was 13 years old. She was only 16 when the poet Kenneth REXROTH spotted her talent and included her in an anthology, *Four Young Women* (1973). She produced her first collection of poetry, *Dangerous Music,* in 1975. Hagedorn studied acting in San Francisco and worked as a lyricist for a band. New York producer Joseph Papp selected *Mississippi Meets the Amazon* (1977), a play she wrote in collaboration with Thulani Davis and Ntozake SHANGE, for performance at the Public Theater. She then moved to New York and wrote *Mango Tango,* which Papp produced in 1978. Other productions in other New York venues followed, including *Tenement Lover* (1981), and *Holy Good* (1988), and, in San Francisco, *Teenytown* (1990). Hagedorn's plays derive from her early days as a performance artist, so that the style of her drama tends to be based on speech and musical rhythms—as the titles suggest. Her characters often come from the lowest rungs of society, but their verve and imaginative energy represent a celebration of Third World culture. She won the American Book Award for a novella, *Pet Food and Tropical Apparitions* (1981). Her novel *Dogeaters* (1990), like *Pet Food,* is a comic and almost surrealistic story featuring West Indians, Filipinos, and the mingling of ethnic and racial characters that is a hallmark of Hagedorn's work. She has also edited *Charlie Chan is Dead: An Anthology of Contemporary Asian American Fiction* (1993). Her recent short fiction includes *Danger and Beauty* (1993). *Visions of a Daughter, Foretold: Four Poems (1980–1993)* appeared in 1994. *The Gangster of Love* (1996), a novel, is set in the Philippines, San Francisco, and New York. It tells of Rocky Rivera and her boyfriend, Elvis, who is part of a band called The Gangsters of Love.

Sources

San Juan, Epifanio, Jr. "Mapping the Boundaries: The Filipino Writer in the U.S.A." *Journal of Ethnic Studies* 19 (1991): 117–132.

Mosaic. "An Interview with Jessica Hagedorn." Mosaic. Available on-line. URL: http://dolphin.upenn.edu/~mosaic/fall93/page25.html.

Haines, John (1924–) *poet*

Born in Norfolk, Virginia, Haines was educated in art schools and homesteaded in Alaska for 20 years. He has been praised for his strikingly visual imagination, especially his descriptions of places and landscapes. He published *News from the Glacier: Selected Poems 1960–1980* in 1982; *New Poems: 1980–1988* (1990); and *At the End of This Summer: Poems, 1948–1954* (1997). He has also written several volumes that shift between the essay and memoir form, including *Living Off the Country: Essays on Poetry and Place* (1981); *The Stars, the Snow, the Fire: Twenty-five Years in the Northern Wilderness* (1989); and *Fables and Distances: New and Selected Essays* (1996).

Sources

Bezner, Kevin and Kevin Walzer, eds. *The Wilderness of Vision: On The Poetry of John Haines.* Brownsville, Oreg.: Story Line Press, 1996.

Haley, Alex Palmer (1921–1990) journalist

The author of two American classics, *The Autobiography of Malcolm X* (1965) and *Roots* (1976), which won the Pulitzer Prize, Alex Haley was born in Ithaca, New York. He grew up in Henning, Tennessee, and attended Hawthorn College in Mississippi and Elizabeth City State Teachers College in North Carolina. In 1939 he joined the Coast Guard, where he had a 20-year career: He gradually worked his way up from messboy and became chief journalist in 1950. He wrote short articles for *Coronet* magazine in the 1950s and then placed longer pieces in READER'S DIGEST, THE ATLANTIC, and HARPER'S. By the 1960s he was writing high-profile pieces for THE SATURDAY EVENING POST and conducting interviews for *Playboy*. His work brought him into contact with the prominent African Americans of his time, including Martin Luther King Jr., Muhammad Ali, and most important, MALCOLM X. The popular and critical success of the Malcolm X autobiography, which was quickly adopted in college classrooms, provided Haley with a platform, which he used brilliantly in orchestrating his search for his ancestors in *Roots*. More than 130 million viewers in 1977 and 1979 watched the television series based on Haley's book, which stimulated a nationwide interest in genealogy as well as in the legacy of slavery. *Roots* is suspect as both history and autobiography: The extent to which Haley actually recovered the history of his family is difficult to assess, since he clearly shaped his book to read like a novel. What is indisputable, however, is the urgency and energy Haley brought to a study of the past and to racial, political, and social issues that have haunted American life.

Sources

Bloom, Harold, ed. *Alex Haley & Malcolm X's The Autobiography of Malcolm X.* New York: Chelsea House, 1996.
Gonzales, Doreen. *Alex Haley: Author of Roots.* Hillside, N.J.: Enslow Publishers, 1994.
Shirley, David. *Alex Haley.* New York: Chelsea House, 1994.
Williams, Sylvia B. *Alex Haley.* Edina, Minn.: Abdo & Daughters, 1996.

Hall, Donald Andrew (1928–   ) poet, editor, critic

Hall was poetry editor of THE PARIS REVIEW and a professor of English at the University of Michigan before retiring to rural New Hampshire. His first book of poems, *Exiles and Marriages* (1955), won several awards, including the Edna Vincent Millay Award of the Poetry Society of America. Donald Hall is a traditionalist who uses conventional forms with great skill. He edited an important anthology, *The New Poets of England and America* (1957), introducing the work of poets born between 1917 and 1935. Among his poetry collections are *The Alligator Bride: Poems New and Selected* (1969), *Kicking the Leaves* (1978), *The Twelve Seasons* (1983), *The Happy Man: Poems* (1986), *Old and New Poems* (1990). Hall also has been a tireless promoter of poetry, and his crit-

ical prose and anthologies include *Goatfoot Milktongue Twinbird: Interviews, Essays, and Notes on Poetry, 1970–76* (1978); *Remembering Poets: Reminiscences and Opinions: Dylan Thomas, Robert Frost, T. S. Eliot, Ezra Pound* (1978); *The Oxford Book of American Literary Anecdotes* (1981); *The Oxford Book of Children's Verse in America* (1985); *Poetry and Ambition: Essays, 1982–88* (1988); *Their Ancient Glittering Eyes: Remembering Poets and More Poets: Robert Frost, Dylan Thomas, T. S. Eliot, Archibald MacLeish, Yvor Winters, Marianne Moore, Ezra Pound* (1992); and *Death to the Death of Poetry: Essays, Reviews, Notes, Interviews* (1994). *Here at Eagle Pond* (1990) is a nonfiction work about the poet's life in New Hampshire. His writing for children includes *The Man Who Lived Alone* (1984) and *I am the Dog, I am the Cat* (1994). A story collection, *Ideal Bakery*, appeared in 1987.

Sources

Rector, Liam, ed. *The Day I Was Older: On The Poetry of Donald Hall.* Santa Cruz, Calif.: Story Line Press, 1989.

Halper, Albert (1904–1984) novelist

Born in CHICAGO, Halper is best known for his PROLETARIAN LITERATURE. *Union Square* (1933) dramatizes the desperate economic plight of working men. *On the Shore* (1934) draws on Halper's own experience in Chicago—as does *The Foundry* (1934), the story of Chicago electrotype workers. *The Chute* (1937) is set in a mail-order house. *Little People* (1942) collects stories about Chicago clothing-store employees. *The Golden Watch* (1953) tells the story of a boy growing up in the city. *Atlantic Avenue* (1956) shifts the setting to Brooklyn and the waterfront. Halper also wrote a memoir, *Good-Bye Union Square* (1970).

Sources

Hart, John E. *Albert Halper.* Boston: Twayne, 1980.

Hamlet, The William Faulkner (1940) novel

With this novel, William FAULKNER introduces his legendary, predatory Snopes clan. The first and best volume of the Snopes trilogy, which also includes *The Town* (1957) and *The Mansion* (1960), *The Hamlet* recounts Flem Snopes's invasion of Yoknapatawpha County, the domain that Faulkner made one of the classic sites of American literature. Flem begins his attack in Frenchman's Bend, a hamlet where Will Varner owns a store. Flem is his clerk, but he connives to become a partner and then to marry the desirable Eula, Will's daughter. Flem advances from Frenchman's Bend to Jefferson, the county seat, where he finds a position in Colonel Sartoris's bank. Eventually he outmaneuvers General De Spain, the bank's president and a member of one of Jefferson's founding families. Even worse, Flem moves into the De Spain mansion, bringing in cousins such as Mink, I.O., Ike, and Eck Snopes. The trilogy deals with a community almost literally infested with the Snopes clan. This novel is also noteworthy for Faulkner's reworking of material used in his short stories, such as the classic "Spotted Horses." Elements of the tall tale and REGIONALISM inform this brilliant modernist work.

Sources

Holmes, Catherine D. *Annotations to William Faulkner's The Hamlet.* New York: Garland, 1996.

Polk, Noel, and John D. Hart, ed. *The Hamlet: A Concordance to the Novel.* Ann Arbor: University Microfilm International, 1990.

Hammett, Dashiell (Samuel Dashiell Hammett) (1894–1961) *novelist*

Dashiell Hammett was born in St. Mary's County, Maryland, and grew up in a Roman Catholic family. He had little early schooling (he did not complete high school) and worked at odd jobs until he was employed by the Pinkerton Detective Agency in his early 20s. He took to the work and did it well, interrupting his career only to serve in the army during World War I. Approaching 30, he began to write, publishing his first Continental Op (Operative) story in 1923. These detective stories of the hardboiled school led Hammett to write novels, beginning with *Red Harvest,* serialized in 1927–28. Using a style similar to Ernest HEMINGWAY's in its use of understatement, Hammett produced in quick succession *The Dain Curse* (1929), *The Maltese Falcon* (1930), and *The Glass Key* (1931). Their main character, Sam SPADE, is a loner, a stoic, and a fatalist who nevertheless does his job well. Hammett is one of the greatest writers of detective fiction because of his economy of language, his deep knowledge of detective work, and the seriousness of his themes. A man of radical political sympathies, he was a savage critic of corrupt society.

Unlike many writers of detective fiction, Hammett was not willing to repeat his success; that is, he did not continue to write novels about Sam Spade. By the mid-1930s, he had taken the genre of detective fiction about as far as he could, managing to produce only one more full-length work, *The Thin Man,* remarkable for its good humor and its creation of the married sleuths Nick and Nora Charles (played charmingly by William Powell and Myrna Loy in the movies). Lillian HELLMAN, who described herself as Hammett's on-again, off-again partner for 30 years, reportedly was the inspiration for Nora, who is one of the few truly witty women to be found in the fiction of male detective writers. Although Hammett lived nearly another 30 years after publishing *The Thin Man,* he did not produce another full-length work of fiction—apparently abandoning all efforts that did not match his own high standards. Virtually every important scholar of the detective story genre—as well as writers who succeeded Hammett in the genre, such as Raymond CHAN-DLER and Ross MACDONALD—have paid tribute to Hammett's example.

Sources

Johnson, Diane. *Dashiell Hammett: A Life.* New York: Fawcett Columbine, 1985.

Metress, Christopher, ed. *The Critical Response to Dashiell Hammett.* Westport, Conn.: Greenwood Press, 1994.

Symons, Julian. *Dashiell Hammett.* San Diego: Harcourt Brace Jovanovich, 1985.

Hansberry, Lorraine Vivian (1930–1965) *playwright*

Lorraine Hansberry grew up in the comfortable well-to-do atmosphere of a middle-class African-American home in Chicago. Both Hansberry's parents were activists who challenged deeds to houses that restricted the occupants to whites only. They established a foundation to further the cause of civil rights for African Americans, and traveled among prominent African Americans such as Langston HUGHES, Joe Louis, and Paul Robeson. Hansberry attended public schools, where she encountered working-class students and learned of their struggle to succeed. She studied journalism at the University of Wisconsin and involved herself in leftist causes. By 1950, she had moved to New York City. She worked at *Freedom,* a newspaper founded by Paul Robeson. She came into contact with Harlem's rich culture and absorbed a good deal of African-American history by reading W. E. B. DU BOIS and Langston HUGHES. By the mid 1950s she had earned an M.A. at New York University and begun work on *A Raisin in the Sun* (1959), a rousing play of an African-American family's struggle to prevail in a racist society. The play, now a staple of the American theater, won a New York Drama Critics Circle Award and made Hansberry, at age 28, the first African-American woman to win the award. Hansberry worked on several plays after her tremendous success, but the only one she completed, *The Sign in Sidney Brustein's Window* (1964), received mixed reviews—a not uncommon result for playwrights whose first work is a hit. Hansberry died of pancreatic cancer the same night as her play closed. The remnants of her last writings were edited for the stage in *To Be Young, Gifted, and Black,* the longest-running show of the 1968–69 OFF-BROADWAY season.

Sources

Carter, Steven R. *Hansberry's Drama: Commitment Amid Complexity.* Urbana: University of Illinois Press, 1991.

Hapgood, Hutchins (1869–1944) *journalist, novelist, autobiographer*

Hapgood was born in Chicago and educated at Harvard. He worked as a journalist in Chicago and New York. He specialized in meticulous accounts of city life—the world of the bohemian, labor agitator, and radical. His books include *The Spirit of Labor* (1907), *An Anarchist Woman* (1909), and *Types from City Streets* (1910). Less important are his novels: *Enemies* (1916) and *The Story of a Lover* (1919). His autobiography, *A Victorian in the Modern World* (1939), provides vivid views of radical Chicago, Provincetown, and Greenwich Village.

Sources

Marcaccio, Michael D. *The Hapgoods: Three Earnest Brothers.* Charlottesville: University Press of Virginia, 1977.

Trimberger, Ellen Kay, ed. *Intimate Warriors: Portraits of a Modern Marriage, 1899–1944: Selected Works by Neith Boyce and Hutchins Hapgood.* New York: Feminist Press, 1991.

Hardwick, Elizabeth (1916–   ) *novelist, critic*

Born in Kentucky and educated there and at Columbia University, Hardwick has spent virtually her entire adult life in NEW YORK CITY. She wrote for *PARTISAN REVIEW,* and thus made herself known to NEW YORK INTELLECTUALS and to writers around the country who regularly read the journal. She is one of the founders of the *NEW YORK REVIEW OF BOOKS* and was married to the poet Robert LOWELL. In the 1960s and 1970s the couple created a kind of salon in New York City, nurturing the talents of many New York writers. Hardwick is a formidable critic, hard-edged and given to withering judgments. Her prose is collected in *A View of My Own* (1962), *Seduction and Betrayal: Women and Literature* (1974), *A New America?: Essays* (1978), *Bartleby in Manhattan and Other Essays* (1983), and *Sight Readings: American Fictions* (1998). She has also written a critical biography, *Herman Melville* (2000).

Her novels have earned critical praise but have not found a wide audience. She began with the autobiographical *The Ghostly Lover* (1945), based on her Kentucky family. *The Simple Truth* (1955), a penetrating psychological analysis of a college student accused of murdering his girlfriend, was largely ignored, but *Sleepless Nights* (1979) earned considerable attention and a National Book Critics Circle award nomination. Hardwick called her novel a "meditation" on a woman's life, calling attention to its unusual form—that of a memoir that has the character analysis and narrative drive of a novel while seeming very close to the grain of Hardwick's own experiences. Hardwick's subjects have been cultural in a very broad sense, since she has written not only about the classics of literature but also about rock concerts, civil rights, and religion. She has not promoted feminism in any orthodox sense, yet the subject of women in a male-dominated world is a recurring theme in her fiction and nonfiction.

Sources

Laskin, David. *Partisans: Marriage, Politics and Betrayal Among the New York Intellectuals.* New York: Simon & Schuster, 2000.

Harjo, Joy (1951–   ) *poet*

A poet and a member of the Creek tribe, Harjo was born in Oklahoma and educated at the University of New Mexico. She learned her craft at the Iowa Writers' Workshop, and she has taught at Arizona State University. Her collections include *The Last Song* (1975), *She Had Some Horses* (1983), *Secrets from the Center of the World* (1989), and *In Mad Love and War* (1990). With Gloria Bird she has produced an anthology, *Reinventing the Enemy's Language: Contemporary Native Women's Writing of North America* (1997). Harjo has acknowledged several influences on her work, including Leslie Marmon SILKO and Flannery O'CONNOR. She has spoken as a feminist with a sensitivity to language that does not reproduce the white male view of the world. Contemporary Native American life is often the subject of her poetry.

Sources

Pettit, Rhonda. *Joy Harjo.* Boise, Idaho: Boise State University, 1998.

"Harlem" Langston Hughes (1951) *poem*

Each line of Langston HUGHES's classic poem about black rage has a cumulative impact, as the poet wonders whether a dream deferred dries up "like a raisin in the sun" or festers "like a sore" or "stink[s] like rotten meat"? The incremental use of similes builds up the pressure in the poem and culminates in the final line, which asks whether the dream deferred explodes. The power of this poem is packed into its extremely short lines, as if the anger is held in and bottled up until the last line. Hughes's simple, precise, and eloquent use of rhyme and alliteration make the poem perfect in its expression of the feeling that the promise of a better future for African Americans has been too long delayed. This poem was published three years before the *Brown v. Board of Education* Supreme Court decision, which outlawed segregation in education. In the years between the end of World War II and 1954, many African Americans expected changes in American society that would fulfill the dream of equal opportunity. Hughes's poem speaks to frustration and anger over the apparent lack of progress. The poem is a warning of what rage can do to African Americans and to America itself. Lorraine HANSBERRY used a line from the poem for the title of her important play about African-American life, *A RAISIN IN THE SUN.*

Harlem Renaissance (1920s–1930s)

Although Harlem developed as a white suburb of New York City, by 1925 it had 175,000 black residents—many of them migrants from the South, the West Indies, and Africa. Painters, writers, actors—artists of all kinds—congregated in a race-conscious community that prompted some commentators to call Harlem the capital of black America. Harlem also attracted white writers interested in exploring African-American life, including the novelists Maxwell Bodenheim (*Naked on Roller Skates* [1929]) and Carl VAN VECHTEN (*Nigger Heaven* [1926]), and the playwright Eugene O'NEILL (*All God's Chillun Got Wings* [1924]).

Several new black organizations located their offices and activities in Harlem, including the NAACP, the National Urban League, the Brotherhood of Sleeping Car Porters and Maids, and Marcus Garvey's Universal Negro Improvement Association. Garvey, in particular, focused the black community's attention on Africa, suggesting that a celebration of blackness was connected to pride in African origins.

The key text associated with the Harlem Renaissance, an outpouring of African-American creative energy, is *The New Negro,* an anthology edited by Alain LOCKE and published in 1925. Locke promulgated the idea of a renaissance—that is, a recovery of African-American creativity. Along with W. E. B. DU BOIS and James Weldon JOHNSON and certain sympathetic whites (Carl Van Vechten in particular), Locke sponsored and mentored a new generation of African-American writers, including Langston HUGHES, Claude MCKAY, Jean TOOMER, Countee CULLEN, and Zora Neale HURSTON.

McKay's novel *Home to Harlem* (1928) evoked the mystique of the Negro, the idea that there was something exotic, sensual, and primitive about African life that contributed to the dynamism of not only American but world culture. The Harlem Renaissance attracted attention in Europe and made possible the careers in Paris of African-American writers such as Richard WRIGHT and James BALDWIN.

Many later African-American writers such as Alice WALKER have explored the feminine consciousness of Hurston, Jessie FAUSET, and other female members of the Renaissance. This period developed the notions of a BLACK AESTHETIC and black power that would resound in the 1960s.

Exactly when the Harlem Renaissance ended is a matter of debate. Some scholars have placed the end as early as 1929, when the stock market crash ended the high-spirited touting of African-American work and writers such as Langston Hughes found it difficult to sustain the support of their white patrons. Other scholars point to the work of Zora Neale Hurston and other African Americans whose work still reflected the spirit of the Harlem Renaissance in the late 1930s.

By 1940, however, with the publication of Richard Wright's *Native Son,* the Renaissance was surely over. Wright presented a grim portrait of African-American marginality and of the failure of even sympathetic whites to understand the anomie of blacks.

Sources

Bontemps, Arna, ed. *The Harlem Renaissance Remembered.* New York: Dodd, Mead, 1962.
Clarke, John Henrik, ed. *Harlem USA.* Brooklyn, N.Y.: A&B Publishers Group, 1998.
Douglas, Ann. *Terrible Honesty: Mongrel Manhattan in the 1920s.* New York: Farrar, Straus and Giroux, 1995.
Huggins, Nathan. *Harlem Renaissance.* New York: Oxford University Press, 1971.
Kellner, Bruce, ed. *The Harlem Renaissance: A Historical Dictionary For the Era.* Westport, Conn.: Greenwood Press, 1984.
Schoener, Allon, ed. *Harlem on My Mind: Cultural Capital of Black America, 1900–1968.* Revised edition. New York: New Press, 1995.
Wall, Cheryl A. *Women of the Harlem Renaissance.* Bloomington: Indiana University Press, 1995.
Wintz, Cary D., ed. *Black Writers Interpret the Harlem Renaissance.* New York: Garland, 1996.

Harris, Mark (1922–   ) *novelist, biographer*

Born in New York City and educated at the University of Minnesota, where he received a Ph.D. in American Studies, Harris taught at several colleges while writing novels about baseball: *The Southpaw* (1953), *A Ticket for Seamstitch* (1957), *It Looked Like Forever* (1979), and the most well known of this series, *Bang the Drum Slowly* (1960), the story of a baseball player dying of Hodgkin's disease and the teammates who rally around him. Harris's other novels include *Wake Up, Stupid* (1959), the account of a professor who writes novels, and *Mark the Glove Boy,* or *The Last Days of Richard Nixon* (1964), which draws on Harris's years in California, as does *Best Father Ever Invented: The Autobiography of Mark Harris* (1976). Harris collected his short nonfiction in *Short Work of It* (1980). *The Self-Made Brain Surgeon, and Other Stories* appeared in 1999. He published an unusual biography, *Saul Bellow, Drumlin Woodchuck* (1980), which recounts his difficulties in researching the life of his hostile subject.

A writer on wide-ranging subjects, Harris has not pursued a single style, although he often returns to the story of naive young men who learn painfully about the nature of the world.

Sources

Lavers, Norman. *Mark Harris.* Boston: Twayne, 1978.

Harrison, James Thomas (1937–   ) *novelist, poet, short story writer*

Jim Harrison grew up in northern Michigan, graduated from Michigan State University, and taught English at the State University of New York. He now lives on a farm in northern Michigan. A versatile author—poet, novelist, short story writer, and screenwriter—he has won both critical praise and popularity. His best-known work is *Legends of the Fall* (1979), three novellas that explore a violent family saga set in Montana but including scenes in Canada, France, Boston, Saratoga, San Francisco, Mexico, Havana, Mombasa, and

Singapore, later made into a major motion picture. Nearly as well known is his other collection of novellas, *The Woman Lit by Fireflies* (1990) similar to *Legends of the Fall* in that Harrison explores tension-filled characters who have both an outlaw sensibility and a sense of the law—a kind of moral compass that informs their fugitive behavior. His other novels include *Wolf: A False Memoir* (1971); *A Good Day to Die* (1973); *Warlock* (1981); *Sundog* (1984, a kind of detective story centered on the mysterious Robert Corvus Strang, who, like many Harrison characters, does not fit easily into society); *Julip* (1994); and *The Road Home* (1998). His poetry is collected in *Plain Song* (1965), *Locations* (1968), *Outlyer* (1969), *Letters to Yesenin* (1973), *Returning to Earth* (1977), and *After Ikkyu and Other Poems* (1996). *Selected and New Poems* appeared in 1982 and *Poems* in 1998. As some of his titles suggest, Harrison's writing has a vein of REGIONALISM and a strong feeling for the land and nature. *Just Before Dark: Collected Nonfiction* appeared in 1991.

Sources

Morgan, Thais. *Men Writing the Feminine: Literature, Theory, and the Question of Genders.* Albany: State University of New York Press, 1994.

Reilly, Edward C. *Jim Harrison.* New York: Twayne, 1996.

Hart, Moss (1904–1961) playwright

A New Yorker, Hart is best known for his collaborations with George S. Kaufman: *Once in a Lifetime* (1930); *You Can't Take It with You* (1936), winner of a Pulitzer Prize; and *The Man Who Came to Dinner* (1939), inspired by the personality of Alexander WOOLLCOTT. Hart's musical comedy, *Lady in the Dark* (1941), was unusual because of his use of psychoanalysis and its impact on his characters. His memoir, *Act One* (1959), is one of the finest accounts of 20th-century commercial theater.

Sources

Bach, Steven. *Dazzler: The Life and Times of Moss Hart.* New York: Alfred A. Knopf, 2001.

Hass, Robert (1941–   ) poet

Born in San Francisco, Hass has made his home in Berkeley, where he is a professor at the University of California. His work has been praised for its sensitive character portraits, its evocation of nature, particularly the California landscape, and the close attention to the nuances of language. His books include *Field Guide* (1973), *Praise* (1979), *Human Wishes* (1989), and *Sun Under Wood: New Poems* (1996). He has collected his essays on poetry in *Twentieth Century Pleasures* (1984). He has also edited several collections, including *Into the Garden: A Wedding Anthology: Poetry and Prose on Love and Marriage* (1993) and *Poet's Choice: Poems for Everyday*

Life (1998). He was named Poet Laureate of the Library of Congress in 1995.

Sources

Gardner, Thomas. *Regions of Unlikeness: Explaining Contemporary Poetry.* Lincoln: University of Nebraska Press, 1999.

Hawkes, John (Clendennin Burne, Jr.)
(1925–1998) novelist

John Hawkes was born in Stamford, Connecticut, but spent his early years in Alaska. His service in World War II as an ambulance driver, like his period in Alaska, contributed to his evocation of bleak and barren environments. He has been known as an experimental novelist who presents a rather entropic view of the world. His novels include *The Cannibal* (1949), *Second Skin* (1964), *The Blood Oranges* (1971)—perhaps his best, most well known work because it best represents his interest in subversive SURREALISTIC narratives, in this case an account of an American couple in Greece who destroy a visiting couple—*Sleep and the Traveler* (1974), *The Passion Artist* (1979), *Adventures in the Alaskan Skin Trade* (1985), *Sweet William: A Memoir of Old Horse* (1993), *The Frog* (1996), *Whistlejacket* (1997), and *An Irish Eye* (1997). *Lunar Landscapes: Stories and Short Novels 1949–1963* appeared in 1969 and *The Universal Fears*, a collection of short stories, in 1978. A *John Hawkes Reader* was published in 1984. He taught writing at Harvard and Brown University and is well regarded among his peers writing American fiction.

Sources

Trachtenberg, Stanley, ed. *Critical Essays on John Hawkes.* Boston: G. K. Hall, 1991.

Hayden, Robert Earl (1913–1980) poet

Hayden had a traumatic childhood in a Detroit ghetto. Beaten by bickering parents and ostracized because of his sensitive, bookish nature, the poet overcame these early obstacles, graduating from Wayne State University in Detroit and working for the FEDERAL WRITERS' PROJECT during the DEPRESSION. His work provided him with a background in history that informs much of his poetry. His first collection, *Heart-Shape in the Dust,* appeared in 1940, and was heavily influenced by Langston HUGHES, Countee CULLEN, and other HARLEM RENAISSANCE figures. The following year Hayden enrolled in the master's program at the University of Michigan, where he studied with W. H. AUDEN. Hayden then taught at the University of Michigan and at Fisk. His mature poetry begins with the publication of *The Lion and the Archer* (1948) and continues with *Figures of Times: Poems* (1955), *A Ballad of Remembrance* (1962), and *Selected Poems* (1966). His *Collected Poems* appeared in 1985. Hayden has been praised for his technical virtuosity and his handing of poetic form. His subject matter has varied from slavery, the slave trade, and the VIETNAM WAR to poems about art and the aesthetic sensibility. Perhaps his most distinctive contribution to modern poetry is his historical consciousness, which seems to have been sparked by Stephen Vincent BENÉT's belief that an African-American writer needed to write the definitive "black epic." "The Ballad of Nat Turner," perhaps his best-known work, represents his effort to come to terms with his African-American heritage—in this case, in a sensitive re-creation of the black man who led the most important slave revolt in U.S. history.

Sources

Williams, Pontheolla. *Robert Hayden: A Critical Analysis of His Poetry.* Urbana: University of Illinois Press, 1987.

Heat-Moon, William Least (William Trogdon)
(1939–) nonfiction writer

Educated at the University of Missouri, William Trogdon adopted his Native American name and took a leave of absence from teaching at Stephens College to tour the country in a recreational vehicle. The result was celebrated best-selling travel book *Blue Highways* (1983), which has been compared to STEINBECK's *Travels with Charley* and Jack KEROUAC's *ON THE ROAD*, because of its picaresque and confessional tone. He has also published *PrairyErth: A Deep Map* (1991) and *River-Horse: Across America By Boat* (1999).

Sources

"William Least Heat-Moon." Available on-line. URL: http://www.heat-moon.com/. Downloaded May 30, 2001.

Hecht, Anthony Evan (1923–) poet, critic

Born in New York City, Hecht has been praised for the fine craftsmanship and eloquent melding of autobiography and philosophy, exemplified in *The Hard Hours* (1967), which won a Pulitzer Prize. Hecht published his *Collected Earlier Poems* in 1989, *The Presumptions of Death* in 1995, and *Flight Among the Tombs: Poems* in 1996. His writing about poetry is collected in *Obbligati* (1986). *The Hidden Law: The Poetry of W. H. Auden* appeared in 1993, *On the Laws of Poetic Art* in 1995.

Sources

German, Norman. *Anthony Hecht.* New York: Peter Lang, 1989.
Lea, Sydney, ed. *The Burdens of Formality: Essays on the Poetry of Anthony Hecht.* Athens: University of Georgia Press, 1989.

Hecht, Ben (1893–1964) journalist, playwright, screenwriter, autobiographer

Hecht was the son of Russian immigrants. He was born in New York City, but his family soon moved to Racine, Wis-consin. Although he had musical talent, Hecht chose to tour with the circus, working as an acrobat during summer vacations. At 16 he ran away from home, got a job in Chicago managing a theater, and by 1910 began working at the *Chicago Journal.* Four years later, he switched to the *Chicago News,* where he wrote daily columns later collected in a book, *1001 Afternoons in Chicago.*

In 1923 he began his own newspaper, which reflected his brash, entrepreneurial personality. He published his first novel, *Erik Dorn,* in 1921. It was based on his experiences as a newspaper correspondent in Berlin, and it won him considerable praise. But Hecht made his greatest mark as a playwright. *The Front Page* (1928), written with Charles MacArthur, is based on Hecht's career in newspapers. In Hollywood, Hecht wrote several classic screenplays, including *Scarface* (1933), *Nothing Sacred* (1937), *Wuthering Heights* (1939), and *Spellbound* (1944), often collaborating with Charles MacArthur and other writers.

Hecht was a master of swift, overlapping dialogue in Hollywood's screwball comedies, but he was equally talented as a writer of fast-paced drama.

Hecht also wrote one of the classics of American autobiography, *A Child of the Century* (1964).

Sources

Fetherling, Doug. *The Five Lives of Ben Hecht.* Toronto: Lester & Orpen, 1977.
MacAdams, William. *Ben Hecht: The Man Behind the Legend.* New York: Scribner, 1990.

Heinlein, Robert Anson (1907–1988) novelist

Robert A. Heinlein is one of the most important science fiction writers of the century. His works include *Stranger in a Strange Land* (1961), a novel that often is considered his most enduring work. Its hero is a human being raised by Martians.

Heinlein was born in Missouri and educated at Annapolis and the University of California, Los Angeles. He wrote his first story in 1939. His work dealt with many themes—especially different forms of totalitarianism—that would pervade post–World War II science fiction. He is known for the boldness of his conceptions and the sometimes prophetic quality of his work. An early novel, *Destination Moon* (1950), was made into a motion picture, for which Heinlein served as a technical adviser. In 1979 a new edition of the novel was published along with Heinlein's account of working on the movie. In 1990 a new version of *Stranger in a Strange Land* appeared with 60,000 words cut from the first edition.

Sources

Olander, Joseph D. and Martin Harry Greenberg, ed. *Robert A. Heinlein.* New York: Taplinger, 1978.
Stover, Leon. *Robert A. Heinlein.* Boston: Twayne, 1987.

Heller, Joseph (1923–1999) *novelist*

A native of Brooklyn, New York, Heller was the son of Russian-Jewish parents. After graduating from high school he served with the U.S. Air Force, flying 60 missions as a B-25 bombardier. He drew on this experience in his classic novel, CATCH-22 (1961). But it took Heller several years to master his style. He studied English at the University of Southern California, New York University, Columbia University, and Oxford University as a Fulbright scholar. During the 1950s he worked for TIME and *McCall's* and wrote stories for *Esquire*, ATLANTIC MONTHLY, and other magazines.

When *Catch-22* was first published in the United States, it was not hailed as a great novel. Indeed, many of the reviews were negative. Not until English critics began touting its merits did Heller's fiction receive a respectful, then an enthusiastic U.S. response. The novel was made into a motion picture in 1970.

Often associated with writers of black humor, Heller wrote several other novels to mixed reviews: *Something Happened* (1974), *Good as Gold* (1979), *God Knows* (1984), *Picture This* (1988), and the sequel to *Catch 22, Closing Time* (1994). *Conversations with Joseph Heller* appeared in 1993. His last novel, *Portrait of the Artist as an Old Man* (2000), was published posthumously.

Sources

Craig, David M. *Tilting at Mortality: Narrative Strategies in Joseph Heller's Fiction.* Detroit: Wayne State University Press, 1997.

Potts, Stephen W. *From Here to Absurdity: The Moral Battlefields of Joseph Heller.* San Bernadino, Calif.: Borgo Press, 1995.

Hellman, Lillian Florence (1905–1984) *playwright, screenwriter, autobiographer*

Lillian Hellman grew up in New Orleans and New York City. Her father, a shoe salesman, traveled a good deal between the North and South, so Hellman was educated half the year in one city and half in the other. This bifurcated existence is reflected in her work, which is set in both parts of the country, and in her memoirs, especially *An Unfinished Woman* (1969) and *Pentimento* (1973). Hellman briefly attended New York University and decided she wanted to be a writer, but she could not find a proper form for her writing. She was encouraged by her husband, Arthur Kober, a successful NEW YORKER magazine writer whom she married in 1925. Kober went to Hollywood, where Hellman began to read play scripts for a movie studio. There she also met her lifelong love, Dashiell HAMMETT, who encouraged her to write for the theater. Her first play, *The Children's Hour* (1934), was a great success and something of a scandal since it dealt with two schoolteachers who were accused of being lesbians.

The success of *The Children's Hour* led to an offer from Hollywood producer Samuel Goldwyn to write screenplays.

Hellman promptly turned her play into *These Three* (1936), a sensitive film that changed the lesbian theme into a love triangle involving the two teachers and a handsome young man. Hellman's screenwriting career prospered, especially with her adaptation of Sidney Kingsley's play *Dead End* (1937).

Hellman solidified her reputation as one of the best playwrights of her generation with another Broadway hit, *The Little Foxes* (1939), an excoriating account of the South she had known in her youth. A product of the DEPRESSION, this play exposed the ruthlessness of capitalists, some of whom were based on members of Hellman's own family. A sequel, *Another Part of the Forest* (1948), is as good, if not better, than *The Little Foxes.* Although Hellman was a Stalinist, she also gained a great reputation as an anti-fascist with her play *Watch on the Rhine* (1941), the story of Kurt Müller, an anti-fascist refugee seeking support in Washington, D.C., which was made into a film in 1943.

Hellman's later plays, especially *The Autumn Garden* (1951) and *Toys in the Attic* (1960), eschew the melodrama of her earlier work. Instead of conflict between the exploiters and the exploited, the plays probe human character and family relationships with more subtlety and ambiguity.

Hellman had a second career when she began to publish her memoirs in the 1960s and 1970s, recounting her life in the South and in New York City, her relationship with Dashiell Hammett, her politics, employment in Hollywood, her life in the theater, and the other important figures in her life. She was heralded as a great survivor of the 1930s and of the blacklist, which had ended her career in Hollywood. She had refused to testify before the House Committee on Un-American Activities, saying she could not inform on her friends, and as a result was both hailed for her courage and condemned for her continuing refusal to speak out against Communist subversion of American institutions. Her story became a part of the COLD WAR that often divided writers into different political camps.

With the publication of *Scoundrel Time* (1976), her defense of her political activities, she provoked massive attacks on her credibility. Her earlier memoirs *An Unfinished Woman* and *Pentimento* were scrutinized for their factual accuracy and were found wanting by a number of commentators. Yet the memoirs remain as vivid narratives and evocations of her period, and her plays have a secure place in the American repertory.

Sources

Griffin, Alice and Geraldine Thorsten. *Understanding Lillian Hellman.* Columbia: University of South Carolina Press, 1999.

Rollyson, Carl. *Lillian Hellman: Her Legend and Her Legacy.* New York: St. Martin's Press, 1988.

Wright, William. *Lillian Hellman: The Image, The Woman.* New York: Simon and Schuster, 1986.

Helprin, Mark (1947–) novelist

Helprin is from Ossining, New York. He was educated at Harvard and served in the Israeli armed forces. His first book, *Ellis Island and Other Stories,* demonstrates his stylish integration of realism and fantasy. His novel, *Winter's Tale* (1983), about New York City and its efforts to combat crime and poverty, brought him critical acclaim. Another story collection, *A Dove of the East,* appeared in 1985, and his first novel, *Refiner's Fire,* appeared in 1977. *A Soldier in the Great War* (1991) is considered his most ambitious work. It is told in flashbacks by an Italian officer who fought on the Austria-Italy front in WORLD WAR I. Now an old man, he provides a young boy with reminiscences of astonishing events during a walk from Rome to a small mountain village. Helprin was praised for both the authenticity of his historical novel and for the vividness of his descriptions and dialogue. He also has published *Memoir From Antproof Case: A Novel* (1995) and *A City In Winter* (1996).

Sources

Linville, James. "Interview with Mark Helprin." *Paris Review* 35 (Spring 1993): 160–199.

Morgan, Keith. "A Mark Helprin Bibliography." Available on-line. URL: http://www.lib.ncsu.edu/staff/kamorgan/helprin-bib.html. Updated November 19, 2000.

Hemingway, Ernest Miller (1899–1961) novelist, short story writer, journalist

Ernest Hemingway was born and grew up in Oak Park, Illinois, the son of a physician and a mother who was a Christian Scientist. Educated in public schools, he first began writing for a student newspaper. In 1918 he gained his first job in journalism at the Kansas City *Star,* but that same year he joined the ambulance corps in Italy. A leg wound put him in a hospital in Milan, where he fell in love with an American nurse. This WORLD WAR I experience would become the subject of his romantic novel, *A FAREWELL TO ARMS,* which featured his deft handling of dialogue and his simple but elegant description of landscapes that evoked mood and theme.

Hemingway's reputation was established with *In Our Time* (1924) and *The Sun Also Rises* (1926). The former is an intricately constructed series of short stories featuring the education of a young man, NICK ADAMS, who learns the facts of life and death in scenes of brilliant understatement and vivid imagery. The latter is a novel about the "LOST GENERATION," a term Gertrude STEIN coined for those Americans in Europe who had become disenchanted with Western values and were seeking in the arts a way to find new meaning in existence. Hemingway was among the writers who frequented Paris cafes and wrote about rootless characters in settings far removed from their American backgrounds. Jake Barnes, the main character of *The Sun Also Rises,* struggles with impotence caused by a war wound. He is in love with Brett Ashley but finds little solace in her company. His mood reflects the bleak, weary aftermath of a war that resolved neither the political nor the social problems of Europe or America.

Although *A Farewell to Arms* is nearly as grim, its romantic dialogue inspired a generation to try to write and act like Hemingway's characters—which meant leaving home and seeking their fortune and happiness on the European continent. Unlike *The Sun Also Rises,* a slight sentimentality and self-pity creeps into Hemingway's second major novel. This tendency toward self-indulgence would mar later novels such as *To Have and Have Not* (1937) and *For Whom the Bell Tolls* (1940), although the audience for Hemingway's work continued to grow.

Indeed, Hemingway was one of the most famous authors of his time. He burnished his own persona as adventurer and sportsman in articles and books on hunting, bullfighting, and fishing. *Death in the Afternoon* (1932) and The *Green Hills of Africa* (1935) became models of the confessional memoir that later such writers as Norman MAILER and Truman CAPOTE would imitate. But later novels such as *Across the River and into the Trees* (1950) revealed a significant diminution of Hemingway's literary powers, as he relied too directly on his own personal experience and settled old scores with ex-wives, including Martha GELLHORN.

Hemingway recovered something of his old form with the long short story, *The Old Man and the Sea* (1952), a somewhat didactic work that nevertheless portrayed the author's sensitive feeling for nature in a contest between man and the elements. This work seems to have prompted the decision to award Hemingway the 1954 Nobel Prize in literature.

Hemingway's greatest contribution to American literature may well be his short stories, several of which, including "The Killers," "Indian Camp," and "Big Two-Hearted River," are included in many anthologies. He brought to the short story a stoic sense of human suffering and a controlled prose that stripped language of sentimentality and verbosity. Much of Hemingway's short fiction has to be read "between the lines": that is, his imagery and simple metaphors evoke but do not articulate overwhelming feeling. To some extent, this style arose out of Hemingway's masculine sensibility, which required males to strictly control their emotions in what he called "grace under pressure."

It became clear only after Hemingway's death and the publication of several biographies that he was at work on an epic series of novels, a group of at least three works that would trace the development of the post–World War II world. These works, which were edited and published after Hemingway's death, have been heavily criticized because they do not reflect the author's final judgments on the texts. Yet a reading of the posthumously published books, *Islands in the Stream* (1970), *The Garden of Eden* (1986), and *True at First Light* (1999), reveals Hemingway's renewed effort to confront the nature of war and of the sexual relationships between men and women.

Among his papers when he committed suicide in 1961—after a prolonged period of depression and psychiatric treatment—Hemingway left a memoir of Paris in the 1920s, published in 1964 as *A Moveable Feast*. It contains portraits of such friends as F. Scott FITZGERALD, as well as an evocation of the mood of the period.

Hemingway's stories have been published in *Three Stories and Ten Poems* (1923), *Men Without Women* (1927), *Winner Take Nothing* (1933), *The Fifth Column* (a play) *and the First Forty-nine Stories* (1938), *The Snows of Kilimanjaro and Other Stories* (1961), and *The Nick Adams Stories* (1972).

Hemingway's journalism is collected in *Byline: Ernest Hemingway, Selected Articles and Dispatches of Four Decades* (1967) and in *Dateline, Toronto: The Complete "Toronto Star" Dispatches, 1920–1924* (1985). *Ernest Hemingway: Selected Letters 1917–1961* was published in 1981.

Sources
Benson, Jackson, ed. *New Critical Approaches to the Short Stories of Ernest Hemingway*. Durham, N.C.: Duke University Press, 1990.

Donaldson, Scott, ed. *The Cambridge Companion to Hemingway*. Cambridge: Cambridge University Press, 1996.

Mellow, James R. *Hemingway: A Life Without Consequences*. Boston: Houghton Mifflin, 1992.

Meyers, Jeffrey. *Hemingway: A Biography*. New York: Harper & Row, 1985.

Wagner-Martin, Linda, ed. *Ernest Hemingway: Seven Decades of Criticism*. East Lansing: Michigan State University Press, 1998.

Henley, Beth Becker (1952–) *playwright*

Raised in Jackson, Mississippi, Henley was introduced to the theater by her mother, who was active in amateur productions. Henley studied drama at southern Methodist University. There she wrote her first and most successful play, *Crimes of the Heart* (1978), a gothic but humorous depiction of three zany sisters in a small southern town, which won a Pulitzer Prize. Henley also wrote the screenplay for the 1986 film adaptation. Her other plays include *Am I Blue* (1982), *The Wake of Jamey Foster* (1983), *The Miss Firecracker Contest* (1985), *The Lucky Spot* (1987), *Abundance* (1991), and *The Debutante Ball* (1991). Henley favors eccentric characters, many of them southern or from southern California, and her work has been praised for its intriguing blend of humor and melodrama.

Sources
Schlueter, June, ed. *Modern American Drama: The Female Canon*. Rutherford, N.J.: Fairleigh Dickinson University Press, 1990.

Herbst, Josephine (1897–1969) *novelist*

Born and raised in Iowa, Herbst was educated at the University of California, Berkeley. She then headed for the writer's life in New York City. By the 1920s she was in Paris, befriending the important American writers there. She has often been associated with PROLETARIAN LITERATURE because her fiction concentrates on the social, economic, and political issues that have an impact on the laboring poor. With her husband, John Herrman, Herbst wrote a good deal of journalism. Herbst is best known for her trilogy on the Trexler family: *Pity Is Not Enough* (1933), *The Executioner Waits* (1934), and *Rope of Gold* (1939). This saga follows the family from the late 19th century to the 1930s, exploring their troubles after they lose their money, grapple with the fast-changing period of the 1920s, and then confront bleak economic times during the GREAT DEPRESSION. Her broad canvas of American life from the Civil War to the 1930s has been compared to DOS PASSOS's U.S.A. TRILOGY. Her later novels are considered less successful. *The Starched Blue Sky of Spain* is an impressive memoir of her days in Spain during the SPANISH CIVIL WAR.

Sources
Langer, Elinor. *Josephine Herbst*. Boston: Northeastern University Press, 1994.

Hergesheimer, Joseph (1880–1954) *novelist*

Born in Philadelphia, Hergesheimer was a best-selling and well-respected novelist of his day. *Java Head* (1919) and *Linda Condon* (1919) are his best-known novels, the former a study of the New England past and of miscegenation, the latter a portrayal of an intense woman. His later books have been deemed more superficial because they forsake REALISM for romance. He favored exotic settings—the West Indies in *The Bright Shawl* (1922), Cuba in *Balisand* (1924), Mexico in *Tampico* (1926). *The Happy End* (1919) is a collection of short stories. His essays on the Civil War are collected in *Swords and Roses* (1929). *From an Old House* (1925) is an essay-memoir.

Sources
Gimmestad, Victor E. *Joseph Hergesheimer*. Boston: Twayne, 1984.

Herr, Michael (1940–) *journalist, novelist*

Herr reported on the war in Vietnam for *Esquire* magazine and then produced *Dispatches* (1977), a book on the conflict, which made his reputation. It is considered one of the best memoirs of the period: Herr is able to relate his personal story to what happened to a whole generation of men who went to fight an unpopular war. Herr also wrote the voice-over narration for Francis Ford Coppola's

Apocalypse Now (1979), one of the major films about Vietnam. Herr has also published a novel, *Walter Winchell* (1990), about the controversial columnist who in his heyday (the 1930s and 1940s) had the power to make and break reputations.

Sources

Beidler, Philip D. *American Literature and the Experience of Vietnam.* Athens: University of Georgia Press, 1982.

Hersey, John Richard (1914–1993) *journalist, novelist*

John Hersey was born while his American missionary parents were in China. He gained his first jobs as a reporter with TIME and the NEW YORKER. As a war correspondent he wrote *Men on Bataan* (1942), a nonfiction account of the U.S. invasion of that island. His second book, *Into the Valley* (1943), was a deft report of combat on Guadalcanal Island and may have influenced war novels such as Norman MAILER's THE NAKED AND THE DEAD. *A Bell for Adano* (1944), which received a Pulitzer Prize, explored the American occupation of Italy with great sensitivity. But it was *Hiroshima* (1946), Hersey's account of the nuclear bombing of Japan, that brought him fame. For many years, this book was required reading in high schools and colleges. An equally ambitious work was Hersey's novel *The Wall* (1950), an account of the uprising in the Warsaw ghetto. His later books received less attention and critical acclaim, but *The Child Buyer* (1960) and *The Algiers Motel Incident* (1968)—set during Detroit's race riots in 1967—demonstrated that he could still write provocative fiction and nonfiction. He published *Fling and Other Stories* in 1990 and a novel, *Antonietta,* in 1991. He lived for many years in Key West. In 1994 *Key West Tales* was published posthumously.

Sources

Huse, Nancy L. *The Survival Tales of John Hersey.* New York: Whitston, 1983.
Sanders, David. *John Hersey Revisited.* Boston: Twayne, 1991.

Hicks, Granville (1901–1982) *critic*

Hicks was born in New Hampshire and educated at Harvard. He is best known for his literary history, *The Great Tradition* (1933), a Marxist interpretation of American literature. This book grew out of his period as editor of the NEW MASSES. He resigned from the Communist Party in 1939, a decision he explains in his memoir *Where We Came Out* (1954). For many years he was an influential reviewer for the SATURDAY REVIEW. He collected his essays in *Literary Horizons* (1970) and *The New Masses* (1974). He published his autobiography, *Part of the Truth,* in 1965.

Sources

Levenson, Leah and Jerry Natterstad. *Granville Hicks: The Intellectual in Mass Society.* Philadelphia: Temple University Press, 1993.
Long, Terry L. *Granville Hicks.* Boston: Twayne, 1981.

Highsmith, Patricia (1921–1995) *novelist*

Born in Fort Worth, Texas, Highsmith was educated at Julia Richmond High School in New York City and studied English, Latin, and Greek at Columbia University. In her teens she wrote stories about deranged characters. Her first published novel, *Strangers on a Train* (1950), the suspenseful story of a psychopathic killer, was published under a pseudonym. It sold more than 1 million copies and was adapted to the screen by Alfred Hitchcock. Her second novel, *The Price of Salt* (1953), the story of two women who fall in love, begun before her first published novel, sold almost as well as *Strangers on a Train.* In many of her novels Highsmith explored disturbed minds and sexual deviants in what critics called "psychological thrillers." For all her popularity, Highsmith avoided the public eye. She lived quietly in isolated surroundings near Locarno on the Swiss-Italian border. Her other noteworthy fiction includes *The Talented Mr. Ripley* (1956). Made into a movie in 1999, it is, in Highsmith's own words, about a "small-time American crook who moves to Europe and kills his way to happiness." Ripley, her favorite character, inspired a series: *Ripley's Game* (1974), *The Boy Who Followed Ripley* (1980), and *Ripley Under Water* (1991). She completed *Small g: a Summer Idyll* (1995), her final novel, just weeks before she died of leukemia. Her only nonfiction book is *Plotting and Writing Suspense Fiction* (1966).

Sources

Harrison, Russell. *Patricia Highsmith.* New York: Twayne, 1997.
Summers, Claude, J. ed. *The Gay and Lesbian Literary Heritage.* New York: Holt, 1995.

Highwater, Jamake (1935–2001) *journalist, novelist, critic*

Part Blackfoot, part Cherokee, Highwater grew up in southern California. He attended North Hollywood High School, where he befriended another precocious student, Susan SONTAG. Highwater went on to study at the University of California, Berkeley, and the University of Chicago. He had a varied career as journalist, music and dance critic, novelist, and filmmaker. He collected traditional Native American tales in *Anpao: An American Indian Odyssey* (1977). His fiction for juveniles includes *The Ceremony of Innocence* (1985) and *I Wear the Morning Star* (1986). His criticism includes *Rock and Other Four Letter Words: Music of the Electric Generation* and *Dance: Rituals of Experience* (1978). Influenced by Joseph CAMPBELL, Highwater published *The Language of*

Vision: Meditations on Myth and Metaphor in 1994. An openly gay writer, he produced an important study, *The Mythology of Transgression: Homosexuality as Metaphor* (1997). He also published *Shadow Show: An Autobiographical Insinuation* in 1986.

Sources

Grimes, Ronald L. "To Hear the Eagles Cry: Contemporary Themes in Native American Spirituality." *The American Indian Quarterly* 20 (June 22, 1996): 433–451.

Hijuelos, Oscar (1952–) *novelist*

Hijuelos was born in New York City to Cuban parents and educated at New York's City College, where he studied writing with Susan SONTAG and Donald BARTHELME. His second novel, *The Mambo Kings Play Songs of Love* (1989), is the story of two brothers who move from Havana to New York in the 1950s in search of stardom. The novel won Hijuelos a Pulitzer Prize and was made into a successful film. His other work includes *Our House in the Last World* (1983), *The Fourteen Sisters of Emilio Montez O'Brien* (1993), *Mr. Ives' Christmas* (1995), and *Empress of the Splendid Season* (1999). Hijuelos has been described as a poet of the Latino/immigrant experience, for his characters sometimes feel lost away from their original homes' beauty and grace. His work is keenly balanced, in other words, between his characters' desires to assimilate and their stubborn pride in their heritage, which is part of their sense of independence.

Sources

Shirley, Paul. "Read Desi Arnaz in *The Mambo Kings Play Songs of Love.*" *Melus* 29 (September 1995): 69–78.

"Featured Author: Oscar Hijuelos." Available on-line. URL: http://www.nytimes.com/books/99/02/01/specials/hijuelos.html. Downloaded July 2001.

Hillerman, Tony (1925–) *novelist*

Born in Sacred Heart, Oklahoma, Hillerman was educated in a Catholic boarding school primarily for American-Indian girls that also accepted non-Indian students from neighboring farms. After brief periods at college and in the U.S. Army, Hillerman returned to the Southwest and to his interest in Navajo life. He graduated from the University of Oklahoma with a degree in journalism in 1948. After various jobs in journalism he began writing mystery fiction in the 1960s, demonstrating an anthropologist's interest in Indian customs and ceremonies. His novels feature Joe Leaphorn and Jim Chee, tribal policeman, both of whom have degrees in anthropology.

Hillerman has won several awards for his writing, including the Edgar Allan Poe Award and the Grand Master Award from the Mystery Writers of America, and the Silver Spur Award from the Center for the American Indian. He has also been honored by the Navajo Tribe with a "Special Friend" award.

Hillerman's most important novels include *The Blessing* (1970), the first in his series on Joe Leaphorn; *Dancehall of the Dead* (1973), *People of Darkness* (1980), *The Dark Wind* (1982), and *The Ghostway* (1984). Later novels such as *The Boy Who Made Dragonfly* (a children's novel) and *Finding Moon* (1995) continue to show his interest in Indian culture but do not include his policemen heroes.

Sources

Erisman, Fred. *Tony Hillerman.* Boise, Idaho: Boise State University Western Writers Series, 1989.

Greenberg, Martin, ed. *The Tony Hillerman Companion: A Comprehensive Guide to His Life and Work.* New York: HarperCollins, 1994.

Himes, Chester Bomar (1909–1984) *novelist*

Himes was born in Jefferson City, Mississippi. His family moved to Cleveland, Ohio, and broke up when he was in his teens. He suffered a bad back injury that left him feeling isolated and alienated for many years. An angry young African-American man, he explored the underworld of Columbus, Ohio, even as he enrolled as a student at Ohio State. Convicted of armed robbery in 1928, he was sent to prison at age 19. In prison he began writing short stories that reflected the hazards of African-American life. Paroled in 1936, Himes tried to make a living as a writer. His most successful work drew on his own experience and included the novels *If He Hollers, Let Him Go* (1945), *Lonely Crusade* (1947), *The Third Generation* (1947), *Cast the First Stone* (1952), and *The Primitive* (1955). These novels explored subjects such as racism in a California defense plant during World War II; a black laborer who faces discrimination in unions and the Communist party; the plights of blacks in prison; and the story of a black author and his white mistress (based on Himes's own experience).

During the mid-1950s Himes, like Richard WRIGHT, went to France to find a new readership and a more hospitable environment in which to write. He turned to detective fiction to support himself. He attracted a wide mainstream readership with mystery novels he set in Harlem: *For Love of Imabelle* (1957), *The Real Cool Killers* (1959), *The Crazy Kill* (1959), *The Big Gold Dream* (1960), *All Shot Up* (1960), *Cotton Comes to Harlem* (1965), *The Heat's On* (1966), and *Blind Man with a Pistol* (1969). Himes's black detectives routinely use violence in a violent world that is inimical to their existence. Whatever genre of fiction he chose, however, Himes nearly always returned to the difficulties of African-American males vying for a place in society. Himes's *Selected Writings* appeared in 1973, and two volumes of autobiography, *The Quality of Hurt* and *My Life of Absurdity*, in 1972 and 1976.

Sources

Fabre, Michel and Robert Skinner, eds. *Conversations with Chester Himes*. Jackson: University Press of Mississippi, 1995.

Margolies, Edward and Michel Fabre. *The Several Lives of Chester Himes*. Jackson: University Press of Mississippi, 1997.

Sallis, James. *Chester Himes: A Life*. New York: Walker, 2001.

Hinton, Susan Eloise (1948–) *novelist*

Born in Tulsa, S. E. Hinton was educated at the University of Tulsa and continues to live in the city. She writes mainly about and for teens. *The Outsiders* (1967), a story about gang violence narrated by a 14-year-old boy, was filmed in 1983. Her other novels about alienated teens have also been successful. *That Was Then, This Is Now* (1971) was filmed in 1985, *Rumble Fish* (1975) in 1983, and *Tex* (1979) in 1982. More recently she has written *Taming the Star Runner* (1988), *Big David, Little David* (1995), and *Puppy Sister* (1995).

Sources

Daly, Jay. *Presenting S. E. Hinton*. Boston: Twayne, 1987.

Hoagland, Edward (1932–) *novelist, short story writer, travel writer*

Hoagland was born in New York City and educated at Harvard. His early novels are about city life, boxing, and the circus; they include *Cat Man* (1956), *The Circle Home* (1960), and *The Peacock's Tail* (1965). He is better known for travel writing, such as *Notes from the Century Before* (1969), *The Courage of Turtles* (1971), *Walking the Dead Diamond River* (1972), *Red Wolves and Black Bears* (1976), and *A Journey to the Sudan* (1979). Complementing his concern for the environment are ecological studies, *The Tugman's Passage* (1982) and *Balancing Acts* (1992). *Seven Rivers West* (1986), a historical novel set on the prairies and in the Rocky Mountains, combines Hoagland's interests in nature and the human character. *City Tales* (1986) is set in New York City. *Tigers and Ice: Reflections on Nature and Life* appeared in 1999.

Sources

Baker, John F. "Edward Hoagland: Frank Memoir by a Hopeful Traveler," *Publishers Weekly*, March 19, 2001. Available on-line. URL: http://www.publishersweekly.com/articles/2001 0319_94905.asp. Downloaded June 2, 2001.

Mudge, Alden. "Edward Hoagland: Relishing a second chance for sight—and speech," Book Page. Available on-line. URL: http://www.bookpage.com/0102bp/edward_hoagland.html. Downloaded June 2, 2001.

Nature Writing. "Edward Hoagland." Nature Writing for Readers and Writers. Available on-line. URL: http://www.naturewriting.com/edhoag.htm. Downloaded June 2, 2001.

Hispanic-American literature

Hispanic or Latino/Latina literature incorporates the writing of Chicanos, or Mexican Americans; Puerto Rican Americans; Cuban Americans; and other Americans whose origins are in Central or South America. Hispanic-American literature also incorporates writing in English and Spanish. This body of work can trace its roots to the early nineteenth century, although recognition of Hispanic-American literature came only with the development of ethnic and multicultural studies beginning in the late 1960s and early 1970s.

The predominant theme in Hispanic-American literature has been the history, folklore, traditions, and family relationships of a minority group within the majority Anglo culture. José Antonio Villareal, the first significant Chicano novelist, for example, explores in *Pocho* (1959) the fate of a Chicano boy who is torn between the values of his parents and the Anglo culture he finds enticing. Similarly, Pedro Juan Soto's Puerto Rican American novel, *Spiks* (1956), tells the story of poor immigrants struggling against the oppression and alienation of New York City.

Cuban-American fiction, however, has developed differently, with much of it focused in the 1960s on political issues, particularly on hostile criticism of Fidel Castro's communist regime in Cuba. These works, such as André Rivera Collado's *Enterrado Vivo* (Buried Alive, 1960), were written in Spanish and idealized pre-revolutionary Cuba. But by the 1970s Cuban-American writers had joined the mainstream of Hispanic-American literature, producing novels such as Celedonio González's *Los Primos* (1971), which centers on Cuban life in this country as well as on the experience of exile from Cuba.

Cuban-American novelist Oscar HIJUELOS became a dynamic force in moving Hispanic-American literature directly into the mainstream of American literature. His work transcends Hispanic-American concerns with exile and alienation in favor of a vibrant celebration of both Hispanic-American heritage and the New World Latinos and Latinas have established in the United States. His novel *The Mambo Kings Play Songs of Love* won the 1990 Pulitzer Prize for fiction and was adapted for film in 1992.

The work of Chicano novelist Rudolfo ANAYA—especially *Bless Me Última* (1972)—reflects the growing sophistication of Hispanic-American literature, and the interest of a new generation of writers in experimenting with different styles, such as magical realism, which blends the myths, folklore, and history of Hispanic-American families and communities. Similarly, Sandra CISNEROS has boldly used shifting points of view, montage techniques, and the other tools of literary MODERNISM to craft complex views of Chicanos and Puerto Ricans in novels such as *The House on Mango Street*. Like Cisneros, the Puerto Rican novelist Nicholasa Mohr has shifted from stories of disaffection with American life to affirm the new emerging identity of Hispanics in *Felita* (1981) and *Rituals of Survival: A Woman's Portfolio* (1985).

Indeed, Cisneros and Mohr represent an explosion of writing by Hispanic-American women. Cherríe MORAGA, a poet and playwright has introduced feminist themes and lesbian subject matter. Her work builds on the example of her teacher, Maria Irene Fornes, a pioneering playwright and director whose work since the early 1960s has encompassed women's issues and Cuba (before and after the revolution) but also a range of themes that go well beyond exclusively ethnic concerns.

Richard Rodriguez's autobiography, *Hunger of Memory*, represents a new generation of Hispanic-American writers who continue to explore the immigrant experience, the problems of assimilation, as well as their desire to shape the American environment out of which they have emerged keenly self-conscious as writers. Rodriguez asks painful questions about the Hispanic-American's place in American life even as he embraces that place as inevitable and appropriate. His controversial work is indicative of a genre of literature that is still very much in the process of formation and debate.

Other important Hispanic-American novelists and short story writers include Gary SOTO, Aristeo Brito, Denise Chavez, Cristina Garcia, Julia Alvarez, Virgil Suarez, and Gina Vald. Soto and Vald are also poets and are frequently represented in anthologies along with Ricardo Sanchez, Luis Omar Salinas, Luis Rodriguez, Demetria Martinez, and Gloria Vando. Representative works of the Hispanic-American theater include Luis Valdez's *Las Dos Caras del Patroneito* (1965) and *Los Vendidos* (1967); Cherríe Moraga's *Giving Up the Ghost* (1986, 1994); and Delores Prida's *Beautiful Senoritas* (1994). Important autobiographers include Floyd Salas, Victor Villasenor, and Sandra Cisneros.

Sources

Christie, John D. *Latino Fiction and the Modernist Imagination: Literature of the Borderlands.* New York: Garland, 1998.

Gish, Robert Franklin. *Beyond Bounds: Cross-Cultural Essays on Anglo, American Indian, and Chicano Literature.* Albuquerque: University of New Mexico Press, 1996.

Horno-Delgado, Anunción, et. al. Ed. *Breaking Boundaries: Latina Writings and Critical Readings.* Amherst: University of Massachusetts Press, 1989.

Shirley, Carl, and Paula W. Shirley. *Understanding Chicano Literature.* Columbia: University of South Carolina Press, 1988.

Hollander, John (1929–) *poet, critic*

Born into a Jewish family in New York City, Hollander was educated at the Bronx High School of Science and Columbia University. His teachers included Lionel TRILLING. He began to publish his poetry in 1954. After a series of academic appointments, he settled in 1986 in New Haven, where he is A. Bartlett Giametti Professor of English at Yale. Hollander credits W. H. AUDEN as the major influence on his first collection of poetry, *A Cracking of Thorns* (1958), published in the YALE SERIES OF YOUNGER POETS, edited that year by Auden. Hollander was quickly recognized as a poet who employs the most sophisticated techniques, elaborate rhyme schemes, unusual numbers of syllables, and intricate free verse—sometimes to the detriment of the poetry, which can seem opaque. His *Selected Poems* appeared in 1972 and 1993, *Harp Lake: Poems* in 1988, *Tesserae: & Other Poems* in 1993, and *Figurehead & Other Poems* in 1999. He has also published a formidable body of literary criticism, including *Visions and Resonance: Two Senses of Poetic Form* (1975), *Rhyme's Reason: A Guide to English Verse* (1981), *Melodius Guide: Fictive Pattern in Poetic Language* (1988), and *The Poetry of Everyday Life* (1998). With Lionel TRILLING, Harold Bloom, and others he edited *The Oxford Anthology of English Literature* (1973) and with Harold Bloom, *Poetics of Influence.*

Sources

Honig, Edwin. *The Poet's Other Voice.* Amherst: University of Massachusetts Press, 1985.

Holmes, John Clellon (1926–1988) *poet, autobiographer*

Holmes was born in Massachusetts and served in the navy during World War II. He began to publish poetry, collected much later in *The Bowling Green Poems* (1977). He is better known for his novel *Go* (1952), an early look at the BEATS as they congregated in New York City. Another novel, *The Horn* (1958), focuses on a black saxophonist in decline. Holmes wrote several memoirs about the Beat scene, including *Nothing More to Declare* (1967), *Gone in October* (1985), and *Representative Men* (1988). *Displaced Persons* (1987) is a record of his travels and *Passionate Opinions* (1988) is his commentary on cultural issues. His *Selected Essays* appeared in 1987.

Sources

Knight, Arthur and Kit Knight, eds. *Interior Geographies: An Interview with John Clellon Holmes.* Warren, Ohio: Literary Denim, 1981.

Horgan, Paul (1903–1995) *historian, biographer, novelist*

Born in Buffalo, New York, Horgan spent much of his life in New Mexico. In 1933 he won the Harper Novel Prize for *The Fault of Angels,* a novel about musicians. He won a Pulitzer Prize for his two-volume history, *Great River: The Rio Grande in North American History* (1954). He won a second Pulitzer Prize for *Lamy of Santa Fe* (1975), a biography of Father Jean-Baptiste Lamy. *Of America East & West* (1984) is a collection of essays. *Certain Climate: Essays in History, Arts, and Letters* appeared in 1988. Horgan also wrote a trilogy of novels about a young boy's progress to manhood. His "Richard" novels are *Things as They Are* (1964), *Everything to Live For* (1968), and *The Thin Mountain Air* (1977). *Centuries of Santa Fe* appeared in 1994.

Sources
Gish, Robert. *Nueva Granada: Paul Horgan and the Southwest.* College Station: Texas A & M Press, 1995.
———. *Paul Horgan.* Boston: Twayne, 1983.

Houston, James D. (1933–) *novelist*
Born in San Francisco, James D. Houston has taught creative writing at the University of California, Santa Cruz, since 1969. He is best known for *Continental Drift* (1978), a novel about a journalist's life in Houston, which was made into a movie. *A Native Son of the Golden West* (1971) centers on a California playboy in Hawaii. Houston's earlier novels were also well received, including *Between Battles* (1968) set during a military exercise and *Gig* (1969), the story of a jazz musician. *In the Ring of Fire: A Pacific Basin Journey* appeared in 1997 and *The Last Paradise* in 1998.

Sources
Raskin, Jonah. *James D. Houston.* Boise, Idaho: Boise State University, 1991.

Howard, Richard Joseph (1929–) *poet, critic, translator*
Born in Cleveland, Ohio, and educated at Columbia University and the Sorbonne, Richard Howard is an accomplished translator and poet. He has translated well over 200 titles in French, most notably authors such as Andre Gide and Roland Barthes. His poetry tends toward the erudite, although his more dramatic pieces bear the imprint of a saturation in Robert Browning. *Untitled Subjects* (1966), 15 dramatic monologues, won the Pulitzer Prize. His other collections include *Lining Up: Poems* (1984), *No Traveller: Poems* (1989), *Like Most Revelations: New Poems* (1994), *If I Dream I Have You, I Have You: Poems* (1997), and *Trappings: New Poems* (1999). In 1969 and 1980 he published *Alone With America: Essays on the Art of Poetry in the United States Since 1950.* He has taught generations of poets at Columbia University, the University of Houston, and at several other colleges and universities.

Howard, Sidney Coe (1891–1939) *playwright*
Born in California, Sidney Howard studied at George Pierce Baker's famous 47 Workshop at Harvard, which trained a generation of American playwrights and writers, including Eugene O'NEILL and Thomas WOLFE. After serving in World War I, Howard began writing plays, primarily adaptations

and verse dramas. His first great success, *They Knew What They Wanted* (1924), the story of a love-match by mail, won a Pulitzer Prize. His next important play, *The Silver Cord* (1926), an intense psychological portrayal of a domineering mother, confirmed his reputation as a leading playwright. His later plays include *Alien Corn* (1933), the story of a woman who suppresses her musical talent in her affair with a college president; *Dodsworth* (1934), an adaptation of Sinclair LEWIS's novel; and *Paths of Glory* (1935), an adaptation of Humphrey Cobb's novel.

Sources
Reuben, Paul P. "Chapter 8: American Drama—Sidney Coe Howard (1891–1939)." *PAL: Perspectives in American Literature—A Research and Reference Guide.* Available on-line. URL: http://www.csustan.edu/english/reuben/pal/chap8/howard.html. Downloaded June 2, 2001.
White, Sidney Howard. *Sidney Howard.* Boston: Twayne, 1977.

Howe, Irving (1920–1993) *critic, historian*
Best known for his collection of essays *Politics and the Novel* (1957) and his history of immigration *World of Our Fathers* (1976), Howe also edited *A Treasury of Yiddish Stories* (1955) and *A Treasure of Yiddish Poetry* (1969). One of the NEW YORK INTELLECTUALS clustered around the *PARTISAN REVIEW*, he initially was a member of the far Left, espousing Marxist ideology, but gradually moved away from Communist orthodoxy to adopt a principled socialism that opposed the tyranny of the Soviet Union and other Communist regimes. His two major studies of American writers are *Sherwood Anderson: A Critical Biography* (1951) and *William Faulkner: A Critical Study* (1953). With Lewis Coser he wrote *The American Communist Party: A Critical History* (1957). In 1982 he published *A Margin of Hope: An Intellectual Autobiography.* His essays are collected in *Decline of The New* (1970), *The Critical Point, on Literature and Culture* (1973), *Celebrations and Attacks: Thirty Years of Literary and Cultural Commentary* (1979), *The American Newness: Culture and Politics in the Age of Emerson* (1986), and *A Critic's Notebook* (1994).

Sources
Webster, Grant. *The Republic of Letters: A History of Postwar American Literary Opinion.* Baltimore: Johns Hopkins University Press, 1979.

Howes, Barbara (1914–) *poet*
Born in New York City, reared in Boston, and educated at Bennington College, Howes was mentored by the poet Genevieve TAGGARD. Howes's poetry has been praised for its precise use of form. Her collections include *The Undersea Farmer* (1948), *In the Cold Country* (1954), *Light and Dark*

(1959), *Looking Up at Leaves* (1966), *The Blue Garden* (1972), *A Private Signal* (1977), and *Moving* (1983). Her *Collected Poems 1945–1990* appeared in 1995. She collected her short stories in *The Road Commissioner* (1983).

Sources

"Barbara Howes Papers." Available on-line. URL: http://web-text.library.yale.edu/sgm.html/beinecke.howes.sgm.html.

"Howl" *Allen Ginsberg* (1956) *poem*

This poem is considered one of the quintessential works of the BEAT poets of the 1950s. The poem is dedicated to Carl Solomon, whom Ginsberg befriended when both of them were patients in a psychiatric hospital in 1949. The poem begins by suggesting that some of the "best minds" of Ginsberg's generation have been "destroyed by madness." Ginsberg is speaking of a generation of writers who took drugs and absorbed themselves in city culture—which meant listening to jazz, exploring "negro streets," and living in "cold-water flats." Like Ginsberg himself, these writers found no haven in universities and found the conventional middle-class culture of America stultifying and imprisoning. Like the poet William Blake, whom the poem invokes, these writers had visions of a more heavenly world, drifting from the East Coast to the West—as Ginsberg himself had done. These sensitive souls found no outlet in a culture Ginsburg describes as filled with lifeless poetry, the "iron regiment of fashion & nitroglycerine shrieks of the fairies/of advertising . . ." The poem is a lament, in other words, for all those writers who were trying to find an original way to express themselves and to jettison the slogans of Madison Avenue advertising.

The poem has much in common with the quest of the English romantic poets to find a new language that reflected the concrete reality of people's lives. The poem ends with Ginsberg's apostrophe to Carl Solomon, who, like William Wordsworth's connection with Samuel Taylor Coleridge, represents a fellow poetic soul.

Although much of the imagery of "Howl" is grim and despairing about the state of American life, it is also filled with Ginsberg's characteristic humor and whimsy. Ginsberg makes allusions to an American patriotism and optimism and translates these qualities into the iconoclasm of the Beat consciousness.

Sources

Ehrlich, J. W., ed. *Howl of the Censor.* Westport, Conn.: Greenwood Press, 1976.

Miles, Barry, ed. *Howl: Original Draft Facsimile, Transcript & Variant Versions, Fully Annotated by Author, with Contemporaneous Correspondence, Account of First Public Reading, Legal Skirmishes, Precursor Texts & Bibliography.* New York: Harper & Row, 1986.

Hudson Review (1948–) *periodical*

This literary quarterly is published in New York City and has featured the work of William Arrowsmith, Saul BELLOW, Kenneth Burke, T. S. ELIOT, Herbert GOLD, Marianne MOORE, W. D. SNODGRASS, Allen TATE, Eudora WELTY, and many other significant American writers. The journal also publishes book reviews and literary criticism.

Hughes, Langston (James Langston Hughes)
(1902–1967) *poet, novelist, essayist, playwright, autobiographer, children's book author, editor*

Langston Hughes grew up in Lawrence, Kansas, and demonstrated his literary ability very early. He drew inspiration from his family heritage, especially his maternal grandmother's first husband, who died as part of the group led by the radical abolitionist John Brown in the attack on Harpers Ferry. Hughes took little comfort from his immediate family, however, and later said that he wrote out of a sense of loneliness. He found company in the world of books.

A bright student, Hughes was already a published author when he enrolled at Columbia University. His landmark poem, "The Negro Speaks of Rivers," had been published in *Crisis,* edited by W. E. B. DU BOIS. This poem reflected Hughes's lifelong fascination with the origins of his race, and it heralded the advent of the HARLEM RENAISSANCE, which inspired African Americans with a desire to search out the origins of their creativity.

But in 1922 Hughes found it difficult to find employment. He took odd jobs and worked on a freighter on the west coast of Africa. After a period in Paris, Hughes returned to the United States in 1924. His work was clearly inspired by Walt Whitman and Carl SANDBURG, poets who emphasized that poetry should mimic the voice of the people and deal with their everyday lives. Hughes's lyrical verse often took the form of dramatic monologues, studded with simple yet evocative images and metaphors. "Life for me ain't been no crystal stair" is an example of Hughes taking a phrase that could well have been uttered by a working man or woman and transforming it into an elegant and eloquent evocation of not just an individual's but a people's experience.

Part of Hughes's success stemmed from his great ear for music, especially jazz, so that his poetry had an improvisational and spontaneous quality. His first book of poetry was entitled *The Weary Blues* (1926). Then Hughes resumed his schooling at Lincoln University in Pennsylvania. He was aided by a white patron, Mrs. Charlotte Mason, who also helped him publish his first novel, *Not Without Laughter* (1930), based in part on his own unhappy childhood in the Midwest. But Hughes chafed under Mason's restraining supervision and broke away from her to enter his most radical period. In 1932 Hughes traveled to the Soviet Union, and his poetry began to reflect his leftist political views. He also published a collection of short stories, *The Ways of White*

Folks (1934), which presented a grim assessment of the state of race relations.

In the mid-1930s Hughes turned to playwriting. *Mulatto* (1935), a drama about miscegenation and tensions between parents and children, was produced on Broadway. Other plays, *Little Ham* (1936) and *Emperor of Haiti* (1936), explored the same themes but did not attract mainstream audiences.

Hughes continued to write poetry, which became less political in the 1940s as he began to reflect on his own life in an autobiography, *The Big Sea* (1940). His feelings about racial injustice remained strong, however, in such collections of verse as *Jim Crow's Last Stand* (1943).

One of Hughes's major achievements in the 1940s was his series of columns (short stories) for a black newspaper, the CHICAGO DEFENDER. He developed a character named Jesse B. Semple, or "Simple," who commented on race and other issues of the day in a direct and concrete voice that remains fresh and timely. Hughes collected these columns in *Simple Speaks His Mind* (1950). *Simply Heavenly,* a musical based on the Simple stories, was produced in 1957.

Hughes's next major book of poetry, *Montage of a Dream Deferred* (1951), recaptured his feeling for jazz and for the plight of oppressed African Americans in a vibrant and intense style reminiscent of the Harlem Renaissance period. Like other radicals of the 1930s, Hughes was fiercely criticized for his politics. He was called before Senator Joseph McCarthy's congressional anti-Communist committee to testify about his politics. He denied ever having been a Communist, and said he regretted some of his radical verse. Hughes later wrote about his time in the Soviet Union in *I Wonder as I Wander* (1956). *Good Morning Revolution* (1973) collects much of his protest writing.

Hughes produced more than a dozen books for children. Among the most notable is *Popo and Fifina* (1932), a story set in Haiti.

Sources

Gates, Henry Louis, Jr. and K. A. Appiah, eds. *Langston Hughes: Critical Perspectives Past and Present.* New York: Amistad, 1993.
Rampersad, Arnold. *The Life of Langston Hughes: I, Too, Sing America, 1902–1941.* New York: Oxford University Press, 1986.
———. *The Life of Langston Hughes: I Dream a World, 1941–1967.* New York: Oxford University Press, 1988.

Humanism, the New

A literary and philosophical movement headed by Irving BABBITT and Paul Elmer MORE. The New Humanists emphasized rationality and were opposed to romanticism. They found their source of support in the ancient Greeks. These thinkers believed they were restoring the classical values of civilizations that had been obscured, if not destroyed, by too much emphasis on emotion and subjectivity. They influenced writers such as T. S. ELIOT who believed too much emphasis had been placed on the writer's personality.

Sources

Hoeveler, David J. *The New Humanism: A Critique of Modern America, 1900–1940.* Charlottesville: University Press of Virginia, 1977.
Samson, Leon. *The New Humanism.* New York, I. Washburn, 1930.

humor

The 1920s is the first great period of humorous writing in 20th-century American literature. The writers who assembled around the ALGONQUIN ROUND TABLE—especially Robert Benchley, S. J. PERELMAN, Ring LANDNER, Dorothy PARKER, George S. KAUFMAN, and Alexander WOOLLCOTT—brought a sardonic wit and engaging sense of fun. Their work was often published in the NEW YORKER, which also featured humorists like James THURBER and E. B. WHITE. Thurber specialized in jokes and stories about husbands and wives, and made himself into a character in his fictional autobiography, *My Life and Hard Times* (1933). His classic story "The Secret Life of Walter Mitty" (1939) poked fun at the common man or little guy with delusions of grandeur, who daydreams himself into greatness. Mitty's comic persistence became a model for the sketches Woody ALLEN published in the *New Yorker* and for some of Allen's movie characters.

Will ROGERS brought to the spoken word and the newspaper column a gentle, folksy cowboy style that made him the most beloved humorist of the 1930s, whereas H. L. MENCKEN's humor was savage. Mencken attacked all forms of pretension and delighted in exposing the vacuousness of much of American culture—but he did so with colorful, amusing terms like "booboisie." New York humorist Fran Lebovitz has inherited much of the *New Yorker* tradition, specializing in an urban form of wisecracking and outspokenness designed to entertain rather than offend.

Among America's canonized authors, William FAULKNER and Eudora WELTY have produced comic masterpieces like "Spotted Horses" and "Why I Live at the P.O.," which poke fun at the absurdity of life. Nathanael WEST, on the other hand, wrote a form of black humor that seems nihilistic in its despair. He established a tradition that has been followed by Joseph HELLER, Kurt VONNEGUT, Thomas PYNCHON, John BARTH, and Ken KESEY, among many others.

Langston HUGHES, Ralph ELLISON, and Ishmael REED are probably the finest humorists among African-American writers. Hughes used his character Jesse B. Semple to point out the comic ironies of existence. Hughes also edited *The Book of Negro Humor* (1966). Ellison's *Invisible Man* (1952) pokes fun at his narrator's naivete as well as at the larger white society, which seems unaware of its own absurdity. Reed has poked fun at virtually every American institution as well as at African Americans.

Jewish-American authors like Saul BELLOW, Bernard MALAMUD, Philip ROTH, and Cynthia OZICK have created memorable comic characters. On the lighter, gentler side are books like Leo ROSTEN's *The Joys of Yiddish* (1969) and *Only in America* (1958), which became best-sellers.

In addition to the *New Yorker*, the major humor magazines in America are *Mad* (1952–   ) and *National Lampoon* (1970–   ). Important collections of humor include Nicholas Bakalar's *American Satire: An Anthology of Writings from Colonial Times to the Present*; Bryan B. Sterling and Frances N. Sterling's *Will Rogers' World: America's Foremost Political Humorist Comments on the Twenties and Thirties—and Eighties and Nineties* (1989); and Robert Wechsler's *Here We Are: The Humorists' Guide to the United States* (1991).

Among the most important studies of American humor are Constance Rourke's *American Humor: A Study of the National Character* (1931); Walter Blair's *Native American Humor* (1937); Norris W. Yates's *The American Humorist; Conscience of the Twentieth Century* (1964); Richard Boyd Hauck's *A Cheerful Nihilism: Confidence and the "Absurd" in American Humorous Fiction* (1971); and Nancy Walker's *A Very Serious Thing: Women's Humor and American Culture* (1988).

Humphrey, William (1924–   ) *novelist*

Humphrey's work is set in East Texas, where he grew up. Humphrey belongs to the regionalist (see REGIONALISM) tradition of J. Frank DOBIE, although in novels like *The Ordways* (1958) he dwells more on the violence of back-country people. Many of his novels are family chronicles, including *Proud Flesh* (1973), *Hostages to Fortune* (1984), *No Resting Place* (1989), and *September Song* (1992). His stories are collected in *The Last Husband* (1953) and *A Time and Place* (1968). An avid fisherman, he has published nonfiction works, including *The Spawning Run* (1971) and *My Moby Dick* (1978). He writes about growing up in Texas in *Farther Off From Heaven* (1977).

Sources

Almon, Bert. *William Humphrey: Destroyer of Myths.* Denton: University of North Texas Press, 1998.

Hunter, Evan (Ed McBain) (1926–   ) *novelist*

Born Salvatore A. Lombino in New York City and a product of Cooper Union and Hunter College, this novelist is best known as Ed McBain, author of the 87th Precinct novels. Called "mystery thrillers," they began to appear at the rate of three a year in 1956. He has provided strikingly authentic descriptions of New York City police work and the milieu of the

20th-century city, carrying on the tradition of Dashiell HAMMETT and Raymond CHANDLER, although without their flair for evoking the decadence of urban life. But Hunter's first success as a novelist came with *The Blackboard Jungle* (1954), which exposed the seamy side of a big-city high school. Hunter has written close to 100 novels using different names such as Curt Cannon, Ezra Hannon, Hunt Collins, and Richard Marsten. He is also a playwright and screenwriter. In 1962 he wrote the screenplay for Alfred Hitchcock's *The Birds*. Some of his more noteworthy 87th Precinct novels include *Cop Hater* (1956, filmed 1958), *Fuzz* (1968, filmed 1972), *Widows* (1991), and *Mischief* (1993). Hunter also has written children's stories and stage plays. His later works include *Criminal Conversation* (1994), *Privileged Conversation* (1996), and *Me and Hitch* (1997).

Sources

Dove, George N. *The Boys From Grover Avenue: Ed McBain's 87th Precinct Novels.* Bowling Green, Ohio: Bowling Green University Popular Press, 1985.

Hurst, Fannie (1889–1968) *novelist, short story writer, screenwriter*

Born in Hamilton, Ohio, and raised in St. Louis, Hurst was educated at Washington University and Columbia. In New York City she began to publish short stories, collected in *Just Around the Corner* (1914), *Gaslight Sonata* (1916), and *Humoresque* (1919). Her popular novels became films, especially *Back Street* (1913) and *Imitation of Life* (1933). Her novels concentrated on women, some of whom achieved the American dream of success and marriage while others remained unfulfilled. Hurst's work captured the stories of striving women and was so popular in the 1920s and 1930s that she became the country's highest-paid fiction writer. Hurst also involved herself in social and political causes, campaigning for religious tolerance and civil rights. She published her autobiography, *Anatomy of Me: A Wonderer in Search of Herself* in 1958.

Sources

Kroger, Brooke. *Fannie: The Amazing Rise to Fame of Author Fannie Hurst.* New York: Times Books, 1999.
Ravitz, Abe C. *Imitations of Life: Fannie Hurst's Gaslight Sonatas.* Carbondale: Southern Illinois University Press, 1997.

Hurston, Zora Neale (1891–1960) *novelist, short story writer, playwright, folklorist*

Hurston was one of the first writers whose work displayed an implicit belief in the beauty of African-American culture. She was born and grew up in Eatonville, Florida. Precocious and independent at an early age, Hurston read English classics such as John Milton's *Paradise Lost* and Thomas Gray's "Elegy in a Country Churchyard," which she memorized. She attended the Morgan Academy in Baltimore and then Howard University in Washington, D.C. She published her first story in 1925, and moved to New York City, where she worked as a secretary for the novelist Fannie HURST. She also studied anthropology at Columbia University with the leading scholars of the day, including Franz Boas and Ruth Benedict.

After two brief failed marriages in the late 1920s, Hurston returned to do field research in the South. She wrote scholarly articles, and her first great book, *Mules and Men* (1935), is a collection of tales, song, talk, sermons, and religious practices integrated into an impressive narrative.

Hurston's first novel, *Their Eyes Were Watching God* (1937), is a powerful evocation of a woman's life and her search for fulfillment. It contains comic as well as devastating insights into white and black life, presented with an anthropologist's keen eye.

Although Hurston has been associated with the HARLEM RENAISSANCE, her personality and work were distinctive and often at odds with her male counterparts. In particular, she disliked the exaggerated sense of tragedy she found in the work of Langston HUGHES, although she and Hughes collaborated on a play, *Mule Bone* (1931). Hughes, in turn, found her arrogant.

In later life Hurston became a staunch anti-Communist and opposed the Supreme Court's 1954 ruling against segregated schools. Her work fell into neglect, but was rediscovered by feminists and African-American studies scholars in the 1970s, and she is now considered one of the great writers of her era.

Sources

Bloom, Harold, ed. *Zora Neale Hurston.* New York: Chelsea House, 1986.
Hemenway, Robert. *Zora Neale Hurston: A Literary Biography.* Urbana: University of Illinois Press, 1977.

Hwang, David Henry (1957–) *playwright*

One of the most important figures in Asian-American literature, Hwang is the son of Chinese immigrants. He won an Obie Award for his play *FOB* (1981), which stands for "fresh off the boat." The play explores the way Chinese immigrants survive when they are thrust into American culture without any preparation. *Family Devotions* (1983) continues the immigrant story. *The Dance and the Railroad* (1982) dramatizes an 1867 strike by Chinese immigrant railroad builders. *M. Butterfly* (1988), his most successful play, won a Tony Award for distinguished achievement in theater.

Sources

Street, Douglas. *David Henry Hwang.* Boise, Idaho: Boise State University, 1989.

Ignatow, David (1914–1997) poet

Born in Brooklyn, Ignatow drew on the struggle of his immigrant parents during the GREAT DEPRESSION in his poetry, which is filled with the idioms of Brooklyn and of city speech. His collections include *Poems* (1948), *The Gentle Weight Lifter* (1955), *Say Pardon* (1962), *Figures of the Human* (1964), *Earth Hard* (1968), *Rescue the Dead* (1968), *Poems 1934–1969* (1970), and *New and Collected Poems: 1970–1985*. In *Notebooks* (1973) he writes about his personal life and poetic aspirations. *The One in the Many: A Poet's Memoirs* appeared in 1988; *Shadowing the Ground* in 1991, *Talking Together: Letters of David Ignatow, 1946 to 1990* in 1992; *Against the Evidence: Selected Poems, 1934–1994* in 1994; *At My Ease: Uncollected Poems of the Fifties and Sixties* in 1998; and *Living is What I Wanted: Last Poems* in 1999.

Sources

Terris, Virginia R. *Meaningful Differences: The Poetry and Prose of David Ignatow.* Tuscaloosa: University of Alabama Press, 1994.

I Know Why the Caged Bird Sings Maya Angelou (1970) autobiography

MAYA ANGELOU's autobiography, one of the finest accounts of an African-American woman's experience ever published, is also one of the primary documents in the wave of feminism that marked the early 1970s. The author's title comes from Paul Laurence Dunbar's poem "Sympathy" (1902) and refers to Angelou's painful but necessary recognition of her slavery and her need to articulate her suffering, which also begins her progress toward freedom. Angelou writes of her childhood in Stamps, Arkansas, where she was raised by a grandmother, the owner of a general store. Through this domestic setting Angelou examines the segregated South of the 1930s and 1940s. The book also deals with Angelou's exposure to urban life in St. Louis, where she is raped and loses her innocence. Indeed, she loses her voice until she returns from St. Louis to Stamps, begins the process of educating herself, and discovers the power of the human voice. Part testimony, part social history, *I Know Why the Caged Bird Sings* is also a poetic evocation of African-American folk traditions, the development of an urban blues tradition, and Angelou's awakening literary sensibility.

Sources

Braxton, Joanne M., ed. *Maya Angelou's I Know Why the Caged Bird Sings: A Casebook.* New York: Oxford University Press, 1999.

Megna-Wallace, Joanne, ed. *Understanding I Know Why the Caged Bird Sings: A Student Casebook to Issues, Sources, and Historical Documents.* Westport, Conn.: Greenwood Press, 1998.

I'll Take My Stand: The South and the Agrarian Tradition, by Twelve Southerners (1930) essay collection

These essays by "twelve southerners" object to the trends of modern life and affirm the rural, agrarian traditions of the South. Many of the writers could be termed modernists, yet their social and political views were conservative and in some cases reactionary. Allen TATE, John Gould FLETCHER, Robert Penn WARREN, and Donald DAVIDSON were poets with considerable reputations. Stark YOUNG was a fine theater critic and historical novelist. Many had been members of an avant-garde group called THE FUGITIVES. However, in *I'll Take My Stand* they stood by an anticapitalist position reminiscent of the proslavery apologists of the 19th century who excoriated the wage slavery of the North and promoted a more genteel, humane tradition in the South. They were intellectual aristocrats who had little sympathy for modern, mass democracy. Indeed, some of them despised it and took an idealist position similar to those of Plato and Thomas Carlyle, both of whom believed in government by a privileged class. Of all the AGRARIANS, only Robert Penn Warren later repudiated forthrightly many of the views he expressed in *I'll Take My Stand*. Others modified their views, to be sure, but like Allen Tate they never really accommodated themselves to northern values. Donald Davidson, in fact, went so far as to align himself with the White Citizen's Councils in the South that fought against the introduction of integration. He saw himself—as did other Agrarians—in a states' rights tradition that stemmed from Thomas Jefferson, a tradition that upheld the sovereignty of individual states and distrusted the powers of a central government.

Sources

Duncan, Christopher M. *Fugitive Theory: Political Theory, The Southern Agrarians, and America.* Lanham, Md.: Lexington Books, 2000.

Havard, William C. and Walter Sullivan. *A Band of Prophets: The Vanderbilt Agrarians after Fifty Years.* Baton Rouge: Louisiana University Press, 1982.

imagism *literary movement*

In the first decade of the 20th century, poets such as Ezra POUND, William Carlos WILLIAMS, and Amy LOWELL advanced the idea that poetry should focus on clear, concise images. Imagism was a reaction against the florid rhetoric and emotion of romanticism. Focusing on the image promoted an understated quality in poetry, so that the physical world, not thoughts about it, prevailed. Williams coined the phrase "no ideas but in things," by which he meant the world must be portrayed as directly as possible before interpretation of it commenced. Imagists, in other words, wanted poetry to be more concrete and less abstract.

Lowell published three anthologies of imagist verse, and Pound formulated what he called the three principles of imagism: 1. "Direct treatment of 'the thing.'" 2. "Use absolutely no word that does not contribute to the presentation." 3. "Compose in the sequence of the musical phrase, not in the sequence of a metronome." Pound's second and third principles were intended to wean poetry away from using words that sounded "poetic" yet were in fact abstractions—words that really did not contribute to the poem's power but instead were there to fill out the poetic line, which in turn was often too mechanically conceived. Thinking in terms of musical phrases would inject the variety and natural rhythm to poetry that Pound and other poets of his generation found lacking in their immediate predecessors. Pound did more than any other poet to define what he meant by image: "that which presents an intellectual and emotional complex in an instant of time." His two-line poem, "In a Station of the Metro" (1914), is usually cited as the quintessential imagist poem, for it juxtaposes the "apparition" of faces in a subway crowd to " petals" on a "black bough."

Sources

Gage, John T. *In the Arresting Eye: The Rhetoric of Imagism.* Baton Rouge: Louisiana State University Press, 1981.

Hughes, Glenn. *Imagism & the Imagists: A Study in Modern Poetry.* New York: Biblo and Tannen, 1972.

Pratt, William and Robert Richardson, eds. *Homage to Imagism.* New York: AMS Press, 1992.

Inge, William (1913–1973) *playwright*

Inge was born and grew up in Independence, Kansas. He had a difficult childhood. A precocious boy, he was drawn to the idea of acting and to the theater, but he did not pursue his dream until his late 30s. By then he had also become an alcoholic and was subject to fits of depression that would eventually lead to suicide. Before his death, however, he became one of America's most important playwrights. Many of his plays—*Come Back, Little Sheba* (1950), *Picnic* (1953), *Bus Stop* (1955), *The Dark at the Top of the Stairs* (1957), and his screenplay *Splendor in the Grass* (1961)—are set in small midwestern towns. His characters ache from their loss of ambition or youth, sexual frustration, alcoholic tendencies, and loneliness. Clearly Inge's portraits of family life in the Midwest were based on his own experience, but he also spoke to the anxieties of many middle-class Americans. His characters yearn to feel special—Cherie in *Bus Stop*, for example, dreams of stardom in Hollywood—yet they are often disappointed in themselves and in the world that engulfs them. Although Inge's characters can seem self-pitying, they redeem themselves through self-knowledge or through at least the struggle to understand why their hopes are thwarted, so that they can reconcile themselves to communities and families. All of Inge's important plays were made into memorable films, although the playwright apparently resented the changes Hollywood made in his scripts. Inge was more of a popular than a critical success. New York reviewers, in particular, tended to dismiss dramas they found sentimental or contrived. Inge published *Eleven Short Plays* in 1962. In his later years he turned to fiction, producing two novels, *Good Luck, Miss Wyckoff* (1970) and *My Son is a Splendid Driver* (1971), which are autobiographical and have a thematic resemblance to his plays.

Sources

McClure, Arthur F. *Memories of Splendor: The Midwestern World of William Inge.* Topeka: Kansas State Historical Society, 1989.

Shuman, R. Baird. *William Inge.* Boston: Twayne, 1989.

In Our Time Ernest Hemingway (1925) *short story collection*

HEMINGWAY's greatest collection of short stories, this is Hemingway at his finest, writing in a spare, clean style that revolutionized American literature and made him one of the most imitated writers of his generation. The stories are set in the Michigan woods, where Hemingway himself camped, hunted, and fished as a boy. Between the stories are italicized interchapters that vividly re-create the immediacy and horror of war. Both the war and peace episodes are based on Hemingway's own experiences (he served in the Italian ambulance corps during WORLD WAR I). The stories are a *bildungsroman;* that is, they follow the maturation of their main character, NICK ADAMS, as he is exposed to the fundamental experiences of life and death. In one of the most famous stories, "Indian Camp," Nick tries to come to terms with the death of an Indian who slits his own throat in agony over his wife's cries during childbirth. Even as the Indian dies, Nick is jolted into an adult recognition of mortality. Hemingway avoids any sort of sentimentality by writing in a terse, understated style, and with a reportorial economy that he honed as a reporter for the *Toronto Star.*

Sources

Reynolds, Michael, ed. *Critical Essays on Ernest Hemingway's In Our Time.* Boston: G. K. Hall, 1983.

Tetlow, Wendolyn E. *Hemingway's In Our Time: Lyrical Dimensions.* Lewisburg, Penn.: Bucknell University Press, 1992.

Invisible Man Ralph Ellison (1952) *novel*

Ralph Ellison's masterpiece of the African-American experience describes the experience of an unnamed narrator who is invisible in the sense that white Americans do not see him any more than they see or try to understand other African Americans. In typical Ellison irony, the narrator occupies the basement of a "whites only" building on the edge of Harlem.

The narrator describes how he grew up in the South and was educated at an African-American college, dominated by Dr. Bledsoe, an authoritarian college president. The narrator gets into trouble when he drives Mr. Norton, one of the college's white benefactors, to a brothel. Expelled from college, the narrator makes his way to New York City with some letters of introduction by Dr. Bledsoe. Mr. Emerson, the son of a businessman to whom the narrator presents the president's letter, tells him that Dr. Bledsoe's message is to keep the narrator, an embarrassment, away from the college. The narrator then finds a job in a paint factory, where the newly hired African Americans are regarded as scabs by the union workers about to go on strike. The narrator is attacked by the anti-union African-American foreman, and in the melee the plant explodes. White doctors in the company hospital give the narrator electric shock treatments and then release him. On a Harlem street an African-American woman, Mary Rambo, kindly takes the narrator home to recuperate.

The following winter the narrator emerges as a political activist courted by the Communist Party. He becomes its African-American spokesman. But in a conflict with Ras the Exhorter, an African-American nationalist, the narrator becomes disillusioned with the Communist Party. At the end of the novel he is biding his time, thinking about his next step as he takes refuge in his invisibility.

Ellison's novel is considered one of the great works of American literature: it is an acute analysis of the African-American experience as well as a shrewd portrait of mid-20th-century American society. A master stylist, Ellison was greatly influenced by William FAULKNER and European writers such as Fyodor Dostoevsky, especially the novel *Notes from the Underground,* which is the narrative of a man underground—marginalized—just as Ellison's narrator in *Invisible Man* has deliberately absented himself from society in order to tell his story.

Sources

O'Meally, Robert, ed. *New Essays on Invisible Man.* New York: Cambridge University Press, 1988.

Sundquist, Eric J., ed. *Cultural Contexts for Ralph Ellison's Invisible Man.* Boston: Bedford/St. Martin's, 1995.

Trimmer, Joseph F., ed. *A Casebook on Ralph Ellison's Invisible Man.* New York: Crowell, 1972.

Iowa Writers' Workshop

The University of Iowa in Iowa City was the first important American university to offer a degree program in creative writing. Founded in 1922, The Writers' Workshop has graduated many important writers, such as John IRVING and Flannery O'CONNOR. Before World War II, programs such as Iowa's were rare: Writers were not generally part of college English departments, courses in creative writing were also rare, and contemporary American literature often was not part of the college curriculum. After the war, many independent intellectuals and writers sought university affiliations for the first time, and the idea of producing literature while working on a college campus became one of the primary ways in which writers were able to support themselves. The many general circulation magazines and literary quarterlies that flourished before World War II and could afford to pay writers decently or even generously for their work found themselves competing with other media, especially television, for a general audience. Such magazines as THE

SATURDAY EVENING POST and THE SATURDAY REVIEW lost circulation and could not compete with the immediacy of television as a purveyor of news, pictures, and stories. Meanwhile, colleges and universities were able to subsidize writing programs and small literary magazines. Writers on the faculty could bring prestige and attract students to colleges and universities. The Iowa Writers' Workshop is still one of the most important and prestigious programs of its kind in the country.

The program is divided into a poetry workshop and a fiction workshop. Within those categories, there are also seminars specifically focused on writing and reading literature as well as a graduate poetry workshop and a graduate fiction workshop. The number of credits for each course depends on how much time students allot to their writing. Additional courses titled "Form of Fiction" and "Form of Poetry" are also offered. A translation workshop is scheduled to coincide with the comparative literature program at the university. The Department of Theatre offers playwriting courses, and its Film and Broadcasting program gives introductory and advanced courses.

Irving, John Winslow (1942–   ) novelist

Born in Exeter, New Hampshire, John Irving has often set his fiction in his native region, especially in his renowned *The World According to Garp* (1978), a novel about a writer who struggles with many of the contentious issues of his time, especially the sexual politics that lead to his assassination. Irving's later work has probed similar themes and settings. Irving's style has been called "serio-comic," a term meant to convey his joking exaggeration of the conflicts, absurdities, and contradictions of contemporary manners and values. His other novels include *The Hotel New Hampshire* (1981), *The Cider House Rules* (1985), *A Prayer for Owen Meany* (1989), *A Son of the Circus* (1994), *A Widow for One Year* (1998), and *The Fourth Hand* (2001).

Sources

Campbell, Josie R. *John Irving: A Critical Companion.* Westport, Conn.: Greenwood Press, 1998.

Reilly, Edward C. *Understanding John Irving.* Columbia: University of South Carolina Press, 1991.

Isherwood, Christopher (1904–1986)
autobiographer, novelist

Born in England and educated at Cambridge, Isherwood came to the United States at the beginning of World War II. He settled in Los Angeles and became an inspiration for later generations of American writers, especially the BEATS, who admired his frankness about his homosexuality and emulated his interest in Eastern religions. In 1953 Isherwood published *How To Know God: The Yoga Aphorisms of Patanjali,* one of several books that would inspire the counterculture of the 1960s. Isherwood made his reputation with a collection of stories, *Goodbye to Berlin* (1939), which John VAN DRUTEN adapted into a hit Broadway play, *I Am a Camera* (1954), which in turn evolved into the hit musical and movie, *Cabaret* (1968, 1972). Through all of its transformations Isherwood's Berlin stories retain their focus on a quintessential American character, Sally Bowles, whose last name Isherwood took from his friend Paul BOWLES. Isherwood wrote about his own life and his collaborations with the poet W. H. AUDEN in *Lions and Shadows* (1939). Isherwood and Auden wrote two remarkable plays, *The Dog Beneath the Skin* (1935) and *The Ascent of F6* (1936). Isherwood's novel, *Praeter Violet* (1945), based on his experiences as screenwriter, is still one of the best novels to portray what filmmaking is like in Hollywood. His *Diaries,* a remarkable record of life in southern California, appeared in 1997. In all its different forms, Isherwood's fiction about Berlin provides an evocative portrayal of the rise of Nazism and the corruption and decadence of Germany that contributed to the rise of Hitler.

Sources

Fryer, Jonathan. *Eye of the Camera: A Life of Christopher Isherwood.* London: Allison & Busby, 1993.

Jackson, Charles Reginald (1903–1968) *novelist*

Charles Jackson is best known for his novel *The Lost Weekend* (1944), a terrifying case study of an alcoholic. It became a successful film directed by Billy Wilder and starring Ray Milland. Jackson's other work includes the novels *The Fall of Valor* (1946), which deals with homosexuality; *The Outer Edges* (1948), about the impact of a newspaper article on its readers; and *Earthly Creatures* (1953), a collection of stories. Jackson himself battled alcoholism and a monumental writer's block.

Sources

Breit, Harvey. *The Writer Observed.* Cleveland, Ohio: World Publishing, 1956.

Jackson, Laura Riding

See RIDING, LAURA.

Jackson, Shirley Hardie (1919–1965) *novelist, short story writer*

Born in San Francisco and educated at Rochester University in New York, Shirley Jackson had to leave school because of her parents' difficulties in the GREAT DEPRESSION, but she earned a B.A. from Syracuse University. The year she graduated she married the critic Stanley Edgar Hyman, and later moved with him and their four children to Vermont, where he taught at Bennington College. Jackson published her first novel, *The Road Through the Wall*, in 1948, and followed that immediately with a classic collection of stories, *The Lottery* (1949). The title story has been anthologized frequently and discussed as an example of American gothic. A consummate storyteller, Jackson bridged the gap between serious literary and popular fiction. Another noteworthy novel is *The Haunting of Hill House* (1959). The less known *Hangsaman* (1951) is a novel about a disturbed young girl who speaks with four voices. *The Sundial* (1958) portrays a family awaiting the end of the world. *We Have Always Lived in the Castle* (1962) explores modern witchcraft in the form of a young woman who poisons her family. Jackson also wrote the children's books *The Witchcraft of Salem Village* (1956) and *Nine Magic Wishes* (1963) and a play, *The Bad Children* (1959). Like *The Lottery*, much of Jackson's other work presents disturbed characters and occult experiences within the context of vividly realized domestic, everyday settings. Jackson's fiction and nonfiction is often humorous. She described her life at home with her children in *Life Among the Savages* (1953) and *Raising Demons* (1957). After her death her husband edited two collections: *The Magic of Shirley Jackson* (1966) and *Come Along with Me* (1968), which includes her last, unfinished novel.

Sources

Friedman, Lenemaja. *Shirley Jackson.* Boston: Twayne, 1975.
Hall, Joan Wylie. *Shirley Jackson: A Study of Short Fiction.* New York: Twayne, 1993.
Oppenheimer, Judy. *Private Demons: The Life of Shirley Jackson.* New York: Putnam, 1988.

Jarrell, Randall (1914–1965) *poet, critic*

A native of Nashville, Tennessee, Jarrell was educated at Vanderbilt University, where he was a student of John Crowe RANSOM. When Ransom moved to Kenyon College,

Jarrell followed and taught there for two years. He shared a room with Robert LOWELL, one of the poets of a brilliant generation against which Jarrell would measure himself. He served in the air force in WORLD WAR II, and out of that experience he produced memorable poems, especially the much anthologized "The Death of the Ball Turret Gunner," which appeared in *Little Friend, Little Friend* (1945). This first collection was followed with the impressive *Losses* in 1948. Jarrell was particularly attentive to prosody and has often been compared to Robert FROST for his ability to link traditional forms of poetry to colloquial speech. Like Frost, whom Jarrell wrote about brilliantly, Jarrell excelled in the dramatic monologue, featured in his acclaimed collection, *The Woman at the Washington Zoo* (1960). His later poems, like those of his contemporaries Lowell and John BERRYMAN, became somewhat more confessional, as in "The Lost World" and "Thinking of the Lost World," collected in *The Lost World* (1965). *The Complete Poems* appeared in 1969, and *Selected Poems* in 1990. Jarrell's standing as a literary critic is as high, if not higher, than his ranking as a poet. His reputation is based on two volumes: *Poetry and the Age* (1953) and *A Sad Heart at the Supermarket* (1962), which established sound readings of modern poets, especially Robert Frost. He published one novel, *Pictures From an Institution* (1954), a satire of the academic world. Like Lowell and Berryman, his friends and competitors, Jarrell led an intense, troubled life devoted to poetry and its promulgation. It is still an open question whether his death (the result of being struck by a car) was an accident or a suicide. *No Other Book* (1999) collects the best of Jarrell's nonfiction. Mary Von Schrader Jarrell, Jarrell's wife, has published *Remembering Randall: A Memoir of Poet, Critic, and Teacher Randall Jarrell* (1999).

Sources

Bryant, Jr., J. A. *Understanding Randall Jarrell.* Columbia: University of South Carolina Press, 1986.

Travisano, Thomas. *Midcentury Quartet: Bishop, Lowell, Jarrell, Berryman, and the Making of a Postmodern Aesthetic.* Charlottesville: University Press of Virginia, 1999.

Jazz Age

This term applies to the 1920s and to post–WORLD WAR I period in which young people jettisoned the social restraints of the 19th century, opting for freer relations between the sexes, indulgence in alcohol, and the enjoyment of new music like jazz, which was popular in cities such as New York, Chicago, and Kansas City. F. Scott FITZGERALD captured the period as it was happening in *Tales of the Jazz Age* (1922). The term "the LOST GENERATION" has also been applied to members of the Jazz Age. Some of them, like Fitzgerald and HEMINGWAY, left the United States for Paris and other European cities, where they could escape Ameri-

can provincialism. Dorothy Baker's novel, *Young Man with a Horn* (1938), also captures the period.

Sources

Bogart, Max, ed. *The Jazz Age.* New York: Scribner's, 1969.
Time-Life Books. *The Jazz Age: The 20s.* Alexandria, Va.: Time-Life, 1998.

Jeffers, Robinson (John Robinson Jeffers) (1887–1962) *poet*

Born outside of Pittsburgh, Jeffers was educated in grammar schools in Switzerland and Germany because his father was determined to make him a classical scholar. The family moved to California in 1903, where Jeffers earned a degree at Occidental College and then studied forestry, comparative literature, and medicine at the University of Southern California, University of Zurich, and the University of Washington. Jeffers settled in southern California to lead the bohemian life of a poet, self-publishing his first book, *Flagons and Apples* (1912). Jeffers soon became associated with the central California coast around Carmel, and the natural world became the focus of his poetry, beginning with the publication of *Californians* (1916). His early influences were British, and it was not until *Tamar and Other Poems* (1924) that he developed his own voice, most conspicuous in *The Women at Point Sur* (1927), *Dear Judas* (1929), *Descent to the Dead* (1931), *Thurso's Landing* (1932), *Give Your Heart to the Hawks* (1933), and *Solstice* (1935). Jeffers's immersion in the natural scene was in part a response to his rejection of the Western world's decadence. But this retreat from the modern seem linked to a falling-off of poetic power, so that by 1938, when his *Selected Poetry* appeared, his reputation was in decline. Jeffers's later successes were in verse drama, particularly his translation of *Medea*, which had a successful run with the renowned actress Judith Anderson. Jeffers's narrative poetry has not found favor among later critics, although his place in American literature nevertheless seems secure because of the strength of his early work, which vigorously explores human psychology. *The Collected Poetry of Robinson Jeffers* was published in three volumes in 1988.

Sources

Brophy, Robert, ed. *Robinson Jeffers: Dimensions of a Poet.* New York: Fordham University Press, 1995.

Jewish-American literature

Twentieth-century Jewish-American literature begins with Abraham CAHAN's classic novel, *The Rise of David Levinsky* (1917), which raises the question of assimilation and success: Can Jews still be Jews and fit comfortably into American life? While all immigrant groups have faced the question of assimilation, for Jews, given their history of persecution in so many countries, the idea of finding acceptance in America is both exhilarating and frightening. In America, Jews have the opportunity, should they so wish, to assimilate. Thus in Cahan's novel, David Levinsky comes to America from Russia. A devout student of the Talmud, he decides to compete in secular society. He works in the garment industry and educates himself. With success he achieves the American dream, but at the end of the novel he questions what remains of his Jewishness and of his spiritual life.

Cahan's novel remains a part of the American canon because the author captured the mood of the early 20th century in moving prose. David Levinsky epitomizes the melting pot metaphor that dominated the literature of the American experience, and he took his place among other classic American heroes striving for success in the world of business.

By the 1930s, the Jewish-American novel and the country had changed considerably. The GREAT DEPRESSION challenged American optimism. With millions of people out of work, the promise of American capitalism seemed to vanish. Michael GOLD, editor of the NEW MASSES, the American Communist Party's powerful literary journal, expressed a new radical view of the American economy and its institutions in *Jews Without Money* (1930). Riveting, though sometimes sentimental, portrayals of Jews in tenements on the LOWER EAST SIDE of NEW YORK CITY replaced the melting-pot plot of accomplishment and prosperity. Gold applied a Marxist analysis to society, indicting an America that had betrayed the working class. Most Jews were poor and would remain so, his work implied, until fundamental changes were made in society.

In the theater, playwrights such as Clifford ODETS explored Jewish family life in terms of this new radicalized view of America. In *Awake and Sing!,* for example, a middle-class Jewish Bronx family's fate in linked to its tenuous place in a Depression-era economy. In *Waiting for Lefty* (1934), Odets captured the militancy of striking workers who refuse to accept the status quo. Odets was part of the GROUP THEATRE, a group composed primarily of Jewish writers, directors, and actors who attempted to meld left-wing politics with art. Unlike Cahan's work, however, Gold's and Odets's generation tended to subordinate questions of Jewishness to political questions about working-class life and the exploitation of the poor by the rich capitalist class. Thus what came to be called PROLETARIAN LITERATURE featured working-class heroes. Daniel Fuchs's Williamsburg trilogy follows the lives of Jewish immigrants who settle into the Williamsburg section of Brooklyn, at the time a densely crowded neighborhood of ghetto homes cut off from the riches of Manhattan. In Fuchs, there also emerge certain stereotypical Jewish characters—such as the Jewish mother—who would appear in the significant developments of Jewish literature in the 1950s.

Almost in a special category is Henry ROTH's novel *Call It Sleep* (1934). Roth combined much of the NATURALISM of the 1930s writers who dealt with social and ethnic issues with the modernist attitude of James Joyce. Roth's novel is told from the point of view of a young Jewish boy who grows up in America to watch the painful confrontation of his parents with American life. Unlike Gold, however, Roth does not blame society or focus exclusively on material conditions. On the contrary, his searing psychological portraits suggest a view of society predicated on his awareness that the world is, in good part, what his characters choose to make of it. They are driven by inner demons as much as by outer forces. Certainly environment shapes character in Roth's novel, but it is also character that interprets environment. Roth's novel, poorly received and then forgotten, was rediscovered in the late 1950s when a new generation of Jewish writers was searching for a model of how to express both their Jewishness and their connection to American life.

Even as writers such as Gold, Odets, Fuchs, and Roth concentrated on urban Jews and their plight in an exploitatively political and economic system, others, such as the critic Lionel TRILLING, rose out of a Jewish background to take their places in important institutions of American society. In the late 1930s and 1940s, Trilling embraced the Anglo-Saxon and European tradition in literature, earning tenure at Columbia University and writing a morally engaged and rather traditional literary criticism that conveyed a much more ambiguous view of the world that rejected the militancy of proletarian writers. Trilling and his students—particularly Norman PODHORETZ, the influential editor of COMMENTARY magazine—ambitiously pursued the project of assimilation while maintaining a critical view of American society in the 1950s and 1960s. Among writers of this intellectual generation was Alfred KAZIN, who wrote a series of memoirs about Jewish-American life that includes the classic *A Walker in the City* (1951).

Jewish poets such as Louis ZUKOFSKY, Charles REZNIKOFF, Georg OPPEN, and Muriel RUKEYSER, writing in the Depression and after World War II, did not make Jewishness as such their subject, even though ELIOT's and POUND's anti-Semitism challenged the modern Jewish poet's sense of himself or herself. Oppen's radical activism allied him with the Jewish generation of the 1930s, and Reznifkoff made the Holocaust the subject of one of his books. Karl SHAPIRO, a Pulitzer Prize–winning poet, confronted Jewish themes more directly and criticized the work of Eliot and Pound, which he felt was diminished by their prejudices.

The generation of Jewish-American novelists after World War II came to embody the spirit of Jewish literature. Saul BELLOW, Bernard MALAMUD, and Philip ROTH became virtually synonymous with the Jewish-American literary renaissance. Bellow's *The Adventures of Augie March* (1953), Malamud's *The Assistant* (1957), and Roth's *Goodbye, Columbus* (1959) in quick succession defined what it meant to be Jewish in mid-20th-century America. Bellow's picaresque novel made his Jewish characters a vivid part of the American landscape, comfortable inside of their own identities in a way that previous generations of Jews in literature could only dream of. Malamud's narrative suggested just the opposite: The difficulty of assimilation remained, and the Jew could still be seen as a symbol of the alienated or the other. Most outrageously, Roth wrote stories and novels that made fun of his Jewish characters and savagely criticized them. Paradoxically, the very freedom he expressed to criticize Jews and to show their hypocrisies demonstrated how confident Jewish writers had become.

Not all Jewish writers of the postwar generation wished to deal directly with Jewish themes or to have their Jewishness considered an important part of their identity. Norman MAILER, for example, self-consciously chose subjects that steered clear of his Brooklyn-Jewish upbringing, although in novels such as *The Naked and the Dead* (1948) he provided indelible portraits of Jewish characters and of anti-Semitism. Later Jewish writers such as E. L. DOCTOROW have not made Jewishness itself a subject, and yet their sensibility can be viewed as Jewish and urban. Doctorow sets much of his fiction in New York City, and some of it—such as *World's Fair* (1985)—draws directly on his own experience of growing up in a Jewish family. The poet Allen GINSBERG, usually associated with the BEATS and with Eastern religions, has also drawn on his Jewish heritage in poems like "Kaddish" (1958), his lament for his mother.

Although Jewish-American literature has sometimes been associated most strongly with the 1950s and 1960s, two of its greatest figures—Bellow and Roth—have continued to publish significant work. Indeed, in the case of Bellow and Roth, their work continues to excite significant attention. With *Ravelstein* (2000) and *The Human Stain* (2000) Bellow and Roth continue to write major novels that still raise issues of Jewish and human identity.

Sources

Chametsky, Jules, ed. *Jewish American Literature: A Norton Anthology.* New York: W. W. Norton, 2001.

Wade, Stephen. *Jewish American Literature Since 1945: An Introduction.* Edinburgh: Edinburgh University Press, 1999.

Johnson, Diane Lain (1934–) *novelist, biographer, critic*

Born in Illinois, Diane Johnson has spent much of her professional life in California, where she has taught at the University of California, Los Angeles and Davis. Her novels focus on many different subjects, including Mormonism, Los Angeles, small California towns, Paris, the victimization of women, and Iran on the eve of revolution. Her tone also ranges from the comic to the farcical to the terrifying to the apocalyptic. *Fair Game* (1965) is her first novel, followed by *Loving Hands at Home* (1968), *Burning* (1971), *The Shadow Knows* (1972), *Lying Low* (1978), and *Persian Nights* (1987). She has published two biographies: *Lesser Lives* (1972), a bi-

ography of the wife of novelist George Meredith, and *Dashiell Hammett: A Life* (1983). A frequent contributor to the NEW YORK REVIEW OF BOOKS, she has collected her essays in *Terrorists and Novelists* (1982). *Natural Opium: Some Traveler's Tales* appeared in 1993, *Le Divorce* (a novel), in 1997, *Le Marriage* (2000), and *Changing Paris: A Tour Along the Seine* in 2000. She also wrote the script for *The Shining*, a film adaptation of the Stephen King novel.

Sources

Williams, Donald. "An Interview with Diane Johnson," The C. G. Jung Page. Available on-line. URL: http://www.cgjung-page.org/films/shining.html. Updated January 1, 2001.

Johnson, James Weldon (1871–1938) *novelist, critic*

Johnson grew up in Jacksonville, Florida, and was fortunate to have several early mentors, including his mother, who taught in the public schools, and James Walter, principal of the Stanton School, a private school in Jacksonville. Johnson was only 16 when he enrolled in Atlanta University, graduating in 1894. The next year he established the *Daily American,* a newspaper anchored in the African-American community. Like many such efforts, the newspaper last only a year, but Johnson's industry recommended him to older leaders such as Booker T. Washington and W. E. B. DU BOIS. Johnson then established a successful law practice in Jacksonville and became principal of the Stanton School. Along with his brother, James, he wrote poetry and songs, the most notable "Lift Every Voice and Sing." Just as he had studied law with a white lawyer, Johnson took up the systematic study of literature with a renowned white critic, Brander Matthews. Johnson's breakthrough as a writer came with THE AUTOBIOGRAPHY OF AN EX-COLORED MAN (1912), one of the seminal texts in African-American literature. During the HARLEM RENAISSANCE, Johnson published the anthologies *The Book of American Negro Poetry* (1922), *The Book of American Negro Spirituals* (1925), and *The Second Book of American Negro Spirituals* (1926). This work fed his own creativity, and he produced the moving and beautifully constructed *God's Trombones, Seven Negro Sermons in Verse* (1927), which has often been staged. *Black Manhattan* (1930) is his survey of the cultural scene. Johnson taught at Fisk University for several years and wrote *Negro Americans: What Now?* (1934), which argued vigorously for integration and cooperation among the races. He published his autobiography, *Along This Way* in 1933 and a *Saint Peter Relates an Incident: Selected Poems* in 1934. He died in an automobile accident in Maine.

Sources

Fleming, Robert E. *James Weldon Johnson.* Boston: Twayne, 1987.

Oliver, Lawrence J., ed. *Critical Essays on James Weldon Johnson*. New York: G.K. Hall, 1997.

Johnson, Josephine (1910–) *novelist, short story writer, social critic, autobiographer*

Johnson is a Missouri native whose compelling story of life on a midwestern farm, *Now In November* (1934), won a Pulitzer Prize. Her REGIONALISM is also reflected in her story collection, *Jordanstown* (1937). *The Inland Island* (1969) is a record of her observations of nature and her criticism of contemporary America. She published a memoir, *Seven Houses*, in 1973.

Sources

Kocks, Dorothee E. *Dream a Little: Land and Social Justice in Modern America*. Berkeley: University of California Press, 2000.

Washington University Libraries. Josephine Johnson Papers. Available on-line. URL: http://www.library.wustl.edu/units/spec/manuscripts/mlc/johnson/. Updated November 19, 1999.

Jones, Gayl (1949–) *novelist, playwright*

Born in Lexington, Kentucky, Jones has used the state as a setting for much of her work. She began writing stories in grade school and wrote poetry at Connecticut College, where she won two awards for her work. With M.A. and B.A. degrees from Brown University, she wrote her first two novels, *Corregidora* (1975) and *Eva's Man* (1976), which were edited by Toni MORRISON at Random House. She also published two plays, *Chile Woman* and *The Ancestor* (1974). She left a successful teaching career at the University of Michigan in the early 1980s, retreating from the literary scene but continuing to write about African-American culture, especially its oral traditions. Her work has been compared to Alice WALKER, Ernest HEMINGWAY, and Zora Neale HURSTON—an extraordinary array of writers that reflect Jones's efforts to combine anthropological and literary sensibilities. Her plays have attracted notice for their ritualistic qualities and their reliance on the African-American tradition of call and response used in sermons when the congregation answers or echoes the preacher's words. *Corregidora* remains her signature work because of its comprehensive exploration of the African-American family and the relationship between men and women. She published *White Rat*, a short story collection in 1977, and two other novels, *The Healing* (1998) and *Mosquito* (1999). Her poetry has appeared in *Song for Anninho* (1981), *The Hermit Woman* (1983), and *Xarque and Other Poems* (1985). Jones's poetry is especially attuned to the rhythms of jazz and the blues. As a literary critic, Jones has published *Liberating Voices: Oral Tradition in African American Literature* (1991), in which she discusses the work of Paul Laurence Dunbar, Langston HUGHES, Shirley Anne Williams, Zora Neale Hurston, Jean TOOMER, Ann PETRY, Ralph ELLISON, and Toni Morrison. Jones has been both praised and blamed for her frank criticisms of African-American men, especially in her novels where they often abuse African-American women.

Sources

Coser, Stelamaris. *Bridging the Americas: The Literature of Paule Marshall, Toni Morrison, and Gayl Jones*. Philadelphia: Temple University Press, 1995.

Jones, James (1921–1977) *novelist*

An Illinois native, Jones could not afford to go to college, so he enlisted in the army in 1939. He was sent to Hawaii and saw action on Guadalcanal Island, which provided material for his best-selling and critically acclaimed novel, *From Here to Eternity* (1951). His novel vies with MAILER's *The NAKED AND THE DEAD* for consideration as the best novel of WORLD WAR II. Jones focuses, however, on the events leading to the bombing of Pearl Harbor, whereas Mailer explores the Pacific War in its last stages. After considerable study and reflection, Jones produced a sequel, *The Thin Red Line* (1962), which is a meticulous and riveting study of men in combat during the war. It is often cited as the best novel about men in combat ever written by an American. Jones barely lived long enough to complete the last volume of his trilogy about combat, *Whistle* (1978), which is set in a veterans' hospital. Jones spent much of his later writing career in Paris, and his other novels received mixed to negative reviews. They include *Some Came Running* (1957), *The Pistol* (1959), and *Viet Journal* (1974). *To Reach Eternity: The Letters of James Jones* appeared in 1989.

Sources

Carter, Steven R. *James Jones: An American Literary Orientalist Master*. Urbana: University of Illinois Press, 1998.

Giles, James R. *James Jones*. Boston: Twayne, 1981.

Jones, Le Roy

See BARAKA, AMIRI.

Jong, Erica Mann (1942–) *poet, novelist, autobiographer*

Erica Jong is a product of New York City, raised in Manhattan by Jewish parents, and a graduate of Barnard College. She has written a sizeable and well-regarded body of poetry—*Fruits and Vegetables* (1971), *Ordinary Miracles* (1983), *Becoming Light: Poems New and Selected* (1991)—but she earned fame and fortune with her sensational and controversial novel *Fear of Flying* (1973). The book's unbridled sexuality rivaled the work of such male authors as Henry MILLER.

The explicitness of the language amused and outraged readers. Her humor was brassy and bold and adventurous—again, more akin to what readers expected from males. Jong's other fiction, while widely reviewed, has not added appreciably to her reputation, although *Fanny, Being the True History of Fanny Hackabout Jones* (1980) demonstrates her ambition in invading the territory occupied by Henry Fielding's classic *Tom Jones.* Certainly this is Jong's most accomplished novel, and it reflects her background in 18th-century literature acquired while earning a master's degree at Columbia University. Jong's poetry shows the same desire to transgress on male territory and to make it a woman's. She is at her best when demonstrating her considerable gift for the comic. Her other novels include *How to Save Your Own Life* (1977), *Serenissima: A Novel Of Venice* (1987), and *Any Woman's Blues* (1990). In 1993 she published *The Devil at Large: Erica Jong on Henry Miller,* and in 1994 *Fear of Fifty: A Midlife Memoir.*

Sources

Templin, Charlotte. *Feminism and the Politics of Literary Reputation: The Example of Erica Jong.* Lawrence: University of Kansas Press, 1995.

Jordan, June (1936–) *poet, novelist, biographer*

Born in Harlem and raised in the Bedford-Stuyvesant section of Brooklyn, Jordan attended the Northfield School for Girls in Massachusetts. While at Barnard College she met and married a white student, Michael Meyer, and accompanied him to the University of Chicago, where she studied anthropology. The couple divorced in 1965. Jordan came of age as a writer in the 1960s and 1970s, contributing to periodicals such as EVER-GREEN REVIEW, the *Nation,* PARTISAN REVIEW, the *Village Voice,* the NEW YORK TIMES BOOK REVIEW, as well as African-American publications such as *Black World, Essence,* and *Black Creation.* She established her reputation with her first book, *Who Look at Me* (1969), a probing look at interracial relations in a white-dominated society. In 1970 she edited *Soulscript: Afro-American Poetry,* which included work by young adults as well as by established writers. She began writing novels and biographies for children, including *His Own Where* (1971), *Dry Victories* (1972), and *Fannie Lou Hamer* (1972). She published her *Selected Poetry* in 1977. *Civil Wars* (1981) is a collection of essays, lectures, and articles. *Naming Our Destiny: New and Selected Poems* appeared in 1989, followed by *Technical Difficulties: African-American Notes on the State of the Union* (1992) and *Haruko: Love Poems* (1994). Her plays include *In the Spirit of Sojourner Truth* (produced by the Public Theater in New York City in May 1979) and *For the Arrow That Flies by Day,* a staged reading at New York City's Shakespeare Festival in April 1981. She has taught at the City University of New York, Connecticut College, Sarah Lawrence, the State University of New York at Stony Brook, and the University of California, Berkeley. She is a feminist and an ardently political writer, believing in the efficacy of activism, in instilling pride in African-American children, and in fostering freedom of sexual orientation. Her poetry and essays are generally regarded as her strongest work, which has been compared to Toni MORRISON, Toni Cade BAMBARA, Nikki GIOVANNI, and Amiri BARAKA. Her roots, however, are in the black militancy of the 1960s—as exemplified by Eldridge CLEAVER and MALCOLM X. Her *Affirmative Act: Political Essays* was published in 1998.

Sources

Davis, Thadious and Trudier Harris, eds. *Afro-American Writers after 1955: Dramatists and Prose Writers.* Detroit: Gale Research, 1985.

Josephson, Matthew (1899–1978) *editor, critic, historian, biographer*

Based in New York City, Josephson began his career in Europe as an expatriate, editing *Secession* (1922–1924), which featured expatriate writers of the LOST GENERATION. He established his reputation as a critic with two books, *Zola and His Time* (1928) and *Portrait of the Artist as American* (1930), which argued that Americans like Henry James and James McNeil Whistler had to go abroad to develop their talents. *The Robber Baron* (1934) was an influential history of American industrialists. Josephson later wrote biographies, including *Stendahl* (1956) and *Edison* (1959). Josephson published two memoirs that are invaluable guides to the early literary history of the 20th century: *Among the Surrealists* (1962) and *Infidel in the Temple* (1967).

Sources

Shi, David E. *Matthew Josephson, Bourgeois Bohemian.* New Haven: Yale University Press, 1981.

Justice, Donald Rodney (1925–) *poet*

Born in Florida, Donald Justice has taught at several universities, including the University of Florida since 1982. His poems have often been praised for their calm and discipline even as they treat themes such as depression and subjects such as unfulfilled lives. His collected works include *The Summer Anniversaries* (1960); *Night Light* (1967); *Departures* (1973); *Selected Poems* (1979), which won a Pulitzer Prize; *Tremayne* (1984); *The Sunset Maker* (1987), and *New & Selected Poems* (1995). He collected his essays in *Platonic Scripts* (1984), *A Donald Justice Reader: Selected Poetry and Prose* (1991), and *Oblivion: On Writers & Writing* (1998).

Sources

Gioia, Dana and William Logan, eds. *Certain Solitudes: On the Poetry of Donald Justice.* Fayetteville: University of Arkansas Press, 1997.

K

Kang, Younghill (1903–1972) *autobiographer, novelist*

Born in Korea, Kang came to the United States in the early 1920s. He taught at New York University and produced a scholarly book, *Translations of Oriental Poetry* (1929). He is best known for his fictionalized autobiography *East Goes West* (1937), which explores the lives of Asian Americans. He is also the author of *The Grass Roof* (1931), a novel about his experiences in Europe.

Sources

Kaya Books. "East Goes West: The Making of an Oriental Yankee." Kaya Books. Available on-line. URL: http://www.kaya.com/egw-auth.html. Downloaded June 2, 2001.

Kim, Henry, M. D. "The Korean American Experience." *Korean Journal* (June 1999). Available on-line. URL: http://www.koreamjournal.com/june1999/cover_story1.shtml. Downloaded June 2, 2001.

Kaufman, George Simon (1889–1961) *playwright, director*

Born in Pittsburgh, George Kaufman spent his early career working for newspapers in Pittsburgh and Washington, D.C. He wrote his first successful play, *Dulcy* (1921), with Marc CONNELLY. Kaufman and Connelly wrote seven plays together, often treating the foibles of marriage in comic fashion. Sometimes the wives were the target of humor and sometimes the husbands, as in *To the Ladies,* in which a wife saves her husband's reputation. Two plays, *Merton of the Movies* (1922) and *Beggar on Horseback* (1924), exploit the 1920s fascination with movies stars and making it rich in business. Kaufman, who almost always worked with collaborators, wrote several successful Marx Brothers plays, including *The Cocoanuts* (1925) and *Animal Crackers* (1928). In 1931 Kaufman and his collaborators, Morrie Ryskind and Ira Gershwin, won a Pulitzer Prize for the book of their political musical satire, *Of Thee I Sing.*

In the 1930s Kaufman's collaboration with Moss HART won a Pulitzer Prize for *You Can't Take It With You* (1936), one of the great American comedies about an eccentric family and its friends. They wrote the equally successful *The Man Who Came to Dinner* (1939), based on the career of the writer and radio personality Alexander WOOLLCOTT.

Kaufman had fewer successes in the 1940s and 1950s, although he directed such Broadway hits as *My Sister Eileen* (1940) and *Guys and Dolls* (1950). Throughout his long career, this comic genius of the American stage and screen made many uncredited contributions to plays and movies that were in need of revision, additional scenes, and dialogue. He had a wry, whimsical view of life that enlivened almost everything he wrote or directed.

Sources

Goldstein, Malcolm. *George S. Kaufman: His Life, His Theater.* New York: Oxford University Press, 1979.

Mason, Jeffrey D. *Wisecracks: The Farces of George S. Kaufman.* Ann Arbor, Mich.: UMI Research Press, 1988.

Pollack, Rhoda Gale. *George S. Kaufman.* Boston: Twayne, 1988.

Kazin, Alfred (1915–1998) *literary critic*

Kazin grew up in BROOKLYN, NEW YORK, and wrote about his Jewish-American background in the classic autobiography *A*

Walker in the City (1951), considered one of the key texts in the flourishing of Jewish-American literature in the 1950s. But Kazin first earned renown for his groundbreaking work of literary criticism, *On Native Grounds* (1942), a book breathtaking in its scope and vivid style. Kazin was the first critic to encompass the burgeoning of American literature, beginning in the 1890s. Influenced by PROLETARIAN LITERA-TURE, his book discounted important writers such as William FAULKNER, but Kazin would revise his judgment in later books as he established himself as one of the most important American critics of his period. Although not an academic critic, he taught at several colleges, including the State University of New York at Stony Brook and the City University of New York. Considered one of the NEW YORK INTELLECTUALS, Kazin brought a sophisticated urban sense to his writing about world literature. Unlike the NEW CRITICS, he was concerned not with literature alone but with its social and psychological contexts. His most important books include *Bright Book of Life* (1973), a sequel to *On Native Grounds; Starting Out in the Thirties* (1965); *New York Jew* (1978); *An American Procession* (1984); *A Writer's America: Landscape in Literature* (1988); Writing *Was Everything* (1995); A *Lifetime Burning in Every Moment: From the Journals of Alfred Kazin* (1996); and *God and the American Writer* (1997).

Sources

Rodriguez, Richard. "Cultural Legacy." The NewsHour with Jim Lehrer. Available on-line. URL: http://www.pbs.org/news hour/essays/august98/rodriguez_8–28.html

Rosen, Johnathan "A Bridge to the World." *Slate.* Available on-line. http://slate.msn.com/Obit/98-06-09/Obit.asp. Posted June 9, 1998.

Teres, Harvey M. *Renewing the Left: Politics, Imagination, and the New York Intellectuals.* New York: Oxford University Press, 1996.

Wald, Alan M. *The New York Intellectuals: The Rise and Decline of the Anti-Stalinist Left from the 1930's to the 1980's.* Chapel Hill: University of North Carolina Press, 1987.

Kelley, William Melvin (1937–) *novelist, short story writer*

Kelley is best known for his first novel, *A Different Drummer* (1962), about a black sharecropper, Tucker Calhoun, who destroys his farm and moves north, declaring his independence. In this parable, every black in this mythical southern state follows Calhoun's example, making it the first all-white state in the Union. Kelley grew up in New York City and was educated at Harvard, where he studied with Archibald MACLEISH and John HAWKES. In *Dancers on the Shore* (1964) he explores what it means to be an African-American writer. His other novels include *A Drop of Patience* (1965), *dem* (1967), and *Dunfords Travels Every Wheres* (1970).

Sources

Ro, Sigmund. *Rage and Celebration: Essays on Contemporary Afro-American Writing.* Atlantic Highlands, N.J.: Humanities Press, 1984.

Kennedy, William (1928–) *novelist*

Born and raised in Albany, New York, Kennedy graduated from Siena College and worked on the *Albany Times Union* until 1956. After working in other parts of the country, he returned to Albany in the early 1960s, working again on the *Times Union* and gathering material for fiction set in his native region. *Ironweed* (1983), his fourth novel, earned him the Pulitzer Prize and was made into a movie starring Jack Nicholson. Part of Kennedy's Albany cycle, which also includes *Legs* (1975) *Billy Phelan's Greatest Game* (1978), *Quinn's Book* (1988), *Very Old Bones* (1992), and *The Flaming Corsage* (1996), *Ironweed* exemplifies the author's attention to historical setting, local color, city corruption, immigrant life, and the assorted characters who inhabit an Irish Catholic, proletarian world. *Ironweed* is set in 1938 and centers on Francis Phelan, a homeless man who has lost his family and apparently his purpose in life. Yet the story, while hardly a triumph for Francis, nevertheless affirms the quest for belief and redemption.

Kennedy wrote the screenplay for *Ironweed* and for *The Cotton Club* (1984). He also has written about his native region in *O Albany! An Urban Tapestry* (1983) and *Albany and the Capitol* (1986). *Riding the Yellow Trolley Car: Selected Nonfiction* was published in 1993. His books for children include *Charlie Malarkey and the Belly Button Machine* (1986) and *Charlie Malarkey and the Singing Moose* (1994).

Sources

Michener, Christian. *From Then into Now: William Kennedy's Albany Novels.* Scranton, Penn.: University of Scranton Press, 1998.

Seshachari, Neila C., ed. *Conversations with William Kennedy.* Jackson: University Press of Mississippi, 1997.

Kenyon Review *periodical*

Founded in 1939 by the distinguished poet and critic John Crowe RANSOM, this quarterly published the poetry and essays of distinguished writers such as Marianne MOORE and R. P. BLACKMUR as well as articles on music, painting, and aesthetics. The journal continues to publish noteworthy literary essays and pieces on other genres as well.

Kerouac, Jack (1922–1969) *novelist, poet, and essayist*

The son of French-Canadian parents, Kerouac was born in Lowell, Massachusetts, attended Lowell High School, and gained his first job carrying water buckets for the Works Progress Administration. A bright student and superb athlete, he was recruited for Columbia University's football team. At Columbia he studied under the critic and poet Mark VAN DOREN, made friends with the poet Allen GINSBERG, and then dropped out to travel as a merchant seaman. He began writing novels in this period, the first published being *The Town and the City* (1950). More travels and odd jobs formed much of the experience reflected in his classic novel, *On the Road* (1957), one of the key texts of the BEAT era and a harbinger of the 1960s counter-culture. A heavy drinker, Kerouac died of internal bleeding after writing in rapid succession *The Dharma Bums* (1958), *The Subterraneans* (1958), *Visions of Cody* (1960), *Big Sur* (1962), and several other novels.

On the Road concerns Sal Paradise, a traveler to the West who doubles back to the Midwest and East on a kind of pilgrimage of America. He has an alter ego, Dean Moriarty (based on Kerouac's friend Neal Cassady) whose reckless energy and aesthetic sense come to symbolize the questing individual, the embodiment of America itself. Kerouac's spontaneous prose has been compared to the intense loquacity of Thomas WOLFE and to the picaresque imagination of Mark Twain.

Kerouac also exemplifies Whitman's sensual side, and the later novels—while not as highly regarded as *On the Road*—continue the saga of characters who seek out the solidarity of deep emotional involvement with others. Kerouac's characters search for the best in America, desiring to celebrate rather than criticize the national experience. Yet this optimism is severely undercut by self-destructive behavior and by the quality of novels that tend to sprawl, even though they were severely edited.

Kerouac published three books of poetry: *Mexico City Blues* (1959), *Scattered Poems* (1971), and *Old Angel Midnight* (1976). His nonfiction includes *Lonesome Traveler* (1960), *The Scripture of the Golden Eternity* (1960), *Book of Dreams* (1961), and *Satori in Paris* (1966). In style and subject matter Kerouac's verse is heavily influenced by poet Gary SNYDER, the novelist's close friend and a devotee of Eastern religions.

Sources
Amburn, Ellis. *Subterranean Kerouac: The Hidden Life of Jack Kerouac.* New York: St. Martin's Press, 1998.
Nicosia, Gerald. *Memory Babe: A Critical Biography of Jack Kerouac.* New York: Grove Press, 1983.

Kesey, Ken Elton (1935–2001) *novelist*
Ken Kesey was born in La Junta, Colorado, and attended public schools in Springfield. He was good at sports and wrestled while attending the University of Oregon. He was also good at acting and considered a career in the theater. He married his high school sweetheart in 1956 and wrote an unpublished novel, *End of Autumn,* about college athletics.

By the early 1960s Kesey had met a number of writers, including Larry MCMURTRY and Robert STONE, and began experimenting with drugs, including LSD. It was out of these experiences that he wrote his famous novel, *One Flew Over the Cuckoo's Nest* (1962), in which he portrayed the exuberant but tragic career of Randle Patrick MCMURPHY. A creative and anarchic character, McMurphy is subdued by a repressive society symbolized by the mental institution that destroys him with drugs and a lobotomy. *One Flew Over the Cuckoo's Nest* became one of the signature works of the 1960s, aided by Tom WOLFE's account of Kesey in *The Electric Kool-Aid Acid Test* (1968) and Jack Nicholson's portrayal of McMurphy in the highly successful film of the novel.

Kesey's other important novel, *Sometimes a Great Notion* (1964), was faulted for an incoherent structure, but its powerful evocation of the Stamper family is reminiscent of William FAULKNER's family sagas. Also like Faulkner, Kesey has been praised for his innovative techniques—particularly his use of time shifts and points of view.

After nearly 30 years Kesey published two more novels, *Sailor Song* (1992) and *Last Go Round* (1994). They did not excite the interest given to his earlier work, but they reflect a high level of achievement, emphasizing Kesey's interest in individualism and persistence exemplified in the physical and mental lives of his characters.

Sources
Searles, George J., ed. *A Casebook on Ken Kesey's "One Flew Over the Cuckoo's Nest."* Albuquerque: University of New Mexico Press, 1992.
Tanner, Stephen, L. *Ken Kesey.* Boston: Twayne, 1983.

Killens, John Oliver (1916–1987) *novelist*
Born in Georgia, Killens attended Howard University and Columbia University Law School before his education was interrupted by army service in World War II. His first novel, *And Then We Heard the Thunder* (1962), explores racism in the army. A founder of the Harlem Writers Guild (1952), Killens played a pivotal role in encouraging other African-American writers. His other novels include *'Sippi* (1967), a searing account of struggling African-Americans set in the 1960s, and *Cotillion* (1971), a satirical novel about conflicts within the African-American community. He also wrote *Great Gittin' Up Morning* (1972), a biography of Denmark Vesey, the slave insurrectionist.

Sources
Davis, Thadious and Trudier Harris. *Afro-American Writers After 1955.* Detroit: Gale Research, 1984.

"Killers, The" Ernest Hemingway (1927) short story

This work brought a sense of economy and drama to the modern American short story. George, a lunchroom owner, is talking with his friend Nick ADAMS when two men enter and order dinner. Similarly dressed, the two men, Al and Max, begin to banter in a sinister way. Max picks on George, asking him what he is looking at. They call Nick "bright boy" and order him to go behind the counter with George and the kitchen help. Then the men say they have been sent to kill Ole Andreson, a Swede. George says as little as possible—as do the killers. After more than a hour, Al and Max decide to leave, and George sends Nick to warn Andreson. Nick returns to say that Andreson knows about two men but has no plans to do anything about them. George advises Nick not to think about what will happen to their friend. The story is one of the best examples of Hemingway's understated style and his bleak vision of the world. There is no editorializing in the story, no commentary to soften the harsh fate that awaits Andreson.

Sources

Benson, Jackson, J. ed. New Critical Approaches to the Short Stories of Ernest Hemingway. Durham, N.C.: Duke University Press, 1990.

Smith, Paul, ed. New Essays on Hemingway's Short Fiction. New York: Cambridge University Press, 1998.

Kincaid, Jamaica (Elaine Potter Richardson)
(1949–) short fiction writer, novelist, essayist

Born in St. John's, Antigua, Kincaid left home in 1965 and worked in New York City as an au pair. This experience would become the basis of her acclaimed novel, Lucy (1990).

In New York Kincaid studied photography at the New School for Social Research, attended classes at Franconia College in New Hampshire, and worked as a secretary. In 1973 she found a job at Ingenue Magazine and began to think of a writing career. Her first book, At the Bottom of the River (1983), a collection of short stories, is heavily autobiographical, like much of her later work. Her first novel, Annie John (1985), is a searing account of her adolescence and her agonizing relationship with her mother.

Kincaid's stories and parts of her novels were published in THE NEW YORKER, which helped her attract a broad audience—as did A Small Place (1988), an essay that addressed such issues as colonialism and placed her among a new generation of post-colonialist writers of color.

Kincaid has continued to write about her own life, especially in the frank Autobiography of My Mother (1996) and My Brother (1997). Kincaid's interest in gardening is revealed in My Garden (Book) (1999). She has also edited My Favorite Plant: Writers and Gardeners on the Plants They Love (1999).

Sources

Ferguson, Moira. Jamaica Kincaid: Where The Land Meets the Body. Charlottesville: University Press of Virginia, 1994.

Paravisini-Gebert, Lizabeth. Jamaica Kincaid: A Critical Companion. Westport, Conn.: Greenwood Press, 1999.

King, Stephen (1947–) novelist, short story writer

Stephen King was born in Maine, where he has lived most of his life. His father deserted the family when King was two, and King was brought up by his conservative Methodist mother. King read comic books voraciously and began to write stories for sale by the age of 12. After earning a B.S. degree at the University of Maine, he worked as a teacher at a private school in Hampden, Maine. By the early 1970s his stories began to appear in men's magazines. In 1974 he published the novel Carrie, which became a best-seller and a motion picture starring Sissy Spacek. Carrie reveals King's great strengths as a writer: Not only does he dramatize the full horror of 16-year-old Carrie's telekinetic powers, but also he fuses her own terror to the agony she experiences as a maturing, sexually attractive young woman.

King's range is impressive. In novels such as The Stand (1978, expanded 1990) and The Tommyknockers (1987) he combines a shrewd observation of society with science fiction themes about the fate of the world and of the future. Three of his finest novels, The Shining (1977), Misery (1987), and The Dark Half (1989) investigate the plight of writers and how the imagination interacts with reality.

King has also explored the vampire myth in 'Salem's Lot (1975) and werewolves in Cycle of the Werewolf (1983). Pet Sematary (1983) is a reworking of the Frankenstein story. In The Eyes of the Dragon (1984) he explores the terrain of the fairy tale. The supernatural is often a terrifying presence in his stories and novels.

The novel Dolores Claiborne (1993) demonstrated that King could create strong and sympathetic female characters. Indeed, the appearance of his short stories in the NEW YORKER in recent years suggests that King has transcended the genre-fiction classification that for many years influenced critics who dismissed his work as merely commercial. Although King's work has been uneven, the power of his stories is undeniable.

King's short fiction has been collected in Night Shift (1978), Different Seasons (1982), Skeleton Crew (1985), Four Past Midnight (1990), Nightmares and Dreamscapes (1993), and Hearts in Atlantis (1999).

His published screenplays include Creepshow (1982) and Sleep Walkers (1992). He also wrote the teleplays for The Stand (1994) and Storm of the Century (1999).

In 2000, he published On Writing: A Memoir of the Craft.

Sources

Bloom, Harold, ed. Stephen King. New York: Chelsea House, 1998.

Magistrale, Tony, ed. *The Dark Descent: Essays Defining Stephen King's Horrorscape*. Westport, Conn.: Greenwood Press, 1992.

Kingsolver, Barbara (1955–) *novelist, poet, short story writer*

Kingsolver is from eastern Kentucky, where her father, a physician, had a practice treating the rural poor, and which had an impact on her own sympathetic portrayals of working-class characters. She earned a B.A. degree from DePauw University in Greencastle, Indiana, and then traveled extensively in the United States and Europe.

In *The Bean Trees* (1988), Kingsolver won both critical and popular acclaim with her vivid story of an independent woman, Taylor Greer, who establishes a thriving life with her adopted child, Turtle, a young Cherokee girl. The novel is set in Arizona, and Kingsolver's exquisite sense of place is evident in her wonderful evocations of both urban and desert settings.

Pigs in Heaven (1993) is the sequel to *The Bean Trees*. It is the story of the remarkable cross-country journey made by Taylor and Turtle, and of Taylor's fierce fight to keep Turtle when the legality of her adoption is challenged.

Kingsolver has also published *Animal Dreams* (1990), which is about an independent woman in a small Arizona town, and *Homeland and Other Stories* (1989). *Another America* (1991) collects her poetry about poor women attempting to overcome sexual and political abuse, and confronting war and death.

The Poisonwood Bible (1999) is a departure in both setting and subject matter. The novel deals with a missionary family in the Belgian Congo and explores that colony's struggle for independence. In *Prodigal Summer* (2000), three closely integrated stories, Kingsolver returns to her Kentucky roots.

Kingsolver has also published nonfiction: *Holding the Line: Women in the Great Arizona Mine Strike of 1983* (1989) and *High Tide in Tucson: Essays from Now or Never* (1995).

Sources

"Barbara Kingsolver." http://www.kingsolver.com/. Downloaded June 3, 2001.

DeMarr, Mary Jean. *Barbara Kingsolver: A Critical Companion*. Westport, Conn.: Greenwood, 1999.

Kingston, Maxine Hong (1940–) *novelist, autobiographer*

Kingston was born and grew up in Stockton, California, working in her parents' laundry. She graduated with a degree in English from the University of California at Berkeley and became a high school teacher. Her first book, *The Woman Warrior: Memoirs of a Girlhood Among Ghosts* (1976), won the nonfiction National Book Critics Circle Award and inspired a generation of Asian-American writers to explore both the traditions of their parents' generation and the process of as-

similation in America. The book delved into Kingston's life as a Chinese-American girl, but combined her story with the legends of Cantonese peasants and stories of her female relatives. In 1980 she published a sequel, *China Men*, which also won the National Book Critics Circle Award. This narrative, which combines memoir and story, concentrated on her father and her other male relatives. Her first novel, *Tripmaster Monkey*, (1990) the story of a young Chinese-American playwright, won the PEN West Award for fiction.

Sources

Skandera-Trombley, Laura E., ed. *Critical Essays on Maxine Hong Kingston*. New York: G.K. Hall, 1998.

Skenazy, Paul and Tera Martin, ed. *Conversations with Maxine Hong Kingston*. Jackson: University Press of Mississippi, 1998.

Kinnell, Galway (1927–) *poet*

Born in Providence, Rhode Island, and educated at Princeton University, Kinnell has made a career of teaching and publishing poetry. He is the winner of several prestigious fellowships and awards, including two Guggenheims. Many of his poems, such as "Saint Francis and the Sow" and "Blackberry Eating" are frequently anthologized, the latter revealing his deft and humorous use of poetic techniques such as alliteration. His repetition of consonants in this poem shows his delight not only in the taste of blackberries but also in the making of poetry, which became a delicious exercise. His poetry evokes a highly sensual and material world. His collections include *First Poems 1946–1954* (1970), *What a Kingdom it Was* (1960), and *Body Rags* (1968).

Sources

Tuten, Nancy Lewis. *Critical Essays on Galway Kinnell*. New York: G. K. Hall, 1996.

Kizer, Carolyn (1925–) *poet, translator*

Kizer founded the journal *Poetry Northwest* (1959–1965). Her translations of Chinese and Pakistani poetry have appeared in *The Ungrateful Garden* (1960), *Knock Upon Silence* (1965), and *Midnight Was My Cry* (1971). Her own career as a poet began with *Mermaids in the Basement: Poems for Women* (1984) and *Yin: New Poems* (1984), which won a Pulitzer Prize. Her other poetry collections include *The Nearness of You* (1986). *Carrying Over* (1988) contains an impressive range of translations from languages as diverse as Yiddish and Chinese. *Proses: On Poems & Poets* appeared in 1993.

Sources

Finch, Annie, Johanna Keller, and Candace McClellan, eds. *Carolyn Kizer: Perspectives on Her Life & Work*. Fort Lee, N.J.: CavanKerry Press, 2001.

Knopf, Alfred (1892–1984) and Blanche Wolf (1894–1966) publishers

Founders of the distinguished American publishing house Alfred A. Knopf, which introduced new European writers to Americans, the couple were married in 1916, a year after Alfred Knopf began publishing. They shrewdly sought out the best European and American authors such as Thomas Mann, Willa CATHER, and Langston HUGHES, and were known for producing books elegantly, with many different handsome typefaces and high-quality paper. Random House bought Knopf in 1960, and Knopf ceased to be an independent publisher. Yet the traditions of the company have largely remained intact, and Knopf is still considered one of the most prestigious imprints in publishing.

Sources

Oliphant, Dave, ed. *The Company They Kept: Alfred A. and Blanche W. Knopf, Publishers: An Exhibition Catalog*. Austin: Harry Ransom Humanities Research Center, University of Texas at Austin, 1995.

Knowles, John (1926–2001) novelist

Born in West Virginia and educated at Yale University, Knowles was widely acclaimed *for A Separate Peace* (1960), a novel set in a New England boys' school during WORLD WAR II, which has become required reading on many high school and college syllabi. Like J. D. SALINGER's THE CATCHER IN THE RYE it captures the painful experiences of adolescence with sensitivity and respect. His other novels include *Peace Breaks Out* (1981) the sequel to *A Separate Peace, Spreading Fires* (1974), and a story collection, *Phineas* (1968).

Sources

Bryant, Hallman Bell. *"A Separate Peace": The War Within*. Boston: Twayne, 1990.

Kober, Arthur (1900–1974) playwright, short story writer, screenwriter

Kober was born in Poland, but he was brought to New York City as a child and lived there, except for periods of work in Hollywood, for the rest of his life. He was married to the playwright Lillian HELLMAN from 1930 to 1934. His first great success on Broadway was *Having Wonderful Time* (1937), a comedy about New York City office workers and their experiences on vacation in the Catskills. The play became the basis for a musical, *Wish You Were Here* (1952), and drew on the sketches of city life that he had published for years in THE NEW YORKER. Many of the stories were about a character named Bella. Later she appeared in several collections: *Thunder Over the Bronx* (1935), *My Dear Bella* (1941), and *Bella, Bella, Kissed a Fella* (1951). Kober's tales of Hollywood appear in *Pardon Me For Pointing* (1939) and *That Man is Here Again (1947)*.

Sources

Rollyson, Carl. *Lillian Hellman: Her Legend and Her Legacy*. New York: St. Martin's Press, 1988.

Koch, Kenneth Jay (1925–) poet

Born in Cincinnati, Kenneth Koch is a product of Harvard and Columbia Universities, and he has taught at Columbia for many years. He is associated with the NEW YORK SCHOOL OF POETS, which also includes John ASHBERY and Frank O'HARA. He has written in a variety of styles: SURREALISM in *Poems* (1953), octava rima (eight syllable lines) in *Ko*, and the comic epic in *The Duplications* (1977). *The Burning Mystery of Anna in 1951* (1979) experiments with using prose and poetry together. Koch has also achieved renown for his books about teaching children to write poetry, especially *Wishes, Lies and Dreams: Teaching Children to Write Poetry* (1970). Koch's collections of his own poetry include *Ko, or A Season on Earth* (1959) and *Selected Poems 1950–1982* (1985), and *The Art of Poetry: Poems, Parodies, Interviews, Essays, and Other Work* (1996).

Sources

Auslander, Philip. *The New York School Poets as Playwrights: O'Hara, Ashbery, Koch, Schuyler, and the Visual Arts*. New York: Peter Lang, 1989.

Kolodny, Annette (1941–) critic

An influential feminist scholar, Kolodny is the author of *Dancing Through the Minefield: Theory, Method, and Politics in Feminist Literary Criticism* (1983). She takes a radical perspective on sexuality and literature, taking her inspiration from the 1960s counterculture. She is also the author of *Westering Women: Fantasies of the American Frontiers, 1630–1860* (1983).

Sources

Kolodny, Annette. "Some Notes on Defining a 'Feminist Literary Criticism,'" *Critical Inquiry* 2, no. 1 (Autumn 1975). Available on-line. URL: http://www.uchicago.edu/research/jnl-crit-inq/vl-v19/v2n1.kolodny.html. Downloaded July 26, 2001.
Kolodny, Annette. "The Feminist as a Literary Critic," *Critical Inquiry* 2, no. 4 (September 1976). Available on-line. URL: http://www.uchicago.edu/research/jnl-crit-inq/vl-v19/v2n4.kolodny.html. Downloaded July 26, 2001.

Kopit, Arthur (1937–) playwright

A New York native whose plays border on the absurd even as they probe domestic settings and family life, Kopit is best known for *Oh Dad, Poor Dad, Mama's Hung You in the Closet and I'm Feeling So Sad* (1960). His later plays include *Indians* (1968) and *Wings* (1978).

Sources

Auerbach, Doris. *Sam Shepard, Arthur Kopit, and the Off Broadway Theater.* Boston: Twayne, 1982.

Korean War

Communist North Korean troops invaded South Korea on June 25, 1950, in an effort to overthrow the government and reunite a country that had been divided at the end of WORLD WAR II when the Japanese occupying forces had been forced out. Under U.S. leadership the United States launched a police action to repel the invasion, which then seemed part of the Soviet Union's COLD WAR strategy to put the entire country under the Communist rule of the North. (Much later it was learned that the North Koreans had acted independently of Soviet influence).

U.S. forces did push back the Koreans, but General Douglas MacArthur's aggressive actions provoked a Chinese attack, and President Truman relieved MacArthur of command. On July 27, 1953, a truce was signed, although the two Koreas remained officially at war and tensions between them have continued.

Novels written about the conflict include James Michener's *The Bridges at Toko-ri* (1953), Duane Thorin's *Ride to Panmunjon* (1956), A. M. Harris's *Tall Man* (1958), Ernest Frankel's *Band of Brothers* (1959), and Quentin Reynolds's *Known But to God* (1960). In *The Martyred* (1964), Richard Kim provides a riveting account of Seoul, the capital of South Korea, during the North Korean occupation. The film *M*A*S*H* is a black comedy set in a U.S. army mobile surgical hospital during the war. It was also made into a successful television series.

Sources

Goldstein, Donald M. and Harry J. Maihafer. *The Korean War.* New York: Brasseys, 2000.

Jason, Philip K., ed. "Novels of the Korean War," The Korean War in Literature: Biographies of the Korean War. Available on-line. URL: http://www.illyria.com/Korea_html. Updated June 2001.

———. "Short Fiction of the Korean War," The Korean War in Literature: Biographies of the Korean War. Available on-line. URL: http://www.illyria.com/Korea_top.html. Updated June 28, 2001.

Varhola, Michael J. *Fire and Ice: The Korean War, 1950–1953.* New York: Stackpole Books, 2000.

Kosinski, Jerzy Nikodem (1933–1991) *novelist, sociologist*

Born in Lodz, Poland, Jerzy Kosinski spent a harrowing childhood in rural Poland. He described his ordeal in a novel, *The Painted Bird* (1965). He was later attacked for exaggerating and perhaps inventing much of his suffering as a Jewish child during the Holocaust. But certainly Kosinski felt the tensions of anti-Semitism in Poland and saw the dangers of collectivist society, which he wrote about in *The Future Is Ours, Comrade* (1960) and *No Third Path* (1962), two sociological studies which he published under the name of Joseph Novak.

With degrees in history and political science from the University of Lodz, Kosinski arrived in NEW YORK CITY in 1957. He studied English intensely and became fluent. He married Mary Haward Weir, the young widow of a steel magnate. She died in 1968, by which time Kosinski had turned to fiction.

Kosinski's second novels, *Steps* (1968), won the National Book Award, and like his first novel it blends the real and surreal, historical events, autobiography, and phantasmagoric scenes that reflected a powerful imagination. *The Painted Bird* is the story of a boy's education about life, his struggle to survive among cruel Polish peasants, and his ability to absorb even the most brutal behavior and conditions. *Steps,* on the other hand, is much more elusive, with its succession of 50 individual scenes, with characters repeating themselves but with no central narrative consciousness explicitly tying the episodes together. What binds Kosinski's two early novels together, however, is an exploration of human deceit, manipulation, and revenge.

Of Kosinski's later novels, *Being There* (1971) is the most successful. Its portrayal of Chance, a man without personality who takes on the features of whatever setting or events he is exposed to, is a carefully crafted comment on a contemporary world dominated by television. Chance simply acts as he has seen people do on television, and he is remarkably successful. The novel was made into a brilliant film starring Peter Sellers.

Kosinski's later novels received less praise and seem to represent a decline in energy and creativity, although his work continued to sell well. His later novels include *Cockpit* (1975), *Blind Date* (1977), *Passion Play* (1979), and *Pinball* (1982).

Kosinski was active in New York City's social life. He played polo and taught at Yale, Princeton, and Wesleyan Universities. He married Katherian von Frauenhofer in 1987, and served a term as president of PEN (Poets, Playwrights, Editors, Essayists, and Novelists). Beset with attacks on the veracity of his experience in Poland and on the authorship of his fiction (he was accused of employing others to write his books), along with failing health and an inability to concentrate on his writing, Kosinski committed suicide. His *Passing By: Selected Essays, 1962–1991* was published in 1992.

Sources

Lavers, Norman. *Jerzy Kosinski.* Boston: Twayne, 1982.

Sloan, James Park. *Jerzy Kosinski: A Biography.* New York: Dutton, 1996.

Tepa Lupack, Barbara, ed. *Critical Essay on Jerzy Kosinski.* New York: G. K. Hall, 1998.

Kramer, Larry (1935–) *novelist, playwright, journalist*

Kramer grew up in Bridgeport, Connecticut, earned a B.A. degree from Yale in 1957, served in the army, and began work at the William Morris Agency in 1958. He later worked for Columbia Pictures. His first writing credit was a screenplay for the 1969 adaptation of D. H. Lawrence's novel *Women in Love*. But Kramer built his reputation as an outspoken writer about gay life and as an advocate for gay rights. His novel *Faggots* (1978) is a satiric attack on gay life in New York City and its environs as well as an exposé of the drug culture and the promiscuous and sadomasochistic practices of his characters. The novel was attacked by both mainstream and gay critics, but it also sold well and established Kramer's credentials as an authority on gay life. By 1987 Kramer's involvement in gay life had changed radically, largely because of the devastating impact AIDS had on the gay community. Kramer became one of the strongest advocates for prompt treatment of the disease and for the search for a cure. His play *The Normal Heart* (1986), one of the first important responses to the AIDS epidemic, won the Dramatists Guild Marton Award and the City Lights Award, the Sarah Siddons Award for the best play of the year, and a nomination for an Olivier Award. The play explored many responses to AIDS, including the possibility of abstinence from sex. Like *Faggots*, *The Normal Heart* proved controversial, although the play received better reviews than the novel and is now regarded as a major contribution to the theater. A second play, *The Destiny of Me* (1992), continues the themes of *The Normal Heart*. Kramer's nonfiction includes *Reports from the Holocaust: The Making of an AIDS Activist* (1989). *Brilliant Windows: Poems* was published in 1998.

Sources

Kramer, Larry. "His Brilliant Career." *The Advocate*. May 16, 1995. Available on-line. URL: http://www.advocate.com/html/stories/811/811_laurents_kram.asp. Downloaded June 3, 2001.

Mass, Lawrence, ed. *We Must Love One Another or Die: The Life and Legacies of Larry Kramer*. New York: St. Martin's Press, 1998.

Krutch, Joseph Wood (1893–1970) *literary critic, social commentator*

Krutch was born in Tennessee, studied at the state university and received a Ph.D. from Columbia University in 1923, where he taught for several years while also serving on the editorial staff of the *Nation*. His most influential work is *The Modern Temper* (1929), a grim assessment of contemporary culture: it suggests that science has deprived the modern intellectual of confidence. His work complemented the sense of decadence apparent in T. S. ELIOT and Ezra POUND. Krutch provided critics with a handy definition of the early 20th century, a definition they could ratify or repudiate. Krutch's biographies include *Samuel Johnson* (1944) and *Thoreau* (1948). After Krutch moved to Arizona in the 1950s, he wrote about human nature, the environment, and nature in *The Desert Year* (1952) and *Human Nature and the Human Condition* (1959). *More Lives Than One* (1962) is a memoir.

Sources

Margolis, John. *Joseph Wood Krutch: A Writer's Life*. Knoxville: University of Tennessee Press, 1980.

Kumin, Maxine Winokur (1925–) *novelist, poet*

Born in Philadelphia, Kumin won the Pulitzer Prize for *Up Country: Poems of New England* in 1972. Her first novel. *Through Dooms of Love* (1965), draws on her experience at Radcliffe College. Other novels include *Passions of Export* (1968) and *The Designated Heir* (1974). She is considered a superb nature poet. Kumin's work is noteworthy for the ways it integrates descriptions of family life, nature, and the cycle of existence as well as issues of Jewish identity and farm life. Her later collections include *Our Ground Times Will be Brief* (1982) and *Nurture* (1989). She has also published essay collections: *To Make a Prairie* (1979) and *In Deep* (1987).

Sources

Grosholz, Emily, ed. *Telling the Barn Swallow: Poets on the Poetry of Maxine Kumin*. Hanover, N.H.: University Press of New England, 1997.

Kunitz, Stanley Jasspon (1905–) *poet*

One of the most long-lived poets of the 20th century, Stanley Kunitz was born in Worcester, Massachusetts, and educated at Harvard. He has been influential as both a translator and anthologist. He won the Pulitzer Prize for *Selected Poems* in 1958. One of his signature poems, "Father and Son," collected in *Passport to the War*, is about a son's search for his father. He has been praised for his translation of Anna Akhmatova's poetry in *Antiworlds and the Fifth Ace* (1967). In *The Testing Tree* (1971) he experiments with unrhymed verse of differing line lengths and explores the theme of imagination and its relationship to memory. In his 90s, Kunitz continues to produce poetry of a high order. His anthologies include *Contemporary Poetry in America* (1973) and *The Essential Blake* (1987).

Sources

Orr, Gregory. *Stanley Kunitz: An Introduction to the Poetry*. New York: Columbia University Press, 1985.

Kushner, Tony (1956–) *playwright*

Kushner was born in New York City but reared in Lake Charles, Louisiana. Encouraged by his parents, he studied drama at both Columbia University and New York University. He began writing and producing plays in the 1980s. His desire to write epics that deal with broad historical canvases is apparent in his first play, *A Bright Room Called Day* (1985), which shifts between Germany in the 1930s and America in the 1980s.

Kushner's two-part play, *Angels in America* (*Millennium Approaches,* 1991; *Perestroika,* 1993) took him from regional theater to the New York stage. Subtitled *A Gay Fantasia on National Themes,* the play won a Pulitzer Prize in 1993. It explored the advent of AIDS in the gay community and its impact on American culture. The play's humor and its blend of REALISM and EXPRESSIONISM made Kushner the worthy heir of European and American models such as Bertolt Brecht and Eugene O'NEILL.

Tony Kushner in Conversation, a series of interviews, appeared in 1998. Kushner has published *Thinking About the Longstanding Problems of Virtue and Happiness: Essays, A Play, Two Poems, and a Prayer* (1995) and *Death & Taxes: Hydriotaphia & Other Plays* (2000) and *Homebody/Kabul* (2002).

Sources

Aull, Felice. "Kushner, Tony: Angels in America." Theatre Communications Group (New York). Available on-line. URL: http://mchip00.nyu.edu/lit-med/li-med/db/webdocs/webdescrips/kushner1050-des-.html. Updated July 13, 1998.

Brask, Per, ed. *Essays on Kushner's Angels.* Winnipeg: Blizzard Publishing, 1995.

Vorlicky, Robert, ed. *Tony Kushner in Conversation.* Ann Arbor: University of Michigan Press, 1997.

La Farge, Oliver (1901–1963) *novelist, short story writer*

Born in New York City, La Farge graduated from Harvard with a degree in anthropology and archaeology and a fascination with Native American life. He won a Pulitzer Prize for his novel *The Laughing Boy* (1929), which reflected his experiences as an archaeologist working with Navajo Indians. His other books include a collection of short stories, *All the Young Men* (1935); *A Pictorial History of the American Indian* (1956); *The Enemy Gods* (1937), a novel about the Navajo; *As Long as the Grass Shall Grow* (1940), a history of the American Indian; and *Raw Material* (1945), a memoir of his intellectual development.

Sources
Gillis, Everett A. *Oliver La Farge.* Austin, Tex.: Steck-Vaughn, 1967.

L'Amour, Louis (1910–1988) *novelist, short story writer*

Born in North Dakota, L'Amour spent much of his life in Los Angeles writing vastly popular novels about the American West. He published at least 200 novels and 14 books of stories. A memoir, *Education of a Wandering Man* (1989), was published shortly after his death. See also WESTERNS.

Sources
Gale, Robert L. *Louis L'Amour.* New York: Twayne, 1992.

Lardner, Ringgold Wilmer (1885–1933) *short story writer, journalist*

Born in Niles, Michigan, Ring Lardner began his career as a newspaper columnist and sportswriter. He had a gift for capturing American speech—usually in humorous stories and sketches. He wrote satire and peopled his stories with unforgettable characters: baseball players, boxers, songwriters, stockbrokers, stenographers, chorus girls. His first significant book, *You Know Me, Al* (1916), a collection of stories still anthologized, demonstrates his gift for vividly rendering American slang in his accounts of a baseball team. *Gullible's Travels* (1917) was just as good and exhibited Lardner's talent for parody. He lampooned writing guides in *How to Write Short Stories (With Samples)* (1924). *The Love Nest and Other Stories* (1926) includes the classic "Haircut." Lardner also wrote a humorous autobiography, *The Story of a Wonder Man* (1927).

Sources
Patrick, Walton R. *Ring Lardner.* New York: Twayne, 1963.
Yardley, Jonathan. *Ring: A Biography of Ring Lardner.* New York: Random House, 1977.

Lardner, Ringgold Wilmer, Jr. (1915–2000) *screenwriter, novelist, biographer*

A son of Ring LARDNER, he had a distinguished career as a screenwriter. He won an Academy Award for *Woman of the Year* (1942) and wrote the screenplay for *M*A*S*H* (1970). He was sent to prison for refusing to testify about his Communist affiliations before the House Committee on

Un-American Activities. He later turned this experience into a novel, *The Ecstasy of Owen Muir* (1955), and a memoir, *I'd Hate Myself in the Morning* (2000). He also wrote a biography/memoir about his family, *The Lardners* (1976).

Sources

Dick, Bernard F. *Radical Innocence: A Critical Study of the Hollywood Ten.* Lexington: University Press of Kentucky, 1989.
Dmytryk, Edward. *Odd Man Out: A Memoir of the Hollywood Ten.* Carbondale: Southern Illinois University Press, 1996.

Larsen, Nella (1891–1964) *novelist*

Larsen was born in Chicago, the daughter of a West Indian man and a Danish woman. She divided her early years between Denmark and the United States. Her first novel, *Quicksand* (1928), is autobiographical. Set in Alabama, it deals with an African-American woman who marries an evangelist and is horrified by the racist South. Larsen's other novel, *Passing* (1929), is a tragedy about an African-American woman with fair skin who tries to live as a white woman with a white man. It is comparable to James Weldon JOHNSON's novel, THE AUTOBIOGRAPHY OF AN EX-COLORED MAN (1912). Larsen was associated with the figures in the HARLEM RENAISSANCE. She has been criticized for writing like a white and not writing more in the idiom of African Americans, although other critics discount this attitude as narrow-minded.

Sources

Wall, Cheryl A. *Women of the Harlem Renaissance.* Bloomington: Indiana University Press, 1997.

Laughlin, James (1914–1997) *poet, publisher*

Laughlin is best known for founding NEW DIRECTIONS in 1936, which has published modernist and contemporary writers of distinction, as well as literary criticism and literature in translation. Laughlin's creative work is collected in *Wild Anemone and Other Poems* (1957) and *Selected Poems* (1960). His *Collected Poems* appeared in 1994. His correspondence with the writers he published is extensive. W. W. Norton has published series of letters between Laughlin and William Carlos WILLIAMS (1989), Kenneth REXROTH (1991), Delmore SCHWARTZ (1993), Ezra POUND (1994), Henry MILLER (1996), and Thomas MERTON (1997).

Sources

Carruth, Hayden. *Beside the Shadblow Tree: A Memoir of James Laughlin.* Port Townsend, Wash.: Copper Canyon Press, 1999.
Dana, Robert, ed. *Against the Grain: Interviews with Maverick American Publishers.* Iowa City: University of Iowa Press, 1986.

Lawson, John Howard (1895–1977) *dramatist, screenwriter*

Lawson grew up in New York City. His early expressionist plays include *Roger Bloomer* (1923) and *Processional* (1925). His later work reflects his interest in PROLETARIAN LITERATURE and radical politics. *Marching Song* (1937), for example, is the dramatization of a sit-down strike. Lawson was one of the Hollywood Ten, a group of screenwriters who refused to testify about their political affiliations and were jailed during the COLD WAR period. Lawson spent a year in prison and had to write scripts under pseudonyms. He also published *Theory and Technique of Playwriting* (1936), *Film in the Battle of Ideas* (1953), and *Film: The Creative Process* (1964).

Sources

Carr, Gary. *The Left Side of Paradise: The Screenwriting of John Howard Lawson.* Ann Arbor, Mich.: UMI Research Press, 1984.
Dick, Bernard F. *Radical Innocence: A Critical Study of the Hollywood Ten.* Lexington: University Press of Kentucky, 1989.
Dmytryk, Edward. *Odd Man Out: A Memoir of the Hollywood Ten.* Carbondale: Southern Illinois University Press, 1996.

Leavitt, David (1961–) *novelist, short story writer*

A Pittsburgh-born writer whose story collection *Family Dancing* (1984) was a finalist for the National Book Critics Circle Award and the PEN/Faulkner Award for fiction, Leavitt began his publishing career with a short story in THE NEW YORKER. His first novel, *The Lost Language of Cranes* (1986), was well received. It explored the sexual coming-out of a young gay man and his father's own struggle with his sexuality. *Equal Affections* (1989), his second novel, drew on Leavitt's family experience in its depiction of a gay lawyer and his family. A third novel, *While England Sleeps* (1993), became controversial when poet Stephen Spender accused Leavitt of drawing too closely on Spender's memoir *World Within World* (1951). Leavitt had to withdraw and rewrite the book for publication in 1995. He has also edited *The Penguin Book of Gay Short Stories* (1994) and published *Arkansas: Three Novellas* (1997); two novels, *The Page Turner* (1998) and *Martin Bauman, or A Sure Thing* (2000), the story of a gay writer; two travel books, *Italian Pleasures* (1996) and *In Maremma: Life and a House in Southern Tuscany* (2001); and a story collection, *A Place I've Never Been* (1990).

Sources

Guscio, Lelia. *We Trust Ourselves and Money, Period: Relationships, Death, and Homosexuality in David Leavitt's Fiction.* New York: Peter Lang, 1995.

Lee, Harper (Nelle Harper Lee) (1926–) *novelist*

Harper Lee's only novel, TO KILL A MOCKINGBIRD (1960), won the Pulitzer Prize for fiction (1961), was made into a major motion picture in 1962, and became a staple in the school curriculum because of its sensitive portrayal of a young white girl whose father defends a black man accused of raping a white woman in a small southern town. Lee is a descendant of the Confederate general Robert E. Lee. She grew up in Monroeville, Alabama, where her father practiced as a lawyer and where she befriended Truman CAPOTE, who became a model for the character Dill in her novel. Her novel has sold over 30,000,000 copies. She has never published another.

Sources
Bloom, Harold, ed. *To Kill a Mockingbird*. Philadelphia: Chelsea House, 1999.

Le Guin, Ursula Kroeber (1929–) *novelist, essayist*

Ursula K. Le Guin was born in Berkeley, California, and credits her anthropologist father for instilling in her a love of stories and of myth. Educated at Radcliffe (B.A., 1951) and Columbia (M.A., 1952), Le Guin married the historian Charles Le Guin in 1953 and had three children. *The Left Hand of Darkness* (1976) is considered her masterpiece in the science fiction genre. *The Word for World is Forest* (1976) combines her interest in fantasy, ecology, and anthropology. Like other science fiction authors, she has produced multiple series of books about alternative worlds, including the Hainish universe, first described in *Rocannon's World* (1966), and the allegorical trilogy for children collected as *Earthsea* (1977). *The Dispossessed: An Ambiguous Utopia* (1974) explores political issues, especially anarchism.

Buffalo Gals, Won't You Come Out Tonight (1994) is a highly praised book of short stories about animals. *Unlocking the Air and Other Stories* was published in 1997. Le Guin has also published a series of "Catwings" novels for children. *Sixty Odd: New Poems* was published in 1999.

Le Guin's later novels include an omnibus edition of *City of Illusions, Rocannon's World,* and *Planet of Exile* (1996), *The Eye of the Heron* (1999), and *The Telling* (2000), a continuation of the Hainish cycle.

Le Guin has also published *The Language of the Night* (1979), a collection of her writing on feminism. She discusses her way of writing and other women writers in *Dancing at the Edge of the World* (1989).

Sources
Bloom, Harold, ed. *Ursula Le Guin*. New York: Chelsea House, 2000.
Reid, Suzanne Elizabeth. *Presenting Ursula K. Le Guin*. New York: Twayne, 1997.

Leithauser, Brad (1953–) *poet, novelist, essayist*

Leithauser was born in Detroit, educated at Harvard, and a resident of Japan for several years. His first book of poetry, *Hundreds of Fireflies* (1982), showed an impressive handling of verse and vocabulary that reminded critics of James MERRILL, one of Leithauser's influences. Leithauser's later collections of poetry include *Between Leaps: Poems 1972–1985* (1987) and *The Odd Thing She Did* (1998), praised for its strong narrative drive.

Leithauser has also drawn on his Japanese sojourn in an impressive novel, *Equal Distance* (1985). He has published four other novels, *Hence* (1989); *Seaward* (1993), the story of Terry Seaward, a Washington, D.C., lawyer; *A Few Connections* (2001), the story of the late Wes Sulton, a Rotarian in Restoration, Michigan, the subject of his son Luke's investigations; and *Friends of Freeland* (1993), is the story of a fictitious country between Iceland and Greenland. *Penchants and Places: Essays and Criticism* was published in 1995.

Sources
Flowers, Charles. "The Friend of Freeland." Available online. URL: http://www.bookpage.com/970lbp/fiction/friendsoffreeland.html
Kirsch, Adam. "Tales and Meditations." Available online. URL: http://www.nytimes.com/books/98/10/11/reviews/981011.11kirscht.html

Le Sueur, Meridel (1900–1996) *journalist, novelist*

Le Sueur was born in Iowa and reared in Texas, Oklahoma, and Kansas. Her father was a radical lawyer, and she absorbed his politics, moving to New York and befriending socialists. She wrote for the *Daily Worker* and *The NEW MASSES*. Her novel, *The Girl* (1939), and a collection of stories, *Salute to Spring* (1940), concentrate on the hardships of women during the GREAT DEPRESSION and reflect her sympathetic connections to PROLETARIAN LITERATURE. Like many radicals she was investigated during the COLD WAR period. She wrote fiction sporadically and made her living as a journalist. *Ripening: Selected Work 1927–1980* appeared in 1982.

Sources
Boehnlein, James M. *The Sociocognitive Rhetoric of Meridel Le Sueur: Feminist Discourse and Reportage of the Thirties*. Lewiston, N.Y.: Edwin Mellen Press, 1994.
Coiner, Constance. *Better Red: The Writing and Resistance of Tillie Olsen and Meridel Le Sueur*. New York: Oxford University Press, 1995.

Let Us Now Praise Famous Men James Agee (1941)

James AGEE's powerful account of sharecropping families in GREAT DEPRESSION–era America, with photographs by the famous photographer Walker Evans, began in 1936 as a series of articles for FORTUNE magazine, but the articles were not printed because they were not conventional reporting. The text and pictures aimed, instead, to present an all-encompassing view of hardy but suffering rural people enduring the worst of the Depression. Both the text and the photographs created a degree of intimacy and contact with the poor perhaps not equaled since Jacob Riis's classic books of pictures and text about the urban poor, *How the Other Half Lives* (1890). Agee and Evans presented a compelling and compassionate portrait of rural poverty through Agee's poetic writing style and Evans's carefully composed photographs. This profoundly sympathetic account of the poor is reminiscent of other works of PROLETARIAN LITERATURE, especially John STEINBECK's novel *THE GRAPES OF WRATH* (1939).

Sources

Böger, Astrid. *Documenting Lives: James Agee's and Walker Evans's Let Us Now Praise Famous Men.* New York: Peter Lang, 1994.

Maharidge, Dale and Michael Williamson. *And Their Children After Them: The Legacy of Let Us Now Praise Famous Men: James Agee, Walker Evans, and The Rise and Fall of Cotton in the South.* New York: Pantheon Books, 1989.

Levertov, Denise (1923–1998) *poet, essayist*

Born in England, the daughter of a Russian Jewish father and Welsh mother, Levertov served as a nurse in World War II, married an American, Mitchell Goodman, and settled in the United States in 1948. She became a U.S. citizen in 1955 and regarded herself as an American poet. Levertov had one son before divorcing in the 1970s.

Influenced by William Carlos WILLIAMS and H.D., Levertov also became associated with Charles OLSON, Robert DUNCAN, and the BLACK MOUNTAIN POETS. A prolific poet, Levertov has been praised for capturing the rhythms of colloquial speech as well as for her political awareness (the VIETNAM WAR figures largely in her work). Her poetry has also explored the horrific possibility of nuclear holocaust and America's involvement in countries such as El Salvador.

Given its high quality and consistency, Levertov's work is frequently anthologized, with selections of her poetry ranging from the 1950s to the 1980s. Her books include *Overland to the Islands* (1958), *The Sorrow Dance* (1967), *The Freeing of the Dust* (1975), *Collected Poems 1960–1974* (1976), *Collected Poems 1940–1960* (1979), *Breathing the Water* (1987), *Door in the Hive* (1993), and *The Life Around Us: Selected Poems on Nature* (1997), and *This Great Unknowing: Last Poems* (1999). She published two books about poetry: *The Poet in the World* (1973) and *Light Up the Cave* (1981), and a memoir, *Tesserae: Memories & Suppositions* (1995).

Sources

Brooker, Jewel Spears, ed. *Conversations with Denise Levertov.* Jackson: University Press of Mississippi, 1998.

Marten, Harry. *Understanding Denise Levertov.* Columbia: University of South Carolina Press, 1988.

Wagner-Martin, Linda, ed. *Critical Essays on Denise Levertov.* Boston: G. K. Hall, 1991.

Levin, Ira (1929–) *novelist, playwright*

Levin was born in New York City and educated at New York University. He served in the army and then wrote his first horror novel, *A Kiss Before Dying* (1953). His most popular work is *Rosemary's Baby* (1967), about a woman impregnated by the devil. The novel became a successful motion picture directed by Roman Polanski and starring Mia Farrow. Levin's other horror/fantasy novels include *The Perfect Day* (1970), about a nightmarish computerized world; *The Stepford Wives* (1972), the story of robot women; and *The Boys from Brazil* (1976), the story of Josef Mengele, a Nazi doctor who attempts to create clones of Adolf Hitler.

Levin has also produced several popular plays, including *No Time for Sergeants* (1955) and *Deathtrap* (1978).

Levin's later work includes *Sliver: A Novel* (1991) and *Son of Rosemary: The Sequel to Rosemary's Baby* (1997).

Sources

Fowler, Douglas. *Ira Levin.* San Bernardino, Calif.: Borgo Press, 1989.

Levine, Philip (1928–) *poet*

Levine was born, raised, and educated in Detroit, Michigan, the setting for many of his finest poems. As a young man he worked in automobile factories and at other menial jobs. His work celebrates his fellow workers and tries to express the poetry of their experience. Levine's most important book is *They Feed They Lion* (1972), a collection that, in the words of the title poem, explores the "acids of rage" that provoked the Detroit race riot of 1967.

Levine also writes about his own experience in Detroit and of his family in books like *1933* (1974), which is the year his father, a Russian-Jewish immigrant, died. "Letters to the Dead" recalls his father's but also the past of "all the dead fathers." Levine has been called the poet of the midcentury city.

Levine is a memory poet, constantly returning to the scene of his life and work in Detroit. He left the city in 1953, and his writing about it did not begin to see publication in book form until 1963 in *On the Edge.* His other important books include *Ashes: Poems New and Old* (1979), *Selected Poems* (1984), and *New Selected Poems* (1991). His poetry collection *What Work Is* (1991) won the National Book Award.

In 1994 Levine published *The Bread of Time: Toward an Autobiography.*

Sources

Buckley, Christopher, ed. *On the Poetry of Philip Levine: Stranger to Nothing.* Ann Arbor: University of Michigan Press, 1991.

Lewis, Janet (1899–1998) *poet, novelist*

Born and raised in Chicago, Lewis graduated from the University of Chicago and married the poet and critic Yvor WIN-TERS. Her books, especially *Poems Old and New, 1918–1978* (1981), have been praised for their clarity and calm. She has written novels about a variety of subjects and settings, including a Michigan family with an Indian heritage in *The Invasion* (1932); 17th-century Denmark in *The Trial of Soren Qvist* (1947); and the France of Louis XIV in *The Ghost of Monsieur Scarron* (1959). Her short stories are collected in *Goodbye, Son* (1946).

Sources

Crow, Charles L. *Janet Lewis.* Boise, Idaho: Boise State University, 1980.

Lewis, Oscar (1914–1970) *anthropologist*

La Vida (1966), Lewis's study of Puerto Ricans, won a National Book Award, and his previous works, *Five Families* (1959) and *Children of Sanchez* (1961), were also acclaimed as sensitive portraits of the poor. The books were based on hundreds of hours of tape-recorded interviews, exquisitely edited so that they created stories of lives that were as dramatic and well crafted as many works of fiction. As an anthropologist Lewis gave a voice to the poor, and the literary power of his books enhanced the prestige of what Truman CAPOTE called the nonfiction novel. Lewis crafted fact into story, and his ability to catch the cadence of his interviewees is comparable to Norman MAILER's orchestration of voices in his fact-based novel, *The Executioner's Song* (1979).

Sources

Teiser, Ruth and Catherine Harroun. *Oscar Lewis—Literary San Francisco: An Interview.* Berkeley: University of California, Bancroft Library/Berkeley, Regional Oral History Office, 1965.

Lewis, Richard Warrington Baldwin (1917–) *critic, biographer*

Born in Chicago, educated at Harvard and the University of Chicago, R. W. B. Lewis established his reputation with *The American Adam* (1955), a stimulating treatment of 19th-century American literature that focused on the idea of America as a new paradise. His biography, *Edith Wharton* (1975), won a Pulitzer Prize and helped to renew interest in Wharton's work. He also published *The Jameses* (1991) and *The City of Florence: Historical Vistas and Personal Sightings* (1995).

Lewis, Sinclair (Harry Sinclair Lewis) (1885–1951) *novelist*

Born in Sauk Centre, Minnesota, Sinclair Lewis graduated from Yale University in 1908 and began work as a journalist. He published his first novel, *Hike and the Aeroplane,* an adventure story intended for young boys, in 1912. His other early novels, *Our Mr. Wrenn: The Romantic Adventures of a Gentle Man* (1914) and *The Job: An American Novel* (1917), reveal a writer still searching for a style and tone appropriate to his satirical talents.

Main Street (1920), Lewis's first mature novel, caused great controversy. He had found his subject: the complacency of small-town life set in the Midwest. In the prosperous decade of the 1920s, Lewis portrayed the energy, the comedy, and the pathos of American commercial culture. The American businessman had found his poet, who treated the business world with intense focus and eloquence, albeit an astringent one who mocked the country's pieties and go-getter enthusiasm. At the heart of all money-making, Lewis suggested, was an emptiness. Thus his most famous character, George Babbitt (BABBITT, 1922), in his heart of hearts yearns for a sense of fulfillment and of romance that is sorely lacking in his successful career as realtor and Rotarian.

A succession of brilliant novels—*Arrowsmith* (1925), the study of a small-town doctor; *Elmer Gantry* (1927), about a philandering preacher; and *Dodsworth* (1929), detailing the European adventures of an American automobile manufacturer—revealed Lewis's comprehensive grasp of his country's manners and mores. Although he was highly critical of his characters and country, the lavish detail of his settings and characters (Lewis's experience as a reporter served him well) implied affection for his creations as well. No American writer before Lewis had commented on such a wide range of American types and institutions in such a precise, entertaining, and shrewd style.

At the height of his powers Lewis was awarded the 1930 Nobel Prize in literature. Unfortunately, none of his subsequent work matched the quality of his great decade of creativity. Critics found that such novels as *Ann Vickers* (1933) lacked Lewis's trademark satire. His characterizations softened and became sentimentalized. He recovered his role as social and political critic, however, in the novel *It Can't Happen Here* (1935), which warned that conditions in the United States were ripe for a fascist dictator.

Lewis found the Nobel Prize more of a burden than an inspiration: He is said to have believed that there were other American writers who deserved the honor more. How much his devastating alcoholism contributed to the uninspired later novels such as *Cass Timberlane* (1945) and *Kingsblood Royal* (1947) is debatable.

Lewis's stormy marriage to the journalist Dorothy THOMPSON ended in divorce in 1942, and Lewis spent his later years pursuing a career as an actor.

Sources

Bloom, Harold, ed. *Sinclair Lewis.* New York: Chelsea House, 1987.

Bucco, Martin, ed. *Critical Essays on Sinclair Lewis.* Boston: G. K. Hall, 1986.

Lingeman, Richard. *Sinclair Lewis: Rebel from Main Street.* New York: Random House, 2002.

Schorer, Mark. *Sinclair Lewis: An American Life.* New York: McGraw Hill, 1961.

Liberator, The

See MASSES, THE.

Liebling, Abbott Joseph (1904–1963) *journalist*

Expelled from Dartmouth College, A. J. Liebling began a successful career writing for newspapers and then for the NEW YORKER. *The Road Back to Paris* (1944) recounts his adventures as a war correspondent. *The Wayward Pressman* (1947) is a memoir of his early days as a journalist. One of his best books is *The Sweet Science: A Ringside View of Boxing* (1956). He also wrote a biography of the Louisiana governor Earl Long (the brother of Huey Long, inspiration for ALL THE KING'S MEN), *The Earl Of Louisiana* (1961). *Liebling at Home* (1982) is a representative sampling of his work.

Sources

Sokolov, Raymond. *Wayward Reporter: The Life of A. J. Liebling.* New York: Harper & Row, 1980

Light in August William Faulkner (1932) *novel*

This epic novel, one of William FAULKNER's finest, raises many important issues about race and American identity.

The novel shifts among three stories: the journey of Lena Grove (orphaned, pregnant, and unmarried) in search of Lucas Burch, the father of her child; the tormented life of Joe Christmas, also an orphan, who suspects but will never know if he is of mixed blood, and his involvement with Joanna Burden, the ostracized descendent of Northern abolitionists; and the plight of Gail Hightower, the obese and reclusive widower who has forfeited his place in the community. These three stories intersect when Hightower delivers Lena's baby because the doctor does not arrive in time, and when Joe Christmas, on the run from a lynch mob, seeks refuge in Hightower's house.

Light in August is about the alienation of individuals and about the conflicts and tensions within a community. In retrospect Faulkner reportedly saw that his novel, published the year before the Nazis took power in Germany, was a political prophecy. In Percy Grimm, the man who catches and castrates Joe Christmas, Faulkner had created a kind of Nazi, a white supremacist who would use the paranoia of a community to pervert its sense of justice.

Gail Hightower represents the ineffectuality of the good man whose resistance to evil is only passive: He refuses to leave the community even after he is hounded by the Ku Klux Klan. Joanna Burden seems to represent a spirit of reform that degenerates into sexual and religious dementia. Christmas, tortured by his lack of identity, his anomie, reacts against Burden's effort to reform him, to make him pray, and to educate him.

But even as the racist atmosphere and community breakdown in the novel intensifies, Lena Grove is served well by Byron Bunch, a common man. Lena initially rejects his love for her, but Byron patiently persists and ultimately wins the day.

Light in August is Faulkner's most comprehensive and balanced portrayal of southern society, and the implications of the novel transcend a regional focus to address the fate of the modern world on the eve of another world war.

Sources

Bloom, Harold, ed. *William Faulkner's Light in August.* New York: Chelsea House, 1988.

Millgate, Michael, ed. *New Essays on Light in August.* New York: Cambridge University Press, 1987.

Pitavy, Francois L., ed. *William Faulkner's Light in August: A Critical Casebook.* New York: Garland, 1982.

Lindbergh, Anne Spenser Morrow (1906–2001) *autobiographer, poet, novelist*

The wife of the famed aviator Charles Lindbergh, Anne Morrow Lindbergh wrote about their flights together in *North to the Orient* (1935) and *Listen! The Wind* (1938). *Gift from the Sea* (1955) marked her as a sensitive writer about marriage and women's issues. *The Unicorn* (1956) is a collection of her poetry. Her novel, *Dearly Beloved* (1962), is a family saga. But her literary reputation rests on a series of volumes containing her diaries and letters: *Bring Me a Unicorn* (1972); *Hour of Gold, Hour of Lead* (1973); *The Flower and the Nettle* (1976); *Locked Rooms and Open Doors* (1974); and *War Within and Without* (1980). These memoirs, which explore her marriage, the role of a wife married to a famous man, and the nature of a modern woman's life, have made her work important.

Sources

Herrman, Dorothy. *Anne Morrow Lindbergh: A Gift for Life.* New York: Ticknor & Fields, 1992.

Lindbergh, Reeve. *No More Words: A Journal of My Mother.* New York: Simon and Schuster, 2001.

Lindsay, Nicholas Vachel (1879–1931) *poet*

A native of Springfield, Illinois, Vachel Lindsay had an early ambition to be a missionary. His poetry reflects a certain proselytizing zeal (he lectured for the Anti-Saloon League in

1912). Writing poetry at an early age, he roamed Illinois as a kind of troubadour-poet, exchanging verses for meals. He achieved his first recognition when his work was published in POETRY magazine.

Lindsay never lost his affection for his native town and state, publishing "Abraham Lincoln Walks at Midnight" (1914) and *The Golden Book of Springfield* (1920). His most frequently anthologized poem is "Congo" (1914). In this poem and in much of his other work he tried to incorporate the speech rhythms of Americans and of hymns and revivalist sermons.

A populist poet who believed that poetry should be accessible to all people and reflect the way they spoke and lived, Lindsay eventually succumbed to bitterness and disillusionment and committed suicide. His other books include *In Praise of Johnny Appleseed* (1921) and *Collected Poems* (1923).

Sources

Galtz, Engler. *Poetry and Community.* Tübingen, Germany: Stauffenburg, 1990.

Massa, Anna. *Vachel Lindsay, Fieldworker for the American Dream.* Bloomington: Indiana University Press, 1970.

Literary Digest periodical

Founded in 1890, the magazine had its best years from 1905 to 1933, when its articles emphasized current events and profiled living persons. The *Digest* printed excerpts from other newspapers and magazines, assembling vivid quotations and cartoons, often to humorous effect. It reached a high of 2 million in circulation and became a favorite resource in the classroom. The *Digest* merged with the *Review of Reviews* in 1937 before becoming absorbed by TIME in 1938.

little magazines

This term applies to short-lived, usually avant-garde periodicals published in the 19th and 20th centuries. In the 20th century, the heyday of the little magazine was the 1920s, with the appearance of *The Criterion* (1922–1939), *transition* (1927), and THE DIAL (1880–1929). Although some of these magazines were published in Europe, they included a good deal of American literature by modernist writers such as T. S. ELIOT, William Carlos WILLIAMS, and Gertrude STEIN.

Among the other important little magazines were *The Egoist* (1911–19), *Blast* (1914), the LITTLE REVIEW (1914–1929), *The Double Dealer* (1921–1926), and *Contact* (1930–1932). These were journals that emphasized literature and created literary movements. Other little magazines, such as the MASSES (1911–1917), the LIBERATOR (1918–1926), the NEW MASSES (1926–1948), and PARTISAN REVIEW (1934–   ), had a more political orientation.

Some little magazines became part of academic life—such as the HUDSON REVIEW (1948–   ), KENYON REVIEW (1939–   ), and the PARIS REVIEW (1953–   )—while publishing interviews and more general articles aimed at a sophisticated literary audience. Other little magazines have been identified specifically with literary movements or with groups of writers. *The Fugitive* (1922–1925) featured the work of the FUGITIVE poets; *The Black Mountain Review* (1954–1957), the work of the BLACK MOUNTAIN POETS; and *Yugen* (1958–1962) the work of BEAT writers.

In the 1960s and 1970s, what used to be called little magazines were transformed into the alternative press movement, featuring both magazines and books by writers who were not published by mainstream publishers, and tend to publish books and periodicals for a small, literary-minded readership.

Little Review, The periodical

Founded in 1914 under the editorship of Margaret ANDERSON, this periodical published the foremost modern authors, including Sherwood ANDERSON, Vachel LINDSAY, and Kenneth BURKE. It was part of the LITTLE MAGAZINE movement, which can be compared to the alternative press today. Anderson and other editors of literary publications with small circulation published what they considered to be the finest new and established authors regardless of whether these authors had a popular following. The aim of such "little magazines" was to foster a literary culture and a sense of community among writers.

little theater

This term has been applied to regional and local theater and is often associated with amateur productions. Such little theaters were established in small towns and cities throughout the United States in the 19th century. In the 20th century, the little theater movement was often associated with an attack on the mainstream, commercial theater and its fare of melodramas, light comedies, and musicals. Certain little theaters, clustered together in New York, Chicago, and other large cities, encouraged the work of new playwrights whose work was experimental or delved into subjects considered too serious or controversial for the Broadway stage. Some little theaters also staged the classics such as Shakespeare, attempting to preserve theater traditions and the canon of Western literature.

In the teens and 1920s, the little theater movement became associated with great playwrights such as Eugene O'NEILL. Many of O'Neill's one-act plays were produced at the Provincetown Playhouse by the PROVINCETOWN PLAYERS.

Some little theaters became thriving community theaters and were able to build their own playhouses and feature local talent. Cities such as New York and Detroit also established "players' clubs," organizations where both professional and amateur actors performed and which attracted wealthy patrons of the arts.

In large cities the little theater movement survives by subscription to small companies that present a repertory of the classics, or a mixture of contemporary and classical drama. To some extent modern universities have also incorporated parts of the little theater movement by establishing artists-in-residence programs. Many of these programs feature professional actors or a mix of student, amateur, and professional performers.

Contemporary playwrights such as Edward ALBEE, Sam SHEPARD, David RABE, and Ed BULLINS have had their works first performed in little theaters, often with a university affiliation.

Sources
Mackay, Constance D'Arcy. *The Little Theatre in the United States.* New York: Henry Holt, 1917.

Shervey, Beth Conway and Peter Palmer. *The Little Theatre on the Square: Four Decades of a Small-Town Equity Theatre.* Carbondale: Southern Illinois University Press, 2000.

Liveright, Horace (1886–1933) *publisher*

Innovative owner of the publishing firm Boni and Liveright, which published the early work of William FAULKNER and Ernest HEMINGWAY as well as Theodore DREISER, Sherwood ANDERSON, Hart CRANE, E. E. CUMMINGS, Ezra POUND, T. S. ELIOT, and Eugene O'NEILL. Liveright enjoyed publishing provocative authors but paid little attention to the finances of his firm. His partnership with Alfred Boni was an attempt to recover from massive debts. His lasting contribution to publishing was his development of the Modern Library series, later purchased by Random House. Several generations of Americans grew up reading this reasonably priced series of great books.

Sources
Dardis, Tom. *Firebrand: The Life of Horace Liveright.* New York: Random House, 1995.

Locke, Alain LeRoy (1886–1954) *editor, writer*

HARLEM RENAISSANCE writer best known for his seminal book, *The New Negro* (1925), which argued that a new innovative and creative spirit had emerged in the Negro community. Locke grew up in Philadelphia in a prosperous African-American family. He majored in philosophy at Harvard and studied as a Rhodes scholar in 1907 at Oxford University and the University of Berlin. He returned to the United States in 1911 and began teaching at Howard University. He earned a Ph.D at Harvard in 1917. Locke became the leading intellectual figure of the Harlem Renaissance, writing not only *The New Negro* but also editing *Four Negro Poets* (1927), which featured the work of Claude MCKAY, Jean TOOMER, Countee CULLEN, and Langston HUGHES. *Plays of Negro Life* (1929) solidified Locke's contention that African Americans were in a position to claim their cultural heritage and to make a significant impact on American civilization. His contributions to *Negro Art: Past and Present* (1936) and *The Negro and His Music* (1936) showed the impressive range of African-American artists. This work was followed by an illustrated *The Negro in Art* (1940).

Locke's work provided an alternative to the idea of the melting pot. He demonstrated that African Americans had a distinctive contribution that enriched American life, but that such a contribution could not be completely absorbed by the mainstream. Locke's work established the groundwork for later writers who explored a BLACK AESTHETIC.

Sources
Harris, Leonard, ed. *The Philosophy of Alain Locke: Harlem Renaissance and Beyond.* Philadelphia: Temple University Press, 1989.

Linneman, Russell J., ed. *Alain Locke: Reflections on a Modern Renaissance Man.* Baton Rouge: Louisiana State University Press, 1982.

Posnock, Ross. *Color & Culture: Black Writers and the Making of the Modern Intellectual.* Cambridge: Harvard University Press, 1998.

Loman, Willy *character*

Arthur MILLER's DEATH OF A SALESMAN portrays the common man as tragic hero. Willy Loman is an aging salesman who believes in the American dream that he and his sons will be successful. But Willy is tired of life on the road. He has not achieved his dreams, and his sons are disappointments. He is bitter, yet tries to maintain his illusion that to be "well liked" is to triumph. Loman embraces the American idea of competition and yet is one of its greatest victims. He eventually commits suicide, hoping his insurance money will provide for his family. He represents the yearning of the common man for greatness, and like the greatest heroes of tragedy, he is a flawed man.

Sources
Bloom, Harold, ed. *Willy Loman.* New York: Chelsea House, 1991.

Long Day's Journey into Night Eugene O'Neill (1956) *play*

Eugene O'NEILL's best play and perhaps the greatest play of the American stage is set on a hot summer day in a New England summer cottage. James Tyrone, an old actor nearing retirement, heads a family composed of a drug-addicted wife, a feckless first-born son, Jamie, and an ailing younger son, Edmund, who dreams of escaping home for the sea. Although Tyrone has earned his share of fame and fortune, he is stingy and has tried to skimp on his wife's medical treatment. This harrowing play peels away the family's layers of self-justification and blame to reveal their yearning for a kind of paradise lost, a vision of happiness and security. It is a harsh, unforgiving play, but also an honest one, for it refuses to sentimentalize family life. It also courageously avoids melodrama, so that each character, within his or her limits, confronts his or her own demons. Although the family is rent with dissension, the sons still seek approval from their father, and the father desperately wishes to gain the respect of his sons. On this long day, family secrets, jealousies, rivalries, and disappointments are all revealed, so that the drama provides its own justification: The play comes to terms with the fundamental dynamics of family life, and of the tensions between the characters' craving for independence and their indissoluble ties to one another.

Sources

Barlow, Judith E. *Final Acts: The Creation of Three Late O'Neill Plays.* Athens: University of Georgia Press, 1985.

Loos, Anita (1893–1981) *novelist*

Loos is best known for her novel *Gentlemen Prefer Blondes* (1925), the story of two beautiful women in search of wealthy husbands. It was made into a successful movie directed by Howard Hawks and starring Jane Russell and Marilyn Monroe. Loos wrote less successful sequels. More important are her memoirs of life in New York and Hollywood: *Twice Over Lightly* (1972) and *The Talmadge Girls* (1979).

Sources

Carey, Gary. *Anita Loos: A Biography.* New York: Alfred A. Knopf, 1988.

Lorde, Audre Geraldin (Gamba Adisa) (1934–1992) *poet, autobiographer*

Lorde was born in Harlem to Grenadan parents. She received her B.A. degree from Hunter College and a master's degree from Columbia University. She worked as a librarian at the City University of New York while publishing her first poems in journals. *First Cities* (1968), her first book of poetry, led to various awards and fellowships, including the National Book Award in 1974. Lorde's works celebrates the love of women, protests against racism and sexism, and deftly explores the way language shapes social and individual behavior. Her work often draws upon African myths.

Lorde's collections of poetry include *Cables to Rage* (1970), *New York Head Shop and Museum* (1975), *The Black Unicorn* (1978), *Chosen Poems* (1982), and *Our Dead Behind Us: Poems* (1986). She also wrote several autobiographical books: *The Cancer Journals* (1980), *Zami: A New Spelling of My Name* (1988), and *A Burst of Light* (1988). *The Audre Lorde Compendium: Essays, Speeches and Journals* was published in 1996.

Sources

Perreault, Jeanne. *Writing Selves: Contemporary Feminist Autobiography.* Minneapolis: University of Minnesota Press, 1995.
Tate, Claudia. *Black Women Writers at Work.* New York: Continuum, 1983.

Lost Generation

This term is often applied to young expatriate writers of the 1920s such as Ernest HEMINGWAY, who quoted Gertrude STEIN's observation, "you are all a lost generation," and F. Scott FITZGERALD who were living abroad and feeling disaffected from American life and embittered after the experience of WORLD WAR I, which did not fulfill President Wilson's aim to "make the world safe for democracy." Their heroes, somewhat like themselves, often live in Europe searching for a meaningful life, a culture that is more cosmopolitan than the provincial America of their youth. THE SUN ALSO RISES is perhaps the greatest work of this "lost generation," because it captures the bleak, alienated attitude that made a return to postwar American seem impossible.

Sources

Dolan, Mark. *Modern Lives: A Cultural Re-reading of the "Lost Generation."* West Lafayette, Ind.: Purdue University Press, 1996.

Lovecraft, Howard Phillips (1890–1937) *short story writer, novelist*

Born in Providence, Rhode Island, H. P. Lovecraft published only two books in his lifetime, *The Shunned House* (1928) and *The Shadow Over Unsmooth* (1936). Largely because of his writing in *Weird Tales*, a PULP magazine, he acquired a devoted following of readers who relished his gift for writing in the fantasy and horror genre. Steeped in 18th-century lore, the reclusive Lovecraft wrote stories that extended Edgar Allan Poe's use of the grotesque. Lovecraft has also inspired many science fiction writers attracted to his ambivalent attitude toward modern science.

Lovecraft's stories have been collected in *The Outside and Others* (1939), *Beyond the Wall of Sleep* (1943), *Marginalia* (1944), *The Lurker at the Threshold* (1945), *Dreams and Fancies* (1962), *Dagon and Other Macabre Tales* (1965), and *The Dark Brotherhood* (1966).

Sources

Burleson, Donald R. *H. P. Lovecraft: A Critical Study.* Westport, Conn.: Greenwood Press, 1983.
De Camp, L. Sprague. *Lovecraft: A Biography.* Garden City, N.Y.: Doubleday, 1975.

"Love Song of J. Alfred Prufrock, The" *T. S. Eliot* (1915) *poem*

First published in POETRY magazine, this poem later appeared in ELIOT's collection *Prufrock and Other Observations* (1917). The poem is a dramatic monologue in the modernist mode. Prufrock, an aging, timid man, may be speaking to an intimate, to himself, or to the reader when he extends an invitation: "Let us go then, you and I." Certainly the poem's fragmentary nature—the interruption of lines of thought, the quick shifts from one setting to another, and the allusions to many historical figures and works of literature—suggest the STREAM-OF-CONSCIOUSNESS style developed by James Joyce, William FAULKNER, and other modernist writers.

In a fashion similar to Shakespeare's Hamlet, Prufrock muses on his existence but also on existence itself and whether life is worth living. Prufrock acknowledges that he is no hero, and his thoughts "no great matter": He stands for a 20th-century consciousness confronting itself and its awareness of the world. Prufrock wonders if he will have the strength to "force the moment to its crisis." This suggestive line has sexual connotations—he suggests that he is courting a woman—but also connotations of failure of nerve, of an inability to accomplish anything.

What makes Eliot's poem such a significant representation of modernist literature is its grappling with the nature of existence. The poem is not so much a quest for the meaning of life as it is a lament for the fact that life may have no meaning at all.

Sources

Poetry In and Out of the Classroom: Essays from the ACLS Elementary and Secondary Schools Teacher Curriculum Development Project. New York: American Council of Learned Societies, 1995.

Wain, John, ed. *Interpretations: Essays on Twelve English Poems.* London: Routledge and Kegan Paul, 1955.

Lowell, Amy Lawrence (1874–1925) *poet*

Lowell, a writer and advocate of IMAGISM, was born and died in the same house in Brookline, Massachusetts. The descendant of a distinguished New England family, she turned to poetry with a passion that the skeptical Ezra POUND called "Amygism." Her most important collections are *Sword Blades and Poppy Seed* (1914) and *Pictures of the Floating World* (1919). "Lilacs" (1925) and "Patterns" (1916) are two of her poems that are frequently anthologized, for they demonstrate both her lyrical gifts and her creation of crisp images. In her lifetime she was as famous for her personality as for her politics. She was flamboyant, smoked cigars, and kept a large pack of dogs. She was outspoken and wrote lesbian love poems that shocked the public of her time. She also published a well-received two-volume biography, *John Keats* (1925). Her *Complete Poetical Works* was published in 1955.

Sources

Benvenuto, Richard. *Amy Lowell.* Boston: Twayne, 1985.

Lowell, Robert Traill Spence, Jr. (1917–1977) *poet*

Descended from a literary family that included James Russell Lowell and Amy LOWELL, Robert Lowell formed the ambition to be a great poet while he was an undergraduate at Harvard. He left New England and spent a summer with the poet Allan TATE and his wife, Caroline GORDON, who became his mentors. They recommended that Lowell transfer to Kenyon College in Ohio, where the poet and critic John Crowe RANSOM taught. Lowell became one of Ransom's protégés and also a kind of ambassador between North and South, between the NEW YORK INTELLECTUALS and the southern AGRARIANS.

Lowell's first book of poetry, *Land of Unlikeness* (1944), was a traditional and rather formal production that revealed his exquisite skill with meter and highly symbolic language. His second book, *Lord Weary's Castle* (1946), revealed the influence of Allan Tate and of Lowell's conversion to Catholicism. Lowell won the Pulitzer Prize and was hailed as the finest poet of his generation—a reputation he sustained with the difficult modernist (see MODERNISM) verse of his third volume, *The Mills of the Kavanaughs* (1951).

During the late 1940s and 1950s Lowell struggled to find a new style for his poetry, since he believed he had exhausted the resources of the modernist sensibility, which depended on sophisticated allusions to the classics of world literature—the tradition that T. S. ELIOT described in his essay "Tradition and the Individual Talent." A contentious marriage to Jean STAFFORD, a fine short story writer and novelist, complicated Lowell's feelings—which verged toward madness. During his second marriage to Elizabeth HARDWICK, he was hospitalized nearly every year for disturbing outbreaks of manic behavior followed by deep depressions.

Out of his suffering, however, Lowell developed an entirely new style—more personal and less polished. This "CONFESSIONAL POETRY" made a dramatic impact with the publication of *Life Studies* (1959), a volume that constituted a kind of spiritual autobiography in verse. At the same time, Lowell became involved in protests against the VIETNAM WAR, drawing on his prestige as a poet and public figure. His poems in *History* (1973) and *For Lizzie and Harriet* (1973) reflected his public and private selves. "Lizzie" was Lowell's wife, Elizabeth Hardwick, whose letters he would quote virtually verbatim in his verse—causing a storm of controversy over the appropriateness of exposing such intimacies in print. Harriet was his and Hardwick's only child.

Despite fierce criticism of the morality of Lowell's confessional poetry, his stature as a poet steadily increased with the publication of *Selected Poems* (1976) and other volumes.

His last book, *Day by Day* (1977), published just before he died of a heart attack in a taxi, seemed to many critics his best work in the confessional mode.

Sources

Axelrod, Steven Gould, ed. *The Critical Response to Robert Lowell.* Westport, Conn.: Greenwood Press, 1999.

Doreski, William. *Robert Lowell's Shifting Colors: The Poetics of the Public and the Personal.* Athens: Ohio University Press, 1999.

Hamilton, Ian. *Robert Lowell: A Biography.* New York: Random House, 1982.

Mariani, Paul. *Lost Puritan: A Life of Robert Lowell.* New York: W. W. Norton, 1994.

Lower East Side

A part of NEW YORK CITY near the East River and the Bowery, a section often frequented by derelicts. At the turn of the 20th century it teemed with immigrants (primarily Jews), crowded tenements, pushcarts, and all the elements of ghetto life. It has been the subject of JEWISH-AMERICAN and PROLETARIAN LITERATURE and has featured prominently in the work of Clifford ODETS, Elmer RICE, Waldo FRANK, Michael GOLD, Alfred Kreymborg, Alfred KAZIN, Bernard MALAMUD, and Henry ROTH.

Luce, Clare Boothe

See BOOTHE, Clare.

Luhan, Mabel Dodge   (1879–1962)   *patron of the arts, memoirist*

Dodge's memoirs help to chart the development of American literature in the 20th century. Most important is her trilogy, *Background* (1933), *European Experiences* (1935), and *Movers and Shakers* (1936), which provide portraits of the American writers she befriended. Born in Buffalo, New York, into the wealthy Ganson family, Luhan married architect Edwin Dodge, divorced him, and moved to Taos, New Mexico, marrying Pueblo Indian Tony Luhan. She established salons in Italy (1902–1912) and New York City (1912–1918). Among the writers she cultivated were Gertrude STEIN, John REED, Carl VAN VECHTEN, and most notably D. H. Lawrence.

Sources

Frazer, Winifred, L. *Mabel Dodge Luhan.* Boston: Twayne, 1984.

Hahn, Emily. *Mabel: A Biography of Mabel Dodge Luhan.* Boston: Houghton, Mifflin, 1977.

Lurie, Alison   (1926–   )   *novelist*

Lurie was born and grew up in Chicago. From an early age, her parents encouraged her to be a writer. She graduated from Radcliffe College with a B.A. degree in 1947 and married Jonathan Peal Bishop, a college professor. They were divorced in 1985. She published her first novel, *Love and Friendship*, in 1962. A novelist of manners, Lurie has often been compared to Jane Austen. Lurie's most important and most well-known novel is *The War Between the Tates* (1974), filmed in 1976, which dramatizes both marital and intergenerational conflict during the VIETNAM WAR era. *Foreign Affairs* (1984) won a Pulitzer Prize for its study of the sexual life of the middle-aged in a story about two professors on sabbatical. *The Truth About Lorin Jones* (1988) depicts a feminist biographer's disillusionment with her subject. Lurie's other novels include *The Nowhere City* (1965); *Imaginary Friends* (1967); *Real People* (1969); and *Only Children* (1979), which is narrated from the children's point of view.

Lurie also published *The Language of Clothes* (1981), a deft treatment of female and male fashion that reflects the kind of precise observation of dress that is found in her novels.

Lurie has also published children's books: *Clever Gretchen and Other Forgotten Folktales* (1980) and *The Heavenly Zoo* (1980). *Don't Tell the Grown-ups: Subversive Children's Literature* appeared in 1990.

Sources

Costa, Richard Hauer. *Alison Lurie.* New York: Twayne, 1992.

Lytle, Andrew   (1902–1995)   *novelist*

One of the group of southern AGRARIANS who wrote *I'll Take My Stand* (1930), a rejection of modern urban life, Lytle was educated at Vanderbilt University in Nashville and remained in the South except for brief periods at Harvard and in New York City. His novels include *The Long Night* (1936) and *The Velvet Horn* (1957). A Tennessee native, Lytle for many years was editor of SEWANEE REVIEW.

Sources

Bradford, M. E., ed. *The Form Discovered: Essays on the Achievement of Andrew Lytle.* Jackson: University Press of Mississippi, 1973.

McAlmon, Robert (1896–1956) *poet, novelist, autobiographer*

An expatriate of the LOST GENERATION, McAlmon knew many of the principal American figures, such as Ernest HEMINGWAY, who settled in Paris after WORLD WAR I. McAlmon published his free verse in *Portrait of a Generation* (1926), *North America, Continent of Conjecture* (1929), and *Not Along Lost* (1937). In *Village: As It Happened Through a Fifteen-Year Period* (1924) he presents a picture of small-town American life reminiscent of Sherwood ANDERSON's *WINESBURG, OHIO*. His memoir of the post-World War I period, *Being Geniuses Together,* appeared in 1938, with additions by Kay BOYLE in 1968. He extended his reminiscences in a self-portrait, *McAlmon and the Lost Generation* (1962), edited by Robert E. Knoll.

Sources

Knoll, Robert E. *Robert McAlmon: Expatriate Publisher and Writer.* Lincoln: University of Nebraska Press, 1957.

Smoller, Sanford J. *Adrift Among Geniuses: Robert McAlmon, Writer and Publisher of the Twenties.* University Park: Pennsylvania State University Press, 1975.

McCarthy, Cormac (1933–) *novelist*

McCarthy was born in Providence, Rhode Island, but grew up in Tennessee and attended the University of Tennessee. In college he formed his ambition to be a writer. In 1965 his first novel, *The Orchard Keeper,* won the William Faulkner Foundation Award. His subsequent novels, *Outer Dark* (1968), *Child of God* (1973), *Suttree* (1979), and *Blood Meridian* (1985) were highly praised by critics, although his work did not attract a popular audience. His subjects—the violence of the border states and the seamy side of family life—were apparently too lurid for some readers. Critics, however, thought the stories reflective of an exquisite stylist with an uncompromising sense of morality and humanity. With the publication of *All the Pretty Horses* (1992), which won the National Book Award, McCarthy began to attract a broader audience. This novel's terse account of cowboy adventures set against an austere western landscape is a captivating tale reminiscent of Ernest HEMINGWAY's understated style. *All the Pretty Horses* is part of *The Border Trilogy,* which also includes *The Crossing* (1994) and *Cities of the Plain* (1998).

Sources

Arnold Edwin T. and Dianne C. Luce, eds. *Perspectives on Cormac McCarthy.* Oxford: University Press of Mississippi, 1993.

Jarrett, Robert L. *Cormac McCarthy.* New York: Twayne, 1997.

McCarthy, Mary Therese (1912–1989) *novelist, essayist, short story writer, travel writer*

Mary McCarthy was born in Seattle, but after her parents died during the World War I influenza epidemic she was cared for by relatives in Minneapolis. She describes her unhappy childhood and abusive guardians in one of her best books, *Memories of a Catholic Girlhood* (1957). McCarthy developed her literary aspirations at Vassar College. Her generation at Vassar included such distinguished writers as Elizabeth BISHOP, Eleanor CLARK, and Muriel RUKEYSER. McCarthy satirized Vassar and its students in her best-selling and controversial novel, *The Group* (1963).

Early on, McCarthy developed a reputation for a sharp tongue and a tendency to include her friends and enemies in her fiction. Her first publications, however, were nonfiction. She wrote savage theater reviews for PARTISAN REVIEW, the premier intellectual journal of its time. She also followed the journal's fierce anti-Stalinist line. She was one of the few women to be included in the journal's inner circle of writers, which included William PHILLIPS, Philip RAHV, Delmore SCHWARTZ, Dwight MACDONALD, and Harold ROSENBERG.

After an early marriage to and divorce from Harold Johnsrud, an actor, McCarthy married the celebrated critic Edmund WILSON. Although it was a stormy marriage that also ended in divorce, Wilson convinced McCarthy to turn to fiction. She began by producing stories notable for their depiction of a promiscuous young woman and her adventures in bohemian circles. The sexual explicitness of McCarthy's fiction brought her much attention and criticism. Her first novel, *The Company She Keeps* (1942), included portraits of nearly every important male figure in her early career, exposing the rivalry and competitiveness of New Yorkers.

McCarthy's other novels, *The Oasis* (1949), *The Groves of Academe* (1952), *Birds of America* (1971), and *Cannibals and Missionaries* (1979), explored the worlds of college life, politics, and terrorism. They were not considered as successful and certainly were not as popular as her early fiction and *The Group*. McCarthy's addiction to gossip and her handling of plot and characterization were cited as her chief weaknesses.

McCarthy was a forceful opponent of the VIETNAM WAR, and she published two accounts of her trips to the scene of fighting in *Vietnam* (1967) and *Hanoi* (1968).

McCarthy was an excellent travel writer, with two notable books, *Venice Observed* (1956) and *The Stones of Florence* (1959).

An astringent critic, she collected her literary and political essays in *Sights and Spectacles* (1956), *On the Contrary* (1961), *The Mask of State* (1975), a study of Watergate, *Ideas and the Novel* (1980), and *Occasional Prose* (1985).

Although McCarthy's later autobiographical writing, *How I Grew* (1987) and *Intellectual Memoirs* (1992), does not match the riveting narrative of *Memories of a Catholic Girlhood*, these later books are important contributions to American intellectual and literary life, and McCarthy herself has proven to be an inexhaustible subject for biographers and critics. Part of her correspondence, *Between Friends: The Correspondence of Hannah Arendt and Mary McCarthy, 1949–1975*, was published in 1995.

Sources

Gelderman, Carol, ed. *Conversations with Mary McCarthy.* Jackson: University Press of Mississippi, 1991.

Kiernan, Mary. *Seeing Mary Plain: A Life of Mary McCarthy.* New York: W. W. Norton, 2000.

Swertka, Eve and Margo Vicusi, eds. *Twenty-four Ways of Looking at Mary McCarthy: The Writer and Her Work.* Westport, Conn.: Greenwood Press, 1996.

McClure, Michael Thomas (1932–) *poet*

Born in Kansas but associated for most of his career with the BEATS and the SAN FRANCISCO RENAISSANCE, Michael McClure had had a long association with Oakland's California College of Arts and Crafts. His poetry is intensely personal and passionate. Among his collections are *Passage* (1956), *For Artaud* (1959), *Dark Brown* (1961), *Thirteen Mad Sonnets* (1965), *Star* (1970), *September Blackberries* (1974), *Jaguar Skies* (1975), and *Fragments of Perseus* (1983). His *Selected Poems* appeared in 1986. He has written several verse plays, including *The Beard* (1967) and *Gorf* (1976). *Scratching the Beat Surface* (1982) is a collection of essays. *The Adventures of a Novel in Four Chapters* appeared in 1991, *Lighting the Corners: On Art, Nature, and the Visionary: Essays and Interviews* in 1994, *Three Poems* in 1995, *Huge Dreams: San Francisco and Beat Poems* and *Rain Mirror: New Poems* in 1999.

Sources

Kherdian, David. *Six Poets of the San Francisco Renaissance: Portraits and Checklists.* Fresno, Calif.: Giligia Press, 1967.

McCoy, Horace (1897–1955) *novelist, screenwriter*

Born in Tennessee, McCoy became a journalist after service in WORLD WAR I. He became a Hollywood screenwriter in 1931 and in 1935 published his first novel, *They Shoot Horses, Don't They?*, set during one of the marathon dance contests of the period, and made into a film in 1969 starring Jane Fonda. Considered an existentialist, McCoy had a remarkable following in France, where his later novels met with success. His subjects are crime, corruption, and Hollywood decadence. His other novels include *No Pockets in a Shroud* (1937), *I Should Have Stayed Home* (1938), *Kiss Tomorrow Good-Bye* (1948), and *Scalpel* (1952).

Sources

Winchell, Mark Royden. *Horace McCoy.* Boise, Idaho: Boise State University, 1982.

McCullers, Carson Smith (1917–1967) *novelist, short story writer, playwright*

A native of Columbus, Georgia, the precocious Carson McCullers was writing fiction and drama by the age of 15. She studied music in New York City and creative writing at Columbia University. She published her first story in 1936 and the following year married Reeves McCullers, also an aspiring writer. The marriage proved stormy, but McCullers continued to write, producing an impressive first novel, *The*

Heart is a Lonely Hunter (1940), a work that is sometimes called an exercise in the southern GOTHIC or grotesque. She was attracted to characters who physically and mentally did not fit into conventional society, and she usually set her work in the South.

In 1941 McCullers divorced her husband and published *Reflections in a Golden Eye* (1941), a novel about a homosexual army officer stationed in a southern camp, filmed in 1967 with Elizabeth Taylor and Marlon Brando. McCullers was a close friend of Tennessee WILLIAMS, and their writing shares an interest in people whom society finds offensive.

McCullers's most famous work is *The Member of the Wedding* (1946), which Williams helped her turn into a successful play. Both the novel and the play concentrate on Frankie, a young girl growing up in the South with a sense of alienation.

Many of McCullers's novels and stories have a melodramatic quality that lend themselves to dramatization. All of her novels except *Clock Without Hands* (1957) have been filmed, and in 1963 Edward ALBEE wrote a dramatization of her novella *The Ballad of the Sad Cafe* (1952), which features a relationship between a hunchback and a tall, powerful woman.

McCullers remarried her ex-husband in 1945, but there were more separations, and she attempted suicide in 1948. She was also plagued by illness, including cancer. *The Mortgaged Heart,* a collection of essays, appeared in 1971, and *Collected Stories* in 1987. Her journals, *Autumn Light: Illuminations of Age,* were published in 1978. *Illumination and Night Glare: The Unfinished Autobiography of Carson McCullers* was published in 1999.

Sources

Carr, Virginia Spencer. *The Lonely Hunter: A Biography of Carson McCullers.* Garden City, N.Y.: Doubleday, 1975.
———. *Understanding Carson McCullers.* Columbia: University of South Carolina Press, 1990.
Clark, Beverly Lyon and Melvin J. Friedman, eds. *Critical Essays on Carson McCullers.* New York: G. K. Hall, 1996.

Macdonald, Dwight (1906–1982) *critic, editor*

A literary and social critic, Macdonald also was an editor at *FORTUNE, PARTISAN REVIEW,* and the *NEW YORKER,* and the founder of *Politics.* Macdonald is an important figure among the NEW YORK INTELLECTUALS and is usually grouped with such writers as Philip RAHV, William Phillips, and Irving HOWE, in any discussion of the liberal left. Macdonald is often cited, as well, for his groundbreaking essays on popular culture, especially those collected in *Against the American Grain* (1963).

Sources

Wrezin, Michael. *A Rebel in Defense of Tradition: The Life and Politics of Dwight Macdonald.* New York: Basic Books, 1994.

———— ed. *A Moral Temper: The Letters of Dwight Macdonald.* Chicago: Ivan R. Dee, 2001.

MacDonald, John Dann (1916–1986) *novelist*

The author of taut mystery novels featuring the detective Travis McGee, John D. MacDonald sets many of these mysteries in Key West, where McGee moors a boat. He has been identified as a descendant of the tough, tight-lipped detectives created by Dashiell HAMMETT and Raymond CHANDLER. But unlike his predecessors, he has a softer, somewhat more relaxed side, reflecting the easygoing life of Key West. He is less intense but just as dogged as Sam SPADE.

Sources

Geherin, David. *John D. MacDonald.* New York: Ungar, 1982.
Hirshberg, Edgar, W. *John D. MacDonald.* Boston: Twayne, 1985.

MacDonald, Ross (Kenneth Millar) (1915–1983) *novelist*

Born in California, Ross MacDonald served in the navy and earned a Ph.D. from the University of Michigan. He is most well known for a series of detective novels featuring private investigator Lew Archer. Some of Archer's cases have an EXISTENTIALIST aspect, particularly the highly praised *The Underground Man,* the title of which echoes Dostoyevsky's *Notes from Underground.* Archer is akin to the classic detective in HAMMETT's novels, but he has a greater concern with the psychological nuances of the people in his cases. *Self-Portrait* (1982) features essays and reminiscences. Some of MacDonald's other titles are *The Galton Case* (1959), *The Goodbye Look* (1964), and *The Far Side of the Dollar* (1965).

Sources

Mahan, Jeffrey Howard. *A Long Way From Solving That One: Psycho/Social and Ethical Implications of Ross Macdonald's Lew Archer Tales.* Lanham, Md.: University Press of America, 1990.
Schopen, Bernard. *Ross MacDonald.* Boston: Twayne, 1990.

McElroy, Joseph (1930–) *novelist*

Born in Brooklyn, New York, McElroy earned a B.A. degree from Williams College in 1951 and an M.A. degree from Columbia University in 1952. He taught for many years at Queens College and the City University of New York. Compared to the work of contemporaries like Robert Coover, Thomas PYNCHON, and William GADDIS, McElroy's fiction is viewed as experimental and demanding. His narrator protagonists struggle to define the nature of reality against the ambiguous landscapes of their own minds. In perhaps his best novel, *Lookout Cartridge* (1974), McElroy is able to harness his cerebral style to a sharply crafted plot of a mystery-thriller hinging on a terrorist explosion in New York City. *Women and Men* (1987) is recognized as his most ambitious novel. Set in New York, where most of McElroy's fiction unfolds, the novel centers on James Mayn, a journalist specializing in science, technology, and economic issues, and on Grace Kimball, an extreme feminist leader. They live in the same apartment building and eventually come together in a pattern of coincidences. Like *Lookout Cartridge,* this novel develops McElroy's vision of the order, chaos, and contingency of modern life.

McElroy's other novels include *A Smuggler's Bible* (1966), *Hind's Kidnap: A Pastoral on Familiar Airs* (1969), *Ancient History: A Paraphrase* (1971), *Plus* (1974), and *The Letter Left to Me* (1988).

Sources

Hanke, Steffen. *Conspiracy and Paranoia in Contemporary American Fiction: The Works of Don DeLillo and Joseph McElroy.* New York: Peter Lang, 1994.

McGuane, Thomas Francis, III (1939–) *novelist*

Thomas McGuane was born in Wyandotte, Michigan, and received a B.A. degree from Michigan State University and an M.F.A. from the Yale School of Drama. Giving up the idea of an academic career, he concentrated on writing novels and screenplays. *Ninety-Two in the Shade* (1973) is among his best and most characteristic works. The novel centers on Thomas Skelton, who pursues his desire to be a fishing guide in the face of a woman's vow to kill him if he continues to work on the land she considers hers. Skelton's determination to act according to his own values, even though he risks his life in doing so, is typical of McGuane's skill at portraying characters who pursue their own dreams at great risk. Much of McGuane's fiction is set in the West. *Nobody's Angel* (1982), for example, explores Deadrock, Montana, a listless environment of farmers and cowboys where Patrick Fitzpatrick wrestles with a stymied life on his family's ranch after an intense period in the tank corps of the army. McGuane's other protagonists confront similar challenges: how to cope with conventional life when the more romanticized versions of the West and of the past elude the characters' grasp. McGuane's other novels include *The Sporting Club* (1969), *The Bushwhacked Piano* (1971), *Panama* (1978), *Something to Be Desired* (1984), *Keep the Change* (1989), and *Nothing But Blue Skies* (1992).

McGuane has also had a significant career as a screenwriter with *Rancho DeLuxe* (1973), *Ninety-two in the Shade* (1975), *The Missouri Breaks* (1975), and *Tom Horn* (1980). His short fiction has been collected in *To Skin a Cat* (1986). His nonfiction includes *An Outside Chance: Essays on Sport* (1980), *The Longest Silence: A Life in Fishing* (1999), and *Some Horses* (1999).

Sources

Westrum, Dexter. *Thomas McGuane.* Boston: Twayne, 1991.

McInerney, Jay (1955–) *short story writer, novelist*

Born in Connecticut and educated at Williams College, McInerney first worked as a fact checker at the NEW YORKER. Virtually all of his fiction is set in NEW YORK CITY and is practically regionalist in its attention to settings and characters shaped by the Manhattan milieu. His first and greatest success, *Bright Lights, Big City* (1984), made into a motion picture, is the story of a young man coming to terms with New York City, struggling with his mother's death, and succumbing to drug addiction. Told in the second person, so that "you" is always the subject, McInerney makes his readers feel directly involved in his unnamed character's fate. His other novels, comic and satirical, are *Story of My Life* (1988), *Brightness Falls* (1992), *The Last of the Savages* (1996), and *Model Behavior: A Novel and 7 Stories* (1998). *Bacchus & Me: Adventures in the Wine Cellar,* a collection of essays about wine, appeared in 2000. He has also edited *Cowboys, Indians and Commuters: The Penguin Book of New American Voices* (1994).

Sources

Hogan, Ron. "The Beatrice Interview: Jay McInerney." 1996. Available on-line. URL: http://www.beatrice.com/interviews/mcinerney/.

Garner, Dwight. "The Salon Interview: Bright Lights, Bad Reviews." 1996. Available on-line. URL: http://www.salon.com/weekly/mcinerney1960527.html.

The New York Times. "Featured Author: Jay McInerney." (Articles by and about Jay McInerney, 1984–2001). *New York Times* on the Web: Books. Available on-line. URL: http://www.nytimes.com/books/98/09/27/specials/mcinerney.html.

McKay, Claude (1890–1948) *poet, novelist*

McKay grew up in Jamaica. At the age of seven, while still in Jamaica, he went to live with his brother, a schoolteacher. McKay studied English literature, science, and theology. He was also encouraged to write poetry, and he attracted the attention of Walter Jekyll, a white British expatriate and folklorist, who urged McKay to write about his land and people. *Songs of Jamaica* (1912) portrayed the peasant life his parents had lived. He also experimented with local dialects and perfected his diction as a poet.

By 1914 McKay was living in New York City. He began to associate with radicals and became famous for his protest poem, "If We Must Die," published in 1919. *Spring in New Hampshire* (1920) dealt with both his experience in America and his memories of Jamaica. *Harlem Shadows* (1922) reflects his increasing interest in the urban experience of

African Americans. Evidence of his radicalized consciousness and the influence of Marxism on his thought is demonstrated in *Negroes in America* (1923), a collection of essays. He traveled widely in Europe and the Soviet Union in the 1920s.

McKay worked at various jobs, including a stint on the Pennsylvania Railroad. He drew on this experience in his first novel, *Home to Harlem* (1929), one of the key texts of the HARLEM RENAISSANCE. Although McKay's poetry became increasingly radical and reflective of a black consciousness, he remained conservative in his use of English verse forms, including the sonnet.

Banjo (1929), McKay's second novel, draws on his travels abroad and comments on colonialism. Moving on to Morocco in 1932, he published *Gingertown*, a collection of short stories. He returned to the United States in 1934, suffering ill health and struggling to write. In 1937 he published an autobiography, *A Long Way From Home*. In 1944 he converted to Catholicism and repudiated his Communist beliefs in *Harlem: Negro Metropolis* (1940), which argued that African Americans should concentrate on home-grown leaders and a set of indigenous beliefs born of their urban and racial experience.

The Selected Poems of Claude McKay was published in 1953, and the memoir *My Green Hills of Jamaica* did not appear until 1979. McKay, a central figure in the Harlem Renaissance, is renowned for both the high quality of his poetry and the historical importance of his novels and memoirs. Like his contemporary Langston HUGHES, he strove to make a close connection between politics and art.

Sources

Gayle, Addison. *Claude McKay: The Black Poet At War*. Detroit: Broadside Press, 1972.

Giles, James, R. *Claude McKay*. Boston: Twayne, 1976.

Tillery, Tyrone. *Claude McKay: A Black Poet's Struggle for Identity*. Amherst: University of Massachusetts Press, 1992.

MacKaye, Percy Wallace (1875–1956) *playwright*

Born in New York City and educated at Harvard, Percy MacKaye is best known for his career as a verse dramatist and champion of community-based pageant dramas. In this respect, his work is regionalist and comparable to Paul GREEN's. Among his verse pageants are *Canterbury Pilgrims* (1909), *Sanctuary, a Bird Masque* (1913), *Caliban, by the Yellow Sands* (1916), and *The Evergreen Tree* (1917). Similarly he wrote folk plays based on his travels in Kentucky: *This Fine-Pretty World* (1923) and *Kentucky Mountain Fantasies* (1928).

Sources

Ege, Arvia MacKaye. *The Power of the Impossible: The Life Story of Percy and Marion MacKaye*. Falmouth, Me.: Kennebec River Press, 1992.

Percy MacKaye: A Symposium on his Fiftieth Birthday, 1925. Hanover, N.H.: The Dartmouth Press, 1928.

MacLeish, Archibald (1892–1982) *poet*

Born in Illinois and educated at Harvard Law School and Yale, MacLeish served in World War I and began his career teaching law at Harvard. By 1923 he had moved to Paris to pursue a career as a poet. In the 1930s he returned to America and worked as an editor at several magazines, then for the U.S. government as Librarian of Congress and in the Office of War Information. A confidant of many writers, including Ernest HEMINGWAY and Robert FROST, MacLeish won the Pulitzer Prize in 1932, 1952, and 1958 for poetry. His *Collected Poems, 1917–1982* was published in 1985. *Uphill with Archie: A Son's Journey* appeared in 2001. MacLeish's style changed over his long career. In the 1920s his work—greatly influenced by T. S. ELIOT and Ezra POUND—portrayed alienated individuals adrift in a postwar wasteland. But beginning in the 1930s, as MacLeish took a much more active role in public affairs, his poetry became more focused on social and political values and how to sustain a cultural heritage. By the late 1930s in collections of poetry such as *America Was Promises* (1939) he eloquently advocated his country's involvement in world affairs. Of his later work, his verse play, *J. B.*, a retelling of the story of Job, is most famous, winning a Pulitzer Prize and much praise for the way it brings this biblical episode to life in contemporary language.

Sources

Donaldson, Scott and R. H. Winnick. *Archibald MacLeish: An American Life*. Boston: Houghton Mifflin, 1992.

Falk, Signi Lenea. *Archibald MacLeish*. New York: Twayne, 1966.

McMurphy, Randle Patrick *character*

Ken KESEY's rowdy hero in ONE FLEW OVER THE CUCKOO'S NEST, McMurphy is incarcerated in an Oregon mental institution. This dissolute gambler refuses to play by institutional rules. Gradually he wins over other patients with his irreverent, subversive behavior. His main opponent is "Big Nurse," Miss Ratched, who rules the ward and has McMurphy declared "disturbed." He is forced into electric shock treatments and then is given a lobotomy. A fellow patient, the Chief, suffocates McMurphy with a pillow so that he does not have to suffer the indignity of having his vibrant personality suppressed.

Sources

Kappel, Lawrence, ed. *Readings on One Flew Over the Cuckoo's Nest*. San Diego, Calif.: Greenhaven Press, 2000.

Searles, George J., ed. *A Casebook on Ken Kesey's One Flew Over the Cuckoo's Nest*. Albuquerque: University of New Mexico Press, 1992.

McMurtry, Larry Jeff (1936–) *novelist*

Born in Wichita Falls, Texas, Larry McMurtry has made the Southwest the focus of most of his highly praised fiction. He grew up on a ranch, the grandson of a pioneer cattleman. He received a B.A. from North Texas State University in 1958 and began writing his first novels. He later supported himself by working for and then owning bookstores.

Although McMurtry's setting is the Southwest, he did not write a traditional western until *Lonesome Dove* (1985), now considered one of the finest examples of the genre and perhaps his best novel. It was later filmed—as were *The Last Picture Show* (1966), *Terms of Endearment* (1975), and *Buffalo Girls* (1990). His novels are often set in moribund small towns and decrepit ranches in north and west Texas. The excitement of frontier days has vanished, and his characters struggle to make a living and to find a purpose in life. His early work—*Horseman, Pass By* (1961) and *Leaving Cheyenne* (1963)—best exemplifies his sense of a dying way of life.

Like William FAULKNER, McMurtry often revives his characters and continues their stories through several novels, which gives his work a sagalike effect. *Duane's Depressed* (1999), for example, returns to the locale and characters of *Texasville* (1987) and *The Last Picture Show* (1966). August McCraw and Woodrow Call, the main characters of *Lonesome Dove*, figure prominently in *Streets of Laredo* (1993), *Dead Man's Walk* (1995), and *Comanche Moon* (1997). Like Faulkner, as well, the revivals of characters do not follow chronological order; that is, later novels often deal with periods before the characters' initial appearances in earlier novels. Although some readers have found McMurtry's time shifts confusing, he seems to take the Faulknerian view that fiction demands such latitude—indeed it requires of the author a godlike creativity that reorders history and previous interpretations of the past.

McMurtry has published several works of nonfiction: *In a Narrow Grave: Essays on Texas* (1968), *It's Always We Rambled: An Essay on Rodeo* (1974), *Film Flam: Essays on Hollywood* (1987), *Crazy Horse* (1999), and *Walter Benjamin at the Dairy Queen: Reflections at Sixty and Beyond* (1999).

Sources

Busby, Mark. *Larry McMurtry and the West: An Ambivalent Relationship.* Denton: University of North Texas Press, 1995.

Reynolds, Clay, ed. *Taking Stock: A Larry McMurtry Casebook.* Dallas: Southern Methodist University Press, 1989.

McNally, Terrence (1939–) *playwright*

McNally grew up in Corpus Christi, Texas. At age 17 he enrolled at Columbia University in New York City. After graduating Phi Beta Kappa, McNally traveled to Mexico, wrote a play, and worked at the Actors Studio in New York, learning stagecraft. His first original play, *Things That Go Bump in the Night* (1964), was produced at the Tyrone Guthrie Theater in Minneapolis but received poor reviews. *Next* (1967), a one-act play, was well received. It concerns an overweight middle-aged man mistakenly drafted into the army. But McNally's subsequent full-length plays drew little critical enthusiasm, but his one-acts *Ravenswood* (1971) and *Dunlawn* (1971) won a *Village Voice* Obie award for off-Broadway theater. Set in sanatoriums, the plays show McNally's comic gift for presenting absurd situations, a talent well suited to the short play format.

McNally's popular and critical breakthrough came with *Frankie and Johnnie in the Clair de Lune* (1987). McNally's development of characters with seemingly little to offer is extraordinary: This play shows that any human character can be intrinsically interesting. Even though the play's characters are middle-aged and apparently too fearful to make a commitment, the play convincingly draws them together in comic and moving detail.

McNally then embarked on a string of successes: *Lips Together, Teeth Apart* (1991), a comic and moving exploration of the AIDS crisis; *Love! Valour! Compassion!* (1994), a superb ensemble cast of characters delving into the lives of eight gay men; and *The Master Class* (1995), a riveting re-creation of a day in the life of diva Maria Callas.

McNally wrote the screenplay for *Frankie and Johnnie* (1991). He also has written scripts for television, including *The Five Forty-Eight* (1979), an adaptation of a John CHEEVER story, and *Andre's Mother* (1990).

Sources

Bryer, Jackson R., ed. *The Playwright's Art: Conversations with Contemporary American Dramatists.* New Brunswick, N.J.: Rutgers University Press, 1995.

McPhee, John Angus (1931–) *nonfiction writer*

After graduation from Princeton University, where he has taught journalism, John McPhee became a staff writer for the *NEW YORKER* and wrote books that proved not only popular but also influential. *The Pine Barrens* (1968), his loving depiction of the unspoiled wilderness in the heart of New Jersey, was instrumental in forestalling plans to develop the area as a major airport. One of his finest narratives is *Coming into the Country* (1977), an account of his journeys in Alaska. His other important books include *The Crofter and the Laird* (1970), an account of Scotland; *The Curve of Binding Energy* (1974), an investigation of nuclear energy; *Rising from the Plains* (1986), the formation of the Rocky Mountains; *Looking for a Ship* (1990), stories of the seafaring life; and *Annals of the Former World* (1998), a study of geology. *Irons in the Fire* (1997) collects his essays on various subjects.

Sources

Pearson, Michael. *John McPhee.* New York: Twayne, 1997.

Mailer, Norman Kingsley (1923–) *novelist, journalist, biographer*

Born in Long Branch, New Jersey, where his relatives had a seaside resort business, Norman Mailer moved with his parents and sister to Brooklyn, New York, where he attended public schools before going to Harvard to earn a bachelor's degree in engineering. In college Mailer realized that he wanted to be a writer, but to please his parents he continued with his engineering studies. By the time he was drafted in 1944, he had already written several short stories—including an impressive depiction of combat in war—and two novels. Influenced by James T. FARRELL and John DOS PASSOS, Mailer was determined to write a great war novel that would portray not only the realities of war but also the underlying social and political significance of events, related in a gritty naturalistic style. Mailer experienced limited but valuable periods of combat, and when his first novel, *The Naked and the Dead,* was published in 1948, he was hailed as one of America's great new writers. The novel became a best-seller, and overnight Mailer became a celebrity author, a reputation he has maintained throughout his career regardless of the positive and negative reactions to his work.

Mailer's next novel, *Barbary Shore* (1951), was a COLD WAR allegory set in Brooklyn. It did not have the narrative drive of *The Naked and the Dead,* and the novel's disturbing politics (it excoriated both the United States and the Soviet Union) found little favor with critics. Part of Mailer's problem had to do with his conclusion that his first success was undeserved. He regarded *The Naked and the Dead* as a derivative novel, a kind of pastiche of the novelists he admired. He sought a less naturalistic and more supple and intense style that he associated with such writers as William FAULKNER. Mailer's third novel, *The Deer Park* (1955), a study of Hollywood, received better reviews than *Barbary Shore,* yet it did little to fulfill his promise as the great American novelist.

Beginning in the mid-1950s, Mailer turned increasingly to short fiction and nonfiction as ways of testing out new styles and ideas. This period culminated in the groundbreaking *Advertisements for Myself* (1959), a collection that included the full range of Mailer's fiction and nonfiction, including his much debated essay, "The White Negro" (1956), which many critics took as a rationale for urban violence. In the italicized sections of *Advertisements,* Mailer developed a quirky, egotistical voice that became the signature of his later, mature style. He treated "Mailer" as a character, a center of controversy, a persona that he had worked hard to develop.

In the 1960s as a full-time journalist, Mailer covered the major political conventions and treated politics with the imagination of a novelist. This work culminated in two books that secured his reputation as an innovator in nonfiction: *The Armies of the Night* (1969), an account of the anti–Vietnam War protest at the steps of the Pentagon, and *Miami and the Siege of Chicago* (1969), an empathetic account of Richard Nixon and the 1968 Republican Convention. Both books showed off Mailer the journalist and novelist interacting with the key personalities and issues of American life. These exhilarating books displayed a keen balance between the subjectivity of the novelist and the objectivity of the journalist. Mailer proved capable of writing about public events with great sensitivity even as he was writing a kind of autobiography.

Mailer was also writing innovative novels in the 1960s. *An American Dream* (1964) featured a hero, Stephen Rojack, who had served in Congress with John F. Kennedy, but who had, like Mailer himself, derailed his career. Rojack murders his wife and gets away with it—a fact that outraged many reviewers of the novel. Mailer himself was attacked, in part because his personal life came close to replicating his fiction: In 1960 Mailer had stabbed his second wife at a party that was supposed to be the launching point for his campaign to be mayor of New York.

Mailer's other novel of this period, *Why Are We in Vietnam?* (1967), is a brilliant, scatological story of a big game hunt in Alaska. His narrator, D.J., speaks like a radio disk jockey, but D.J. is also an alienated, hip narrator akin to the narrator in Ralph ELLISON's *INVISIBLE MAN.* The high energy of Mailer's novel and the beautiful evocation of wilderness scenes represent a high point in Mailer's search for a new style.

In the 1970s Mailer continued to innovate. He produced an experimental biography, *Marilyn* (1972), which raised fundamental questions about biography—how it is possible to understand another person's life, especially when individuals have many different sides or selves—as a form as well as elevating the importance of Monroe as a key figure in the American imagination. By this point, Mailer was being attacked as a male chauvinist by Kate MILLET and other feminists, and his book on Monroe was dismissed by some critics as simply an exploitative, commercial enterprise. Mailer responded to his feminist critics in *The Prisoner of Sex* (1971), an uneven work of autobiography and literary criticism.

Throughout the 1970s Mailer wrote substantial books, including *Of a Fire on the Moon* (1971), an account of U.S. astronauts' voyage to the moon, and *The Fight* (1975), a brilliant piece of reportage on the George Foreman–Muhammad Ali heavyweight championship bout. But his crowning achievement, and perhaps his greatest book, is *The Executioner's Song* (1979), a nonfiction novel reminiscent of Truman CAPOTE's *In Cold Blood.* Mailer's work was hailed for its astonishing grasp of the western milieu of Utah and for his comprehensive and sensitive portrayal of murderer Gary Gilmore, his family, friends, and victims.

The reception of Mailer's later work has been shadowed by his biography. Married six times and the father of eight children, he has been attacked from many different political and literary standpoints. Although his reputation has suffered, he has continued to produce outstanding work, especially *Oswald's Tale* (1995), his investigation of Lee Harvey Oswald and the Kennedy assassination.

Mailer's later fiction, such as *Ancient Evenings* (1983), a novel set in ancient Egypt, *Tough Guys Don't Dance* (1984), a crime novel, and *Harlot's Ghost* (1991), a novel about the CIA, do not seem equal in stature to his earlier fiction, although *The Gospel According to the Son* (1997) is a well-wrought, sensitive first-person account of the life of Jesus.

Mailer has also worked as a filmmaker, but his films—*Beyond the Law* (1968), *Wild 90* (1971), *Maidstone* (1971)—have had little impact on cinema history, although he has demonstrated considerable prowess as a film theoretician. Mailer's film of his novel *Tough Guys Don't Dance* was a critical and box office failure.

Mailer adapted his novel *The Deer Park* as a play in 1960, and it had a limited run in New York City. He collected his poems in *Deaths for the Ladies and Other Disasters* (1962). He has collected his essays in *Cannibals and Christians* (1963), *Existential Errands* (1972), and *Pieces and Pontifications* (1982).

Sources

Bloom, Harold, ed. *Norman Mailer*. New York: Chelsea House, 1986.

Dearborn, Mary. *Mailer: A Biography*. Boston: Houghton Mifflin, 1999.

Lennon, J. M., ed. *Conversations with Norman Mailer*. Jackson: University Press of Mississippi, 1985.

Manso, Peter, ed. *Mailer: His Life and Times*. New York: Simon & Schuster, 1985.

Rollyson, Carl. *The Lives of Norman Mailer: A Biography*. New York: Paragon House, 1991.

Major, Clarence (1936–) *poet, short story writer, essayist, editor, novelist*

Born in Atlanta, Georgia, Major divided his youth between that city and Chicago, where he studied modern art and which has had an important influence on his experimental novels, especially *Reflex and Bone Structure* (1975) and *Emergency Exit* (1979).

Major's delight in thwarting the conventions of narrative fiction—including the abandoning of plot, stable characters, and point of view—has been compared to the work of Ishmael REED, Thomas PYNCHON, and Donald BARTHELME. In novels such as *All-Night Visitors* (1969), *No* (1973), *My Amputations* (1986), and in the short story collection *Fun and Games* (1988), fiction is explored as a resource in itself—a kind of alternative reality—not as a report on reality. At the same time, he seconds Reed in believing that fiction is nevertheless a comment on the disjunctions of contemporary culture and the difficulties of achieving a sound identity.

Such Was the Season (1987) and *Painted Turtle: Woman with Guitar* (1988) are more realistic in style and structure and have been compared to the work of Ernest J. GAINES and Gloria NAYLOR, who explore African-American community life and folkways. Major's later fiction includes *Dirty Blues* (1996).

Major's subjects are by no means only African American. He explores the lives of Americans in Venice in his poetry collection *Surfaces and Masks* (1988), and of Native Americans in another poetry collection, *Some Observations of a Stranger at Zuni in the Latter Part of the Century* (1989). His later poetry is collected in *Poems* (1998).

Major's essays are collected in *The Dark and Feeling* (1974), where he argues for judging literature by its quality not its message. His work as editor and lexicographer is reflected in the *Dictionary of Afro-American Slang* (1970) and in *Juba to Jive* (1994). He has also edited three influential anthologies: *The New Black Poetry* (1969), *Calling the Wind: Twentieth-Century African-American Short Stories* (1993), and *The Garden Thrives: Twentieth-Century African-American Poetry* (1996).

Sources

Byerman, Keith E. *Fingering the Jagged Grain: Tradition and Form in Recent Black Fiction*. Athens: University of Georgia Press, 1985.

Johnson, Charles. *Being & Race: Black Writing Since 1970*. Bloomington: Indiana University Press, 1988.

Malamud, Bernard (1914–1986) *novelist, short story writer*

A native of Brooklyn, New York, the son of Russian-Jewish immigrants, Malamud grew up in New York City, attended City College and Columbia University, and taught for many years at Bennington College in Vermont.

Malamud, along with Saul BELLOW and Philip ROTH, has had an enormous impact on post–WORLD WAR II American literature. All three were members of a large group of Jewish-American writers who wrote about their ethnic identity and about the tensions of assimilation in a post-Holocaust world.

Malamud's most important novels, *The Assistant* (1957), *The Fixer* (1966), and *The Tenants* (1971), explore the nature of Jewish suffering, the legacy of the shetl, and contemporary tensions between Jews and African Americans. In all his novels, even those like *The Natural* (1952) that do not feature Jewish characters, his protagonists must reckon with the past and take responsibility for their own actions. Roy Hobbs, a "natural" athlete, destroys his career by collaborating in a scheme to intentionally lose the league playoffs. He commits a crime against himself, so to speak, by denying his God-given gifts. In much of Malamud's work there is a biblical simplicity, a reworking of Adam's fall from paradise.

Equally important in Malamud's work is the nature of human suffering, which can sometimes lead to redemption in an almost religious sense. Indeed, some critics have faulted Malamud for making his moral parables too schematic and didactic.

Malamud's other novels include *A New Life* (1961), *Dubin's Lives* (1979), *God's Grace* (1982), and *The People*

(1989). The last work was left uncompleted at the author's death. In this novel Malamud continues an old theme—the story of a Jewish refugee trying to adjust to American life—but this time Malamud put his protagonist among a group of Native Americans who make him their chief and advocate.

Malamud's achievement in short fiction surpasses his work in the novel. He wrote many love stories, often about old men and women, as well as accounts of the strong bonds between men. Here his penchant for parables and fables fits well into the form of the short story. Many of his stories are at once whimsical and moving. In the classic "The Jewbird," a skinny crow flies into the Cohens' apartment window in the Bronx. The Yiddish-speaking bird irritates the father, who eventually kills it even though it has proven helpful with his son's homework. This portrait of self-destructiveness among certain Jews and their inability to cope even with those who would help them is characteristic of Malamud's darker moods. Similarly, "Angel Levine" mixes reality and fantasy and calls upon Jewish folklore. "The Magic Barrel," often cited as one of Malamud's most characteristic stories, explores the life of Leo Finkle, who is studying to be a rabbi. He knows more about books than he does about life. When his parents propose that he be married, he puts himself in the hands of a professional matchmaker—with comic results. This adventure shows Finkle how constricted his life has become. Like many of Malamud's characters, Finkle is awakened to a much greater knowledge of the world and an identification with the joy and the suffering of others.

Malamud's stories have been collected in *The Magic Barrel* (1958), *Idiots First* (1963), *Pictures of Fidelman: An Exhibition* (1969), *Rembrandt's Hat* (1973), *The Stories of Bernard Malamud* (1983), and *The People and Uncollected Stories* (1989).

Sources

Abramson, Edward A. *Bernard Malamud Revisited.* New York: Twayne, 1993.

Ochshorn, Kathleen. *The Hearts Essential Landscape: Bernard Malamud's Hero.* New York: Peter Lang, 1990.

Salzberg, Joel, ed. *Critical Essays on Bernard Malamud.* Boston: G. K. Hall, 1987.

Malcolm X (Malcolm Little) (1925–1965) *political activist*

Born in Omaha, Nebraska, Malcolm X moved as a small boy with his family to Lansing, Michigan. His father was murdered when he was six, and his mother had a mental breakdown, so that Malcolm and his sister were declared wards of the state. Attracted to the nightlife of the city, where he went to live with his half sister, Ella, he got to know the criminal element and worked as a drug dealer in Harlem. He was arrested for armed robbery in 1946 and was sent to prison.

Out of this rather ordinary criminal experience, a new man was fashioned. In prison, Malcolm absorbed the teachings of the Black Muslims. From 1952 to 1963 he served as a minister in the Nation of Islam, headed by Elijah Muhammad. A fiery speaker and charismatic leader, he contributed forcefully to the calls for black power in the 1960s.

But Malcolm X's growing celebrity caused a rift within the Nation of Islam, and Malcolm himself became disenchanted with the movement when he discovered its leader did not follow the religion's strict moral code in his personal life. Malcolm X then began to develop his own brand of black nationalism and an internationalist philosophy often called Pan-Africanism, since it rested on the belief that people of color should unite across national boundaries.

Much of Malcolm X's story is told in THE AUTOBIOGRAPHY OF MALCOLM X (1965), published the year he was assassinated. Based on two years of interviews with the writer Alex HALEY, this autobiography became an instant best-seller and a fixture in the canon of African-American literature. The autobiography's account of Malcolm X's spiritual journey, especially his realization that the Black Muslim ideology did not accurately represent Islam—a religion embraced by people of many different colors, including white—has given Malcolm's story a currency and relevance well beyond his original race-based and nationalistic ideology.

Malcolm X's speeches were collected in *Malcolm X Speaks* (1965) and in *Malcolm X: The Last Speeches* (1989).

Sources

Dyson, Michael Eric. *Making Malcolm: The Myth and Meaning of Malcolm X.* New York: Oxford University Press, 1994.

Gallen, David, ed. *Malcolm A to X: The Man and His Ideas.* New York: Carroll & Graf, 1992.

———. *Malcolm X: As They Knew Him.* New York: Carroll & Graf, 1992.

———. ed. *A Malcolm X Reader.* New York: Carroll & Graf, 1994.

Maltz, Albert (1908–1985) *playwright, screenwriter, novelist*

The Brooklyn-born Maltz graduated from Columbia University and studied at the Yale School of Drama. He wrote plays such as *Merry-Go-Round* (1932) that dealt with political corruption. A man of radical and pacifist convictions in the early 1930s, he wrote *Peace on Earth* (1933), an antiwar drama. He entered the field of PROLETARIAN LITERATURE with his one-act play, *Black Pit* (1935), the story of a coal miners' strike. His novel *The Underground Stream* (1940) focused on the effort to unionize auto workers. Throughout this period he also wrote for Hollywood and left-wing publications. During the COLD WAR he became suspect because of his Communist affiliations, and when, like other screenwriters, he declined to testify before Congress about his political activities, he was jailed, becoming one of the Hollywood Ten. Maltz's stories are collected in *The Way Things Are* (1938) and *Afternoon in the Jungle* (1970). *The Citizen Writer* (1950) is a collection of essays.

Sources
Salzman, Jack. *Albert Maltz.* Boston: Twayne, 1978.

Mamet, David Alan (1947–) *playwright*
David Mamet was born and raised on the Jewish South Side of CHICAGO. After completing his undergraduate work at Goddard College in Vermont, he studied acting at the Neighborhood Playhouse and worked in OFF-BROADWAY theater. He returned to Chicago in 1972, having written several short plays. *Sexual Perversity in Chicago* (1974), his third produced play, first attracted major notices and was later made into a film, *About Last Night . . .* (1986). *American Buffalo* (1975), with a characteristic mixture of profanity and insight, made Mamet, along with Sam SHEPARD, one of the contemporary theater's most provocative playwrights. Mamet's next major play, *Glengarry Glen Ross* (1983), set in a sales office with a group of men desperately trying to peddle worthless Florida swampland, featured an array of male characters as impressive as Eugene O'NEILL's barroom bunch in *The Iceman Cometh.* Indeed, the critic Robert Brustein deemed the play better than Arthur MILLER's classic *Death of a Salesman.* The brutal, competitive world of business is also the subject of Mamet's well-received *Speed-the-Plow* (1988). *Oleanna* (1992) is one of his most controversial plays: It concerns a smug college professor who is accused of sexual harassment by one of his earnest female students. The play has already become a staple of college anthologies.

Mamet has written several experimental plays, including *A Life in the Theatre* (1977), which features a play within a play and comments from the characters on the theater and acting. Mamet has collected some of his shorter works in *Short Plays and Monologues* (1981), *Three Childrens' Plays* (1986), *Three Jewish Plays* (1987), *Oh Hell: Two One-Act Plays* (1991), *A Life With No Joy in It, and Other Plays and Pieces* (1994).

Mamet has been active as a screenwriter, producing original scripts for *House of Games* (1987), *Things Change* (1988), and *Homicide* (1992). He also adapted *Glengarry Glen Ross* (1992) and *Oleanna* (1994). His other film credits include *The Postman Always Rings Twice* (1981), *The Verdict* (1982), *The Untouchables* (1985), *We're No Angels* (1989), *Hoffa* (1992), and *Vanya on 42nd Street* (1994). *The Spanish Prisoner: and The Winslow Boy: Two Screenplays* was published in 1999. He has collected his writing for television in *Five Television Plays* (1990) and *A Life in the Theatre* (1993).

Mamet is also a prolific essayist and has published the following collections: *Writing in Restaurants* (1986), *Some Freaks* (1989), *On Directing Film* (1991), *The Cabin: Reminiscence and Diversions* (1992), *The Village* (1994), *A Whore's Professions: Notes and Essays* (1994), *Make-Believe Town: Essays and Remembrances* (1996), *3 Uses of the Knife: On the Nature and Purpose of Drama* (1998), and *Jafsie and John Henry: Essays* (1999).

His writing for children includes *The Owl* (1987), *Warm and Cold* (1988), and *Passover* (1995).

Sources
Kane, Leslie, ed. *David Mamet: A Casebook.* New York: Garland, 1992.
———. *Weasels and Wisemen: Ethics and Ethnicity in the Work of David Mamet.* New York: St. Martin's Press, 1999.

Manfred, Frederick Feikema (1912–1994) *novelist*
Born in Iowa, Frederick Manfred became a journalist and then a prolific novelist, writing under the names Frederick Feikema and Feike Feikema. His fiction is set in the upper Middle West from Minnesota to South Dakota and is often about the Sioux. His rough regionalist style portrays the hard life of the land in such novels as *This is the Year* (1947), *The Chokecherry Tree* (1948), *The Primitive* (1949), *The Brother* (1950), and *The Giant* (1951). His protagonist is often a young man at odds with his environment. A later novel, *Scarlet Plume* (1964), is about a white woman captured by the Sioux. A companion novel is *The Manly-Hearted Woman* (1976), which also deals with Sioux life. His stories are collected in *Arrow of Love* (1961) and *Apples of Paradise* (1968). *The Wind Blows Free* (1980) is based on his hitchhiking from Iowa to the Rockies in the 1930s. Manfred's essays and reminiscences were published in *Prime Fathers* (1987). *Selected Letters* appeared in 1989.

Sources
Wright, Richard C. *Frederick Manfred.* Boston: Twayne, 1979.
"The Frederick Manfred Homepage." Available on-line. URL: http://usd.edu/engl/manfred.html.

Marquand, John Phillips (1893–1960) *novelist*
Born in Wilmington, Delaware, John Marquand began his literary career as the author of light romantic novels, including *The Unspeakable Gentleman* (1922), *The Black Cargo* (1925), *Warning Hill* (1930), and *Ming Yellow* (1935). He also created a Japanese detective, Mr. Moto, in a series of popular short stories that were made into equally popular movies. Marquand sharpened and deepened his portrait of society in his exquisite satirical novel of manners, *The Late George Apley* (1937), which won a Pulitzer Prize. This mock memoir of a Boston Brahmin was succeeded by other fine novels that skewered the New England sensibility, including *Wickford Point* (1939) and *H. M. Pulham, Esquire* (1941). Marquand's later novels added little to his reputation. *Thirty Years* (1954) contains stories and articles.

Sources

Bell, Millicent. *Marquand: An American Life.* Boston: Little, Brown, 1979.

Gross, John J. *John P. Marquand.* New York: Twayne, 1963.

Wires, Richard. *John P. Marquand and Mr. Moto: Spy Adventures and Detective Films.* Muncie, Ind.: Ball State University, 1990.

Marshall, Paule (1929–) *novelist, short story writer*

Marshall was born in Brooklyn, New York, the daughter of Barbadian immigrants. Marshall attributes her affinity for fiction to her mother's storytelling powers. Early on, Marshall grew to appreciate the rhythms of language and the delight of capturing speech in stories.

Marshall graduated from Brooklyn College in 1953 and taught in many college creative writing programs. Her novel *Brown Girl, Brownstones* (1959) draws on the experience of her family and community, and the tensions that result when her main characters interact with whites in New York City. *Clap Hands and Sing* (1961) collects the stories of Marshall's childhood. *The Chosen Place, The Timeless People* (1969) explores divided peoples on a Caribbean Island. Marshall has slowly accumulated an audience and much critical praise for her elegant prose. Her later work includes the novels *Praisesong for the Widow* (1983), *Daughters* (1991), and *The Fisher King* (2000). She has also published *Reena and Other Stories* (1983), short fiction set in both Brooklyn and Barbados.

Sources

Delamotte, Eugenia C. *Places of Silence, Journeys of Freedom: The Fiction of Paule Marshall.* Philadelphia: University of Pennsylvania Press, 1998.

Denniston, Dorothy Hamer. *The Fiction of Paule Marshall: Reconstructions of History, Culture and Gender.* Knoxville: University of Tennessee Press, 1995.

Mason, Bobbie Ann (1940–) *novelist, short story writer*

Raised in Kentucky, Mason has shown an affinity for presenting the lives of characters in small southern towns, many of whom feel trapped by their environment while others find a way out. Both types of characters earn her sympathy because of her ambivalent feelings about the modern world.

Mason's first collection of short fiction, *Shiloh and Other Stories* (1982), won the PEN/Faulkner Award. Her first novel, *In Country*, won the PEN/Hemingway Award and was later filmed. Her other fiction includes *Spence & Lila* (1988), *Love Life* (1989), a collection of stories, and *Feather Crowns* (1993). She has also published nonfiction: *Nabokov's Garden: A Nature Guide to Ada* (1974) and *The Girl Sleuth: A Feminist Guide to the Bobbsey Twins, Nancy Drew, and Their Sisters* (1975). In 1999 she published *Clear Springs: A Memoir.*

Sources

Wilhelm, Albert. *Bobbie Ann Mason: A Study of the Short Fiction.* New York: Twayne, 1998.

Masses, The periodical

An influential leftist magazine published between 1911 and 1918, Max EASTMAN became its editor in December 1912 and published articles that presaged the rise of PROLETARIAN LITERATURE in the United States. Writers such as Michael GOLD, John REED, and Floyd Dell made the magazine a cutting-edge publication read by intellectuals wishing to keep up with the latest thinking about literature and politics. Federal authorities shut down the magazine in 1917 after the post office barred it from the mails in August of that year because of its radical Communist articles.

In March 1918 Eastman brought out a new version of *The Masses* under the title *The Liberator*, which continued publication until 1924, when it became *The Workers' Monthly*. Two years later it became a weekly under the title *The New Masses*. In 1948 the magazine changed its name again, becoming *Masses and Mainstream*, a monthly publication. In this guise, it published important progressive and Communist writers such as John Howard LAWSON, Howard FAST, and W. E. B. DU BOIS.

Masters, Edgar Lee (1868–1950) *poet*

Born in Garnett, Kansas, Masters grew up in Lewistown, Illinois, not far from the area he fictionalized as Spoon River, the setting of his most famous collection of poetry. *Spoon River Anthology* (1915) is a series of dramatic monologues that create a vivid picture of small-town life: Spoon River residents who have died reflect wistfully on their lives and times. The book was an instant success and went through several editions. An expanded *The New Spoon River* (1924) included intertwined monologues that explored 243 lives. Masters's method inspired other writers such as Sherwood ANDERSON (*WINESBURG, OHIO*) and Thornton WILDER (*Our Town*) to do similar collections of short stories and theater pieces.

Masters's later poetry collections include *Starved Rock* (1919), *Poems of People* (1936), and *Illinois Poems* (1941). He also wrote nonfiction: *Lincoln, the Man* (1931), *Whitman* (1937), and *Mark Twain: A Portrait* (1938). He published *Across Spoon River: An Autobiography* in 1936.

Sources

Flanagan, John T. *Edgar Lee Masters: The Spoon River Poet and His Critics.* Metuchen, N.J.: Scarecrow Press, 1974.

Wrenn, John H. and Margaret M. *Edgar Lee Masters.* Boston: Twayne, 1983.

Matthiessen, Francis Otto (1902–1950) *literary critic*

With a B.A. from Yale and a Ph.D. from Harvard, F. O. Matthiessen was one of the most influential literary critics of his day. An active liberal, he sought to promote the progressive tradition in American literature. His most outstanding book is *American Renaissance* (1941), which explored, as the subtitle says, "art and expression in the age of Emerson and Whitman." Matthiessen also wrote groundbreaking books such as *The Achievement of T. S. Eliot* (1935, revised 1947) and *Theodore Dreiser* (1951). A man tormented about his homosexuality and deeply disturbed by the developing COLD WAR, Matthiessen committed suicide.

Sources

Gunn, Giles B. *F. O. Matthiessen: The Critical Achievement.* Seattle: University of Washington Press, 1975.

Stern, Frederick C. *F. O. Matthiessen, Christian Socialist as Critic.* Chapel Hill: University of North Carolina Press, 1981.

Matthiessen, Peter (1927–) *novelist, journalist*

Matthiessen is best known for his fiction about indigenous cultures and their confrontation with exploitative outsiders. He began work in this genre with *At Play in the Fields of the Lord* (1965), set in the Amazon, and *Far Tortuga* (1975). Other books range through South America, including *The Cloud Forest* (1961), *Under the Mountain Wall* (1963), and then on to Africa in *The Tree Where Man Was Born* (1972) and *The Snow Leopard* (1978), which won the National Book Award. Matthiessen's blistering attack on the way Native Americans have been treated engendered a rancorous lawsuit, filed by a former South Dakota governor who felt he had been libeled, after the publication of *In the Spirit of Crazy Horse* (1983). Matthiessen's later work includes *Indian Country* (1984), *Midnight Turney Gray: Short Stories* (1984), *African Silences* (1991), *Baikal: Sacred Sea of Siberia* (1992), *Lost Man's River* (1997) and *Bone by Bone* (1999), novels set in pioneer Florida. *The Peter Matthiessen Reader: Nonfiction, 1959–1991* appeared in 2000.

Sources

Dowie, William. *Peter Matthiessen.* Boston: Twayne, 1991.

Maxwell, William (1908–2000) *short story writer, novelist*

Maxwell was born in Illinois and educated at Harvard. He worked at the NEW YORKER, editing writers such as John O'HARA, John UPDIKE, J. D. SALINGER, and Harold BRODKEY. His novels include *Bright Center of Heaven* (1934), *They Came Like Swallows* (1937), *The Folded Leaf* (1945), *Time Will Darken It* (1948), *The Chateau* (1961), *The Old Man at the Railroad Crossing* (1966), and *So Long, See You Tomor-*

row (1979). A good deal of this fiction is set in the Midwest of Maxwell's youth. *Over by the River* (1977) is a story collection. *Ancestors* (1971) deals with his family background. He wrote one study of fiction, *The Writer as Illusionist* (1955). His essays and books reviews are contained in *The Outermost Dream* (1989). *Billy Dyer and Other Stories* appeared in 1992 and *The Happiness of Getting It Down Right: Letters of Frank O'Connor and William Maxwell, 1945–1966* in 1996.

Meltzer, David (1937–) *poet*

Born in New York, Meltzer is associated with the BEATS. *Ragas* (1959), his first book, reflects the Beat interest in Indian and other Eastern forms of art and religion. Meltzer has also published *The Process* (1965), *The Dark Continent* (1967), *Tens* (1973), and *The Name* (1984), *Arrows: Selected Poetry, 1957–1992* (1994), *No Eyes: Lester Young* (2000). He has also edited critical anthologies, including *Reading Jazz* (1993) and *Writing Jazz* (1999).

Sources

Kherdian, David. *Six Poets of the San Francisco Renaissance: Portraits and Checklists.* Fresno: Giligia Press, 1967.

Mencken, Henry Louis (1880–1956) *journalist, editor, literary critic*

A coeditor of *The Smart Set* and, in 1924, cofounder of *The American Mercury*, H. L. Mencken wrote numerous books, the most influential of which was *The American Language* (1919).

Mencken began his journalistic career with the *Baltimore Sun* in 1906 and remained at that newspaper for the rest of his life as a reporter and columnist. A savage satirist, Mencken coined such terms as the "booboisie" to express his contempt for America's ignorant middle class. He was just as critical, though, of Communists, conservatives, Christians, Jews, the Ku Klux Klan, and virtually any individual or group that he thought merited attack. Vitrolic is not too strong a word to apply to many of Mencken's writings.

Mencken's outspoken opinions and his interest in the American language have made him a central figure in American culture of the 20th century. He published three autobiographies: *Happy Days* (1940), *Newspaper Days* (1941), and *Heathen Days* (1943). His newspaper columns were collected in *A Book of Burlesques* (1916), *A Book of Calumny* (1917), and six volumes of *Prejudices* (1919–1927, reprinted in 1977).

Sources

Hobson, Fred C. *Mencken: A Life.* Baltimore, Md.: Johns Hopkins University Press, 1995.

Williams, William H. A. *H. L. Mencken Revisited.* New York: Twayne, 1998.

"Mending Wall" Robert Frost (1914) poem

One of the great examples of Robert FROST's use of understatement and irony in his probing of the New England sensibility, this poem begins with Frost's famous first line: "Something there is that doesn't love a wall." The first part of the poem seems to ratify the speaker's idea, reticently expressed, that walls divide people from each other and that they are unnatural. Nature itself breaks down walls, and each spring the speaker has to mend the gaps. The wall between the speaker's and his neighbor's property seems unnecessary since there is a natural division made by their different trees. But the neighbor replies, "Good fences make good neighbors." This rebuttal, a typical example of what has been called New England understatement, implies that people do need a distance between one another, a privacy that walls help to support. To the neighbor the wall is not a metaphor for dividedness but instead for respect of the individual's rights. Walls are necessary for human community. Because spring puts new energy or "mischief" in the speaker, he wonders what his neighbor is "walling in or walling out." His neighbor, the speaker suggests, is atavistic—an "old-stone savage" armed with the rocks he uses to rebuild his wall. In the speaker's mind the neighbor is not merely a supporter of tradition, but a conservative. Although the speaker may seem to have the better of the argument, the poem holds together only as a dialogue or tension between points of view; the argument between neighbors, after all, only occurs in the context of their mending the wall when they "walk the line" between them. It is a line that separates them, but it also a line that joins them, where they meet to talk and express their differences. To abolish the wall, in other words, is to abolish the idea of differences. The neighbor is suggesting that walls stand for the respect paid to differences. The poem itself respects those differences by ensuring that neither speaker nor neighbor convinces the other of his point of view.

Sources

Bloom, Harold, ed. *Robert Frost.* New York: Chelsea House, 1999.

Faggen, Robert, ed. *The Cambridge Companion to Robert Frost.* New York: Cambridge University Press, 2001.

Meredeth, William Morris (1919–) poet

A New York City native, William Meredeth graduated from Princeton University and then served in the navy as an aviator. His first book of poetry, *Letter from an Impossible Land* (1944), was selected for the YALE SERIES OF YOUNGER POETS. His naval experience permeates *Ships and Other Figures* (1948), *Open Sea* (1958), and *The Wreck of the Thresher* (1964). Robert FROST's influence is also evident in *Earth Walk* (1970). Indeed much of Meredeth's finest verse evokes the natural world and the human response to it. *Hazard the Painter* (1975) creates a fictional artist and his thoughts

about life and art. *Partial Accounts* (1987), which combines a selection of poems from earlier books with new poems, won a Pulitzer Prize. Meredeth's later work includes *Effort At Speech: New and Selected Poems* (1997). *Poems Are Hard to Read* (1991) contains his writing about poetry.

Sources

Rotella, Guy. *Three Contemporary Poets of New England: William Meredith, Philip Booth, and Peter Davison.* Boston: Twayne, 1983.

Merrill, James Ingram (1926–1995) poet

Merrill was born in New York City, the son of one of the founders of the Merrill Lynch brokerage firm, and was educated at private schools. Merrill was fortunate that his father recognized his literary talent and provided the financial security that allowed Merrill to pursue a literary career.

Merrill earned recognition early for his fluency, wit, humor, and intensity. He won the National Book Award for *Nights and Days* (1966), a Pulitzer Prize for *Divine Comedies* (1976), and another National Book Award for *Mirabell: Books of Number* (1978). His work is autobiographical and deals with his day-to-day life.

One of the most accessible of modern poets, Merrill wrote love poetry that was explicit about his homosexuality. Merrill was also quite open about his intensely social life. The old-fashioned term "playboy" has often been applied to him. Yet his work is rarely trivial or hedonistic, although some critics have found certain poems silly. His best work, though, is elegant and philosophical, probing the complications of human relationships.

In 1982 Merrill published *From the First Nine: Poems 1946–1976.* His later collections include *Late Settings* (1985), *The Inner Room* (1988), and *A Scattering of Salts* (1995). His *Collected Poems* appeared in 2001 along with a memoir of Merrill and his longtime companion, David Jackson, by Alison LURIE entitled *Familiar Spirits.*

Merrill had one play, *The Immortal Husband,* produced OFF BROADWAY. He also wrote a novel, *The Seraglio* (1957).

Sources

Adams, Don. *James Merrill's Poetic Quest.* Westport, Conn.: Greenwood Press, 1997.

Rotella, Guy, ed. *Critical Essays on James Merrill.* Boston: G. K. Hall, 1996.

Merton, Thomas (1915–1969) poet, autobiographer

Merton's most representative writing can be found in *The Seven Storey Mountain* (1948), which became a best-seller. It recounts his conversion to the Catholic faith, his decision to abandon his literary career in New York, and how he committed himself to a religious life.

Merton became an ordained Catholic priest in 1949 and chose the vocation of a Trappist monk. A prolific author, he wrote more than 50 books, including *The Collected Poems of Thomas Merton* (1977) and *Mystics and Zen Masters* (1967), the latter exemplifying his broad and profound understanding of spirituality, which won him many readers regardless of their attitude toward religious faith per se. Merton brought a critical and even satirical perspective to religious writing that made him a key figure for those interested in the intersection between the spiritual and secular worlds. His poetry tends to be aphoristic and autobiographical.

Sources

Cooper, David D. *Thomas Merton's Art of Denial: The Evolution of A Radical Humanist.* Athens: University of Georgia Press, 1989.
Kramer, Victor A. *Thomas Merton.* Boston: Twayne, 1984.

Merwin, William Stanley (1927–) *poet, translator*

W. S. Merwin grew up in Union City, New Jersey, and Scranton, Pennsylvania. His father was a Presbyterian minister, and Merwin wrote his first verses (for hymns) at age five.

Merwin graduated from Princeton University and turned to translating other poets, beginning with *The Poem of the Cid* (1959), and Perseus's *Satires* (1961). Merwin has also translated *The Song of Roland* (1963), Pablo Neruda's *Twenty Love Poems and a Song of Despair* (1969), *Asian Figures* (1973), Osip Mandelstam's *Selected Poems* (1989), and Dante's *Purgatorio* (2000).

Yet Merwin achieved recognition as a poet early. His *A Mask for Janus* (1952) was selected for the YALE SERIES OF YOUNGER POETS by W. H. AUDEN, who was impressed with Merwin's expert grasp of traditional verse forms and patterns as well as his profound understanding of myth. This aspect of his work, however, made Merwin feel his work was derivative, not original.

Merwin developed a different style with later books of poetry such as *The Moving Target* (1963), which critics praised for its epigrammatic style. He won the Pulitzer Prize for *The Carrier of Ladders* (1970), a deeply introspective volume that explores the presence of the past in the poet's life. *Finding the Islands* (1982), inspired by Merwin's move to Hawaii, experimented with haiku. *Opening the Hand* (1983) portrayed the poet's childhood. Merwin published his *Selected Poems* in 1988. His later collections include *Koa* (1988), *The Second Four Books of Poems* (1993), *Travels* (1993), *The Vixen* (1996), *Flower & Hand: Poems, 1977–1983* (1997), *The Folding Cliffs: A Narrative* (1998), and *The River Sound: Poems* (1999).

Merwin's fiction is also strongly poetical. He has collected his short stories in *The Miner's Pale Children* (1970), *Houses and Travellers* (1977), *Unframed Originals* (1982), and *The Lost Upland* (1992).

Regions of Memory: Uncollected Prose, 1949–1982 was published in 1987.

Sources

Hix, H. L. *Understanding W. S. Merwin.* Columbia: University of South Carolina Press, 1997.
Nelson, Cary and Ed Folsom, eds. *W. S. Merwin: Essays on the Poetry.* Urbana: University of Illinois Press, 1987.

middlebrow

A term often applied to literature that is considered neither of the highest order nor of the lowest, "middlebrow" art is popular in that it appeals to a broadly defined middle-class audience but not necessarily to mass culture. Thus a play like DEATH OF A SALESMAN has sometimes been called "middlebrow" by critics who consider it a good, if not a great, play. To some critics, middlebrow works are flawed because they are sentimental or didactic, enforcing a message rather than allowing the style and content of the work of art speak for itself.

Miles, Josephine Louise (1911–1985) *poet*

Educated at the University of California, Josephine Miles became a professor at Berkeley and began producing highly precise and witty poetry. Her books include *Lines at Intersection* (1939), *Poems on Several Occasions* (1941), *Local Measures* (1946), *Prefabrications* (1955), *Poems 1930–1960* (1960), *Kinds of Affection* (1967), *Fields of Learning* (1968), *To All Appearances* (1974), and *Coming to Terms* (1979). Her scholarly work includes *The Vocabulary of Poetry* (1946), *The Continuity of English Poetic Language* (1951), *Eras and Modes in English Poetry* (1957), *Renaissance, Eighteenth Century and Modern Language in Poetry* (1960), and *Poetry and Change* (1974).

Sources

Larney, Marjorie, ed. *Josephine Miles, Teaching Poet: An Oral Biography.* Berkeley, Calif.: Acacia Books, 1993.

Millay, Edna St. Vincent (1892–1950) *poet*

Millay was born in Rockland, Maine, the daughter of a nurse and a schoolteacher. She graduated from Vassar College in 1917 and published her first book of poetry, *Renascence and Other Poems*, that year. She went to GREENWICH VILLAGE and acted with the PROVINCETOWN PLAYERS. They produced one of her plays, *Aria da Capo* (1920). Her second book of poems, *Few Figs from Thistles* (1920), extolled the bohemian life with lines such as "My candle burns at both ends," which glorified the idea of a short but intense existence. Her next book of poetry, *The Harp Weaver and Other Poems* (1923), won a Pulitzer Prize. As the first woman to win this award, Millay became the most famous poet of her time, praised for her lyrical and elegant style.

As a public figure Millay participated in the protest over the SACCO-VANZETTI CASE, making it her subject in "Justice

Denied in Massachusetts," "Hangman's Oak," "The Anguish," and "To Those Without Pity," collected in *The Buck in the Snow* (1928). She distinguished herself in the sonnet form in *Fatal Interview* (1931) and *Conversation at Midnight* (1937).

Millay wrote little in the 1940s, and much of her work became so identified with her period that it has not won many new readers. Her *Collected Poems* was published in 1956.

Sources

Epstein, Daniel Mark. *What My Lips Have Kissed: The Loves and Love Poems of Edna St. Vincent Millay.* New York: Henry Holt, 2001.

Freedman, Diane P., ed. *Millay at 100: A Critical Reappraisal.* Carbondale: Southern Illinois University Press, 1995.

Milford, Nancy. *Savage Beauty: The Life of Edna St. Vincent Millay.* New York: Random House, 2001.

Thesing, William, B., ed. *Critical Essays on Edna St. Vincent Millay.* New York: G.K. Hall, 1993.

Miller, Arthur (1915–) *playwright*

Miller was born in Harlem and raised in Brooklyn, New York. He was a teenager when the stock market crashed, and this event's devastating impact on his father (a successful businessman who was ruined) and his family left an indelible scar on Miller that marks many of his dramas.

Miller went to the University of Michigan, where his talent as a playwright was recognized early. He won the prestigious Hopwood Prize for plays that explored societal conditions that could wreck people's lives. His second play on Broadway, *All My Sons* (1947), was successful and was made into a motion picture. It concerned an airplane manufacturer who had produced shoddy parts that led to the death of his own son in the war. Although melodramatic and sentimental, this play also showcases Miller's strengths: his uncompromising vision of what a moral society should stand for and the failures of individuals to abide by or to find their own standards of integrity.

DEATH OF A SALESMAN (1949) is considered Miller's masterpiece. A popular and critical success, it established him as the major voice in the postwar American theater, rivaled only by Tennessee WILLIAMS. In the story of WILLY LOMAN, Miller believed he had created the tragedy of the common man. Willy stands for every American who wants to get ahead, to dream that he and his sons will be well liked and prosperous. The problem is that his only standards are popularity and success. In other words, Willy had no moral code, no bedrock of standards on which he can rely to face adversity.

Miller's play was also noteworthy for the way it melded different styles, from REALISM to EXPRESSIONISM, so that his audience could both identify with the social consequences of what was happening to Willy and his family and also appre-

ciate the play as a psychological study. It was Miller's ability to project a sense of both objective and subjective reality that made his work so rich and so ripe for study in the classroom.

While no other play by Miller has achieved the same level of acclaim, several have achieved success and have become fixtures in the American repertory of plays and of college texts. *The Crucible* (1953), a vivid reenactment of the Salem witch hysteria, has proven an enduring work (it has been made into a major motion picture). At the time of its first production, it was thought that Miller was drawing a parallel between the 17th century and his own time, a period when Senator Joseph McCarthy labeled certain Americans as Communist subversives in what many called a witch-hunt.

Similarly, *A View From the Bridge* (1956) is considered vintage Miller in that the play once again poses the struggle of a tormented man against the values of his own society. Eddie Carbone, a longshoreman who harbors incestuous feelings for his daughter, comes into conflict with the illegal immigrant he has welcomed into his house and who courts his daughter. Eddie turns informer and has the police apprehend the immigrant. The personal and political implications of Eddie's tragedy were ones Miller was familiar with, since the playwright had been called before Congress and asked to betray friends who had been Communists. Miller revisited this theme in *After the Fall* (1964), which directly addresses the COLD WAR hysteria over Communism and deals with his own troubled marriage to Marilyn Monroe, which ended in divorce in 1961, just a year before her death. As in *A View From the Bridge, After the Fall* has a narrator, a device that reflects Miller's tendency in some of his work to direct his audience's attention a little too strenuously to the message of his plays. When the didactic side of Miller's work surfaces, his plays lose dramatic tension and persuasiveness.

Miller's later plays have received at best mixed reviews, except for *The Price* (1968), a taut drama about two brothers who struggle with each other for the meaning of their lives and their family history. *The Creation of the World and Other Business* (1972), a comic reworking of the Adam and Eve story, excited little interest—as did *The American Clock* (1980), Miller's portrayal of the GREAT DEPRESSION, and *The Ride Down Mt. Morgan* (1992), although the latter received favorable notices in England. *Broken Glass* (1994), the most recent Broadway production of a new Miller play, was a failure, largely due to its trite, melodramatic, and sentimental treatment of the Holocaust.

Collected Plays was published in 1957 and *Collected Plays, Volume II* in 1981. The latter includes Miller's screenplay, *The Misfits* (1961), a film that starred Clark Gable and Marilyn Monroe. Although a valiant effort to write a sophisticated western, the film is undone by Miller's efforts to idealize Monroe and to make all his male characters revolve around her. He published the screenplay for *Everybody Wins* in 1990 and for *The Crucible* in 1996. His one play for television is *Playing for Time* (1980).

Miller published one provocative novel, *Focus* (1945), a study of anti-Semitism. His short fiction is included in *I Don't Need You Anymore* (1967) and *Homely Girl, A Life, and Other Stories* (1995).

Miller's nonfiction includes several travel books that include photographs by his wife, Inge Morath: *In Russia* (1969), *In the Country* (1977), and *Chinese Encounters* (1979). He wrote a memoir about the Chinese production of his most famous play, *Salesman in Beijing* (1984). *Conversations with Arthur Miller* was published in 1987, *The Theater Essays of Arthur Miller* in 1978, and his memoirs, *Timebends: A Life,* in 1987.

Sources

Bigsby, Christopher, ed. *The Cambridge Companion to Arthur Miller.* New York: Cambridge University Press, 1997.

Murphy, Brenda and Susan C. W. Abbotson. *Understanding Death of a Salesman: A Student Casebook to Issues, Sources, and Historical Documents.* Westport, Conn.: Greenwood Press, 1999.

Siebold, Thomas, ed. *Readings on Arthur Miller.* San Diego, Calif.: Greenhaven Press, 1997.

Miller, Henry (1891–1980) *novelist, essayist*

Born in New York City, Henry Miller grew up in Brooklyn, attended City College, dropped out, worked at odd jobs, traveled west, and then settled down to four years of work at Western Union, starting in 1920. His first marriage ended in divorce, and he quit his job. In the mid 1920s Miller began to make notes for what would be his first novel, *Tropic of Cancer* (1934), an exhilarating work that portrays Miller himself as a prodigious sexual athlete and includes sexual scenes so explicit that the book was considered pornographic. Miller's works were banned in the United States and Great Britain until the 1960s, but many readers admired the author for his energetic style and exploration of the sensuous side of life. His work was clearly inspired by D. H. Lawrence, and Miller was recognized by many European writers as a novelist of genius, especially after the publication of *Tropic of Capricorn* (1939), generally regarded as his most ambitious work.

In 1957 Miller was elected to the National Institute of Arts and Sciences. In 1961 Grove Press published *Tropic of Cancer* in the United States and successfully defended the novel in court. Miller then moved from Europe to a home in Pacific Palisades, California, where he lived until his death in 1980.

Miller employed first-person narrators in narratives that were highly descriptive and apparently realistic, yet clearly the product of fantasy. While he amused readers with his sexual braggadocio and bawdy humor from the 1930s to the early 1960s, he came under heavy attack in the 1970s from feminists such as Kate MILLET, who deemed Miller's work demeaning to women. Miller has been defended not only by male writers such as Norman MAILER in *The Prisoner of Sex* (1981), but by female writers such as Erica JONG in her book *The Devil at Large: Erica Jong on Henry Miller* (1993).

Miller's other major work of fiction in his trilogy, entitled *The Rosy Crucifixion,* which includes *Sexus* (1949), *Plexus* (1953), and *Nexus* (1960).

Miller wrote a considerable body of nonfiction, including *The Colossus of Marousssi: Or, The Spirit of Greece* (1941), *The Air-Conditioned Nightmare* (1945), *Big Sur and the Oranges of Hieronymus Bosch* (1957), and *Selected Prose* (1965).

There have been several collections of Miller's letters, including *Letter to Anaïs Nin* (1965), *Letters of Henry Miller and Wallace Fowlie 1943–1972* (1975), and *The Durrell-Miller Letters 1935–80* (1988).

Sources

Dearborn, Mary. *The Happiest Man Alive: A Biography of Henry Miller.* New York: Simon & Schuster, 1991.

Gottesman, Ronald, ed. *Critical Essays on Henry Miller.* New York: G. K. Hall, 1992.

Millhauser, Steven (1943–) *novelist, short story writer*

Born in New York City and reared in Connecticut, Millhauser earned a B.A. degree from Columbia University. One of the most inventive of contemporary novelists, he made his debut with *Edwin Mullhouse: The Life and Death of an American Writer 1943–1954 by Jeffrey Cartwright* (1972), an inspired parody of biography especially as practiced by such biographers as Leon EDEL. Millhauser excels in the novella form as exemplified by *In the Penny Arcade* (1986) and *The Barnum Museum* (1990), two delightful re-creations of 19th-century America. *Little Kingdoms* (1994) is a collection of novellas that also shows his gift for creating fantasy literature, some of it again set in the 19th century, some of it in the 1920s. *Martin Dressler* (1996) is about an entrepreneur in turn-of-the-20th-century New York City.

Sources

Faulkner, Donald. "Stephen Millhauser, American Dreamer." Writers Online, Vol. 2, No. 1 (Fall 1997), New York State Writers Institute, State University of New York. Available on-line. URL: http://www.albany.edu/writers-inst/olv2n1.html millhauser.

minimalism

A term often applied to such writers as Ernest HEMINGWAY, Raymond CARVER, and Donald BARTHELME, who have favored simplicity of form and language, avoiding florid romantic and philosophical terms in order to provide a more direct, lifelike feel to their prose. Such writers make spare use of adjectives and qualifying phrases. In some cases, sentence structure is also pared down to the use of simple connectives such as "and" instead of complex conjunctions and transitions. The term has also been applied to other arts, so that in dance it may mean a reduction of movement or in music a use of pure, isolated tones in contrast to sophisticated harmonies.

Sources
Hallett, Cynthia Whitney. *Minimalism and the Short Story—Raymond Carver, Amy Hempel, and Mary Robison.* Lewiston, N.Y.: Edwin Mellen Press, 1999.

Mitchell, Margaret (1900–1949) *novelist*
A Georgia native, Mitchell won the Pulitzer Prize for her immensely popular novel, *Gone With the Wind* (1936), made into a major motion picture in 1939. She presented a highly romanticized version of the old South, topped off by the burning of Atlanta during the Civil War. Mitchell evoked strong sympathies for her southern characters, especially the strong-willed Scarlett O'Hara. In the background were the slaves, who served (especially in the film version) only to recapitulate the stereotypes of slaves devoted to their masters. The aura of the plantation, of a relaxed way of southern living, captured the national imagination and distorted the period of Civil War and Reconstruction in which African Americans struggled to forge their own identities even as the states imposed segregation statutes that made African Americans second-class citizens.

Sources
Pyron, Darden Asbury. *Southern Daughter: The Life of Margaret Mitchell.* New York: Oxford University Press, 1991.

Taylor, Helen. *Scarlett's Women: Gone with the Wind and Its Female Fans.* New Brunswick, N.J.: Rutgers University Press, 1989.

Mitty, Walter *character*
James Thurber's daydreamer in his classic short story "The Secret Life of Walter Mitty" (1942). This average man with a seemingly vague manner actually leads a very rich life of the imagination. He shows remarkable prowess in a hurricane, performs a rare and ingenious surgical procedure, and engages in other heroic feats—all in his mind. In every instance he is indomitable, a hero to himself even as he goes about performing the most innocuous errands and chores. Mitty has become the figure of the classic American daydreamer.

Sources
Holmes, Charles S., ed. *Thurber: A Collection of Critical Essays.* Englewood Cliffs, N.J.: Prentice Hall, 1974.

Tobias, Richard C. *The Art of James Thurber.* Athens: Ohio University Press, 1970.

modernism
Modernism in literature is usually ascribed to 20th-century works that are experimental and innovative. The modernist canon includes such writers as William FAULKNER, T. S. ELIOT, and Eugene O'NEILL. Modernists favor ambiguity and multiple interpretations of events—especially in novels such as *THE SOUND AND THE FURY* and poems such as "The Waste Land." These highly symbolic works question the meaning of literary genres and the stability of history. They experiment with such techniques as STREAM OF CONSCIOUSNESS, flashbacks, and other manipulations of time. Radical skepticism and the quest to write in different styles are characteristic of the modernist mentality.

Sources
Barbour, Scott, ed. *American Modernism.* San Diego, Calif.: Greenhaven Press, 2000.

Hegemen, Susan. *Patterns for America: Modernism and the Concept of Culture.* Princeton, N.J.: Princeton University Press, 1999.

Hoffman, Michael J. and Patrick D. Murphy, eds. *Critical Essays on American Modernism.* New York: G. K. Hall, 1992.

Momaday, Navarre Scott (1934–) *novelist, poet, historian*
Born in the Kiowa nation in Lawton, Oklahoma, N. Scott Momaday moved to New Mexico, where he worked with the Jemez Indians, and earned a B.A. from the University of Mexico. A fine scholar, he earned an M.A. and Ph.D. from Stanford University and has held professorships at California universities and the University of Arizona. He won a Pulitzer Prize for *House Made of Dawn* (1968), the story of a young Indian who cannot come to terms with either his native people or American culture. His later work evokes Native American myths as well as the modern material world that often comes into conflict with traditional Native American values. Much of his fiction is autobiographical, reflecting his feeling for family and for the land. *Angle of Geese and Other Poems* (1974) and *The Gourd Dancer* (1976) demonstrate his exquisite grasp of traditional verse (iambic pentameter) as well as of modern free verse and prose poems. Momaday published *The Ancient Child*, a novel, in 1989, a moving memoir, *The Way to Rainy Mountain* (1969), and *The Names: A Memoir* (1976).

Sources
Isernhagen, Hartwig. *Momaday, Vizenor, Armstrong: Conversations on American Indian Writing.* Norman: University of Oklahoma Press, 1999.

Monroe, Harriet (1860–1936) *editor, poet*

A Chicago native, Monroe first gained fame as the author of the *Columbian Ode* for the Chicago Exposition of 1893, but her founding of POETRY: A MAGAZINE OF VERSE earned her a place in the history of American literature. She encouraged young poets and published poetry that was experimental and innovative. In effect, she subsidized a new generation of American poets, making sure they had a platform for their work, which was sometimes difficult and unappealing to a general audience. At the same time, Monroe maintained her respect for traditional verse forms, so that she never made poetry merely an avant-garde venture. Not only did she publish great American poets such as T. S. ELIOT, Carl SANDBURG, Ezra POUND, and Robert FROST, she also inspired others to publish LITTLE MAGAZINES and to foster difficult but important writing in prose and verse. She published an influential anthology, *The New Poetry*, in 1917 (revised in 1932). She collected her own poems in *Chosen Poems* (1935) and published her autobiography, *A Poet's Life*, in 1937.

Sources

Cahill, Daniel J. *Harriet Monroe*. New York, Twayne, 1973.
Williams, Ellen. *Harriet Monroe and the Poetry Renaissance: The First Ten Years of Poetry, 1912–22*. Urbana: University of Illinois Press, 1977.

Moore, Marianne Craig (1887–1972) *poet, critic, editor*

Marianne Moore was born in Kirkwood, Missouri, but moved to Carlisle, Pennsylvania, when she was seven. She graduated from Bryn Mawr College, where she published poems in the college literary magazines. After teaching school in Carlisle, she moved to GREENWICH VILLAGE, befriending such writers as William Carlos WILLIAMS, Kenneth BURKE, and Wallace STEVENS. Her poems were published in THE DIAL and her second book of poetry, *Observations* (1924), won *The Dial* prize. She served as editor of *The Dial* from 1925 to 1929, when the magazine ceased publication. Moore's *Selected Poems* (1935) sealed her reputation as an important modern American poet. Her *Collected Poems* (1951) won the Pulitzer Prize, the Bollingen Prize, and the National Book Award. *The Complete Poems of Marianne Moore* appeared in 1981, and *The Complete Prose of Marianne Moore* in 1986. She published one work of nonfiction: *Predilections* (1955), essays on her favorite writers.

Moore's poetry has sometimes been called OBJECTIVIST, a term that has also been associated with the work of her contemporary, William Carlos Williams. This kind of poetry concentrates on images and objects in as concrete a fashion as possible. Moore's affinity for this kind of poetry may have stemmed, in part, from her devotion to painting, which she also considered as an artistic avocation. She wanted to delineate the world as clearly as possible. She eschewed confessional, autobiographical verse in favor of wit, irony, and compact, metrical forms and patterns. She took much of her imagery from the animal world.

No anthology of American poetry could be considered complete without several selections from Moore. The titles of her poems reflect her style and subjects: "To a Steam Roller," "No Swan so Fine," "The Fish." This last poem, which begins "wade/through black jade," immediately captures the fish's suddenness of movement. The "black jade" is explained in the third line with its reference to mussel shells. Like an IMAGIST, Moore used words to present the immediacy of images and motion. The poem is about the human fascination with such uninhibited, spontaneous creatures, but this idea arose out of words that attempt to mimic what the poet sees and thinks.

The subtext of many of Moore's poems is a theory of what poetry should be. Sometimes she made that theory explicit, as in "Poetry." Moore was also fascinated with the way the mind works, and she often explored its working by drawing analogies between the mind and nature, as in "The Mind Is an Enchanted Thing," which compares the mind to "the glaze on a/katydid-wing."

Sources

Molesworth, Charles. *Marianne Moore: A Literary Life*. New York: Atheneum, 1990.
Parisi, Joseph, ed. *Marianne Moore: The Art of a Modernist*. Ann Arbor, Mich.: UMI Research Press, 1990.
Willis, Patricia, ed. *Marianne Moore: Woman and Poet*. Orono, Me.: National Poetry Foundation, 1990.

Moore, Merrill (1903–1957) *poet*

Born in Tennessee and educated at Vanderbilt University, Moore became part of the group of poets who published *The Fugitive*, a literary magazine. Although he pursued a career as a psychiatrist in Boston, he also published poetry that has the fluency and formality associated with his mentor, John Crowe RANSOM. Moore's books include *The Noise That Time Makes* (1929), *It is a Great Deal Later Than You Think* (1934), *Six Sides to a Man* (1935), *M: One Thousand Autobiographical Sonnets* (1939), and *Clinical Sonnets* (1949).

Sources

Fitts, Dudley. *The Sonnets of Merrill Moore*. Sewanee, Tenn.: University of the South, 1939.
Wells, Henry Willis. *Poet and Psychiatrist: Merrill Moore, M.D.; A Critical Portrait with an Appraisal of Two Hundred of His Poems*. New York: Twayne, 1955.

Moraga, Cherríe (1952–) *poet, playwright, editor*

Moraga was born in Whittier, California, the daughter of Joseph Lawrence and a Chicana mother, Elvira Moraga. She identified with her Spanish heritage and pursued feminist writing in her graduate studies at San Francisco State University. She edited an influential anthology, *This Bridge Called My Back: Writings by Radical Women of Color* (1981). Her first book of poetry, *Loving in the War Years: (Lo que nunca pasó por sus labios)* (1983) explored her Chicana and lesbian identities in both Spanish and English. Her play *Giving Up the Ghost* (1986) has been cited as the first explicitly lesbian play by a Chicana. Constructed as a series of monologues by three women, the repression—indeed the invisibility—of lesbian and Chicana women is emphasized as these characters try to work through their sense of confusion and separateness.

Moraga has also edited *Cuentos: Stories by Latinas* (1983) and *The Sexuality of Latinas* (1993). She is the author of *The Last Generation: Prose and Poetry* (1993), *Heroes and Saints & Other Plays* (1994), and *Waiting in the Wings: Portrait of a Queer Motherhood* (1997).

Sources

Horno-Delgado, Asuncion, ed. *Breaking Boundaries: Latina Writing and Critical Readings.* Amherst: University of Massachusetts Press, 1989.

More, Paul Elmer (1864–1937) *critic*

Born in St. Louis, More was educated at Washington University. He continued his studies at Harvard and then became an editor at *The Nation* from 1909 to 1914. He later taught at Princeton University and produced 14 volumes of his *Shelburne Essays* (1904–1936), commentaries on literature and culture. His name is often linked with Irving BABBITT as one of the founders of the New HUMANISM movement, which emphasized the importance of Greek classicism. Among More's other books are *Platonism* (1917) and *Pages from an Oxford Diary* (1937), an autobiography.

Sources

Duggan, Francis X. *Paul Elmer More.* New York: Twayne, 1967.
Hoeveler, Jr., J. David. *The New Humanism: A Critique of Modern America, 1900–1940.* Charlottesville: University Press of Virginia, 1977.

Morris, Wright (1910–1998) *novelist, short story writer, photographer, critic*

Born in Nebraska, Wright set much of his fiction in the Midwest and can be defined as a regionalist. He has been called the writer of situations, around which he builds perceptive character studies. He has also been referred to as a "writer's writer" because his novels are crafted so carefully. His early work includes *My Uncle Dudley* (1942), *The Man Who Was There* (1945), *The World in the Attic* (1949), and *Man and Boy* (1951). *The Field of Vision* (1956), which won a National

Book Award, is set in Mexico and concerns a group of Americans watching a bullfight. *Ceremony in Lone Tree* (1960) has a Nebraska setting and deals with a family reunion. *One Day* (1965) explores different characters' reactions to the assassination of John F. Kennedy. *Plains Song: For Female Voices* explores the lives of midwestern women. *Collected Stories 1948–1986* appeared in 1986. His later work includes *Three Easy Pieces* (1993) and *The Loneliness of the Long Distance Writer* (1995).

Morris also published several autobiographical volumes: *Will's Boy* (1981), *Solo: An American Dreamer in Europe* (1983), and *A Cloak of Light: Writing My Life* (1985).

A distinguished photographer, Wright published several books in which prose and pictures are carefully integrated: *The Inhabitants* (1946), *The Home Place* (1948), *God's Country and My People* (1968), *Love Affair* (1972), *Photographs and Words* (1982), and *Wright Morris: Origin of a Species* (1992).

Morris wrote extensively about American themes and issues in *The Territory Ahead* (1958), *A Bill of Rites, a Bill of Wrongs, a Bill of Goods* (1968), *About Fiction* (1975), and *Earthly Delights, Unearthly Adornments* (1978).

Sources

Crump, G. B. *The Novels of Wright Morris: A Critical Interpretation.* Lincoln: University of Nebraska Press, 1978.
Wydeven, Joseph J. *Wright Morris Revisited.* New York: Twayne, 1998.

Morrison, Toni (Chloe Anthony Wofford) (1931–) *novelist*

Born in Lorain, Ohio, the daughter of a shipyard welder, Morrison proved to be a precocious student, later earning a B.A. degree at Howard University, working in important New York publishing houses, and holding prestigious professorships at the State University of New York and Princeton University. She is the first African-American woman to win the Nobel Prize in literature (1993).

In all of her fiction, Morrison explores the forces that impede and shape individuals. History in the form of the legacy of slavery of racism can be a crushing burden, yet her black families persevere and sometimes even triumph over misfortune.

The Bluest Eye (1970), Morrison's first novel, confronts the blond-haired, blue-eyed standard that has predominated in American culture. Romantic love—not to mention lust—has focused on white film stars who exemplify this single, repressive vision of the ideal woman. Claudia, the young black girl who becomes the central character of the novel, rejects the Shirley Temple doll she is given for Christmas, recognizing that it represents a denial of any other kind of beauty. Later, she understands how her community has victimized Pecola, a young woman raped by her father. Claudia realizes that

Pecola, who is ugly by society's standards, becomes society's scapegoat, a convenient displacement of its own inadequacies.

Sula (1973) continues Morrison's exploration of African-American marginality. Bottom, a hillside community where blacks have been relegated, suddenly becomes the site of suburban expansion, which results in the destruction of a black community. As in *The Bluest Eye,* a black woman is the victim of the black community's inability to deal with its own experience of oppression. Instead, it attacks Sula, a proud black woman who rejects the passive female role.

Song of Solomon (1977), fittingly one of Morrison's most lyrical works, is about a young black man, Milkman. Although he grows up in comfort, the young man learns that his father attempted to kill him before he was born. Later, his best friend, Guitar (thinking Milkman has a hoard of gold), also tries to kill him—making his last name, "Dead," apparently prophetic. The very fact of Milkman's survival in such circumstances creates a kind of biblical sense of wonder in the novel and instills in him a desire to create himself anew.

Tar Baby (1981) represents an expansion of Morrison's range, since it includes not only her exploration of black-white relationships but also of family dynamics and the tensions between black men and women. These themes are brought to life against a broad historical canvas in *Beloved* (1987), arguably Morrison's most ambitious work. This wrenching story of a runaway slave who kills her own children rather than see them returned to slavery exemplifies the agonizing choices that Morrison's characters have always had to make.

Jazz (1992) brings the world of African-American culture explored in *Beloved* into the 1920s, when southern blacks arrive in Harlem. *Paradise* (1998) shifts between the 1970s and the 1870s, telling the story of freed slaves who tried to build a utopian community and of their descendants. Once again the hostility between black men and women becomes a major theme in Morrison's work—this time with ambiguous results, since the women have decided to isolate themselves in a convent, thus inviting the anger and the attacks of black men.

Like Ralph ELLISON, Morrison portrays the major themes of American and African-American life, and creates universal stories that probe the psyches of men and women in superbly realized geographical and historical settings.

Morrison's nonfiction includes *Playing in the Dark: Whiteness and the Literary Imagination* (1992) and *Birth of a Nation'hood: Gaze, Script, and Spectacle in the O. J. Simpson Case* (1997). In 1992 she also edited a collection of essays: *Race-ing Justice, En-gendering Power: Essays on Anita Hill, Clarence Thomas, and the Construction of Social Reality.*

Sources

Furman, Jan. *Toni Morrison's Fiction.* Columbia: University of South Carolina Press, 1996.
Kubitschek, Missy Dehn. *Toni Morrison: A Critical Companion.* Westport, Conn.: Greenwood Press, 1998.
Peach, Linden, ed. *Toni Morrison.* New York: St. Martin's Press, 1998.

Mourning Dove (Christine Quintasket McLeod Galler; Hum-Ishu-Ma) (1888–1936) *novelist, autobiographer*

Born in Idaho to an Okanogan father and a Colville mother, Mourning Dove attended the Sacred Heart Convent in Ward, Washington, and business school in Calgary, Alberta, Canada. She is the author of a novel *Cogewea the Half Blood: A Depiction of the Great Montana Cattle Range* (1927). Mourning Dove is considered the first Native American novelist. Her work was especially concerned with Native Americans of mixed blood, especially women who were abused by white men. Her short fiction was collected in *Coyote Stories* (1990) and in *Mourning Dove's Stories* (1991). *Mourning Dove: A Salishan Autobiography* was published in 1990.

Sources

Clifton, James. A., ed. *Being and Becoming Indian: Biographical Studies of North American Frontiers.* Chicago: Dorsey Press, 1989.

Mukherjee, Bharati (1940–) *novelist*

Born and educated in Calcutta, Mukherjee came to the United States to study at the IOWA WRITER'S WORKSHOP. Her first two novels, *The Tiger's Daughter* (1972) and *Wife* (1975), are autobiographical and concentrate on Indian women adjusting to U.S. culture. A third novel, *Jasmine* (1989), expands on her first two works of fiction by following the odyssey of an Indian woman across the North American continent. Out of her own immigrant experience, Mukherjee has fashioned a body of work demonstrating both the separateness and interconnections of different societies.

Mukherjee has also published *The Middleman and Other Stories* (1988) and another novel, *The Holder of the World* (1993). Her nonfiction includes *Days and Nights in Calcutta* (1977) and *The Sorrow and the Terror* (1987), an account of an Air India plane crash off the Irish coast.

Sources

Alam, Fakul. *Bharati Mukherjee.* Boston: Twayne, 1995.
Dlaska, Andrea. *Ways of Belonging: The Making of New Americans in the Fiction of Bharati Mukherjee.* Wien, Austria: Braumüller, 1999.

Mumford, Lewis (1895–1990) *critic, biographer, urbanist*

Born in New York City, Mumford studied at City College, Columbia, and New York University, although he never received a degree. He first wrote for magazines. *Herman*

Melville (1929), a biography that came at a time when the 19th-century author was being rediscovered, was his first important book. Equally important was *The Brown Decades* (1931), a study of U.S. post–Civil War culture. The heart of Mumford's reputation, however, rests on four volumes: *Technics and Civilization* (1934), *The Culture of the Cities* (1938), *The Condition of Man* (1944), and *The Conduct of Life* (1951). Mumford's great achievement was to apply his aesthetic sensibility to architecture, to city living, and to a vision of the city as a construct built on a human scale. The impact of Mumford's ideas stretched well beyond the United States and influenced European thinkers and public figures who rebuilt Europe after WORLD WAR II. Mumford's later books consolidate his thinking, but they do not advance it much beyond what these four volumes achieved. His later work, especially *The Urban Prospect* (1968), expresses his dismay at the way city planners have deprived cities of their human scale.

Mumford's essays are collected in *Interpretations and Forecasts* (1973). His autobiographical books include *Findings and Keepings* (1975), *My Works and Days* (1978), and *Sketches From Life* (1982).

Sources
Hughes, Thomas P. and Agatha C. Hughes. *Lewis Mumford: Public Intellectual.* New York: Oxford University Press, 1990.
Wojtowicz, Robert. *Lewis Mumford and American Modernism: Eutopian Theories for Architecture and Urban Planning.* Cambridge: Cambridge University Press, 1996.

Mura, David Alan (1952–) *poet*
A third-generation Japanese American (*sansei*), Mura was born and raised in Great Lakes, Illinois, a Chicago suburb. He grew up hearing more Yiddish in his neighborhood than Japanese, and his reading was primarily in white male writers. His parents did not discuss their heritage, not even that they had been in U.S. detention camps during WORLD WAR II.

In *A Male Grief: Notes on Pornography and Addiction* (1987), Mura has traced his difficulties as a young adult—his indulgence in drug use and sexual promiscuity—to the absence of an identity, or rather to the repression of his *sansei* identity. His first book of poetry, *After We Lost Our Way* (1989), explores the way he came to accept and cherish his heritage. His suggestive, open-ended poems have been compared to Japanese verse forms.

Turning Japanese: Memoirs of a Sansei (1991) is an account of Mura's trip to Japan, during which he recognized that he could not live in such a restrictive culture and that he could not call himself Japanese.

The Colors of Desire (1994) examines Mura's personal responsibility for condoning racism, for not dealing honestly with his sexuality, and with his concerns about his daughter's ability to handle similar issues.

Mura has also published *Listening* (1992), a collection of poetry, and another memoir/study, *Where the Body Meets Memory: An Odyssey of Race, Sexuality, and Identity* (1995). His work is remarkable for its sophisticated melding of introspection and social analysis.

Sources
Mura, David. "How America Unsexes the Asian Male." *New York Times.* August 22, 1996. Available online. URL: http://www.nytimes.com.
Friedman, Paula. "Where The Body Meets Memory." *New York Times Book Review.* July 28, 1996. Available online. URL: http://www.nytimes.com.

musicals
The modern American musical theater stems from the work of Jerome Kern, especially from his score for *Showboat* (1927), one of the first works to integrate drama, music, and the portrayal of contemporary life with a modicum of realism. Before *Showboat,* operas and operettas tended to be fanciful, and little effort was made to craft a play that unified the words and music.

The first musical to win the Pulitzer Prize, *Of Thee I Sing* (1931), words by Ira Gershwin and music by George Gershwin, not only had a satirical edge to its presentation of American institutions, but also relied on the bluesy, jazzy language of indigenous American music. *Pal Joey* (1940) and *Oklahoma!* (1943) advanced the structure of the musical by creating "books," carefully written texts that crafted spoken dialogue as carefully as the songs. *Oklahoma!* also featured superb dances choreographed by the renowned Agnes de Mille. Her work presaged the complex work of Jerome Robbins and Bob Fosse, both of whom made dance and music advance the story of the musical as much as its "book" did.

Many of America's most successful musicals have been based on novels and dramatic plays, including Cole Porter's *Kiss Me Kate* (1948), based on Shakespeare's *The Taming of the Shrew; South Pacific* (1949), based on James Michener's *Tales of the South Pacific; My Fair Lady* (1956) based on George Bernard Shaw's *Pygmalion;* and Leonard Bernstein's *West Side Story* (1957), based on Shakespeare's *Romeo and Juliet.* This last play, set on the streets of New York, confronted urban realities and the immigration of Puerto Ricans in daring and dramatically charged dance scenes, songs, and dialogue.

Just as musicals of the 1930s and 1940s incorporated the styles of jazz and the blues, so musicals of the 1970s—such as *Hair* (1968), *Godspell* (1971), and *Jesus Christ Superstar* (1971)—used rock music and explored religious themes that could not have been addressed in an earlier generation. In the early days of Broadway, musicals had also been the province of middle-class, middle-aged audiences, whereas a significant number of musicals like *Cats* (1981), based on

T. S. ELIOT's poetry, and *Les Miserables,* based on Victor Hugo's novel, appealed to a broader audience, including adolescents and children.

American composers such as Stephen Sondheim in the Pulitzer Prize–winning *Sunday in the Park with George* (1985) expanded the range of subjects that musicals can treat—in Sondheim's case, the French painter George Seurat. *Rent* (1996), a Pulitzer Prize winner, is narrated by a filmmaker, Mark, who cannot pay his rent and who guides the audience through a tour of contemporary New York City. Through the stories of his friends, who protest the plight of the homeless, the effects of AIDS, and the difficulties of making a living in the city, the play becomes an operatic Puccini-inspired epic that uses the genre of the musical to comment on the many different forms of friendship and social activism in contemporary American society.

Sources

Bordman, Gerald. *American Musical Theatre: A Chronicle.* Third Edition. New York: Oxford University Press, 2000.

Kislan, Richard. *The Musical: A Look at the American Musical Theater.* Revised, expanded edition. New York: Applause, 1995.

Mordden, Ethan. *Better Foot Forward: The History of American Musical Theatre.* New York: Grossman, 1976.

Swain, Joseph P. *The Broadway Musical: A Critical and Musical Survey.* New York: Oxford University Press, 1990.

N

Nabokov, Vladimir (1899–1977) *novelist, short story writer, poet, autobiographer*

Nabokov was born in St. Petersburg, Russia. He grew up in a well-to-do family and learned English at an early age from his father, an Anglophile. As a young student he developed a penchant for chess and for collecting butterflies. By his teenage years he was writing poetry, but after the failure of the provisional government in 1917, his father, a government official, took the family to live in exile. Nabokov studied at Trinity College, Cambridge, graduating with honors in French and Russian literature in 1923. His father was assassinated in Berlin in 1922. Nabokov moved to that city in 1925 and the next year published his first novel, *Mary*. Throughout this period he published stories and poems in journals edited by Russian exiles and began to make plans to immigrate to the United States. On the way, while in Paris, he began writing his first novel in English, *The Real Life of Sebastian Knight* (1941), the story of a biographer and his brother—a typical Nabokov fiction, in that the narrator begins to project himself into the life of his brother to such an extent that his brother's life becomes the narrator's own. Thus the way the imagination and the world interact make it difficult, sometimes, to tell one from the other.

Still relatively unknown in the United States, Nabokov supported himself by teaching at several colleges and universities, including Stanford, Wellesley, Harvard, and Cornell. His novel *Bend Sinister* (1945) focused on Paul Krug, an influential intellectual whose ideas helped to found a postwar Eastern European state. Krug remains aloof from politics and refuses to pledge his loyalty to the state, provoking a regime of repression that eventually takes his life. The novel is a testament to Nabokov's uncompromising belief in the autonomy of the imagination. He himself resisted several invitations from the Soviet government to return to his native land.

Lolita (1955) is the novel that made Nabokov's American reputation. Scandalous at the time, it meticulously presented the obsession of a middle-aged man, Humbert Humbert, with a 12-year-old girl. In this novel Nabokov demonstrated his startling grasp of American idioms and manners. The novel celebrates the postwar American landscapes and its panoply of fast-food restaurants and motels. This savage but affectionate satire of America outraged some readers and delighted others. Nabokov challenged moralistic justification for fiction, refusing to suggest any noble motives for the creation of *Lolita*. His screenplay for Stanley Kubrick's film of *Lolita* preserves the novel's delight in human eccentricity and perversity.

Later novels, such as *Pale Fire* (1962), deepen the Nabokovian sense of irony and experimentation. "Pale Fire" is presented as a long poem by John Shade with a commentary by the biographer and critic Charles Kinbote, who believes that Shade was writing a poem about Kinbote's obsession with Charles Xavier Vselav, the King of Zembla, who was forced to flee the revolution that replaced him. Is Kinbote turning literary criticism into autobiography? Is he substituting his sense of reality for Shade's? Nabokov leaves these questions open to several different answers, thus emphasizing the ambiguity of literature.

After the success of *Lolita* and later novels, such as *Ada or Ardor: A Family Chronicle* (1969), Nabokov translated his earlier Russian novels into English. Thus a whole new Nabokov corpus entered the English language with *The Gift* (1963), *King, Queen, Knave* (1968), *Glory* (1971), and other titles.

Nabokov collected his short fiction in *Nine Stories* (1947), *Nabokov's Dozen: A Collection of Thirteen Stories* (1958), *Nabokov's Quartet* (1966), *A Russian Beauty and Other Stories* (1975), and *Details of a Sunset and Other Stories* (1976).

A remarkable poet, Nabokov published his verse in English in *Poems* (1952) and *Poems and Problems* (1970).

A formidable man of letters, his literary criticism has been collected in *Nikolai Gogol* (1944), *Conclusive Evidence: A Memoir* (1951), *Strong Opinions* (1973), *Lectures on Literature: British, French, and German* (1980), *Lectures on Russian Literature* (1981), and *Lectures on Don Quixote* (1983). His extended arguments with the critic Edmund WILSON were recorded in *The Nabokov–Wilson Letters, 1940–1971* (1979). *Vladimir Nabokov: Selected Letters, 1940–1977* was published in 1989.

Sources

Bloom, Harold, ed. *Vladimir Nabokov.* New York: Chelsea House, 1987.

Boyd, Brian. *Vladimir Nabokov: The Russian Years.* Princeton, N.J.: Princeton University Press, 1990.

———. *Vladimir Nabokov: The American Years.* Princeton, N.J.: Princeton University Press, 1991.

Foster, John Burt. *Nabokov's Art of Memory and European Modernism.* Princeton, N.J.: Princeton University Press, 1993.

Naked and the Dead, The   Norman Mailer   (1948) *novel*

Based in part on Norman MAILER's brief experience in combat in the Pacific during WORLD WAR II, this novel became a best-seller and made Mailer's reputation as a promising new novelist. Heavily influenced by John Dos PASSOS's *USA TRILOGY*, the work of James T. FARRELL, and Ernest HEMINGWAY, Mailer created a cross section of American characters who must blend into one unit on a combat patrol. The core conflict of the novel is between idealistic Robert Hearn, a second lieutenant, and his commanding officer, General Cummings, a quasi fascist. As punishment for insubordination, Cummings sends Hearn on a dangerous mission on a Japanese island, Anopopei. Hearn then has to vie with Sergeant Croft, who has command of the platoon. Croft eventually leads Hearn into an ambush that takes Hearn's life. In the end, the mission itself has proven unnecessary, since the Japanese have exhausted their resources and capitulate without much opposition. The novel is notable for its portraits of Wilson, the easygoing southerner; Roth, a graduate of New York's City College who dislikes dwelling on his Jewishness; Gallagher, an anti-Semitic Boston Irishman; and other ethnic Americans.

Sources

Bloom, Harold, ed. *Norman Mailer.* New York: Chelsea House, 1986.

Merrill, Robert. *Norman Mailer Revisited.* New York: Twayne, 1992.

Nash, Ogden Frederick   (1902–1971) *poet*

A New York City native, Ogden Nash specialized in light verse with a slight satiric bite. He often employed the mannerisms of bad poetry, such as excessive rhyming, to comic effect. His books include *The Bad Parents' Garden of Verse* (1936), *Parents Keep Out* (1951), *You Can't Get There From Here* (1957), and *Everyone But Thee and Me* (1962). His correspondence with his family, *Loving Letters,* appeared in 1990.

Sources

Crandell, George W. *Ogden Nash: A Descriptive Bibliography.* Metuchen, N.J.: Scarecrow Press, 1990.

Nathan, George Jean   (1882–1958) *theater critic*

Born in Indiana, Nathan graduated from Cornell in 1904. By 1908 he was associated with *Smart Set,* a literary magazine, and later founded AMERICAN MERCURY with H. L. MENCKEN. An influential reviewer of Broadway plays, he also published several books, including *The Critic and the Drama* (1922), *Materia Critica* (1924), *Art of the Night* (1928), *The Morning After the First Night* (1938), and *Encyclopaedia of the Theatre* (1940). Nathan was instrumental in helping to establish Eugene O'NEILL's reputation as the theater's greatest living playwright. *"As ever, Gene": The Letters of Eugene O'Neill to George Jean Nathan* appeared in 1987, and *My Very Dear Sean: George Jean Nathan to Sean O'Casey, Letters and Articles* in 1985.

Sources

Connolly, Thomas F. *George Jean Nathan and the Making of Modern American Drama Criticism.* Madison, N.J.: Fairleigh Dickinson University Press, 2000.

Nathan, Robert Gruntal   (1894–1985) *novelist, poet, playwright*

A New York native, Robert Nathan was a prolific author of short novels. *Peter Kindred* (1919) is set in a boy's prep school and at Harvard. Several of his works are fantasies, such as *The Puppet Master* (1923), in which puppets come to life; *The Bishop's Wife* (1928), the story of an angel who falls in love with a bishop's wife; and *There is Another Heaven* (1929), in which a Jew finds himself in a Christian heaven. Other novels have a parablelike quality: *One More Spring* (1933), *Road of Ages* (1935), *Mr. Whittle and the Morning Star* (1947), *Sir Henry* (1955). Still others are romances and travel stories, such as *Mia* (1970) and *The Elixir* (1971).

Nathan's poetry is collected in *Youth Grows Old* (1922), *A Cedar Box* (1929), *A Winter Tide* (1940), *Darkening Meadows* (1945), *The Green Leaf* (1950), and *Evening Song* (1973).

Nathan's plays include *Jezebel's Husband & the Sleeping Beauty* (1953) and *Juliet in Mantua* (1966).

Sources

Sandelin, Clarence K. *Robert Nathan*. New York: Twayne, 1968.

Native American literature

Twentieth-century Native American literature is marked by an increasing number of novels, the most important of which address the problem of the mixed-blood Indian who is caught between tribal ways and mainstream society. In *Cogewea, the Half Blood* (1927), MOURNING DOVE, a Cristal Quintasket Indian, created a strong heroine who ultimately rejects the temptation to forsake her Indian heritage. Similar novels by John Joseph Matthews told the story of his tribe, the Osage, their battle to keep their identity, the depredations of alcoholism, and the demoralizing life of reservations. His most important novels include *Wah-Kon-Tah* (1932) and *Sundown* (1934). In *The Surrounded* (1936), D'Arcy McNickle, a Creek-Salish Indian, creates one of the finest narratives of an Indian rediscovering his culture.

Native Americans also drew on American genres such as the western (in Mourning Dove's case) and the regional novel. In *Brothers Three* (1935) John Oskison, a Cherokee, evokes the Indian feeling for his Oklahoma land and his effort to maintain Indian values. Todd Downing, a Choctaw, wrote mystery and detective fiction, including *Murder on Tour* (1933), *The Cat Screams* (1934), and *Night Over Mexico* (1937).

Very little drama and poetry by Native Americans was published in the early part of the 20th century. An exception is Lynn Riggs, who published his nature poetry in *Iron Dish* (1930) and the folk drama *Green Grow the Lilacs* (1931), which was transformed into the musical *Oklahoma!*

By the 1960s, however, Native American literature erupted with the success of N. Scott MOMADAY, whose novel *The House Made of Dawn* (1968) won a Pulitzer Prize. His themes showed the continuity of Native American literature, for the primary subject once again was an Indian's quest to regain his sense of self and community. Momaday explored Native American traditions even more deeply in *The Ancient Child* (1989), the story of Set, an artist whose breakdown eventually turns him more strongly toward his family and heritage.

Other outstanding Native American writers in this new generation include Leslie Marmon SILKO and Paula Gunn ALLEN, whose work introduces a strongly feminist perspective in Native American literature. Allen's novel, *The Woman Who Owned the Shadows* (1983) resembles the efforts of African-American women writers in that like them she harshly criticizes the role men have played in suppressing women's aspirations. In *Winter in the Blood* (1975), *The Death of Jim Loney* (1979), and *Fools Crow* (1986), James Welch, a Blackfoot-Gros Ventre Indian, created a trilogy that shifts between the 19th and 20th centuries as his protagonists cope with white settlement and search for the sources of their own identity, which includes a reckoning with their white heritage.

Like Welch, Louise ERDRICH, an Ojibwa, has published several novels that have earned her national recognition and a place in the mainstream of American literature. Novels like *Love Medicine* (1984), *Beet Queen* (1986), and *Tracks* (1988) provide comprehensive treatments of Indian families and communities, both on and off reservations.

The Native American novel toward the end of the 20th century expanded to include the satire of Gerald VIZENOR's (Ojibwa) *Griever: An American Monkey King in China* (1987); the humor of Thomas King's (Cherokee) *Medicine River* (1990); the fate of urban Indians in Janet Campbell Hale's (Coeur d'Alene-Kootenai) *Owl Song* (1974) and *The Jailing of Cecilia Capture* (1985). Martin Cruz Smith, a Senecu del Sur-Yaqui, has written several best-selling novels, including two mystery novels with Indian themes: *Nightwing* (1977) and *Stallion Gate* (1986). Jamake HIGHWATER (Blackfoot and Cherokee) has made brilliant use of myth in his novel *Journey to the Sky* (1978), which concerns the lost kingdom of the Mayas, and in *The Sun, He Dies* (1980), about the demise of the Aztecs.

The most important Native American poets include Joy HARJO (Creek), Louise Erdrich, N. Scott Momaday, Leslie Silko, James Welch, Gerald Vizenor, Jamake Highwater, and Joseph Bruchac (Abnakie). Bruchac and many others have written for children, concentrating on creation myths and traditional stories that feature talking animals and the sacred presence of nature.

Collections of Native American writing include Patricia Riley's *Growing up Native American: An Anthology* (1993); Arlene B. Hirschfelder and Beverly R. Singer, eds., *Rising Voices: Writings of Young Native Americans* (1992); and William S. Yellow Robe Jr's. *Where the Pavement Ends: Five Native American Plays* (2000).

Some of the more important studies of Native American literature include *The Primal Mind: Vision and Reality in Indian America* (1981) by Jamake Highwater; *Critical Essays on Native American Literature* (1985), edited by Andrew Wiget; *The Sacred Hoop: Recovering the Feminine in American Indian Tradition* (1986) by Paula Gunn Allen; *The Voice in the Margin: Native American Literature and the Canon* (1989) by Arnold Krupat; *Critical Perspectives on Native American Fiction* (1993), edited by Richard F. Fleck; and *Feminist Readings of Native American Literature: Coming to Voice* (1998) by Kathleen M. Donovan.

Native Son Richard Wright (1940) *novel*

Richard Wright's groundbreaking novel of African-American life is a major contribution to the literature of American NATURALISM. The novel centers on Bigger Thomas, who lives in the CHICAGO ghetto and is looking for work. Wright opens the novel with a grim scene in which Bigger kills a rat that has invaded his family's apartment.

Bigger has promised his mother he will go to an interview for a chauffeur's job. His life is severely circumscribed. He belongs to a gang that engages in petty crime. Knowing only his neighborhood, Bigger is intensely fearful of whites and uncertain how to behave with them. He gets the job and is immediately in trouble—not sure how to react to Mary Dalton, an attractive white girl who associates with Communists and includes Bigger in her conversations as he drives her to her meetings.

Mary does not realize how not only her attention but also her lack of understanding of Bigger contributes to his growing sense of panic. When he takes the drunken Mary home, he is aroused by her body and fondles her. When Mary's blind mother enters the room, the hysterical Bigger puts a pillow over Mary's face to keep her from making any noise. By the time her mother leaves, Mary is dead.

Insanely afraid of what he has done, Bigger tries to dispose of Mary's body in the house furnace. He flees when the body is discovered, and he later murders his girlfriend Bessie in sheer terror that she will reveal his hideout. The last section of the novel focuses on Bigger's trial, and on the racism directed at him even as he acknowledges that he is a murderer, albeit one who has killed out of his enormous fear of white society.

Wright's novel is comparable to other great works of American naturalism such as Theodore DREISER's *AN AMERICAN TRAGEDY* or John STEINBECK's *Of Mice and Men*. In the former, Clyde GRIFFITHS murders his poor girlfriend because her pregnancy thwarts his plans to marry a high society girl. In the latter, Lennie strangles a young woman in his confusion over her advances to him. As in Wright's novel, these men are trapped by the intense feelings and conditions (both societal and biological) that compel them to act irrationally and to abandon control over their own will. The naturalistic novel emphasizes the ways in which individuals are driven by circumstances to commit crimes. The environment, in a sense, selects their actions or brings out certain impulses in them that otherwise might not be acted out. In Wright's novel the overwhelming racism in American society virtually guarantees that Bigger will be treated like a cornered rat and that he will strike out at his persecutors.

Sources

Bloom, Harold, ed. *Bigger Thomas*. New York: Chelsea House, 1990.

Kinnamon, Kenneth, ed. *Critical Essays on Richard Wright's Native Son*. New York: Twayne, 1997.

naturalism

This movement in fiction developed in the late 19th century as an outgrowth of REALISM. Naturalists like Theodore DREISER and Jack London dealt with characters who came from the lower and middle classes and were, like the characters of realistic novels, "common people," not great heroes. Unlike the realists, however, the naturalists did not focus solely on the concrete details of their characters' lives; on the contrary, naturalism evolved out of a deterministic view of society. Naturalistic novels suggest that individuals are shaped by society, and that their actions have to be understood in terms of how their society and their biology formed them. The idea that characters behave in accord with their social standing or class influenced the PROLETARIAN LITERATURE of the 1930s. The writings of Charles Darwin and Karl Marx had an enormous impact on naturalists such as Dreiser, Richard WRIGHT, James T. FARRELL, and John STEINBECK, all of whom to varying degrees attributed their characters' actions to their psychology (determined from childhood) and their environment (the family and neighborhood, which dictated, to a large extent, the range of their actions). Naturalism thus challenges the concept of free will and shows how the material conditions of the past and present largely control the behavior of individuals.

Sources

Condor, John J. *Naturalism in American Fiction: The Classic Phase*. Lexington: University of Kentucky Press, 1984.

Pizer, Donald, and Earl N. Harbert, eds. *American Realists and Naturalists*. Detroit: Gale, 1982.

Pizer, Donald, ed. *The Cambridge Companion to American Realism and Naturalism: Howells to London*. New York: Cambridge University Press, 1995.

Naylor, Gloria (1950–) *novelist*

Gloria Naylor was born and grew up in New York City. Her literary tastes developed early. She read 19th-century British novelists and took a creative writing course at Brooklyn College. Toni MORRISON's novel *The Bluest Eye* was an early influence and convinced Naylor of the need to write about African-American women in fiction. *The Women of Brewster Place* (1982), Naylor's first and best-known novel, was published the year after she graduated from Brooklyn College. The novel immerses the reader in the African-American experience with an intensity that approaches melodrama and gothic (see GOTHICISM) fiction. Naylor, who was once a Jehovah's Witness, writes with missionary fervor about her female characters and their environments. Her novel *Linden Hills* (1985) explores the problems of African-American middle-class identity with grim realism, while *Mama Day* (1988) returns to a more optimistic view of the prospects for African-American women. *Bailey's Cafe* (1992) has been called Naylor's most ambitious work, because it combines her concern for the lives of African-American women with more global concerns, including the story of Mariam, who is both Ethiopian and Jewish. Male characters also play more dominant roles in this novel. *The Men of Brewster Place* (1998) not only marks a return to Naylor's fictional beginnings but also allows her to recast her views of males as presented in her first novel.

Sources
Kelley, Margot Anne, ed. *Gloria Naylor's Early Novels.* Gainesville: University Press of Florida, 1999.

Whitt, Margaret Earley. *Understanding Gloria Naylor.* Columbia: University of South Carolina Press, 1998.

"Negro Speaks of Rivers, The" *Langston Hughes* (1920) *poem*

One of the classic works of the HARLEM RENAISSANCE, dedicated by Langston HUGHES to W. E. B. DU BOIS, this poem evokes a sense of the Negro as part of an ancient history. The ancient rivers of the world—the Euphrates, the Nile, as well as the Mississippi—are evoked to suggest the abiding nature of the Negro. The dedication to Du Bois reflects Hughes's acknowledgment that Du Bois had done more than any other African American to promulgate a sense of the Negro's past, that a whole race of people were not merely slaves but instead belonged to a much greater history going back to the founding of civilization in Africa and Egypt (both of which are alluded to in the poem). The sonorous lines of the poem evoke a feeling of calm and permanence, of a people who have endured over centuries.

The poem also appealed to white readers and writers who flocked to Harlem to experience its music and literature, to absorb from African Americans an instinctive—and what was then called primitive—feeling for life itself. Certain American writers such as Carl VAN VECHTEN and Sherwood ANDERSON (especially in his novel *Dark Laughter*) suggested that African Americans were closer to nature and were less stilted than their white counterparts.

Sources
Jemie, Onwuchekwa. *Langston Hughes: An Introduction to the Poetry.* New York: Columbia University Press, 1976.

Mullen, Edward, J., ed. *Critical Essays on Langston Hughes.* Boston: G. K. Hall, 1986.

Neihardt, John Gneisenau (1881–1973) *poet, novelist*

Born in Illinois, John Neihardt was both a teacher and farmer, but his formative experience was living with the Omaha Indians from 1901 to 1907. Absorbing their experience, he published a five-part poem about the Plains Indians and their defeat during the white conquest of the continent: *The Song of Hugh Blas* (1915), *The Song of Three Friends* (1919), The *Song of the Indian Wars* (1925), *The Song of the Messiah* (1935), and *The Song of Jed Smith* (1941). These five books were collected as *A Cycle of the West* (1949). Neihardt published his *Collected Poems* in 1926.

Indian Tales, and Others appeared in 1926, and other novels followed, although Neihardt's greatest achievement was *Black Elk Speaks, Being the Life Story of a Holy Man of the Oglala Sioux* (1932), his transcription of the dreams and stories told to him. This text has become central in Native American studies because it appears to render the Indian's voice in such unmediated clarity.

Two memoirs of Neihardt's early years have been published: *All Is but a Beginning* (1972) and *Patterns and Coincidences* (1978).

Sources
Aly, Lucille F. *John G. Neihardt.* Boise: Boise State University, 1976.

Deloria, Vine, Jr., ed. *A Sender of Words: Essays in Memory of John G. Neihardt.* Salt Lake City: Howe Brothers, 1984.

Nemerov, Howard (1920–1991) *poet*

Nemerov, a Harvard graduate, taught for many years at Washington University. Although he wrote fiction, including *The Melodramatists* (1949), *Federigo, or The Power of Love* (1954), and *The Homecoming Game* (1957), his major reputation was built on his subtle poetry. His *Collected Poems* (1977) won a Pulitzer Prize, a National Book Award, and a Bollingen Prize. Nemerov was named Poet Laureate in 1988. *Trying Conclusions: New and Selected Poems, 1961–1991* appeared in 1991.

Nemerov's criticism and essays have been collected in *Poetry and Fiction* (1963), *Journal of the Fictive Life* (1966), *Reflections on Poetry and Poetics* (1972), *New and Selected Essays* (1985), and *The Oak in the Acorn: On Remembrance of Things Past, and on Teaching Proust, Who Will Never Learn* (1987).

Sources
Labrie, Ross. *Howard Nemerov.* Boston: Twayne, 1980.

Mills, William. *The Stillness in Moving Things: The World of Howard Nemerov.* Memphis, Tenn.: Memphis State University Press, 1975.

New Criticism

This school of analysis of the elements—metaphor, imagery, semantics, and so on—of a poem or other forms of literature, concentrates on the work itself and not on its historical, biographical, or cultural context. The New Critics were especially influential from 1940 to 1960.

Cleanth BROOKS and Robert Penn WARREN established and spread the methodology of New Criticism through textbooks such as *Understanding Fiction* and *Understanding Poetry* (1938). These critics emphasized the multiple meanings of great works of literature. In their view, a poem or a novel has an organic form that can be analyzed and interpreted, although any interpretation would have to recognize the ambiguity and often the irony inherent in art. Literature is by definition paradoxical, and style and form are unified, so that the meaning of a work of literature cannot be separated from its inner organization. In other words, the work of art stands for itself, not for some message or content extracted from the work.

Other critics, such as W. K. Wimsatt and Monroe Beardsley, added to the method of New Criticism by emphasizing the dangers of the "intentional fallacy"—the idea that a work of literature can be interpreted in terms of the author's stated intentions. From the New Criticism standpoint, the author is not the privileged interpreter of his or her work, because the work itself has an independent life.

These ideas of organic form and the intentional fallacy drew on the long tradition of criticism in England. Samuel Taylor Coleridge, for example, developed the idea of organic form in the *Biographia Literaria* (1817) D. H. Lawrence expressed his own understanding of the intentional fallacy when he advised readers to "trust the tale, not the teller."

In *The New Criticism* (1941), John Crowe RANSOM (closely associated with Brooks and Warren) codified the critical credo of the New Critics. Other English critics who contributed to the methodology of New Criticism include William Empson in *Seven Types of Ambiguity* (1930) and I. A. Richards in *Practical Criticism* (1929).

Sources

Royden, Mark. *Cleanth Brooks and the Rise of Modern Criticism.* Charlottesville: University Press of Virginia, 1996.
Young, R. V. *At War with the Word: Literary Theory and Liberal Education.* Wilmington, Del.: ISI Books, 1999.

New Directions *publisher*
Established in 1936 by James LAUGHLIN, New Directions has become one of the major publishers of avant-garde and innovative literature. Among its distinguished list of authors are Ezra POUND, William Carlos WILLIAMS, Djuna BARNES, and Tennessee WILLIAMS.

New England
Many of New England's finest writers draw on the region's distinguished 18th- and 19th-century heritage as one of the main sources of American literature. The early poetry of Robert LOWELL, for example, is steeped in New England traditions and in the poet's consciousness of carrying on a distinguished family name. Edwin Arlington ROBINSON and Robert FROST are the region's most important 20th-century poets. Each reflects New England's Puritan inheritance, its brooding on a tragic world view, its inclination toward understatement, and its treatment of many subjects with a religious intensity. Eugene O'NEILL, who grew up in New London, Connecticut, set his modern Greek tragedy, *Mourning Becomes Electra,* in New England. The use of New England as a decaying or decadent culture with declining moral and religious values is reflected not only in O'Neill's work but also in George Santayana's *The Last Puritan,* J. P. MARQUAND's *The Late George Apley,* John CHEEVER's *The Wapshot Chronicle,* and in many of John UPDIKE's stories and novels.

New Masses, The
See MASSES, THE.

New Republic, The *periodical*
Founded in 1914, this news magazine and journal of opinion has a distinguished history of commentary on literature and politics. Its contributors have included Rebecca West, Malcolm Cowley, James AGEE, Edmund WILSON, and Walter Lippmann. For much of its history, the *New Republic* was identified with liberal and progressive politics. Since the 1980s the journal has become more conservative, although it retains its progressive character and maintains a strong pro-Israel political stance.

Sources

Peterson, Merrill D. *Coming of Age with the New Republic, 1938–1950.* Columbia: University of Missouri Press, 1999.
Seideman, David. *The New Republic: A Voice of Modern Liberalism.* New York: Praeger, 1986.

New York City
In the 20th century, Manhattan replaced Boston as the literary capital of the United States. Many of the writers associated with the *NEW YORKER* held court at the Algonquin Hotel. Known collectively as the ALGONQUIN ROUND TABLE, such writers as Robert Benchley, Alexander WOOLLCOTT, and Dorothy PARKER set the tone for literary life in the 1920s. Their witticisms were reported in the newspapers, and as reviewers they shaped the literary and theatrical taste of a generation.

At the same time, more avant-garde poets, novelists, and playwrights settled in the GREENWICH VILLAGE neighborhood. Uptown, Harlem became the center of another literary renaissance not only for African Americans but for all writers interested in new, exciting work.

By the late 1930s, still other pockets of literary activity solidified New York's preeminence. At Columbia University, Lionel TRILLING presided as one of the most important literary critics in the *New York Times* and other newspapers and periodicals not only for his book reviews but for his more general essays on culture. Trilling was also part of a group of NEW YORK INTELLECTUALS associated with *PARTISAN REVIEW,* a journal of literary and political comment that set the tone for intellectuals throughout the country.

With such writers as George S. KAUFMAN, Moss HART, Eugene O'NEILL, Clifford ODETS, Lillian HELLMAN, Arthur MILLER, Tennessee WILLIAMS, Edward ALBEE, and virtually every important playwright from the 1930s to the 1960s presenting plays on Broadway, New York maintained its position as the theater capital of the country as well.

All of the major publishing houses, including firms like Boni & Liveright, Random House, and Alfred A. Knopf, were located in Manhattan and dominated the publication of the best literature in the first half of the 20th century. After World War II they were joined by such firms as Farrar, Straus & Giroux, which introduced into American literature the work of many foreign authors, most notably Isaac Bashevis SINGER.

Although literature and the theater have become much more regionalized in the last two decades, New York remains a magnet for creative talent in the arts. Success in New York is still regarded as the pinnacle of a literary career.

The different sections and societies of New York City have been portrayed in many works of fiction, including the novels of E. L. DOCTOROW, Louis AUCHINCLOSS, and Tom WOLFE, as well as the plays of Jack Richardson, Arthur Miller, and Edward Albee, and the poetry of Frank O'HARA, Muriel RUKEYSER, and Hart CRANE.

Sources

Douglas, Ann. *Terrible Honesty: Mongrel Manhattan in the 1920s.* New York: Farrar, Straus & Giroux, 1995.
Stansell, Christine. *American Moderns: Bohemian New York and the Creation of a New Century.* New York: Metropolitan Books, 2000.

New Yorker, The periodical
Founded in 1925 by Harold Ross, this weekly magazine of current events, literature, criticism, and humor has had a significant impact on the cultural life of the United States. Its long list of distinguished contributors includes James THURBER, John HERSEY, Janet FLANNER, John UPDIKE, and Donald BARTHELME. Although the magazine published a wide range of writers with many different styles, the "*New Yorker* story" became a recognizable genre featuring witty, elegant elaborations of minor events, which are elevated in significance by the writer's subtle style. Its cartoons often become classics. It has published as much important nonfiction as fiction. Since the decline of general circulation magazines in the last decades of the 20th century, however, the magazine has struggled to retain its audience, its advertising revenue, and its importance as a cultural icon.

Sources
Kunkel, Thomas. *Genius in Disguise: Harold Ross of the New Yorker.* New York: Random House, 1995.
Yagoda, Ben. *About Town: The New Yorker and the World It Made.* New York: Scribner, 2000.

New York intellectuals
This influential group of writers radicalized by the GREAT DEPRESSION included many, such as William Phillips and Philip RAHV, editors of *PARTISAN REVIEW* (the premier journal of the New York intellectuals), who began as Communists, but by the mid-1930s opposed Stalinism and often favored Communist dissenters such as Leon Trotsky. Like Phillips and Rahv, many of the New York intellectuals came from immigrant Jewish backgrounds. Irving HOWE, one of this group, wrote about their backgrounds in *World of Our Fathers* (1972). While Phillips, Rahv, Harold Rosenberg, Clement Greenberg, Lionel TRILLING, Alfred KAZIN, Diana TRILLING, and others were primarily literary critics, art historians, and political commentators, others such as Delmore SCHWARTZ, Mary MCCARTHY, and Elizabeth HARDWICK wrote fiction.

McCarthy and Hardwick were exceptions to the rule, however, both as women and as creative artists. They were not from New York, and they were not Jewish, but they became a part of the New York intellectual milieu by espousing the views of the anti-Stalinists and by writing fiction and criticism that had the argumentative edge favored by a group of writers who passionately debated writing and personal beliefs. As Alfred Kazin put it, "writing was everything."

Through the *Partisan Review,* the New York intellectuals introduced European MODERNISM to America and formed the terms of intellectual debate about ABSTRACT EXPRESSIONISM and popular culture. European exiles such as Hannah ARENDT became part of the New York intellectual group. A devotion to high literary standards allowed the New York intellectuals to make connections with southern writers such as Allan TATE and Caroline GORDON. These writers in turn mentored such figures as Robert LOWELL, who became a kind of ambassador between North and South and between modern and traditional conceptions of literature.

What united the New York intellectuals and won them adherents outside New York was their commitment to works of art. They were allied with critics and poets such as Tate, Robert Penn WARREN, and John Crowe RANSOM, who advocated what came to be called the NEW CRITICISM, a form of literary commentary that concentrated exclusively on the structure and style of the literary work, eschewing discussion of the author's intentions, life, and historical background.

As Norman PODHORETZ has pointed out, the New York intellectuals were a kind of family rife with conflict, jealously, and competitiveness as well as a mission to elevate literary and political discussion to the highest levels. In later years, some members of the group, such as Irving Kristol and Nathan

Glazer, became more conservative and rejected not only communism but all forms of Marxism and socialism. Others, like Irving Howe, remained lifelong socialists. Still others like Lionel and Diana Trilling, Mary McCarthy, and Elizabeth Hardwick retained a set of liberal, anti-Communist beliefs.

The New York intellectuals as a group began to break up after World War II when the United States became engaged in a COLD WAR with the Soviet Union. Some members of the group became anti-anti-Communists—that is, they rejected an ideology that led to witch-hunts and the rise of Senator Joseph McCarthy, who made his reputation searching out Communist subversives in American institutions. Other members of the group, while deploring McCarthy's tactics of smearing people with the Communist label so that they were blacklisted and lost their jobs, supported the idea that communism was indeed a threat to American institutions.

The Vietnam War also helped to fragment the New York intellectuals. Lionel and Diana Trilling, for example, were appalled by the student riots, even though the Trillings opposed the war itself. Hannah Arendt, on the other hand, supported student protests and opposed the war. Mary McCarthy, one of the most outspoken members of the group, not only opposed the war but supported the North Vietnamese Communists.

As the New York intellectuals began to divide along political lines, their journal, *Partisan Review,* which had united their conflicting personalities under the banner of anti-Stalinism, lost influence. Arguments about popular culture and politics did not advance beyond positions the group had taken in the 1930s and 1940s. A new generation of writers, such as Susan SONTAG, acknowledged the importance of critics such as Lionel Trilling and Harold Rosenberg while trying to forge a new unity between high and low art, thereby recasting the definition of modernism.

In the 1960s members of the old New York intellectual/ *Partisan Review* group—particularly Elizabeth Hardwick and Mary McCarthy—reassembled and established the NEW YORK REVIEW OF BOOKS, which quickly became the favored organ of New York intellectuals for political and cultural commentary. Philip Rahv and others moved away from New York and severed ties with *Partisan Review.* Irving Howe established his own journal, *Dissent,* which hewed more closely to the socialist/leftist line, and William Phillips stubbornly carried on the traditions of the journal he helped to establish.

Sources
Dorman, Joseph. *Arguing the World: The New York Intellectuals in Their Own Words.* New York: Free Press, 2000.
Laskin, David. *Partisans: Marriage, Politics, and Betrayal Among the New York Intellectuals.* New York: Simon & Schuster, 2000.

New York Review of Books, The periodical
Founded in 1963 during a New York City newspaper strike, this biweekly book review is considered the foremost intellectual organ of its kind in the United States. It was founded by the novelist and critic Elizabeth HARDWICK, the publisher Jason Epstein, and his wife, Barbara, one of the review's editors, although the driving force has been editor Robert Silvers. *The New York Review of Books* features long, analytical essays—often not book reviews but independent pieces of research and opinion—by distinguished contemporary writers such as Susan SONTAG, Gore VIDAL, and Norman MAILER. The publication has often been praised and blamed for its Anglophilia because of its reliance on British writers. In many ways, *The New York Review of Books* grew out of and has surpassed the tradition established by PARTISAN REVIEW.

Sources
Nobile, Philip. *Intellectual Skywriting: Literary Politics & The New York Review of Books.* New York: Charterhouse, 1974.

New York School of Poets
A group of poets writing in New York City during the 1950s and 1960s, they wrote in different styles but shared an affinity for the urban landscape and for the energy inherent in the ABSTRACT EXPRESSIONISM of Jackson Pollock and others visual artists. Kenneth KOCH, John ASHBERY, and Frank O'HARA, the key figures in the group, met as students at Harvard University and shared an interest in the relationship between poetry and painting. Just as painters could juxtapose images and create disjunctive styles, so poetry could assemble radically different images in a manner similar to the surrealists (see SURREALISM) of the 1920s.

An Anthology of New York Poets was published in 1970.

Sources
Ward, Geoff. *Statutes of Liberty: The New York School of Poets.* New York: St. Martin's Press, 1993.

New York Times Book Review
The book review section of *The New York Times* has the greatest cultural impact on readers and literary opinion of any of the American newspaper review magazines. Certain periods have been marked by high excellence—when John Leonard was editor in the 1950s, for example—and other periods have shown a marked decline, when critics such as Elizabeth HARDWICK termed the reviews insipid. The *Book Review* tends to favor nonfiction, with a special emphasis on biography.

New-York Tribune periodical
Founded in 1841 by Horace Greeley, this daily newspaper was known for its strong support of abolitionism and women's rights and the fine journalists it attracted. In 1924 it became the *Herald Tribune* and was noteworthy for its cov-

erage not only of news events but also of the theater and books. It was absorbed by *The New York Times* in 1966, although an international edition of the *Herald Tribune* is still published.

Nightwood Djuna Barnes (1936) novel

Djuna Barnes's innovative and influential novel of 1920s Paris, American expatriates, and bisexual lovers centers on Robin Vote, an unstable young woman who attracts and destroys a series of lovers. Men and women alike are drawn to her with physical craving. An alcoholic with a boylike body and a sensuous aura, Robin marries Felix Volkbein, an Austrian. Although she agrees to have a child with him, she is absent from home for long periods and he realizes he cannot control her. She gives birth to a son but rejects the role of mother, deserts Felix, and moves to America. There she takes up with Nora Flood, noted for her salon of artists, radicals, and practitioners of black magic. Robin again wanders off and engages in lesbian affairs and alcoholic binges. Finally, Robin leaves Nora for Jenny Petherbridge, a middle-aged woman who is an old hand at breaking up couples and stealing lovers. This time Jenny deserts Robin, and the latter—now entirely without moorings—wanders into a chapel and gets down on all fours, evidently more comfortable with animals than with human beings.

Robin represents the unattainable love object. She is as much a creation of other characters' fantasies as she is of her own actions. Without a stable identity—sexual or otherwise—she cannot remain attached to anyone or fixed to a single locale. Barnes herself rejected the idea that her book was a lesbian novel, perhaps because the novel itself resists the simple labeling of sexuality and the confinement of individuals to single roles.

Quite aside from the sensational sexual material, the novel is a modernist (see MODERNISM) work that raises important questions about the composition of institutions such as marriage and of society itself.

Sources
Plumb, Cheryl J., ed. *Nightwood: The Original Version and Related Drafts.* Normal, Ill.: Dalkey Archive Press, 1995.
Scott, Bonnie Kime. *Refiguring Modernism.* Bloomington: Indiana University Press, 1995.

Nordhoff, Charles (1887–1947) novelist

After serving in World War I, Nordhoff accompanied James N. Hall to Tahiti, where they wrote the immensely popular novels *Mutiny on the Bounty* (1932), *Men Against the Sea* (1934), and *Pitcairn's Island* (1934). The story of the mutiny against Captain Bligh (played by Charles Laughton in the movie) and the leader of the mutiny Fletcher Christian (Clark Gable) is one of the most romantic and tragic popular stories of the 20th century, because it sets a principled but harsh captain against a compassionate but insubordinate officer. The conflict between duty, order, discipline, and a sense of humanity is a riveting feature of a trilogy based on actual events.

Sources
Briand, Paul L. *In Search of Paradise: The Nordhoff-Hall Story.* New York: Duell, Sloan & Pearce, 1966.

Norman, Marsha (1947–) playwright

Born in Louisville, Kentucky, Norman grew up in a fundamentalist Christian family and attended local schools. After graduation from Agnes Scott College in Decatur, Georgia, she returned home in 1969, married Michael Norman, a high school English teacher, and earned an M.A. degree at the University of Louisville. She worked with disturbed children at Kentucky Central State Hospital and taught adolescents at the Brown School. She also wrote articles and reviews for the *Louisville Times* and later divorced her husband.

Norman turned to playwriting in 1976, when she formed a relationship with the Louisville Actors Theatre through its artistic director, Jon Jory. Her first play, *Getting Out* (1977), won the Theatre's first prize and was well reviewed. The play focuses on Arlene, a former prostitute attempting to move on—even though her only alternative seems to be a menial job. She has no job skills, but almost any job, in the end, seems worth it if she manages to maintain some degree of control over her life.

Norman has said that all of her plays are the same essential issue: Will the characters have the fortitude to overcome their liabilities? In each play characters confront a range of debilitating experiences such as child abuse and other family disorders, yet they ultimately have to take responsibility for their own lives.

Norman experienced several critical failures before her fifth play, *'night, Mother* (1982), won a Pulitzer Prize and confirmed her position as one of the important playwrights of her era. This play suggests there is nothing certain about her characters' efforts to prevail over their weaknesses. Indeed, the main character, Jessie, commits suicide. What is extraordinary about the play is that Jessie makes the right choice for herself. She has run out of options, and she faces ending her life with enormous courage and insight. As a work for the theater, it is brilliantly compelling because the audience, bowled over by Jessie's mesmerizing monologues, wants her to succeed, and in an ironic, heartbreaking way, she does.

None of Norman's subsequent plays—*Traveler in the Dark* (1984), *Sarah and Abraham* (1987), *D. Boone* (1993)—has achieved the same acclaim as *'night, Mother,* but her 1991 adaptation of a children's classic, Frances Hodgson Burnett's *The Secret Garden,* to the musical stage won a Tony Award.

Sources

Brown, Linda. *Marsha Norman: A Casebook.* New York: Garland, 1996.

Kintz, Linda. *The Subject's Tragedy: Political Poetics, Feminist Theory, and Drama.* Ann Arbor: University of Michigan Press, 1992.

North American Review *periodical*

From 1815 to 1939, this magazine served as a significant forum for men of letters based in the Northeast. In the 1920s it was known for spirited articles on political subjects as well. In 1963 the University of Northern Iowa established a journal with the same name, but it did not draw on the tradition of the earlier publication, and it has not achieved anything like the same degree of prominence.

Notes of a Native Son James Baldwin (1955) *essay collection*

The title of James BALDWIN's elegant collection of essays about race and important African-American authors refers to Richard WRIGHT's novel *NATIVE SON* (1940), one of the great achievements of African-American literature and of NATURALISM. Baldwin brought a special authority to his writing not only because of his achievement as a novelist but also because he related his observations of literature and society to his own autobiography. In other words, he tested his perceptions of history against his own experiences, and he opened up a view of the individual African-American writer and his society that had not been previously accessible to whites or blacks. In examining Harriet Beecher Stowe's *Uncle Tom's Cabin* (1852), for example, Baldwin faulted the novel for its sentimentality and crude employment of protest literature. Stowe's characters were stereotypes, he argued, created to manipulate and move the reader to accept her propagandistic aims. To this analysis Baldwin added a startling and disturbing analysis of Richard Wright's fiction, especially *Native Son,* which had inspired a generation of African-American writers. Baldwin argues that Wright actually perpetuates stereotypes even as he excoriates white society. Like Ralph ELLISON, Baldwin reacted against Wright's determinism because it did not allow for individual growth or for the changing of history. Indeed, much of *Notes of a Native Son* suggests that the world is changing and the African American's central place in it is being recognized. "This world is white no longer, and it will never be white again," Baldwin concludes.

Sources

Bloom, Harold, ed. *James Baldwin.* New York: Chelsea House, 1986.

McBride, Dwight A., ed. *James Baldwin Now.* New York: New York University Press, 1999.

novel *genre*

REALISM dominated the late 19th- and early 20th-century novel. Writers at the beginning of the century, such as Edith WHARTON and Willa CATHER, wrote well-observed social and historical novels that concentrated on the development of character, of manners, and of communities. But within this realistic tradition, such writers as Theodore DREISER, John Dos PASSOS, James T. FARRELL, John STEINBECK, and Richard WRIGHT took what came to be viewed as a naturalistic view of society and the individual. They showed how industrialism, capitalism, and the whole economic structure of society determined the lives of masses of people. For the naturalist, the individual is not simply free to exert his own will, and the novelist cannot simply describe society as if it were composed of individuals at liberty to do as they like. On the contrary, the ethnic enclaves of Farrell's Chicago, or the migrant labor camps set up by California growers in Steinbeck's *THE GRAPES OF WRATH* force families, communities, and individuals to react to material conditions that shape human behavior.

The naturalists were influenced by Marxist thought, which suggested that matter shapes minds. The Communist organizer in Steinbeck's novel *In Dubious Battle,* for example, knows that society has to be changed if millions of people are to be able to change or take control of their lives. In *NATIVE SON,* Bigger Thomas does not murder because he is an evil man but because of conditions that cause him to panic and that foreclose the choices open to him.

Writers like Sinclair LEWIS, who were less driven by ideological concerns, used the realistic novel to satirize society. Lewis's work exposes the flaws in American society and punctures its surface complacency, but is not the protest fiction that Michael GOLD, Daniel Fuchs, and other writers of the 1930s published in order to arouse social and political action.

Although both naturalism and realism pervaded novels about working people in the first three decades of the 20th century, at the same time a modernist impulse began to radically alter the features of the American novel. Dos Passos is a pivotal figure, because the techniques of his fiction took his work well beyond naturalism and realism. The "Camera Eye" sections of *U.S.A.,* for example, experimented with STREAM-OF-CONSCIOUSNESS passages that reflected the author's sensibility and the artist's way of shaping reality. The author's juxtaposition of newsreels and headlines also suggested reality had to be of reorganized and reinterpreted.

Indeed, Dos Passos was part of a new generation that reinvented the style of the American novel. F. Scott Fitzgerald infused realism with a romantic and mythic aura, exemplified by *THE GREAT GATSBY.* Ernest HEMINGWAY pared down the novel, preferring the compound to the complex sentence not so much to simplify meaning as to understate it, to strip fiction of verbosity and sentimentality. William FAULKNER, on the other hand, tended to write long paragraphs, trying to capture all of reality in one complex sentence. He experimented with point of view, employing multiple narrators who were often in conflict over what happened and why. Faulkner, in other words, attacked the idea that the novel needed to have one stable point of view. Much of his work, like Fitzgerald's, has a romantic intensity influenced by Joseph Conrad and D. H. Lawrence.

Cultural movements that impinged on the development of the American novel added an ethnic and moral dimension. Such writers as Langston HUGHES and Claude MCKAY wrote poetry and novels that dealt with the lives of working-class urban blacks. Hughes, McKay, and Jean TOOMER wrote fiction with a poetic intensity and an attention to African-American diction that fused realism with the modernist esthetic—which drew attention to the artist and to the autonomy of art.

The 19th-century tradition of the regional or local color novel was perpetuated in the work of Eudora WELTY, Sherwood ANDERSON, and William Faulkner. REGIONALISM would continue to develop in the later novels of Flannery O'CONNOR, William KENNEDY, and such Native American writers as Leslie Marmon SILKO. Indeed, every regional subgenre of the American novel continues to flourish—from the westerns of Cormac MCCARTHY to the New Orleans settings of Anne RICE's vampire novels.

Novelists such as Saul BELLOW, Bernard MALAMUD, and Philip ROTH brought to the American novel a Jewish-American sense of irony and self-consciousness and a questioning of ethnic values. Similarly, Alice WALKER and Toni MORRISON energized the novel with an African-American feminist consciousness that analyzed the failings of both black and white society.

A whole group of novelists—perhaps best represented by William GASS, John BARTH, Robert COOVER, and Donald BARTHELME—rejected realism, naturalism, and virtually any esthetic that made the novel subordinate to the reality it depicted. According to Gass, their novels were about literature. As Susan SONTAG argued, art should be appreciated for its form, not its content. Art, in other words, should not be converted into something else: It was about itself, about its own way of experiencing the world.

Even so, the realistic tradition has hardly been exhausted, and even writers like Sontag who rejected it in the 1960s have returned not only to realism but to even older genres such as the historical novel. In the tradition of the American novel, as in the tradition of literature itself, different styles and conceptions of fiction do not reflect progress—that is, a moving away from the past—but rather a recapitulation and refinement of earlier modes of narrative.

Sources

Bradbury, Malcolm. *The Modern American Novel.* New York: Oxford University Press, 1992.

Elliott, Emory, ed. *The Columbia History of the American Novel.* New York: Columbia University Press, 1991.

Wagner-Martin, Linda. *The Mid-century American Novels, 1935–1965.* New York: Twayne, 1997.

✂◈✂

Oates, Joyce Carol (1938–   ) *novelist, short story writer, poet, playwright, critic*

Joyce Carol Oates was born in Lockport, New York, the setting for many of her stories and novels. A precocious child, she wrote stories and short books, publishing her first story in 1959. After receiving her B.A. degree from Syracuse University, she married Raymond Smith and the couple moved to various academic positions. Oates taught at the University of Detroit and wrote about the city's riots of 1967 in her much-acclaimed novel, *them* (1969), which won the National Book Award. She had already published three earlier novels, which demonstrated a range of style and subject matter reminiscent of William FAULKNER and John DOS PASSOS; she combined a sensitivity to social reality with a gothic and romantic sensibility.

The author of more than 40 novels, Oates is a writer of enormous ambition. In *The Assassins: A Book of Hours,* she explores the world of politics and political assassination; in *Wonderland* (1971) she delves into the intense world of medical practice; *Bellefleur* (1980) is a combination of gothic grotesquerie and REALISM; *The Mysteries of Winterthurn* (1984) is not only a gothic mystery story but also a searing study of a male-dominated society. *Blonde* (1999) not only re-creates the biography of Marilyn Monroe, it introduces new fictional characters to her biography and posits a way of understanding the males of Monroe's life with startling freshness, because Oates provides a more complete sense of the male universe that Monroe had to confront and placate.

More than any of her contemporaries Oates has been willing to directly confront political and historical events while showing—as Dos Passos did—how private lives and public figures intersect. Among her other important novels are *With*

Shuddering Fall (1964), her first novel, which announces one of her primary themes: the individual's struggle with heritage, environment, and his or her own conflicting impulses; *Expensive People* (1968), a devastating attack on the tradition of nihilism in American fiction, a novel that excoriates important American writers from Ernest HEMINGWAY to John BARTH for their facile notions that life is meaningless and formless; *Childwold* (1976), a clever reworking of NABOKOV's *Lolita; Foxfire: Confessions of a Girl Gang* (1993), the finest expression of Oates's feminism; *What I Lived For* (1994), a diverting story on the quest for success in America; *My Heart Laid Bare* (1998), a panoramic novel ranging over the American experience from the late 19th century to the present day.

Early on in Oates's career, critics began to criticize her for writing too much. They found her novels uneven, but such reservations seemed almost beside the point as Oates produced volume after volume of work that continued to challenge readers.

Oates is a master of the short story. She has published more than 16 volumes of short stories, many of which have won O. Henry Awards and have been anthologized. These stories confront a variety of subjects from surprising angles. Thus "In the Region of Ice," a college teacher who is a nun engages her recalcitrant, disturbing Jewish student. In "Where Are You Going, Where Have You Been?" one of Oates's most famous stories, a teenage girl confronts a sinister visitor who finds her at home. Female juvenile delinquency is treated with both seriousness and humor in "How I Contemplated the World from the Detroit House of Correction and Began My Life Over Again." "Assault" is a vivid and shocking account of the aftermath of a rape. Other stories are based on Oates's travels abroad, particularly in Eastern Europe.

Among Oates's most important story collections are *By the North Gate* (1963), *Upon the Sweeping Flood* (1966), *The Wheel of Love* (1970), *Marriages and Infidelities* (1972), *The Hungry Ghosts* (1974), *Last Days* (1984), and *The Collector of Hearts* (1994).

An accomplished poet, Oates has collected her verse in *Women in Love* (1968), *Anonymous Sins* (1969), *Love and Its Derangements* (1970), *The Fabulous Beasts* (1975), *Women Whose Lives are Food, Men Whose Lives Are Money* (1978), *Invisible Woman: New and Selected Poems, 1970–1982* (1982), and *Tenderness* (1996).

Several of Oates's plays have been produced. She has published *Three Plays* (1980), *In Darkest America: Two Plays* (1991), *Twelve Plays* (1991), and *New Plays* (1998).

Oates has also continued her teaching career. Since 1987 she has been a professor at Princeton University. Her books of literary criticism include *The Edge of Impossibility: Tragic Forms in Literature* (1972), *The Hostile Sun: The Poetry of D. H. Lawrence* (1973), *New Heaven, New Earth: The Visionary Experience in Literature* (1974), *Contraries: Essays* (1981), *The Profane Art: Essays and Reviews* (1983), and *On Boxing* (1987).

Sources

Creighton, Joanne V. *Joyce Carol Oates.* Boston: Twayne, 1979.
———. *Joyce Carol Oates: Novels of the Middle Years.* New York: Twayne, 1992.
Johnson, Greg. *Invisible Writers: A Biography of Joyce Carol Oates.* New York: Penguin Putnam, 1998.
———. *Joyce Carol Oates: A Study of the Short Fiction.* New York: Twayne, 1991.
Wesley, Marilyn. *Refusal and Transgression in Joyce Carol Oates's Fiction.* Westport, Conn.: Greenwood Press, 1993.

objectivism

This term was used in the 1930s by the poet William Carlos WILLIAMS and others to express their belief that the primacy of the image, rather than ornamental language, should govern the form of poetry. Along with the poets Louis ZUKOFSKY, George OPPEN, Carl Rakosi, and Charles REZNIKOFF, Williams cultivated a poetry that was pared down to essentials (sometimes only a few words per line), making a poem a brief but intense experience, a moment of perception akin to what Amy LOWELL called "IMAGISM"—poetry that concentrates on the impact of a single image or a cluster of images. But objectivists, like Williams, often isolated individual words in a cluster of two or three, as if the words themselves were objects shaped by the special dimensions of the page.

Objectivist poets were first recognized as such in the February 1931 issue of *POETRY* where Louis Zukofsky presented an objectivist manifesto. In 1934 Williams's poems were published by the Objectivist Press. Later such poets as Allen GINSBERG took Williams as a model, and Williams's central tenet "no ideas but in things" has had an enormous influence on modern poetry.

Sources

DuPlessis, Rachel Blau and Peter Quartermain, ed. *The Objectivist Nexus: Essays in Cultural Poetics.* Tuscaloosa: University of Alabama Press, 1999.

O'Brien, Tim (William Timothy O'Brien) (1946–) *novelist*

Tim O'Brien, a Minnesota native, was sent to Vietnam (see VIETNAM WAR) as soon as he graduated from high school. Wounded in action, he used the experience for three highly regarded novels: *If I Die in a Combat Zone, Box Me Up and Ship Me Home* (1973); *Going After Cacciato* (1978), winner of a National Book Award; and *The Things They Carried* (1990). Often compared to Joseph HELLER's CATCH-22, O'Brien's work has been praised for its evocative scenes of war's absurdity. Like Norman MAILER's THE NAKED AND THE DEAD O'Brien concentrates on the platoon experience in war. His style can shift from the ultra-realistic to a kind of magical, mythical dimension. His other novels are *In the Lake of the Woods* (1994) and *Tomcat in Love* (1998).

Sources

Herzog, Tobey C. *Tim O'Brien.* New York: Twayne, 1997.
Kaplan, Steven. *Understanding Tim O'Brien.* Columbia: University of South Carolina Press, 1995.

O'Connor, Flannery (Mary Flannery O'Connor) (1925–1964) *novelist, short story writer*

O'Connor was born in Savannah, Georgia, and moved to Milledgeville, Georgia, in 1938. After graduating from Women's College of Georgia in 1945, she attended the IOWA WRITERS' WORKSHOP and graduated in 1947 with an M.F.A. "The Geranium" (1946) was her first published story. The next year she won the Rinehart-Iowa fiction prize for her first novel, *Wise Blood.* Throughout her career she suffered from lupus erythematosus, which restricted her travel and cut short her life.

O'Connor has sometimes been called a practitioner of southern gothic, and certainly her novels and stories do evoke the darker strains of southern history associated with writers of the southern Renaissance, a term associated with the work of the FUGITIVES and writers such as William FAULKNER, Robert Penn WARREN, and Caroline GORDON. But violence in her work is merely the sign of a corrupt and fallen world, which O'Connor sees partly through an intense Roman Catholic vision of evil. Her work does not reflect specific religious dogma, but it does articulate the spiritual vision of a devout believer and an intense writer.

The Baptist, fundamentalist South spawned characters and stories that naturally appealed to O'Connor's theological sensibility. If readers of all beliefs and persuasions have been attracted to O'Connor's vision, it is because she grounds it so specifically in everyday reality and in precise language. Her characters speak and act with utter conviction, and are driven by a spiritual sense even if they do not lead religious lives. Thus Hazel Motes, the protagonist of *Wise Blood,* is a "Christian *malgre lui*" (despite himself). The idea that Christianity speaks to a world that might even reject the doctrines of Christianity—that this is a Christian world in spite of itself—endows O'Connor's story with tremendous irony and an uncanny feeling that unbelievers often find compelling.

The Violent Bear It Away (1960), O'Connor's second novel, hinges on a verse in Matthew 11:12: "From the days of John the Baptist until now, the kingdom of heaven suffereth violence and the violent bear it away." This is the quintessential dilemma for the world O'Connor creates: On the one hand, there is the consciousness of a kingdom of heaven, of salvation; on the other, there is the constant desire of a flawed, evil humanity to "bear it away," to cancel out the Christian message through violence.

The impact of O'Connor's imagery and language is even more apparent in short such stories as "The Enduring Chill," "The Artificial Nigger," "Good Country People," and "The Lame Shall Enter First." Each of O'Connor's stories is a study of the human will caught in a tension between desire and duty, passion and belief, feeling and faith. These dichotomies reflect the internal conflicts of her characters and her compassionate handling of paradox.

O'Connor's short fiction has been collected in two classic volumes, *A Good Man Is Hard to Find* (1955) and *Everything That Rises Must Converge* (1965). *The Complete Stories* was published in 1971.

O'Connor's eloquent commentary on the craft of fiction was collected in *Mystery and Manners* (1969). Her letters have been collected in *The Habit of Being: Letters* (1979), *The Presence of Grace* (1983), and *The Correspondence of Flannery O'Connor* (1986).

Sources

Enjolras, Laurence. *Flannery O'Connor's Characters.* Lanham, Md.: University Press of America, 1998.

Paulson, Suzanne Morrow. *Flannery O'Connor: A Study of the Short Fiction.* Boston: Twayne, 1988.

Rath, Sura P., and Mary Neff Shaw, eds. *Flannery O'Connor: New Perspectives.* Athens: University of Georgia Press, 1996.

Odets, Clifford (1906–1963) *playwright, screenwriter*

Odets was born in Philadelphia but grew up in New York City. Much of his work draws on his Jewish background. He began his work in the theater as an actor, but with his work at the GROUP THEATRE he achieved recognition as a playwright concerned with ethnic and proletarian themes. The Group staged his first significant play, *Waiting for Lefty* (1935), which is about a group of striking taxi drivers. His first Broadway success came with *Awake and Sing!* (1935), a lyrical but somber play about Jewish family life set in the GREAT DEPRESSION, and *Till the Day I Die* (1935), the story of German Communists.

On the strength of his New York fame, Odets was offered screenwriting assignments in Hollywood. His play *Golden Boy* (1937), which recounts the life of an aspiring Italian boy who forsakes the violin for a boxing career, was made into a film in 1939 starring William Holden. *Clash by Night* (1941), set in the gritty atmosphere of a California fish cannery, was made into a film by renowned director Fritz Lang.

Odets's other plays include *Paradise Lost* (1935), *Rocket to the Moon* (1938), and *Night Music* (1940). *The Big Knife* (1949), also filmed, is an attack on Hollywood. *The Country Girl* (1950), centering on the decline of an alcoholic actor, was made into a fine film starring Bing Crosby.

Throughout his career Odets created memorable working-class characters, but his plays were often marred by sentimentality and preachiness. In later years, Odets also wrote for television.

Sources

Cantor, Harold. *Clifford Odets, Playwright-Poet.* Lanham, Md.: Scarecrow Press, 2000.

Miller, Gabriel, ed. *Critical Essays on Clifford Odets.* Boston: G. K. Hall, 1991.

Schiff, Ellen, ed. *Awake and Singing: 7 Classic Plays from the American Jewish Repertoire.* New York: Mentor, 1995.

Off-Broadway

This term came into regular use after World War II. It refers to small theaters that are not located in the Broadway-Times Square section of New York City. Some Off-Broadway theaters are located in former lofts, churches, and other commercial buildings. Productions are modest, although most employ professional actors. Successful Off-Broadway productions are sometimes moved to Broadway theaters. Among the most important Off-Broadway theaters and groups have been Circle in the Square, La Mama, the Living Theater, and the Negro Ensemble Company. The works of many important playwrights, including Samuel Beckett, Sam SHEPARD, and Jean Genet, have been produced Off-Broadway.

Sources

Greenberger, Howard. *The Off-Broadway Experience.* Englewood Cliffs, N.J.: Prentice Hall, 1971.

Off-Off-Broadway

This term came into regular use during the 1960s. It refers to theaters that are even smaller than Off-Broadway houses. Off-Off-Broadway productions are cheaper and often more experimental than Off-Broadway plays.

O'Hara, Frank (1926–1966) *poet, critic, playwright*

Associated with the NEW YORK SCHOOL OF POETS and artists that also included Kenneth KOCH, John ASHBERY, Jackson Pollock, and Jasper Johns, O'Hara bridged the worlds of literature and art in his job at the Museum of Modern Art in New York City. His first book of poetry, *A City in Winter* (1952), demonstrated his urbane, witty and sometimes recondite style. O'Hara's included many details from his own life and reveled in the details of living in the hectic, stimulating world of Manhattan. His essays and reviews for *Art News* also established him as an important critic and impresario of modern art. O'Hara most distinctive volumes of poetry include *Meditations in an Emergency* (1956) and *Lunch Poems* (1964). *Collected Poems* appeared in 1971 and *Collected Plays* in 1978.

Sources

Elledge, Jim, ed. *Frank O'Hara: To Be True to a City.* Ann Arbor: University of Michigan Press, 1990.
Gooch, Brad. *City Poet: The Life and Times of Frank O'Hara.* New York: Alfred A. Knopf, 1993.

O'Hara, John Henry (1905–1970) *novelist, short story writer*

John O'Hara was born in Pottsville, Pennsylvania, and got his start as a writer for local newspapers. He then moved to New York City and began writing for *Newsweek*. His stature as a writer grew as he became one of the *NEW YORKER*'s featured short story writers. With the popular and critical success of his first novel, *Appointment in Samarra* (1934), he had the means to concentrate on his fiction full time.

O'Hara is known for his ironic, often scathing stories of the country club set. The very rich fascinated and appalled him. He was also obsessed with questions of social status and class. Although he was so often critical of the wealthy and the snobbish, his work and his life also reveal a certain envy of the privileged and an anxiety about his own place in society.

O'Hara's most important novels include *Butterfield 8* (1935), which contrasted the world of fashionable New York City nightclubs with the underworld of gangsters and criminals and was made into a major motion picture with Elizabeth Taylor; *Ten North Frederick* (1955); and *From the Terrace* (1958). O'Hara's high standing as a short story writer is reflected in the collections *The Doctor's Sun* (1935), *Sermons and Soda Water* (1960), *The Cape Cod Lighter* (1962),

The Hat on the Bed (1963), and *The Good Samaritan* (1974). In *Sweet and Sour* (1954) he collected his journalism—primarily on literary subjects.

Sources

Eppard, Philip B., ed. *Critical Essays on John O'Hara.* New York: G. K. Hall, 1994.
MacShane, Frank. *The Life of John O'Hara.* New York: Dutton, 1980.

Olsen, Tillie Lerner (1913–) *novelist, short story writer, nonfiction writer, poet*

Olsen was born in Wahoo, Nebraska, the daughter of Russian-Jewish immigrants. She was brought up a socialist and attended Omaha public schools. A member of the Young Communist League, she was imprisoned briefly twice for participating in strikes. She married Jack Olsen, a warehouseman and printer, in San Francisco in 1943. She is the mother of four daughters.

In the 1930s Olsen wrote political articles about striking workers and literary life, as well as poetry that explored the lives of poor women. She wrote part of a novel, *Yonnondio: From the Thirties,* which she did not complete and publish until 1974.

In the 1950s Olsen began to publish the short fiction that would place her in anthologies of the best American writing. "I Stand Here Ironing" and "Tell Me a Riddle" explored the consciousness of women (especially mothers and daughters), not only their devotion to domestic life, but also their quest to establish their own identities.

Olsen's memoir, *Silences* (1972), which explores the difficult choices a woman has to make between domestic life and her urge to write, won Olsen instant acclaim. In 1984 Olsen published two anthologies, *Mother to Daughter* and *Daughter to Mother.* In 1987 she published a memoir about her mother: *Mothers and Daughters: That Special Quality* (1987).

Sources

Nelson, Kay Hoyle and Nancy Huse, eds. *The Critical Response to Tillie Olsen.* Westport, Conn.: Greenwood Press, 1994.
Pearlman, Mickey and Abby H. P. Werlock. *Tillie Olsen.* Boston: Twayne, 1991.

Olson, Charles (1910–1970) *poet*

Olson was born and grew up in Worcester, Massachusetts. Educated at Wesleyan University, where he earned his B.A. and M.A. degrees, he left a Ph.D. program at Harvard to work for the Office of War Information during World War II. After the war he turned to a career in literature, producing his first book in 1947, *Call Me Ishmael: A Study of Melville,* a stimulating study of Shakespeare's influence on Melville. Olson's first important writing about poetry appeared in an essay, "Projective Verse" (1950), in which he argued that a poem should reflect the poet's perceptions in lines that naturally followed his own system of breath control. Meter, rhythm, line length, stanza structure—all the traditional tools of poetry—should be a projection of the poet's own energy. Olson's views influenced such poets as William Carlos WILLIAMS, Robert CREELEY, Robert DUNCAN, Ed DORN, and Denise LEVERTOV—all of whom wrote poetry that was not bound by conventional definitions.

Many of these poets congregated around Olson at Black Mountain College in North Carolina, where they became known as the BLACK MOUNTAIN POETS. Olson's own poetry, which he began publishing in the late 1940s, received increased attention with the appearance of *The Maximus Poems 1–10* (1953), followed by *The Maximus Poems 11–22* (1956). Written in letter form, the speaker Maximus addresses the citizens of Gloucester, Massachusetts, where Olson spent his summers as a child. Maximus writes in incredible detail about the town—its streets, people, sights—evoking its beauty as well the urban decay that prompted urban renewal which, in turn, destroyed much historic housing. Other editions of the Maximus poems appeared in 1960, 1968, 1975, and 1983. In their entirety the series has been compared to Ezra POUND's *Cantos* (1917) and William Carlos Williams's *Paterson* (1946–1948) as among the most ambitious poems of the 20th century.

Olson's other poetry collections include *The Collected Poems of Charles Olson: Excluding "The Maximus Poems"* (1987) and *A Nation of Nothing but Poetry: Supplementary Poems* (1989).

The *Selective Writings of Charles Olson* was published in 1966; *On Black Mountain* in 1971; *Additional Prose: A Bibliography on American, Proprioception, and Other Notes and Essays* in 1974; *Charles Olson and Ezra Pound: An Encounter at St. Elizabeth's* in 1975; *Muthologos: The Collected Lectures and Interviews* (two volumes) in 1978 and 1979; *Charles Olson and Robert Creeley: The Complete Correspondence* (nine volumes) from 1980 to 1990.

Sources

Clark, Tom. *Charles Olson: The Allegory of a Poet's Life.* New York: W. W. Norton, 1991.

Merrill, Thomas F. *The Poetry of Charles Olson: A Primer.* Newark: University of Delaware Press, 1982.

One Flew Over the Cuckoo's Nest Ken Kesey (1962) novel

Ken KESEY's second-generation BEAT novel pits his hero against the conformism of American society.

The novel focuses on Randle Patrick MCMURPHY, a rough-and-tumble misfit sent to an Oregon mental institution. The men around him are sedated and incapable of asserting their will. McMurphy is all will, and for some time only pretends to take his pills. McMurphy is a gambler and sets up several games. His biggest gamble is to thwart "Big Nurse," Miss Ratched, who prizes law and order. McMurphy, the anarchist, is determined to undermine her authority. Gradually the men begin to admire McMurphy's stubborn, fearless resistance to the regime of control, and they join him in a sit-down strike.

McMurphy escalates his defiant actions and also gets into a fight—which leads Nurse Ratched to sequester him and then apply electric shock treatments. When he proves even more defiant, he is given a lobotomy. In a rage over the destruction of McMurphy's identity, one of the men, an Indian called "The Chief," suffocates McMurphy with a pillow and then goes on a rampage and escapes confinement.

The novel can be seen as a parable about a repressive society and its demand that individuality be crushed. Indeed, the eccentric person is quickly identified as insane. The mental hospital, in other words, is merely an extreme example of a society that values control above all else. To the Beat sensibility, to be "cuckoo" may be the only way to remain a creative individual. The society that Kesey and fellow Beats criticized had become, in their view, too complacent and conformist. It needed shaking up, and it was most likely to be challenged by the McMurphys of the world—the gamblers who rejected the status quo.

Sources

Pratt, John Clark, ed. *One Flew Over the Cuckoo's Nest: Text and Criticism.* New York: Penguin Books, 1996.

O'Neill, Eugene Gladstone (1888–1953)
playwright

The winner of four Pulitzer Prizes and the 1936 Nobel Prize in literature for his dramas, Eugene O'Neill brought a profound sense of realism and tragedy to an American stage dominated by melodrama and light musical comedies.

O'Neill was born in New York City, but as a child he toured the country with his actor father, James O'Neill, who was most famous for his starring role in *The Count of Monte Cristo.* An actor of great talent, James O'Neill bought the rights to the play and turned it into a money machine, thereby losing the respect of his son, who knew his father was capable of performing the great Shakespearean roles. His father's corruption of his talent became the theme of O'Neill's greatest play, *Long Day's Journey Into Night,* first produced in 1956.

As a young man Eugene O'Neill was troubled by ill health, including tuberculosis. He had trouble staying in school and often caroused with his older brother, Jamie, who also figures in several of O'Neill's plays. As he recovered from illness, Eugene O'Neill went to sea and read Joseph Conrad, whose stories of the sea influenced O'Neill's first plays, including *Bound East for Cardiff* (1916) and *Fog* (1917).

At first O'Neill shied away from the commercial theater, preferring to stage his one-act plays with the PROVINCETOWN PLAYERS. He had also been influenced by a playwriting class taught at Harvard by George Pierce Baker. Baker helped O'Neill immerse himself in the craft of play construction, which O'Neill worked on both in GREENWICH VILLAGE and in Provincetown.

By 1920 O'Neill had written several intense, short plays, which culminated in the full-length *Beyond the Horizon* (1920), which won him his first Pulitzer Prize. This drama of a young man's yearning to leave home and explore the world draws from O'Neill's own troubled youth. At the same time, O'Neill was exploring provocative racial and political issues, producing THE EMPEROR JONES (1920) the story of an African-American pullman porter who becomes the tyrant of a West Indies island; *Anna Christie* (1921), the story of a fallen woman presented with extraordinary sympathy, insight, and somberness; and *The Hairy Ape* (1922), the story of a coal stoker on a luxury liner who becomes tragically involved with a beautiful woman and the exploitative society on which her wealth is built. Indeed, there seemed to be no subject—no matter how controversial—that O'Neill would not confront.

In subject and style, O'Neill's plays were groundbreaking. He gave his African-American characters dramatic monologues composed of both colloquial speech and a kind of grandeur that hearken back to Shakespeare and other classic playwrights. In *The Great God Brown* (1926) O'Neill experimented with masks, adapting the dramatic devices of the ancient Greeks to the modern stage. The use of the mask was in part influenced by O'Neill's reading of Sigmund Freud. The mask dramatized not only the face individuals showed to society; it also was the tool of repression, underneath which individuals expressed their true feelings. O'Neill took this method to the greatest extreme with his experimental drama *Strange Interlude* (1928), in which characters speak their true feelings not by taking off masks but by using asides—as characters do in Shakespeare's plays.

O'Neill's Civil War trilogy, *Mourning Becomes Electra* (1931), drew directly on Aeschylus's *Orestia* as he melded modern psychological notions with the Greek concept of fate and the furies. Like the naturalistic novelists of this period—Theodore DREISER in particular—O'Neill probed the extent to which human behavior is determined or predestined. He confronted America's Calvinist heritage and its questioning of free will.

Throughout his career, the prolific O'Neill produced both triumphs and failures. Even his greatest plays show some haste and considerable verbosity. Yet the epic impact of his plays, and their social and psychological profundity, depends in part on their length and on the playwright's willingness to incorporate themes that a novel would need several hundred pages to explore.

Illness prevented O'Neill from completing the lengthy cycle of history plays that he had projected. He completed only *A Touch of the Poet*, produced in 1957, and *More Stately Mansions*, produced in 1967. In both plays he conflated his own family's history with the American past.

In his maturity O'Neill produced two plays that are considered his greatest. In *The Iceman Cometh* (1946), Hickey, a traveling salesman, addresses the meaning of life itself, exhorting a group of saloon derelicts to forsake their illusions. This long, garrulous play mimics the circularity of human consciousness itself and of the dialogues human beings have with themselves and others. In *Long Day's Journey into Night* (1956), O'Neill confronts directly his feelings about his family: his powerful yet fatally flawed father, his weak, drug-addicted mother, his engaging but feckless brother, and his own earnest, struggling efforts to forge an identity. (*A Moon for the Misbegotten*, produced in 1957, continues the family story, focusing on his older brother.)

These two plays are O'Neill's most original: They represent O'Neill at the height of his powers as a searing dramatist of America's promise and its tragedy.

Sources

Bogard, Travis. *Contour in Time: The Plays of Eugene O'Neill.* New York: Oxford University Press, 1988.

Gelb, Arthur and Barbara. *O'Neill: Life with Monte Cristo.* New York: Putnam, 2000.

Manheim, Michael, ed. *The Cambridge Companion to Eugene O'Neill.* New York: Cambridge University Press, 1998.

Scheaffer, Louis. *O'Neill: Son and Playwright.* Boston: Little, Brown, 1968.

———. *O'Neill: Son and Artist.* Boston: Little, Brown, 1973.

On the Road Jack Kerouac (1955) novel

Jack KEROUAC's classic BEAT novel focuses on Dean Moriarity and Salvator Paradise, friends who believe they "understand each other on other levels of madness." Dean is the sexual athlete who uses up lovers and wives and leaves behind a trail of children. He has engaged in petty crimes, but he tells Sal he wants to be a writer. In New York, Dean meets Carlo Marx, a moody thinker, and they become intellectual soulmates. Dean abandons his wife, Marylou, and drives to Denver with Carlo. There he meets another woman, Camille, who becomes his second wife. They embark for San Francisco. Dean suddenly appears at Carlo's home in New Jersey with Marylou; after a week, Dean departs by himself. When Sal next travels to San Francisco, he finds Dean once again living with Camille, but the marriage is unsatisfactory. Dean proposes that he and Sal take a trip, which they do, stopping off in Chicago on the way back to New York. When Dean hears that Camille is about to have a baby, he returns to San Francisco, but then persuades Sal and another friend to travel with him to Mexico. Predictably, Dean leaves his friends and shows up later in New York, looking for Marylou. He does not find her, and receives word that Camille is awaiting his return. The novel ends with Dean's preparations for yet another trip west.

This peripatetic novel expresses the restlessness of the Beat sensibility, the desire to head out for new territory and to break conventional rules. Most of the Beats came from the Northeast, and although they did create the SAN FRANCISCO RENAISSANCE, they, like Dean, continued to travel back east, alternating between the unconventional and the conventional, challenging the status quo but never quite overturning it. Kerouac's achievement was to evoke the excitement of the Beat quest, the refusal to settle for less than one's dreams. At the same time, the reader senses an element of futility and self-destructiveness in Dean's search for fulfillment.

Sources

Hunt, Tim. *Kerouac's Crooked Road: Development of a Fiction.* Hamden, Conn.: Archon Books, 1981.

Swartz, Omar. *The View from On The Road: The Rhetorical Vision of Jack Kerouac.* Carbondale: Southern Illinois University Press, 1999.

Oppen, George (1908–1984) poet

The least well known member of the Objectivist school of poets (see OBJECTIVISM), Oppen was a protégé of Ezra POUND and a close confidant of William Carlos WILLIAMS. Oppen's poetry has been praised for its remarkable terseness and the stark vividness of his imagery. Although he was an unapologetic supporter of the Communist Party, his work rarely addresses overt political themes. He won the Pulitzer Prize for *Of Being Numerous* (1968). His *Collected Poems* appeared in 1975, and his last collection, *Primitive*, in 1978.

Sources

Hatlen, Burton, ed. *George Oppen, Man and Poet.* Orono, Me.: National Poetry Foundation, 1981.

Ortiz, Simon (1941–) poet, short story writer

A Pueblo Indian born in Albuquerque, New Mexico, Ortiz published his first major poetry collection, *Going for the Rain*, in 1976. This work retells the creation myth of the Acomas while also dealing with the present. *A Good Journey* (1977) is deeply immersed in Acoma culture. *Rising in the Heart Which Is Our America* (1981) is an emotional work that draws parallels between massacres of Native Americans and the VIETNAM WAR. *Woven Stone* (1991) and *After and Before the Lightning* (1991) are both set on the Great Plains. Ortiz has collected his stories in *Howbah Indians* (1978), *Fightin'* (1983), and *Men on the Moon* (1999). The latter collection emphasizes his interest in spiritual conflicts between

Indian and white cultures. Like his poetry, his fiction re-creates the rhythms of an oral tradition of storytelling. He has also edited *Speaking for the Generations: Native Writers on Writing* (1998).

Sources

Wiget, Andrew. *Simon Ortiz.* Boise, Idaho: Boise State University, 1986.

Ox-Bow Incident, The Walter Van Tilburg Clark (1940) novel

In this riveting story of a lynching, rancher Larry Kincaid is murdered, and the community, suspecting the culprits are cattle rustlers, forms a posse. Arthur Davies, a local store owner, objects to this vigilante justice and the mob psychology it promotes. Davies urges a local judge to declare the posse illegal, but when the judge meets with the posse, he stipulates only that the rustlers should be apprehended and returned to his authority.

When the posse captures the rustlers, Davies is again alone in his protests against a lynching. The posse decides to hang all three rustlers in spite of Davies's plea for a fair trial. The men are hanged mainly at the instigation of Major Tetley, a former Confederate officer who carries out his mission with brutal efficiency.

One of the rustlers, Donald Martin, is allowed to write a letter to his wife before his execution. In the letter he protests his innocence. After Tetley and the posse return to their community and their passions have cooled, Tetley is overcome with a sense of guilt and hangs himself. His father, hearing of his son's suicide, impales himself on his sword.

In the category of the WESTERN, Clark's novel has a special place for its intense realism and unflinching portrayal of frontier and mob violence. In an important introduction to the novel, Wallace STEGNER observed that the work's theme was civilization itself and the way a new country had to establish sound principles of justice.

Sources

Laird, Charlton, ed. *Walter Van Tilburg Clark: Critiques.* Reno: University of Nevada Press, 1983.

Ozick, Cynthia (1928–) short story writer, novelist, essayist

Ozick was born and brought up in the Bronx, where her parents, Russian-Jewish immigrants, owned a pharmacy. She went to public school and then to New York University and Ohio State University, where she wrote a master's thesis on Henry James, one of the principal influences on her fiction. Indeed, Ozick's first novel, *Trust* (1966), explores James's favorite theme, the interaction of Europeans and Americans.

By the early 1970s Ozick had begun to explore in her work the ramifications of the Jewish-American experience. *The Cannibal Galaxy* (1983) focuses on Joseph Brill, a Holocaust survivor. *The Messiah of Stockholm* (1987) is a fascinating study of Lar Andemening, a Polish refugee who claims to be the son of Bruno Schulz, the great Polish Jew who wrote about the Holocaust. *The Puttermesser Papers* (1997) is a novel developed out of short stories about Ruth Puttermesser, a retiring, literary-minded woman who works for New York City's Department of Receipts and Disbursements. She lives in the Bronx and is keenly absorbed in her Jewish identity, which estranges her from her assimilated parents.

Ozick is renowned for her experimentation with point of view and her explorations of the meaning of art in both her fiction and nonfiction. Many critics consider her short stories to be superior to her novels. Her important collections of short fiction include *The Pagan Rabbi and Other Stories* (1971), *Bloodshed and Three Novellas* (1976), *Levitation: Five Fictions* (1982), and *The Shawl* (1989).

Ozick is a formidable essayist, elaborating a sophisticated theory of fiction with probing discussions of writers' careers. Her nonfiction is collected in *Art and Ardor* (1983), *Metaphor and Memory: Essays* (1989), *What Henry James Knew and Other Essays on Writers* (1993), *Portrait of the Artist as a Bad Character and Other Essays on Writing* (1994), *Fame and Folly: Essays* (1996), and *Quarrel and Quandary: Essays* (2000).

Sources

Bloom, Harold, ed. *Cynthia Ozick.* New York: Chelsea House, 1986.

Kauvar, Elaine M. *Cynthia Ozick's Fiction.* Bloomington: Indiana University Press, 1993.

Pack, Robert (1929–) poet

A New York City native, Pack earned a B.A. degree from Dartmouth College and an M.A. from Columbia University. He has taught at Middlebury College. His poetry has been praised for its humor and satire, governed by a sharp sense of form. His books include *A Stranger's Privilege* (1959), *Guarded by Women* (1963), *Home from the Cemetery* (1969), *Nothing but Light* (1973), *Keeping Watch* (1976), *Waking to My Name* (1980), *Faces in a Single Tree: A Cycle of Monologues* (1984), *Minding the Sun* (1996), and *Rounding It Out: A Cycle of Sonnetelles* (1999).

Pack has collected his nonfiction in *Affirming Limits: Essays on Morality, Choice, and Poetic Form* (1985) and *The Long View: Essays on the Discipline of Hope and Poetic Craft* (1991).

Pack has also edited *The Breadloaf Anthology of Contemporary American Poetry* (1985), *The Breadloaf Anthology of Contemporary American Short Stories* (1987), *The Breadloaf Anthology of Contemporary American Essays* (1989), and *Introspections: American Poets on One of their Own Poems* (1997).

Sources

Bain, David Haward and Sydney Landon Plum, eds. *At an Elevation: On the Poetry of Robert Pack*. Middlebury, Vt.: Middlebury College Press, 1994.

Paglia, Camille (1947–) critic

Educated at Yale University, where she was mentored by Harold Bloom, Paglia has taught at Bennington College and the University of Arts in Philadelphia. Her landmark book, *Sexual Personae: Art and Decadence from Nefertiti to Emily Dickinson* (1990), brought her both popular and critical success. The book defies categorization: It draws on many different disciplines, including anthropology, history, literary criticism, and developments in feminist and gender studies. Unlike many of her academic colleagues, Paglia has rejected much of contemporary literary theory, especially the influence of the French Deconstructionists. Although she is an outspoken lesbian and feminist, she is also opposed to many of the developments in feminist politics and in feminist critiques of literature.

Paglia's second book, *Sex, Art, and American Culture* (1992), continued her provocative examination of all forms of art and entertainment. *Vamps and Tramps* (1994) collects additional essays as well as notices and reviews of her career as a critic and public intellectual.

Sources

Synnevåg, Marit. "Camille Paglia—Feminist Fatale." Available on-line. URL: http://privat.ub.uib.no/bubsy/nomore.htm. Downloaded June 13, 2001.

Paley, Grace Goodside (1922–) short story writer

Paley was born in the Bronx, New York, the child of Jewish socialist immigrant parents. She began writing poetry at an early age, but eventually turned to the short story after she realized that her verse lacked originality. Her first story collection, *The Little Disturbances of Man: Stories of Men and Women* (1959), created characters that would appear in later books in a rich texture of social and political life that reflects Paley's own experience as a political activist and antiwar protestor. Paley established her reputation with another collection, *Enormous Changes at the Last Minute* (1974), which won praise for its shrewd humor and deft handling of family relationships. Paley's other books include *Later the Same Day* (1985), *Long Walks and Intimate Talks: Poems and Stories* (1991), and *Begin Again: Collected Poems* (2000). In 1998 she published a memoir, *Just as I Thought.*

Sources

Arcana, Judith. *Grace Paley's Life Stories: A Literary Biography.* Urbana: University of Illinois Press, 1993.
Bach, Gerhard and Blaine H. Hall, eds. *Conversations with Grace Paley.* Jackson: University Press of Mississippi, 1997.

Paris Review, The periodical

Founded by George Plimpton in 1953 as a quarterly journal, *The Paris Review* publishes fiction, poetry, criticism, and interviews with renowned writers. Its contributors have included Jack KEROUAC, Philip ROTH, W. D. SNODGRASS, and Susan SONTAG. Plimpton published *The Paris Review Anthology* in 1990, and the magazine regularly publishes a series of interviews with writers, titled *Writers at Work.*

Parker, Dorothy Rothschild (1893–1967) *short story writer, poet, critic, screenwriter*

Dorothy Parker grew up in West End, New Jersey, where her father, a wealthy garment manufacturer, brought her up after her mother's early death. By 1916 she was publishing poems in *Vogue* and writing picture captions for the magazine. She married Edwin Pond Parker II in 1917 and divorced him in 1928. *Enough Rope,* her first volume of poetry, was published in 1926.

Like her poetry, Parker's prose was distinguished by her wit and satire. Her amusing book reviews were published in *The Constant Reader* (1930, 1933). Parker became a public figure, a member of the famous ALGONQUIN ROUND TABLE, and a celebrated short story writer. One of her most famous stories, "Big Blonde," won the O. Henry Award in 1929.

In 1933 Parker married Alan Campbell and they became a screenwriting team, working on important films such as *The Little Foxes* (1941), a movie based on the Lillian HELLMAN play. Much of Parker's best work is collected in *The Portable Dorothy Parker* (1974).

Sources

Kinney, Arthur F. *Dorothy Parker: Revised Edition.* New York: Twayne, 1998.
Meade, Marion. *Dorothy Parker: What Fresh Hell Is This?* New York: Villard, 1988.

Parrington, Vernon Louis (1871–1929) *literary scholar*

Vernon Parrington, who taught at the University of Washington, is best known for his three-volume study, *Main Cur-*

rents in American Thought* (1927–1930), for which he won a Pulitzer Prize. His work was primarily historical; that is, there was little discussion of literary form or style, but instead an explanation of the content and ideas that informed works of literature. He was more concerned with the material conditions of society that produced or provided the context for literature. Parrington became a favorite target of the NEW CRITICISM and of Lionel TRILLING, who believed Parrington's conception of literature was too narrow and paid insufficient attention to aesthetics. Nevertheless, Parrington was the first scholar in the academy to provide an overarching interpretation of the national literature.

Sources

Hall, H. Lark. *V. L. Parrington: Through the Avenue of Art.* Kent, Ohio: Kent State University Press, 1994.
Hofstadter, Richard. *The Progressive Historians: Turner, Beard, Parrington.* New York: Alfred A. Knopf, 1968.

Partisan Review periodical

Established in 1934 as a radical Marxist-oriented journal, *Partisan Review* was reorganized in 1937 when the editors, William Phillips and Philip RAHV, broke with the Communist Left. It was arguably the most influential intellectual journal of the 1930s, and its impact on American cultural life continued into the 1960s. It promoted some of the most important European and American writers, including Hannah ARENDT, Dwight MACDONALD, Mary MCCARTHY, Lionel TRILLING, Saul BELLOW, and Susan SONTAG. The journal's influence began to wane in the 1950s and was supplanted by *THE NEW YORK REVIEW OF BOOKS* was established in 1962. Phillips published his memoir, *A Partisan View,* in 1983.

Sources

Cooney, Terry A. *The Rise of the New York Intellectuals: Partisan Review and Its Circle.* Madison: University of Wisconsin Press, 1986.
Laskin, David. *Partisans: Marriage, Politics, and Betrayal Among the New York Intellectuals.* Chicago: University of Chicago Press, 2001.

Patchen, Kenneth (1911–1972) *poet*

The Ohio-born Patchen was educated at the University of Wisconsin, then moved to New York and later to California. He is often described as a metaphysical poet and praised for his subtle use of religious symbolism, although his poetry is less structured than traditional metaphysical verse. His *Selected Poems* appeared in 1958 and his *Collected Poems* in 1969.

Patchen wrote distinguished prose as well, especially *The Journal of Albion Moonlight* (1941), which employs a STREAM-OF-CONSCIOUSNESS technique. *The Memoirs of a Shy*

Pornographer (1945) is a satirical novel. *Patchen's Lost Plays* (1977) is a collection of unproduced drama.

Sources

Nelson, Raymond. *Kenneth Patchen and American Mysticism.* Chapel Hill: University of North Carolina Press, 1984.

Smith, Larry. *Kenneth Patchen: Rebel Poet in America.* Huron, Ohio: Bottom Dog Press, 2000.

Percy, Walker (1916–1990) *novelist*

Born in Birmingham, Alabama, Percy was brought up by his father's cousin William Alexander Percy, a distinguished writer best known for his autobiography, *Lanterns on the Levee* (1941). Walker Percy's father committed suicide when his son was 11, and the boy lost his mother two years later in a car crash. Percy grew up with the memory of visits from such writers as William FAULKNER and Langston HUGHES. Although trained as a doctor, Percy never practiced. He struggled for years to find his voice as a writer and then succeeded with his first novel, *The Moviegoer* (1962), which won a National Book Award. The novel is the story of an alienated young man who seeks refuge in an obsession with the movies. A devout Roman Catholic interested in moral issues, Percy wrote elegant, understated, and often comic prose. Like other southern writers, he had a tragic sense of history, but his work is buttressed with a high philosophical mentality that questions the nature of existence and the ambiguity of human motivations. His other novels include *The Last Gentleman* (1966), *Lancelot* (1977), *Love in the Ruins* (1971), *The Second Coming* (1980), and *The Thanatos Syndrome* (1986). His nonfiction includes *The Message in the Bottle* (1975) and *Novel Writing in an Apocalyptic Time* (1986).

Sources

Samway, Patrick. *Walker Percy: A Life.* New York: Farrar, Straus & Giroux, 1997.

Tolson, Jay. *Pilgrim in the Ruins: A Life of Walker Percy.* New York: Simon & Schuster, 1992.

Perelman, Sidney Joseph (1904–1979) *humorist*

The Brooklyn-born S. J. Perelman graduated from Brown University, where he made friends with Nathanael WEST. Perelman, the master of the short comic sketch, became a lifelong contributor to THE NEW YORKER. His pieces poked fun at contemporary institutions, and he liked to satirize virtually anything that was popular and successful—such as novels, Hollywood, and advertising. He published many collections. Titles like *Strictly from Hunger* (1937) adopt contemporary Jewish expressions. Other titles like *Westward Ha!* (1948) mocked American values by giving them a twist, in this case poking fun at the American pioneering ethos encapsulated in the expression "Westward Ho!" He parodied travel literature in titles such as *Eastward Ha!* (1977). By the 1970s Perelman's brand of man-about-town New York City humor had gone out of fashion.

Perelman wrote two comic plays, *One Touch of Venus* (1943), a musical coauthored with Ogden NASH, and *The Beauty Part* (1963). *The Last Laugh* (1981) collects his comic sketches and his unfinished autobiography. *Don't Tread On Me: The Selected Letters of S. J. Perelman* appeared in 1987, and a collection of interviews, *Conversations with S. J. Perelman,* in 1995.

Sources

Gale, Steven H., ed. *S. J. Perelman: Critical Essays.* New York: Garland, 1992.

Herrman, Dorothy. *S. J. Perelman: A Life.* New York: Putnam, 1986.

Perkins, Maxwell (William Maxwell Evarts Perkins) (1884–1947) *editor*

Maxwell Perkins spent his entire career at Charles Scribner's Sons editing Ring LARDNER, F. Scott FITZGERALD, Ernest HEMINGWAY, Thomas WOLFE, and James JONES among other significant writers. He was legendary for the care he took with manuscripts. Indeed, his editing of Wolfe led to assertions that Perkins was responsible for shaping his author's often chaotic prose. Wolfe acknowledged Perkins's key role but became so sensitive about the charges that he was not the master of his own work that he changed publishers.

Perkins is often cited as the ideal of what an editor should be—always working for the best literary interests of a book. It is sometimes forgotten, however, that he also made decisions on a commercial basis and considered the market for books very carefully. He worked on his share of potboilers as well as on aesthetic triumphs.

Editor to Author: The Letters of Maxwell E. Perkins appeared in 1950.

Sources

Berg, A. Scott. *Max Perkins, Editor of Genius.* New York: Dutton, 1978.

Cowley, Malcolm. *Unshaken Friend: A Profile of Maxwell Perkins.* Boulder, Colo.: Roberts Rinehart, 1985.

Petry, Ann (1908–1997) *novelist*

Born in Connecticut, Petry earned critical praise for her novel *The Street* (1946), which depicts the struggle of a woman determined to make a decent life for herself and her son in the midst of the poverty and frustration of Harlem. Petry was one of the first African-American women novelists to achieve fame. Her later work includes *Miss Muriel* (1971), a collection of short stories, and several children's books: *The Drugstore Cat* (1949), *Harriet Tubman:*

Conductor on the Underground Railway (1955), and *Tituba of Salem Village* (1964), the story of a Caribbean woman accused of stirring up witchcraft.

Sources

Holladay, Hilary. *Ann Petry.* New York: Twayne, 1996.

Phillips, Jayne Anne (1952–) *short story writer, novelist*

Born in Buckhannon, West Virginia, Phillips earned a B.A. degree in 1974 from West Virginia University and an M.F.A from the University of Iowa in 1978. *Sweethearts* (1976), her first novel, draws on her West Virginia background with evocative portraits of rural families. *Counting* (1978) has an urban setting and deals with sex and politics. *Black Tickets* (1979) expanded Phillips's audience and is her most experimental work, developing a number of different narrators and a cast of characters who have been called "urban grotesques." The novel *Machine Dreams* (1984) is an expansive canvas of social and popular history set in West Virginia from the GREAT DEPRESSION to the VIETNAM WAR. *Shelter* (1994) is a novel set in a girls camp in West Virginia in 1963. *Fast Lanes* (1987) depicts the extremes of urban existence. *Motherkind* (2000) is about a mother dying of cancer and her daughter's visit home to tell her mother she is going to have a baby.

Sources

Kephart, Beth. "Mothers Who Think: Crossing Over," SALON. Available on-line. URL: http://www.salon.com/mwt/feature/2000/04/28/phillips/index.html. Posted on April 28, 2000.

Phillips, Jayne Anne. "Jayne Anne Phillips: American Writer." Available on-line. URL: http://www.jayneannephillips.com/. Downloaded June 13, 2001.

Piercy, Marge (1936–) *novelist, poet*

Piercy was born and raised in a working-class section of Detroit. She earned degrees from the University of Michigan (B.A. 1957) and Northwestern University (M.A. 1958). She traveled and wrote many unpublished works of fiction in the late 1950s and early 1960s, most of them with political and feminist themes reflecting her experience as a political activist in New York City. She later called her first efforts at writing fiction "too feminist and too political" to be published. In the novels *Going Down Fast* (1969), *Dance the Eagle to Sleep* (1971), and *Vida* (1980) Piercy developed her distinctive mix of characters who are politically committed and sexually liberated. Piercy has experimented with different genres of fiction, including science fiction in *Woman on the Edge of Time* (1976), which has a Chicana protagonist, and in *He, She, and It* (1993) a fascinating amalgam of science fiction and Jewish mysticism. *Gone to Soldiers* (1987) is an ambitious attempt to create an encyclopedic narrative of the different peoples affected by WORLD WAR II. In *City of Darkness, City of Light* (1997), Piercy explores the French Revolution, concentrating on neglected female figures.

Piercy has also been a prolific poet. The titles of her collections reflect her radical sentiments: *Hard Loving* (1969), *Living in the Open* (1976), *The Moon is Always Female* (1980), *My Mother's Body* (1985), and *What Are Big Girls Made Of?* (1997). She published *Early Grrrl: The Early Poems of Marge Piercy* in 1999. Her essays have been collected in *The Grand Coolie Dam* (1970) and *Parti-Colored Blocks for a Quilt* (1982). She has edited *American Women's Poetry Now* (1988).

Piercy's later fiction includes *Storm Tide* (1998) and *Three Women* (1999).

Sources

Shands, Kerstin W. *The Repair of the World: The Novels of Marge Piercy.* Westport, Conn.: Greenwood Press, 1994.

Thielmann, Pia. *Marge Piercy's Women: Visions Captured and Subdued.* Frankfurt, Germany: R. G. Fischer, 1986.

Pinksy, Robert (1940–) *poet, critic, translator*

A New Jersey native and graduate of Rutgers, Pinsky has taught at several universities, including the University of California at Berkeley and Boston University. He is one of America's more deeply read poets in history, and his learning is revealed in poetry volumes such as *An Explanation of America* (1979), *History of My Heart* (1984), *The Want Bone* (1990), and *Jersey Rain* (2000). His work has been influenced by jazz, and Pinsky maintains that he has tried to make words into the harmonic structures of musicians such as Charlie Parker and Dizzy Gillespie.

Pinsky's books of criticism include *The Situation of Poetry* (1977), *Poetry and the World* (1988), and *The Sounds of Poetry: A Brief Guide.*

Pinksy has also edited collections of poetry, including *The Handbook of Heartbreak: 101 Poems of Lost Love and Sorrow* (1998) and *Americans' Favorite Poems: The Favorite Poem Project Anthology* (2000). He received great acclaim for his translation of Dante's *Inferno* (1994). Seeking to come as close to the original as possible, he used slant rhyme and near-rhyme so as not to force the meaning of the poem into the metrical structure of the English language. His bilingual edition allows readers to compare the translation and the original side by side.

Sources

"Robert Pinsky." The Academy of American Poets. Available on-line. URL: http://www.poets.org/poets/poets.cfm?prm ID=204. Downloaded June 13, 2001.

Pirsig, Robert Maynard (1928–) novelist

Robert Pirsig is the author of the acclaimed cult novel *Zen and the Art of Motorcycle Maintenance* (1974), which combines a sustained philosophical argument with a narrative of a motorcycle trip across America. Pirsig drew on many actual figures for his characters, including his professors at the University of Chicago.

Sources

Hayles, Katherine. *The Cosmic Web: Scientific Field Models and Literary Strategies in the Twentieth Century.* Ithaca, N.Y.: Cornell University Press, 1984.

Plath, Sylvia (1932–1963) poet, novelist

Sylvia Plath was born in Boston. Her father, a faculty member at Boston University, died when she was eight.

At a very early age, the idea of a writing career and of achieving fame fused in Plath's imagination. She wanted to be both a highly regarded poet and a popular writer of fiction. Even before entering Smith College, she published her first story in *Seventeen* magazine.

Plath's comprehensive ambition took its toll early. After a summer guest editorship at *Mademoiselle* magazine in 1953, Plath attempted suicide and was saved only because her hiding place was discovered. She returned to Smith and graduated summa cum laude in June 1955.

Plath then went to study at Oxford University, where she met the English poet Ted Hughes. The couple married and had two children. They worked on their poetry, taking teaching positions in the United States and then in England.

By early 1962 the couple separated, and Plath took a flat in London with her two children. She was writing her greatest poetry then but was terribly depressed about the failure of her marriage. Her poetry reflected her suicidal tendencies, the grip of the past—her need to have a powerful male figure in her life—and an absolute commitment to poetry itself, even though her verse often opened emotional wounds.

During a very cold winter, Plath turned on the gas in her London flat (after carefully shielding her children from the fumes), put her head in the oven, and was found dead many hours later.

At the time of Plath's death she was just beginning to achieve her mark as a poet and novelist. Her novel, *The Bell Jar* (1963), which deals with her emotional breakdown in 1953, had just been published anonymously. It bears comparison with J. D. SALINGER's THE CATCHER IN THE RYE as a brilliant evocation of the sensitive adolescent mind. Plath was able to show the peculiar pressures placed on a young woman of genius, and the conflict between her own ambitions and her desire to please men in a male-dominated society. Plath's final and best-known poems were collected in *Ariel* (1965), published after her death.

Interest in Plath's life and career has increased year by year as one biography after another has appeared. Plath has been treated as feminist martyr; her husband, Ted Hughes, has been demonized. Hughes presented his own view of Plath and their marriage in *Birthday Letters* (1998), a volume of verse published shortly after he died. The poet Anne Stevenson in *Bitter Fame* (1989) attempted to rehabilitate Hughes and to show Plath as a deeply disturbed woman whom Hughes had no hope of saving.

The intense interest in Plath's biography is likely to continue because her poems are so outspokenly autobiographical. Their intensity makes it inevitable that readers will want to consider the biographical sources of her work—abetted by the publication of *The Unabridged Journals of Sylvia Plath, 1950–1962* (2000).

But Plath as poet is more than the sum of her biography. In poems like "Lady Lazarus" she fuses myth, history, and the universal theme of self-destructiveness and resurrection with her personal experience. Thus this CONFESSIONAL poet speaks of more than her own suicidal tendencies when she begins the poem with a reference to skin "Bright as a Nazi lampshade." The reference to the Nazis—which recurs in the poem "Daddy"—suggests how intricately Plath suffused her personal suffering with the suffering of the 20th century, so that her poetry and the age have become indissoluble.

The Collected Poems of Sylvia Plath was published in 1981 and *Selected Poems* in 1985. *Letters Home*, an expurgated edition of her letters to her mother, Aurelia Plath, appeared in 1975, and the expurgated *Journals of Sylvia Plath* in 1982. Plath's short fiction has been collected in *Johnny Panic and the Bible of Dreams* (1977). She wrote two books for children: *The Bed Book* (1976) and *The It-Doesn't-Matter Suit* (1996).

Sources

Alexander, Paul, ed. *Ariel Ascending: Writings About Sylvia Plath.* New York: Harper & Row, 1985.

Hall, Caroline King Barnard. *Sylvia Plath Revised.* New York: Twayne, 1998.

Stevenson, Anne. *Bitter Fame: A Life of Sylvia Plath, with additional material by Lucas Myers, Dido Merwin, and Richard Murphy.* New York: Viking, 1989.

Wagner-Martin, Linda, ed. *Critical Essays on Sylvia Plath.* Boston: G. K. Hall, 1984.

———. *Sylvia Plath: A Biography.* New York: Simon & Schuster, 1987.

Podhoretz, Norman (1930–) critic, editor

Born in Brooklyn, New York, Podhoretz studied with Lionel TRILLING at Columbia University. Podhoretz's long tenure as editor of COMMENTARY magazine made him an important arbiter of cultural affairs in New York City, and later on—as his politics shifted—of Jewish concerns as well. A liberal with sympathies for the radical left, Podhoretz championed writers such as Norman MAILER, who became a close friend, and Hannah ARENDT. Podhoretz published the best of his literary and cultural essays in *Doings and Undoings: The Fifties and After in American Writing* (1967).

Podhoretz's politics and literary tastes began to change when he published his autobiography, *Making It* (1967), a candid revelation of his own ambitions and of his connections with the NEW YORK INTELLECTUALS. When his frank account received cool, if not hostile reviews, Podhoretz began to rethink the hegemony of the Left over cultural and political matters in New York City. *Breaking Ranks* (1979) is an account of his turn toward conservatism and the ostracism he experienced as soon as his political views began to diverge from those of the liberal intelligentsia.

By the early 1980s Podhoretz emerged as a staunch conservative, a scourge of the New Left, an adamant defender of Israel and of U.S. COLD WAR policy in Vietnam, as evidenced in *Why We Were in Vietnam* (1982).

Podhoretz has subsequently produced a series of memoirs, expanding on his change of politics and aesthetics: *The Bloody Crossroads: Where Literature and Politics Meet* (1986), *Ex-friends: Falling Out with Allen Ginsberg, Lionel & Diana Trilling, Lillian Hellman, Hannah Arendt, and Norman Mailer* (1999), and *My Love Affair With America: The Cautionary Tale of a Cheerful Conservative* (2000).

Sources

Winchell, Mark Royden. *Neoconservative Criticism: Norman Podhoretz, Kenneth S. Lynn, and Joseph Epstein.* Boston: Twayne, 1991.

poetry *genre*

Twentieth-century American poetry begins with the work of regionalist poets such as Edwin Arlington ROBINSON, Edgar Lee MASTERS, and Robert FROST. Like Sherwood ANDERSON in *WINESBURG, OHIO* (1919), these poets examined nature and small-town life with a precision, irony, and humor that rejected the sentimental vision of America and focused on individuals who felt alienated from their communities or sought an alternative identity. Robinson's poem "Richard Cory," about a well-to-do man who seems to have everything and who commits suicide, represents this new tone in American poetry. The community envies Cory, and yet this elegant man's life has seemed to him a sham.

While Frost's poetry would seem to embrace New England life much more than Robinson's, much of his poetry in fact contains dark intimations. Nature soothes but also troubles the poet, whose embrace of America is much more ambivalent than Walt Whitman's. Frost's verse seems traditional in use of meter and rhyme, yet it is also ambiguous and fraught with uncertainty when it speaks of a humankind that can see "neither far out nor in deep."

Frost's poetry heralds a kind of restraint and understatement in American literature that also pervades the work of fiction writers such as Ernest HEMINGWAY. Indeed, Hemingway is more typical of American poets such as Ezra POUND, T. S. ELIOT, and H. D., who forsake America for Europe and its greater cosmopolitanism and sense of history. Like Henry James a generation earlier, these poets are seeking a sophistication in which they can ground their work. They are part of a MODERNISM that in part celebrates the writer as exile. Eliot's and Pound's poetry of the 1920s and 1930s evokes feelings of doom and decadence. America, in their view, is provincial and inhospitable to the literary sensibility.

At the same time, William Carlos WILLIAMS and Carl SANDBURG carry on Whitman's tradition of embracing America and finding in its people and places the inspiration for great poetry. Williams rejected Eliot's pro-European attitude. He was, however, greatly influenced by Pound's view of poetry as a concrete, hard-edged, imagist medium that can express not only the poet's feelings but also render with great clarity the objects of this world.

It is through Williams and Pound, indeed, that later generations of poets, spearheaded by Charles OLSON, published "projectivist" verse, which maintains that it is possible for the poet to express himself while drawing very directly on American culture and its greatest authors, especially Herman Melville. Olson's great task was to reunify the classical and romantic conceptions of literature; that is, that the poem could be a unique expression of the poets's voice (romanticism) and at the same time be a precise, almost scientific description of the world and of the world of literature.

Other American poets such as Allen TATE, John Crowe RANSOM, and Robert Penn WARREN brought traditionalist southern sensibilities to modernism. They emphasized irony and used well-wrought poems—to borrow the phrase of southern-born critic Cleanth Brooks—to evoke and critique not only their southern heritage but also the cultural climate of the modern world. These poets attempted to correct the excesses of emotionalism in modern poetry. Like Frost, their way of exploring deep feeling was to become less explicit and more understated.

Outside of or parallel to this modernist tradition of poetry were poets such as Vachel LINDSAY and Langston HUGHES, who explored what might be called the folklore of American life. Hughes, in particular, was able to mimic and intensify the speech of African Americans into exquisitely crafted poems—deft dramatic monologues of both comic and tragic power.

Quite apart from other poets of era, Wallace STEVENS took poetry to a level of abstraction that is still difficult to comprehend. His poems seem often to be about art, which he called the "supreme fiction." Unlike Williams and other poets who saw poetry in the world, the poem to Stevens seemed to be hermetic, an object the world could not penetrate. Whether an "emperor of ice cream" or a "jar in Tennessee," the objects and images Stevens names often have little to do with the world outside of the poem. This is largely because Stevens was hostile to the idea of a poem being about something besides itself. It was the poem that created its own order; it was not the world that gave order to art. His work is much praised by poets who find Stevens's use of metaphor intriguing and admire his ability to keep his art separate from the world in a kind of parallel universe. His poetry marks a refusal to submit to ordinary forms of expression. But it is partly the highly original nature of Stevens's poetry that makes it difficult to understand. There is nothing else quite like it.

In the 1940s a new generation of poets—including Robert LOWELL, Randall JARRELL, and John BERRYMAN, all taught or influenced by Ranson and Tate—shifted the modernist interest back to the poet, creating what came to be called CONFESSIONAL POETRY. The poet's life and psychology became the primary subject matter. Lowell was the most daring in this respect, including excerpts from his wife's letters in some of his poems.

In the 1950s BEAT poets such as Allen GINSBERG and Gary SNYDER experimented with Whitman's long lines, free verse, and effort to comment on virtually any aspect of American life that captured the poet's attention. Even more than Whitman, the Beats drew on Eastern philosophy, which they melded with the sounds of jazz in such poems as Lawrence FERLINGHETTI's "A Coney Island of the Mind."

In the 1960s Robert Lowell had two brilliant students: Anne SEXTON and Sylvia PLATH, both of whom continued the confessional tradition. Plath in particular aimed to reunite poetry and prose, and to reconfigure the image of the poet. Although she wrote in the high modernist tradition, she also wanted to be a popular writer and to blend high art and popular art, the poet and her audience. Her early death by suicide and her stormy marriage to the poet Ted Hughes ensured that she would survive, not only because of the quality of her work but also because of the myth she made of her life.

Other poets like Adrienne RICH transformed the incipient feminist themes of Plath's work into a vision of poetry and society that emphasizes the female poet's need to unburden herself of the demands of a patriarchal society. The female psyche in and of itself became a subject for the poet in a way that earlier generations of women poets such as Elizabeth BISHOP and Marianne MOORE had not contemplated.

Beginning in the 1970s, American poetry saw the explosion of work among Native Americans, Asian Americans, Chicano and Chicanas, and other ethnic groups. This abundant diversity of new voices has yet to be fully integrated into an understanding of the trajectory of 20th-century American poetry.

Although this new American poetry is still evolving, certain authors and key works are emerging as representative of a new American canon. Works such as Sonia SANCHEZ's "Womanhood," Rita DOVE's "Jiving," Robert HAYDEN's "Middle Passage," Audre LORDE's "The Woman Thing," Louise ERDRICH's "Dear John Wayne," N. Scott MOMADAY's "Carrier of the Dream Wheel," and Li-Young Lee's "Persimmons"—all of which are frequently anthologized—reflect poetic sensibilities that are multicultural and styles that blend Native American and other ethnic tones into mainstream language. At the same time, the language of poetry is being modified by the oral traditions of its ethnic writers. Gwendolyn BROOKS and Langston HUGHES, poets from an earlier generation, initiated this new developing poetry by incorporating the rhythms of African-American speech—as in Brooks's brilliant "We Real Cool." Their sense of the contemporary language has been deepened and extended in the anthropological and historical perspectives of poets such as Momaday and Hayden. What has not changed, however, is the perennial American concern with expressing both the distinctiveness of the individual voice and a desire—dating back at least as far as Walt Whitman—to find a common, universal ground of experience no matter what the poet's ethnicity, race, or sexual orientation may be.

Sources

Gray, Richard. *American Poetry of the Twentieth Century.* New York: Longman, 1990.
Perkins, David. *History of Modern Poetry.* Two volumes. Cambridge, Mass.: Harvard University Press, 1976, 1987.
Rexroth, Kenneth. *American Poetry in the Twentieth Century.* New York: Herder & Herder, 1971.
Von Hallberg, Robert. *American Poetry and Culture.* Cambridge, Mass.: Harvard University Press, 1985.

Poetry: A Magazine of Verse periodical

Founded in 1912 by Harriet MONROE, this magazine has published many of the great poets of the 20th century, including Ezra POUND, T. S. ELIOT, Wallace STEVENS, William Carlos WILLIAMS, Edna St. Vincent MILLAY, Elinor WYLIE, Robinson JEFFERS, and Marianne MOORE. *Poetry* championed IMAGIST verse, published controversial literary criticism, and generally served as a platform for modernist (see MODERNISM) statements about the function of literature. Monroe died in 1936, but the magazine has continued to publish new and established poets.

Sources

Cahill, Daniel J. *Harriet Monroe.* New York: Twayne, 1973.
Williams, Ellen. *Harriet Monroe and the Poetry Renaissance: The First Ten Years of Poetry, 1912–22.* Urbana: University of Illinois Press, 1977.

Poole, Ernest (1880–1950) *novelist*

Born in Chicago and educated at Princeton University, Poole pursued his literary career in New York. His first major novel is *The Harbor* (1915), set on the LOWER EAST SIDE. He explored the changing conditions of family life in his next novel, *His Family* (1917), which won a Pulitzer Prize. A succession of novels—*The Dark People* (1918), *The Village* (1918), and *Blind* (1920)—treated the Russian Revolution (which Poole had reported on firsthand), tenement life, and WORLD WAR I. His later novels, such as *With Eastern Eyes* (1926), *Silent Storms* (1927), and *The Car of Croesus* (1930) deal with the reactions of European visitors to America.

Poole published an autobiography, *The Bridge* (1940).

Sources
Keefer, Truman Frederick. *Ernest Poole.* New Haven, Conn.: Yale University Press, 1966.

Porter, Katherine Anne (Callie Lee Russell Porter) (1890–1980) *short story writer, novelist*

Katherine Anne Porter was born in Indian Creek, Texas. Her early life was spent in small Texas towns. She was a precocious child and married early, although she purposely obscured the details of these years and they are hard to verify. Porter worked for a time in Chicago as a reporter. Then she visited Hollywood and made trips back to Texas, where she worked for newspapers there. She settled in New York in 1919, having recovered from a near fatal case of influenza during the epidemic of 1918, but later went to Mexico and Texas again. This varied experience in different locales contributed significantly to her first short story collection, *Flowering Judas and Other Stories* (1930).

The title story, set in Mexico, is a modern classic. It reflects Porter's own disillusionment with the Mexican revolution and her desire to probe the limits of idealism as a way of dealing with the world. Many of Porter's later stories deal with the old South, or as she calls it in one story, "The Old Order," which depicts a southern grandmother's firm hold on her family (a situation Porter experienced with her own grandmother after her mother died). "The Fig Tree" (1930), "The Circus" (1935), "The Grave" (1935), "Old Mortality" (1938), and "Pale Horse, Pale Rider" (1938) trace the gradual initiation of a woman into the world. The stories are frequently anthologized and are considered prime examples of Porter's exquisite craftsmanship.

Porter published one novel, *Ship of Fools* (1962), which garnered enormous attention as a long-awaited masterpiece. Critical opinion divided on this ambitious work—some readers found it too schematic and pretentious, while others lauded the breadth of Porter's social and political vision. The novel, set in 1931 aboard a ship with American, Danish, Mexican, Cuban, German, Swiss, and Swedish passengers, portrayed the lives of more than 40 characters representing a cross section of modern civilization. In a corrupt, deeply sensual world clearly headed toward a clash with fascism, these characters seem to share real intimacy only in the act of sex.

Porter produced a relatively small body of work and allowed only a small fraction of the stories she wrote to see print. *The Collected Stories of Katherine Anne Porter* was published in 1965.

Porter demonstrated her radical politics in a book on the SACCO-VANZETTI CASE, *The Never-Ending Wrong* (1977). Her interviews were collected in *Conversations with Katherine Anne Porter* (1987). The *Letters of Katherine Anne Porter* appeared in 1990 her *Collected Essays and Occasional Writings* in 1970.

Sources
Givner, Joan. *Katherine Anne Porter: A Life.* New York: Simon & Schuster, 1982.
Hendrick, George and Willene Hendrick. *Katherine Anne Porter.* Boston: Twayne, 1988.
Stout, Janis. *Katherine Anne Porter: A Sense of the Times.* Charlottesville: University Press of Virginia, 1995.

Portis, Charles McColl (1933–) *novelist*

Born in Arkansas, educated at the University of Arkansas, and a resident of Little Rock, Charles Portis published his first novel, *Norwood*, in 1966. It has been called a southern version of Jack Kerouac's ON THE ROAD. His second novel, *True Grit* (1968), established an original voice. It is a comic narrative by Mattie Ross, a 14-year-old girl seeking revenge for her father's murder. She hires the broken-down Rooster Cogburn, played by John Wayne with great relish in the movie version. Mattie's telling of her story pits her innocent but dogged quest against the Western roughs on the trail. Like Mark Twain's *Huckleberry Finn*, *True Grit* captures the nature of frontier anarchy while affirming the integrity of the individual and a sense of justice. *The Dog of the South* (1979) and *Gringos* (1991) confirm Portis's gift for writing picaresque fiction.

Sources
"Charles (McColl) Portis." Available on-line. URL: http://www.emory.edu/ENGLISH/Bahri/Portis.html. Downloaded June 14, 2001.
Rosenbaum, Ron. "Our Least-Known Great Novelist." *Esquire* 129.1 (1998): 30.

postmodernism

In literature, this movement rejects 18th-century Enlightenment thought, particularly the emphasis on rationality and objectivity. Postmodern critics and writers see these values as false, and argue that "reality" must be filtered through race, gender, class, and other variables.

Postmodernism can also be distinguished from MODERNISM in that the former tends to collapse the distinction between elite and mass culture, between what is high art and popular art; the postmodern sensibility is anti-elitist. The term was used as early as 1946, in Randall JARRELL's review of

Robert LOWELL's *Lord Weary's Castle.* Charles OLSON also used the term in his essays of the 1950s. Susan SONTAG's essays of the 1960s have often been cited as postmodern. Novelists such as Walter ABISH, Kathy ACKER, Robert COOVER, Thomas PYNCHON, Ishmael REED, and Ronald SUKENICK have all been put into the postmodern camp. The postmodernists tend to think of art as self-referential—work that is designed to revel in immediacy and sensuality, the hallmarks of what Sontag calls "the new sensibility."

Important studies of postmodernism include Ihab Hassan's *The Postmodern Turn: Essay in Postmodern Theory and Culture* (1987); Linda Hutcheon's *A Poetics of Postmodernism: History, Theory, Fiction* (1988); Peter Brooker's *Modernism/Postmodernism* (1992); Perry Anderson's *The Origins of Postmodernity* (1998); and Niall Lucy's *Postmodern Literary Theory: An Anthology* (2000).

Pound, Ezra Weston Loomis (1885–1972) *poet, critic*

Born in Hailey, Idaho, Ezra Pound grew up in a suburb of Philadelphia, but his lifelong devotion to Europe was established in 1898, when he traveled for three months on the Continent with his great-aunt. Pound studied at Hamilton College in upstate New York and then at the University of Pennsylvania, where he made a lifelong friend of fellow poet William Carlos WILLIAMS. By then Pound had formed the ambition to learn everything worth knowing about poetry. This meant not only becoming a scholar of the genre, a translator of great poetry, and a poet of genius himself, but also an impresario of poetry, furthering the careers of T. S. ELIOT, Robert FROST, Ernest HEMINGWAY, and many other writers whom Pound deemed part of the great tradition of literature and who extended the possibilities of MODERNISM.

After a brief teaching stint at Wabash College, Pound left for Italy in 1907 and then went on to London, befriending the Irish poet W. B. Yeats. By 1912 Pound championed IMAGISM, a movement in poetry that favored verse with a concrete, objective style that was the opposite of the florid romanticism and the elaborate rhetoric of 19th-century English and American literature.

Pound himself did not achieve poetic brilliance until *Hugh Selwyn Mauberly* (1920), a long poem occasioned by the disillusionment with Western values following WORLD WAR I, a disillusionment that also marked Eliot's "The Waste Land," a poem Pound helped to edit into a masterpiece. In *Mauberley,* Pound compressed allusions to works of art and literature and to the history of ancient Greece while invoking the events of World War I, in order to create a sense of a declining civilization and the exhaustion of the individuals within it.

Pound, like many other modernists, evinced in his poetry a disgust with bourgeois society, democratic institutions, and conventional culture. By the late 1920s he was a fervent sup-

porter of Mussolini, and during WORLD WAR II he made radio broadcasts supporting the fascist cause. In the meantime he published installments of his *Cantos,* often brilliant but also uneven commentaries on ancient China, Renaissance Italy, and Jeffersonian America woven into anti-Semitic and fascist theories.

In 1945 Pound was arrested for treason and incarcerated in St. Elizabeth's Hospital in Washington, D.C. Deemed insane, he escaped a trial that could have led to his execution. Writers like Robert Frost and Ernest Hemingway, who deplored Pound's politics, nevertheless acknowledged his greatness as a writer and campaigned for his release from St. Elizabeth's. In 1948 Pound won the Bollingen Prize for *The Pisan Cantos,* a recognition that split the literary community over whether a fascist and anti-Semite should be honored and whether his literary achievement could be separated from his politics.

Released from the hospital in 1958, Pound returned to his home in Italy and continued to write poetry. He rarely spoke in public or private, although he was visited by such notable poets as Charles OLSON and Allen GINSBERG. Pound did acknowledge to his visitors that many of his statements had been foolish. However his politics are ultimately judged, his central place in 20th-century literature as a critic and poet seems secure.

The Cantos of Ezra Pound I–CXVII was published in 1970, his *Selected Poems: 1908–1959* in 1975, and *Collected Early Poems* in 1976. Other important early collections include *Personae: The Collected Poems of Ezra Pound* (1926) and *The Translations of Ezra Pound* (1953).

Pound produced a considerable body of nonfiction, including *How to Read* (1931), *ABC of Reading* (1934), *The Letters of Ezra Pound, 1907–1941* (1960), *Literary Essays* (1954), *Pound/Joyce: The Letters of Ezra Pound to James Joyce* (1967), *Selected Prose, 1909–1965* (1973), *"Ezra Pound Speaking": Radio Speeches of World War II* (1978), *Pound/Ford: The Story of Literary Friendship* (1982), *Ezra Pound and Dorothy Shakespear: Their Letters, 1909–1914* (1984), *The Letters of Ezra Pound and Wyndham Lewis* (1985), *Pound/Williams: Selected Letters of Ezra Pound and William Carlos Williams* (1996).

Sources

Carpenter, Humphrey. *A Serious Character: The Life of Ezra Pound.* London: Faber, 1988.

Gibson, Andrew, ed. *Pound in Multiple Perspective: A Collection of Critical Essays.* Basingstoke, England: Macmillan, 1993.

Kenner, Hugh. *The Pound Era.* Berkeley: University of California Press, 1971.

Wilson, Peter. *A Preface to Ezra Pound.* New York: Longman, 1997.

Powell, Dawn (1897–1965) *novelist, journalist*

Powell was born in Mount Gilead, Ohio. Her mother died when she was a young child, and she was reared on various farms and in small towns. She began writing early, producing stories when she was only 12, although her stepmother disapproved and burned them. Powell edited a school magazine and graduated from Lake Erie College in 1918. She published her first novel, *Whither*, in 1924. She also collaborated on radio scripts and musical plays. She used her Ohio background in such novels as *A Time to Be Born* (1942) and *My Home is Far Away* (1944).

Powell's reputation was enhanced when she started writing for THE NEW YORKER. She found her true subject in writing about New York City life and as a satirist of the middle class. Although she wrote 20 novels, her work fell into obscurity until such writers as Gore VIDAL began writing about her as a neglected American classic.

Many of Powell's best novels have been reissued, including *Angels on Toast* (1940, 1990), her hilarious burlesque of New York City businessmen; *The Locusts Have No King* (1948, 1996), a satire set in the New York publishing industry; *The Wicked Pavilion* (1954, 1990), which centers on a Manhattan cafe; *and The Golden Spur* (1962, 1990), set in GREENWICH VILLAGE. *Sunday Morning, and Always* (1952) collects her short stories.

The Diaries of Dawn Powell, 1931–1965 was published in 1995 and her *Selected Letters* in 1999.

Sources

Page, Tim. *Dawn Powell: A Biography.* New York: Henry Holt, 1998.

Rice, Marcelle Smith. *Dawn Powell.* New York: Twayne, 2000.

Powers, James Farl (1917–1999) *novelist*

An Illinois native, J. F. Powers has most often dealt in his fiction with the lives of Catholic priests, beginning with *Prince of Darkness* (1947) and *The Presence of Grace* (1956). In 1962 he won a National Book Award for *Morte d'Urban*, the story of Father Urban, a worldly man who is nevertheless committed to his religious vocation. *Wheat that Springeth Green* (1988) returns to similar themes and characters, this time from a comic point of view.

Sources

Derbyshire, John. "Sub specie aeternitatis: J. F. Powers, 1917–1999." *The New Criterion* 18: 1 (September 1999). Available on-line. URL: http://www.newcriterion.com. Downloaded June 14, 2001.

Hagopian, John F. *J. F. Powers.* New York: Twayne, 1968.

Price, Reynolds (Edward Reynolds Price)
(1933–) *novelist, short story writer, playwright, essayist*

Price was born in Macon, a small rural town in North Carolina. He was educated at Duke University and has taught there for many years. Price's debut novel, *A Long and Happy Life* (1962), draws on his family experience and explores the comic and romantic adventures of its younger characters, Rosacake Mustion and Wesley Beavers, lovers who have considerable trouble sorting out their feelings. *Kate Vaiden* (1986), one of Price's most important novels, explores through its main character the degree to which individuals bear a responsibility to their families. Kate Vaiden must cope with her father's murder of her mother and then his own suicide. Other novels, such as *Love and Work* (1968), have grown out of Price's experience as a college professor. In this novel, Thomas Eborn, a novelist and professor, suddenly confronts the full force of his family's history when his mother dies unexpectedly. A dutiful son, he nevertheless has felt the tension of trying to be his own man and to keep faith with his writing.

Other novels, such as *The Surface of the Earth* (1975) and *The Source of Light* (1981), continue Price's concern with family destinies and sibling relationships, as do *A Generous Man* (1966), *Good Hearts* (1988), and *The Promise of Rest* (1995).

Price has also published important work in other genres. His *Collected Stories* was published in 1993. Among his published plays are *Early Dark* (1977) and *Full Moon and Other Plays* (1993). His poetry is collected in several volumes, including *Vital Provisions* (1982), *The Laws of Ice* (1986), and *The Use of Fire* (1990).

A wide-ranging essayist who is concerned with literature, autobiography, and the Bible, Price has published *Things Themselves: Essays and Scenes* (1972), *A Common Room: Essays 1954–1987* (1987), *Clear Pictures: First Loves, First Guides* (1989), *A Whole New Way of Life* (1994), and *Three Gospels* (1996).

Sources

Schiff, James, ed. *Critical Essays on Reynolds Price.* New York. G. K. Hall, 1998.

———. *Understanding Reynolds Price.* Columbia: University of South Carolina Press, 1996.

Prohibition

A concerted campaign against the dangers of alcohol began in 1826 with the founding of the American Temperance Society. By 1838 one million Americans had taken a pledge to abstain from alcohol. In 1846 Maine became the first state to outlaw alcohol, and it was followed by 13 other states by 1855. The strength of the anti-alcohol movement was such that by 1917, when Congress passed the Eighteenth Amendment outlawing alcohol, 75 percent of American counties had already passed their own prohibition laws.

As literary works of the 1920s show, however, Americans continued to drink alcohol in enormous numbers, catered to by an illegal industry dominated by gangsters. Drinking is a central activity in the novels of F. Scott FITZGERALD and Ernest HEMINGWAY. Other writers of the 1920s and 1930s glamorize drinking, making it a way of life, as in Dashiell HAMMETT's novel *The Thin Man* (1934).

Congress eventually recognized that Prohibition as a national policy had failed, and the Eighteenth Amendment was repealed by the Twenty-first Amendment in 1933, which returned the regulation of alcohol back to the states.

Sources

Kyvig, David E. *Repealing National Prohibition.* Second edition. Kent, Ohio: Kent State University Press, 2000.

Merz, Charles. *The Dry Decade.* Second Edition. Seattle: University of Washington Press, 1969.

Prokosch, Frederic (1908–1989) *novelist*

Born in Wisconsin, Prokosch made fiction out of his travels: *The Asiatics* (1935); *The Seven Who Fled* (1937), set in the Russian exile community; *Night of the Poor* (1939), the story of a boy on the move from Wisconsin to Texas; *The Skies of Europe* (1941), set on the eve of WORLD WAR II; *The Conspirators* (1943), a spy tale set in Lisbon; *Storm and Echo* (1948), about men traveling in Africa in search of values they can live by; *The Dark Dancer* (1964), a historical novel about the prince who built the Taj Mahal; and *The Missolonghi Manuscript* (1968), a fictional version of George Gordon, Lord Byron's autobiography.

In *Voices* (1983) Prokosch wrote about himself, his literary contemporaries, his friends, and famous people he knew.

Sources

Squires, Radcliffe. *Frederic Prokosch.* New York: Twayne, 1964.

proletarian literature

This term describes novels about the poor and working-class life in the 1930s. The term *proletarian* refers to the Marxist analysis of society, in which the workers, the proletariat, are exploited by the capitalist owners of industry, or the means of production. In America during the GREAT DEPRESSION, Marxist-inspired authors created novels with heroes who came from the proletariat. Plays such as *Waiting for Lefty* (1935) by Clifford ODETS dramatized the conditions in which the working class would rise up and strike against the status quo. In plays like Lillian HELLMAN's *Days to Come* (1936), union organizers became the heroes. In some cases proletarians were shown as victims of society, as in Michael GOLD's *Jews Without Money* (1930), which emphasized the Marxist view of economic determinism, of a society shaped almost exclusively by the power of money. Many proletarian novels were set in urban environments, but the spirit of proletarian fiction spread to other kinds of writers who were not necessarily Marxist but who saw in proletarian fiction a way to address the shortcomings of society. Thus John STEINBECK's *Grapes of Wrath* (1939) features a hero, Tom Joad, who

comes to the conclusion that he must fight for all men, especially the downtrodden, against the rich and powerful.

Proletarian literature also became associated with the fight for the rights of minorities and for any class or group that could be considered a part of the underprivileged. James T. FARRELL's classic Studs Lonigan trilogy, with its riveting portrayal of the urban Irish poor, has been associated with proletarian fiction—as has Richard WRIGHT's powerful naturalistic study of Bigger Thomas, an African-American young man who is suddenly overwhelmed by his proximity to the wealth and privileges of the upper class. Other classic proletarian novels include Josephine HERBST's *Pity is Not Enough* (1933), Henry ROTH's *Call It Sleep* (1934), and John DOS PASSOS's *U.S.A.* (1938).

After 1939 few proletarian novels were written. WORLD WAR II helped to erase some of the grievances that proletarian novels addressed. Some writers also became disenchanted with the idea of proletarian literature, finding it sentimental in its glorification of the working class. Marxist influence on writers waned after Stalin formed his pact with Hitler in 1939, establishing an alliance between Germany and Russia that left Hitler free to attack Poland from the west while Stalin invaded the country from the east. The idea that writers of all kinds on the left were contributing to a literature that spoke the truth about social and political injustice was destroyed by conflicts between liberals and Communists over the sudden alliance between fascism and its hitherto arch opponent, communism. Many liberals could no longer support Communists and the Communist idea of literature.

Sources

Aaron, Daniel. *Writers on the Left: Episodes in American Literary Communism.* New York: Harcourt, Brace & World, 1961.

Hicks, Granville, ed. *Proletarian Literature in the United States.* New York: International Publishers, 1935.

Prouty, Olive Higgins (1882–1974) *novelist*

Prouty wrote popular fiction for women. *Stella Dallas* (1922) was her greatest success. It was made into a popular movie starring Barbara Stanwyck. Prouty endowed a scholarship at Smith College, which Sylvia PLATH won. Prouty later served as the model for Philomea Guinea in Plath's novel, *The Bell Jar.*

Sources

Hughes, Lynn Gordon. "Olive Higgins Prouty." Dictionary of Unitarian Universalist Biography. Available online. URL: http://www.duub.org/. Downloaded October 25, 2001.

Provincetown Players *organization*

From 1915 to 1929 this small company of theater people performed important plays by Eugene O'NEILL, Susan

GLASPELL, Paul GREEN, and more than 40 other writers. Located in Provincetown, Massachusetts, this group encouraged young new talent who wrote experimental and provocative plays that challenged the conventional drama popular on the New York stage. Productions in Provincetown were modest and staged in an old, derelict fish house on a pier. One of the group's notable successes was O'Neill's *Bound East for Cardiff* (1916), a riveting play about a seaman's last hours aboard a tramp steamer. The play signaled a new seriousness in the American theater—recognized in New York City when the Players moved to a theater, the Provincetown Playhouse, in GREENWICH VILLAGE. Its productions there in the mid-1920s had a transformative impact on the New York stage, providing O'Neill in particular with the opportunity to have his more ambitious, experimental, full-length plays produced for larger audiences.

Sources

Deutsch, Helen and Stella Hanau. *The Provincetown; A Story of the Theatre.* New York, Russell & Russell, 1972.

Sarlós, Robert Károly. *Jig Cook and the Provincetown Players: Theatre in Ferment.* Amherst: University of Massachusetts Press, 1982.

Pulitzer Prizes

In 1917 the newspaper publisher Joseph Pulitzer set aside $500,000 to be awarded to books that advanced the cause of American literature, education, and public service and morality. Prizes go to journalists as well as to literary figures in poetry, drama, and the novel. A nonfiction category was added in 1962. A music award is also made. The prizes are awarded under the auspices of the Columbia University School of Journalism.

Sources

Bates, J. Douglas. *The Pulitzer Prize: The Inside Story of America's Most Prestigious Award.* New York: Carol Publishing, 1991.

Hohenberg, John. *The Pulitzer Diaries: Inside America's Greatest Prize.* Syracuse, N.Y.: Syracuse University Press, 1997.

pulps

This term applies to cheap magazines that published mystery fiction and other genres such as science fiction and horror, primarily in the 1920s and 1930s. The name refers to the very cheap paper on which these magazines and books were printed. A kind of escapist fiction, the pulps were full of adventure and melodrama. Although much of the writing was conventional and hastily constructed, certain writers like Dashiell HAMMETT emerged from the pulps with distinctive styles.

Sources

Goodstone, Tony, ed. *The Pulps: Fifty Years of American Pop Culture.* New York: Chelsea House, 1976.

Gunnison, John, ed. *Adventure House Guide to the Pulps.* New York: Adventure House, 2000.

Purdy, James (1923–) *novelist, poet, playwright*

Purdy was born in Fremont, Ohio, and educated at the University of Chicago and the University of Puebla in Mexico. He taught at Lawrence College in Appleton, Wisconsin, and at New York University, but since 1953 has devoted himself to writing full time.

Purdy's work often features grotesque characters, and his novels explore the relationship between parents and children. Sex, love, and violence are often intertwined in his plots. *Malcolm* (1959), the novel that established his reputation, is about an orphan in search of a father. Many of the characters the orphan meets resemble stereotypical comic-book figures, and the novel itself questions the substantiality of the world Malcolm confronts. *The Nephew* (1960), Purdy's next novel, also focuses on an orphan, this time a man missing in action in Korea. One of the families he lives with attempts to reconstruct the story of his life, learning in the process how difficult it is ever to fathom another individual.

Much of Purdy's writing, as in his third novel, *Cabot Wright Begins* (1964), takes a dim view of American life, seeing it as dominated by the media, big business, and popular culture. Cabot Wright, yet another orphan, asserts himself through raping a woman. Purdy's later novels—*Eustace Chisholm and the Works* (1967), *Jeremy's Version* (1970), and *The House of the Solitary Maggot* (1974)—heighten Purdy's perception of violence at the core of the American family.

Purdy's subsequent novels—*In a Shallow Grave* (1976), *Narrow Rooms* (1977), *Mourners Below* (1981), *On Glory's Course* (1984), *In The Hollow of His Hand* (1986), *Garments the Living Wear* (1989), *Out With the Stars* (1992), and *Gertrude of Stony Island Avenue*—show no lessening of his pessimistic probing of the ambiguous and often SURREALISTIC nature of American life.

Purdy has collected his short fiction in *Selected Stories, 1956–1987* (1991). He has published several plays, including *Proud Flesh: Four Short Plays* (1980) and *Scrap of Paper, and the Berry-Picker* (1981). He has also published several volumes of poetry: *The Running Sun* (1971), *Sunshine Is an Only Child* (1973), *She Came Out of the Mists of Morning* (1975), *Lessons and Complaints* (1978), and *The Brooklyn Branding Parlors* (1986).

Sources

Chudpack, Henry. *James Purdy.* Boston: Twayne, 1975.

Ladd, Jay L., ed. *James Purdy: A Bibliography.* Columbus: Ohio State University Libraries, 1999.

Pyle, Ernie (1900–1945) *journalist*

Pyle covered WORLD WAR II in North Africa, Europe, and the Pacific. His syndicated articles made the war a story with which millions of Americans could identify. No other journalist had quite the same impact, and Pyle himself became a beloved figure who brought the news home. He died on Iwo Jima, the victim of Japanese machine-gun fire, fusing his story and the end of the war in the public imagination. His books follow the course of American involvement in the war: *Ernie Pyle in England* (1941), *Here is Your War* (1943), *Brave Men* (1944), and *Last Chapter* (1946).

Sources

Miller, Lee G. *The Story of Ernie Pyle.* New York: Viking, 1950.
Tobin, James. *Ernie Pyle's War: America's Eyewitness to World War II.* New York: Free Press, 1997.

Pynchon, Thomas (1937–) *novelist*

Pynchon was born in Glen Cove, New York. He has guarded his privacy zealously, and little is known about his life except that he was an excellent literature student in high school and was one of Vladimir NABOKOV's students at Cornell University. Pynchon lives in New York City.

One of the most challenging and innovative of contemporary novelists, Pynchon's novels make demanding reading. They are suffused with details from the periods he writes about. Sometimes the modern world looks like a vast conspiracy in his paranoid vision of modern science, culture, and politics. In *V* (1963), his first novel, he shifts between the mid 1950s and a period that ranges from 1880 to 1943. V is the initial of a woman variously identified as Victoria Wren, Veronica Manganes, Ver Meroving, and other names. She has a habit of turning up at crucial moments in history—she appears, for example, in various scenes leading to both world wars. In the more surrealistic parts of the novel she actually loses her body parts, a metaphor for a civilization that is be-coming increasingly fragmented and dominated by the search for precious metals and other materials that are used, in turn, to dismember civilization.

Gravity's Rainbow (1973), Pynchon's next novel, is set in London during the landing of the V-2 rockets in WORLD WAR II. The main character is Tyrone Slothrop, an American army lieutenant assigned to an Allied intelligence unit. Strangely, the pattern of his sexual conquests coincides with the V-2 bombing sites, and his erections are good predictors of incoming rockets. Dense with historical detail and a multitude of characters, the novel is a disturbing picture of a world run amok over technical inventions and sexual chaos.

Vineland (1989) again sets up a dual historical focus—this time, 1984 and the 20 years that precede it. Less well structured than Pynchon's earlier novels, *Vineland* is also more hopeful about America's future. It tells the story of the reuniting of several families or clans and ends with a sense of reunification, as if the country itself could be renewed and fulfill the promise of discovery that caused the Vikings to call the North American continent Vineland. *Mason and Dixon* (1997) is named after the men who established the Mason Dixon line, the basic division of the United States between North and South. Spanning the 18th century, Pynchon once again pursues his main theme: the battle between the spiritual world and material forces. Within this historical novel, Pynchon injects many allusions to 20th-century history and popular culture, thus helping to measure the developments in the 18th century by their consequences in the 20th.

In 1984 Pynchon published *Slow Learner: Early Stories.* He is also the author of a short novel, *The Crying of Lot 49* (1966).

Sources

Berressem, Hanjo. *Pynchon's Poetics: Interfacing Theory and Text.* Urbana: University of Illinois Press, 1993.
Chambers, Judith. *Thomas Pynchon.* New York: Twayne, 1992.

Rabe, David William (1940–) *playwright*

David Rabe was born in Dubuque, Iowa, and educated there in Catholic schools. After graduating from Loras College, he attended the graduate theater program at Villanova University. He completed his M.A. degree in 1968. His studies were interrupted by two years in the army, which included 11 months in Vietnam.

Rabe's writing for the theater has been greatly determined by his period of service in a hospital unit in Vietnam. He was struck by the way very young, inexperienced men had to deal with an overwhelming situation. His own troubled reentry into civilian society intensified his understanding of the VIETNAM WAR as a watershed even in the nation's history.

Sticks and Bones (1969) and *The Basic Training of Pavlo Hummel* (1971) were written while Rabe was still in graduate school. Both concerned disillusioned veterans confronting their own mortality and the absurdity of war. The second play was actually produced first and won Rabe an Obie Award and a Drama Desk Award. *Sticks and Bones* enhanced Rabe's reputation when it won a Tony Award and Outer Circle Award in 1972. Rabe had in this short period established his reputation as one of America's most promising playwrights.

Rabe's next two plays were *The Orphan* (1973), which sought to draw parallels between the Trojan War and the Vietnam War, and *In the Boom Boom Room,* a departure in subject matter (it probed the life of deteriorating nightclub performers), did little better in terms of popularity, although it did receive a Tony nomination.

But *Streamers,* which returned Rabe's focus to Vietnam, was an enormous success, winning the New York Drama Critics Circle Award for the best play of 1976, and earning praise for Rabe's ability to use an army barracks as a microcosm of the divided America of the 1960s. *Hurly Burly* (1984), a play about a society deteriorating in the wake of the Vietnam War, was his next successful play.

Although Rabe's plays have been interpreted as antiwar dramas, he has resisted that label and argued that he is exploring an event and the reactions to it—not presenting his interpretation of it. Certainly Rabe's portrayal of civilian society is no more flattering than that of the military in wartime, and the playwright treats civilian life with the same blend of realistic detail and symbolic evocations of the chaos that threatens to tear human communities apart.

Rabe has written several screenplays, including *I'm Dancing as Fast as I Can* (1982), *Streamers* (1983), *Casualties of War* (1989), and *The Firm* (1993). He has published one novel, *The Crossing Guard* (1995).

Sources

Kolin, Philip C. *David Rabe: A Stage History and a Primary and Secondary Bibliography.* New York: Garland, 1988.

Zinman, Toby Silverman, ed. *David Rabe: A Casebook.* New York: Garland, 1991.

Rabbit, Run John Updike (1960) *novel*

This novel by John UPDIKE epitomizes the demoralization of the white American male of the 1950s.

Harry "Rabbit" Angstrom, a former high school basketball hero, does not know what to do with himself. Contrary to the cliché about sports building character, all basketball has done for him is improve his running and shooting skills. Rabbit's inability to find a worthwhile career is paralleled by his wife, Janice's alcoholism: She stays home, drinks, and watches television. All Rabbit can think to do is run away and live with Ruth Leonard, who has from time to time worked as a prostitute. Rabbit returns home briefly after Janice gives birth to a second child, but she will not have sex with him, and he leaves her again for Ruth. In an alcoholic stupor, Janice drowns the baby in a bathtub. Rabbit blames Janice, but Ruth calls Rabbit "Mr. Death himself." When Ruth tells him she is pregnant, Rabbit runs away again.

Rabbit, Run is the first of four novels to chart the development of Rabbit and his family. Although the first novel ends on a bleak note, at least Rabbit is still running, still searching for a solution to his sense of emptiness and lack of direction.

This novel, published at the end of the 1950s, was interpreted as the latent manifestation of a restlessness that would infect the 1960s, when not only youths but also older adults began to question the conventional arrangements of society.

Sources

Broer, Lawrence R., ed. *Rabbit Tales: Poetry and Politics in John Updike's Rabbit Novels.*

O'Connell, Mary. *Updike and the Patriarchal Dilemma: Masculinity in the Rabbit Novels.* Carbondale: Southern Illinois University Press, 1996.

Rahv, Philip (1908–1973) *editor, literary critic*

The cofounder of *PARTISAN REVIEW*, Rahv was born in Russia, came to the United States as a child, and was educated in Rhode Island. He began his writing career as a Marxist political theorist, but by the late 1930s he and his colleague, William Phillips, had become anti-Stalinist. They worked together to create a journal that would publish the best critics and creative writers in the world. Although many of their contributors were leftists, the journal pursued a consistent anti-Communist position. Rahv in his later years became an influential literary critic. He published several collections of his essays, including the influential *Image and Idea* (1949) and *Literature in America* (1957).

Sources

Edelstein, Arthur, ed. *Images and Ideas in American Culture: The Functions of Criticism: Essays in Memory of Philip Rahv.* Hanover, N.H.: Brandeis University Press, 1979.

Raisin in the Sun, A Lorraine Hansberry (1959) *play*

Lorraine Hansberry's classic drama about the African-American experience appeared on Broadway in 1959 and won the New York Drama Critics Circle Award. An instant popular success, the play concentrates on several generations of African-American family life. The Younger family lives in a small apartment on Chicago's South Side. They are torn over a dispute concerning Walter Senior's insurance benefit. Mother and son are at odds about how the money should be used, provoking a generational conflict about human values and society's materialistic ethos. Part of Hansberry's success was her transformation of this African-American drama into the story of the American dream—of the aspirations that all Americans have for a better life and the way each generation defines itself by protesting against its predecessor. Hansberry's title comes from Langston HUGHES's famous line questioning what happens to a dream deferred: Does it, the poet asks, like a raisin shrivel in the sun? In this play one generation does shrivel or exhaust itself when the dream (the promise of success, of achieving freedom and individual identity) is deferred. Another generation explodes in rage when its aspirations are thwarted. The play dramatizes the tensions between these differing reactions to disappointment.

The play was made into a film and is still frequently produced, having been translated into more than 30 languages. It is noteworthy for its excellent construction and deft use of stage realism. Some critics have called the play a "black soap opera," but the play's confrontation with social issues hardly seems to merit that description.

Sources

Carter, Steven R. *Hansberry's Drama: Commitment Amid Complexity.* Urbana: University of Illinois Press, 1991.

Domina, Lynn, ed. *Understanding A Raisin in the Sun: A Student Casebook to Issues, Sources, and Historical Documents.* Westport, Conn.: Greenwood Press, 1998.

Rand, Ayn (Alyssa Rosenbaum) (1905–1982) *novelist, playwright, philosopher*

Born Alyssa Rosenbaum in St. Petersburg, Russia, Rand grew up and was educated in her native country before immigrating to the United States in 1926. Her reaction against the Russian Revolution inspired her staunch belief in individualism and capitalism.

Rand got her first job as a screenwriter in Hollywood. Her first play, *Night of January 16th*, had a successful Broadway run in 1935. But her fame and reputation rest on her novels *The Fountainhead* (1943) and *Atlas Shrugged* (1957). The former was said to be loosely based on the life of architect Frank Lloyd Wright, although Rand disputed that claim. The latter novel is Rand's most complete statement of her philosophy, which she called "Objectivism." In both her fiction and nonfiction, Rand argued for the idea of "rational self-interest" rather than altruism. Only when the individual's needs were satisfied, she argued, could society expect to benefit.

Although Rand attained no standing among scholars in philosophy and literature, her books continue to attract a large and devoted following.

Rand's earlier novels include *We the Living* (1936) and *Anthem* (1938). Her nonfiction includes *The Virtue of Selfishness* (1964) and *Introduction to Objectivist Epistemology* (1979).

Sources
Gladstein, Mimi. *The New Ayn Rand Companion.* Westport, Conn.: Greenwood Press, 1999.

Randall, Dudley (1914–2000) *poet*
Trained as a librarian at the University of Michigan, Randall, an African American, founded the BROADSIDE PRESS in Detroit in 1963, publishing his own poems on single sheets or broadsides. Over the next 15 years, he published more than 50 books of poetry, giving new African-American writers an opportunity to begin or sustain their writing careers. His most important author was Gwendolyn BROOKS. His collections include *More to Remember: Poems of Four Decades* (1971).

Sources
Thompson, Julius E. *Dudley Randall, Broadside Press, and the Black Arts Movement in Detroit, 1960–1995.* Jefferson, N.C.: McFarland, 1999.

Ransom, John Crowe (1888–1974) *poet, critic*
A native of Tennessee, Ransom was an editor of the literary magazines *The Fugitive* (1922–1925) and *Kenyon Review* (1939–1959). His *Selected Poems* was published in 1963.

Educated at Vanderbilt University, Ransom became a Rhodes scholar and returned to the university to teach and to write poetry and criticism. He became known as one of the FUGITIVES, a group of poets and critics that included Allen TATE and Robert Penn WARREN. This group advocated what they saw as the superior values of the southern AGRARIAN tradition, and were the guiding lights of the agrarian-inspired collection of essays *I'LL TAKE MY STAND*, which was their response to the country's growing industrialization and urbanization.

A fastidious poet whose body of work is small, Ransom is known for exquisite diction and understatement. His poetry has been called spare and classical. He believed in the integrity of the work of literature and that its meaning should not be violated by extraneous discussions of history, of the poet's biography, or of anything that might detract from a close reading of the work. He codified his view of literary criticism in *The New Criticism* (1941). His literary essays appear in *God Without Thunder* (1930), *The World's Body* (1938), and *Beating the Bushes 1914–1970* (1972).

Although Ransom's agrarianism failed to attract many followers after the 1930s, his critical views and his work as a poet greatly influenced the next generation, particularly such poets as Robert LOWELL and Randall JARRELL.

Sources
Young, Thomas Daniel. *Gentleman in a Dustcoat: A Biography of John Crowe Ransom.* Baton Rouge: Louisiana State University Press, 1976.
———. ed. *John Crowe Ransom: Critical Essays and a Bibliography.* Baton Rouge: Louisiana State University Press, 1968.

Rawlings, Marjorie Kinnan (1896–1953) *novelist, short story writer*
Rawlings was born in Washington, D.C. In 1914 her parents moved to Madison, Wisconsin, where she graduated from the university and married the journalist Charles A. Rawlings in 1919. She worked as a reporter for the Louisville *Courie-Journal* until 1928. While working at other newspapers she tried to sell her stories to magazines. She divorced her husband in 1933 and moved to Florida to write full time, achieving some success when her work was published in *Scribner's* magazine.

Rawlings is chiefly remembered for her Pulitzer Prize–winning second novel, *The Yearling* (1938), which is about a young boy growing up in the South. It was adapted for the screen in 1946 and became a movie classic.

Rawlings's other important work includes a novel, *Cross Creek* (1942), and a collection of stories, *When a Whipporwill* (1930).

Sources
Silverthorne, Elizabeth. *Marjorie Kinnan Rawlings: Sojourner at Cross Creek.* Woodstock, N.Y.: Overlook Press, 1988.

Reader's Digest
Founded by DeWitt and Lila Acheson Wallace in 1922 as a monthly journal, *Reader's Digest* has helped to shape the literary taste of several generations. The *Digest* supplied condensations of articles from other magazines, and tended to be conservative and MIDDLEBROW. It was staunchly anti-Communist and appealed to a very broad audience of general readers who shared the magazine's confidence in America. It also sponsored a book club, which offered volumes that were condensations of popular fiction and nonfiction books. The magazine continues to publish in the same format. It also continues to produce a wide range of books, such as *Our Living History (Exploring America)* (2001), *Secrets of the Seas* (2000), and *The Reader's Digest Children's Atlas of the Universe* (2000).

Sources
Sharp, Joanne P. *Condensing the Cold War: Reader's Digest and American Identity.* Minneapolis: University of Minnesota Press, 2000.

realism

As a movement in American literature, realism is associated with the 19th century, primarily the 1870s, and with the rise of such novelists as Mark Twain, Henry James, and William Dean Howells.

In novels like *The Adventures of Tom Sawyer* and *Adventures of Huckleberry Finn*, Twain sought to render colloquial American language, to capture the rhythms of American speech that accurately reflected regional differences. In Huckleberry Finn, he also created a narrator different from the literary, formal first- or third-person narrators of earlier American fiction. Huck's style is informal and critical. He sizes up the mores and manners of his society from his adolescent perspective: He is a social critic without knowing it and "realistic" in the sense that he reports phenomena as he sees it. Thus Twain creates the illusion that his novel is not shaped by a literary sensibility but rather by a fresh, unaffected sensibility.

Henry James developed a realism that probed both the manners of his society and his character's states of mind. James's famous later style, convoluted and allusive, was meant to capture the complexities and meanderings of his characters' consciousness. James dramatizes the way the mind perceives reality, so that he has often been called a psychological realist. He took realism into new areas in his short stories of the supernatural. Ghosts appear, or seem to appear, in tales such as "The Jolly Corner" and "The Turn of the Screw" in vivid, haunting scenes; yet James leaves open the possibility that this "reality" is only what his characters imagine or project onto their environment.

William Dean Howells wrote novels that were almost sociological in their emphasis on everyday details, on how people dressed, spoke, ate, and so on. He strove to avoid melodrama and sought a plain style aimed at recording, rather than heightening, reality. Like Twain, he was interested in notating regional differences with quirky humor. Howells thought of himself as writing what was true, not what was worked up for entertainment or moral uplift.

The limitations of Howells's methods were apparent to writers of the naturalistic school. He tended to avoid the dark side of life, the intense impulses that lead to violence and alienation from society. Even James and Twain, who had a more complex and ambiguous view of society, did not go so far as naturalists like Theodore DREISER and Frank Norris, whose characters are often crushed under the weight of economic, social, and psychological forces. Realism tended to uphold the virtues of individualism—no matter how flawed human beings might be. NATURALISM questioned the American confidence and pride in self reliance.

As a literary movement, realism waned in the early 20th century. But as a mode of writing fiction, it has persisted. Writers such as John O'HARA, Ernest HEMINGWAY, John CHEEVER, Ann BEATTIE, Alison LURIE, and Toni MORRISON—to mention a small, noteworthy sample—have continued to produce stories and novels that are "realistic" in the sense that they describe in minute detail their characters' milieu and manners and attempt to faithfully record actual patterns of speech and modes of expression. These same authors and others have produced works that are in part realistic while adding a symbolic or mythic dimension. Bernard MALAMUD, for instance, has produced authentic accounts of Jewish-American life even while inventing fantastic tales such as "The Jewbird."

Sources

Kolb, Harold H., Jr. *The Illusion of Life: American Realism as a Literary Form.* Charlottesville: University Press of Virginia, 1969.

Pizer, Donald and Earl N. Harbert, eds. *American Realists and Naturalists.* Detroit: Gale, 1982.

Smith, Christopher, ed. *American Realism.* San Diego, Calif.: Greenhaven Press, 2000.

Reed, Ishmael Scott (1938–) *novelist, poet*

Born in Chattanooga, Tennessee, Ishmael Reed, an African American, moved with his mother to Buffalo, New York, when he was four. After graduation from high school, he went to night school at the University of Buffalo and worked in the public library. His writing attracted the attention of an English professor, but an early marriage and family responsibilities plunged him into a two-year period in a public housing project, a miserable experience that helped to fuel his intense feelings about race and American history. After five years of active involvement in the Black Power movement in New York City, Reed moved to Berkeley, California, in 1967 and began teaching at the University of California.

Reed's first novel, *The Free-Lance Pallbearers* (1967), heralded his penchant for outlandish titles and satirical thrusts. The novel parodies the traditional African-American confessional memoir, which itself (in Reed's view) hews too closely to American and European models of autobiography. As one commentator put it, the novel turns the Horatio Alger myth inside out—as if it were written by Nathanael WEST.

In later novels, Reed became a master at poking fun at mainstream conventional fiction. *Yellow Back Radio Broke-Down* (1969) features the Loop Garoo Kid, a wacky protagonist in a novel that mocks the traditional western. The novel's villain, Drag Gibson, is a wife-murdering degenerate cattle baron who is called on by the town of Yellow Back Radio to destroy its children's attempts to "create [their] own fictions." Drag Wilson represents the myth of America that stifles every new generation's efforts to define itself through its own myths or fictions. Reed's own fiction is a profound argument against REALISM as a reactionary ideology. The realist describes the status quo, the so-called "reality" which, to Reed, is at war with the human capacity to imagine better worlds.

Mumbo Jumbo (1972) extends Reed's case against America through a new mythology based on voodoo, Egyptian mythology, and jazz. The novel also provides a hilarious critique of the HARLEM RENAISSANCE, which in Reed's view failed to sustain its own artistic vision. Reed is just as hard on African Americans as he is on the dominant white culture—a point repeatedly made in *The Last Days of Louisiana Red* (1974).

Flight to Canada (1976) is at once a brilliant re-creation of the Civil War South and a parody of historical novels that claim to portray the past authentically. Thus Reed studs his novel with anachronisms, breaking the time frame and ridiculing such American icons as Abraham Lincoln and Harriet Beecher Stowe.

Reed satirizes the Reagan administration in *The Terrible Twos* (1982); in *Reckless Eyeballing* (1986), he excoriates feminists (black and white) and manages to insult Jews as well. Reed has been charged with both sexism and antifeminism, but his attacks on all forms of ideology and on dominant groups mitigates the idea that he is prejudiced against any particular group. In *The Terrible Threes* (1989) and *Japanese by Spring* (1993), Reed takes on American capitalism and the academic establishment.

Reed is one of the most important contemporary African-American fiction writers, but his poetry also is regarded highly. He published *Conjure: Selected Poems 1963–1970* in 1972 and *New and Selected Poems* in 1988. His provocative essays have been collected in *Shrovetide in New Orleans* (1978), *God Made Alaska for the Indians* (1982), *Writin' Is Fightin'* (1988), and *Airing Dirty Laundry* (1993). *Conversations with Ishmael Reed,* a collection of interviews, appeared in 1995.

Sources
McGee, Patrick. *Ishmael Reed and the Ends of Race.* New York: St. Martin's Press, 1997.
Martin, Reginald. *Ishmael Reed and the New Black Aesthetic Critics.* New York: St. Martin's Press, 1988.

Reed, John (1887–1920) *journalist, poet*
Reed grew up in a wealthy family in Portland, Oregon. After he graduated from Harvard in 1910, he worked for newspapers, befriended the muckraking journalist and editor Lincoln STEFFENS, and went to work for Max EASTMAN at THE MASSES in 1913. Reed first achieved recognition for his reports on the Mexican Revolution, which he published in *Insurgent Mexico* (1914). His dispatches on WORLD WAR I were collected in *The War in Eastern Europe* (1916).

As Reed gained a reputation as a socialist and progressive journalist, he was also writing poetry and associating himself with avant-garde cultural movements like the PROVINCETOWN PLAYERS. He published *Tamburlaine and Other Poems* in 1916.

Reed's fame rests on his eyewitness reports on the Russian Revolution, which he crafted into the classic book *Ten Days That Shook the World* (1919). Reed purported to give the inside news on this great event, befriending Lenin and other Bolshevik leaders. The story of his political reporting and activism is told in Warren Beatty's film *Reds* (1972).

Reed was a founding member of the American Communist Party and edited its newspaper, *The Voice of Labor.* He died of typhus in Russia in 1920.

Sources
Duke, David C. *John Reed.* Boston: Twayne, 1987.
Lamont, Corliss, ed. *The John Reed Centenary.* New York: John Reed Centenary Committee, 1988.

regionalism
Certain American writers have always been associated with certain regions of the country because their work provides detailed and dramatic portraits that draw on the characteristic speech and manners of localities. Sherwood ANDERSON, for example, is associated with the Midwest, which inspired some of his greatest fiction, especially *WINESBURG, OHIO* (1919). To Anderson, the more specific a writer was about the setting of his story the more believable he could make his characters; for him, the particular led to the universal. William FAULKNER was fond of quoting Anderson's advice to create fiction out of his "little postage stamp of native soil."

In addition to Anderson, Edgar Lee MASTERS, Carl SANDBURG, and Willa CATHER have been associated with the Midwest—small-town, urban, and farming settings, respectively. Cather's Scandinavian immigrants, for example, suggest the difficult yet durable quality of American pioneers. But even contemporary novelists such as Joyce Carol OATES, who provides detailed descriptions of both upstate New York and the city of Detroit, can be said to be a regionalist because her observations of characters in these settings are virtually sociological and historical.

Other writers not only set their novels in a particular region, they also narrow the focus to a single place, as William KENNEDY does with his novels set in Albany, New York. Similarly, detective novelist Raymond CHANDLER writes as a regionalist by developing in one novel after another a full portrait of Los Angeles and southern California. Anne RICE's vampire novels seem most persuasive when she can anchor them in New Orleans, one of the few American cities with a complex past involving many different European peoples, races, and ethnic groups. John STEINBECK concentrates on a single California valley in many of his short stories and novels. Writers such as John CHEEVER and John UPDIKE have probed the suburban Northeast, and their works often show how these communities and regions are changing under enormous economic, social, and political pressures.

The American West carries an even greater mythic impact, for it embodies the American myth of the self-made man, the loner, and the adventurer heading out for new territory and exploring the frontier. The novels of Owen Wister and Zane Grey made the cowboy a staple of the American mythos, while Larry MCMURTRY, among others, shows how that myth has degenerated in the modern world.

The SOUTH has been remarkably successful in producing writers who have viewed it as a distinct region. The legacy of the Civil War has left the South the only part of the United States to have been invaded and to have lost a war. This sense of southern tragedy pervades the work of William Faulkner. He often presents a decadent society that is failing itself, although his later work seems more hopeful as a new generation takes on the burden of the race problem in novels such as *Intruder in the Dust* (1948). A later generation of southern writers—Flannery O'CONNOR and Carson MCCULLERS, for example—carried on the southern gothic tradition, creating a melancholy and mysterious world of extremists with a sense of life as an apocalypse. Other southern writers such as Eudora WELTY and Reynolds PRICE, have used elements of grotesquerie in the southern novel for comic purposes.

Although critics have suggested that regionalism as a force in literature has diminished as the country becomes more unified by mass education, the mass media, and a global culture, the regionalist impulse still seems quite vital in a new generation of ethnic writers—ranging from Sherman ALEXIE to Amy TAN to Ishmael REED. Although none of these writers identify themselves as regionalist, their work is grounded in specific communities that have an intrinsic interest for the author: The characters and the environment mesh, and one is not conceivable without the other.

Sources

Burke, John Gordon, ed. *Regional Perspectives: An Examination of America's Literary Heritage.* Chicago: American Library Association, 1973.
Kowalewski, Michael, ed. *Reading the West: New Essays on the Literature of the American West.* New York: Cambridge University Press, 1996.
Quantic, Diane Dufva. *The Nature of the Place: A Study of Great Plains Fiction.* Lincoln: University of Nebraska Press, 1995.
Turner, Frederick. *Spirit of Place: The Making of an American Literary Landscape.* San Francisco: Sierra Club Books, 1989.
Watkins, Floyd C. *In Time and Place: Some Origins of American Fiction.* Athens: University of Georgia Press, 1977.

Rexroth, Kenneth (1905–1982) *poet, critic*

Born in Indiana, Rexroth established himself as a writer in San Francisco in 1927 and later became part of the SAN FRANCISCO RENAISSANCE and the BEAT movement. His work reflects a rugged nonconformity. A radical individualist, he attacked the status quo and the establishment, arguing for a grassroots way of life in books such as *Communalism* (1975). His collections include *In What Hour* (1940), *The Phoenix and the Tortoise* (1944), *The Signature of All Things* (1949), *In Defence of the Earth* (1956), *Natural Numbers* (1963), *Shorter Poems* (1966), *Longer Poems* (1968), and *New Poems* (1974).

A great promoter of contemporary poetry, Rexroth published several collections of essays: *Bird in the Bush* (1959), *Assays* (1961), and *Classics Revisited* (1969).

His autobiographical work is contained in *An Autobiographical Novel* (1966) and *Excerpts from a Life* (1981). After his death a group of essays appeared as *World Outside the Window* (1987). *Kenneth Rexroth and James Laughlin: Selected Letters* appeared in 1991.

Sources

Gibson, Morgan. *Revolutionary Rexroth: Poet of East-West Wisdom.* Hamden, Conn.: Archon Books, 1986.
Hamalian, Linda. *A Life of Kenneth Rexroth.* New York: W. W. Norton, 1991.

Reznikoff, Charles (1894–1976) *poet*

A New York poet associated with the Objectivists (see OBJECTIVISM), Reznikoff reflected both a Jewish and imagist (see IMAGISM) sensibility, best shown in his lyric poems. His collections include *Inscriptions* (1959), *By the Waters of Manhattan* (1962), *Testimony: The United States 1885–1915* (1965), *Holocaust* (1975). *Family Chronicle* (1969) is an account of ghetto life in New York City. *Selected Letters of Charles Reznikoff, 1917–1976* appeared in 1997.

Sources

Hindus, Milton. *Charles Reznikoff: A Critical Essay.* Santa Barbara, Calif.: Black Sparrow Press, 1977.

Rhodes, Eugene Manlove (1869–1934) *short story writer*

A native of Nebraska and longtime resident of New Mexico, Eugene Rhodes drew on his experience as a cowboy to write WESTERNS. Many of his stories were published in the SATURDAY EVENING POST and then collected in *Good Men and True* (1910), *The Desire of the Mother* (1916), *Stepsons of Light* (1921), *Copper Streak Trail* (1922), *Once in the Saddle* (1927), *The Trusty Knaves* (1933), *Beyond the Desert* (1934), and *The Proud Sheriff* (1935). Rhodes, a careful writer, often revised and expanded his stories, which dealt with ranch life and cowboys on the range. Rhodes was not only popular but also respected as a writer of authentic regionalist REALISM. In the main, he avoided the sentimentality and melodrama that weakened most cowboy stories. *Sandpapers: The Lives and Letters of Eugene Manlove Rhodes and Charles Fletcher Lummis* appeared in 1994.

Sources

Gaston, Edwin W., Jr. *Eugene Manlove Rhodes: Cowboy Chronicler*. Austin, Tex.: Steck-Vaughn, 1967.

Hutchinson, W. H. *A Bar Cross Man: The Life & Personal Writings of Eugene Manlove Rhodes*. Norman: University of Oklahoma Press, 1956.

Rice, Anne (Howard Allen Frances O'Brien)
(1941–) *novelist*

Anne Rice was born Howard Allen Frances O'Brien in New Orleans, Louisiana, the setting for many of her vampire novels. She took the name of Anne, finding her masculine first name unbearable. While in high school, Anne moved with her family to Richardson, Texas, where she met her husband, Stan Rice, a poet. They were married in 1961 and settled in San Francisco, moving in 1988 to New Orleans, where Rice continues to live.

Early on, Rice aspired to be a great writer. She tried many different forms of literature but did not find success until *Interview with the Vampire* (1976), a riveting and refreshing novel that turned the horror story into the moving autobiography and contest between Lestat, the vampire, and Louis, the vampire Lestat has "made." Much of the story is told from Louis's point of view, detailing his struggle against the clutches of Lestat. The other side of the story is told in *The Vampire Lestat* (1985). Throughout her vampire chronicles—which include *The Queen of the Damned* (1988), *The Tale of the Body Thief* (1992), *Memnoch the Devil* (1995), *The Servant of the Bones* (1996), *Pandora: New Tales of the Vampires* (1998), *The Vampire Armand* (1998), and *Vittorio the Vampire: New Tales of the Vampires* (1999)—Rice has built a mythic structure that encompasses the struggle to be human and the struggle to be immortal. The corruption of the flesh, which vampires transcend, also leads, unfortunately, to the corrupt behavior of supernatural beings because there are no physical or moral limits to the fulfillment of their desires. Rice's elaborate mythology can sometimes be tiresome, as in *Queen of the Damned*, but she is also able to tell a taut story, as in *Servant of the Bones*. Her vampire tales clearly come out of a sensibility steeped in romantic literature that emphasizes the questing self— at once a noble figure and, taken to extremes, a self-destructive one.

Rice has written erotic novels under the name of A. N. Roquelaure, including *The Claiming of Sleeping Beauty* (1983), *Beauty's Punishment* (1984), and *Beauty's Release: The Continued Erotic Adventures of Sleeping Beauty* (1985). She has also written the Mayfair Witches series, beginning with *The Witching Hour* (1985) and continued with *Lasher* (1993) and *Taltos* (1994). These novels are noteworthy for their historical authenticity and Rice's deft employment of gothic conventions.

Sources

Hoppenstand, Gary and Ray B. Browne, ed. *The Gothic World of Anne Rice*. Bowling Green, Ohio: Bowling Green State University Press, 1996.

Ramslund, Katherine, ed. *The Anne Rice Reader*. New York: Ballantine, 1997.

Rice, Elmer (Elmer Reizenstein) (1892–1967)
playwright

Born in New York City, Rice studied law and practiced briefly, putting his experience to work in *The Trial* (1914), which made deft use of flashbacks to contrast with courtroom testimony. Rice followed his initial success with two more courtroom dramas, *For the Defense* (1919) and *It Is the Law* (1922). But Rice earned a place in the history of American drama with *The Adding Machine*, an expressionist, experimental play that posed questions about what modern technology was doing to human identity. Rice's other major success was *Street Scene* (1929), which won a Pulitzer Prize, and was made into an opera, *Dream Girl* (1945). Unlike *The Adding Machine*, *Street Scene* is a deft piece of REALISM set in New York City.

Rice had 24 plays produced in New York with an impressive range of styles and subject matter. *The Left Bank* (1931) dramatizes the life of American expatriates in Paris; *Dream Girl* (1941) is a light comedy. During the 1930s he wrote a number of earnest, didactic political plays, such as *We, the People* (1932) and *American Landscape* (1938).

Rice published his autobiography, *Minority Report*, in 1963.

Sources

Durham, Frank. *Elmer Rice*. New York: Twayne, 1970.

Palmieri, Anthony F. R. *Elmer Rice: A Playwright's Vision of America*. Rutherford, N.J.: Fairleigh Dickinson University Press, 1980.

Rich, Adrienne Cecile (1929–) *poet*

Adrienne Rich was born in Baltimore, Maryland. Her father, a physician at Johns Hopkins University, encouraged her affinity for poetry, guiding her to an understanding of metrical forms. Her mother, a pianist, attuned Rich to the nature of lyrics and the use of rhythm.

Rich graduated from Radcliffe College in 1951, and that same year W. H. AUDEN chose her first book of poetry, *A Change of World*, for the YALE SERIES OF YOUNGER POETS. This early work reflected the influence of Wallace STEVENS, Robert FROST, and other modernist poets.

In the 1950s Rich married and had three sons while continuing to publish poetry. *The Diamond Cutters and Other Poems* (1955) won the Ridgely Torrence Memorial Award of the Poetry Society of America. This volume described many powerful women figures and elaborated an image of the poet as a diamond cutter—a careful craftsman bringing light to lives just as the cutter carves out the diamond from a dark stone.

In the 1960s Rich taught at several colleges and universities, including Swarthmore and Columbia, while producing vivid poems that reflected an emerging feminist consciousness. *The Will to Change* (1971) demonstrated her desire to merge the personal and the political, to change her own life as she began to focus on the oppression of women and question her own choices to marry and have a family. Her husband committed suicide in 1970, although Rich has never treated that event in her work, yet her work did become more revealing, more CONFESSIONAL.

Rich's poetry collection *Diving into the Wreck* (1974) won the National Book Award. One of her boldest works, it directly explores the patriarchal nature of society. Rich's belief that women had long suppressed a part of their own desires merged for a time with the ideas of the women's movement in the 1970s, so that Rich conceived the idea of writing, for a time, only for other women—particularly in *The Dream of a Common Language* (1978). The shift in her poetic consciousness mirrors a change in her personal life, which reflected her lesbian identity and involvement in lesbian, feminist, antiwar, and civil rights causes.

Rich has continued to write eloquent poetry, although none of her work has struck quite the same powerful chord as her collections of the 1960s and 1970s. Her *Collected Early Poems, 1950–1970,* was published in 1993. Later collections of her poetry include *Time's Power: Poems 1985–1988* (1989), *An Atlas of the Difficult World, Poems 1988–1991* (1991), *Dark Fields of the Republic: Poems 1991–1995* (1995), *Selected Poems 1950–1995* (1996), and *Midnight Salvage: Poems 1995–1998* (1999).

Rich has had an important role in writing about the women's movement and the rise of feminist criticism. Her nonfiction includes *Of Woman Born: Motherhood as Experience and Institution* (1976), *On Lies, Secrets and Silence, Selected Prose 1966–1978* (1979), *Blood, Bread, and Poetry: Selected Prose 1979–1985* (1986), and *What is Found There: Notebooks on Poetry and Politics* (1993).

Sources

Cooper, Jane Roberta, ed. *Reading Adrienne Rich: Reviews and Re-visions, 1951–81.* Ann Arbor: University of Michigan Press, 1984.

Gelpi, Barbara Charlesworth and Albert Gelpi, eds. *Adrienne Rich's Poetry and Prose: Poems, Prose, Reviews, and Criticism.* New York: W.W. Norton, 1993.

Richter, Conrad Michael (1890–1968) *novelist*

Born in Pennsylvania, Conrad Richter was a longtime resident of New Mexico. A regionalist writer, he is best known for his historical novels about pioneers, including a family he follows through three novels: *The Trees* (1940), *The Fields* (1946), and *The Town* (1950), which won a Pulitzer Prize. His other important work is *Sea of Grass* (1937), which centers on an Eastern woman who settles in the Southwest.

Early Americana (1936) collects Richter's stories about the Southwest, and *The Rawhide Knot* (1978) features stories about frontier marriages. Richter wrote about the regionalist imagination in *The Mountain and the Desert* (1955). His notebooks and autobiographical writings were published posthumously as *Writing to Survive* (1988) and *Private Notebooks* (1988).

Sources

Gaston, Edwin W., Jr. *Conrad Richter.* Boston: Twayne, 1989.

LaHood, Marvin J. *Conrad Richter's America.* The Hague Netherlands: Mouton, 1975.

Johnson, David R. *Conrad Richter: A Writer's Life.* University Park: Pennsylvania State University Press, 2001.

Riding, Laura (Laura Riding Jackson)

(1901–1991) *poet, critic, short story writer, novelist*

The daughter of socialist Jewish parents, Riding grew up in New York City and attended Cornell University. Beginning in the 1920s, her poems began to appear in such important LITTLE MAGAZINES as *The Fugitive* and POETRY. Leonard and Virginia Woolf published her first volume of poetry, *The Chaplet* (1926), which is typical of her humor, philosophical outlook, and sometimes rather obscure thoughts. The Woolfs also published her *Voltaire: A Biographical Fantasy* (1927).

Riding has been written about extensively, in part because of her relationship with the English writer Robert Graves. Like him, she was fascinated by the ancient world. She published two novels, *A Trojan Ending* (1937) and *Lives of Wives* (1939), which deals with the views on marriage expressed by Aristotle, Alexander the Great, and others.

Riding's strong personality and independent streak often put her at odds with her contemporaries. In *Love as Love* and *Death as Death,* both published in 1928, she advised poets to rely on their own experience and perceptions and to beware of aligning themselves with any movement or group.

Riding's *Collected Poems* (1938) were reprinted in 1980. She published *Progress of Stories* in 1982.

Sources

Baker, Deborah. *In Extremis: The Life of Laura Riding.* New York: Grove Press, 1993.

Wexler, Joyce Piell. *Laura Riding's Pursuit of Truth.* Athens: Ohio University Press, 1979.

Riesman, David (1909–) *sociologist*

Philadelphia-born Riesman became one of the most influential sociologists of the Chicago school, a group of academics clustered at the University of Chicago. In 1950 he produced the landmark study *The Lonely Crowd,* which became famous for its thesis that Americans had emerged from an "inner-directed" individualistic society to an "other-directed" society based on conformity to the status quo. Literature of the 1950s took up the issue of conformism and was heavily influenced by Riesman's statement of the problem. Novels such as John UPDIKE's *RABBIT, RUN* (1960), and the stories and essays in Norman MAILER's *Advertisements for Myself* (1959) explore the causes and consequences of conformity in a society on the verge of massive change in the 1960s.

Riesman followed up his initial study with *Faces in the Crowd* (1952), written with Nathan Glazer. His essays are collected in *Individualism Reconsidered and Other Essays* (1954) and *Abundance for What and Other Essays* (1964).

Sources

Lipset, Martin, and Leo Lowenthal, eds. *Culture and Social Character: The Work of David Riesman Reviewed.* New York: Free Press of Glencoe, 1961.

Riggs, Lynn (1899–1954) *playwright*

An Oklahoma native who wrote in the regionalist tradition, Riggs concentrated on the people of the Plains in such plays as *Roadside* (1930) and *Green Grow the Lilacs* (1931), his best-known work, set in 1900 in Indian territory, and the source of the groundbreaking Broadway musical *Oklahoma! The Cherokee Night* (1936) is his most explicit outcry against the shameful treatment of Native Americans when the U.S. government took their lands in Oklahoma.

Sources

Braunlich, Phyllis Cole. *Haunted by Home: The Life and Letters of Lynn Riggs.* Norman: University of Oklahoma Press, 1988.

Erhard, Thomas. *Lynn Riggs, Southwest Playwright.* Austin, Tex.: Steck-Vaughn, 1970.

Rinehart, Mary Roberts (1876–1958) *novelist, playwright*

Born in Pittsburgh, Mary Roberts Rinehart became one of the most important mystery writers of her day. In both her plays and novels she developed a memorable protagonist, "Tish," an idiosyncratic spinster. The first in the series, *Tish,* appeared in 1916, followed by *More Tish* (1921), *Tish Plays the Game* (1926), and *Tish Marches On* (1937).

Her other titles include *Miss Pinkerton* (1932), *Mr. Cohen Takes a Walk* (1934), *The Yellow Room* (1945), and *The Swimming Pool* (1952).

Her short fiction has been collected in *Love Stories* (1919), *Affinities: And Other Stories* (1920), and *Alibi for Isabel and Other Stories* (1944).

Roberts wrote an autobiography, *My Story* (1931), revised in 1948.

Sources

Cohn, Jan. *Improbable Fiction: The Life of Mary Roberts Rinehart.* Pittsburgh: University of Pittsburgh Press, 1980.

MacLeod, Charlotte. *Had She But Known: A Biography of Mary Roberts Rinehart.* New York: Mysterious Press, 1994.

Robbins, Tom (Thomas Eugene Robbins) (1936–) *novelist*

A quirky and popular author, the Seattle-based Robbins first wrote about a hot dog stand in Seattle in *Another Roadside Attraction* (1971). *Even Cowgirls Get the Blues* (1976), his best-known work, is about a health ranch for cowgirls. *Still Life with Woodpecker* (1980) is about the daughter of a exiled king who falls in love with a Seattle radical. Robbins's other novels include *Jitterbug Perfume* (1984), the story of a janitor whose perfume bottle is believed to hold the essence of the universe; *Skinny Legs and All* (1990), set in New York City; *Half Asleep in Frog Pajamas* (1994), narrated by a 29-year-old Filipino woman, a stockbroker who deals hilariously with a stock market crash; and *Fierce Invalids Home from Hot Climates* (2000). His whimsical, ironic work has been compared to the fiction of Richard BRAUTIGAN, Kurt VONNEGUT, and Thomas PYNCHON.

Sources

Hoyser, Catherine E. and Lorena Laura Stookey. *Tom Robbins: A Critical Companion.* Westport, Conn.: Greenwood Press, 1997.

Siegel, Mark. *Tom Robbins.* Boise, Idaho: Boise State University, 1980.

Roberts, Elizabeth Madox (1881–1941) *poet, novelist*

A Kentucky native who graduated from the University of Chicago in 1921, Roberts began her literary career as a poet and published several volumes of verse—collected in 1940 in *Song in the Meadow.* But she made her mark as a novelist, especially with *The Time of Man* (1926), set in rural Kentucky and portraying the lives of the pioneers and the poor. In the regionalist tradition her work conveys with meticulous authenticity the speech and manners of her characters in such novels as *My Heart and My Flesh* (1927), *The Great Meadow* (1930), and *He Sent Forth a Raven* (1935). *Not by Strange Gods* (1941) is a collection of stories concentrating on Kentucky women.

Sources

McDowell, Frederick P. W. *Elizabeth Madox Roberts.* New York: Twayne, 1963.

Rovit, Earl H. *Herald to Chaos: The Novels of Elizabeth Madox Roberts.* Lexington: University of Kentucky Press, 1960.

Roberts, Kenneth Lewis (1885–1957) novelist

After graduating from Cornell University in 1908, Kenneth Roberts settled in Maine and published a series of lively and authentic historical novels, including *Arundel* (1930), the story of Benedict Arnold; *The Lively Lady* (1931), set during the War of 1812; *Northwest Passage* (1973), the story of Robert Rogers's efforts to find a Northwest Passage to China; *Oliver Wiswell* (1940), set during the American Revolution; and *Lydia Bailey* (1947), the story of a young Maine lawyer, his romance with a young girl, and his involvement in the Haitian Revolution.

Roberts published several collections of literary essays and memoirs, including *For Authors Only* (1935), *Trending into Maine* (1944), and *I Wanted to Write* (1949).

Sources

Bales, Jack. *Kenneth Roberts.* New York: Twayne, 1993.

Robinson, Edwin Arlington (1869–1935) poet

Robinson spent his childhood in Gardiner, Maine, which became the model for his Tilbury Town, the setting for much of his poetry about NEW ENGLAND and the New England character. *The Children of the Night* (1897), his second book of poetry, contains many of his classic poems, including "Luke Havergal" and "Richard Cory," the latter a riveting, dramatic, and ironic portrait of a "gentleman," a man who has everything and is envied by everyone and yet commits suicide. Robinson's deft use of understatement and his mimicking of the laconic New England temper was much admired by Robert FROST, who modeled some of his dramatic monologues on Robinson's.

The much-anthologized "Miniver Cheevy," "born too late," laments the lack of romance in the present day compared to earlier times "When swords were bright." This poem appeared in *The Town Down the River* (1910), a poetry collection so successful that Robinson was able to make his living as a poet. *The Man Against the Sky* (1916) was an ambitious philosophical poem heavily influenced by the mass destruction of WORLD WAR I and the development of modern science. The book reflected Robinson's stoicism, laced with irony and pessimism. Robinson won the Pulitzer Prize three times: for *Collected Poems* (1921), *The Man Who Died Twice* (1924), and *Tristram* (1927), the latter a long poem that formed part of an Arthurian trilogy that also included *Merlin* (1917) and *Lancelot* (1920).

Sources

Franchere, Hoyt C. *Edwin Arlington Robinson.* New York: Twayne, 1968.

Murphy, Francis, ed. *Edwin Arlington Robinson: A Collection of Critical Essays.* Englewood Cliffs, N.J.: Prentice-Hall, 1970.

Rocky Mountain Review periodical

A quarterly literary magazine founded in Utah in 1937 as the *Intermountain Review.* Its contributors included Wallace STEGNER, Harvey SWADOS, and William Carlos WILLIAMS. It ceased publication in 1959 after it had been moved, first to Lawrence, Kansas, in 1946, and then to the State University of Iowa in 1949.

Rodman, Seldon (1909–) editor, poet, playwright, critic

A New York City native and graduate of Yale, Rodman was a coeditor of *Harness Hoot* (1930–1931), an avant-garde literary journal, and editor of *Common Sense* (1932–1943), a liberal review of contemporary affairs. His long association with Haiti and his interest in Haitian art is reflected in *Renaissance in Haiti* (1948); *Haiti: The Black Republic* (1954); *The Revolutionists* (1942), a play set in revolutionary Haiti of 1791; *Haiti* (1984), and *Where Art is Joy* (1988).

Rodman has published two long narrative poems: *Lawrence: The Last Chronicle* (1937), the story of the English soldier and writer T. E. Lawrence; and *The Airmen* (1941), in praise of the human yearning to fly.

Rodman has also written a biography of the artist Ben Shahn, *Portrait of the Artist as an American* (1951), and *Tongues of Fallen Angels* (1974), an account of his talks with Allen GINSBERG, Norman MAILER, and other American writers.

Roethke, Theodore (1908–1963) poet

Roethke was born in Saginaw, Michigan. His wonderful poetry about nature stems from his early experience in his father's greenhouse. Roethke attended the University of Michigan and Harvard, and taught at Lafayette College, Pennsylvania State University, and Bennington College.

Although Roethke began writing poetry in the 1940s, he did not achieve recognition until *The Waking: Poems 1933–1953*, which won a Pulitzer Prize. *The Far Field* (1964) received a National Book Award shortly after Roethke died. *The Collected Poems of Theodore Roethke* was published in 1966.

Roethke's poems "Cuttings" and "Root Cellar" are found in most comprehensive anthologies of American literature. "Root Cellar" has the feel of a man who has dug his hands in dirt and whose very life was awakened by the smells of the earth. The poet's use of alliteration captures his delight in growing things and his effort to evoke the exuberance of life itself: "Even the dirt kept breathing a small breath."

Sources

Kalaidjian, Walter B. *Understanding Theodore Roethke.* Columbia: University of South Carolina Press, 1987.

Seager, Allan. *The Glass House: The Life of Theodore Roethke.* New York: McGraw Hill, 1968.

Rogers, William (1879–1935) *humorist*

Born in Claremore, Oklahoma, Will Rogers toured with various groups of entertainers, including a Wild West show, to hone his skills as a comic monologuist. By 1913 he had achieved considerable success performing with the Ziegfeld Follies. By 1919 he began appearing in movies. His humor was in the 19th-century cowboy tradition of the folksy philosopher, but like Mark Twain, Rogers had a knack for poking fun at the pretensions of public figures and at anyone who took himself too seriously. His writing in newspaper columns was distinguished by his use of aphorisms. His comic material is included in *The Cowboy Philosopher on Prohibition* (1919), *The Illiterate Digest* (1924), and *Letters of a Self-Made Diplomat to His President* (1927). Rogers was at the height of his fame and national influence when he died in a plane crash in Alaska.

Sources

Robinson, Ray. *An American Original: A Life of Will Rogers.* New York: Oxford University Press, 1996.

Yagoda, Ben. *Will Rogers: A Biography.* New York: Alfred A. Knopf, 1993.

Rölvaag, Ole Edvard (1876–1931) *novelist*

O. E. Rölvaag came to the United States from Norway in 1896 and settled in Minnesota. He wrote the semi-autobiographical *Letters From America* (1912) about the adjustment to a new country. Other notable works include *Giants in the Earth* (1927) and *The Father's God* (1929). His work has been praised for its REALISM and its psychological portrayals of Norwegian immigrants on the Northwest frontier.

Sources

Haugen, Einar. *Ole Edvart Rölvaag.* Boston: Twayne, 1983.

"Rose for Emily, A" *William Faulkner* (1930) *short story*

William FAULKNER's most famous story, often treated as the quintessential example of southern gothic (see GOTHICISM), is told by a townsman of Jefferson, Mississippi. He gradually reveals a gruesome story of the aristocratic Emily Grierson and her obsession with a lover, Homer Barron, a Northerner who, people believe, jilted the proud Emily. In fact, by the end of the story it appears that Emily murdered her lover and slept beside his corpse in her decaying house. The narrator assembles the story from the clues and signs slowly revealed to add insight and speculation to Miss Emily's character and motivations.

Sources

Inge, M. Thomas, ed. *A Rose for Emily.* Columbus, Ohio: Merrill, 1970.

Rosenbaum, Alyssa

See RAND, Ayn.

Rosten, Leo Calvin (1908–1997) *humorist*

Born in Poland, Leo Rosten was brought to the United States as a child. He was educated at the University of Chicago, where he earned a Ph.D. in 1937 and initially worked as a sociologist. He is much better known, however, as the author of popular fiction and nonfiction, including *The Education of H*Y*M*A*N* K*A*P*L*A*N* (1937), comic stories about immigrant night-school students in New York. There were two sequels: *The Return of H*Y*M*A*N K*A*P*L*A*N* (1959) and *O K*A*P*L*A*N! MY K*A*P*L*A*N!* (1976). Rosten also published *Captain Newman, M.D.,* a popular and highly praised novel about an army psychiatrist. He published a collection of his work, *The Many Worlds of L*E*O R*O*S*T*E*N,* in 1964.

Rosten became even more popular with *The Joys of Yiddish* (1968). The versatile Rosten drew on his Yiddish books in detective novels such as *Silky* (1978) and *King Silky* (1981).

Rosten also has written about travel in *The 3:10 to Anywhere* (1976). *Passions and Prejudices* (1978) is a collection of his essays.

Sources

Cohen, Debra Nussbaum. "Writer Leo Rosten dies; Popularized Yiddish in U.S." *Jewish Bulletin of Northern California.* Available on-line. URL: http://www.jewishsf.com/bk970228/obrosten.htm. Posted February 28, 1997.

Roth, Henry (1906–1995) *novelist*

Roth was born in the Galician region of the Austro-Hungarian Empire and immigrated to the United States with his family at age two. The family settled on the Lower East Side of New York City and later lived in Harlem. Roth went to high school and then on to City College, where he began to demonstrate his literary talent by writing for a student magazine. Edna Lou Walton, a City College professor, encouraged him to write and later became his lover. She helped him find a publisher for *Call It Sleep* (1934), his brilliant, searing, semi-autobiographical account of growing up as an immigrant child in New York City.

Call It Sleep is a classic American novel. Not only is it the story of a boy growing up in the mode of other American coming-of-age stories, it also contains elements of a gritty RE-ALISM, a profound understanding of proletarian life, and an eloquence of language that has been compared to the work of James Joyce and other European and American modernists. Unlike many of his contemporaries who were writing PROLE-TARIAN LITERATURE, Roth did not concentrate solely on the social and political conditions of the GREAT DEPRESSION. On the contrary, his novel is psychological, presenting the STREAM OF CONSCIOUSNESS of his protagonist, David Schearl. Roth also explores in great depth and intensity the tensions between husband and wife, father and son, as well as the bond between mother and son.

Call It Sleep was recognized as an important achievement when it first appeared, but Roth's publisher went out of business, and his inability to write another novel for nearly 60 years plunged him and his work into obscurity. In despair, he attempted suicide. It was not until 1964, when critics such as Alfred KAZIN rediscovered *Call It Sleep,* that Roth's book began to take its place in the American canon.

By the late 1960s Roth again tried to resurrect his writing career. After several false starts, he was able to resume the production of a series of novels, which he completed at the age of 89, just before he died.

The collective title of these novels is *Mercy of a Rude Stream.* They were published separately as *A Star Shines over Mt. Morris Park* (1994), *A Diving Rock on the Hudson* (1995), *From Bondage* (1996), and *Requiem for Harlem* (1998).

Although Roth changed the name of his protagonist to Ira Stigman, the character has been viewed as an extension of *Call It Sleep*'s David Schearl. Like *Call It Sleep,* the later novels are autobiographical. They address Ira's sexual life, including incest with his sister. *Mercy of a Rude Stream* gathers the experiences that take Ira through his college years and to the brink of his major work as a writer, mirroring Roth's own pilgrimage and his 60-year meditation on the experiences that drove him to create *Call It Sleep.*

Critics have suggested that *Mercy of a Rude Stream* lacks the intensity of Roth's first great novel, but it remains, nevertheless, an important contribution to proletarian literature.

Sources

Lyons, Bonnie. *Henry Roth: The Man and His Work.* New York: Cooper Square, 1976.

Wirth-Nesher, Hana, ed. *New Essays on "Call It Sleep."* New York: Cambridge University Press, 1996.

Roth, Philip Milton (1933–) *novelist*

Philip Roth was born and raised in Newark, New Jersey, the setting for several of his stories and novels. He went to public schools in Newark and worked at the Newark Public Library. After a year at the Newark branch of Rutgers University, he transferred to Bucknell University in Pennsylvania. He received an M.A. in English from the University

of Chicago, enlisted in the U.S. Army, then returned to teach at Chicago, an experience he drew on for his first novel, *Letting Go* (1962). He has also taught at the University of Pennsylvania and Hunter College.

Roth made his mark with a collection of stories, *Goodbye, Columbus* (1959), many of which dealt with the fate of American Jews in contemporary America. Stories like "Defender of the Faith" and "Epstein" were, by turns, comic, ironic, and critical. Indeed, Roth's probing of the hypocrisy of his fellow Jews led to charges that he was a "self-hating Jew." In his long and productive career, however, Roth has targeted many different groups and individuals (including President Richard Nixon) for savage satire.

Early novels like *Letting Go* and *When She Was Good* (1967) were fairly conventional in style, the work of a young writer greatly influenced by Henry James's kind of psychological novel. As with much of his fiction, Roth drew on his own experience—his childhood in Newark, his graduate school years at Chicago, and a failed early marriage. Not until *Portnoy's Complaint* (1969) did Roth demonstrate the kind of bawdy, outlandish style that made him a controversial and celebrated writer. The clichés of Jewish life—the dominating mother, the guilty son, the Jewish boy's yearning for the shiksa (blond gentile)—are vividly brought to life in this STREAM-OF-CONSCIOUSNESS novel. *Portnoy's* exuberant prose transformed Roth into the realm of comic genius, stimulated in part by the throwing off of inhibitions that characterized the 1960s. Although Roth has shown that he can write in different styles, his penchant for evoking manic sexuality remains a steady feature of his work and is on display most notably in *Sabbath's Theater* (1995).

In the middle and later stages of his career Roth has developed an alter ego, the writer Nathan Zuckerman, who appears in *The Ghost Writer* (1979)—a remarkable story that contemplates what would have happened if Anne Frank had survived the concentration camps—*Zuckerman Unbound* (1981), *The Anatomy Lesson* (1983), *The Prague Orgy* (1985), *The Counterlife* (1986), and *Deception* (1990). "Philip" is identified in *Deception* as having written about Zuckerman.

Roth's fiction has continually grown stronger, with many critics hailing *Sabbath's Theater* (1995), *American Pastoral* (1997), *I Married a Communist* (1998), and *The Human Stain* (2000) as his best work. Certainly *The Human Stain,* in which Zuckerman appears once again, is one of the most provocative novels of Roth's career. It concerns a white college professor who is accused of racism—only, as Zuckerman learns, the professor is not white. Zuckerman traces the story of his accused friend's roots right back to the Newark where Philip Roth got his start.

Roth has written 19 novels, including *Our Gang* (1971), a satirical attack on Richard Nixon, *The Great American Novel* (1973), *My Life as a Man* (1974), *The Professor of Desire* (1977), and *Operation Shylock* (1993).

Roth has also written eloquently about the craft of fiction in *Reading Myself and Others* (1975, expanded edition 1985) and *The Facts: A Novelist's Autobiography* (1988). He has also published a memoir, *Patrimony: A True Story* (1991), which deals with his relationship with his father.

Sources

Cooper, Alan. *Philip Roth and the Jews.* Albany: State University of New York Press, 1996.

Halio, Jay L. *Philip Roth Revisited.* New York: Twayne, 1992.

Rodgers, Bernard F., Jr. *Philip Roth.* Boston: Twayne, 1978.

Rourke, Constance Mayfield (1885–1941)
historian

After graduating from Vassar College, Constance Rourke began writing her influential studies of American life, beginning with *Trumpets of Jubilee* (1927), which combine history, biography, and literary criticism in a study of 19th-century religion and entertainment. *Troupers of the Gold Coast* (1928) was a vivid study of actresses of the California frontier. Rourke's most well known book is *American Humor: A Study of the National Character* (1931). *Roots of American Culture, and Other Essays* (1942) appeared shortly after her death.

Sources

Bellman, Samuel I. *Constance Rourke.* Boston: Twayne, 1981.

Rubin, Joan Shelley. *Constance Rourke and American Culture.* Chapel Hill: University of North Carolina Press, 1980.

Rukeyser, Muriel (1913–1980) *poet, translator, essayist, critic, novelist*

Rukeyser was born and raised in New York City and educated in Manhattan private schools, then at Vassar College and Columbia University. At an early age she wanted to be a writer. She also had a keen interest in politics, associating herself with Communist Party causes. Later in life she participated in anti–Vietnam War demonstrations and in 1975 campaigned for the release of imprisoned writers during her term as president of the PEN American Center.

Rukeyser's first book of poetry, *Theory of Flight* (1935), won the YALE SERIES OF YOUNGER POETS Prize. Several more volumes of poetry followed, culminating in *Elegies, Orpheus* (1949) and *The Life of Poetry* (1949), mature poetry and criticism that dealt with the place of poetry in society. Rukeyser wrote a very social poetry that has been compared to Walt Whitman's work: She rejected the vision of the poet as a loner alienated from family and community. American history and political issues often figure importantly in Rukeyser's poetry, especially in *The Soul and Body of John Brown* (1940), an exploration of the militant abolitionist who led the attack on Harpers Ferry, and in *One Life* (1957), an unusual mixture of poetry and prose that delves into the career of Wendell Willkie, who ran for the presidency in 1940 and was defeated by Franklin Roosevelt.

Rukeyser produced distinguished translations of Octavio Paz's *Early Poems* (1973) and Bertolt Brecht's *Uncle Eddie's Mustache* (1974). She published one novel, *The Orgy* (1966). *The Collected Poems of Muriel Rukeyser* was published in 1979.

Sources

Kertesz, Louise. *The Poetic Vision of Muriel Rukeyser.* Baton Rouge: Louisiana State University Press, 1980.

Runyon, Alfred Damon (1884–1946) *short story writer, columnist*

Damon Runyon wrote about classic American characters in such books as *Guys and Dolls* (1932). Born in Kansas and raised in Colorado, Runyon served in the Philippines during the Spanish-American War and then got a job as a sportswriter at *The New York American* in 1911. There he began to develop his racy writing style and glib characterizations of Broadway and New York City types that also began appearing in THE SATURDAY EVENING POST. *The Best of Runyon* was published in 1938.

Sources

D'Itri, Patricia Ward. *Damon Runyon.* Boston: Twayne, 1982.

Russ, Joanna (1937–) *novelist, critic*

Born in New York City, educated at Cornell and Yale, Russ has worked as a college professor while creating a series of science fiction novels that explore feminist and gay issues in political and social contexts. Her books include *Picnic in Paradise* (1968), *And Chaos Died* (1970), *The Female Man* (1975), *The Adventures of Alyx* (1983), and *Extraordinary People* (1984).

She has also published forceful nonfiction: *How to Suppress Women's Writing* (1983); *To Write Like a Woman: Essays in Feminism and Science Fiction* (1995); and *What Are We Fighting For?: Sex, Race, Class, and the Future of Feminism* (1998).

Sources

Cortiel, Jeanne. *Demand My Writing: Joanna Russ, Feminism, Science Fiction.* Liverpool, England: Liverpool University Press, 1999.

Freedman, Carl. *Critical Theory and Science Fiction.* Hanover, N.H.: University Press of New England, 2000.

ᥴᥰᥱᥰᥲ

Sacco-Vanzetti case *historical event*

The case of two Italian immigrants accused of murder touched off a series of protests by American writers. Their trial and execution prompted books and articles by Edna St. Vincent MILLAY, John DOS PASSOS, Maxwell ANDERSON, and Katherine Anne PORTER, along with plays, poems, and paintings by other writers and artists.

Sacco and Vanzetti were tried and convicted for the murder of a paymaster and a guard in South Braintree, Massachusetts, on April 15, 1920. The two men were anarchists, and many writers at the time assumed their execution was a result of prejudice against their political beliefs and their ethnicity. Many immigrants at the time were involved in radical politics, and the Russian Revolution of 1917 had provoked a "Red Scare" and hostility against labor unions such us the International Workers of the World. Both men denied any involvement in the murders. In 1961 tests on Sacco's gun seemed to confirm his complicity in the crime, although the case continues to be debated.

The case epitomized for many American writers a country that had still not fulfilled its promise to welcome immigrants and to establish a truly democratic and just society. Anger and grief over the fate of these two men poured out in works such as John Dos Passos's *U.S.A.* (1938), Maxwell Anderson's *Winterset* (1935), James T. FARRELL's *Bernard Clare* (1946), and Katherine Anne Porter's *The Never Ending Wrong* (1977).

Vanzetti learned English during his imprisonment, and his letters in Italian and English demonstrated considerable literary power. His final appeal and defense of his innocence has become a classic. The *Letters of Sacco and Vanzetti* were published in 1928.

Sources

Avich, Paul. *Sacco and Vanzetti: The Anarchist Background.* Princeton, N.J.: Princeton University Press, 1991.

Felix, David. *Protest: Sacco-Vanzetti and the Intellectuals.* Bloomington: Indiana University Press, 1965.

Young, William and David E. Kaiser. *Postmortem: New Evidence in the Case of Sacco and Vanzetti.* Amherst: University of Massachusetts Press, 1985.

Sackler, Howard (1929–1982) *playwright*

A New York native, Sackler spent his career writing and directing for film and the stage. His best-known work is *The Great White Hope* (1967), a stirring play about Jack Johnson, the first African-American heavyweight boxing champion. The play won a Pulitzer Prize and was made into a major film starring James Earl Jones. Sackler's other dramas include *Mr. Welk and Jersey Jim* (1960) and a collection of one-act plays, *The Nine O'Clock Mail* (1965), published under the title *A Few Enquiries* (1970).

Sources

Weber, Bruce. "Power, Pitfalls, and 'The Great White Hope.'" September 14, 2000. Available on-line: URL: http://nytimes.com. Downloaded October 25, 2001.

Salinger, Jerome David (1919–) *novelist, short story writer*

J. D. Salinger was born and raised in New York City. He attended private schools and several colleges, including Columbia University, where he took a writing course with Whit

Burnett, the editor of STORY magazine. *Story* published Salinger's first story, "The Young Folks." Salinger enlisted in the U.S. Army in 1940 and continued to write, placing his stories in magazines such as *Collier's*, THE SATURDAY EVENING POST, and THE NEW YORKER, where most of his work would appear after World War II.

Salinger's most famous and controversial work is THE CATCHER IN THE RYE (1951), his only published novel. It concerns a young man, Holden Caulfield, who finds it difficult to adjust to American life. Indeed, Caulfield is filled with loathing at the hypocrisy he sees at school and in society at large. Confused, extremely sensitive, and highly critical, he is searching for a code of conduct and a set of values he can believe in. Even worse, there are very few people to whom he can communicate his anxieties. The novel follows him throughout a visit to New York City. At one point, like Huck Finn, he dreams of abandoning civilization, yet Holden's suffering ultimately brings him closer to humanity, and some critics have suggested that he becomes a Christ figure.

Salinger has also published three volumes of short fiction: *Nine Stories* (1953), *Franny and Zooey* (1961), and *Raise High the Roof-Beam, Carpenters, and Seymour: An Introduction* (1963). These stories show the influence of Ernest HEMINGWAY in that they are carefully crafted and achieve their power through understatement. "Last Day of the Last Furlough," "A Boy in France," "This Sandwich Has No Mayonnaise," and "The Stranger" are stories that reflect Salinger's experiences during the war, as well as his obsession with childhood innocence and the search for savior figures. Other stories, such as "A Perfect Day for Bananafish," "Uncle Wiggily in Connecticut" and "To Esmé, with Love and Squalor" express an almost Zen-like or transcendental contemplation of the world that is counterposed to the American obsession with self. *Franny and Zooey* is a chronicle of the Glass family, which is shadowed by the suicide of Seymour Glass and the search for a redemptive vision of the world.

By the early 1960s Salinger was so disgusted at the way writers were publicized and written about in American society that he stopped publishing and refused to appear in public. Although two biographies of him have been published, he continues to resist any inquiries about his life or work, although it is reported that he has continued to write.

Sources

Belcher, William F. and James W. Lee, eds. *J. D. Salinger and the Critics.* Belmont, Calif.: Wadsworth, 1962.
French, Warren. *J. D. Salinger, Revisited.* New York: Twayne, 1988.
Hamilton, Ian. *In Search of J. D. Salinger.* New York: Random House, 1988.

Salmagundi periodical

Founded in 1965 as a quarterly literary journal that would publish some of the best writing by and interviews with contemporary artists and critics, the journal has been sponsored by Skidmore College since 1969. The editor, Robert Boyers, has concentrated on one issue a year that focuses on an important author or theme.

Sanchez, Sonia (1934–) poet

Sanchez was born in Birmingham, Alabama, and educated at Hunter College in New York City. She has written extensively as a protest poet, enraged over the "neoslavery" of African Americans and decrying sexism, violence, and child abuse. Her work deftly captures the speech of African Americans. Her reliance on dialect suggests how closely she feels her art should mirror and speak to the attitudes of her milieu: *We a BaddDDD People* (1970), *It's New Day: Poems for Young Brothas and Sistuhs* (1971), *Ima Talken bout the Nation of Islam* (1972), *A Blues Book for Blue Black Magical Women* (1973), *I've Been A Woman: New and Selected Poems* (1978), *Homegirls and Handgrenades* (1984), *Generations: Poetry, 1969–1985* (1986), *Under a Soprano Sky* (1987), *Wounded in the House of a Friend* (1995), *Does Your House Have Lions?* (1997), *Like the Singing Coming Off the Drums: Love Poems* (1998), and *Shake Loose My Skin: New and Selected Poems* (1999).

Sanchez has also published *A Sound Investment: Short Stories for Young Readers* (1980) and an anthology, *Three Hundred and Sixty Degrees of Blackness Comin' at You* (1971).

Sources

Joyce, Joyce Ann. *Ijala: Sonia Sanchez and the African Poetic Tradition.* Chicago: Third World Press, 1996.

Sandburg, Carl August (1878–1967) poet, historian, novelist

Carl Sandburg was born and raised in Galesburg, Illinois. He left the town while quite young to try his hand at many different jobs, including newsboy, milkman, bottle washer, scene shifter, potter's helper, hobo, icehouse worker, and painter's apprentice. He returned to Galesburg in 1898, but he almost immediately enlisted in the army after the beginning of the Spanish-American War. Home from war, he entered Lombard College and took to writing, editing the school paper. But the restless Sandburg was off again on travels across the United States. In 1904 he published *Reckless Ecstasy*, 22 poems, and in 1908 married Lillian Steichen, the sister of the prominent photographer Edward Steichen.

Not until 1914 did Sandburg begin to find his poetic voice. In Chicago he wrote "Chicago" ("City of the Big Shoulders") and published his work in POETRY magazine. Sandburg's free verse and long lines, as well as his populism, are reminiscent of Walt Whitman's poetry. In quick succession Sandburg published his best books of poetry:

Chicago Poems (1916), *Cornhuskers* (1918), and *Smoke and Steel* (1920).

By 1920 Sandburg had become a successful lecturer and wandering troubadour, singing folk songs, reading his poetry, and talking philosophy. He collected ballads and published them in *The American Songbag* (1927). Through the 1920s and 1930s Sandburg published a six-volume life of Abraham Lincoln, for which he won a Pulitzer Prize in 1940. In 1954 he combined the six volumes into *Abraham Lincoln: The Prairie Years and the War Years*. This work was less of a contribution to history than to the evolving myth of Lincoln in the American consciousness.

Although Sandburg continued to publish poetry after 1920—including his *Complete Poems* in 1950—his best work of this period was his children's fiction: *Rootabaga Stories* (1922), *Rootabaga Pigeons* (1923), and *Potato Face* (1930). Charming and whimsical, the stories were well received.

Sandburg's only novel, *Remembrance Rock*, is a huge family saga ranging from the beginnings of America at Plymouth Rock to the 1940s. Sandburg also published a lively autobiography, *Always the Young Strangers*, in 1953. *The Sandburg Range* (1957) is an excellent sampling of his work. *Letters of Carl Sandburg* was published in 1968.

Certain classic Sandburg poems—"Fog," "Chicago," "Cool Tombs"—continue to be published in comprehensive anthologies of American literature. Virtually all of Sandburg's noteworthy poems are from the 1914–1920 period, when Sandburg brought a robust new voice to urban life and made poems sound as strong and as energetic as the city and the people they celebrated.

Sources

Crowder, Richard. *Carl Sandburg*. New York: Twayne, 1964.

Niven, Penelope. *Carl Sandburg: A Biography*. New York: Scribner's, 1991.

Yanella, Philip R. *The Other Carl Sandburg*. Jackson: University Press of Mississippi, 1996.

Sandoz, Marie Susette (1896–1966) *novelist, biographer, historian*

A Nebraska native, Mari Sandoz wrote about her Swiss father and his frontier farm in *Old Jules* (1935). Her novels, *Slogum House* (1937), *Capital City* (1939), and *The Tom-Walker* (1947), are also about midwestern pioneers. Her greatest work may be her biography *Crazy Horse* (1942), one of the finest reconstructions of an American Indian life ever written. She also wrote history, including *These Were the Sioux* (1961), *The Battle of Little Big Horn* (1978), and a history of the fur trade, *The Beaver Men* (1964). *Love Song to the Plains* (1961) mixes autobiography and history. She also wrote a memoir, *The Christmas of Phonograph Records* (1966). The *Letters of Mari Sandoz* appeared in 1992.

Sources

Kocks, Dorothee E. *Dream a Little: Land and Social Justice in Modern America*. Berkeley: University of California Press, 2000.

Stauffer, Helen Winter. *Mari Sandoz: Story Catcher of the Plains*. Lincoln: University of Nebraska Press, 1982.

San Francisco Renaissance (1955–1965)

Several poets congregated in San Francisco and around the CITY LIGHTS BOOKSTORE, owned by the poet Lawrence FERLINGHETTI. They rejected what they saw as the conformism of the Eisenhower years, and lamented and celebrated the reckless and romantic gestures of artists who sought a more intense way of living. Allen GINSBERG's "Howl" exemplified the keening, yearning, outrage of the period, as did Ferlinghetti's mellow, jazzy *A Coney Island of the Mind*. Jack KEROUAC celebrated the San Francisco scene in his famous novel *ON THE ROAD*. Many of the San Francisco poets were also BEATS. They rejected the idea of the tightly structured work of art that the NEW CRITICISM had espoused. They wanted to be more expressive and freer of form. Their extroverted poetry was often read in public, making poetry a communal event.

An earlier generation of poets and novelists had made San Francisco a bohemian or countercultural capital, beginning with Jack London and Robinson JEFFERS. While some of the San Francisco Renaissance poets moved to New York, Ferlinghetti, Gary SNYDER, and Kenneth REXROTH continued to make the city their base even after the Renaissance per se had subsided.

Studies of the San Francisco Renaissance include David Meltzer's *The San Francisco Poets* (1971), Lawrence Ferlinghetti's and Nancy Peters's *Literary San Francisco* (1980), and Michael Davidson's *The San Francisco Renaissance* (1989).

Sources

Davidson, Michael. *The San Francisco Renaissance: Poetics and Community at Mid-Century*. New York: Cambridge University Press, 1989.

Santayana, George (1863–1952) *philosopher, essayist*

Born in Spain, Santayana was brought to the United States in 1872, studied in Germany and England, and earned a Ph.D. from Harvard in 1889, where until 1912 he taught philosophy. He wrote about aesthetics in *The Sense of Beauty* (1896); a play in verse, *Lucifer: A Theological Tragedy* (1899, revised 1924); a book of poetry, *A Hermit of Carmel* (1901); and a five-volume work of philosophy, *The Life of Reason* (1905–1906). Much of Santayana's work in philosophy and literature has to do with attempts to reconcile the materialist and idealist views of life—that is, the conflict between those who see the world in terms of matter and motion and those who see it as immaterial or as a projection of the mind.

Although Santayana wrote many other works of philosophy, his standing in American literature is due primarily to his novel *The Last Puritan* (1935), which explores the decline of Calvinism and the Puritan mentality in American culture. Of equal importance is his memoir, *Persons and Place,* also published as separate volumes: *The Backgrounds of My Life* (1944), *The Middle Span* (1945), and *My Host the World* (1953). His essays, lectures, and reviews were published in *Obiter Scripta* (1936). A collected edition of his works was published in 14 volumes (1936–1937). *The Letters of George Santayana* appeared in 1955.

Sources

Dawidoff, Robert. *The Genteel Tradition and the Sacred Rage: High Culture vs. Democracy in Adams, James, and Santayana.* Chapel Hill: University of North Carolina Press, 1992.

Price, Kenneth M. and Robert C. Letiz III, ed. *Critical Essays on George Santayana.* Boston: G. K. Hall, 1991.

Saroyan, William (1908–1981) *short story writer, novelist, playwright*

Saroyan was born and grew up in Fresno, California. From his immigrant Armenian parents he absorbed a sense of rootlessness that is almost anarchic. Saroyan was a master of the comic impression and of a style that at its best expressed a freewheeling vitality. His first success was the exuberant collection of stories *The Daring Young Man on the Flying Trapeze* (1934). He then embarked on a stunning string of successes in the theater, including *My Heart's in the Highlands* (1939), the story of a poor poet, his son, and a visiting actor who is dying. *The Time of Your Life* (1939), set in a San Francisco bar, won a Pulitzer Prize. Subsequent plays were failures, however, and critics chastised Saroyan for his inability to write coherent drama.

Saroyan's most notable novels are *The Human Comedy* (1943) and *The Laughing Matter* (1953). His memoirs and other short prose are collected in *My Name is Aram* (1940), *The Bicycle Rider in Beverly Hills* (1952), and *Here Comes, There Goes, You Know Who* (1961).

Sources

Keyishian, Harry, ed. *Critical Essays on William Saroyan.* New York: G. K. Hall, 1995.

Lee, Lawrence and Barry Gifford. *Saroyan: A Biography.* New York: Harper & Row, 1984.

Sarton, May Eleanor (1912–1995) *poet, novelist, memoirist*

May Sarton was born in Wondelgem, Belgium, where her mother was a designer and her father, the son of a Belgian upper middle-class family, worked as a historian of science. During World War I, the family moved to Cambridge, Massachusetts. Sarton attended the Cambridge Latin High School and then studied at the Boston Repertory Theater, followed by work in summer stock and trips to Paris. She began writing poetry and fiction in her mid-20s as she struggled over whether to consider herself a European or an American.

Sarton did not find her stride as a writer until *The Bridge of Years* (1946), her second novel, was published. Based on her years in Belgium and on her family's history, the novel focuses on a Belgian family experiencing the changing phases of Europe—from World War I and the postwar period to the subsequent depression, the rise of fascism, and the outbreak of World War II.

The Birth of a Grandfather (1957), which has been compared in style to the work of Henry James, drew on Sarton's experiences in Cambridge and explored the issues of generational change. *Mrs. Stevens Hears the Mermaids Singing* (1965) concentrated on the development of a female artist, and *A Reckoning* (1978) on a female novelist.

The prolific Sarton published 19 novels, including *Kinds of Love* (1970), *As We Are Now* (1973), and *Crucial Conversations* (1975)—three novels that continue her exploration of what it means to be female and to be an artist. Sarton's first novel, *The Single Hound* (1938), was a fictionalized account of her love affair with the English writer Elizabeth Bowen. The theme of lesbianism occurs throughout Sarton's work in different genres.

A formidable poet, Sarton published her *Collected Poems, 1930–1973* in 1974. Although critics paid little attention to her verse in the early part of her career, her direct and lyrical style earned favor in the 1970s during a period when women's writing was reevaluated.

Sarton has been read as much for her autobiographies as for her fiction and poetry. Her nonfiction volumes include *I Knew a Phoenix: Sketches for an Autobiography* (1959), *Journal of a Solitude* (1973), *A World of Light: Portraits and Celebrations* (1976), *Recovering: A Journal* (1980), *At Seventy: A Journal* (1984), *After the Stroke: A Journal* (1988), *Endgame: A Journal of the Seventy-ninth Year* (1992), *Encore: A Journal of the Eightieth Year* (1993), and *At Eighty-two* (1996).

Sources

Evans, Elizabeth. *May Sarton Revisited.* Boston: Twayne, 1989.

Peters, Margot. *May Sarton: A Biography.* New York: Alfred A. Knopf, 1997.

Saturday Evening Post, The *periodical*

Founded in 1821, the magazine was originally literary, with such contributors as Edgar Allan Poe, James Fenimore Cooper, and Harriet Beecher Stowe. In the 20th century it broadened its popular appeal, although it continued to publish serious fiction by such writers as William FAULKNER and F. Scott FITZGERALD. By 1909 the magazine's circulation had reached 1 million. Under the ownership of Cyrus Curtis it doubled in the next five years by emphasizing articles about sports and adventure, often told humorously. Later editors emphasized nonfiction, and circulation climbed to 6 million. By the early 1960s, however, the *Post* began to experience a lost of readership—as did other general circulation magazines, which found it increasingly difficult to compete with television that offered the same brand of pictures, cartoons, news, and other forms of entertainment. The magazine ceased publication in 1969, but was revived in 1971, appearing less frequently and concentrating on specific topics, anniversaries, and cultural events around which whole issues could be constructed. It is now published six times a year.

Saturday Review, The periodical

Established in 1924 as *The Saturday Review of Literature,* the magazine shortened its title in 1952 to reflect the magazine's inclusion of world events, recordings, drama, radio, television, and travel. Several of the magazine's departments developed a strong following: "Trade Winds," "Broadway Postscript," "Booked for Travel" and "Manner of Speaking," a column on language by the poet John Ciardi. Norman Cousins was the most influential editor of the magazine, serving from 1940 to 1980, when the magazine ceased publication—a victim to changing public interests and a new media world dominated by television.

Schaefer, Jack (1907–   ) *novelist*

A Cleveland native and graduate of Oberlin College, Schaefer studied English at Columbia University before becoming a journalist and novelist. His first novel, *Shane* (1949), was also his most important. A classic western that features a hero enmeshed in a battle between homesteaders and cattlemen, the novel was translated into more than 30 languages and became a classic motion picture, written by A. B. GUTHRIE and starring Alan Ladd. Schaefer's later fiction includes *The Canyon* (1953), the story of the Cheyenne. *The Collected Stories of Jack Schaefer* appeared in 1966. *Monte Walsh* (1963) and *Mavericks* (1967) are later novels.

Sources

Haslam, Gerald. *Jack Schaefer.* Boise, Idaho: Boise State University, 1975.
Work, James C., ed. *Shane: A Critical Edition.* Lincoln: University of Nebraska Press, 1984.

Schulberg, Budd Wilson (1914–   ) *novelist, screenwriter*

Born in New York City but brought up in Hollywood, where his father was a movie studio executive, Schulberg satirized Hollywood in his classic novel *What Makes Sammy Run?,* which provides authentic detailed descriptions of film pro-

ducers and other opportunists. *The Disinherited* (1950) features a main character partly modeled on F. Scott FITZGER-ALD, who also inspired the novel's style. Schulberg's greatest success as a screenwriter came with *On the Waterfront,* starring Marlon Brando. In 1981 he published an autobiography: *Moving Pictures: Memories of a Hollywood Prince* (1981), and in 1995, *Sparring with Hemingway and Other Legends of the Fight Game.*

Schuyler, James Marcus (1923–1991) *poet, playwright, novelist*

Born in Chicago, James Schuyler became part of the NEW YORK SCHOOL OF POETS. *Salute* (1960), a poetry collection, showed the influence of the ABSTRACT EXPRESSIONIST painting that other members of the group also promoted. Schuyler has been highly praised for his use of understatement and his delicate observations of city and rural life. His collections include *May 24th or So* (1966); *Freely Espousing* (1969); *The Crystal Lithium* (1972); *Hymn to Life* (1974); *The Morning of the Poet* (1980), which won a Pulitzer Prize; *A Few Days* (1985); and *Selected Poems* (1988).

Schuyler's experimental plays and prose are collected in *The Home Book* (1977). He also wrote three novels: *Arthur and Guinevere* (1958), *A Nest of Ninnies* (1969), and *What's For Dinner* (1979). The subjects of these works range from a brother and sister on a summer holiday to comic stories of suburbanites, both sane and unbalanced. *The Diary of James Schuyler* appeared in 1997.

Sources

Ward, Geoff. *Statutes of Liberty: The New York School of Poets.* New York: St. Martin's Press, 1993.

Schwartz, Delmore (1913–1966) *poet, editor, short story writer, critic*

A native of Brooklyn, Schwartz is often included in histories of the NEW YORK INTELLECTUALS. He was an editor at PARTISAN REVIEW from 1943 to 1955. Although his body of work is small, he had a knack for writing pieces that captured the spirit of his times—as in his first book of poetry, *In Dreams Begin Responsibilities* (1938). His short stories, many of which deal with urban Jewish life, are collected in *The World is a Wedding* (1948).

Schwartz has been praised for the lyrical quality of his poetry and prose. In both forms, he was a poet of alienation, evoking his characters' sense of isolation and defeat in poignant terms. His life was the stuff of legend—in part because he made such witty and biting remarks about his fellow writers. In Saul BELLOW's novel *Humboldt's Gift* (1975), he figures as the character Von Humboldt Fleisher. Schwartz's *Last and Lost Poems* appeared in 1979 and *Delmore Schwartz and James Laughlin: Selected Letters* in 1993.

Sources

Atlas, James. *Delmore Schwartz: The Life of an American Poet.* New York: Farrar, Straus & Giroux, 1977.

science fiction and fantasy

American science fiction is largely a product of the second half of the 20th century. Between 1950 and 1960 a large number of popular and critically successful novelists established the genre at a level of creativity comparable to English counterparts such as H. G. Wells. Robert HEINLEIN (*The Green Hills of Earth* [1951] and *Stranger in a Strange Land* [1961]), the prolific Isaac ASIMOV (*The Caves of Steel* [1953]), Ray BRADBURY (*The Martian Chronicles* [1950] and *Fahrenheit 451* [1953]) became modern masters of science fiction and fantasy. They created, on the one hand, superbly realized worlds that were extrapolations from the findings of science, and on the other, alternative realities that had much in common with similar works of fantasy in English literature.

Two of the most innovative writers in what might be called the second generation of science fiction and fantasy writers are Ursula LE GUIN and Samuel R. DELANY. Le Guin's masterpiece, *The Left Hand of Darkness* (1969), creates a world in which individuals have more than one sex, thus making a comment, by indirection, about a world where everyone has only one sexual identity. Delany, perhaps the most deeply read of all American science fiction writers—his work constantly alludes to the great writers of the century—has also been the most experimental. His Neveryon fantasy series explores the roots of writing and of civilization itself. *Triton* (1976), set on a moon of Neptune in 2112, creates a world in which individuals can change their sex as easily as their residences and exchange one set of psychological attributes for another in pursuit of a satisfactory identity. That even such complete freedom does not result in happiness is clearly a comment on the present as much as a projection into the future.

Sources

Banks, Michael A. *Understanding Science Fiction.* Morristown, N.J.: Silver Burdett Co., 1982.

Davin, Eric Leif, ed. *Pioneers of Wonder: Conversations with the Founders of Science Fiction.* Amherst, N.Y.: Prometheus Books, 1999.

Scott, Evelyn (1893–1963) *novelist*

Born in Tennessee but brought up in New Orleans, Scott achieved her first great success with *The Wave* (1929), a superb Civil War novel. *A Calendar of Sin* (1935) is a generational saga, and even more notable is *Eva Gay* (1933), a brilliant evocation of a woman's life and loves. *Bread and Sword* (1937) focuses on a writer's effort to sur-

vive in the modern economy. One of the best southern novelists of her generation, Scott's work has been sadly neglected. In *Background in Tennessee* (1937) she recounts her early childhood.

Sources

Callard, D. A. *Pretty Good for a Woman: The Enigmas of Evelyn Scott.* London: Jonathan Cape, 1985.

White, Mary Wheeling. *Fighting the Current: The Life and Work of Evelyn Scott.* Baton Rouge: Louisiana State University Press, 1998.

Scott, Winfield Townley (1910–1968) *journalist, novelist*

Born in Massachusetts and educated at Brown University, from which he graduated in 1931, Scott worked on the staff of *The Providence Journal* and began writing poetry of a distinctly regionalist (see REGIONALISM) flavor, influenced by Edwin Arlington ROBINSON and Robert FROST. Scott's poetry collections include *Elegy for Robinson* (1936), *Wind the Clock* (1941), *Mr. Whittier* (1948), and *Collected Poems* (1962). After his death his notebooks were published as *A Dirty Hand* (1969).

Sources

Donaldson, Scott. *Poet in America: Winfield Townley Scott.* Austin: University of Texas Press, 1972.

Scottsboro case *historical event*

The trials (1931–1937) of nine young African-American men charged with the rape of two white women galvanized the protests of the literary community and became the subject of protests by poets such as Langston HUGHES and Lincoln STEFFENS.

The "Scottsboro boys" ranged in age from 13 to 19, and only one of them was not sentenced to death. All served prison sentences. The cases were brought to the U.S. Supreme Court twice. The Court found that the defendants had not received fair trials because African Americans had been excluded from serving on the juries. The case became a cause célèbre for the Communist Party and for other groups and individual protesting American racism and injustice. One of the defendants, Clarence Norris (1912–1989), published *The Last of the Scottsboro Boys* (1979), a memoir of his ordeal.

Sources

Goodman, James E. *Stories of Scottsboro.* New York: Pantheon Books, 1994.

Carter, Dan T. *Scottsboro: A Tragedy of the American South.* Revised edition. Baton Rouge: Louisiana State University Press, 1979.

Scribner's Magazine *periodical*

Founded in 1887, this magazine emphasized literary fiction, biography, and cultural criticism. Beginning in 1914 under the editorship of critic Robert Bridges, *Scribner's* featured Edith WHARTON and Theodore Roosevelt as its important contributors. In the 1920s and 1930s it published the fiction of Ernest HEMINGWAY, Thomas WOLFE, William FAULKNER, and others. It went out of business in 1938.

Sedgwick, Anne Douglas (1873–1935) *novelist*

Born in New Jersey, Sedgwick lived most of her life abroad. She early on took up Henry James's international theme, the relationship between Americans and old-world Europeans. *Franklin Winslow Kane* (1910), for example, hinges on the contrast between an American and an English couple. *Adrienne Toner* (1922) portrays a young American woman who fascinates her English friends. Sedgwick's stories are collected in *The Nest* (1913) and *Christmas Roses* (1920). *Anne Douglas Sedgwick: A Portrait in Letters* appeared in 1936.

Sources

Forbes, Esther. *Anne Douglas Sedgwick. An Interview by Esther Forbes and Appreciations by William Lyon Phelps, Dorothy Canfield, Hugh Walpole and Others.* Boston: Houghton, Mifflin: n.d.

Selby, Hubert, Jr. (1928–   ) *novelist*

Selby is best known for *Last Exit to Brooklyn* (1964), a look at the seamy urban life of gays, prostitutes, and criminals often involved in violent altercations. The novel was the subject of an obscenity trial in England. Selby's other novels are *The Room* (1971), *The Demon* (1976), and *Requiem for a Dream* (1978).

Sources

Giles, James R. *Understanding Hubert Selby, Jr.* Columbia: University of South Carolina Press, 1998.

Separate Peace, A John Knowles (1960) *novel*

John KNOWLES's classic coming-of-age novel is set at Devon, a New Hampshire boys' school in the early 1940s. During the summer session, as some of the school's graduates go off to war, Gene Forrester and his roommate Phineas (Finny) are two 16-year-olds more interested in boyhood adventures. Each day they jump from a high tree into the river. Their friendship is strained, however, because Gene thinks Finny is envious of Gene's academic success and is doing his best to set him back. An enraged Gene pushes Finny out of the tree one day, and the unprepared Finny shatters his leg, ending his participation in the sports at which he excels. Overwhelmed with guilt, Gene is stunned when Finny does not blame him but instead tries to make Gene a superior athlete.

Gradually, the news of the war has an impact on the boys, who learn that their friend Elwin has enlisted. When Elwin returns, he has had a mental breakdown. He overwhelms Gene with the story, and with his disclosure that he knows Gene was responsible for Finny's accident. When Gene tells Finny about Elwin's breakdown, Finny finally accepts the fact of the war, a fact he had been trying to avoid in order to preserve his innocent world.

Brinker, an officious boy, holds an inquisition about the circumstances of Finny's accident, getting Elwin to testify that Gene was the cause. Finny is so upset that he runs away, falls down a flight of stairs, and breaks his leg again. Although Finny forgives Gene, Finny suffers a heart attack and dies as his leg is being set. Gene enlists in the navy, but the war has ended. Many years later, Gene realizes that he fought his own war at school and killed an enemy, Finny.

This powerful novel is a kind of parable about innocence and experience, about the human desire to hide from the truth and the desire to prosecute those who are guilty. Finny demonstrates the human capacity for forgiveness and Gene the capacity for guilt. Even more important, Knowles shows that what is at stake in war is also what is at stake in peace, and that the passions that start wars are the same passions that can lead to peace—although at enormous cost to the individual and to society.

Sources

Bryant, Hallman Bell, ed. *Understanding A Separate Peace: A Student Casebook to Issues, Sources, and Historical Documents.* Westport, Conn.: Greenwood Press, 2001.

Karson, Jill, ed. *Readings on A Separate Peace.* San Diego, Calif.: Greenhaven Press, 1999.

Seven Arts (1916–1917) *periodical*

This LITTLE MAGAZINE, published monthly, promoted American talent and printed works considered too radical for conventional literary magazines. It had distinguished editors, including Waldo FRANK and Van Wyck Brooks. Among its contributors were Vachel LINDSAY, Sherwood ANDERSON, John REED, John DOS PASSOS, Theodore DREISER, Robert FROST, and H. L. MENCKEN. The magazine's pacifist stance, however, led to its demise during WORLD WAR I.

Sewanee Review *periodical*

Established in 1892 and housed at the University of the South, the *Sewanee Review* is the nation's oldest literary quarterly. Under the editorship of the poet Allen TATE from 1944 to 1946, the journal attained widespread influence in the literary community. Since Tate's time a succession of academic editors have maintained the journal's high quality. It is respected for its publication of southern literature and its promulgation of the NEW CRITICISM.

Sexton, Anne Gray Harvey (1928–1974) *poet*

Born in Newton, Massachusetts, to upper middle-class parents, Anne Sexton had an abusive childhood that later became a subject of her poetry. After an early marriage and the birth of a daughter, Sexton tried to commit suicide. She was frequently hospitalized in the late 1950s, but she returned to school and studied with distinguished writers such as Robert LOWELL. She also met contemporary poets such as Maxine KUMIN and Sylvia PLATH. Under Lowell's influence she began to write CONFESSIONAL POETRY, drawing deeply on her own disturbing experiences, including her suicidal impulses. Her second collection, *All My Pretty Ones* (1962), was nominated for a National Book Award, and her third collection, *Live or Die* (1966), won a Pulitzer Prize.

A daring, experimental poet, Sexton became a leading figure in contemporary poetry and in women's studies. She was hailed for her candor not only about her own experience but also about the issues women confront in marriage and in modern society. *Complete Poems* was published in 1981.

Sexton also wrote a one-act play, *45 Mercy Street* (1969), and, with Maxine Kumin, several children's books, including *Eggs and Things* (1963) and *Joey and the Birthday Present* (1971). *No Evil Star: Selected Essays, Interviews, and Prose* appeared in 1985.

Sources

Middlebrook, Diane Wood. *Anne Sexton: A Biography.* Boston: Houghton Mifflin, 1991.

Wagner-Martin, Linda, ed. *Critical Essays on Anne Sexton.* Boston: G. K. Hall, 1989.

Shange, Ntozake (Paulette Linda Williams) (1948–) *novelist, poet, playwright*

An African-American writer committed to documenting the struggle of women and African Americans, Ntozake Shange grew up in a middle-class family in Trenton, New Jersey. She enjoyed a conventional upbringing that included exposure to jazz and the work of important African-American authors such as Langston HUGHES and Paul Laurence Dunbar as well as to classic writers such as Shakespeare and T. S. ELIOT.

When her family moved to St. Louis, Missouri, eight-year-old Williams was one of the first black children to integrate the public school system. She experienced racism firsthand and began to write when her family moved back to New Jersey, where she attended high school.

Williams graduated from Barnard College in 1970 and shortly afterward chose a new name for herself. Ntozake means "she who brings her own things" and Shange "one who walks with lions." In Oakland, California, she be-friended several writers, and her first play, *for colored girls who have considered suicide/when the rainbow is enuf* (1974), received acclaim on Broadway for its depiction of seven black women who confront their lives and articulate their need for self-definition. She regards her work as being about the lives of all women who have to struggle to maintain their independence and integrity. Like her later work, her first play features unusual punctuation, dialect, slang, and rhythms that come close to everyday speech.

Shange's other plays include *From Okra to Greens* (1978), *Boogie Woogie Landscapes* (1979), and *Three Pieces* (1981).

Shange has published several books of poetry, including *Nappy Edges* (1978) and *Ridin' the Moon in Texas* (1989). Like her plays, her poems emphasize an active engagement with society and an assertion of the individual's worth. Critics have sometimes referred to her as a warrior-writer.

Shange's collections of essays include *A Daughter's Geography* (1983) and *See No Evil: Prefaces, Essays, and Accounts, 1976–1983* (1984). Her emphasis on black women's search for wholeness is comparable to Alice WALKER's essays and novels.

Her novel *Sassafras, Cypress and Indigo* (1982) reflects her musical style and the importance of music itself in her writing. It is the story of three women in search of the sources of creativity. She has published two other novels, *Betsey Brown* (1985) and *Liliane: Resurrection of the Daughter* (1994). She has also published a novel for children, *Whitewash* (1997), based on the true story of a young African-American girl who was terrorized by a gang that attacked her and spray-painted her face white.

Sources

David, Thadious M. and Trudier Harris, eds. *Afro-American Writers After 1955: Dramatists and Prose Writers.* Detroit: Gale Research, 1985.

Lester, Neal A. *Ntozake Shange: A Critical Study of the Plays.* New York: Garland, 1995.

Shapiro, Karl Jay (1913–2000) *poet, novelist, critic*

Born in Baltimore, Karl Shapiro made his career in New York. He began to publish poetry in the 1930s, but he established his reputation with *V-Letter and Other Poems* (1944), a winner of the Pulitzer Prize. An outspoken poet, he became acutely conscious of his Jewish identity during WORLD WAR II, when Ezra POUND's pro-fascists radio broadcasts radicalized him. He published *Trial of a Poet* in 1947 and *Poems of a Jew* in 1958. His *Selected Poems* appeared in 1968 and *The Wild Card: Selected Poems, Early and Late* in 1998. A poet of enormous range, Shapiro wrote intense love lyrics and satirical verse, often engaging with political, social, and ethnic issues as well as the nature of war.

Shapiro taught at the University of Nebraska and the University of California at Davis, an experience he put to use in a novel, *Edsel* (1971), which concerns a poet-professor at a midwestern university.

Shapiro's literary criticism includes *Beyond Criticism* (1953), a study of poetry, *In Defense of Ignorance* (1960), an argument against excessive intellectualism in art, and *The Bourgeois Poet* (1964), an exploration of the poet's relation to society.

Shapiro published his autobiography in two volumes, *Poet* (1988) and *Reports of My Death* (1990).

Sources
Bartlett, Lee. *Karl Shapiro: A Descriptive Bibliography 1933–1977.* New York: Garland, 1979.

Reino, Joseph. *Karl Shapiro.* Boston: Twayne, 1981.

Shaw, Irwin (1913–1984) *short story writer, playwright, novelist*

Born in Brooklyn, New York, Shaw first gained prominence with his plays *Bury the Dead* (1936), *Siege* (1937), *The Gentle People* (1939), *Retreat to Pleasure* (1940), and *Sons and Soldiers* (1944). His dramas confront social and political issues with considerable intensity, yet he does not sacrifice his stories for his messages.

Shaw became much better known after WORLD WAR II for his fiction, especially his war novel, *The Young Lions* (1948). This work focuses on two soldiers, one Jewish and one Gentile, and a Nazi, who kills the Jew and is killed by the Gentile. Shaw's other important achievement is *Rich Man, Poor Man* (1970) an epic novel set in various locations from New York City to the French Riviera, which tells the story of two brothers and of the period between the 1940s and the 1970s. *Evening in Byzantium* (1973) is set in Hollywood and follows the fate of a producer. *Beggarman, Thief* (1977) is a sequel to *Rich Man, Poor Man.*

Shaw's short fiction has often been anthologized, for it constitutes some of his best writing. A master of the compact plot, Shaw created stories with narratives that seemed to flow naturally in the realistic style graced by sharp character portraits. *Five Decades* (1978) collects his stories. *Paris! Paris!* (1977) is a collection of essays.

Sources
Giles, James R. *Irwin Shaw.* Boston: Twayne, 1983.

———. *Irwin Shaw: A Study of the Short Fiction.* Boston: Twayne, 1991.

Shnayerson, Michael. *Irwin Shaw: A Biography.* New York: Putnam, 1989.

Sheed, Wilfrid John Joseph (1930–) *critic, novelist*

Wilfrid Sheed was born in England but has resided in the United States since 1947. He has been much admired for his satirical novels, particularly *A Middle Class Education* (1961),

the story of a student at Oxford; *The Hack* (1963), the life of a writer who confects inspirational verse and fiction for American Catholic magazines; *Max Jamison* (1970), a novel about critics; and *People Will Always Be Kind* (1973), an account of an Irish-American politician's successes.

A prolific essayist, Sheed has collected his work in *Essays in Disguise* (1990). He has also written biographical profiles: *Muhammad Ali* (1976) and *Clare Boothe Luce* (1982). *Frank and Maisie* (1985) is a memoir of Sheed's parents. *In Love with Daylight: A Memoir of Recovery* (1995) is a humorous account of how Sheed has recovered from several severely debilitating illnesses.

Sources
Duncan, Erika. "Encounters: Beset by Illnesses Yet Making the Most of the Literary Life." February 4, 1996. Available on-line. URL: http://nytimes.com. Downloaded October 25, 2001.

Shepard, Samuel (1943–) *playwright, screenwriter*

Born in Fort Sheridan, Illinois, Sam Shepard moved frequently from base to base as the son of an Air Force bomber pilot. The family finally established a home on a ranch in Duarte, California, where Shepard—in spite of liking the rugged, simple outdoor life—longed for a more exciting outlet. He loved the movies and jazz and read BEAT poets such as Gregory CORSO and Lawrence FERLINGHETTI.

By the early 1960s Shepard had situated himself in New York City's East Village as an OFF-OFF-BROADWAY playwright. His early plays, *Cowboys* (1964) and *The Rock Garden* (1964), focus on tensions between father and son and on western settings that derived from his own background. The stripped-down—virtually bare—stages of these early plays suggest place as a state of mind, a work of the imagination. Shepard's characters in these plays are disruptive and explosive, fiercely defending their individuality in terms reminiscent of the Beat poets, though in a far more violent fashion. Later plays such as *La Turista* (1966) and *Mad Dog Blues* (1971) present an apocalyptic America from which Shepard's characters restlessly seek escape through their own destructive acts. In *La Turista*, a character swings from a rope and crashes through the stage set—an example of Shepard's effort to shake up his audience and to make the stage itself an extension of his characters' anarchism.

In *The Tooth of Crime* (1972), a drama about a rock star, the effort to escape societal definition of the self is shown to be illusory: the rock star kills himself, realizing he cannot escape the role of star except as he is replaced by other stars. *Curse of the Starving Class* (1976) suggests it is not society but the self that should be criticized; that is, there is a shift in political consciousness that demands more from Shepard's characters and makes them more responsible for their own actions.

As Shepard's politics shifted, his plays became more accessible, including *Buried Child* (1979), a drama about a family that must come to terms with its secrets, which won the Pulitzer Prize. Shepard's ability to create complex characters in such plays as *True West* (1980), *Fool For Love* (1983), and *A Lie of the Mind* (1985) make his earlier work seem cartoonish and dated—the work of a clever young writer determined to shock and outrage. The later plays continue to deal with physical and psychological violence, but with more sophistication. The tension between the two brothers in *True West*, for example, is presented with greater skill and humor than the earlier, angrier Shepard could manage.

Critics also have noted that in Shepard's later plays the female characters are more fully realized. Even as Shepard continues to probe the male need to dominate, women are stronger and simply more present on the stage.

Like Eugene O'NEILL, Shepard is an uneven playwright but a relentlessly experimental one. He has been willing to risk more onstage than most American playwrights, although certainly the frenzy of creativity that marked his early period as a playwright is over. Since *A Lie of the Mind*, he has produced only *States of Shock* (1991) and *Simpatico* (1995).

Shepard has also had a successful career as a movie actor, beginning with a remarkable performance in *Days of Heaven* (1978). He often plays the kind of laconic Westerner presented in his plays. He has also made notable appearances in *Resurrection* (1980), *Frances* (1982), *Country* (1984), *Fool for Love* (1985), *Crimes of the Heart* (1986), and *The Right Stuff* (1983), which earned him an Academy Award as best supporting actor.

As a screenwriter, Shepard won a Golden Palm Award at the Cannes Film Festival for *Paris, Texas* (1984). He has also written screenplays for *Me and My Brother* (1967), *Zabriskie Point* (1969), *Ringaleevio* (1971), and *Far North* (1988).

Shepard's short fiction and poetry have been collected in *Hawk Moon: A Book of Short Stories, Poems, and Monologues* (1973), *Motel Chronicles* (1982), and *Cruising Paradise* (1996).

Sources

Bottoms, Stephen J. *The Theatre of Sam Shepard: States of Crisis.* New York: Cambridge University Press, 1998.
Wade, Leslie A. *Sam Shepard and the American Theatre.* Westport, Conn.: Greenwood Press, 1997.
Wilcox, Leonard, ed. *Rereading Shepard: Contemporary Critical Essays on the Plays of Sam Shepard.* New York: St. Martin's Press, 1993.

Sherwood, Robert Emmet (1896–1955)
playwright, biographer

Robert Sherwood was born and grew up in New Rochelle, New York. He was educated at Harvard and served in World War I. In 1919 he became the drama critic for VANITY FAIR and then an editor at *Life* magazine, where he reviewed films with a notable seriousness, applying to this new art standards then reserved for the theater. In New York, he was associated with the writers of the ALGONQUIN ROUND TABLE. Although he wrote several plays that earned some praise and popularity in the early 1930s—especially *The Petrified Forest* (1935)—he shot to the forefront of the American theater later in the decade with two Pulitzer Prize–winning dramas: *Idiot's Delight* (1936) and *Abe Lincoln in Illinois* (1938). These plays and others are notable for their direct and realistic portrayal of important public figures and issues. Sherwood's earnest, liberal point of view now makes his work seem too didactic, too forced.

Sherwood also achieved great success in Hollywood, writing the screenplay for *Rebecca* (1940), Alfred Hitchcock's classic film based on the Daphne du Maurier novel, and *The Best Years of Our Lives* (1946), an ambitious film about American soldiers returning home.

The public-spirited Sherwood served in the Franklin Delano Roosevelt administration during WORLD WAR II. In *Roosevelt and Hopkins* (1948), he wrote about his experience in the Office of War Information and earned another Pulitzer Prize.

Sources

Brown, John Mason. *The Worlds of Robert E. Sherwood: Mirror to His Times, 1896–1939.* New York: Harper & Row, 1965.
Shuman, R. Baird. *Robert E. Sherwood.* New York: Twayne, 1964.

Shirer, William Lawrence (1904–1993) *journalist*

Born in Illinois, William Shirer spent much of his life as a war correspondent. He is best known for his writings on Germany: *Berlin Diary* (1941) and *The Rise and Fall of the Third Reich* (1960). Along with Vincent Sheean, Dorothy THOMPSON, and John GUNTHER, he is one of the most important American journalists of the 20th century. He wrote three volumes of memoirs: *20th Century Journey* (1976), *Nightmare Years* (1984), and *20th Century Journey: A Native's Return 1945–1988* (1990).

Sources

Widner, James F. "Commentators: William L. Shirer." Radio Days: Broadcast Journalism and Historical Events. Available on-line. URL: http://www.otr.com/shirer.html. Updated January 15, 2000.

short story *genre*

The modern American short story has its beginnings with Sherwood ANDERSON, whose stories in WINESBURG, OHIO (1919) marked a movement away from 19th-century REALISM in order to explore in greater psychological depth the inner lives of characters and their ambiguous relationships with their communities and environment. Anderson's characters are often isolated and alienated. They are regarded by their contemporaries as grotesques, a point Anderson emphasizes in titling a chapter of *Winesburg* "The Book of the Grotesque."

In Anderson's sensitive and probing exploration of misfits can be found the origins of William FAULKNER's gothic and eccentric characters in stories such as "A Rose for Emily" (1931). Faulkner paid tribute to Anderson as his mentor, pointing out that it was Anderson who provided the model for both the themes and techniques of modern short fiction. Anderson's sense of place and his re-creation of small-town life, for example, clearly inspired Faulkner to explore—as he put it—his "postage stamp of native soil."

Similarly, Ernest HEMINGWAY saw in Anderson a harbinger of characters like Nick ADAMS, the central character in Hemingway's first short story collection, *In Our Time*. Nick is a version of Anderson's George Willard in *Winesburg, Ohio*, although Nick's view of existence is bleaker than George's. *In Our Time* also emulated *Winesburg* by constructing short stories so interrelated in terms of theme, technique, and character that they were virtually an episodic novel. Faulkner created this kind of innovative, integrated short story collection in *Go Down, Moses* (1942).

Both Hemingway and Faulkner perceived that Anderson had invented a supple form of short story collection that elevated fiction to the heights of the most sophisticated music, employing contrapuntal effects akin to the work of European masters like James Joyce and D. H. Lawrence. In *Winesburg, Ohio*, for example, each story examines a character's life in the town, a story that implicitly comments on and sometimes provides a counterpoint to the protagonist George Willard's aspirations and beliefs.

F. Scott FITZGERALD took many of Anderson's themes and techniques and applied them to urban settings and the world of the rich. An early story such as "Winter Dreams" (1922) centers on Dexter Green, whose life declines from early youthful enthusiasm to an early, disenchanted middle age. As a youth, Dexter caddies in the summer for wealthy patrons and has winter dreams of enjoying their status, power, and privilege. Caddying for Judy Jones, Dexter views her as an embodiment of his American dream of success. (Critics have pointed out how this story foreshadows Fitzgerald's masterpiece, THE GREAT GATSBY). The irony is that as soon as Dexter becomes a successful businessman, his illusions about Judy are shattered: He realizes that she is vain and superficial, and that his own material prosperity cannot sustain him. America becomes, in this story, a kind of wonder that is unfulfilled.

Fitzgerald, Hemingway, and Faulkner all used the short story form in the 1920s and early 1930s to portray post–WORLD WAR I disillusionment. Dorothy PARKER used the life of a party girl to explore similar themes in "Big Blonde" (1929). Hazel Morse, for all her good times, suffers from despair. She cannot find meaning in her life. Her husband deserts her. She descends into long periods of drinking and drug use. Parker's exquisite sense of the short story form and her powers of observation are so precise that Hazel's story is not merely tawdry or pathetic. In fact, Hazel is keenly aware of her predicament, and confronts her disillusionment. Parker's style has often been compared to Hemingway's, and there is no doubt that she felt his influence and paid tribute to it. Like other modern masters of the short story, Parker dramatizes the telling moments in her characters' lives, avoiding both melodrama and sentimentality. Hazel, for example, does not commit suicide; she does not die of drink; instead she persists, coping as best she can with the shambles of her life.

In stories such as "Flowering Judas" (1930), Katherine Anne PORTER exhibited a command of the intricate detail of short fiction. Eminent critics such as Robert Penn WARREN praised Porter for her "rich surface detail" that contributed to the overall unity of her work, her pairing of physical reality and moral significance. Porter went beyond Parker, however, in exploring not only the fate and the psychology of individuals but also how their plight reflected the nature of existence itself. Thus in "Flowering Judas" the main character, Laura, confronts her realization that the Mexican Revolution will not fulfill her political ideals. What is more, she sees that there is something inherent in idealism itself that dooms it to destruction. This realization is strikingly portrayed in the figure of the fat revolutionary leader, Braggioni, whose sloppy posture indicates a careless grasp of life itself. The story's climactic scene—when Laura, in a dream, eats leaves from the Judas tree—symbolizes not only Laura's self-destructive failure to affirm a noble cause, but also of her withdrawal from life itself. There is a grandeur in Porter's vision, a sweeping view of civilization, that give her stories an unrivaled sense of authority and expands the form of the short story itself.

In "Petrified Man" (1941), Eudora WELTY demonstrated that she was a brilliant disciple of Porter's and a master of dialogue that becomes the voice of a community. Like Porter, Welty's stories read like economical summations of civilization—although Welty tends to have a lighter touch. She uses the short story form in "Petrified Man" to explore the environs of a beauty shop, in which each character is revealed almost exclusively by the cruel words she uses. Like Parker, Welty is a master of irony, describing the run-down shop in which these women seek to beautify themselves. But there is a good deal of comedy in the way the characters speak, which is itself a mark of what Welty has contributed to the short story genre: the use of satire for purposes of both social criticism and good-natured celebration of an infinite variety of human types.

In the 1930s and early 1940s, such writers as John STEINBECK, Richard WRIGHT, and Ralph ELLISON introduced proletarian, ethnic, sexual and racial themes to the American short story. Steinbeck's "The Chrysanthemums" (1938), set in the Salinas Valley of California during the DEPRESSION years, creates in Elisa Allen a vibrant woman stimulated by sexual and creative impulses. Unlike Hemingway, however, whose characters are usually uprooted and living apart from their native land, Steinbeck's characters seem to emerge from their environment almost as part of the natural landscape. In "Big Boy Leaves Home" (1938), Wright takes "Big Boy" through a 24-hour period, recreating African-American speech patterns and adapting his theme—white hostility to blacks—to the mainstream American short story's probing of a youth's initiation into life, as exemplified by Anderson's George Willard and Hemingway's Nick Adams. Wright, however, shows the lurking violence and the explosive nature of racism that few white authors, except William Faulkner in "Dry September" (1930), portrayed as vividly in this period. In "King of the Bingo Game," Ralph Ellison showed how he had absorbed Richard Wright's social criticism and applied it to a somewhat broader, more universal study of the alienated or underground man. As in Ellison's masterpiece, the novel *INVISIBLE MAN,* the protagonist of Ellison's story is a southerner confronting the alien environment of the North. He has trouble as much with other African Americans as with whites, and like the narrator of Ellison's novel, the self-named Bingo King is searching for an identity that draws on but surmounts the liabilities of both races.

In the 1950s the American short story benefited from the still flourishing renaissance in southern literature, dominated then by Flannery O'CONNOR and Carson MCCULLERS, and from an explosion of challenging stories from Jewish writers such as Saul BELLOW, Bernard MALAMUD, and Philip ROTH. O'Connor and McCullers continued the tradition of southern gothic, often presenting bizarre and grotesque characters, but with a brilliance of style, moral commentary, and in O'Connor's case, religious intensity that equaled the best writing of Katherine Anne Porter. McCullers achieved poetic intensity with *The Ballad of the Sad Cafe* (1951), a long short story, or novella, the story of an improbable match between a male hunchbacked dwarf and a female giant. O'Connor's stories are savagely ironic. In "Good Country People," for example, she demolishes pastoral notions associated with rural and small-town life, finding a monstrosity in so-called good country people that is reminiscent of but more astringent than Sherwood Anderson's view. There is a hard-edged intellectuality that separates O'Connor both from Anderson and from her contemporaries Eudora Welty and Carson McCullers, the former seldom as bleak as O'Connor, and the latter far more romantic and sensationalistic.

In the effort to use the short story as a way to explore ideas about human character, Saul Bellow is probably O'Connor's closest match in the flood of great Jewish-American literature in the 1950s. *Seize the Day* (1956), a novella, is a masterpiece that capitalizes on the short story's compression of setting and theme. The story takes place on New York City's West Side and focuses on a few hours in the life of its protagonist, Tommy Wilhelm. Although Tommy is a passive hero—even what might be called a "loser"—Bellow endows him with a questing sensibility: He has to "believe that he can know why he exists." Bernard Malamud, Bellow's Jewish-American contemporary and a virtuoso of the short story form, develops similar characters but with an exquisite comic touch and a blending of realism and fantasy in such works as "The Jewbird" and "The Magic Barrel," which probe the fate of being Jewish and American with moral intensity. J. D. SALINGER, in stories such as "A Perfect Day for Bananafish" (1953), explored his Jewish background less overtly and developed a whimsical, idiosyncratic style that blended tragedy and comedy—Salinger's response to the traumas of WORLD WAR II and the efforts to Americans to adjust to postwar life. A slightly younger Philip Roth applied the techniques of Bellow and Malamud to both city settings and ethnic themes in his groundbreaking collection of stories, *Goodbye, Columbus* (1959). In stories like "The Conversion of the Jews" he brought a zany humor and ironic criticism of Jewish-American chauvinism that made him a controversial literary figure.

Influenced by avant-garde European and South American writers such as Franz Kafka and Jorge Luis Borges, a new generation of American short story writers in the 1960s such as Donald BARTHELME and John BARTH explore themes that double back, so to speak, on the short story form itself. The story becomes a contrivance, a fiction the writer explores for the sheer pleasure and inventiveness of it. Stories like Barth's "Lost in the Funhouse" have been called metafiction because they are about writing fiction. These stories have been lauded for their experimental quality and also condemned by such critics as Gore VIDAL for their sterile, rather academic tone that cuts fiction off from a general readership.

Since the 1970s it is arguable that the major energy in short fiction has come from women writers such as Toni Cade BAMBARA, Ann BEATTIE, and Cynthia OZICK, who explore a range of class and race and ethnic issues. The master of the form in this period has been Grace PALEY. In her work women's issues, family issues, and political issues fuse in the subtle handling of themes and of dialogue. Raymond CARVER, especially in his early work, revives a minimalist style that recalls the spareness and elegance of Hemingway's early stories.

In every generation major American writers have contributed to the evolution of the short story. Among the classics of the 20th-century American short story are Ring LARDNER's "Haircut" (1929); Zora Neale HURSTON's "Sweat" (1926); Erskine CALDWELL's "Saturday Afternoon" (1931); Willa CATHER's "Neighbour Rosicky" (1932); Langston HUGHES's "The Blues I'm Playing" (1934); William SAROYAN's "The Daring Young Man on the Flying Trapeze" (1934); Conrad Aiken's "Silent Snow, Secret Snow" (1934);

Kay Boyle's "Astronomer's Wife" (1936); William Carlos Williams's "The Use of Force" (1938); James Thurber's "The Secret Life of Walter Mitty" (1942); Nelson Algren's "How the Devil Came Down Division Street" (1945); Shirley Jackson's "The Lottery" (1949); Jean Stafford's "The Interior Castle" (1953); John Cheever's "The Country Husband" (1958); Mavis Gallant's "My Heart is Broken" (1961); Tillie Olson's "Tell Me a Riddle" (1961); John Updike's "A & P" (1962); James Baldwin's "Sonny's Blues" (1965); Leslie Marmon Silko's "The Man to Send Rain Clouds" (1969); Joyce Carol Oates's "Where are You Going, Where Have You Been?" (1970); Alice Walker's "To Hell with Dying" (1973); Louise Erdrich's "The Red Convertible" (1974); Raymond Carver's "What We Talk About When We Talk About Love" (1981); Bobbie Ann Mason's "Shiloh" (1982); and Sandra Cisneros's "Mexicans" (1991).

Sources

Gelfant, Blanche H. and Lawrence Graver, eds. *The Columbia Companion to the Twentieth-Century American Short Story.* New York: Columbia University Press, 2001.

Peden, William Harwood. *The American Short Story: Continuity and Change, 1940–1975.* Boston: Houghton Mifflin, 1975.

Ross, Danforth. *The American Short Story.* Minneapolis: University of Minnesota Press, 1961.

Stevick, Philip, ed. *The American Short Story 1900–1945.* Boston: Twayne, 1984.

Voss, Arthur. *The American Short Story: A Critical Survey.* Norman: University of Oklahoma Press, 1973.

Werlock, Abby H. P. *The Facts On File Companion to the American Short Story.* New York: Facts On File, 2000.

Silko, Leslie Marmon (1948–) *novelist, poet, playwright, critic*

Born in Albuquerque, New Mexico, Silko grew up in a mixed-heritage family (Laguna, Mexican, and white). She absorbed her family's rich tradition of storytelling and tribal leadership. She rode horses and hunted in the traditional way, but she also attended the University of New Mexico, where she became interested in writing. She graduated from college in 1969 and entered law school, but abandoned it for graduate study in English. After an early marriage and divorce, she lived in Alaska and wrote poetry and short fiction. *Laguna Woman,* her first book of poetry, immediately established her as a major voice in Native American writing. *Storyteller* (1981), with its innovative amalgam of short fiction, poetry, family photographs, commentary, and autobiography, so enhanced her reputation that she won a MacArthur "genius" award in 1981. Her stories and poems are frequently anthologized.

Silko's first novel, *Ceremony* (1977), explores the life of a young veteran, part Laguna and part white, who returns home from Vietnam and tries to adjust to pueblo life. *Al-* *manac of the Dead* (1991) is an epic novel with multiple subplots concerning the uprising of America's deracinated indigenous peoples. *Gardens in the Dunes* (1999), set in the 1890s, follows the lives of two sisters who are separated and then reunited, seeking some way to still live on the land while coping with the encroachment of the capitalist world.

Silko has written one play, *Lullaby* (1976), and several volumes of nonfiction: *The Delicacy and Strength of Lace: Letters Between Leslie Marmon Silko and James Wright* (1986); *Sacred Water: Narratives and Pictures* (1993); and *Yellow Woman and a Beauty of the Spirit: Essays on Native American Life Today* (1996).

Sources

Salyer, Greg. *Leslie Marmon Silko.* New York: Twayne, 1997.

Simic, Charles (1938–) *poet*

Born in Yugoslavia of Serb parents, Simic was brought to Chicago in 1954. He began writing poetry in high school, already having mastered English. He studied at the University of Chicago and New York University and served in the army. He published *Selected Poems 1963–1983* in 1985. His poems are brief, highly concentrated mixtures of REALISM, myth, and occasionally SURREALISM. He won a Pulitzer Prize for *The World Doesn't End* (1989). His other collections include *Selected Poems, 1963–1983* (1990), and *Jackstraws: Poems* (1999).

Simic has also been a prolific translator. Among his titles are *Four Yugoslav Poets: Ivan V. Lalic, Branko Miljkovic, Milorad Pavic, Ljubomir Simovic* (1970), *The Little Box: Translations from the Serbian* (1980), and *The Horse Has Six Legs: An Anthology of Serbian Poetry* (1992).

The Uncertain Certainty: Interviews, Essays, and Notes on Poetry appeared in 1985; *Wonderful Words, Silent Truth: Essays on Poetry and a Memoir* in 1990; and *The Unemployed Fortune-Teller: Essays and Memoirs* in 1994.

Sources

Stitt, Peter. *Uncertainty & Plenitude: Five Contemporary Poets.* Iowa City: University of Iowa Press, 1997.

Weigl, Bruce. *Charles Simic: Essays on the Poetry.* Ann Arbor: University of Michigan Press, 1996.

Simon, Neil (Marvin Neil Simon) (1927–) *playwright, screenwriter, television writer*

Neil Simon was born in the Bronx and educated in New York City public schools and at New York University. He served in the Army Air Force reserve during World War II and then, in 1946, went to work at CBS as a comedy writer. For the next 15 years he worked on scripts for the *Phil Silvers Arrow Show* (1948), the *Tallulah Bankhead Show* (1951), the *Sid Caesar Show* (1956–1957), and the *Garry Moore*

Show (1959–1960). One of Simon's later plays, *Laughter on the 23rd Floor* (1993), deals with his television career.

In 1960 Simon turned to writing for the stage and produced a series of commercial successes, light comedies that feature jokes and one-line gags reminiscent of his television writing but with increasingly sophisticated stories and well-rounded characters. Among his early hits are *Come Blow Your Horn* (1960), *Barefoot in the Park* (1963), *The Odd Couple* (1965), *Sweet Charity* (1966), *Plaza Suite* (1968), *Promises, Promises* (1968), and *Last of the Red Hot Lovers* (1969).

Beginning with *Plaza Suite*, Simon's comedies grew darker, more poignant, and not so easily resolved as the situation comedy plots of his earlier work. *The Sunshine Boys* (1972), about a vaudeville team, two aging comedians who had split up years before and are attempting a reunion, drew not only on Simon's understanding of show business and its people, but also on a desire to dramatize human conflicts that cannot be erased simply with humor. These two old pros have to go beyond "routines" to get at the nub of what bothers them.

Simon drew directly on his own experience in his trilogy *Brighton Beach Memoirs* (1982), *Biloxi Blues* (1984), and *Broadway Bound* (1986). The plays shift from scenes of Simon's own childhood and family relationships to his basic training in Mississippi to his career on Broadway. For the first time, critics began to treat Simon as a serious artist. *Lost in Yonkers* (1991), the story of two brothers that bears some resemblance to Arthur MILLER's *The Price*, was awarded a Pulitzer Prize.

No playwright has written more insightfully about the world of show business and the role of Jews in the entertainment industry. Simon is perhaps the last of a generation of writers who inherited the traditions of vaudeville, television, and Broadway, then lost their hold in the 1980s. Simon's disenchantment with the changes in Broadway culture led to his decision to produce *London Suite* (1994) OFF-BROADWAY, although *Little Me* (1999) did receive a Broadway production. Like other playwrights of his generation, Simon has found it increasingly difficult to write plays that can be both hilarious and serious, appealing to Broadway audiences who want to be entertained as well as to critics who want modern American drama to treat serious issues. However, plays such as *Proposals* (1997), *Dinner Party* (2000), and *45 Seconds From Broadway*, have had Broadway productions.

Simon has had a successful career adapting his plays for the screen, writing the scripts for *Barefoot in the Park* (1967), *The Odd Couple* (1968), *Plaza Suite* (1971), *The Last of the Red Hot Lovers* (1972), *The Sunshine Boys* (1975), *California Suite* (1981), *Brighton Beach Memoirs* (1987), *Biloxi Blues* (1998), and *Lost in Yonkers* (1993). He has also produced original screenplays, including *The Out-of-Towners* (1970), *The Heartbreak Kid* (1972), *The Goodbye Girl* (1977), and *Chapter Two* (1979).

Simon's plays for television include *Broadway Bound* (1992) and *Jake's Women* (1996). Simon has also published two memoirs: *Rewrites* (1996) and *The Play Goes On* (1999).

Sources

Johnson, Robert K. *Neil Simon.* Boston: Twayne, 1983.
Konas, Gary, ed. *Neil Simon: A Casebook.* New York: Garland, 1997.

Simpson, Louis Aston Marantz (1923–) *poet, critic, novelist*

Louis Simpson was born in Jamaica and came to the United States to attend Columbia University. He served in the army in World War II and returned to complete his education at Columbia and to work in publishing. He earned a Ph.D. from Columbia and began a teaching career at the University of California at Berkeley; he retired from the State University of New York at Stony Brook in 1993.

Simpson's earliest work was traditional in form and content. *At the End of the Open Road* (1963) signaled a new approach to poetry, featuring a more concrete, spare, and open verse that won him a Pulitzer Prize. One of his later major collections, *People Live Here: Selected Poems, 1949–1983* (1983), delves into his WORLD WAR II experience, his exploration of America, Russia (where his Jewish mother's family lived), and the contrasts between his down-to-earth father and his romantic mother. The collection also reflects his great feeling for nature in poems like "As Birds Are Fitted to the Boughs."

Simpson's range is impressive. He writes with the precision and understatement of Chekhov, an obvious influence on Simpson's work, and the expansiveness of Walt Whitman, who has also clearly been an inspiration for an immigrant keenly intent on finding his place in America.

Simpson published *Collected Poems* in 1988. His later collections include *In the Room We Share* (1990), *Jamaica Poems* (1993), and *There You Are* (1995).

Simpson has published two novels: *Riverside Drive* (1962) and *North of Jamaica* (1972).

Simpson also has a considerable reputation as a learned and provocative critic. His nonfiction includes *Three on a Tower: The Lives and Works of Ezra Pound, T. S. Eliot and William Carlos Williams* (1975); *A Revolution in Taste: Studies of Dylan Thomas, Allen Ginsberg, Sylvia Plath, and Robert Lowell* (1978); *A Company of Poets* (1981); *The Character of the Poet* (1986); and *Ships Going into the Blue: Essays and Notes on Poetry* (1994).

Simpson published his autobiography, *The King My Father's Wreck*, in 1995. His *Selected Prose* appeared in 1989.

Sources

Lazer, Hank, ed. *On Louis Simpson: Depths Beyond Happiness.* Ann Arbor: University of Michigan Press, 1988.

Sinclair, Upton Beall (1878–1968) *journalist, novelist*

An activist writer, Upton Sinclair was an outspoken Socialist and critic of American society. His most famous book is *The Jungle* (1906), a novel that exposed the primitive and brutal conditions in the CHICAGO stockyards. Its main character, Jurgis Rudkus, a Slavic immigrant, is radicalized by the degrading environment and becomes a crusading Socialist. The novel is said to have influenced the passage of the Pure Food and Drug Act (1906). Sinclair was part of the muckraking movement—so termed in 1906 by President Theodore Roosevelt because writers like Sinclair "raked the muck"—that is, sought out instances of corruption in politics and business and exaggerated (in Roosevelt's view) what was wrong with American life.

In 1934 Sinclair ran as the Democratic nominee for governor of California. He called for an end to poverty and was defeated in a close election bitterly contested by opponents funded by the movie studios. Undoubtedly, his muckraking reputation fueled the efforts to defeat him.

Sinclair's later novels include *King Coal* (1917); *Boston* (1928), based on the SACCO-VANZETTI CASE; and *World's End* (1940), the first of several novels featuring Lanny Budd, who uses his family fortune to fight injustice throughout the world. Sinclair wrote about his career in journalism in *The Brass Check* (1919) and *American Outpost: A Book of Reminiscences* (1932). He published his *Autobiography* in 1962.

Sources

Heims, Dieter, ed. *Upton Sinclair: Literature and Social Reform.* New York: Peter Lang, 1990.

Yoder, Jon A. *Upton Sinclair.* New York: Unger, 1975.

Singer, Isaac Bashevis (1904–1991) *novelist, short story writer*

Singer was born in Leoncin, Poland, and spent most of his boyhood in Warsaw. Although he trained as a rabbi, Singer was attracted to literature and was mentored by his older brother, Israel Joshua, also a writer. Isaac loved Jewish mysticism and supernatural tales, while his brother was more of a rationalist. Isaac began publishing his work in 1925. By 1935 he had settled in America, well aware of what Hitler's accession to power would mean to the Jews in Europe.

Singer's work in America was published in the *Jewish Daily Forward* in Yiddish. *The Family Moskat*, a novel, was translated into English in 1950, but it was not until 1953, with Saul BELLOW's translation of "Gimpel the Fool" in the PARTISAN REVIEW, that Singer attracted the attention of critics and general readers. Thereafter his stories appeared in COMMENTARY, the NEW YORKER, *Harper's*, and *Esquire*.

A sentence from "Gimpel the Fool" has often been cited to explain Singer's approach to fiction: "No doubt the world is entirely an imaginary world, but is only once removed from the real world." Singer has been praised for his uncanny ability to combine fantasy and reality, the imaginative world and the world of reason, in his stories and novels. Although he was not a devout believer, he draws on Jewish faith to challenge the rationalistic view of the world. *Satan in Goray*, Singer's first novel, published in Yiddish in 1935 and translated into English in 1955, typifies his use of the gothic, historical, and mystical elements of the Jewish tradition. This work also reflects the influence of Edgar Allan Poe and Dostoevsky, for Singer was deeply read in European and American literature. The novel centers on two historical events: the Cossack rebellion of 1648–1649, which resulted in the deaths of 100,000 Jews, and the messianic movement called Shabbeteanism, named after the self-proclaimed messiah Shabbetai Avi of the same period. The novel traces the fate of the Jewish survivors of the Cossack pogrom. In 1666 they moved back to the village of Goray, seeking redemption but also divided into opposing factions, which in turn led to a degradation of spiritual values and even demonoic possession. In some ways, the novel is prophetic of the forces in Singer's own time that would degrade religion, tear apart the fabric of society, and shake the faith of individuals.

The Magician of Lublin (1960) is a more symbolic novel but also a more psychological study, focusing on a single individual, Yasha Mazur, who becomes, like every individual, a magician in the sense that he walks a "tightrope merely inches from disaster." In spite of this sense of impending doom, Mazur is an exuberant character, battling the evil within himself. He says "everything is fate," yet he is constantly making choices and exercising his will.

These two novels, like Singer's other major works—*The Manor* (1967), *The Estate* (1969), *The Slave* (1962), and *Enemies: A Love Story* (1972)—express the sensibility of a man fully engaged in 20th-century history. At the same time Singer sought a perspective on that history by searching a more remote past and calling on the forces of the supernatural to define the limitations of the modern world found in the Enlightenment values of reason and humanistic standards. The demonic imagery of his stories and novels is a constant reminder of how difficult it is for human beings to control their irrational impulses. At the same time, the sheer charm, humor, and fetching ironies of Singer's stories make them entertainment of the highest order.

Singer collected his stories in several classic volumes, including *Gimpel the Fool and Other Stories* (1957), *The Spinoza of Market Street* (1961), and *A Friend of Kafka and Other Stories* (1970). His *Collected Stories* was published in 1982.

Singer wrote a memoir about his life in Poland, *In My Father's Court* (1966). He also published several volumes of fiction for children, including *Zlateh the Goat and Other Stories* (1966), *When Shlemiel Went to Warsaw and Other Stories* (1968), *Why Noah Chose the Dove* (1974), *The Golem* (1982), and *Stories for Children* (1984).

Sources

Farrell, Grace, ed. *Critical Essays on Isaac Bashevis Singer.* New York: G. K. Hall, 1996.

Hadda, Janet. *Isaac Bashevis Singer: A Life.* New York: Oxford University Press, 1997.

Singer, Israel Joshua (1893–1944) *novelist*

Like his brother, Isaac, I. J. Singer was born in Poland, where he began his career as a Polish-Yiddish novelist. He came to the United States in 1934 sponsored by Abraham CAHAN, the father of the modern Jewish-American novel. Although Israel and his brother continued to write about Poland in Yiddish, translations of their work have a significant impact on American literature. Israel's *The Brothers Ashkenazi* (1936) is a magnificent saga of the Polish Jews, and as its title suggests, it is a serious work that merits comparison with Dostoevsky. Singer also published *In Die Berg* (1942), a novel set in the United States, and *The Family Carnovsky* (1943), the story of a Jewish family wandering across Europe.

Sources

Norich, Anita. *The Homeless Imagination in the Fiction of Israel Joshua Singer.* Bloomington: Indiana University Press, 1991.

Sinclair, Clive. *The Brothers Singer.* New York: Schocken Books, 1983.

Smith, Betty (1904–1972) *novelist*

A native New Yorker, Smith is best known for her novel *A Tree Grows in Brooklyn* (1943), made into a successful film and musical. The novel evokes the early 20th-century city and the life of Frances Nolan, who overcomes poverty and other hardships to become as stalwart as the tree that grows through cracks in the sidewalk. Smith's other novels include *Tomorrow Will Be Better* (1948) and *Maggie-Now* (1958), stories of slum girls growing up in the city.

Smith, David Jeddie (1942–) *poet*

Born in Portsmouth, Virginia, Dave Smith was educated at the University of Virginia. After four years of service in the air force, he established a poetry magazine, *Back Door,* in 1969. He is an inventive, experimental poet, often probing the raw limits of human experience in such books as *The Fisherman's Whore* (1974) and *Drunks* (1975). He published *The Roundhouse Voices: Selected and New Poems* in 1985. His later work includes *Cuba Night: Poems* (1990), *Fate's Kite: Poems, 1991–1995* (1995), and *Floating on Solitude: Three Volumes of Poetry* (1996).

Sources

DeMott, Robert J. *Dave Smith: A Literary Archive.* Athens: Ohio University Libraries, 2000.

Smith, Lillian Eugenia (1897–1966) *novelist, social critic*

Lillian Smith was born in Florida and was employed as a social worker in Georgia. Her most notable work is *Strange Fruit* (1944), the story of a mulatto girl in love. Smith successfully dramatized her novel in 1945. She also wrote several nonfiction works about the Civil Rights movement and the menace of racism: *Killers of the Dream* (1949, revised 1961), *The Journey* (1954), and *Now Is the Time* (1955), a plea to implement the 1954 Supreme Court school desegregation decision swiftly. Smith wrote one memoir, *Memory of a Large Christmas* (1962). *How Am I to Be Heard?: Letters of Lillian Smith* appeared in 1993.

Sources

Blackwell, Louise. *Lillian Smith.* New York: Twayne, 1971.

Loveland, Anne C. *Lillian Smith: A Southerner Confronting the South: A Biography.* Baton Rouge: Louisiana State University Press, 1986.

Smith, Thorne (1892–1934) *humorist*

Smith made his name writing about his WORLD WAR I experiences in *Biltmore Oswald: The Diary of a Hapless Recruit* (1918). He followed this enormously popular book with the creation of an American original in *Topper* (1926), the fantasy tale of a man who returns from death to haunt the straitlaced banker Cosmo Topper. He wrote a sequel, *Topper Takes a Trip* (1932), and the character of Cosmo Topper appeared in both movies and a television series.

Sources

Thorne Smith: Haunts and By-Paths. Available on-line. URL: http://members.tripod.com/~JCHOMA/THORNE.html. Downloaded June 15, 2001.

"The Rebold Page: A Tribute to Thorne Smith." Available on-line. URL: http://www.geocities.com/Athens/Forum/9904/ Downloaded June 15, 2001.

Snodgrass, William DeWitt (1926–) *poet, translator*

Born in Wilkinsburg, Pennsylvania, W. D. Snodgrass grew up in Beaver Falls, another town in the western part of the state. He earned his B.A., M.A., and M.F.A. degrees from the University of Iowa and served in the navy during World War II. At Iowa he studied with Robert LOWELL, who became one of his great influences. Snodgrass has taught at the University of Rochester, Wayne State University, Syracuse University, Old Dominion University, and the University of Delaware.

His most influential collection of poetry is *Heart's Needle* (1959), his debut book, which won a Pulitzer Prize. Robert Lowell admitted that Snodgrass's form of CONFESSIONAL POETRY influenced him, and later Anne SEXTON, also a student of Lowell's, testified to the importance of Snodgrass's example. He led the way for poets who wanted to confront their emotional pain—in his case, the death of his daughter and tender memories of her—directly.

Snodgrass's later poetry seemed to many critics less groundbreaking, even though he continued in the confessional vein with his next book, *After Experience: Poems and Translations* (1968). Snodgrass's third book, *The Fuhrer Bunker: A Cycle of Poems in Progress* (1977) is a series of dramatic monologues—important Nazis who speak in different styles of verse according to their personalities. Josef Goebbels, for example, speaks in rhymed couplets. Snodgrass's deft handling of the dramatic monologue has been compared to Robert Browning's technique. *The Fuhrer Bunker: The Complete Cycle* was published in 1995.

Snodgrass published *Selected Poems, 1957–1987* in 1987, *Autumn Variations* in 1990, and *Each in His Season* in 1993. His translations include *Six Troubadour Songs* (1977), *Traditional Hungarian Songs* (1978), *Six Minnsinger Songs* (1983), *Selected Translations* (1998), and *Five Folk Ballads* (1999).

In Radical Pursuit: Critical Essays and Lectures was published in 1975 and *After-Images: Autobiographical Sketches* in 1999.

Sources

Haven, Stephen, ed. *The Poetry of W. D. Snodgrass: Everything Human.* Ann Arbor: University of Michigan Press, 1993.

Raisor, Philip, ed. *Tuned and Under Tension: The Recent Poetry of W. D. Snodgrass.* Newark: University of Delaware Press, 1998.

Snopes, Flem *character*

Snopes is the most prominent member of the predatory clan that dominates William FAULKNER's last novels, especially *The Hamlet, The Town,* and *The Mansion,* as well as several short stories. He is one of the most nefarious characters in American literature and also one of the most intriguing and mysterious, since he actually speaks very few times in Faulkner's fiction. It is what others say about him and how they react to him that makes Flem and the spread of Snopesism—connivance and economic skulduggery—so fascinating, threatening, and insidious. Flem seems inhuman in his coldness and calculation. He is ruthless and devious, driving men out of business. He preys on the respectable and makes them do his dirty work. He marries Eula Varner, the daughter of a respectable farmer, but the marriage is simply another bid for power. As soon as he attains power, he seeks social acceptance. Eventually, he is murdered by one of his relatives, Mink Snopes.

Sources

Beck, Warren. *Man in Motion: Faulkner's Trilogy.* Madison: University of Wisconsin Press, 1961.

Snyder, Gary Sherman (1930–) *poet*

Born in San Francisco, Gary Snyder grew up in the state of Washington and later moved to Portland, Oregon. He attended Reed College and there became interested in literature, anthropology, Native American myths, Buddhism, and Chinese calligraphy. By the late 1950s he was part of a group of poets that included Kenneth REXROTH, Lawrence FERLINGHETTI, Allen GINSBERG, and Jack KEROUAC, who were part of what came to be called the *beat* movement. These poets—also called BEATS—shared many of Snyder's interests. He appears as the character Japhy Ryder in Kerouac's novel *The Dharma Bums* (1958).

Snyder spent most of the 1960s in Japan studying Buddhism and keeping journals that he later transformed into a collection of poetry, *Regarding Wave* (1970). For Snyder, poetry is a form of spiritual discipline, even a kind of healing, since he traces the roots of poetry to shamanistic cults. His poetry is political in that he often criticizes Western values and their tendency to dominate the world.

Snyder won a Pulitzer Prize in 1974 for his collection *Turtle Island*. In 1992 he published *No Nature: New and Selected Poems*, which brought together work from eight previous collections. His subjects range from community to family to religion and an apocalyptic vision of a unified world. *Mountains and Rivers Without End* (1996) is a long poem Snyder worked on beginning in 1963.

Although he has often drawn from Asian forms of poetry, Snyder's work is also in the tradition of Henry David Thoreau, Carl SANDBURG, William Carlos WILLIAMS, and Ezra POUND, who introduced into English and American poetry an intense consciousness of Chinese literature.

Snyder has also written about his philosophy of life and about poetry in several nonfiction volumes: *Earth House Hold: Technical Notes and Queries to Fellow Dharma Revolutions* (1969); *The Old Ways* (1977); *He Who Hunted Birds in His Father's Village: The Dimension of a Haida Myth* (1979); *The Real Work: Interviews and Talks 1964–1979* (1980); *Passage Through India* (1983); *The Practice of the Wild* (1990); *Gary Snyder Papers* (1995); *A Place in Space: Ethics, Aesthetics, and Watersheds* (1995); and *The Gary Snyder Reader: Prose, Poetry, and Translations, 1952–1998* (1999).

Sources

Murphy, Patrick D. *A Place for Wayfaring: The Poetry and Prose of Gary Snyder.* Corvallis: Oregon State University Press, 2000.

Schuler, Robert. *Journeys Toward the Original Mind: The Long Poems of Gary Snyder.* New York: Peter Lang, 1994.

Sontag, Susan Lee (1933–) *essayist, novelist, dramatist, filmmaker*

Born in New York City, Susan Sontag grew up in Arizona and California. She earned a B.A. degree from the University of Chicago and an M.A. degree in philosophy from Harvard. She became a national intellectual figure with the publication of her essay "Notes on 'Camp,'" a brilliant report on how elite and popular works of contemporary art could be appreciated for both their style and sensuousness—a key term Sontag also employed in her signature essay, "Against Interpretation." Sontag's first two books of criticism, *Against Interpretation* (1966) and *Styles of Radical Will* (1971), established her reputation as an outspoken and controversial critic. She wrote from a deep immersion in European literature and on a wide range of subjects—from literature to film to theater to politics. Her early novels, *The Benefactor* (1963) and *Death Kit* (1967), were less well received and regarded as derivative of the French New Novel, which she had extolled in her essays. *On Photography* (1977) and *Illness as Metaphor* (1978) are her two best books of nonfiction, for they raise provocative questions about photography's relationship to REALISM and the documentary, and the way cancer has been used as a metaphor in literature and viewed in American culture. In 1992 Sontag resurrected her career as a novelist with *The Volcano Lover,* a well-received romantic novel about the story of Horatio Nelson, and William and Emma Hamilton. *In America* (2000), another historical novel, was respectfully reviewed but did not generate the same level of critical or popular acclaim. Sontag's other books include *Under the Sign of Saturn* (1980), *AIDS and Its Metaphors* (1989), and the published scripts of her films, *Duet for Cannibals* (1969) and *Brother Carl* (1974). Her play, *Alice in Bed,* which is about Alice James, the sister of William and Henry James, was published in 1993.

Sources

Poague, Leland, ed. *Conversations with Susan Sontag.* Jackson: University Press of Mississippi, 1995.

Rollyson, Carl and Lisa Paddock. *Susan Sontag: The Making of an Icon.* New York: W. W. Norton, 2000.

Rollyson, Carl. *Reading Susan Sontag.* Chicago: Ivan R. Dee, 2001.

Sorenson, Virginia (1912–) *novelist*

Born in Utah, Sorenson is best known for her fiction about Mormon life: *A Little Lower Than the Angels* (1942), *On This Star* (1946), *The Evening and the Morning* (1949), *Many Heavens* (1954), *Kingdom Come* (1960). *Man with the Key* (1974) is a departure, for it deals with the love of an older white woman for an African-American handyman. Sorenson has also written books for children. *Where Nothing is Long Ago* (1963) is a memoir of her Mormon childhood.

Sources

Geary, Edward A. "Virginia Sorensen." Available on-line. URL: http://www.media.utah.edu/UHE/s/SORENSEN%2CVIRGINIA.html. Downloaded June 15, 2001.

Sorrentino, Gilbert (1929–) *poet, novelist*

Sorrentino is known as an experimental writer. His books rarely have plots, and they often parody literary genres. *Steelwork* (1970) is set in BROOKLYN from the 1930s to WORLD WAR II. *Imaginary Qualities of Actual Things* (1971) is a savage send-up of New York literary life. *Mulligan Stew* (1979), Sorrentino's most notable work, is a comic novel about a novelist. Sorrentino experiments with four different points of view in a novel set in a New Jersey boardinghouse, *Aberration of Starlight* (1980), based partly on his own experience.

Sorrentino's poetry collections—*The Darkness Surrounds Us* (1960), *Black and White* (1964), *The Perfect Fiction* (1968), *Corrosive Sublimate* (1971), and *The Orangery* (1978)—demonstrate the influences of Ezra POUND, William Carlos WILLIAMS, and Robert CREELEY. Like them, his work treats the poem as an object in itself, a form. As he has stated, "form not only determines content but form *invents* content." Sorrentino's *Selected Poems* appeared in 1981. He has also written a book about the nature of the poet, *Splendide-Hotel* (1973).

Sorrentino's essays have been collected in *Something Said* (1984). From 1956 to 1960 he edited the LITTLE MAGAZINE *Neon,* publishing writers in the BEAT tradition.

Sorrentino's later work includes *Blue Pastoral* (1983); *Odd Number* (1985); *A Beehive Arranged on Humane Principles* (1986), a text based on the poems of Wallace STEVENS; *Rose Theatre* (1987); *Misterioso* (1989), a postmodern mystery story; *Under the Shadow* (1991); *Red the Fiend* (1995), about a child abuser; *Pack of Lies* (1997); and *The Sky Changes* (1998), a psychological novel.

Sources

Mackey, Louis. *Fact, Fiction, and Representation: Four Novels by Gilbert Sorrentino.* Columbia, S.C.: Camden House, 1997.

McPheron, William. *Gilbert Sorrentino: A Descriptive Bibliography.* Elmwood Park, Ill.: Dalkey Archive Press, 1991.

Soto, Gary (1952–) *poet, critic, short story writer*

A Chicano and native Californian, Soto has taught at the University of California, Berkeley, and produced several volumes of Chicano literature, including *The Elements of San Joaquin* (1977), *Black Hair* (1985), *Who Will Know Us?* (1990), *New and Selected Poems* (1995), *A Natural Man* (1999), *Nickel and Dime* (2000). *Lesser Evils* (1988) is a collection of essays, and *A Summer Life* (1990) recounts his early years.

His stories for young Chicanos are collected in *Baseball in April* (1990). For children he has also written *The Cat's Meow* (1987), the story of a cat who speaks Spanish; *Pacific Crossing* (1992), about a Chicano boy who spends a summer in Japan with a Japanese family; and *Snapshots From the Wedding* (1997), the story of a Chicana flower girl at a wedding.

Soto has also edited *California Childhood: Recollections and Stories of the Golden State* (1988) and *Pieces of the Heart: New Chicano Fiction* (1993).

Sources

McDougal Littell. "Author Spotlight: Gary Soto," Language Arts. Available on-line. URL: http://www.mcdougallittell. com/lit/guest/soto/index.htm. Downloaded June 15, 2001.

Sound and the Fury, The *William Faulkner* (1929)
novel

William FAULKNER's difficult but experimental novel about the Compson family and the South is among the author's most important works. The novel is divided into four sections: a STREAM-OF-CONSCIOUSNESS view of the Compsons by Benjy, then two very different views from his brothers Quentin and Jason, followed by a final section narrated in the third person.

The Compsons are an old southern family in decline. Mr. Compson, the father, is a tired, cynical man who speaks a great deal about the futility of human endeavor. His son Quentin is a brilliant student at Harvard, but Quentin is tortured by his inability to protect his sister, Caddy, who has been seduced by Dalton Ames. Quentin lives by an outmoded chivalric code and is embarrassed when he cannot stand up to Ames. He is also plagued with incestuous feelings toward Caddy. Conflicted over his inability to protect his sister or to assert his manhood, Quentin eventually commits suicide. His interior monologue or stream of consciousness is a record of his last day of life and of the thoughts that drive him to his last desperate act.

Caddy does not have her own section of the novel and is seen only through the eyes of her three brothers. First there is Benjy, an idiot who has been three years old for 30 years. He registers the world in sensory terms. He is, in fact, a kind of IMAGIST poet. He can accept Caddy on her own terms, not those of the chivalric Quentin or the cynical Jason. Caddy's tragedy is that there is no way she can assert her independence except through her sexuality. She chafes at the idea that she must represent the ideal of chaste southern womanhood.

Jason is the crudest and funniest of the brothers. His section of the novel is more comic monologue than stream of consciousness. It is as if Jason does not think, he just talks. He is fed up with the Compson air of superiority, especially since it has led to selling off the property so that Quentin can go to college while Jason stays home and works in a local store. The bitter Jason feels he is the only one who is keeping the family in some semblance of order.

The novel ends with a fourth section narrated in the third person. It begins with a magnificent description of Dilsey, the black family servant, who represents a life of endurance and self-respect in spite of the degrading conditions she has had to cope with. She is a strong, loving woman who embodies the values of family and community. This fourth section puts into perspective the subjective and fragmentary perspectives of the preceding monologues.

The novel is a prime example of the modernist ethos, in which the writer strives to find new forms of expression and to explore the threats to individual identity in the modern world. Faulkner's work also probes the reactions of characters in a changing society. Some, like Quentin, resist those changes, even though their consciousness is itself the product of change, for he knows that his family is in decline and that his chivalric view of the world is outmoded. Others, like Jason, cope with life and yet ironically have virtually no understanding of how or why their society is changing. Jason is the supreme rationalist, finding reasons for all of his self-serving behavior. At the other end of spectrum, there is Dilsey, a woman of faith who serves others selflessly. Faulkner's achievement is to weld his brilliant style—his ability to portray different voices and states of mind—with an abiding moral vision of the individual and society.

Sources

Minter, David, ed. *The Sound and the Fury: An Authoritative Text, Backgrounds and Contexts, Criticism.* New York: W. W. Norton, 1987.
Polk, Noel, ed. *New Essays on The Sound and the Fury.* New York: Cambridge University Press, 1993.
Ross, Stephen M. and Noel Polk. *Reading Faulkner: The Sound and the Fury: Glossary and Commentary.* Jackson: University Press of Mississippi, 1996.

South, the

Twentieth-century southern literature has been dominated by the figure of William FAULKNER. No other writer has presented more beautiful and more scathing representations of his native region. Faulkner's fiction confronts the legacy of the Civil War, of racism, and of family traditions in both tragic and comic terms. Most of all, however, his major work shows a South in the midst of changes that might seem regrettable in certain respects but that are also inevitable, as Faulkner implies in such works as his Snopes trilogy. In his moral concerns and his sheer brilliance of language and original handling of the novel and short story forms, Faulkner set the highest possible standard for southern and indeed, all American writers.

Other southern writers of Faulkner's generation recognized his greatness. Some, like Robert Penn WARREN, were in the vanguard of those explaining Faulkner's work to the puzzled public. Warren's novels, especially ALL THE KING'S MEN (1946), and his poetry are suffused with the same keen Faulknerian sense of the impact of the past on the present. Warren's achievement has been to extend that consciousness to a direct confrontation with politics. Unlike other southerners of the same period—such as Allen TATE or Stark

YOUNG—Warren does not use the historical novel merely to celebrate or sentimentalize the southern past and its lost causes. Instead, through the figure of Willie STARK, he shows that history must reckon with but also transcend the values of the past.

Eudora WELTY, who has perhaps come closest to matching Faulkner's brilliance of language if not his originality in the novel form, has fastened much more on the lighter, comic side of southern culture, although her work too has acknowledged the darker aspects of her community. Like her mentor, Katherine Anne PORTER, Welty's South is most vivid in her short stories.

Later southern writers, including Flannery O'CONNOR and Carson MCCULLERS, have emulated many of Faulkner's gothic techniques while also focusing on female characters and religious themes, adding a great depth to southern fiction as a whole.

The post–World War II southern generation of writers is typified by William STYRON, whose first novel, *Lie Down in Darkness* (1951), is written with a sensitivity, intensity, and technical brilliance that recalls Faulkner's THE SOUND AND THE FURY. Still later southern writers like Reynolds PRICE have toned down the gothic elements and followed Welty's lead.

By the 1980s southern literature had become too diverse to speak of it any longer as a uniform phenomenon. Although writers such as Walker PERCY, Reynolds PRICE, and William STYRON remained steeped in the South and the tradition of southern literature, there has been no single writer with the authority to rival, let alone replace, Faulkner's example.

Sources
Cash, W. J. *The Mind of the South.* New York: Alfred A. Knopf, 1941.

Escott, Paul D., ed. *W. J. Cash and the Minds of the South.* Baton Rouge: Louisiana State University Press, 1992.

Rubin, Louis D., ed. *History of Southern Literature.* Baton Rouge: Louisiana State University Press, 1985.

Woodward, C. Vann. *The Burden of Southern History.* Baton Rouge: Louisiana State University Press, 1960.

South Atlantic Quarterly periodical
Founded in 1902, the journal is sponsored by Duke University Press. Traditionally it covered southern history and culture. In recent years, it has reflected changes in the Duke English department, which has used the journal as a way to promote more innovative and controversial theories of literary criticism.

Southern Review periodical
Founded and edited Cleanth Brooks and Robert Penn WARREN between 1935 and 1942, this journal featured some of the best writing by Caroline GORDON, Eudora WELTY, and Katherine Anne PORTER. It also championed the NEW CRITICISM and printed essays by notable critics such as F. O. MATTHIESSEN, Yvor WINTERS, and Randall JARRELL. Brooks and Warren published *Stories from the Southern Review* in 1953.

Southwest, the
Discussions of the Southwest and its literature traditionally have focused on Arizona, New Mexico, and western Texas. This is the land of the cowboys described in Zane Grey and Owen Wister in their WESTERNS. Other major Southwestern writers include J. Frank DOBIE, Katherine Anne PORTER, and Conrad RICHTER, who describe the settlement of the land, the exploration of the wilderness, and the efforts to establish new communities. Occasionally writers from other regions have set their work in the Southwest, including Willa CATHER, who describes the work of Catholic missionaries in New Mexico in her novel *Death Comes for the Archbishop* (1927). Paul HORGAN and Larry MCMURTRY have contributed the most toward updating the idea of the western so that it serves as a setting for a commentary on contemporary life. Native American writers such as N. Scott MOMADAY have also made a major contribution to the literature of the Southwest.

Sources
Anderson, Eric Gary. *American Indian Literature and the Southwest: Contexts and Dispositions.* Austin: University of Texas Press, 1999.

Gish, Robert Franklin. *Beyond Bounds: Cross-Cultural Essays on Anglo, American Indian, and Chicano Literature.* Albuquerque: University of New Mexico Press, 1996.

Powell, Lawrence Clark. *Southwest Classics: The Creative Literature of the Arid Lands: Essays on the Books and Their Writers.* Los Angeles: W. Ritchie Press, 1974.

Spade, Sam character
One of the quintessential examples of the hard-boiled detective, invented by Dashiell HAMMETT in *The Maltese Falcon*, Spade is a private investigator in San Francisco in the 1920s. Skeptical about most people, he lives by his own practical code of justice. In *The Maltese Falcon*, Spade is involved with a shady cast of characters all bent on gaining possession of a precious statuette of a falcon. The intricate plot involves the detective in a love affair with Brigid O'Shaughnessy, also known as Miss Wonderly, who has hired Spade and his partner Miles Archer to follow a man named Floyd Thursby. When Archer is murdered, the case becomes a matter not only of Spade's service to his client but also of his quest to find out what happened to Archer— even though Spade disliked his partner and was having an affair with his wife. Spade learns how to play one nefarious

figure against another and recovers the statuette—only to be betrayed by Brigid. When he realizes that she has deceived him and that she is the one who shot his partner, he turns her over to the police—although until the very last moment Brigid thinks she can soften Spade because he loves her. Spade reveals no regrets, even when his faithful secretary, Effie, revolted at what he has done, refuses to let him touch her. His only emotion is a shiver when Effie announces that Archer's widow has come to see him.

Spade is arguably the most influential detective in American literature. Certainly detectives like Ross MACDONALD's Lew Archer and John D. MACDONALD's Travis McGee owe a considerable debt to Spade's stoical yet romantic temperament. Hammett created the model for the aloof, independent detective whose taciturnity masked intense emotions and a dogged desire to see justice done while recognizing, at the same time, a corrupt world that can never be entirely reformed or set right. These detectives persist in spite of a skepticism about human nature verging on cynicism. They are heroic because they act even though they have doubts about the effectiveness of their action.

Sources

Dooley, Dennis. *Dashiell Hammett*. New York: Ungar, 1984.
Laymon, Richard. *The Maltese Falcon*. Detroit: Gale, 2000.

Spanish Civil War (1936–1939)

In 1936 the Spanish Republic was attacked by the forces of General Francisco Franco. Franco was supported by the Roman Catholic Church and the fascist dictators Adolf Hitler and Benito Mussolini. The Republicans, a diverse group that included liberals, Socialists, Communists, anarchists, and Catalan and Basque regionalists, put up a fierce resistance aided by the Soviet dictator Joseph Stalin. The conflict was widely viewed as a prelude to WORLD WAR II. Volunteers from America went to fight on behalf of the Republic. They regarded the war as a noble cause, a fight for freedom and an effort to stop fascism before it took over Europe. Other European powers kept out of the conflict, and in the United States President Roosevelt kept his distance from the conflict—in part because of the American public's sentiment that it should not get involved in foreign wars, in part because of the influence of the Catholic Church and reports that the Republican government had condoned the massacre of priests (there was an anticlerical element in the Republican cause).

By the autumn of 1936 Franco had seized most of the northwest part of Spain and part of the southwest, but his forces could not capture Madrid until March 1939, by which time the Republic was cut in two and the war was ended.

John DOS PASSOS, Martha GELLHORN, Lillian HELLMAN, and most famously Ernest HEMINGWAY all wrote about their experiences in the Spanish Civil War. Hemingway published

a novel, *For Whom the Bell Tolls*, which centers on Robert Jordan, an idealistic American who dies fighting for a noble cause. Gellhorn's reports were collected in her famous book of war reportage, *The Face of War*. Hellman describes Hemingway in Spain in her memoir, *An Unfinished Woman* (1969).

Sources

Benson, Frederick R. *Writers in Arms: The Literary Impact of the Spanish Civil War*. New York: New York University Press, 1967.
Pérez, Janet and Wendell Aycock eds. *The Spanish Civil War in Literature*. Lubbock: Texas Tech University Press, 1990.

Spencer, Elizabeth (1921–) novelist

In her early novels *Fire in the Morning* (1948), *The Crooked Way* (1952), and *The Voice at the Back Door* (1956), Spencer, a Mississippi native, explored the contrast between the old and new South. When she moved to Italy with her husband in 1958, she produced two novels about Americans in Italy, *The Light in the Piazza* (1960) and *Knights and Dragons* (1965). Her work has been praised for its careful craftsmanship and plots that are shaped to reveal human character. *The Snare* (1972), a long, ambitious novel, is set in New Orleans.

The Stories of Elizabeth Spencer appeared in 1981 and *Conversations with Elizabeth Spencer* in 1991. Her later work includes *Jack of Diamonds* (1988), *The Night Travellers* (1991), and *Landscapes of the Heart: A Memoir* (1998).

Sources

Prenshaw, Peggy Whitman. *Elizabeth Spencer*. Boston: Twayne, 1985.
Roberts, Terry. *Self and Community in the Fiction of Elizabeth Spencer*. Baton Rouge: Louisiana State University Press, 1994.

Speyer, Leonora (1872–1956) poet

A New York native, Speyer was highly praised for her lyrics in *A Canopic Jar* (1921). Her themes often center on the nature of a woman's consciousness. Her work combines a superb sense of form with intense emotion. *Fiddler's Farewell* won a Pulitzer Prize and was lauded for its insight into the female psyche. Subsequent volumes such as *Naked Heel* (1931) and *Slow Wall* (1939, expanded in 1946), were less well received, with some critics suggesting that her sense of form had become rigid and sapped the intensity of her verse.

Sources

"Women's History" http://womenshistory.about.com/homework/womenshistory/library/etext/pindx/blp_aindex_speyer_leonora.htm. Downloaded June 15, 2001.

Spicer, Jack (1925–1965) *poet*

Associated with California for his entire career, Spicer published *After Lorca* (1957), a tribute to the Spanish poet Federico Garcia Lorca, who was killed in the SPANISH CIVIL WAR and had become a hero to the literary Left. The book contains translations of Lorca's poems, imaginary letters from Spicer to Lorca, and Spicer's original poems. Spicer's collection *Billy the Kid* (1959) celebrates the western hero; *The Heads of the Town Up to Aether* (1962) includes short snippets of poetry about literature and writers. *The Collected Books* (1975) arranges poems written to suit various literary journals. *The House that Jack Built: The Collected Lectures of Jack Spicer* appeared in 1998.

Sources

Ellingham, Lewis and Kevin Killian. *Poet Be Like God: Jack Spicer and the San Francisco Renaissance.* Hanover, N.H.: Wesleyan University Press, 1998.

Foster, Edward Halsey. *Jack Spicer.* Boise, Idaho: Boise State University, 1991.

Spillane, Mickey (Frank Morrison Spillane) (1918–) *novelist*

The prolific Spillane writes novels of the hard-boiled detective school. His series detective is Mike Hammer, who operates in a violent, sadistic world. Typical Spillane titles are *I, The Jury* (1947), *My Gun is Quick* (1950), and *The Big Kill* (1951). Spillane stopped publishing in the 1970s but resumed his work with *Tomorrow I Die* (1984), *The Killing Man* (1989), *The Twisted Thing* (1994), and *Back Alley* (1996).

Sources

Collins, Max Allan and James L. Traylor. *One Lonely Knight: Mickey Spillane's Mike Hammer.* Bowling Green, Ohio: Bowling Green State University Popular Press, 1984.

Van Dover, J. Kenneth. *Murder in the Millions: Erle Stanley Gardner, Mickey Spillane, Ian Fleming.* New York: Ungar, 1984.

Stafford, Jean (1915–1979) *short story writer, novelist*

Stafford was born in Covina, California, and grew up in San Diego and Boulder, Colorado. She started writing poems and stories at the age of six and a novel at age 11. In 1936 and 1937 she earned B.A. and M.A. degrees from the University of Colorado and studied philosophy for a year at the University of Heidelberg.

By the late 1930s Stafford had met the poet Robert LOWELL, who would become her first husband. She taught briefly at Stephens College and then at the IOWA WRITERS' WORKSHOP. She and Lowell married in 1940 and divorced in 1948.

Stafford's first great success was her best-selling novel *Boston Adventure* (1944), a sophisticated study of a woman who learns to become independent by rejecting the dictates of society. The novel reflected the tensions Stafford herself felt in being married to a poet who demanded her full attention even as he devoted himself full time to his own career.

In 1947 Stafford published her masterpiece, *The Mountain Lion*, which is autobiographical in that it explores the western environment of her childhood. The novel also established Stafford's reputation as one of America's finest stylists. Her third novel, *The Catherine Wheel* (1952), has been considered her most carefully structured work, delving once again into the peculiar problems of women of ambition who come into conflict with patriarchal society.

Although Stafford was extremely sensitive to the plight of women, she resisted the label of feminist and yearned to have a conventional marriage. In 1950 she married Oliver Jenson, but their union lasted a matter of months. Somewhat more successful was her marriage to the writer A. J. LIEBLING, who died in 1963.

By the mid-1950s Stafford found it increasingly difficult to write. Her most successful efforts were in the short story form. An alcoholic for most of her adult life, she gradually drifted away from writing at the beginning of the 1960s. Her reputation grew steadily, however, because the work that she did produce was of such high quality. *The Collected Stories of Jean Stafford* won a Pulitzer Prize in 1970.

Stafford's strong sense of irony and precise social observations have been compared to the work of Henry James and Mark Twain. Like them, she writes without sentimentality. Even though she rejected for herself the term *feminist*, her stories indict a society that strictly limits the possible roles women can play.

Sources

Walsh, Mary Ellen Williams. *Jean Stafford.* Boston: Twayne, 1985.

Wilson, Mary Jean. *Jean Stafford: A Study of the Short Fiction.* New York: Twaye, 1996.

Stafford, William Edgar (1914–1993) *poet*

Born in Kansas, William Stafford spent much of his career at Lewis and Clark College in Portland, Oregon. He favored the short lyric. His second volume of verse, *Traveling Through the Dark* (1962), won a National Book Award. He published *Stories That Could Be True: New and Collected Poems* in 1977. His later collections of poetry include *The Quiet of the Land* (1982), *A Glass Face in the Rain* (1982), *An Oregon Message* (1987), *My Name is William Tell: Poems* (1992), and *The Way It Is: New and Selected Poems* (1998).

Stafford's nonfiction includes *Writing the Australian Crawl* (1978), a collection of his essays about poetry, and *Crossing Unmarked Snow: Further Views on the Writer's Vocation* (1998). *Down in My Heart* (1947) recounts his experience as a conscientious objector in WORLD WAR II. Robert BLY published an anthology of Stafford's work, *The Darkness Around Us Is Deep*, in 1994.

Sources

Andrews, Tom, ed. *On William Stafford: The Worth of Local Things.* Ann Arbor: University of Michigan Press, 1993.

Kitchen, Judith. *Writing the World: Understanding William Stafford.* Corvallis: Oregon State University Press, 1999.

Stallings, Laurence (1894–1968) *novelist, playwright*

Born in Georgia, Stallings served in WORLD WAR I, out of which he created a novel, *Plumes* (1924), and the play that made his reputation, *What Price Glory* (1924). Written in collaboration with Maxwell ANDERSON, the drama was part of the wave of revulsion against modern war. Other plays, such as *First Flight* (1925) and *The Bucaneer* (1925)—collected in *Three American Plays* (1926)—were less successful. Stallings also wrote scripts for motion pictures and dramatized the Ernest HEMINGWAY novel *A Farewell to Arms* (1930).

Sources

Brittain, Joan T. *Laurence Stallings.* New York: Twayne, 1975.

Stark, Willie *character*

In Robert Penn WARREN's *ALL THE KING'S MEN*, Stark is a southern governor modeled after the legendary Huey Long of Louisiana.

Known as "the Boss," Willie is an ambitious politician who has come from poor people and wants to represent them. The trouble is that he is willing to use bribery and graft in order to achieve his virtuous goals. Self-educated, he had taken on the corrupt forces of the state in the early part of his career and won election as governor. His magnetism and idealism are what initially attract characters like Sadie Burke (who is in love with him) and Jack Burden, the novel's narrator. Willie builds massive public works in the state and a new hospital, but by his second term it is too late for him to reform his own government. He is killed by Adam Stanton, a doctor who believes Willie has used him and his sister to cleanse his reputation. Willie dies telling Burden, "It might have been different."

Warren taught in Louisiana during Huey Long's days in power. Long was also assassinated by a doctor, although there was no connection between the doctor and Long as there is between the doctor and Stark in the novel. Warren used Long's example to create a moral parable about the uses of power and the ease with which even noble aspirations can become corrupted in the world of politics. But politics itself is treated rather sympathetically in the novel; Warren implies that only through politics—through a direct dealing with the world as it is—can the world be made into a better place. Idealism without a grounding in and knowledge of human fallibility is doomed; indeed, it is self-destructive.

Sources

Chambers, Robert H., ed. *Twentieth Century Interpretations of All the King's Men: A Collection of Critical Essays.* Englewood Cliffs, N.J.: Prentice Hall, 1977.

Woodell, Harold. *All the King's Men: The Search for a Usable Past.* New York: Twayne, 1993.

Stearns, Harold Edmund (1891–1943) *critic*

Harold Stearns helped to articulate the attitude of the post–WORLD WAR I generation in *America and the Young Intellectual* (1921). The book excoriated the present leadership of the country and figures of authority whose ideas were bankrupt. This view was reiterated in the symposium he edited, *Civilization in the United States: An Inquiry by Thirty Americans* (1922). By 1935, however, his position had shifted from one of disgust to a deepening concern about the GREAT DEPRESSION and the need for social and political action. This new sense of engagement was reflected in *The Street I Know* (1935) and another symposium edited by Stearns: *America: A Re-Appraisal.* (1937).

Sources

Ford, Hugh. *Four Lives in Paris.* San Francisco: North Point Press, 1987.

Steel, Danielle (1947–) *novelist*

Born in New York, Steel has lived much of her life in San Francisco. She spent her early career in journalism and public relations. Her fast-paced novels with contemporary settings and bold characters have made her a popular mass-market author whose work has often been adapted for television and films. She has written about many professions—from jewelers to women journalists and aviators to scientists. She has dealt with the detention of Japanese Americans in WORLD WAR II, the VIETNAM WAR, politics, sexual abuse, marriage, and cloning. Her novels include *The Ring* (1980), *Remembrance* (1981), *Crossings* (1982), *Changes* (1983), *Full Circle* (1984), *Family Album* (1985), *Wanderlust* (1986), *Zoya* (1988), *Star* (1989), *Message from Nam* (1990), *Heartbeat* (1991), *No Greater Love* (1991), *Jewels* (1992), *Mixed Blessings* (1992), *Vanished* (1993), *Accident* (1994), *The Gift* (1994), *Wings* (1994), *Malice* (1996), *Silent Honor* (1996) *The Klone and I: A High-Tech Love Story* (1998), *Bittersweet* (1999), *Irresistible Forces* (1999), *The House on Hope Street* (2000), *Journey* (2000), and *The Wedding* (2000).

Sources

Bane, Vickie L. and Lorenzo Benet. *The Lives of Danielle Steel: The Unauthorized Biography of America's #1 Best-Selling Author.* New York: St. Martin's Press, 1994.

Steffens, Lincoln (Joseph Lincoln Steffens)
(1866–1936) *journalist*

Lincoln Steffens was born in San Francisco and spent a restless youth traveling and studying in Europe before finally settling in New York City in 1892. He was managing editor of *McClure's Magazine* from 1902 to 1906 before going on to work at other magazines and to establish his reputation as a muckraker alongside writers such as Ida TARBELL and Upton SINCLAIR. His articles on the corruption of urban life were collected in *The Shame of the Cities* (1904), his best and most well-known book of journalism. He also published *The Struggle for Self-Government* (1906) and *The Upbuilders* (1909). His most important literary contribution is undoubtedly his *Autobiography* (1931) because of his profound grasp of modern liberal and radical movements that did so much to shape his view of the world.

Sources
Kaplan, Justin. *Lincoln Steffens: A Biography.* New York: Simon & Schuster, 1974.

Stegner, Wallace Earle (1909–1993) *novelist*

Born in Lake Mills, Iowa, Wallace Stegner led a peripatetic childhood as his father, a gambler, moved the family across the Midwest and the West. Stegner's feel for the American landscape developed in these years. He graduated from the University of Utah and earned M.A. and Ph.D. degrees from the University of Iowa. His speciality was the history of the American West, and he taught at the University of Utah and later at the University of Wisconsin before settling at Stanford University in 1945, where he taught until 1971.

Stegner has often been called a regional writer because of his close identification with the West. His work is concerned with the way place shapes human character and how personality arises out of history. His exploration of frontier values inevitably results in fiction about the tensions between the East and the West. *The Big Rock Candy Mountain* (1943), one of his most memorable novels, is in part based on his family experience. Bo Mason, the tyrannical head of the Mason family, inspired by the myth of the West, searches for a pot of gold that forever eludes him. In *Angle of Repose* (1971), considered by many critics to be Stegner's greatest novel, he juxtaposes western expansiveness with eastern conservatism, the rugged, anarchic individualism of the West with the sense of cooperation and community in the East. The Mormons, however, represent an exception to the Western myth in so far as Stegner portrays them as family- and community-oriented.

Among Stegner's other important novels are *Recapitulation* (1979) and *Crossing to Safety* (1987). In addition to 14 novels, he published two collections of short fiction: *The Women on the Wall* (1950) and *The City of the Living and Other Stories* (1956). The *Collected Stories of Wallace Stegner* was published in 1990.

Stegner was also a prolific author of nonfiction, including *Mormon Country* (1942); *Look at America: The Central Northwest* (1947); *The Writer in America* (1951), a collection of essays; *Beyond the Hundreth Meridian; John Wesley Powell and the Second Opening of the West* (1954); *The Gathering of Zion: The Story of the Mormon Trail* (1964); *The American West as Living Space* (1987); and *Where the Bluebird Sings to the Lemonade Springs: Living and Writing in the West* (1992).

Stegner edited many books relating to his work as a teacher and historian of the West: *An Exposition Workshop* (1939), *The Writer's Art: A Collection of Short Stories* (1950), *The Exploration of the Colorado River of the West* (1957), and *Modern Composition* (1964).

Sources
Benson, Jackson J. *Wallace Stegner: His Life and Work.* New York: Viking, 1996.
Meine, Curt, ed. *Wallace Stegner and the Continental Vision: Essays on Literature, History, and Landscape.* Washington, D.C.: Island Press, 1997.

Stein, Gertrude (1874–1946) *novelist, autobiographer*

Stein was born in Allegheny, Pennsylvania. Her family moved to Oakland, California, when she was seven. She lived a comfortable upper-middle-class life, dominated by her father, a vice president of a municipal railroad company in San Francisco. Both parents had died by the time the 17-year-old Stein entered Radcliffe College, joining her brother, Leo, her confidant, who was enrolled at Harvard. She graduated from Harvard with a B.A. degree and enrolled in medical school at Johns Hopkins University, although by 1901 she had lost interest in becoming a doctor.

For the next few years Stein traveled in America and Europe, engaging in love affairs with women and becoming engrossed, along with her brother, Leo, in modern art. By 1907 Stein had become ensconced in Paris, living with a young American woman, Alice B. Toklas, who would eventually supplant Leo in Stein's life.

Inspired by innovative European art, Stein sought to transform American literature into a more supple, experimental, and challenging form, publishing *Three Lives* (1909), three novellas that explored the nature of human consciousness. She stripped language to its essential, using common, ordinary words to describe poor German immigrants, a young black woman, and other characters who come alive mainly in terms of their speech rhythms and the repetition of certain words. Stein eschewed conventional narration and character description, preferring language that was immediate and concrete over elaborate metaphors and vocabulary. *The Making of Americans* (1925), which Stein had worked on since 1903, expanded the method of *Three Lives* in its portrait of two large immigrant families, the Herslands and the Dehnings, and the many different personality types in America. Stein compared her efforts to the techniques of the cinema: She was writing in effect, a montage of America.

Stein was perhaps even better known as an influence on other writers, especially Ernest HEMINGWAY, who adapted her emphasis on the concrete and the colloquial into novels and stories of compressed and powerful eloquence. Her own later work attracted only an esoteric audience, though many scholars continue to find her example inspiring, citing such books as *Lucy Church Amiably* (1930) and *Ida, a Novel* (1941) as key texts in the formation of the modernist sensibility.

Stein wrote several influential works of nonfiction, including *The Autobiography of Alice B. Toklas* (1933), *Portraits and Prayers* (1934), *Lectures in America* (1935), *Everybody's Autobiography* (1937), *Picasso* (1938), and *What Are Masterpieces* (1940).

She wrote several plays and two operas, the most noteworthy being *Four Saints in Three Acts* (1934, with music by Virgil Thomson). Her most important book of poetry is *Tender Buttons: Objects, Food, Rooms* (1914).

Sources

Bridgeman, Richard. *Gertrude Stein in Pieces.* New York: Oxford University Press, 1970.

Mellow, James R. *Charmed Circle: Gertrude Stein and Company.* New York: Praeger, 1974.

Wineapple, Brenda. *Sister Brother: Gertrude and Leo Stein.* New York: Putnam's, 1996.

Steinbeck, John Ernst (1902–1968) *novelist, short story writer*

John Steinbeck was born in Salinas, California, and graduated from Salinas High School. He ran into academic difficulties at Stanford University and dropped out, working on ranches in the Salinas Valley while forming the ambition to become a writer. He left for New York City in 1925, finding employment as a journalist and freelance writer. But he found it hard to support himself and returned to California, where he began to have some success publishing short fiction. Not until his fourth novel, *Tortilla Flat* (1935), did he begin to attract both a large audience and critical acclaim. His subject matter was the Mexican quarter of Monterey, where he lived.

Steinbeck's next novel, *In Dubious Battle* (1936), which portrayed a violent agriculture strike in the fictional Torgas Valley, established his credentials as a progressive, even radical writer, who had contributed a key text to the PROLETARIAN LITERATURE of the 1930s. Steinbeck revealed compassion and dedication to the downtrodden and featured main characters who are Communist agitators. The novel is hardly straightforward propaganda, however, for it approaches the strike in documentary fashion as a case study of a labor dispute.

Of Mice and Men (1937), which tells the story of Lennie, the retarded but gentle giant, and his friend George, is a beautifully crafted parable of ordinary men who nevertheless have a sensitive and romantic conception of nature and of human existence. Society has no place for these men, who roam from ranch to ranch, until Lennie runs afoul of Curly, a short man with a Napoleonic complex. This short novel is so tautly written in terms of action and dialogue that it was easily adapted for the stage and for a brilliant film staring Burgess Meredith and Lon Chaney Jr. The novel also reveals Steinbeck's deep feeling for nature and for connections between man and nature, a feeling so intense that it amounts to a kind of biological determinism.

The Grapes of Wrath (1939), an American classic often taught in the classroom, combines Steinbeck's empathy for the displaced—in this case the "Okies" of the 1930s, farmers who have been bankrupted by the dust storms that ruined agriculture in Oklahoma and made it a "dust bowl." These hardworking but bewildered people trek across the country in dilapidated automobiles in search of the promised land in California. Instead, they are exploited by farmers who pay below-subsistence wages and crush with violence any attempts by workers to organize. Steinbeck shows his sympathetic understanding of collective action in a scene in a government camp run cooperatively and effectively by its inhabitants. In this epic novel he complements the story of the Joad family's struggles to make a life in California with poetic chapters of social history that put the experience of one family into a national perspective. Steinbeck won the Pulitzer Prize for the novel, and the director John Ford made it into a stirring film memorable for Henry Fonda's performance as Tom Joad, who realizes that his family's struggle is a whole people's struggle and that he will have to organize others if he is to make a place for his own family.

Steinbeck also wrote exquisitely observed short stories. Those collected in *The Long Valley* (1938) explore the lives of American and Mexican characters in the Salinas Valley. His fine screenplays based on his short novels include *The Pearl* (1945) and *The Red Pony* (1949), as well as the classic film *Viva Zapata* (1952).

Steinbeck's later novels, including the ambitious *East of Eden* (1952), were not well received by critics, but he remained a popular author with an international following. He won the 1962 Nobel Prize in literature, the same year he published *Travels with Charley*.

Steinbeck's profound feeling for nature is reflected in his nonfiction, particularly *Sea of Cortez* (1941). *Steinbeck: A Life in Letters* appeared in 1975.

Sources

DeMott, Robert J., ed. *Steinbeck's Typewriter: Essays on His Art.* Troy, N.Y.: Whitston, 1996.

French, Warren. *John Steinbeck Revisited.* New York: Twayne, 1994.
Parini, Jay. *John Steinbeck: A Biography.* New York: Henry Holt, 1996.

Steinem, Gloria (1934–) *journalist*

A feminist writer, Steinem is one of the key figures in the women's liberation movement of the 1970s. Born in Toledo, Ohio, Steinem graduated from Smith College and later moved to New York City, where she published articles in the 1960s in such magazines as *Esquire, Vogue, Glamour, McCall's,* and *Cosmopolitan.* She attracted much notice, especially when she posed as a Playboy bunny and wrote about the experience. In 1968 she demonstrated her savvy understanding of politics in a column for a newly established magazine, *New York.* At this time she also allied herself with the expanding women's movement. In 1972 she founded a new magazine, *Ms.,* which became part of the highly successful organizing movement for women's rights.

Steinem's most important publication is her collection of essays *Outrageous Acts and Everyday Rebellions* (1983). She turned to less political and more personal writing in *Revolution from Within: A Book of Self-Esteem* (1994). She also published *Marilyn* (1986), a biography of Marilyn Monroe that speculated on how the actress might have benefited from the women's movement of the 1970s. Later books, such as *Moving Beyond Words* (1994), have demonstrated Steinem's continuing interest in politics.

Sources

Heilbrun, Carolyn. *The Education of a Woman: The Life of Gloria Steinem.* New York: Dial Press, 1995.
Stern, Sydney Ladensohn. *Gloria Steinem: Her Passions, Politics, and Mystique.* New York: Birch Lane Press, 1997.

Stern, Richard Gustav (1928–) *novelist*

Born in New York City, Richard G. Stern has spent much of his professional life at the University of Chicago. His novels cover a range of subjects: television in *Golk* (1960); post–WORLD WAR II Germany in *Europe; or Up and Down with Baggish and Shreiber* (1961); treason in *In Any Case* (1963); expatriates in *Stitch* (1965); college professors in *Other Men's Daughters* (1973); and journalists in *Natural Shocks* (1978).

Stern's stories are collected in *Teeth, Dying and Other Matters* (1964); *1968: A Short Novel* (1970); *Packages* (1980); and *Noble Rot* (1989).

A shrewd essayist and occasional poet, Stern has collected his shorter pieces in *The Book in Fred Hampton's Apartment* (1973), *The Invention of the Real* (1982), and *The Position of the Body* (1986). He has also published a memoir about his sister and family, *A Sistermony* (1995).

Sources

Schiffer, James. *Richard Stern.* New York: Twayne, 1993.

Stevens, James Floyd (1892–1971) *novelist*

The Iowa-born James Stevens served in WORLD WAR I and then went to live in the Northwest, where his novels, *Brawnyman* (1926) and *Mattock* (1927), are set. Stevens is better known for his creation of pseudo-folk tales, especially *Paul Bunyan* (1925) and *The Saginaw Paul Bunyan* (1932). *Homer in Sagebrush* (1928) contains his western short stories.

Sources

Dorson, Richard. *American Folklore: With Revised Bibliographical Notes.* Chicago: University of Chicago Press, 1977.

Stevens, Wallace (1879–1955) *poet*

Stevens was born in Reading, Pennsylvania. His background does not figure in his poetry except in certain poems like "Dutch Graves in Bucks County," which evoke his Pennsylvania Dutch ancestry. Stevens is, in fact, the least autobiographical of modern American poets.

Stevens attended Harvard and then New York University, where he earned a law degree and practiced in the city between 1904 and 1916. There he met other poets in GREENWICH VILLAGE, including William Carlos WILLIAMS and Marianne MOORE.

Stevens continued to work as a lawyer all his life, becoming a counsel for the Hartford Insurance Company in 1916. In 1934 he became a vice president. Critics have commented on the anomaly of Stevens being both a major poet and a businessman, but Stevens himself found no contradiction or conflict between his two roles—which were not unprecedented, after all, since William Carlos WILLIAMS practiced medicine all his life.

Stevens's reputation as a poet grew slowly. Although he began publishing work in POETRY magazine as early as 1914, he did not publish his first collection of poetry, *Harmonium,* until 1923, when he was 44. That volume received little attention, but his subsequent work, especially *Ideas of Order* (1935), *The Man with the Blue Guitar and Other Poems* (1937), *Parts of a World* (1942), and *Notes Toward a Supreme Fiction* (1942), gradually built for him a respectful and then a devoted audience. *Auroras of Autumn* (1950) won the National Book Award and *Collected Poems* (1954) won another National Book Award and a Pulitzer Prize.

Even sophisticated readers have had trouble with Stevens's verse, which is highly intellectual and elliptical. He has become lionized, especially among scholars of the POSTMODERN, as the harbinger of ideas that are now in vogue—especially the notion that poetry is a self-contained object, a means of expression intact in itself, and not merely a reflection of the world out of which it arises. Part of Stevens's inscrutability seems to stem from his effort to make poetry impregnable, immune to being understood as a message expressing an extractable theme. As the poet remarks in "On Modern Poetry," "It [poetry] has/ To construct a new stage." The words poetry speaks are "that which it wants to hear . . . The poem of the act of the mind."

Stevens also had a brief career in New York City as an experimental playwright. His plays include *Three Travelers Watch a Sunrise* (1916), *Carlos Among the Candles* (1917), and *Bowl, Cat, and Broomstick* (1917).

Although Stevens's public appearances and readings were rare, he published one book of essays that help to explain his aesthetics: *The Necessary Angel: Essays on Reality and the Imagination* (1951).

The *Letters of Wallace Stevens* appeared in 1966 and *Souvenirs and Prophecies: The Young Wallace Stevens* in 1977.

Sources

Bloom, Harold, ed. *Wallace Stevens.* New York: Chelsea House, 1985.

Maeder, Beverly. *Wallace Stevens' Experimental Language: The Lion in the Lute.* New York: St. Martin's Press, 1999.

Sampson, Theodore. *A Cure of the Mind: The Poetics of Wallace Stevens.* New York: Black Rose Books, 2000.

Sukenick, Ronald. *Wallace Stevens: Musing the Obscure: Readings, An Interpretation, and a Guide to the Collected Poetry.* New York: New York University Press, 1967.

Vendler, Helen. *Wallace Stevens: Words Chosen Out of Desire.* Knoxville: University of Tennessee Press, 1984.

Stewart, George Rippey (1895–1980) *historian, novelist, critic*

Rippey was professor of English at the University of California, Berkeley, while he pursued a prolific and versatile publishing career. Among his works are *Ordeal by Hunger* (1936), an account of the ill-fated Donner Party; *Pickett's Charge* (1959), a riveting account of the last attack at Gettysburg; and *The California Trail* (1962), a study of the pioneering treks in the 1840s and 1850s. His novels paralleled his nonfiction. *East of the Giants* (1938) is set in California just before the Gold Rush. His interest in the environment and in ecology led him to write novels about natural disasters, including *Storm* (1941) and *Fire* (1948).

Sources

Caldwell, John. *George Rippey Stewart.* Boise, Idaho: Boise State University, 1981.

Stone, Irving (1903–1989) *novelist*

A California-based author, Stone wrote popular and insightful biographical fiction, including *Lust for Life* (1934), on Vincent van Gogh; *Sailor on Horseback* (1938), on Jack London; *The President's Lady* (1951), on Rachel Jackson (Andrew Jackson's wife); *Love Is Eternal* (1954), on Mary Todd Lincoln; *The Agony and the Ecstasy* (1961) on Michelangelo; *Passions of the Mind* (1971), on Sigmund Freud; *The Origin* (1980), on Charles Darwin, and *Depths of Glory* (1985) on Camille Pissarro.

Sources

Stieg, Lewis F. *Irving Stone: A Bibliography.* Los Angeles: Friends of the Libraries, University of Southern California, 1973.

Stone, Robert Anthony (1937–) *novelist, screenwriter*

Born in Brooklyn, New York, Robert Stone grew up in a fatherless home and became a rebellious student in the Catholic schools into which he was put. He joined the navy and then attended New York University from 1958 to 1960. He worked odd jobs, began to frequent beatnik hangouts, made friends with Jack KEROUAC and Ken KESEY, and by the late 1960s was a freelance writer. *A Hall of Mirrors* (1967), his first novel, won the William Faulkner Foundation Award. The book is an incisive exposure of the racism and right-wing extremism of the 1960s. *Dog Soldiers* (1974), which won a National Book Award, and *A Flag for Sunrise,* which won the John Dos Passos Prize for literature (1981), solidified Stone's reputation as a political and social novelist who has been compared to DOS PASSOS and Nathanael WEST. Both novels deal with the sorry consequences of the VIETNAM WAR and the disaffection among radicals in the 1970s. For Stone, the war corrupted American values and led to a drug culture and cynicism that are a betrayal of the American dream. A later novel, *Children of Light* (1986), takes up the crass commercial world of the 1980s, drawing on Stone's own experience in Hollywood. *Damascus Gate* (1996) shifts attention to the Middle East, focusing on an American journalist, Christopher Lucas, who explores the lives of people who come to Jerusalem in the belief that God has sent them on a mission. Some critics praised Stone's taut plotting, while others dismissed this novel as a superficial thriller.

Stone has written two important screenplays based on his novels: *WUSA* (1970) and *Who'll Stop the Rain* (1978). He collected his short stories in *Bear and His Daughter* (1997).

Sources

Solataroff, Robert. *Robert Stone.* New York: Twayne, 1994.

"Stopping by Woods on a Snowy Evening"
Robert Frost (1923) *poem*

Robert FROST's haunting poem evokes the tensions between the individual and civilization. On the face of it, this famous work is exceedingly simple. The speaker stops to watch snow falling in the woods. He mentions that this property is owned by a man in the village. It is a deserted place, and the speaker imagines that his horse thinks it is a strange place to stop. It is the "darkest evening of the year." The speaker wishes to linger, but he has "promises to keep" and, as he repeats in the poem's closing lines, "miles to go before I sleep."

The poem expresses not only the human sense of duty but also the desire to relinquish that duty. The "lovely, dark and deep" woods evoke a feeling of prehistoric or primitive rootedness in nature itself. The speaker is tempted to rest in this soft ("downy") scene. The emphasis on the darkness suggests death or the cessation of consciousness, a merging with nature, an ultimate rest. The speaker's reassertion of his sense of obligation, however, defines what makes him human and what it means to have a human consciousness that projects itself on the environment.

Sources

Bloom, Harold ed. *Robert Frost.* Broomall, Pa.: Chelsea House, 1999.

Poirier, Richard. *Robert Frost: The Work of Knowing.* Stanford Calif.: Stanford University Press, 1990.

Story periodical

Founded in 1931 by Whit Burnett and his wife, Martha Foley, *Story* was the only magazine of its time devoted solely to the publication of short stories. It published a good many classic American writers, including William FAULKNER and Eudora WELTY. Burnett and Foley divorced, but with his second wife, Hallie, Burnett continued to edit the magazine and produced a collection, *Story: The Fiction of the Forties* (1949). He also published a memoir, *The Story of Story Magazine* (1980).

Stout, Rex Todhunter (1886–1975) novelist

Rex Stout is best known for the creation of Nero Wolfe, a huge (nearly 300-pound) armchair detective who solves crimes mainly by dint of his wits and logic. Wolfe employs the engaging leg man, Archie Goodwin, to check on various details and to run errands. Stout turned to detective fiction after his first three novels were praised by critics but failed to attract an audience. Nero Wolfe appeared in 46 novels, beginning with *Fer-de-Lance* (1934) and ending with *A Family Affair* (1975). *Justice at Home* (1977) collects Stout's unpublished stories written between 1913 and 1917.

Sources

McAleer, John. *Rex Stout: A Biography.* Boston: Little, Brown, 1977.

Strand, Mark (1934–   ) poet

Strand was born on Prince Edward Island in Canada and moved to the United States with his family when he was four. After earning a B.A. degree at Antioch College in Yellow Springs, Ohio, Strand studied at Yale, the University of Florence, and the University of Iowa, where he earned an M.A. He has taught at several colleges, including Columbia, Yale, Princeton, and Harvard.

Strand's poetry has a spare style, sometimes called minimalist. His first book, *Sleeping with One Eye Open* (1964), is renowned for his use of surrealist imagery involving the dismemberment of human bodies and metaphors that evoke something like Edgar Allan Poe's vision of the phantasmagoria of life. Many of Strand's poems are pictorial and express his affinity for painting, an art he considered practicing instead of poetry.

Strand published his *Selected Poems* in 1980. His later collections include *Prose: Four Poems* (1987), *The Continuous Life* (1990), *Dark Harbor* (1993), *Blizzard of One: Poems* (1998), and *Chicken, Shadow, Moon & More* (2000). In 1990 he was selected to succeed Robert Penn WARREN as poet laureate of the Library of Congress.

Strand has written one novel, *The Monument* (1978), and a collection of short fiction, *Mr. and Mrs. Baby and Other Stories* (1985). His writing for children includes *The Planet of Lost Things* (1982), *The Night Book* (1985), and *Rembrandt Takes a Walk* (1986).

Strand has also written two biographical/critical books on artists: *William Bailey* (1987) and *Hopper* (1994). In 2000 he published *The Weather of Words: Poetic Invention.* As an editor he has published *The Contemporary American Poets: American Poetry Since 1940* (1969), *New Poetry of Mexico* (1970), *Another Republic: Seventeen European and South American Writers* (1976), *Art of the Real: Nine American Figurative Painters* (1983), and *The Making of a Poem: A Norton Anthology of Poetic Forms* (2000).

Sources

Kirby, David. *Mark Strand and the Poet's Place in Contemporary Culture.* Columbia: University of Missouri Press, 1990.

stream of consciousness

This style of writing gives the illusion of expressing the uncensored thoughts of the narrator, as in THE SOUND AND THE FURY (1929) by William FAULKNER. This technique was first used toward the end of the 19th century as novelists took an interest in the psychic life of their characters. The term itself was first used by William James in *The Principles of Psychology* (1890). James and, later, Sigmund Freud emphasized the idea of human identity as a constantly shifting consciousness, and not as simply a product of "character" (the sum total of an individual's actions). Stream of consciousness in the novel is an effort to capture a character's thoughts without commentary by the author. The term is often referred to as "interior monologue," although that phrase suggests a higher degree of articulation and order than the spontaneous flow, or stream, of consciousness. The first two sections of *The Sound and the Fury* have the fragmentary quality of stream of consciousness, whereas the third section is closer to a soliloquy or interior monologue—as are many of the sections in AS I LAY DYING. John DOS PASSOS provides a good example of stream of consciousness in his "Camera Eye" sections of *U.S.A.*

Sources

Humphrey, Robert. *Stream of Consciousness in the Modern Novel.* Berkeley: University of California Press, 1954.
Steinberg, Erwin R., ed. *The Stream-of-Consciousness Technique in the Modern Novel.* Port Washington, N.Y.: Kennikat Press, 1979.

Streetcar Named Desire, A   Tennessee Williams (1947) *play*

In this play Tennessee WILLIAMS created two of the most famous dramatic characters, Stanley Kowalski and Blanche DUBOIS, in what has become a staple of the American theater.

Blanche DuBois, who has lost her family's plantation, comes to visit her sister, Stella, in New Orleans. Blanche is a romantic woman who lives in the past. Aging and desperate with nowhere else to go, Blanche has been disappointed in love, but gilds reality with a patina of poetry. Stella's husband, Stanley Kowalski, does not like the airs Blanche puts on, nor her supposition that because his manners are not like hers he is a brute. Stanley aggressively badgers Blanche and eventually rapes her. Blanche's charm appeals to Mitch, Stanley's friend, but Stanley also tells Mitch that Blanche was fired from her teaching job for attempting to seduce a student. Mitch, Blanche's last hope, then rejects her. Driven mad, Blanche is taken away to a psychiatric hospital, uttering the famous line that she has "always depended on the kindness of strangers."

A description of the plot cannot do justice to this sensitive, poetic play. Stanley, for example, is much more than the beast Blanche incites to violence. He represents a new world for Stella, who is not bound by Blanche's self-destructive devotion to the past and to an outdated code of conduct for southern women. At the same time, Blanche is hardly just a victim. She expresses the need for human beings to idealize life and to see the nobility of it even when they cannot live up to their dreams. Neither Stanley the realist nor Blanche the idealist has the last word in this play. Instead, the clash between their personalities and attitudes toward life gives the play a tragically inevitable ending.

The play can be read as a comment on the decline of the South and of an American past giving way to a cruder but also more dynamic time. But Williams does not sentimentalize his characters or turn them into symbols of history. Rather, it is because they are so intensely individual and so memorable in the cadence of their speech that they have come to embody clashing ideas of masculinity and femininity and of what civilization itself should be.

The original New York production of the play ran for 855 performances. Marlon Brando, who played Stanley with such brute force and magnetism, reprised his role in the film directed by Elia Kazan, who was also responsible for the stage direction. Brando's performance created the essential tension of the play, since Blanche must simultaneously reject Stanley's crudeness and yet be attracted to his overwhelming masculine strength. Subsequent productions of the play tend to succeed or fail based on the actor who plays Stanley and who must create the attraction/repulsion dynamic.

Sources

Bloom, Harold, ed. *Tennessee Williams's A Streetcar Named Desire.* New York: Chelsea House, 1988.
Kolin, Philip C., ed. *Confronting Tennessee William's A Streetcar Named Desire: Essays in Critical Pluralism.* Westport, Conn.: Greenwood Press, 1993.

Stuart, Jesse Hilton   (1907–1984) *poet, novelist, short story writer, essayist, autobiographer*

A Kentucky native, Stuart belongs to the regionalist school. His titles include *Kentucky is My Land* (1952), poetry; *Men of the Mountains* (1941), stories; *Trees of Heaven* (1940), a novel set on a Kentucky farm; and *God's Oddling* (1960), an autobiography describing his father and his upbringing in Kentucky. *The Seasons* (1976) and *If I Were Seventeen Again* (1980) are continuations of his autobiography. His essays are collected in *Lonely Skies* (1979).

Sources

LeMaster, J. R. and Mary Washington Clarke, eds. *Jesse Stuart: Essays on His Work.* Lexington: University Press of Kentucky, 1977
LeMaster, J. R. *Jesse Stuart, Kentucky's Chronicler-Poet.* Memphis Tenn.: Memphis State University Press, 1980.

Sturgeon, Theodore Hamilton   (1918–1985) *novelist*

Theodore Sturgeon's science fiction emphasizes human isolation. It is noteworthy for its psychological sophistication and speculative forays into the nature of a consciousness of the universe that transcends individuals. His signature novel is *More Than Human* (1953), but his impact may be even greater in his short story collections: *A Touch of Strange* (1958), *Sturgeon in Orbit* (1964), *Sturgeon Is Alive and Well* (1971), *Visions and Venturers* (1978), and *The Stars Are the Styx* (1979).

Sources

Diskin, Lahna. *Theodore Sturgeon.* Mercer Island, Wash.: Starmont House, 1981.
Menger, Lucy. *Theodore Sturgeon.* New York: Ungar, 1981.

Styron, William Clark (1925–) novelist

William Styron was born in Newport News, Virginia. He came from an old southern family and grew up steeped in southern lore. Styron dropped out of college to enlist in the marines. While in Officers Candidate School he took a creative writing course at Duke University. His first stories resembled William FAULKNER's portrayal of a bigoted South. After the war Styron resumed his education and graduated from Duke in 1947. He then moved to New York to work as an editor and to write his first novel in a Brooklyn boardinghouse.

Lie Down in Darkness (1951), Styron's brilliant debut novel, concerned a decadent southern family that drives it sensitive daughter, Peyton Loftis, to insanity and suicide. The character and the environment are reminiscent of Faulkner's Caddy Compson in THE SOUND AND THE FURY (1929). But the searing power of the novel was Styron's own, and his work was quickly hailed by critics. The novel won a Prix de Rome in 1952.

Equally powerful was Styron's novella, *The Long March* (1956), based on his experience in the marines. The economy and authenticity of the writing equals, if it does not surpass, earlier novels of war written by James JONES and Norman MAILER.

Yet Styron struggled to find a subject and a style commensurate with his ambitions. His next novel, *Set This House on Fire* (1960), proved disappointing. Its account of postwar American intellectuals in Europe contained Styron's trademark eloquence—including lovely descriptions of Italy and harrowing descriptions of its poverty—but the novelist could not find the proper form. Styron later admitted it was a failure.

When Styron returned to the milieu he knew best—the South—he scored another triumph with *The Confessions of Nat Turner* (1967), a fictionalized account of Nat Turner's slave rebellion told by Turner himself. Styron presented Turner as an extraordinarily intelligent and highly imaginative man—not the religious fanatic who had prompted African-American novelists such as Arna BONTEMPS to shy away from depicting Turner's revolt in fiction. Turner was from Styron's region, and Styron had always thought he would one day explore the nation's only successful slave revolt in fiction. Styron worked from a historical document—an interview Turner had given to a white man. The novelist also did considerable historical research but concluded that so much was unknown about Turner himself that he would have to create his own version of Turner's emotional life. In doing so, Styron employs some of the most beautiful prose ever published in American fiction.

The novel, however, provoked the wrath of some African-American historians and critics who saw it as a white southerner's effort to commandeer an African-American rebel's experience. They criticized Styron for endowing Turner with a love for a white woman, and for minimizing the political consequences of Turner's actions. Among prominent African-American writers of the time, only James BALDWIN, a friend of Styron's, endorsed the novel, although Eugene Genovese, one of the most important historians of slavery, defended Styron's interpretation of the historical record.

Not only did Styron withstand attacks on his integrity and his writing, he also produced a subsequent novel, *Sophie's Choice* (1979), which dealt with the dilemma of a Polish woman who survived a Nazi concentration camp but who had to choose which of her two children to save from the gas chamber. Just as he had dared to deal with slavery, so Styron boldy entered the history of the Holocaust—not only dealing with other people's history but suggesting in various passages of the novel parallels between southern and European history. The novel's narrator, Stingo, a callow southern boy, is gradually introduced to the horrors of the Holocaust by becoming involved in the lives of Sophie and her lover, Nathan. Perhaps because of this naive narrator who slowly discovers the enormity of his friends' history, Styron escaped the kind of harsh criticism leveled at *The Confessions of Nat Turner*. The authentic voice of Stingo, based partly on Styron's own experience in a Brooklyn rooming house, provided the author with a valid, unassailable angle of vision.

Styron has not completed another novel, although various novel-length projects have been announced and apparently abandoned. He has published one play, *In the Clap Shack* (1972), and one collection of short fiction, *A Tidewater Morning: Three Tales from Youth* (1993). An eloquent essayist, he published *This Quiet Dust*—the title essay is about how he came to write *The Confessions of Nat Turner*—in 1982. *Darkness Visible: A Memoir of Madness* (1990) is Styron's candid and moving mediation on his lifelong battle with depression and his suicidal impulses. *Conversations with William Styron* was published in 1985.

Sources

Cologne-Brookes, Gavin. *The Novels of William Styron: From Harmony to History*. Baton Rouge: Louisiana State University Press, 1995.

Casciato, Arthur D. and James L. W. West III, eds. *Critical Essays on William Styron*. Boston: G.K. Hall, 1982.

West, James L. W., III. *William Styron: A Life*. New York: Random House, 1998.

Suckow, Ruth (1892–1960) novelist, short story writer

An Iowa regionalist, Suckow is known for *Country People* (1924), a novel detailing three generations of a German-American family. *The Odyssey of a Nice Girl* (1925) shifts focus to the life of a single young girl confronting the provinciality of Iowa life. *Iowa Interiors* (1926) and *Children and Older People* (1931) collect Suckow's short stories. *Some Others and Myself* (1952) includes stories and memoirs.

Sources

Hamblen, Abigail Ann. *Ruth Suckow*. Boise, Idaho: Boise State University, 1978.

Kissane, Leedice McAnelly. *Ruth Suckow.* New York: Twayne, 1969.

Sukenick, Ronald (1932–) *novelist, essayist*

Born in BROOKLYN, NEW YORK, Sukenick was educated at Cornell and Brandeis University, and has directed the creative writing program at the University of Colorado. *Up* (1968) is a comic novel about a young man's attempts to write a first novel. *Out* (1973) explores New Yorkers in the 1960s who move to California in search of a better life. *98.6* (1975) is set in a commune in the West. *Blown Away* (1986) deals with Hollywood. Highly praised as an innovative writer for his style and structure, Sukenick exhibits a self-consciousness about writing fiction that often makes the writing itself the subject of his books. His stories are collected in *The Death of the Novel* (1969) and *The Endless Short Story* (1986). He has also published a critical study, *Wallace Stevens: Musing the Obscure: Readings* (1967) and *In Form* (1985), essays on fiction and poetry.

Sukenick's later work includes *Doggy Bag* (1994) and *Mosaic Man* (2000), novels that deal with politics and Jewish identity.

Sources

Kutnik, Jerzy. *The Novel as Performance: The Fiction of Ronald Sukenick and Raymond Federman.* Carbondale: Southern Illinois University Press, 1986.

Sun Also Rises, The Ernest Hemingway (1926) *novel*

Ernest HEMINGWAY's inimitable novel of post–WORLD WAR I disillusionment focuses on an American journalist in Paris, Jake Barnes. A member of 1920s cafe society, Jake has suffered a mysterious wound in the war that has apparently made him impotent, although the source and the consequences of his disability are never made explicit. Indeed, the point is that the war has incapacitated Jake in a psychic sense, not just a physical one. Jake is aloof and numbed by the horror of war. Although in private he can grieve for himself, he turns a stoic face to the world. Jake is in love with Lady Brett Ashley, a British aristocrat, but because his love cannot be consummated, he leaves Paris for Spain in the hope of relieving his suffering. Jake's behavior is contrasted with that of his wealthy friend Robert Cohn, who also is in love with Brett and indulges in self-pity. Jake so desires Brett's happiness that he encourages her liaison with the bullfighter Pedro Romero. Cohn accuses Jake of becoming a pimp. He knocks Jake out and then, in remorse, apologizes. A resigned Jake accepts Cohn's act of contrition. At the end of the novel, Jake and Brett are reunited but remain suspended in a love they cannot consummate.

Hemingway's novel became the quintessential work of what Gertrude STEIN called the "LOST GENERATION," a group of Americans who had served in the war and settled in Paris, unable to return home because of the devastation they had experienced. Their sense of home, of solid values, has vanished. In their disillusionment, they are stymied. Jake's problem, then, is an intensification of that feeling—that there is no goal worth fighting for again. The novel's style, as much as its theme, make it a disturbing work of art. The despair is understated, and Hemingway uses words so economically that there is also a lingering sense of a significance that the words themselves can only allude to—depths of feeling that no words can quite reach.

Sources

Bloom, Harold, ed. *Ernest Hemingway's The Sun Also Rises.* New York: Chelsea House, 1996.

Nagel, James, ed. *Critical Essays on The Sun Also Rises.* New York: G.K. Hall, 1995.

surrealism

This term usually is associated with a group of artists in 1920s France. Surrealists attacked the notion of a stable reality, of logic, of order, and gave free rein to the subconscious—the images and scenes conjured up by dreamlike landscapes often associated with the paintings of Salvador Dali, for example. But surrealism as American writers such as Susan SONTAG define it can also mean the radical art of juxtaposition—setting one kind of image against another without intrusive commentary by the artist. William Carlos WILLIAMS practiced this kind of surrealism in many of his poems, in which one image is set against another to make a "picture" or "object." Surrealism often focuses on the strange or incongruous that breaks through ordinary reality. In this sense, surrealistic elements appear throughout American literature, from the stories of Edgar Allan Poe to the work of William FAULKNER ("A ROSE FOR EMILY," for example) and in contemporary novels such as Sontag's *Death Kit* (1967) and Thomas PYNCHON's *Gravity's Rainbow* (1972).

Sources

Josephson, Matthew. *Life Among the Surrealists.* New York: Holt, Rinehart & Winston, 1962.

Matthews, J. H. *An Introduction to Surrealism.* University Park: Pennsylvania State University Press, 1965.

Sharma, R. K. *Contemporary Black Humour: American Novels from Nathanael West to Thomas Berger.* Delhi: Ajanta Publications, 1988.

Swados, Harvey (1920–1972) *novelist, short story writer, essayist*

Swados was born in Buffalo, New York, and educated at the University of Michigan. His novels reflect a strongly socialist point of view that has much in common with the

PROLETARIAN LITERATURE of the 1930s, although Swados's characters include artists and industrialists, not only the poor or laboring classes. In *False Coin* (1959), for example, the theme is the artist's struggle to maintain his principles in a consumer society. *Standing Fast* (1970), generally considered his best work, focuses on a small group of dedicated Marxists. Also notable is his short story collection, *The Line* (1957), which details the lives of auto assembly workers. His essays are collected in *A Radical's America* (1962).

Sources

"Swados, Harvey." Valencia Community College West Campus Learning Resources Center. Available on-line. URL: http://www.valencia.cc.fl.us/lrcwest/swados.html. Downloaded June 16, 2001.

Swenson, May (1927–1989) *poet*

Swenson was born in Utah and raised there by her Swedish parents, who were Mormons. Swenson was a bold poet, experimenting with typography, striking imagery, and expansive rhetoric. Her collections include *Another Animal* (1954), *A Cage of Spines* (1958), *To Mix with Time* (1963), *Half Sun Half Sleep* (1967), *Iconographs* (1970), and *New and Selected Things Taking Place* (1979). She wrote two books of riddles for children: *Poems to Solve* (1966) and *More Poems to Solve* (1971). She won the Bollingen Prize in 1979. *In Other Words* (1987) is the last collection she put together. Thirteen new poems appeared posthumously in *The Love Poems of May Swenson* (1992). Her writings on poetry have been collected in *Made with Words* (1997).

Sources

Knudson, R. R. *The Wonderful Pen of May Swenson.* New York: Macmillan, 1993.

Taggard, Genevieve (1894–1948) *poet*

Taggard was born in Washington state and grew up in Hawaii. She graduated from the University of California in 1919 and began to publish poetry. *Words for the Chisel* (1926), her third volume of verse, ushered in her mature phase, marked by a metaphysical bent and inspired by Emily Dickinson, about whom Taggard wrote *The Life and Mind of Emily Dickinson* (1930). Taggard's *Collected Poems* appeared in 1938. Later volumes include *Long View* (1942) and *Slow Music* (1946). *May Days* (1925) is her selection of verse from THE MASSES and THE LIBERATOR.

Sources

Berke, Nancy. "Genevieve Taggard." Modern American Poetry. Available on-line. URL: http://www.english.uiuc.edu/maps/poets/s_z/taggard/taggard.htm. Downloaded June 16, 2001.

Tan, Amy (1948–) *novelist*

Amy Tan was born in Oakland, California, the daughter of Chinese immigrants. She grew up very conscious of her Asian appearance among her Caucasian schoolmates. Tan graduated from San Jose State University, got married, and became a successful business writer. This work did not satisfy her, and she turned to fiction, producing her first novel, *The Joy Luck Club* (1989), and achieving virtually instant success as a major new voice in contemporary literature.

The Joy Luck Club, the story of three Chinese mothers and their American-born daughters, explores generational conflicts that center on the degree to which mothers and daughters assimilate American culture. The social club fosters the solidarity of these women, even though they have different orientations toward their communities.

The Kitchen God's Wife (1991), Tan's second novel, continues her exploration of mother/daughter relationships. It concentrates on Winnie Louie and her daughter, Pearl, and shifts between a narrative of Winnie's earlier life in China and Pearl's estrangement from her mother, with which Pearl gradually comes to terms.

The Hundred Secret Senses (1995) differs from Tan's first two novels in that it explores the ties and tensions between sisters. The novel is noteworthy for its creation of Kwan, a dynamic woman with a strong Chinese identity who comes into conflict with her American-born sister, Olivia. Although Olivia would like to jettison her family's Chinese past, Kwan stubbornly finds ways to make her sister confront her Chinese heritage.

The Bonesetter's Daughter (2001) is another generational saga. The novel is divided into three sections. The first, set in contemporary California, concerns Ruth Young, a Chinese American confronted with a failing marriage and a mother who is degenerating into dementia. The second section is Ruth's mother's memoir of life in China, and the third section returns to Ruth's present. The hallmarks of Tan's fiction—the role of memory and language in maintaining and restoring both a sense of the past and of human identity—are paramount in this fully realized novel.

Tan wrote the screenplay for the 1993 film version of *The Joy Luck Club*. She has also written two children's books, *The Moon Lady* (1992) and *The Chinese Siamese Cat* (1994).

Sources

Huntley, E. D. *Amy Tan: A Critical Companion.* Westport, Conn.: Greenwood Press, 1998.

Tarbell, Ida Minerva (1857–1944) *journalist, biographer, historian*

Tarbell was born in Erie County, Pennsylvania, and was educated at Allegheny College. She got her start as a journalist on the *Chautauquan* magazine. By 1895 she was working for *McClure's*, a nationally syndicated magazine. Here she had the opportunity to write about Standard Oil, the company she believed had victimized her father and had dominated American industry through its monopoly on oil. *The History of the Standard Oil Company* (1902) established Tarbell's reputation and earned her a permanent place in the history of American journalism. She became one of several journalists designated "muckrakers"—writers who stirred the muck, investigating improprieties in American business and politics. An activist, Tarbell lectured around the country in favor of progressive policies, including women's rights. She published her autobiography, *All in the Day's Work*, in 1939.

Sources

Brady, Kathleen. *Ida Tarbell: Portrait of a Muckraker*. New York: Putnam, 1984.

Tarkington, Newton Booth (1869–1946) *novelist*

Booth Tarkington, an Indiana novelist, was immensely popular both for his historical romances such as *Monsieur Beaucaire* (1900) and for his tales of life in the Midwest. *The Magnificent Ambersons* (1918), a novel that chronicles three generations of a prominent Indiana family and its decline, won a Pulitzer Prize and was made into a major motion picture by Orson Welles. Similarly, *Alice Adams* (1921), the story of an ordinary girl who aspires to marry above her class, won a Pulitzer Prize and became a successful film starring Katharine Hepburn. Tarkington as an Indiana regionalist is best studied in his novels *The Gentleman from Indiana* (1899) and The *Conquest of Canaan* (1905), which deals in detail with midwestern life. Tarkington also won fame as the author of fiction about adolescents, especially his series *Penrod* (1914), *Penrod and Sam* (1916), and *Penrod Jashber* (1916). *The World Does Move* (1928) is a memoir. Two editions of correspondence have been published: *On Plays, Playwrights, and Playgoers: Selections from the Letters of Booth Tarkington to George C. Tyler and John Peter Toohey, 1918–1925* (1959) and *Dr. Panofsky & Mr. Tarkington: An Exchange of Letters, 1938–1946* (1974).

Sources

Fennimore, Keith J. *Booth Tarkington*. New York: Twayne, 1974.
Woodress, James. *Booth Tarkington: Gentleman from Indiana*. Philadelphia: Lippincott, 1955.

Tate, Allen (John Orly Allen Tate) (1899–1979) *poet, critic*

The southern-bred Allen Tate was a student of John Crowe RANSOM at Vanderbilt University. He was an editor of *The Fugitive* (1922), a magazine of modern poetry established at Vanderbilt. Although a modernist in literary temperament, Tate was also known as one of the Nashville AGRARIANS, a group of writers who looked to the preindustrial South for their model of a society. Tate was hostile to northern, urban civilization, although he maintained close personal contacts with northern poets such as Robert LOWELL and with NEW YORK INTELLECTUALS such as Philip RAHV, one of the editors of *PARTISAN REVIEW*.

Tate's writing about poetry influenced the New Critics (see NEW CRITICISM), and he was able to put his literary tastes into practice by editing *Hound and Horn* (1931–1934) and the *SEWANEE REVIEW* (1944–1946). He taught at Princeton University and other colleges. He was married to the southern novelist Caroline GORDON, who with Tate taught creative writing and mentored generations of writers.

Tate's poems have been frequently anthologized, especially "Ode to the Confederate Dead," "The Mediterranean," and "The Oath"—works that exemplify both his dedication to southern traditions and his modernist use of irony and metaphor. *Essays of Four Decades* was published in 1969. Tate received the Bollingen Prize for Poetry in 1956. *Collected Poems* was published in 1977, and *Memoirs and Opinions 1926–1974* in 1975.

Tate wrote one historical novel, *The Fathers* (1938), a probing psychological study of the Civil War, and two well-received biographies, *Stonewall Jackson* (1928) and *Jefferson Davis* (1929).

Sources

Bishop, Ferman. *Allen Tate*. New York: Twayne, 1967.
Underwood, Thomas A. *Allen Tate: Orphan of the South*. Princeton: Princeton University Press, 2001.

Tate, James Vincent (1943–) *poet*

James Tate's talent was recognized early when his book, *The Lost Pilot* (1967), won the YALE SERIES OF YOUNGER POETS award. Robert LOWELL liked his understated, casual style, laced with self-deprecating humor. Tate's sharp turns of phrase are evident in later collections such as *The Oblivion Ha-Ha* (1970), *Absences* (1972), *Viper Jazz* (1976), *Riven Doggeries* (1979), *Constant Defender* (1983), and *Reckoner* (1986). *Selected Poems* (1992) won a Pulitzer Prize. *Wonderful Company of Fletchers* (1994) won a National Book Award.

Sources

Upton, Lee. *The Muse of Abandonment: Origin, Identity, Mastery, in Five American Poets*. Lewisburg, Pa.: Bucknell University Press, 1998.

Taylor, Peter Hillsman (1917–1994) *short story writer, novelist*

Peter Taylor was born in Trenton, Tennessee, but grew up in Nashville, St. Louis, and Memphis, and was able to witness the changes taking place in the 20th-century South. At Vanderbilt University he was taught by John Crowe RANSOM, who along with Allen TATE and Robert Penn WARREN become important influences on Taylor's writing. He first published his work in the KENYON REVIEW and SEWANEE REVIEW. Taylor was not as well known as other southern writers of his generation, mainly because he concentrated on the short story. His subtle and gentle irony is reminiscent of Ransom's. He generally avoided the gothic violence prevalent in southern fiction. An early novella, *A Woman of Means,* is considered one of his finest works for its sensitive portrayal of a woman's breakdown when her urban sensibility clashes with her father's rural values. Late in his career he published a novel, *A Summons to Memphis* (1986), which was well received. Since his death his reputation has grown. *The Collected Stories of Peter Taylor* was published in 1969, *The Miro District and Other Stories* in 1977, *The Old Forest* in 1985, and *The Oracle at Stoneleigh Court* in 1993. *Conversations with Peter Taylor* was published in 1987.

Sources

McAlexander, Hubert Hurton. *Peter Taylor: A Writer's Life.* Baton Rouge: Louisiana State University Press, 2001.

Robinson, David M. *World of Relations: The Achievement of Peter Taylor.* Lexington: University Press of Kentucky, 1998.

Stephens, C. Ralph and Lynda B. Salamon, ed. *The Craft of Peter Taylor.* Tuscaloosa: University of Alabama Press, 1995.

Taylor, Robert Lewis (1912–1998) *journalist, novelist, biographer*

Taylor wrote many profiles for the NEW YORKER. In that genre is his compact and lively biography, *W. C. Fields: His Follies and Fortunes* (1949) and his more extensive narrative, *Vessel of Wrath* (1966), the life of the temperance agitator Carry Nation. Taylor also wrote satirical novels, the best of which is *The Travels of Jamie McPheeters* (1958), which won a Pulitzer Prize. The story, set in 1849, follows a young boy and his father as they travel from Louisville to California to take part in the gold rush. Taylor's later work includes a novel set during Reconstruction, *A Journey to Matecumbe* (1961); another set during the Mexican War, *Two Roads to Guadalupe* (1964); a western set in the 19th century, *A Roaring in the Wind* (1978); and *Niagara* (1980), a boisterous account of life in a resort town.

Sources

Special Collections, Morris Library. "Robert Lewis Taylor Papers." Southern Illinois University Carbondale. Available on-line. URL: http://www.lib.siu.edu/spcol/SC049.html. Downloaded October 25, 2001.

Teasdale, Sara (1884–1933) *poet*

Born in Missouri, Teasdale settled in New York. She was a traditionalist who favored the sonnet form, although her verse is devoid of rhetorical flourishes and reflects a desire to evoke emotion simply. Her books include *Sonnets to Duse and Other Poems* (1907); *Helen of Troy* (1911); *Rivers to the Sea* (1915); *Love Songs* (1917), winner of a Pulitzer Prize; *Flame and Shadow* (1920); *Dark of the Moon* (1926); *Strange Victory* (1933); and *Collected Poems* (1937).

Sources

Carpenter, Margaret Haley. *Sara Teasdale: A Biography.* Norfolk, Va.: Pentelic Press, 1977.

Drake, William. *Sara Teasdale: Woman & Poet.* San Francisco: Harper & Row, 1979.

Schoen, Carol B. *Sara Teasdale.* Boston: Twayne, 1986.

Terkel, Studs (Louis Terkel) (1912–) *interviewer*

Born Louis Terkel in Chicago, he took the name "Studs" from the main character Studs Lonigan in James T. FARRELL's novels. During a long career in radio as an interviewer Terkel began to publish beautifully crafted collections of interviews. *Hard Times* (1970) created a magnificent oral history of the GREAT DEPRESSION; *American Dreams: Lost and Found* (1980) explores the myth of America, relying on the testimony of people from many different classes, races, and occupations. As with all his books, the interviews became a statement of Terkel's generous and compassionate democratic sensibility. *The Good War* (1984), an oral history of WORLD WAR II, won a Pulitzer Prize. *Talking to Myself: A Memoir of My Times* appeared in 1977.

Terkel's other books include *Working: People Talk About What They Do All Day and How They Feel About What They Do* (1974); *Race: How Blacks and Whites Think and Feel about the American Obsession* (1993); *Coming of Age: The Story of Our Century by Those Who've Lived It* (1996); *My American Century* (1997), a collection of his most memorable interviews; and *Will the Circle Be Unbroken?: Reflections on Death, Rebirth, and Hunger for a Faith* (2001).

Sources

Baker, James T. *Studs Terkel.* New York: Twayne, 1992.

Parker, Tony. *Studs Terkel: A Life in Words.* New York: Henry Holt, 1996.

Theatre Arts periodical

Founded in Detroit in 1916 as a quarterly, *Theatre Arts* became a monthly in 1924. Aimed at a popular audience, its articles were well informed, sophisticated, and illustrated with superb photographs. It ceased publication in 1964.

Theatre Guild

Founded in 1918 as a little theater, a forerunner of OFF BROADWAY and OFF-OFF-BROADWAY, the Guild produced experimental and controversial plays, notably by Eugene O'NEILL and George Bernard Shaw. The Guild's bold and creative management attracted large audiences, and it was able to build a large theater in 1925, premiering O'Neill's *Marco Millions* three years later. The larger venue, however, made each play production more risky, since it depended on attracting large audiences, and yet plays with great commercial potential were also candidates for Broadway. Thus the Guild eventually lost sight of its original impulse and by the 1940s was moribund, but members who got their start in the Guild went on to found other important theatrical enterprises such as THE GROUP THEATRE.

Theroux, Paul Edward (1941–) *novelist, travel writer*

Paul Theroux was born in Medford, Massachusetts. His French-Canadian father encouraged his son's literary interests, even prompting Paul and his brother, Alexander, to start a family newspaper. Theroux graduated from the University of Massachusetts with a B.A. degree in English and served in the Peace Corps in 1963. In Africa he became involved in local politics that led to his expulsion from the Peace Corps and his turn toward writing about places all over the world.

Theroux has alternated between travel books and novels, the former earning him best-seller status with *The Great Railway Bazaar* (1975) and *The Old Patagonian Express: By Train Through the Americas* (1979). Many of his stories and novels are set in postcolonial Africa and Southeast Asia, and explore the meaning of civilization and the interaction of different peoples. His early African novels—*Fong and the Indians* (1968), *Girls at Play* (1969), and *Jungle Lovers* (1971)—explore the absurdity of existence. *Saint Jack* (1973) shifts the action to Singapore and to Jack Flowers, a misfit who typifies Theroux's view of modern, displaced man. *The Mosquito Coast* (1981), a novel of Theroux's middle period, explores the consequences of extreme individualism. Allie Fox is western man gone mad in his belief in his own resources. In the jungle he defeats himself in supposing that civilization can be imposed on alien environments. Theroux's later work has become increasing self-referential, with such novels as *My Secret History* (1989) and *My Other Life* (1996) expressing Theroux's avowed need to fictionalize his own life and make himself a character in his own work.

Theroux's other novels include *The Black House* (1974), *The Family Arsenal* (1976), *O-Zone* (1986), *Chicago Loop* (1990), and *Kowloon Tong* (1997). His other travel books include *The Kingdom by the Sea: A Journey Around Great Britain* (1983); *Sailing Through China* (1983); *The Happy Isle of Oceania: Paddling the Pacific* (1992); and *The Pillars of Hercules: A Grand Tour of the Mediterranean* (1995).

Theroux published *The Collected Stories* in 1997 and in 1998 *Sir Vidia's Shadow: A Friendship Across Three Continents*, a memoir of his mentor turned ex-friend, the writer V. S. Naipaul.

Sources

Coale, Samuel. *Paul Theroux.* Boston: Twayne, 1987.

Thompson, Dorothy (1894–1961) *reporter, newspaper columnist*

Thompson first attained prominence with her eyewitness account *I Saw Hitler* (1932), one of the first American works to warn of Adolf Hitler's menace. After her interview with the Nazi leader she was expelled from Germany. She wrote a syndicated daily column, "On the Record," about domestic and world affairs. Her views were considered influential from 1930s to the 1950s. She was married from 1928 to 1942 to Sinclair LEWIS.

Sources

Kurth, Peter. *American Cassandra: The Life of Dorothy Thompson.* Boston: Little, Brown, 1990.

Thurber, James Grover (1894–1961) *journalist, essayist, short story writer, cartoonist*

James Thurber grew up in Columbus, Ohio, and began his career there as a journalist. He met the writer E. B. WHITE in 1927 and they became friends. White introduced Thurber to Harold Ross, editor of the NEW YORKER, and Thurber joined the magazine's staff, helping to establish its witty and whimsical style. His work exposed the foibles of American characters, especially husbands and wives. His cartoons often summed up his sardonic view of life. His most famous story is "The Secret Life of WALTER MITTY," which recounts the fantasies of an ordinary man who projects himself into heroic roles. It was made into a movie starring Danny Kaye.

Thurber was known for what has been called his "deadpan prose," a kind of writing that was apparently somber, even morose, and yet very funny. The humor arises from ridiculous situations treated with utmost seriousness.

White and Thurber collaborated on *Is Sex Necessary?* (1929), a spoof of pop psychology books. Thurber and Elliot Nugent collaborated on *The Male Animal* (1940), a successful play that became an equally successful film starring Henry Fonda.

Thurber's other books include *The Middle-Aged Man on the Flying Trapeze* (1935) and *The Thurber Carnival* (1945). *The Years with Ross* (1959) is a memoir of Harold Ross and his years as the idiosyncratic editor of *The New Yorker*.

Sources

Kinney, Harrison. *James Thurber: His Life and Times.* New York: Henry Holt, 1995.
Morsberger, Robert E. *James Thurber.* New York: Twayne, 1964.

Time periodical

Founded in 1923 by Henry Luce as a weekly newsmagazine, *Time* pioneered rewriting news reports from other newspapers as sections of the magazine—all written in a brisk style that capsulized the world for readers wishing a quick review of events. Sections on the theater, film, politics, with notable contributors such as James AGEE and Whittaker Chambers made *Time* a popular and influential publication. *Time* merged with THE LITERARY DIGEST in 1938. While still a widely read magazine, its influence has waned with competition from *Newsweek,* other magazines, and the proliferation of media on network and cable television.

To Kill a Mockingbird Harper Lee (1960) novel

This novel, set in Alabama in the GREAT DEPRESSION, raises important issues about race and American justice.

Atticus Finch, a white lawyer, defends Tom Robinson, a black man accused of raping a white woman in a small southern town. At stake is not only Tom's freedom but also Atticus's battle with his community, where racism and violence threaten to overwhelm the justice system. As a father, Atticus must set an example for his own children. How can he instill proper values in them if the courts do not reflect his sense of integrity and truth?

The situation would seem to be hopeless for Atticus. He anticipates not only a guilty verdict but also threats against himself and his family simply because he has taken the case. Atticus's daughter, Jean Louise, a tomboy called "Scout" who narrates the novel, hears her father called a "nigger lover" at school and on his instruction has to defend herself with words, not her fists. In the meantime, Atticus's own sister, Alexandra, criticizes him for ruining the family.

In the trial Atticus brilliantly exposes all of the weaknesses in the prosecution's case. Without a doubt, Robinson is innocent. Nevertheless, the jury returns a predictable guilty verdict. Having lost hope, Robinson tries to escape from prison and is killed. Atticus's children are assaulted by Bob Ewell, the poor white father of the girl Robinson was accused of raping. The children are saved from more serious injury by a neighbor, who kills Ewell. The novel ends with Atticus by the bedside of his son, Jem, whose left arm was broken by Ewell.

A best-seller when it first appeared, Harper LEE's only novel has continued to engage readers because it exposes with such sensitivity the damage racism causes—not only to its victims but also to the communities that allow preju-

dice to rule people's imaginations. The horrific impact on children of a racist society has never been better dramatized than in this novel. At the same time, Lee does not simplify the problem. Indeed, she acknowledges the flaws in the legal system and shows how justice can be perverted. Above all, the novel emphasizes that justice, humanity, and freedom are not to be taken for granted and that they must be earned—sometimes at a tremendous cost to individuals and to families.

Sources

Bloom, Harold, ed. *Harper Lee's To Kill a Mockingbird.* Philadelphia: Chelsea House, 1998.
O'Neill, Terry. *Readings on To Kill a Mockingbird.* San Diego, Calif.: Greenhaven Press, 2000.

Tolson, Melvin Beaunorus (1898–1966) poet

An African-American Missouri native, Melvin Tolson graduated from Lincoln University in Pennsylvania and taught at Langston University in Missouri. He established his reputation with *Rendezvous with America* (1944)—eloquent poetry that draws a stark contrast between European, American, and African-American history—and *Libretto from the Republic of Liberia* (1953). For much of his life he worked on an unfinished epic about the history of African Americans, some of which appears in *Harlem Portraits* (1979), which has been compared to Edgar Lee MASTERS's *Spoon River Anthology. Caviar and Cabbage* (1982) collects his newspaper articles.

Sources

Berube, Michael. *Marginal Forces/Cultural Centers: Tolson, Pynchon, and the Politics of the Canon.* Ithaca, N.Y.: Cornell University Press, 1992.
Farnsworth, Robert M. *Melvin B. Tolson, 1898–1966: Plain Talk and Poetic Prophecy.* Columbia: University of Missouri Press, 1984.
Flasch, Joy. *Melvin B. Tolson.* New York: Twayne, 1972.

Toole, John Kennedy (1937–1969) novelist

Born in New Orleans, educated at Tulane and at Columbia University, where he earned an M.A. degree, Toole served in the army and then taught at several colleges. He set to work on a robust comic novel, *A Confederacy of Dunces,* about the French Quarter of New Orleans. After many futile efforts to find a publisher, he committed suicide. His mother gave the book to the novelist Walker PERCY, who persuaded Louisiana State University Press to publish it in 1980. The novel won a Pulitzer Prize and is now recognized as a contemporary classic. In Percy's words, the novel celebrates the life of a "fat Don Quixote," a phrase that captures the novel's creation of a modern picaresque myth.

Sources

Nevils, René Pol and Deborah George Hardy. *Ignatius Rising: The Life of John Kennedy Toole.* Baton Rouge: Louisiana State University Press, 2001.

Toomer, Jean (1894–1967) *writer*

Born in Washington, D.C., Toomer, an African American, graduated from Paul Laurence Dunbar High School in 1914. With the support of his grandmother and uncle, he cultivated his intellectual interests, beginning work on the first sections of his innovative book *Cane* (1923), one of the key texts of the HARLEM RENAISSANCE. The book was stimulated by his first visit to the South in 1921. Struck by Georgia's landscape and the legacy of slavery and segregation, Toomer also explored the vitality of African-American storytelling and myth. *Cane* is an impressive amalgam of his sophisticated style and the folklore he absorbed on his travels, with passages of almost pure poetry, suggestive character sketches, and lush evocations of nature. *Cane* demonstrated how African-American writers could combine poetry and prose and a concern for the manners and sensibilities of diverse characters.

But *Cane* initially sold fewer than 500 copies, and Toomer abandoned fiction to undertake a lifelong philosophical search for an understanding of human development. Even though *Cane* was a groundbreaking work that influenced many writers—Gloria NAYLOR and Alice WALKER have paid Toomer homage—Toomer himself seemed unable to build upon it in literary terms. *Essentials* (1931) is a collection of aphorisms on human identity. *A Jean Toomer Reader: Selected Unpublished Writings* appeared in 1993.

Sources

O'Daniel, Therman B., ed. *Jean Toomer: A Critical Evaluation.* Washington, D.C.: Howard University Press, 1988.

Torrence, Frederic Ridgely (1875–1950) *poet, dramatist, journalist*

A New York native, Ridgely Torrence collected his best poetry in *Poems* (1941, 1952), which evokes a sense of the spiritual and the dignity of life. *Granny Maumee, The Rider of Dreams,* and *Simon the Cyrenian* are plays about African Americans, all published in 1917, just before the advent of the HARLEM RENAISSANCE. Torrence also wrote the biography of a black educator, *The Story of John Hope* (1948). A friend of Edwin Arlington ROBINSON, he edited his friend's correspondence, publishing *Selected Letters* in 1940.

Sources

Clum, John M. *Ridgely Torrence.* New York: Twayne, 1972.

Traven, B. (Berick Traven Torsvan) *novelist*

Virtually nothing certain is known about this author, although he was apparently born in 1890 in Chicago to Swedish parents. At different times, he lived in the United States, Germany, and Mexico. His most famous novel is *The Treasure of Sierre Madre* (1935), the story of three Americans searching for a gold mine in the Mexican mountains. The story was filmed by John Huston and became a classic, starring Walter Huston and Humphrey Bogart. Traven's shorter fiction has been collected in *Stories by the Man Nobody Knows* (1961) and *The Night Visitor* (1973). Traven's fiction reveals strong radical sympathies. He identifies with the downtrodden, but he is also acutely aware of the terrible flaws in human nature.

Sources

Mezo, Richard E. *A Study of B. Traven's Fiction: The Journey to Solipaz.* Lewiston, N.Y.: Edwin Mellen Press, 1993.
Zogbaum, Heidi. *B. Traven: A Vision of Mexico.* Wilmington, Del.: SR Books, 1992.

Trillin, Calvin (1935–) *journalist*

Born in Kansas City, Missouri, and educated at Yale, Trillin worked as a reporter at TIME and as a staff writer at the NEW YORKER. He has written a wide range of books that reflect his political interests and satirical temper. *Education in Georgia* (1964) is an account of the first African Americans to be admitted to the state's university. *U.S. Journal* (1971) surveys various sections of the country. *American Fried* (1974) is about American cuisine, as is *Alice, Let's Eat* (1978), *Third Helpings* (1983), and *Travels With Alice* (1989). Trillin's mastery of the comic is on display in *Uncivil Liberties* (1982), *With All Disrespect* (1985), and *If You Can't Say Something Nice* (1987). For many years Trillin has published his doggerel about politics in *The Nation* and written about his work in *Deadline Poet: My Life as a Doggerelist* (1994).

Trillin's later work includes *Remembering Denny* (1993), the story of a friend who committed suicide; *Messages From My Father* (1996) and *Family Man* (1998), both memoirs; and a novel, *Tepper Isn't Going Out* (2001). He has collected his sketches and essays in *Too Soon to Tell* (1995).

Sources

"The Salon Interview: Calvin Trillin." Salon. Available on-line. URL: http://www.salon.com/weekly/interview960624.html. Downloaded June 17, 2001.

Trilling, Diana (1905–1996) *essayist*

A New York City native, Trilling began her career as a singer, then married the critic Lionel TRILLING and became a reviewer for the *Nation* and other periodicals. Her *Claremont Essays* (1964) established her as one of the most important essayists of her generation, with a range of social, political, and literary concerns that surpassed her husband's. More outspoken than her husband, her staunch anti-Communist politics are evident in *We Must March My Darlings* (1977), a collection of essays. Trilling's biographical profile, *Mrs. Harris* (1981), about the private school teacher and administrator who murdered her lover, a famous diet doctor, is a good example of Trilling's scorching sense of morality and of her mandarin style. She wrote a candid and painful memoir about her marriage, *The Beginning of the Journey: The Marriage of Diana and Lionel Trilling* (1993).

Sources

Laskin, David. *Partisans: Marriage, Politics, and Betrayal among the New York Intellectuals.* Chicago: University of Chicago Press, 2001.

Trilling, Lionel (1905–1975) *literary critic, short story writer, novelist*

Trilling grew up in New York City and was educated at Columbia University. He became one of the first Jews to earn tenure at Columbia. He then became one of the university's most prominent teachers in its Great Works of Literature program. Trilling's first book, *Matthew Arnold* (1939), an intellectual biography of the English poet and critic, established Trilling's credentials as a sensitive interpreter of writers' careers. Unlike the NEW CRITICISM Trilling did not concentrate on a writer's work alone but also considered the writer's psychology, social background, and political beliefs. Trilling's signature work, *The Liberal Imagination* (1950), solidified his reputation as one of the leading critics of his generation.

This collection of essays, ranging in subject matter from the fiction of Henry James and Theodore DREISER to the psychology of Sigmund Freud, called for liberals to reevaluate their ideology. Although not a conservative himself, Trilling found much in the conservative worldview that appealed to him, because it tempered the liberal belief in progress. Trilling argued for a darker, more complex view of literature and society than he found in most liberal critiques of culture. His book was all the more powerful because it argued within, not against the liberal tradition; Trilling was offering a corrective to other liberals.

Trilling's novel, *The Middle of the Journey,* is a thinly disguised account of Whittaker Chambers and of the postwar COLD WAR world of anti-Communism, in which Chambers won fame for accusing Alger Hiss, a prominent ex-government official, of having been a Communist spy. Trilling knew Chambers and was able to write sympathetically about his friend's involvement in the Communist cause while at the same time revealing the duplicity of the Communist Party and its agents.

Trilling has remained a touchstone figure in American criticism and has been the subject of continuing study be-

cause of the subtlety and ambiguity of his critical stance. Trilling often stood between warring factions, pointing out the flaws in all positions. His other books include *E. M. Forster* (1943), *The Opposing Self* (1955), and *Sincerity and Authenticity* (1972). In such works as *Freud and the Crisis of Our Culture* (1955) he stands as one of the most shrewd and probing critics of Freud's contribution to contemporary culture.

Sources

Rodden, John, ed. *Lionel Trilling and the Critics: Opposing Selves.* Lincoln: University of Nebraska Press, 1999.
Trilling, Diana. *The Beginning of the Journey: The Marriage of Diana and Lionel Trilling.* New York: Harcourt Brace, 1993.

Trumbo, Dalton (1905–1976) *screenwriter, novelist*

Born in Colorado, Trumbo became involved in the political movements of the 1930s, seeking a better form of government than capitalism seemed to offer during the GREAT DEPRESSION. His finest work is *Johnny Got His Gun* (1939), a powerful antiwar novel about a soldier who has lost all of his limbs and is deaf. The soldier has only his brain, so to speak, and moves his head to simulate Morse code signals.

Trumbo was blacklisted in the 1950s when he became part of the Hollywood Ten, a group of screenwriters who refused to testify before Congress about their political affiliations, specifically whether they had been members of the Communist Party. During this period of ostracism, Trumbo wrote scripts under other names. He was hired by courageous directors to write scripts for *Exodus* (1960) and *Spartacus* (1960) just as the blacklist was ending. *Additional Dialogue* (1970) collects his letters.

Sources

Cook, Bruce. *Dalton Trumbo.* New York: Scribner's, 1977.

Tuchman, Barbara Wertheim (1912–1989) *journalist, historian*

A New York native, Barbara Tuchman published several books under her maiden name of Wertheim: *The Lost British Policy* (1938), *Bible and Sword* (1956), and *The Zimmerman Telegram* (1958). The latter demonstrates her mature style of narrative drama and historical synthesis as it recounts the role of an intercepted German telegram in the United States entry into WORLD WAR I.

Writing as Barbara Tuchman, she earned a Pulitzer Prize for her brilliant book on the start of World War I, *The Guns of August* (1962). Few narrative historians have surpassed Tuchman's riveting description of how the German army planned its flanking movement and invasion of Belgium in the first days of the war. Tuchman also won a Pulitzer Prize for *Stilwell and the American Experience in China 1911–1945*

(1971), a brilliant synthesis of biography and history. Her other books include *A Distant Mirror* (1978), about Europe in the 14th century; *The March of Folly* (1984), about political ineptitude; *The First Salute* (1988), about the American Revolution; and *Practicing History* (1981), a collection of essays.

Sources

"Tuchman, Barbara Wertheim." Women in American History by Encyclopedia Britannica. Available on-line. URL: http://www.eb.com/women/articles/Tuchman_Barbara_Wertheim.html. Downloaded June 17, 2001.

Tyler, Anne (1941–) *novelist, short story writer*

Tyler was born in Minneapolis, Minnesota, to Quaker parents, and spent her early years in several rural Quaker communes. Her penchant for telling stories to herself developed early, and at Duke University her writing teacher Reynolds PRICE encouraged her to develop her talent.

Tyler's early novels—*If Morning Ever Comes* (1964), *The Tin Can Tree* (1965), *A Slipping Down Life* (1970), *The Clock Winder* (1972), *Celestial Navigation* (1974)—attracted relatively little notice, even though they are full of Tyler's hallmarks: eccentric characters, an emphasis on family relationships, the burden of the individual's isolation from community, and the journeys her characters must undertake to discover their identities. Only with *Searching for Caleb* (1976) did Tyler begin to receive national attention and praise for her sense of wonder and her fresh perceptions. Perhaps it was the ambition of this novel, a five-generation family saga, that stirred admiring critical comment. Except for the mixed reception of *Earthly Possessions* (1977), Tyler's subsequent novels, especially *Morgan's Passing* (1980), *Dinner at the Homesick Restaurant* (1982), *The Accidental Tourist* (1985), and *Breathing Lessons* (1988), were highly praised, calling forth comparisons to Flannery O'CONNOR for their wit and irony. The whimsical nature of Tyler's middle period, however, gave way to darker strains in such novels as *Saint Maybe* (1991), *Ladder of Years* (1995), and *A Patchwork Planet* (1998). *Back When We Were Grownups* (2001), Tyler's 15th novel, is the story of a 53-year-old woman who is the head of a large family. Now a widow, she reflects on her life, searching for an earlier, more authentic self but finding that such a search proves elusive, prompting her to think more deeply about the life she has made for herself.

Sources

Salwak, Dale, ed. *Anne Tyler as Novelist*. Iowa City: University of Iowa Press, 1994.

Stephens, C. Ralph, ed. *The Fiction of Anne Tyler*. Jackson: University Press of Mississippi, 1990.

Uhry, Alfred (1937–) *playwright*

Born in Atlanta, Georgia, Uhry graduated from Brown University and began his career in the theater. He wrote lyrics and librettos for *Here's Where I Belong* (1968); *The Robber Bridegroom* (1976), an adaptation of Eudora WELTY's novel; and *Little Johnny Jones* (1980). His first full-length play, *Driving Miss Daisy*, a poignant drama about an elderly southern white woman and her African-American chauffeur, won a Pulitzer Prize in 1988 and was made into a fine film, the screenplay published in 1989. *The Last Night of Ballyhoo* (1997) is a play about anti-Semitism in the South. His work is unified by his sensitive portrayals of southern culture and character, dramatized in a realistic and gently comic mode. Uhry wrote the book for the musical *Parade* (1999).

Sources

Chelsea Forum. "Alfred Uhry." The Chelsea Forum, Inc. Available on-line. URL: http://www.chelseaforum.com/speakers/Uhry.htm. Downloaded June 17, 2001.

Untermeyer, Jean Starr (1886–1970) *poet*

Praised for the austerity and simplicity of her work, Untermeyer married the poet and anthologist Louis UNTERMEYER, and collected her poems in *Love and Need* (1965). She also published an autobiography, *Private Collection* (1965).

Sources

Untermeyer, Jean Starr. "Autumn (To My Mother)." Available on-line. URL: http://www.bartleby.com/br/104.html. Posted January 1999.

Womack, T. Michael. "Jean Star Untermeyer, 1886–1970," Jean Starr Untermeyer Papers, Yale Collection of American Literature, Beinecke Rare Book Room and Manuscript Library. Available on-line. URL: http://webtext/library.yale.edu/sgml2html/beinecke.unter.sgm.html. Updated January 1998.

Untermeyer, Louis (1885–1977) *poet, biographer, critic, anthologist*

A New York native, Untermeyer earned praise for the lush, romantic quality of his early poetry. He later collected poems from this phase of his career in *Long Feud: Selected Poems* (1962). A considerable scholar of the history of poetry, he published *Collected Parodies* (1926), deft imitations of both ancient and modern poets. In 1937 he published a biography, *Heinrich Heine: Paradox and Poet* (1937). His anthologies, such as *Modern American Poetry* (1919, revised in many subsequent editions) were quite influential, since Untermeyer provides accessible introductions to a broad range of modern poetry informed by his own work as a poet and his associations with great poets such as Robert FROST. His work as a critic is exemplified in *Play in Poetry* (1938). His collection of biographical portraits, *Lives of the Poets,* appeared in 1960. He published two autobiographies: *From Another World* (1939) and *Bygones* (1965). *The Letters of Robert Frost to Louis Untermeyer* was published in 1963.

Sources

"Louis Untermeyer Papers: Biographical Note," University of Delaware Library, Special Collections Department. Available on-line. URL: http://www.lib.udel.edu/ud/spec/findaids/untermey.htm. Updated March 8, 2000.

Updike, John Hoyer (1932–   ) *novelist, short story writer, poet, essayist*

John Updike was born in Shillington, Pennsylvania, attending the local high school and then going to Harvard University, where he majored in English. He graduated in 1954 with the highest honors. After a year in Oxford, studying at the Ruskin School of Drawing and Fine Art, he became a staff writer for the NEW YORKER. He wrote the "Talk of the Town" column and honed his skills as a social observer. His second novel, RABBIT, RUN (1960), was the first in a series of novels that would follow the protagonist, Harry "Rabbit" ANGSTROM, through five decades of American history in *Rabbit Redux* (1971), *Rabbit Is Rich* (1981), and *Rabbit at Rest* (1990).

Updike's third novel, *The Centaur* (1963), won the National Book Award. Drawing on his Pennsylvania background, Updike updated the myth of Chiron the centaur by fusing it with the story of an adolescent boy and his father in the winter of 1947. The narrator is a 30-year-old artist, a painter who calls himself a "second-rate ABSTRACT EXPRESSIONIST." He hopes that by confronting his past he can redeem his dedication to art. His father represents Chiron, part man, part stallion, the mentor of Greek heroes. In the myth, as in Updike's novel, the Centaur/father sacrifices his power (in the myth his immortality) so that the son will be free to succeed. Critics are divided on the extent to which Updike successfully integrates the myth with contemporary reality, but the novel's power to suggest a meaning beyond the everyday strivings of its characters is undeniable.

One of the great strengths of the Rabbit novels is the way Updike demonstrates that human character can change over time. The Rabbit Angstrom of *Rabbit, Run* is an ex-basketball player who cannot equal in the world of work and family the success he had in high school sports. He runs away from responsibility in a novel that presents a rather bleak, existential view of the late 1950s. Yet Rabbit's running is also a metaphor for his seeking a better life, a sign that he is redeemable.

In *Rabbit Redux,* the 1960s Angstrom seems more resilient, if less an active searcher for the truth. He experiences a certain resignation to life, even as his wife, Janice, awakens to a sense of her own autonomy and takes a lover. As in *Rabbit, Run,* however, the rocky marriage does not disintegrate. On the contrary, the end of the novel brings a kind of reconciliation that suggests the Angstroms are on the verge of even greater changes, perhaps even improvements, in their relationship.

In *Rabbit Is Rich,* Angstrom's running has become a symbol of his new energy as well as the fitness craze of the 1970s. He is a successful Toyota dealer and reads *Consumer Reports.* He sees his son, Nelson, making some of the same mistakes he made in early adulthood. But Rabbit himself is not immune to the moral laxity of the times, as he shows in a wife-swapping episode. Indeed, his grip on fundamentals is

slipping, and leads in *Rabbit At Rest* to a confrontation with his own profligacy, which has left him with a bloated body in an intensive care unit—returning to the questions he posed about the meaning of life in *Rabbit, Run.*

The prolific Updike has published 22 novels in a variety of styles that have engaged many of the social, religious, and political issues of his era. In another novel series—*Bech: A Book* (1970), *Bech Is Back* (1982), and *Bech at Bay: A Quasi-Novel* (1998)—Updike has chartered the career of Jewish novelist Henry Bech, following him on his worldwide travels and commenting on the American literary scene. Other novels—especially *Couples* (1968) with its portrayal of wife-swapping, and *The Witches of Eastwick* (1984), with its demonic character Darryl Van Horn and his coven of female lovers—have earned Updike a reputation for dwelling on randy sexuality.

A Month of Sundays (1975), *Roger's Version* (1986), and *S* continue Updike's concern with love, marriage, and adultery, but with a religious intensity, a Puritan focus, that treats sexuality with profound seriousness. Indeed, *Roger's Version* is a rewriting of *The Scarlet Letter* from the point of view of Roger Chillingworth, Hester Prynne's betrayed husband. Updike's desire to rewrite the classics of Western literature is also evinced in *Gertrude and Claudius* (2000), a new version of *Hamlet.*

Updike has addressed the subject of biography in *Memories of the Ford Administration* (1992). In *Buchanan Dying* (1974), he imagines the last words of the president who preceded Abraham Lincoln into office.

Updike has been just as prolific and important as a short story writer. Indeed, in some way his elegant turns of phrase sometimes work even better in short stories, where a single sentence carries significance that other writers take paragraphs to express. Updike has used short story collections to extend and link the lives of his characters, as in *Too Far to Go: The Maples Stories* (1979) and *Your Lover Just Called: Stories of Joan and Richard Maple* (1980).

Many of Updike's stories have become classics, especially "A & P," "Lifeguard," and "Flight"—all from his second collection, *Pigeon Feathers and Other Stories* (1962). They have been called urbane, witty, and sensitive—quintessential *New Yorker* stories. His other story collections include *The Same Door* (1959), *Olinger Stories: A Selection* (1964), *The Music School* (1966), *Museums and Women and Other Stories* (1972), *Trust Me* (1987), and *The Afterlife and Other Stories* (1994).

Updike is also an accomplished poet specializing in light verse. His poetry collections include *The Carpentered Hen and Tame Creatures* (1958); *Telephone Poles and Other Poems* (1963); *Midpoint and Other Poems* (1969); *Tossing and Turning* (1977); *Facing Nature* (1985); *Mites and Other Poems in Miniature* (1990), and *A Helpful Alphabet of Friendly Objects* (1995).

A complete man of letters, Updike has written a considerable body of commentary on literature and art. His principal collections are *Assorted Prose* (1965); *Picked-Up Pieces* (1975); *Hugging the Shore: Essays and Criticism* (1983); *Just Looking: Essays on Art* (1989); *Odd Jobs: Essays and Criticism* (1991); *Gold Dreams: Writing on Gold* (1996); and *More Matter: Essays and Criticism* (1999).

To forestall a biography that Updike learned was in the works, he published *Self-Consciousness: Memoirs* (1989).

Sources

Luscher, Robert M. *John Updike: A Study of the Short Fiction.* New York: Twayne, 1993.

Macnaughton, William R., ed. *Critical Essays on John Updike.* Boston: G.K. Hall, 1982.

Pritchard, William H. *Updike: America's Man of Letters.* South Royalton, Vt.: Steerforth Press, 2000.

Schiff, James A. *John Updike Revisited.* New York: Twayne, 1998.

Uris, Leon (1924–) *novelist*

Born in Baltimore, Maryland, Uris has published several popular novels, beginning with *Battle Cry* (1953), the story of U.S. Marines in WORLD WAR II, based on his own experience in the service. *Exodus* (1958) is the story of Israel's creation against overwhelming odds. *Mila 18* (1961) recounts the Warsaw ghetto uprising in World War II. *Topaz* (1967) is a COLD WAR spy story. *Trinity* (1976) is a comprehensive treatment of the troubles in Ireland from 1840 to 1916. Both *The Haj* (1984) and *Mitla Pass* (1988) return to the story of Israel, the plight of the Palestinians and the Sinai War of 1956. *Redemption* (1995) is set in Ireland and New Zealand between 1910 and 1921.

Sources

Cain, Kathleen Shine. *Leon Uris: A Critical Companion.* Westport, Conn.: Greenwood Press, 1998.

U.S.A. John Dos Passos (1930–1936) *novels*

This trilogy of novels—*The 42nd Parallel* (1930), *1919* (1932), *The Big Money* (1936)—provides a political and social record of American life from the turn of the last century to the 1930s, including capsule biographies of historical figures such as Theodore Roosevelt, Henry Ford, and Woodrow Wilson as well as accounts of historic events. DOS PASSOS's own development is explored in his "Camera Eye" sections, which use the STREAM-OF-CONSCIOUSNESS technique.

Throughout the three novels Dos Passos also traces the fate of several interrelated fictional characters. Charley Anderson's career takes him from his beginnings as a simple worker to the world of international capitalism as the owner of an airplane factory. Corrupted by success, he eventually loses $400,000 and is caught in bed with a chorus girl. He loses his wife and his position, and becomes an alcoholic

making money on inside information in the stock market. He wrecks his car and dies of medical complications.

Margo Dowling grows up in Queens, a child actress with the dream of becoming a movie star. Abandoned by her widower alcoholic father and raped by her stepmother's boyfriend, she marries and moves to Havana at age 16, then returns to New York City and works as a chorus girl. Margo meets Charley Anderson at a diner, and he takes her to Miami. When they return to New York, she gets a job as a model. She meets a producer, takes money from Charley, and takes off to California, expecting to make it big in films. After yet another sexual assault in a Hollywood house, Margo does become a star, although her career is threatened because she does not have a good voice for talking pictures.

Mary French grows up in a mining town in Colorado. She is influenced by her socialist father and eventually goes to work at a settlement house in Chicago, but there she is seduced by a philandering labor leader. In Cleveland and Pittsburgh she finds newspaper work and reports on labor organizers in the steel industry. When the newspaper disapproves of her work, she goes to work for the union. She becomes pregnant, has an abortion, and goes to New York City, where she works for another union and associates with Ben Compton, a fugitive Communist. He leaves her after a tempestuous love affair. Although Mary meets various "successful people" in New York such as Margo Dowling and Eveline Hutchins, their lives seem empty to her, and she rededicates herself to radical politics.

Eveline Hutchins grows up in Chicago and develops an interest in art and men with aesthetic interests. She goes to New York City with her friend Eleanor Stoddard, designs stage sets, and then accompanies her ailing brother to Santa Fe, New Mexico, where she has her first real love affair, with Jose O'Riely, an artist who uses her as a model. She later falls in love with a political activist, but her work drives her to an association with J. Ward Moorhouse, a public relations man with whom she has a brief affair while also pursuing others. While working in Europe for the Red Cross during WORLD WAR I she meets a soldier, has his baby, and marries him.

But Eveline can't settle down, and back in New York she entertains figures such as Margo Dowling, Mary French, another public relations man, Richard Ellsworth Savage, and the aviator Charley Anderson. Eveline meanwhile seems at a loss—her infidelities merely mask her desperation. Though she tries to go back to stage design, it is not fulfilling, and she takes an overdose of sleeping pills after one of her parties.

Mac McCreary moves from his home in Middletown, Connecticut, to Chicago, where he goes to work for his uncle Timothy, a printer and a socialist. When his uncle's business goes under, Mac tours the country with Doc Bingham, selling religious pamphlets and sensationalist booklets about white slavery. Then Mac meets Ike Hall, a socialist from Duluth, and later works for a socialist printer in San Francisco. Mac meets Maisie Spencer and would like to settle down with her, but he is also dedicated to the labor movement. Eventually they marry, but the marriage falls apart over Mac's continued loyalty to the labor movement. Mac goes to Mexico, where he stays with his new love, Concha, and develops his ties to the revolutionary movement there.

J. Ward Moorehouse, born on July 4th, begins his career in real estate. He marries Annabelle Strang, a socialite, and they travel in Europe while he picks up business contacts. Determined to rise as a young executive in advertising, he leaves Annabelle and settles in Pittsburgh. He joins a country club and meets Gertrude Staple, the daughter of a wealthy industrialist. They marry, and she bankrolls his public relations firm. Moorehouse plays both sides of the street, befriending business tycoons and labor leaders to become an international businessman. He seems driven only by ambition, but even after he becomes a "national institution" he is lonely, without much of a personal or emotional life. After a heart attack, Moorehouse relies more heavily on his secretary, Richard Ellsworth Savage.

Savage grows up in Trenton, New Jersey, and is sent to Harvard by a wealthy benefactor. He volunteers for the ambulance service in World War I, even though his politics are antiwar. He sympathizes with the idea of a workers' revolution, and loses his job as a result. He seduces Anne Elizabeth Trent, who commits suicide after she becomes pregnant and he refuses to marry her.

Back home, he meets Eleanor Stoddard and J. Ward Moorehouse, who hires Savage and makes him his confidant. The success goes to Savage's head, and for a period he almost wrecks his career with drink and carousing, but he pulls himself together and is last seen courting the daughter of a home-remedy magnate.

Eleanor Stoddard grows up in Chicago. Disgusted with her father, a stockyard worker, she gravitates toward the world of art. At the Chicago Art Institute she meets Eveline Hutchins. Eleanor works as a decorator at the department store Marshall Fields, and Eveline, an interior decorator, joins her in New York City to work in the theater. Eleanor meets J. Ward Moorehouse, and they become great friends, though not lovers.

When the war begins, Eleanor goes to Paris and volunteers for the Red Cross. Her friendship with Moorehouse turns amorous, although Eleanor later forsakes Moorehouse and seems about to marry Prince Mingraziali, an exile Russian nobleman.

Elizabeth Trent is an idealistic, naive young American girl, the daughter of a Dallas lawyer. She is sent to boarding school in Pennsylvania but runs away. With her father's approval she enrolls in Columbia University and gets involved in social work. She becomes increasingly involved in political activism and Communist agitation.

When World War I begins, Elizabeth goes to Europe to work for the Red Cross. She meets Richard Ellsworth Savage and falls in love with him. When she becomes pregnant, he urges her to get an abortion. She tries unsuccessfully to end her pregnancy through a horse riding accident, but in another reckless episode she dies in a plane crash.

Each of these characters presents Dos Passos's bitter and ironic portrayal of American life in the early 20th century. The country Dos Passos portrays is in the grip of a capitalist menace: Such forces as advertising and interior decoration represent a culture in which the tastes of the masses will be formed for them. Individuality is under attack. In the novels only a few radicals manage to maintain their integrity, and it is doubtful that even they can make fundamental improvements in the American way of life.

Sources

Dickson, David. *The Utterance of America: Emersonian Newness in Dos Passos' U.S.A. and Pynchon's Vineland.* Göteborg, Sweden: Acta Universitatis Gothoburgensis, 1998.

Pizer, Donald. *Dos Passos' U.S.A.: A Critical Study.* Charlottesville: University Press of Virginia, 1988.

Sanders, David S., ed. *The Merrill Studies in U.S.A.* Columbus, Ohio: Merrill, 1972.

Valentine, Jean (1934–) poet

Valentine was born in Chicago and graduated from Radcliffe College. Her first book, *Dream Barker and Other Poems* (1965), exudes a sophisticated handling of literary allusion and was selected for the YALE YOUNG POETS SERIES. Valentine's other collections include *Pilgrims* (1969), *Ordinary Things* (1974), *The Messenger* (1979), *Deep Blue, New and Selected Poems* (1989), *Night Lake* (1992), *The River at Wolf* (1992), *The Under Voice: Selected Poems* (1995), *Growing Darkness, Growing Light* (1997), and *The Cradle of the Real Life* (2000). Her work has been compared to Emily Dickinson's for its compact, profound brevity; to Adrienne RICH's for its use of fragmented forms; and to Amy LOWELL's for its tight focus on images.

Sources

Upton, Lee. *The Muse of Abandonment: Origin, Identity, Mastery, in Five American Poets.* Lewisburg, Pa.: Bucknell University Press, 1998.

Van Doren, Carl Clinton (1885–1950) biographer, critic

Carl Van Doren was a professor at Columbia University from 1911 to 1934 while also serving as literary editor of *The Nation* (1919–1922) and CENTURY MAGAZINE (1922–1925). He wrote several works of literary criticism, including *The American Novel* (1921, revised 1940), *Contemporary American Novelists 1900–1920* (1922), *James Branch CABELL* (1925), *Swift* (1930), and *Sinclair LEWIS* (1933). Van Doren won a Pulitzer Prize for his biography *Benjamin Franklin* (1938). A companion volume is *The Great Rehearsal* (1948), a history of how the Constitution was created. *Three Worlds* (1936) is his autobiography.

Sources

Van Doren, Carl. *The American Novel.* New York: Macmillan, 1921. Available on-line. URL: http://www.bartleby.com/187/. Posted May 2000.

Van Doren, Mark Albert (1894–1972) critic, novelist, short story writer, poet

Like his brother Carl VAN DOREN, Mark Van Doren was a professor at Columbia University (1920–1959) and an editor of *The Nation* (1924–1928). *Private Reader* (1942) collects his literary criticism. Mark Van Doren also wrote about the state of American education in *Liberal Education* (1942). His novels include *The Transients* (1935) and *Windless Cabins* (1940). His *Collected Stories* appeared in 1962.

Van Doren's strength as a creative writer lay in poetry. His *Collected Poems* (1939) won a Pulitzer Prize. Later collections such as *The Mayfield Deer* (1941), *Our Lady Peace* (1942), and *The Country New Year* (1946) reflect his interest in pastoral poetry, rural life, and war. He published *Collected and New Poems* in 1963 and an *Autobiography* in 1958. Van Doren in his time was an example of the consummate man of letters and a man of the academy who could also appeal to a broader literate audience. *The Selected Letters of Mark Van Doren* appeared in 1987.

Sources

Ledbetter, J. T. *Mark Van Doren.* New York: Peter Lang, 1999.

Van Druten, John William (1901–1957)
playwright, screenwriter

Born in England, Van Druten became a United States citizen in 1944. He established his career in the United States in 1925 with his first play, *Young Woodley*. Although he continued to write his own plays, including *The Voice of the Turtle* (1943), a romantic comedy, he spent much of his career adapting the works of others for the stage and screen. Two of his most notable successes were *I Remember Mama* (1944), a play based on the amusing reminiscences of a San Francisco family by Kathryn Forbes, and *Bell, Book, and Candle* (1950), a comedy about witchcraft, which was later made into a movie with Kim Novak and Jack Lemmon.

Sources
New York Public Library Digital Library Collection. "Van Druten (John) Papers, 1920–1957, Biographical Sketch." New York Public Library. Available on-line. URL: http://dig-ilib.nypl.org/dynaweb/ead/human/mssvandrute/@Generic_BookView. Downloaded June 17, 2001.

Van Duyn, Mona (1921–) *poet*

Van Duyn was born in Waterloo, Iowa. An avid reader from a young age, she earned B.A. and M.A. degrees from the University of Iowa. She has taught at the University of Iowa, the University of Louisville, and Washington University. With her husband, Jarvis Thurston, she founded and edited *Perspective*, a literary journal.

Van Duyn's first two books of poetry, *Valentines to the Wide World* (1959) and *A Time of Bees* (1964), were highly praised, and her third volume, *To See, to Take* (1970), won a National Book Award. In 1991 she won the Pulitzer Prize for *Near Changes* (1991), and in 1992 Van Duyn became the first woman named as Poet Laureate to the Library of Congress.

Van Duyn is a master of domestic detail, a poet of the household. Although her work often includes details about her family, she is not an autobiographical or confessional poet, nor does she see her subject as especially feminine, as men also write about their home lives. She has regularly employed conventional forms such as the sonnet and has used rhyme. She pursues what she calls a "minimalist" style that makes sparing use of traditional meters and genres. Van Duyn's poetry can range from the cosmic to gossip, alluding to Plato and Alexander Pope along the way. For her, poetry is a vehicle of understanding, a way of relating to the world.

Sources
Burns, Michael, ed. *Discovery and Reminiscence: Essays on the Poetry of Mona Van Duyn*. Fayetteville: University of Arkansas Press, 1998.

Vanity Fair periodical

Edited from 1914 to 1935 by Frank Crowninshield, *Vanity Fair* became an elegant magazine that published some of the finest writers of the age, including Ezra POUND and Ernest HEMINGWAY. In 1960 Cleveland Amory and Frederic Bradless edited a selection of articles, stories, and pictures from the magazine entitled *Vanity Fair: A Cavalcade of the Twenties*. In 1983, under the editorship of Tina Brown, the magazine was revived, and after a shaky start, found a niche with celebrity profiles and articles about politics and the arts.

Van Vechten, Carl (1880–1964) *novelist, photographer, critic*

Born in Iowa, Van Vechten graduated from the University of Chicago in 1903 and went to work for the *New York Times*. His dramatic criticism and other articles from this period are collected in *Red* (1925) and *Excavations* (1926). He then turned to creative writing—novels that satirized and celebrated the activities of the sophisticated crowd in New York City. His best work in this vein is *Firecrackers* (1925) and *Parties* (1930). *Nigger Heaven* (1926) is probably his most lasting work, if only for its historical importance, for it reflected the excitement generated by the HARLEM RENAISSANCE. Van Vechten treated life in Harlem sympathetically. Like Eugene O'NEILL and other white authors, he saw artistic material worth preserving and celebrating in the African-American community.

Much of Van Vechten's work after 1930 involved photography. He took fine portraits of many of America's greatest writers. His last book was an autobiography, *Sacred and Profane Memories* (1932).

Several collections of Van Vechten's correspondence have been published: *The Letters of Gertrude Stein and Carl Van Vechten, 1913–1946* (1986), *Letters of Carl Van Vechten* (1987), *Remember Me to Harlem: The Letters of Langston Hughes and Carl Van Vechten, 1925–1964* (2001).

Sources
Coleman, Leon. *Carl Van Vechten and the Harlem Renaissance: A Critical Assessment*. New York: Garland, 1998.

Lueders, Edward G. *Carl Van Vechten*. New York: Twayne, 1965.

Variety periodical

Established in 1905 as a trade publication for the theater and movies, *Variety* has also been noted for its humor and coinages such as "eatery," "vamp," and "scram." Published daily, it remains the publication to consult for news about the business of Hollywood, its products and personalities. *Variety* also reviews books about film, theater, and other aspects of the entertainment/culture industry.

Vidal, Gore (Eugene Luther Vidal) (1925–   )
novelist, playwright, essayist, critic

Born at West Point, New York, Eugene Luther Vidal (he took his mother's surname, Gore, at the age of 14) grew up in Washington, D.C., where his father worked for the Franklin Delano Roosevelt administration. His mother was the daughter of the influential senator Thomas P. Gore of Oklahoma. The young Vidal developed an interest in politics that would become the major concern of his novels, plays, and essays. Indeed, Vidal is unique among American novelists of his generation in that he not only grew up at the seat of power but also has run for political office—first for a U.S. congressional seat in upstate New York and then for a U.S. senatorial seat in California. Vidal also played a U.S. senator in the film *Bob Roberts* (1992).

Vidal had a privileged education at St. Albans School and Philips Exeter Academy. He refused to go to college, however, and enlisted, instead, in the U.S. Army in 1943. By 1946 he had published his first novel, *Williwaw* (1946), which is about his military experience in the Aleutians.

But it was Vidal's third novel, *The City and the Pillar* (1948, revised 1965), which brought him notoriety and trouble. Never reticent about his homosexuality, he explored the issue in this novel, which some critics have called a study of obsession because of its intense focus on a young man whose homosexuality isolates him from others. Unlike most earlier writing about homosexuality, Vidal did not treat it as a misfortune or an aberration. Readers assumed that his main character, Bob Ford, reflected Vidal's own view on sexuality, and Vidal believed that a not-so-subtle prejudice against him soured the reception of his subsequent novels, *The Season of Comfort* (1949), *A Search for the King: A Twelfth Century Legend* (1950), *Dark Green, Bright Red* (1950), *The Judgment of Paris* (1952, revised 1965), and *Messiah* (1954). By 1953 Vidal was largely ignored as a novelist, and he turned to television writing to support himself. He also wrote potboiler detective novels under the name Edgar Box.

Not until *Julian* (1964), a novel about Julian the Apostate and the Roman world, did Vidal again attract critical attention and popular approval. As with his later novels about American history, Vidal was able to develop a main character who mirrored many of the author's own heterodox political, social, and religious ideas. Vidal enticed readers by making the novel a memoir, a kind of confession written by Julian. Here Vidal discovered his major gift, an ability to write convincing, entertaining, and sometimes profound historical fiction.

Burr (1973), which some critics consider Vidal's masterpiece, is a thoroughgoing revisionist account of America's Founding Fathers told from the point of view of a dissenter—a man who has been at the seat of power and seen its corruption. Like Vidal himself, Burr is a fierce critic of the establishment and realizes he will be punished for revealing the secrets of the powerful. By 1973 Vidal had written extensively about his own family's background and his forays

into politics, so many readers of *Burr* had the satisfaction of reading history through the lens of a contemporary commentator on the national scene. The novel reflected Vidal's harsh judgment that America began to decline as soon as it tried to become an empire rather than a republic. From his study of the ancient world, Vidal argues that early America was following the same course as Rome, which fell because the Empire betrayed the ideals of the Republic. For Vidal, this American decline began very early, with Thomas Jefferson's quasi-legal Louisiana Purchase.

Burr is one of the finest novels in a series of works by Vidal that span American history. In terms of historical chronology, *Burr* comes first, followed by *Lincoln* (1984), *1876* (1976), *Empire* (1987), *Hollywood: A Novel of America in the 1920's* (1990), *The Golden Age* (2000), and *Washington, D.C.* (1967). These novels are written with extraordinary wit and an awesome command of historical sources. They also reflect a heavy ideological bias against the conventional, patriotic view of the American past and present. In *The Golden Age,* for example, Vidal sees Franklin Roosevelt as a politician who schemed, indeed invited the attack on Pearl Harbor to get the nation into war. Virtually the only exception to Vidal's cynical view of American history is his treatment of Abraham Lincoln. Although Vidal points out Lincoln's violations of the U.S. Constitution during the Civil War, he portrays Lincoln as a political giant, a man far wiser than his cabinet colleagues or the press.

No other American novelist has presented so many memorable portraits of American figures such as William Randolph Hearst (in *Empire, Hollywood,* and *The Golden Age*), Harry Hopkins (in *The Golden Age*), Henry Adams, Henry James, and Theodore Roosevelt (in *Empire*), Harry Truman (in *The Golden Age* and *Washington, D.C.*), and a fictionalized John F. Kennedy, named Clay Overbury in *The Golden Age* and *Washington, D.C.*. From presidents to very minor historical figures, Vidal portrays a vivid past and revisits historical issues in a provocative, if not always balanced, way.

Vidal also has continued to publish contemporary novels, such as *Myra Breckenridge* (1968) and *Myron* (1974), that challenge conventional notions of sexuality. Like Vidal's essays, these novels are acid on the subject of America's heterosexual tyranny. Myra Breckenridge, for example, is a transsexual who is fiercely proud of her femininity and contemptuous of men: "To be a man in a society of machines is to be an expendable, soft auxiliary to what is useful and hard." Later Myra rapes the all-American stud Rusty with a dildo. In *Myron*, a surrealistic novel and an even fiercer attack on American sexual identity, Myra and her husband, Myron, fight for control over the body they share.

Messiah (1954), *Kalki* (1978), and *Creation* (1981), all set in the ancient world, represent Vidal's most expansive thoughts on the nature of civilization and the prospects for the future.

Vidal won a 1993 National Book Award for *United States: Essays: 1952–1992*, a massive collection of criticism about

American literature and history. Vidal's satirical wit and deep grounding in politics have prompted many critics to prefer his nonfiction, which gives full rein to Vidal's most iconoclastic opinions. In an essay on the avant-garde novelist Susan SONTAG, for example, he suggests that her quest to be different does not reflect (as she thinks) the sophisticated European taste for experimental fiction but instead the values of Detroit, which demand a new model car every year.

Vidal's plays *The Best Man: A Play About Politics* (1960) and *An Evening with Richard Nixon* (1972) were well received in New York when first produced. Vidal also wrote screenplays for *The Catered Affair* (1956) and *Suddenly Last Summer* (1959), adapted from Tennessee WILLIAMS's play.

Views from a Window: Conversations with Gore Vidal appeared in 1980. *Palimpsest: A Memoir* appeared in 1995, *Gore Vidal, Sexually Speaking: Collected Sex Writings* in 1999, and *The Essential Vidal*, a collection of his most important writings, also in 1999.

Sources

Baker, Susan and Curtis S. Gibson. *Gore Vidal: A Critical Companion.* Westport, Conn.: Greenwood Press, 1997.

Dick, Bernard F. *The Apostate Angel: A Critical Study of Gore Vidal.* New York: Random House, 1974.

Kaplan, Fred. *Gore Vidal: A Biography.* New York: Doubleday, 1999.

Parini, Jay, ed. *Gore Vidal: Writing Against the Grain.* New York: Columbia University Press, 1992.

Viereck, Peter (1916–) *historian, poet*

A professor of history at Mount Holyoke College since 1948, Viereck has published several books of intellectual history, including *Conservatism Revisited—The Revolt Against Revolt—1815–1949* (1949), *Shame and Glory of the Intellectuals* (1953), and *Dream and Responsibility: The Tension Between Poetry and Society* (1953).

Viereck also enjoys a considerable reputation as a lyric poet. *Terror and Decorum* (1948) won a Pulitzer Prize. He published his *New and Selected Poems* in 1967 and *Tide and Continuities: Last and First Poems, 1995–1938* in 1995.

Sources

Henault, Mary. *Peter Viereck.* New York: Twayne, 1969.

Weinstein, Michael A. "Peter Viereck: Reconciliation and Beyond." *Humanitas* 10:2 (1997). Available on-line. URL: http://www.nhumanities.org/WEIN.htm. Updated April 8, 2000.

Vietnam War

United States forces first entered Vietnam in 1954 and finally withdrew in 1973. In 1954 Vietnam had been split into two opposing sections: The North became Communist, and the South was an ally of the U.S. and other Western powers. The Communists had defeated a French colonial army in 1954, and the United States had to decide to what extent it would resist the spread of Communism. (For a view of America's early involvement in Vietnam, see Eugene Burdick and William Lederer's *The Ugly American* [1958].)

COLD WAR politics made Vietnam a crucial test of U.S. determination to prevent the Soviet Union and China from using the North Vietnamese Communists to their advantage. However, by the mid-1960s, serious doubts were raised about the wisdom of President Johnson's decision to send in more American troops. Those Americans opposed to the country's involvement in Vietnam saw the conflict there as essentially a civil war, not a proxy war between Communists and anti-Communists. Writers such as Mary MCCARTHY and Susan SONTAG visited North Vietnam, expressed sympathy for the North's effort to unify the country, and condemned the U.S. bombing of the country—even suggesting it was tantamount to genocide.

Supporters of the war included John STEINBECK and James JONES, who wrote essays and books about their visits to the war scene. In *Green Berets* (1965), Robin Moore tried to recover the heroic idea of the American mission in Vietnam by making the special forces (Green Berets) seem like cowboys, a point reinforced by John Wayne's 1968 movie version of the novel.

But the overwhelming tenor of the literature on Vietnam has been antiwar. In *Dog Soldiers* (1974), Robert STONE explores the seamy side of the war, the corruption and drug use rife in Vietnam during the U.S. occupation. In *Dispatches* (1977), one of the finest memoirs of the war, Michael HERR squarely faces his own violent tendencies exacerbated by the war. Francis Ford Coppola's film *Apocalypse Now* (1979) viewed the war though an elaborate parallel with Joseph Conrad's *Heart of Darkness,* one of the key texts about the horror and the corruption of imperialism.

Memoirs by other returning soldiers seemed to confirm Coppola's view. Among the most memorable accounts are Ron Kovic's *Born on the Fourth of July* (1976); Wallace Terry's *Bloods: An Oral History of the Vietnam War by Black Veterans* (1982); Tim O'BRIEN's *If I Die in a Combat Zone* (1973) and *Going After Cacciato* (1978); and Philip Caputo's *A Rumor of War* (1977).

Other important novels about the war include Bobbie Ann MASON's *In Country* (1985); Philip Caputo's *Indian Country* (1987); and Tim O'Brien's *The Things They Carried* (1990).

Robert Olen BUTLER has explored the war and its effects in several works. *The Alleys of Eden* (1981) is the story of an American deserter who falls in love with a Vietnamese prostitute. *On Distant Ground* (1985) is about a veteran returning to Vietnam in search of his lover and son. *A Good Scent from a Strange Mountain* (1993), a collection of stories about Vietnamese emigrés in a Louisiana town, won a

Pulitzer Prize. *They Whisper* (1994) is a novel about a Vietnam veteran and his wife.

Several anthologies of poetry have been published about the war, including *Carrying the Darkness* (1985), edited by E. D. Ehrhart, and *Winning Hearts and Minds* (1972), edited by Larry Rottman. *Writing Fire* (1978) is a collection of short stories edited by Jerome Klinkowitz and John Somers.

David RABE (*Sticks and Bones* [1971] and *Streamers* [1976]) is the important dramatist to emerge out of the war and to dramatize it and its aftermath. Other plays about the conflict include Barbara Garson's *Macbird* (1967) and Megan Terry's *Viet Rock* (1967).

Sources

Bates, Milton J. *The Wars We Took to Vietnam: Cultural Conflict and Storytelling.* Berkeley: University of California Press, 1996.
Jason, Philip K. *Acts and Shadows: The Vietnam War in American Literary Culture.* Lanham, Md.: Rowman & Littlefield, 2000.

Virginia Quarterly Review periodical

Founded in 1925, this literary and current events journal has published work by Allen TATE, Robert FROST, Sherwood ANDERSON, and many others. It continues to publish articles and reviews of interest to a broad audience concerned with the arts, culture, and politics. The magazine's focus is more national than regional.

Vizenor, Gerald (1934–) poet, novelist

Born in Minneapolis of Ojibway and French parents, Vizenor later became a member of the Chippewa. His poetry, collected in *Raising the Moon* (1964), *Two Wings the Butterfly* (1967), and *Matushima Haiku* (1984), has been praised for its formal qualities.

Vizenor writes about contemporary Indian life in his novels: *Darkness in St. Louis Bearheart* (1978), *Trickster of Liberty* (1988), *Hotline Healers: An Almost Browne Novel* (1997), and *Chancers* (2000). His short fiction has been collected in *Landfill Meditation: Crossblood Stories* (1991).

Vizenor's essays are collected in *Cross Bloods* (1990). *Interior Landscapes: Autobiographical Myths and Metaphors* also appeared in 1990. His other studies of Native American literature and culture include *Dead Voices: Natural Agonies in the New World* (1992), *Manifest Manners: Postindian Warriors of Survivance* (1994), and *Fugitive Poses: Native American Indian Scenes of Absence and Presence* (1998).

Vizenor's interviews have been collected in *Postindian Conversations* (1999) and in *Momaday, Vizenor, Armstrong: Conversations on American Indian Writing* (1999). He has also edited *Narrative Chance: Postmodern Discourse on Native American Indian Literatures* (1993) and *Summer in the Spring: Anishinaabe Lyric Poems and Stories* (1993).

Sources

Krupat, Arnold. *The Turn to the Native: Studies in Criticism and Culture.* Lincoln: University of Nebraska Press, 1996.
Lee, Robert, ed. *Loosening the Seams: Interpretations of Gerald Vizenor.* Bowling Green, Ohio: Bowling Green State University Popular Press, 2000.

Vogue periodical

Founded in 1892, *Vogue* today is primarily a fashion magazine, but in its history it has published many important writers, including Katherine Anne PORTER, Ernest HEMINGWAY, and Susan SONTAG. In 1935 it absorbed *VANITY FAIR*, which later was revived as a separate magazine. One of the magazine's important editors, Edna Woolman Chase, published her autobiography, *Always in Vogue* (1954), which reveals how the magazine helped shaped American tastes. Frank Crowninshield edited *Vogue's First Reader* (1942).

Vonnegut, Kurt, Jr. (1922–) novelist, short story writer

Born in Indianapolis, Indiana, Kurt Vonnegut grew up in 1930s America, a world of democratic values that he saw challenged in WORLD WAR II and its aftermath. Vonnegut's own family suffered through the GREAT DEPRESSION, and his father forced him to study science instead of the arts to improve his chances for a safe career. In 1943 Vonnegut left Cornell University and enlisted in the army, even though on principle he was opposed to the war.

A prisoner of war, Vonnegut came home after World War II and studied anthropology at the University of Chicago. He then worked as a publicist with General Electric, and began writing novels and essays, all with his unsparing views of American society and modern life.

Vonnegut's novels, using wit, humor, and the devices of science fiction and fantasy, demonstrate his concern over the fate of humanity and the perversion of basic human values. In *Player Piano* (1952), his first novel, he conceives of Ilium, New York, a fictional city divided between the important, professional people, and the downtrodden, who live on the other side of the river. The novel is set in an unspecified time not so distant from the present. Paul Proteus, the protagonist, grows disenchanted with his managerial duties at the Ilium works. Not even a beautiful wife makes him happy. He protests—as does Vonnegut—the increasing automatism of modern life. The choice Proteus faces is machinelike conformity or alienation.

In *Mother Night* (1961), Howard W. Campbell Jr., a successful writer and producer, allows himself to be recruited by Major Frank Wirtanen as an American double agent. His role is that of a Nazi radio propagandist in Germany. As so often happens in stories of double agents, Campbell loses track of who he is and what he truly believes in. When he dies, it is for what he calls "crimes against himself," an interesting variation on "crimes against humanity," the phrase used at the Nuremberg trials of Nazi war criminals.

Cat's Cradle (1963) ridicules both religion and science, both of which, in Vonnegut's view, human beings use to further their immoral quest for power, which in turn leads to a confusion about what is real and what is an illusion. *Slaughterhouse-Five* (1969) is perhaps Vonnegut's most important work, which features Vonnegut himself as one of the characters and draws on his wartime experience in the bombing of Dresden, a firestorm that destroyed the city. The novel shifts between vivid realistic scenes and time travel fantasies that include such disruptive events as the assassinations of Robert Kennedy and Martin Luther King Jr.

Vonnegut's later novels, including *Breakfast of Champions* (1973), *Slapstick* (1976), *Jailbird* (1979), and *Deadeye Dick* (1982), are also autobiographical but without the deep seriousness and historical weight of his earlier work. By the publication of *Timequake* (1997), Vonnegut said that he had just about run out of ideas for novels, although he published *God Bless You, Dr. Kevorkian*, a novella, in 1999.

Vonnegut's short stories are collected in *Canary in a Cat House* (1961), *Welcome to the Monkey House* (1968), and *Bagombo Snuff Box: Uncollected Short Fiction* (1999). He published one play, *Happy Birthday, Wanda June* (1970), and one teleplay, *Between Time and Timbuktu: Or, Prometheus-5, a Space Fantasy* (1972).

Vonnegut's nonfiction is collected in *Wampeters, Foma, and Granfalloons (Opinions)* (1974), *Palm Sunday: An Autobiographical Collage* (1981), and *Fates Worse than Death: An Autobiographical Collage of the 1980's* (1991).

Sources

Allen, William Rodney. *Understanding Kurt Vonnegut.* Columbia: University of South Carolina Press, 1991.

Klinkowitz, Jerome. *Vonnegut in Fact: The Public Spokesmanship of Personal Fiction.* Columbia: University of South Carolina Press, 1998.

Merrill, Robert, ed. *Critical Essays on Kurt Vonnegut.* Boston: G.K. Hall, 1990.

Vorse, Mary Marvin Heaton (1874–1966)
novelist

Associated for many years with the PROVINCETOWN PLAYERS, which she describes in *Time and the Town* (1942), Mary Heaton Vorse also published several proletarian novels: *The Prestons* (1918), *Passaic* (1926), *Second Cabin* (1928), and *Strike!* (1930). Her autobiography is titled *Footnote to Folly* (1935).

Sources

Garrison, Dee. *Mary Heaton Vorse: The Life of an American Insurgent.* Philadelphia: Temple University Press, 1989.

Wagoner, David Russell (1926–) *poet, novelist*

The work of Ohio-born Wagoner has been praised for its lyrical power and understated tone. He often writes about the Northwest, and his titles reflect his grounding in nature and geography. One of his major influences is Theodore ROETHKE, whose notebooks Wagoner edited and published as *Straw for the Fire* (1972).

Wagoner's poetry collections include *Dry Sun, Dry Wind* (1953), *A Place to Stand* (1958), *The Nesting Ground* (1963), *New and Selected Poems* (1969), *Riverbed* (1972), and *Sleeping in the Woods* (1974). He published his *Collected Poems* in 1976. Later collections include *Broken Country* (1979), *Landfall* (1981), *First Light* (1983), *Through the Forest* (1987), *Walt Whitman Bathing: Poems* (1996), and *Traveling Light: Collected and New Poems* (1999).

His novels tend to be set in 19th-century America and have been described as light in tone and picaresque. The titles suggests a whimsical sense of life as a quest for success and companionship: *Money Money Money* (1955), *The Escape Artist* (1965), *Baby, Come on Inside* (1968), *Where is My Wandering Boy Tonight?* (1970), *The Road to Many a Wonder* (1974), *Tracker* (1975), *The Whole Hog* (1976), *The Hanging Garden* (1980).

Wagoner has also published a book of poetry based on the legends of Northwest Indians, *Who Shall Be the Sun?* (1978).

Sources

McFarland, Ron. *The World of David Wagoner*. Moscow: University of Idaho Press, 1997.

Pinsker, Sanford. *Three Pacific Northwest Poets: William Stafford, Richard Hugo, and David Wagoner*. New York: Twayne, 1987.

Wakoski, Diane (1937–) *poet*

Born in Whittier, California, Wakoski began writing poetry at age seven. Her father left the family when she was 15. At the University of California at Berkeley she was taught by the poets Thom Gunn and Josephine MILES. Her work was also influenced by a wide range of writers, including Gertrude STEIN and Wallace STEVENS.

Wakoski took various jobs—bookstore clerk, temporary teacher—after graduating from college in 1960, then published her first poetry collection in 1962. *Coins and Coffins* features dramatic narrative poems in the style of what has been called CONFESSIONAL POETRY, although Wakoski says she dislikes the term. *The Motorcycle Betrayal Poems* (1971)—her best-known title—is representative of her work in that it deals with failed marriages and love affairs. The book's dedication is striking: "to all those men who betrayed me at one time or another, in hopes they will fall off their motorcycles and break their necks."

Although Wakoski's later poetry collections have not achieved the same level of notoriety or recognition, she was awarded the Poetry Society of America's William Carlos Williams Award for *Emerald Ice: Selected Poems, 1962–1987*.

Wakoski has often presented herself as the poet of places—especially California and Las Vegas. In these settings the poet employs free verse to explore her quest for beauty, love, and romance. A certain rawness pervades many of her poems, an outspoken need for sex and other sensual pleasures.

Wakoski has published more than 40 books of poetry, including *The George Washington Poems* (1967); *Dancing on the Grave of a Son of a Bitch* (1973); *Looking for the King of Spain* (1974); a four-volume series, *Archaeology of Movies and Books: Medea the Sorceress* (1991), *Jason the Sailor* (1993), The *Emerald City of Las Vegas* (1995), and *Argonaut Rose* (1998).

Wakoski's nonfiction includes *Creating a Personal Mythology* (1975) and *Toward a New Poetry* (1980).

Sources

Newton, Robert. *Diane Wakoski: A Descriptive Bibliography.* Jefferson, N.C.: McFarland, 1987.

Walker, Alice Malsenior (1944–) *poet, novelist,*
short story writer, biographer, educator

Walker was born in Eatonto, Georgia. A childhood accident in which her right eye was scarred by a BB pellet drove her into a reticence relieved only by her omnivorous reading, especially her love of poetry. She graduated from high school as valedictorian and went on first to Spellman College and then to Sarah Lawrence. She visited Africa during one summer, became pregnant, and, feeling suicidal, sought an abortion. Her first poems, collected in *Once* (1968), deal with this period. She overcame her despair and wrote a short story, "To Hell With Dying" (1967), which was later published as a children's book in 1988.

After graduation from college, Walker became actively involved in the civil rights struggle. She taught in Mississippi at Jackson State College (1968–1969) and Tougaloo College (1970–1971). She published *Five Poems* (1972), her second book of poetry, and her first novel, *The Third Life of Grange Copeland* (1970), a dark tale of self-conflicted African Americans and their struggle with oppression. She expressed her growing identification with the plight of black women in a collection of short fiction, *In Love and Trouble: Stories of Black Women* (1973). *Revolutionary Petunias and Other Poems* (1973) won the Lillian Smith Award of the southern Regional Council. In 1974 Walker published two biographies for children: *Langston Hughes, American Poet* and *The Life of Thomas Hodge.*

Meridian (1976), Walker's second novel, has been called a "woman-centered" perspective on the civil rights movement. It concentrates on African-American mothers and clearly grows out of Walker's struggle with her own first pregnancy.

Through anthologies of African-American writing and by creating her own company, Wild Tree Press, Walker promulgated new writers while also teaching women's studies at Wellesley College, Brandeis University, Yale, and the University of California at Berkeley.

Walker came to national attention with her novel THE COLOR PURPLE (1982), the riveting story of Celia, who overcomes a rape and the oppression of African-American men. The novel won a Pulitzer Prize and a National Book Award and was made into a major motion picture directed by Steven Spielberg. At the same time, Walker herself became a focal point for the ire of African-American men—including writers like Ishmael REED—who believed her depiction of them was biased and demeaning.

Undeterred, Walker published a memoir, *In Search of Our Mother's Gardens* (1983), which reiterated her commitment to black feminism while emphasizing her dedication to the renewal of an entire people. Her next two novels, *The Temple of My Familiar* (1989) and *Possessing the Secret of Joy* (1992), received much negative criticism from reviewers who regarded her work as too ideological and didactic. She addressed this criticism in *The Same River Twice* (1996), acknowledging the painfulness of the attacks on her. She did not recover critical favor with a sixth novel, *By the Light of My Father's Smile* (1998).

Walker's *Complete Stories* appeared in 1994, *Living by the Word: Selected Writings, 1973–1987* in 1988, *Warrior Marks: Female Genital Mutilation and the Sexual Blinding of Women* in 1993, and *Anything We Love Can Be Saved: A Writer's Activism* in 1997.

Sources

Dieke, Ikenna, ed. *Critical Essays on Alice Walker.* Westport, Conn.: Greenwood Press, 1999.

Gates, Henry Louis and K. A. Appiah, eds. *Alice Walker: Critical Perspectives Past and Present.* New York: Amistad, 1993.

Winchell, Donna Haisty. *Alice Walker.* New York: Twayne, 1992.

Walker, Margaret Abigail (1915–1998) *poet,*
novelist, essayist, educator

Margaret Walker was born in Birmingham, Alabama, and grew up in a middle-class family that moved to New Orleans in 1925. She finished high school at age 14 and went on to two years of college in New Orleans. At an early age she met important African-American writers such as W. E. B. DU BOIS and Langston HUGHES, who read her poetry and encouraged her to attend Northwestern University, where she received a degree in English in 1935. Her first poems were published in CRISIS magazine in 1934.

Walker worked for the Works Progress Administration during the GREAT DEPRESSION. As part of the Writer's Project she worked on a guide for the state of Illinois. She also met Richard WRIGHT, Nelson ALGREN, and other important writers. Walker developed slowly as a writer, completing one unpublished novel, "Goose Island," and publishing *For My People* (1942), her first collection of poetry. Much of her time was taken up with a teaching career, including a 30-year tenure at Jackson State College in Mississippi.

Walker's greatest contribution to African-American literature came with the publication of *Jubilee* (1966), her epic novel about slavery, written with dramatic flair and an impressive command of historical sources. This novel touched off a creative spurt, for Walker quickly published two new volumes of poetry, *Prophets for a New Day* (1970) and *October Journey* (1973). In 1988 she published the long-awaited biography *Richard Wright: Daemonic Genius,* and in 1989, her *Collected Poems.* In 1990 she published *How I Wrote Jubilee and Other Essays on Life and Literature* (1990).

Sources

Giovanni, Nikki. *A Poetic Equation: Conversations between Nikki Giovanni and Margaret Walker.* Washington, D.C.: Howard University Press, 1974.
Tate, Claudia, ed. *Black Women Writers at Work.* New York: Continuum, 1983.

Wallant, Edgar Lewis (1926–1962) *novelist*

Born in New Haven, Connecticut, Wallant is best known as the author of a classic novel, *The Pawnbroker* (1961), which dramatizes the life of a concentration camp survivor, and was filmed in 1965. Wallant began publishing stories in 1955 after a career in advertising and service in the U.S. Navy. His first novel. *The Human Season,* appeared in 1960. Two other novels, *The Tenants of Moonbloom* (1963) and *The Children at the Gate* (1962), were published after his death.

Sources

Galloway, David. *Edward Lewis Wallant.* Boston: Twayne, 1979.

Warren, Robert Penn (1905–1989) *poet, novelist, essayist*

Warren was born in a small town in Guthrie, Kentucky. His father, a banker, encouraged his son's literary propensities, which were stimulated by his identification with his southern roots and the legacy of the Civil War. Warren's talent was recognized by the poet and teacher John Crowe RANSOM, and Warren became part of THE FUGITIVES, a group of poets at Vanderbilt University that also included Donald DAVIDSON and Allen TATE.

Warren continued his education at the University of California, Berkeley, and at Yale and Oxford, where he was a Rhodes scholar. He published his first book, *John Brown: The Making of a Martyr,* in 1929. At this point Warren was very much a southern conservative and AGRARIAN who criticized northern values, especially industrialism and its destructive impact on individual freedom. He contributed to *I'll Take My Stand* (1930), a defense of the Old South and the agrarian tradition.

But at Louisiana State University, where Warren taught between 1934 and 1936 and edited the prestigious literary quarterly SOUTHERN REVIEW, his political views began to change—principally because he began to see the complexity of politics in the progressive and yet corrupt administration of governor and later senator Huey Long. Warren wrote about Long, calling him WILLIE STARK, in his Pulitzer

Prize–winning novel, ALL THE KING'S MEN (1946). In this novel, narrated by Jack Burden, a Ph.D. student in history, Warren explores the problem of whether ends can ever justify means; can Willie Stark resort to expediency and corruption to achieve laudable ends such as the improvement of the state's roads and the health of its people? The novel suggests that immoral means can never yield moral ends, and Willie dies with regret, saying it all could have been different.

None of Warren's other novels—except perhaps his first, *Night Rider* (1939), which is steeped in Kentucky history—ever equaled the achievement of *All the King's Men.* Novels such as *World Enough and Time: A Romantic Novel* (1950) and *Band of Angels* (1955) seemed too baroque, too lush in their language to be integrated into sound narrative construction. Warren's later fiction includes *Wilderness: A Tale of the Civil War* (1961), *Meet Me in the Green Glen* (1971), and *A Place to Come To* (1977). His short fiction has been collected in *Blackberry Winter* (1946) and *The Circus in the Attic and Other Stories* (1947).

Warren's reputation rests on his poetry and his literary and social criticism. As a poet he excelled in both the short forms of the lyric and in long narrative poems, such as *Brother to Dragons: A Tale in Verse and Voices,* which begins with a historical event—the murder of a slave by Thomas Jefferson's nephew Lilburne Lewis. This is the starting point for one of Warren's most important themes: the fallen nature of man, the flaw in human character that makes such crimes inevitable. Warren won a Pulitzer Prize for *Promises: Poems 1954–1956* (1957) and another for *Now and Then: Poems 1976–1978* (1978). His other notable award-winning volumes of verse include *Selected Poems: New and Old, 1923–1966* (1966) and *Audubon: A Vision* (1969). He was named the first Poet Laureate of the United States in 1986. His poetry is distinguished by his vivid imagery, metaphors, and brilliant descriptions. No American poet has better integrated an understanding of American history and of historical incidents into his poetry.

Warren's nonfiction includes two distinguished volumes of social criticism: *Segregation: The Inner Conflict in the South* (1956) and *Who Speaks for the Negro?* (1965).

As one of the century's finest literary critics and teachers of literature, Warren along with critic Cleanth Brooks published *An Approach to Literature* (1936), *Understanding Poetry* (1938), *Understanding Fiction* (1943), and *Modern Rhetoric* (1949). Much of his important literary criticism is included in *Selected Essays* (1958) and *New and Selected Essays* (1989).

Sources

Blotner, Joseph. *Robert Penn Warren: A Biography.* New York: Random House, 1997.
Bohner, Charles. *Robert Penn Warren* Boston: Twayne, 1981.
Madden, David, ed. *The Legacy of Robert Penn Warren.* Baton Rouge: Louisiana State University Press, 2000.

Wasserstein, Wendy (1950–) *playwright*

Born in Brooklyn, New York, Wasserstein moved to Manhattan with her family at age 13. She attended the Calhoun School, where she began writing plays. She continued her education at Mount Holyoke College, where she earned a B.A. degree and went on to a creative writing program at the City University of New York. Her first play, *Any Woman Can't* (1973), produced OFF BROADWAY was a satire about a tap dancer and her involvement with a sexist husband. Then Wasserstein enrolled at the Yale Drama School, collaborating there with the playwright Christopher Durang on a parody of beauty contests, *When Dinah Shore Ruled the Earth* (1977).

Her next play written at Yale, *Uncommon Women and Others,* was produced Off Broadway in 1977. A far more realistic drama, it concerned a reunion of five women who were at college together six years earlier. Her superb delineation of different female personalities and her writing for a superb ensemble of actors led to the play's broadcast on television with a cast that featured Meryl Streep and Swoosie Kurtz. Critics recognized Wasserstein as a promising new playwright.

Wasserstein's play *Isn't It Romantic* (1983) was a great success, followed by the even more successful *The Heidi Chronicles* (1988), a stunning dramatic tour de force that covers the history of the contemporary women's movement through the life of a single woman. It won several prizes, including a Pulitzer.

The Sisters Rosensweig (1992) explores the lives of three Jewish-American sisters and deftly integrates contemporary social and political history into their relationships. Nominated for a Tony Award, the play further enhanced Wasserstein's reputation as one of the finest contemporary playwrights. Less well received has been *An American Daughter* (1997), which deals with a woman who is nominated for a cabinet position by the president of the United States.

Wasserstein has also published a collection of essays, *Bachelor Girls* (1990).

Sources

Ciociola, Gail. *Wendy Wasserstein: Dramatizing Women, Their Choices and Their Boundaries.* Jefferson, N.C.: McFarland, 1998.

Waters, Frank (1902–1995) *novelist*

The Colorado-born Waters has centered virtually all of his work in the West and Southwest, exploring the lives of Indians, miners, hunters, and the interrelationships of these peoples. He published a trilogy about a young man's career in mining: *Wild Earth's Nobility* (1935), *Below Grass Roots* (1937), and *Dust Within the Rock* (1940). Novels centering on Indian life include *The Man Who Killed the Deer* (1942) and *Flight from Fiesta* (1986).

Waters wrote several nonfiction books that complement his fiction: *The Colorado* (1946), *Book of the Hopi* (1964), and *Mountain Dialogues* (1982), a collection of reminiscences.

Waters took a special interest in Mexico, writing its history in *Mystique* (1975) and setting a novel there, *The Yogi of Cockroad Court* (1947).

Sources

Blackburn, Alexander. *A Sunrise Brighter Still: The Visionary Novels of Frank Waters.* Athens: Swallow Press/Ohio University Press, 1991.

Deloria, Vine, Jr., ed. *Frank Waters.* Athens: Swallow Press/Ohio University Press, 1993.

Watts, Alan (1915–1973) *religion writer*

Watts was born in England, but settled in the United States in 1938 and became a citizen in 1943. His name is often associated with the BEAT writers because Watts wrote and lectured widely on the subject of Zen Buddhism, which in America became a form of dropping out from conventional, conformist society. Watts blended this Buddhist sensibility with an interest in drug use, which presaged much of the "counterculture" movements of the 1960s. His books include *The Spirit of Zen* (1936), *Behold the Spirit* (1947), *The Way of Zen* (1957), and *Beat Zen, Square Zen and Zen* (1967). *In My Own Way* (1973) is his autobiography.

Sources

Furlong, Monica. *Genuine Fake: A Biography of Alan Watts.* London: Heinemann, 1986.

Hoyt, E. P. *Alan Watts.* Radnor, Pa.: Chilton Book Co., 1976.

Webb, Walter Prescott (1888–1963) *historian*

Born in Texas, Webb taught at the University of Texas from 1918 until his death. His work on the American West is eloquent and profound and has influenced generations of writers. His two greatest works are *The Great Plains* (1931) and *The Great Frontier* (1952). Excerpts from these works are often anthologized.

Sources

Frantz, Joe, ed. *Essays on Walter Prescott Webb.* Austin: University of Texas Press, 1976.

Furman, Necah Stewart. *Walter Prescott Webb: His Life and Impact.* Albuquerque: University of New Mexico Press, 1976.

Weidman, Jerome (1913–1998) *novelist, playwright*

A New York native, Weidman created blunt portraits of mercenary and acquisitive Jewish characters, especially in novels such as *I Can Get It For You Wholesale* (1937) and *What's In It For Me* (1938), both probing stories of the garment industry on New York City's LOWER EAST SIDE. Many of his subsequent novels extended the same themes and also explored the Jews' ambivalent attitudes toward gentile society as in the aptly titled *The Enemy Camp,* Weidman's 1958 novel. *Fourth Street East* (1971) is a fiction account of Weidman's own experience on the Lower East Side.

Weidman has had a successful career as a dramatist, winning a Pulitzer Prize for his musical, *Fiorello!* (1960), written in collaboration with George Abbott. Weidman also dramatized *I Can Get It For You Wholesale* in 1962.

The Captain's Tiger (1947) and *The Death of Dickie Draper* (1965) are short story collections. *Back Talk* (1963) contains Weidman's magazine pieces. He wrote a candid memoir, *Praying for Rain* (1986), which describes his relationships with many important writers.

Sources

Levin, Bob. "He Can Get It for You Wholesale," *The Magpie,* Vol. 22, No. 1 (January 1938), p. 55. Available on-line. URL: http://newdeal.feri.org/magpie/docs/3801p55.htm.

Welch, James (1940–) *poet, novelist*

Welch was born in Browning, Montana, the son of a Blackfoot father and a Gros Ventre mother. Although he attended reservation schools, he graduated from high school in Minneapolis and earn bachelor's and master's degrees from the University of Montana in Missoula.

Riding the Earthboy 40 (1971, revised 1975) is a collection of 54 poems about a family named Earthboy who live on a 40-acre ranch. The poems reflect a deep feeling for the land and the spirits that inspire its inhabitants.

Welch attracted national attention with his novel *Winter in the Blood* (1974), about a young American Indian who discovers that his roots include a grandfather who saved his ostracized grandmother, a member of a different tribe, from starving. Like Welch's poetry, the novel evokes the spirits of Indian ancestors with uncanny power.

Welch's other novels, *The Death of Jim Loney* (1979), *Fools Crow* (1986), and *The Indian Lawyer* (1990), range in mood from the despair of Jim Loney, who actively seeks his own death, to a powerful historical novel about the Blackfoot tribe, to an Indian who earns a partnership in a prestigious law firm.

Welch is also the author of *Killing Custer* (1994), a historical account of the events leading up to General George Armstrong Custer's death at Little Big Horn and the aftermath of his battle with the Sioux.

Sources

McFarland, Ron. *Understanding James Welch.* Columbia: University of South Carolina Press, 2000.

Welty, Eudora (1909–2001) *short story writer, novelist*

Welty spent most of her life in her native Jackson, Mississippi, leaving only to attend the University of Wisconsin, where she obtained a B.A. degree in 1929, and to live briefly in New York City. She returned home shortly before her father died in 1931. Her interest in literature developed early, and her first short story was published in 1936, the same year her photographs were exhibited in New York City. Employed by the Works Progress Administration in Mississippi, she took many photographs of white and black poor people and, in the process, gathered ideas for her stories. Her highly praised photographs have been published in *One Time, One Place: Mississippi in the Depression, a Snapshot Album* (1971) and *Eudora Welty: Photographs* (1989).

In 1941 Welty published her story "Why I Live at the P.O.," a comic tour de force narrated by a woman who complains about her family with gusto. The story shows off Welty's keen ear for the speech of her fellow southerners as her characters reveal themselves through dialogue. Unlike southern writers like William FAULKNER, Welty usually shied away from violent subjects, although her work does subtly show the dark as well as the light sides of the South.

In 1941 Welty also published her much-acclaimed short story collection, *A Curtain of Green,* and the next year her novella, *The Robber Bridegroom,* which features her characteristic mix of folklore and realistic portraiture. Welty did not write a novel until 1946, but *Delta Wedding* proved to be a rousing success, as did *The Ponder Heart* (1957), which was successfully dramatized for Broadway. Two of Welty's later novels, *Losing Battles* (1970) and *The Optimist's Daughter* (1972), enhanced her reputation, with the latter winning a Pulitzer Prize. Both novels extended her portraits of southern characters into family dramas and sagas depicting life in the 1930s and the present. *The Collected Stories of Eudora Welty* was published in 1980.

Welty's nonfiction is also impressive. She commented incisively on her own work and the nature of fiction in *The Reading and Writing of Short Stories* (1949), *Place in Fiction* (1957), *Three Papers on Fiction* (1962), and *The Eye of the Story: Selected Essays and Reviews* (1978). *A Writer's Eye: Collected Book Reviews* appeared in 1994. Her popular and beguiling memoir, *One Writer's Beginnings,* was published in 1984.

Sources

Champion, Laurie, ed. *The Critical Response to Eudora Welty's Fiction.* Westport, Conn.: Greenwood Press, 1994.
Kreyling, Michael. *Understanding Eudora Welty.* Columbia: University of South Carolina Press, 1999.
Vande Kieft, Ruth M. *Eudora Welty.* Boston: Twayne, 1987.
Waldron, Ann. *Eudora: A Writer's Life.* New York: Doubleday, 1998.

Wescott, Glenway (1901–1987) *novelist, short story writer*

Wescott came from Wisconsin and wrote often about his native state, although he was also a world-class traveler and wrote a good deal about life in Europe as well. He began as a poet with *The Bitterns* (1920), but he soon found his forte with prose. *The Apple of the Eye* (1924) is about a boy in the frontier West, and *The Grandmothers* (1927) is about the Midwest but told by a young man who has escaped the region for Europe. Wescott's masterpiece is the novella *The Pilgrim Hawk* (1940), a perfectly told story set near Paris, where three couples come to represent three different kinds of love.

Wescott's stories were collected in *Like a Lover* (1926) and *Good-Bye Wisconsin* (1928). He collected his essays about his literary friends in *Images of Truth* (1962). *The Best of All Possible Worlds* (1975) includes correspondence and memoirs from 1914 to 1937.

Continual Lessons: The Journals of Glenway Wescott, 1937–1955 appeared in 1990, and *When We Were Three: The Travel Albums of George Platt Lynes, Monroe Wheeler, and Glenway Wescott, 1925–1935* in 1998.

Sources

Johnson, Ira. *Glenway Wescott: The Paradox of Voice.* Port Washington, N.Y.: Kennikat Press, 1971.

Rueckert, William H. *Glenway Wescott.* New York: Twayne, 1965.

West, Jessamyn (1907–1984) *novelist, short story writer*

West was born in Indiana but settled in California, where she attended Whittier College. Her first novel, *The Friendly Persuasion* (1945), evokes her Quaker upbringing in Indiana, and was filmed in 1956. *The Witch Diggers* (1951), also set in Indiana, explores life on a farm in the 1890s. The setting changes to California in *Cress Delahanty* (1953) and *South of the Angels* (1960), two novels that portray the state's ranching and pioneer history. Many of West's later novels, such as *Leafy Rivers* (1967) and *The Massacre at Fall Creek* (1975), return to the Midwest and to 19th-century stories about the settling of the land and the Indians.

West's stories are collected in *Love, Death, and the Ladies' Drill Team* (1959) and *Crimson Ramblers of the World, Farewell* (1970).

West published two autobiographies, *Hide and Seek* (1973) and *The Woman Said Yes* (1976), and a travel diary of 1929, *Double Discovery* (1980).

Sources

Farmer, Ann Dahlstrom. *Jessamyn West.* Boise, Idaho: Boise State University, 1982.

Shivers, Alfred S. *Jessamyn West: Revised Edition.* New York: Twayne, 1992.

West, Nathanael (Nathan Weinstein) (1903–1940) *novelist*

Born in New York City, West was the child of Russian-Jewish immigrants. Undisciplined, he liked to wander the city rather than go to school, yet he earned a B.A. from Brown University in less than three years. West had little interest in his family's background, preferring to immerse himself in American culture. An early satirical novel, *The Dream Life of Balso Snell* (1931), is a spoof on various literary genres, including the lives of saints and biographies of writers. It reveals none of the depth of West's next work, *Miss Lonelyhearts* (1933), about a journalist who dispenses advice to the lovelorn. "Miss Lonelyhearts" is a man who is attracted to and repulsed by his role as confidant. Indeed, this role drives him to hallucinate connections with others. Imagining that he is saving one of his correspondents, he is in fact rushing to his own death.

There is a cartoonish quality to West's characters, who shift between surrealistic and realistic scenes as the world of their imagination collides with the world of business. This phantasmagoria undoes West's heroes—Lemuel Pitkin in *A Cool Million* (1934), a novel that continues West's attack on modern America, including midwesterners, southerners, Jews, capitalists, and socialists.

The Day of the Locust (1939) is West's masterpiece. Tod Hackett, a painter who hopes to find work as a movie set and costume designer, is the epitome of all of West's questing characters. Hackett enters the phantasmagoric modern world through its ultimate product: Hollywood, the make-believe capital of the world. He seeks romance, but he is another of West's dreamers, and movies are depicted as the final absurdity of modern man who cannot find an adequate, let alone satisfying definition of his significance.

It is difficult to assess where West could have taken the modern novel after the bleak vision of his last novel. He died in an automobile accident in 1940.

Sources

Siegel, Ben, ed. *Critical Essays on Nathanael West.* New York: G. K. Hall, 1994.

Veitch, Jonathan. *American Superrealism: Nathanael West and the Politics of Representation in the 1930's.* Madison: University of Wisconsin Press, 1997.

westerns

The 20th-century western begins with Owen Wister's *The Virginian* (1902) and Zane Grey's *Riders of the Purple Sage* (1912). The main characters of these novels, as numerous critics have pointed out, set the pattern for the chivalrous hero, a kind of knight who scrupulously abides by virtuous rules of combat. The western, then, is another form of melodrama and medieval allegory, a parable about the struggle between good and evil. Zane Grey added a detailed portrayal of the rugged environment, a testing ground for the Westerner and the urban visitor alike.

Other writers added an epic quality to the genre. Conrad RICHTER in *Sea of Grass* (1937) portrayed cattle ranching in the Southwest. In *The Big Sky* (1947), A. B. GUTHRIE depicted the journey of a Kentucky man who learns to be a trapper, trader, explorer, and guide. Such resourcefulness of the hero has been a hallmark of the western. Louis L'AMOUR added the element of the family saga to the genre in a story that spans several novels.

Perhaps the one indisputably great work of art to emerge from the popular genre of the western is Walter Van Tilburg Clark's THE OX-BOW INCIDENT (1940), made into a compelling film starring Dana Andrews. This story of a posse that hunts down a group of men and performs vigilante justice is one of the great stories of mob violence, and one of the few westerns to reveal the consequences of anarchic frontier life.

The most recent generation of Native American writers—James WELCH, Louise ERDRICH, N. Scott MOMADAY, Leslie Marmon SILKO, and Sherman ALEXIE—have brought an entirely different perspective to the world evoked by the western. These writers address the Western myth by depicting both the violence and injustice of white settlers and the failures within the Native American community to adapt to changing times. Along with Larry MCMURTRY, who has produced the most impressive body of literature about the contemporary West, these contemporary writers have done much not only to portray the reality behind the western but also to show how the myth of the West as the territory of freedom still stimulates the American imagination.

Sources

Folsom, James K. *The American Western Novel.* New Haven, Conn.: College & University Press, 1966.

Kich, Martin. *Western American Novelists.* New York: Garland, 1995.

Lyon, Thomas J., ed. *The Literary West: An Anthology of Western American Literature.* New York: Oxford University Press, 1999.

Pilkington, William T., ed. *Critical Essays on the Western American Novel.* Boston: G. K. Hall, 1980.

Wexley, John (1907–1985) *dramatist, social critic*

A member of what might be called the New York intelligentsia—liberal and apt to attach himself to progressive causes—Wexley wrote about the social issues of his time. *The Last Mile* (1930) is a drama about the final hours of a man on death row. *They Shall Not Die* (1934) is an impassioned play about the injustice done in the SCOTTSBORO CASE. Wexley's most important work of nonfiction is *The Judgement of Julius and Ethel Rosenberg* (1955), a militant defense of the couple executed for espionage. Wexley's book

presents the full flavor of the times, when many liberals saw the Rosenberg case as nothing more than the reflex action of a COLD WAR U.S. reactionary government intent on finding Communist conspirators.

Whalen, Philip (1923–   ) *poet*

Born in Oregon, Whalen is best known for his association with the BEATS. He often uses STREAM OF CONSCIOUSNESS, and his work reflects the influence of Zen Buddhism. His avant-garde work, often presented in unusual typefaces, has been collected in several volumes: *Self-Portrait from Another Direction* (1959), *Memoirs of an Inter-Glacial Age* (1960), *Like I say* (1960), *Monday in the Evening* (1964), *Every Day* (1965), *Highgrade* (1966), *On Bear's Head* (1966), *Decompressions: Selected Poems* (1978), *Enough Said: Fluctuat Nec Mergitur: Poems 1974–1979* (1980), *Heavy Breathing: Poems, 1967–1980* (1983), *Canoeing up Cabarga Creek: Buddhist Poems* (1996).

Whalen has published three novels, *You Didn't Even Try* (1966), *Imaginary Speech for a Brazen Head* (1972), and *The Diamond Noddle* (1980).

A collection of interviews, *Off the Wall,* appeared in 1978.

Sources

Kherdian, David. *Six Poets of the San Francisco Renaissance: Portraits and Checklists.* Fresno, Calif.: Giligia Press, 1967.

Wharton, Edith Newbold Jones (1862–1937)
novelist, short story writer

Edith Wharton was born in New York City and grew up among elite families who could trace their origins back to the original Dutch and English patricians. She was expected to take her place in genteel society and to make a conventional marriage. Part of her childhood was spent abroad, where she began to learn European languages. When Wharton showed an interest in writing, her mother had her early poetry published privately in 1878. Although Wharton was not expected to have a professional career as a writer, her education, which included private tutoring, helped to make her a sophisticated student of literature and language. In 1879 ATLANTIC MONTHLY published one of Wharton's poems.

Wharton continued her progress as a young lady, taking her place in the fashionable world of Washington Square and Fifth Avenue. She married Edward Wharton in 1885, and the couple first settled on her mother's estate at Newport, Rhode Island, taking off several months each year to travel in Europe. But the marriage was a disaster. Wharton's husband lacked her sophistication and literary interests, and the couple seems to have been sexually incompatible. After a mental collapse, Wharton renewed her dedication to writing and published *The Decoration of Houses,* a nonfiction work, in

1897. That year she suffered another breakdown and consoled herself with literary friendships, especially with Henry James, whom she met in 1887. She also put her energies into building a magnificent new home in Lenox, Massachusetts. Wharton's early fiction, such as "The Fullness of Life" (1891) and *The Greater Inclination* (1899), contains several stories about unhappy marriages.

As Wharton's work matured and began to sell well, she became an embarrassment to her family. Such notoriety was not considered proper for a woman, and so Wharton began to spend more and more time in Europe, treating "Old New York" in her fiction with a mixture of nostalgia and shrewd criticism.

Wharton's growing powers as a novelist, which culminated in her early masterpiece, *The House of Mirth* (1905), and her decision to live permanently in Europe, also led to her divorce—a scandalous event in New York society but absolutely essential to Wharton, whose husband's health deteriorated as she grew stronger and more confident. In much of her greatest work she would fearlessly face what her own terrible marriage had cost her. *Ethan Frome* (1911) and *The Custom of the Country* (1913) are strong novels built on the exploration of unhappy marriages.

Unlike Henry James, whose work is dense with psychological exploration, Wharton took a more sociological and even anthropological view of American and European society. She was keenly interested in how social customs and manners shape the individual's behavior. She analyzed, for example, why Lily Bart in *The House of Mirth* feels she has to sell her beauty. She probed in *The Age of Innocence* (1920) why Newland Archer feels he has to settle for a conventional bride rather than the Europeanized Ellen Olenska, a woman of his class with an unhappy marriage to a Polish nobleman. Wharton treated such complicated relationships with enormous compassion, even though her characters often lack the strength to break with the rules of their society. Wharton's novels also show that most people cannot sever their ties to family and culture and live as independently as she was able to do.

Interest in Wharton's work has intensified in recent decades, not only because of the rise of FEMINIST LITERARY CRITICISM but also because Wharton combines an intense, historical sensibility with an understanding of the universal themes of love, family, and society. A popular novelist in her time, Wharton's career suffered an eclipse after 1920, but later novels such as *The Children* (1928) and the unfinished *The Buccaneers* (1938) have become part of a re-evaluation of her career. Films of *The Buccaneers, Ethan Frome,* and *The Age of Innocence* also testify to Wharton's continuing relevance to contemporary audiences.

Wharton wrote a fine autobiography, *A Backward Glance* (1934)—aptly titled, since it skirts many important events in her life. She also was a superb writer of short fiction. *The Collected Short Stories of Edith Wharton* was published in

1968. Her books on European culture and on travel remain classics of the genre, including *Italian Villas and Their Gardens* (1904), *Italian Backgrounds* (1905), and *French Ways and Their Meaning* (1919). Her work on behalf of WORLD WAR I refugees is reflected in *Fighting France from Dunkerque to Belfort* (1915).

Sources

Bell, Millicent, ed. *The Cambridge Companion to Edith Wharton.* Cambridge: Cambridge University Press, 1995.
Bendixen, Alfred and Annette Zilversmit, eds. *Edith Wharton: New Critical Essays.* New York: Garland, 1992.
Benstock, Shari. *No Gifts From Chance: A Biography of Edith Wharton.* New York: Scribner's, 1994.
Lewis, R. W. B. *Edith Wharton: A Biography.* New York: Harper & Row, 1975.
Wright, Sarah Bird. *Edith Wharton A to Z: The Essential Reference to the Life and Work.* New York: Facts On File, 1998.

Wheelock, John Hall (1886–1978) *poet*

Wheelock was born in New York City and studied at Harvard. His work ranges from the lyrical to the philosophical in such volumes as *The Human Fantasy* (1911) and *The Bright Doom* (1927). He published *Poems 1911–1936* in 1936 and *Poems Old and New* in 1956. *The Gardener* (1961) won a Bollingen Prize and was followed by *Dear Men and Women* (1966), *By Daylight and in Dream* (1970), *In Love and Long* (1971), and *This Blessed Earth* (1978).

Wheelock, who worked as an editor at Charles Scribner's Sons, also wrote a literary study, *Alan Seeger* (1918) and a work of criticism, *What is Poetry?* (1963).

White, Elwyn Brooks (1899–1985) *humorist, playwright, critic, children's author*

E. B. White was born in Mt. Vernon, New York, and received his B.A. degree from Cornell University in 1921. He worked for the NEW YORKER for virtually his entire career, writing the "Talk of the Town" column. He collected many of his amusing sketches and poems in books such as *The Lady is Cold* (1929), *Every Day is Saturday* (1934), and *Here Is New York* (1949).

But White is chiefly known for two very different accomplishments. His superb books for children include *Stuart Little* (1945), a fantasy about a mouse and a human family, and *Charlotte's Web* (1952), the enduring story of a friendship between a spider and a pig.

White's other distinction is *The Elements of Style* (1959), which he cowrote with William Strunk Jr. This essential guide for writers has been revised several times but never surpassed in its soundness or brevity.

White's *Letters* were published in 1976 and his collected *Poems and Sketches* in 1981.

Sources

Elledge, Scott. *E. B. White: A Biography*. New York: W. W. Norton, 1984.

Root, Robert L., Jr., ed. *Critical Essays on E. B. White*. Boston: G. K. Hall, 1994.

White, Edmund (1940–) *novelist, biographer*

White was born in Cincinnati but grew up in Texas. His parents were divorced in 1947, and White lived with his mother in Chicago and in Texas, spending the summers with his father. He was educated at the Cranbrook Academy in Michigan and at the University of Michigan, graduating in 1962. He moved to GREENWICH VILLAGE, already set on a writing career after winning the prestigious Hopwood Award at Michigan. White identified himself as homosexual at an early age and in 1969 witnessed the riots that followed a police raid on a New York City gay bar, the Stonewall Inn—an event that sparked the gay liberation movement and paved the way for GAY AND LESBIAN LITERATURE and criticism.

White worked at TIME magazine in 1969 and then worked as an editor at THE SATURDAY REVIEW from 1972 to 1973. He published his first novel, *Forgetting Elena*, in 1973, which was widely reviewed and praised by such writers as Vladimir NABOKOV, one of White's influences. Between 1977 and 1979 White taught creative writing at Johns Hopkins, Columbia, and other universities. His second novel, the autobiographical *A Boy's Own Story* (1982), established his international reputation. The novel is one of the key works of gay and lesbian literature, as is the sequel, *The Beautiful Room is Empty,* and the last part of this autobiographical trilogy, *The Farewell Symphony* (1997). White's other novels include *Caracole* (1985) and *The Married Man* (2000). *Skinned Alive: Stories* was published in 1995.

White has written many fine essays, included in *The Burning Library* (1993). He has become an important biographer with the publication of *Genet* (1993) and *Marcel Proust* (1999). White has also edited *The Faber Book of Gay Short Fiction* (1991) and *Selected Writings of Jean Genet* (1993).

Sources

Barber, Stephen. *Edmund White: The Burning World*. New York: St. Martin's Press, 1999.

White, Theodore Harold (1915–1986) *journalist*

Theodore H. White graduated from Harvard in 1938 and went to work for *Time* magazine, becoming its bureau chief in China between 1939 and 1945. He correctly observed that the Chinese Communists would take power after WORLD WAR II and thus he came into conflict with the magazine's owner, Henry Luce, a staunch support of Chiang-Kai-Shek, the Nationalist leader who eventually fled to Taiwan.

Although White wrote fiction about his experiences in China and in World War II, it was his groundbreaking account of the 1960 presidential election that won him fame. *The Making of the President 1960* (1961), which won a Pulitzer Prize, brought a novelistic style and level of insight to a presidential campaign not previously attempted by journalists in quite such detail or intimacy. White used the technique in subsequent books, but it was his first that remained a landmark. *In Search of History* (1978) is a memoir of his career.

Sources

Hoffman, Joyce. *Theodore H. White and Journalism as Illusion*. Columbia: University of Missouri Press, 1995.

White, William Allen (1868–1944) *editor*

White grew up in Kansas and made his reputation early as an independent newspaper editor. He was actively involved in Republican politics during Theodore Roosevelt's administration. White is perhaps the best-known newspaper editor in American history, a stature solidified by such books as *The Editor and His People* (1924) and *Forty Years on Main Street* (1937). His *Autobiography* (1946) won a Pulitzer Prize. His *Selected Letters* was published in 1947.

Sources

Dufva, Diane. *William Allen White*. Boise: Boise State University, 1993.

Everett, Rich. *William Allen White: The Man from Emporia*. New York: Farrar & Rinehart, 1941.

Jernigan, E. J. *William Allen White*. Boston: Twayne, 1983.

Whittemore, Edward Reed, II (1919–) *poet, biographer, critic*

Reed Whittemore graduated from Yale University in 1941 and served in World War II. He has taught at several colleges and universities, including Carlton College in Minnesota and the University of Maryland. He has been highly praised for his light and witty verse, collected in such volumes as *An American Takes a Walk* (1956) and *The Self-Made Man* (1959). His *New and Selected Poems* appeared in 1967.

Whittemore also published a well-received biography, *William Carlos Williams* (1975), and two books on the history and nature of biography from ancient times to the present: *Pure Lives* (1988) and *Whole Lives* (1989). *The Poet as Journalist* (1976) collects his essays and reviews.

Sources

Greiner, Donald J., ed. "Reed Whittemore, Maryland Poet Laureate." Available on line: URL: http://www.sailor.lib.us/maryland/art_lit/whittemore.html. Updated February 9, 2001.

Who's Afraid of Virginia Woolf? Edward Albee
(1962) *play*

Edward ALBEE's play, one of the classics of the American repertory, raises issues about American marriage, middle-class life, and middle age.

Martha, the daughter of a college president, is married to George, a history professor who has failed to fulfill her ambitious hopes for him. This bickering couple lacerate each other with their faults in front of a young couple they have invited for an evening of socializing. The young couple, Nick and Honey, soon become a part of the "fun and games." George manages to humiliate Martha, who drinks too much, by talking about their son, who seems to be only an illusion that both have perpetuated. George also manages to manipulate Nick and Honey so that they, too, begin to fall apart and involve themselves in the conflicts of their hosts.

The plot of *Who's Afraid of Virginia Woolf?* resembles another of Albee's plays, *The Zoo Story* (1959), in that the abnormal and normal begin to converge. The savage drama of *Virginia Woolf* is mitigated by moments when George and Martha feel compassion for each other, although they cannot help tearing each other apart.

Sources

Bottoms, Stephen J. *Albee: Who's Afraid of Virginia Woolf?* New York: Cambridge University Press, 2000.

Roudané, Matthew C. *Who's Afraid of Virginia Woolf?: Necessary Fictions, Terrifying Realities.* Boston: Twayne, 1990.

Widdemer, Margaret (1984–1978) *poet*

A Pennsylvania writer, Widdemer first published *The Factories and Other Lyrics* (1915), a passionate expression of outrage at the treatment of workers. *Old Road to Paradise* (1918), much more moderate in tone, won a Pulitzer Prize. Widdemer's later work seems to soften and become even more sentimental. Her work is collected in *Dark Cavalier* (1958). She wrote a memoir, *Golden Friends I Had* (1964).

Sources

Overton, Grant. *Margaret Widdemer.* New York: Farrar & Rinehart, 1930.

Wideman, John Edgar (1941–) *novelist*

Wideman was born in Washington, D.C. A star athlete and scholar, he graduated from the University of Pennsylvania in 1963 with a bachelor's degree in English and subsequently studied at Oxford. He has taught at several colleges, most notably as professor of English at the University of Massachusetts.

Wideman's first novel, *A Glance Away* (1967), is about two drifters attempting to understand their pasts. The individual's involvement in the complex interactions of history is a characteristic theme in much of Wideman's work, and this novel intensifies that theme by shifting from long interior monologues to short conversations, flashbacks, and asides—all of which create the thickly textured context of the drifters' stories.

The search for a usable past is the search for roots—a point that Wideman's next novel, *Hurry Home* (1970), makes. *The Lynchers* (1973) extends this theme to a story dominated by black characters in the inner city. *The Homewood Trilogy* (1985)—*Damballah* (1981), *Hiding Place* (1981), *Sent for You Yesterday*—recasts the same themes in terms of a family saga extending over five generations. Stories are told and retold in a loosely structured way that has been compared to folklore and to jazz. *Philadelphia Fire* (1990) is the fictional account of the 1985 police bombing of a radical African-American group, MOVE. The novel is Wideman's most searching and challenging exploration of African-American urban life, of integration, and urbanization. *The Cattle Killing* (1996), partially set in Africa, and *Two Cities* (1998) read like codas to *Philadelphia Fire,* because they revisit the nexus between racist ideology and the urge to self-destruction while finding reason for hope in communities in Philadelphia and Pittsburgh where Wideman's characters achieve a measure of love and understanding. These novels present blacks and whites as benefactors and oppressors. Wideman feels the urgency of the African-American plight, but he also recognizes the need to treat suffering with compassion and imagination.

Wideman has written sensitive nonfiction on the topics he has covered in his novels. *Brothers and Keepers* appeared in 1984, *Fatheralong: A Meditation on Fathers and Sons, Race and Society* in 1994. *The Stories of John Edgar Wideman* was published in 1992, and *Conversations with John Edgar Wideman* in 1998.

Sources

Coleman, James W. *Blackness and Modernism: The Literary Career of John Edgar Wideman.* Jackson: University Press of Mississippi, 1989.

Mbalia, Doreatha D. *John Edgar Wideman: Reclaiming the African Personality.* London: Associated University Presses, 1995.

Wieners, John (1934–) *poet*

Born in Boston, Wieners was educated at Black Mountain College, where he fell under the influence of Charles OLSON and Robert DUNCAN. He wrote about them in his memoir, *Memory* (1969). Wieners went to San Francisco in the late 1950s and became part of the BEAT scene, which he describes vividly in *The Hotel Wentley Poems* (1958). He published *Selected Poems* in 1971 and issued a revised edition in 1987. *The Journal of John Wieners Is to Be Called 707 Scott Street for Billie Holiday, 1959* appeared in 1996.

Sources

Reed, Jeremy. "To Celebrate This Broken Man: the Poetry of John Wieners." *Angel exhaust*. Available on-line. URL: http://angel-exhaust.offworld.org/html/issue-11/Wieners.html.Downloaded June 17, 2001.

Wilbur, Richard Purdy   (1921–   ) *poet, translator*

Richard Wilbur grew up in rural New Jersey, the son of the artist Lawrence Wilbur. Richard attended Amherst College and served in the U.S. Army in World War II. He continued his education after the war and graduated from Harvard in 1947, teaching there until 1954. Since then he has held teaching posts at Wellesley, Wesleyan, Smith, and other colleges. *The Beautiful Changes* (1947), his first book of poetry, reflects his traditionalist approach. Wilbur has been largely immune to fashions in poetry and has not been influenced much by contemporaries in the BEAT or CONFESSIONAL schools. Wilbur's poetry is elegant and highly polished, prompting some critics to fault him for being too academic and lacking in passion. Yet his poetry does reflect a deep feeling for nature that stems from his childhood upbringing. In addition there is probably no contemporary poet who can surpass Wilbur's sensitive intelligence and grounding in history, based on his deep reading in French and other European texts. *Things of This World* (1957) won both a National Book Award and a Pulitzer Prize. His *New and Collected Poems* was published in 1988.

Wilbur has also had a career as a distinguished translator, especially of Moliere's plays *The Misanthrope* (1955) and *Tartuffe* (1965). His nonfiction includes *Responses: Prose Pieces 1953–1976* (1976), *On My Own Work* (1983), *The Cat Bird's Song: Prose Pieces 1963–1995* (1997). *Mayflies: New Poems and Translations* was published in 2000.

Sources

Butts, William, ed. *Conversations with Richard Wilbur*. Jackson: University Press of Mississippi, 1990.

Hougen, John. B. *Ecstasy Within Discipline: The Poetry of Richard Wilbur*. Atlanta: Scholars Press, 1995.

Wilder, Thornton Niven   (1897–1975) *playwright, novelist*

Born in Madison, Wisconsin, Wilder was the son of a newspaper editor. He spent part of his childhood in China. Educated at Berkeley, Yale, and Princeton, Wilder served in World War I, then from 1921 to 1928 was employed a housemaster at a private school. His first novel, *The Cabala* (1926), was set in Italy and explored the lives of the Italian nobility. His second novel, *The Bridge of San Luis Rey*, won a Pulitzer Prize and established Wilder's international reputation. This philosophical novel, which concerns the collapse of a bridge in Peru in 1704, was a tour de force of learning and narrative skill as it interweaves the lives of five characters and explores their milieu. *Heaven's My Destination* (1934), a picaresque treatment of the adventures of a religious textbook salesman, reflects Wilder's eclectic choice of subjects.

Wilder is perhaps best known for two plays, the Pulitzer Prize–winning *Our Town* (1938), an experimental stage work that is also popular for study in the classroom. Its treatment of small-town life is reminiscent of Sherwood ANDERSON's WINESBURG, OHIO and Edgar Lee MASTERS's *Spoon River Anthology*. *The Skin of Our Teeth* (1942), another Pulitzer Prize winner, is an even more experimental play about world history from prehistoric times to the present, featuring the Antrobus family. This witty play became involved in controversy when Wilder was accused of plagiarizing from James Joyce's *Finnegans Wake* (1939).

Wilder rounded out his career with two important novels, *The Eighth Day* (1967) and *Theophilus North* (1973). A genial and accessible author, Wilder has often been called MIDDLE-BROW and a minor talent. Yet critics such as Edmund WILSON, Malcolm Cowley, and John UPDIKE have praised his work.

Sources

Blank, Martin, ed. *Critical Essays on Thornton Wilder*. New York: G. K. Hall, 1996.

Goldstone, Richard H. *Thornton Wilder: An Intimate Portrait*. New York: Saturday Review Press, 1975.

William, Ben Ames   (1889–1953) *novelist*

A Mississippi native, Williams graduated from Dartmouth College in 1910 and achieved his first great success writing detective stories such as *The Silver Forest* (1926), *The Dreadful Night* (1928), and *Money Musk* (1932). He wrote about various parts of the country, sometimes about the life of newspapermen based on his early experience as a journalist in Boston. *House Divided* (1947) is an epic novel about the Civil War. He collected his popular stories in *Thrifty Stock* (1923).

Sources

Lloyd, James B. *Lives of Mississippi Authors, 1817–1967*. Jackson: University Press of Mississippi, 1981.

Williams, John Alfred   (1925–   ) *novelist, biographer*

John A. Williams was born in Mississippi but grew up in Syracuse, New York. He served in the Navy during World War II. His novel *The Angry Ones* (1960) is a scathing depiction of GREENWICH VILLAGE and the milieu of African-American musicians. Williams achieved considerable attention with *The Man Who Cried I Am* (1967), the fictional autobiography of a dying African-American writer. *Sons of Darkness, Sons of Light* (1969) probes racial tensions in New York

City. *Captain Blackman* (1972) concerns an African-American veteran of the VIETNAM WAR. *!Click Song* (1982) returns to Williams's theme of the conflicts inherent in becoming an African-American writer. *Jacob's Ladder* (1987) deals with the politics of West Africa and its relationship to African Americans. *Clifford's Blues* (1999) deals with the Holocaust and African-American identity.

Williams published his biography of Martin Luther King Jr., *The King God Didn't Save*, in 1970, and his biography of Richard WRIGHT, *The Most Native of Sons*, in the same year. He writes about his travels as an African American in the United States in *This Is My Country Too* (1965). In 1991 he published a biography of the comedian Richard Pryor, *If I Stop I'll Die: The Comedy and Tragedy of Richard Pryor,* and in 1996, *A Street Guide to African Americans in Paris.*

Sources

Cash, Earl A. *John A. Williams: The Evolution of a Black Writer.* New York: Third World Press, 1975.
Muller, Gilbert H. *John A. Williams.* Boston: Twayne, 1984.

Williams, Paulette

See SHANGE, NTOZAKE.

Williams, Tennessee (Thomas Lanier Williams)
(1911–1983) *playwright*

Born in Columbus, Mississippi, Tennessee (or Tom, as his family called him) Williams became interested in writing as he was growing up. His father, a sales manager in a shoe company, scorned his son's literary efforts and made several unsuccessful attempts to start his son on a business career. Williams had the support of his mother, an Ohio woman who projected the style of a southern lady and battled with her husband to preserve that genteel view of life. Her son imbibed much of her romanticism. He was very close to his sister, Rose, a delicate, mentally unbalanced young woman whom he portrayed in his first important play, THE GLASS MENAGERIE (1945).

Williams had trouble staying in school, although he studied with drama teachers at the University of Iowa and had some of his early plays produced—but with great difficulty. His first plays in the 1930s were out of sync with the gritty REALISM of the stage and the PROLETARIAN LITERATURE of the time. He favored a more poetic, romantic theater and was inspired by such writers as D. H. Lawrence, who treated sex and love with a degree of frankness not yet conceivable in the American theater.

By the late 1930s, however, trends in the American theater were beginning to change. The impending war, the exhaustion of New Deal programs, and a renewed interested in psychological drama worked in Williams's favor—although he had not yet learned to discipline his romantic sensibility into

a sound dramatic structures. *Battle of Angels* (1940), his first play produced in New York, suffered from verbosity and Williams's lack of experience with theater directors and actors. But his second play, *The Glass Menagerie,* won the New York Drama Critics' Circle Award and established his reputation. Narrated by a character named Tom (based on Williams himself) and centering on Tom's mother, Amanda Wingfield (a portrait of Williams's mother) and on Tom's sister, Laura, the play captured all the yearning of the playwright's desire to leave home and his guilty feelings about abandoning Rose. The play concerns a family as reflected through a poetic sensibility, a nostalgic yet unsentimental depiction of a mother who had a ridiculous yet admirable sense of grandeur, and of a daughter who represents those sensibilities; both are overwhelmed by life. What makes the play succeed is its language: the lyricism of Tom, the pathos of Laura, the baroque flavor of Amanda's talk.

Williams's evocation of sensitive souls who cannot adjust to society and their clash with the modern world is dramatized in his greatest and most successful play, A STREETCAR NAMED DESIRE (1947), which won a Pulitzer Prize. The indelible portraits of Blanche DuBois, a romantic and decadent southern belle, and Stanley Kowalski, the virile son of Polish immigrants, played on the New York stage and then in film by the electrifying Marlon Brando, sealed Williams's reputation as one of the greatest playwrights of the postwar generation. The play also expanded his range, incorporating not just Williams's sensitivity to human character but also to changes taking place in American society. Stanley, for example, is reminiscent of the coal stoker in Eugene O'NEILL's play *The Hairy Ape* (1922), although Williams shows Stanley's humor and resilience, which Blanche finds both attractive and repellent—since Stanley lacks the genteel qualities that Blanche associates with her lost family plantation, Belle Reve (beautiful dream). Williams's great insight shows that the beautiful dream remains a beautiful dream even when exposed to the harsh realities of modern life.

Williams followed *A Streetcar Named Desire* with several important plays, nearly equal in power to his first two successes. He created remarkably strong roles for women in *Summer and Smoke* (1948), The *Rose Tattoo* (1951), *Cat on a Hot Tin Roof* (1955), a Pulitzer Prize winner, and *The Night of the Iguana* (1961). He explored with considerable daring the obsessiveness of his characters' search for love, for God, and for the meaning of life. His subject was often decadence, and his plays featured characters who had lost the will to succeed but not the ability to critique their faults and the world's failings.

The wistfulness and suffering of his characters arose, in part, out of Williams's own struggle with his homosexuality. He never tried very hard to conceal this aspect of his life, though he also recoiled at labels and never quite reconciled himself to his sexual identity, which perhaps contributes to the tensions his characters express.

After 1961 Williams found success in the theater increasingly difficult to achieve. Later plays such as *The Milk Train Doesn't Stop Here Anymore* (1963) and *The Eccentricities of a Nightingale* (1965), which Williams thought some of his best work, were poorly received. Efforts to resurrect his career in the 1970s and 1980s failed, even though his plays of the 1940s and 1950s continued to be revived and praised by critics.

Williams wrote one novel, *The Roman Spring of Mrs. Stone* (1950). He collected his stories in *Hard Candy* (1954), *The Knightly Quest* (1967), and *Eight Mortal Ladies Possessed* (1975). He published his *Memoirs* in 1975 and a collection of personal essays, *Where I Live*, in 1978.

Sources

Bloom, Harold, ed. *Tennessee Williams*. New York: Chelsea House, 1987.

Falk, Signi. *Tennessee Williams*. Boston: Twayne, 1978.

Leverich, Lyle. *Tom: The Unknown Tennessee Williams*. New York: Crown, 1995.

Spoto, Donald. *The Kindness of Strangers: The Life of Tennessee Williams*. Boston: Little, Brown, 1985.

Williams, William Carlos (1883–1963) *poet, novelist, short story writer, critic, autobiographer, doctor*

Williams was born in Rutherford, New Jersey, to an English father and a Puerto Rican mother. His parents often figure in his poetry. Williams studied medicine at the University of Pennsylvania, where he met his lifelong friend Ezra POUND and the painter Charles Demuth. Painting would become an influence on his writing and the subject matter of his poetry.

Williams began medical practice in Rutherford, New Jersey, in 1912 and would continue as a family doctor for 40 years. He was already dedicated to a career as a poet as well and sometimes wrote poems in haste on prescription blanks. His first poems were quite conventional and imitated 19th-century forms. But influenced by Pound, he soon began writing IMAGIST poems that would lead to his famous pronouncement: "No ideas but in things." Indeed, Williams stripped his poetry of all European characteristics and in *Kora in Hell: Improvisations* (1920) vehemently opposed T. S. ELIOT's emphasis on tradition, which meant steeping poetry in a European context and quoting or alluding to the European masters.

During the 1920s and 1930s Williams achieved little recognition and did not significantly influence the progress of American poetry, although he befriended poets such as Wallace STEVENS and maintained his contacts with Pound. Like Marianne MOORE, he featured a striking visual quality in his poems. At the same time, he explored urban themes in both his poetry and short fiction. "The Use of Force" is a classic American story based on Williams's work as a doctor making a house call. With extraordinary economy this very brief story portrays a doctor's fluctuating emotions as he tries to preserve his professional demeanor while treating a recalcitrant patient.

Williams also published *The Knife of the Times and Other Stories* (1932) and *Life Along the Passaic River* (1938). *The Farmers' Daughters: The Collected Stories of William Carlos Williams* was published in 1961 and *The Doctor Stories* in 1984.

In the 1940s Williams embarked on his great urban epic *Patterson*, published in five volumes from 1946 to 1958. The city, the history of New Jersey, and the poet's sensibility all meld together in a historical and aesthetic work that is reminiscent of Dos PASSOS's U.S.A. in its use of newspaper accounts, letters, and histories. *Patterson* parallels Williams's brilliant collection of essays on American history titled *In the American Grain* (1925). He was far ahead of his time in that book in paying tribute not merely to North American culture but also to the Aztecs and the peoples of Mesoamerica.

Williams's extraordinary output also includes novels, especially his trilogy *White Mule* (1937), *In the Money* (1940), and *The Build-Up* (1952). He provides portraits of women and of events in their lives, such as childbirth, that no other male American writer had ever written about in such detail or with such intense emotion. Here his practice as a doctor who delivered babies brought an authenticity to his prose that is unrivaled by his contemporaries.

Throughout his career, Williams continued to write poetry and essays and books arguing for his poetics. He believed in metrical irregularity and capturing American idioms in the short, often staccato lines of poetry. Language should be less literary, he believed, and grounded in the visual and aural senses. A prolific poet, Williams wrote his share of mediocre verse, but proof of the continuing high level of his work is seen in *Pictures from Brueghel* (1962), which won a Pulitzer Prize.

By the late 1950s Williams's central place in 20th-century American poetry was beginning to be hailed by poets such as Denise LEVERTOV, and Allen GINSBERG and the other BEATS. They saw in Williams the successor to Walt Whitman, who embraced America in all its variety. Williams is now regarded along with Eliot, Pound, and STEVENS as one of the four great American poets of the 20th century. Poems such as "The Red Wheelbarrow," "This is Just to Say," "Between Walls," and "The Yachts" appear in virtually all the standard anthologies of American literature, for they exemplify the poet's use of the compact four- to six-syllable line to present concrete visual images using common, everyday words that evoke a stark, spare beauty—and a clean, crisp view of life without any apparent interference or editorializing. *The Collected Poems of William Carlos Williams: Volume I, 1909–1939* appeared in 1986 and *The Collected Poems of William Carlos Williams: Volume II, 1939–1962* in 1988.

The Autobiography of William Carlos Williams was published in 1951, *Selected Essays of William Carlos Williams* in 1954, and *The Selected Letters of William Carlos Williams* in 1957. Other collections of correspondence include *William Carlos Williams, John Sanford: A Correspondence* (1984), *William Carlos Williams and James Laughlin: Selected Letters* (1989), and *Pound/Williams: Selected Letters of Ezra Pound and William Carlos Williams* (1996).

Sources

Axelrod, Stephen Gould and Helen Deese, eds. *Critical Essays on William Carlos Williams.* New York: G. K. Hall, 1995.

Bloom, Harold, ed. *William Carlos Williams.* New York: Chelsea House, 1986.

Doyle, Charles, ed. *William Carlos Williams: The Critical Heritage.* Boston: Routledge & Kegan Paul, 1980.

Mariani, Paul. *William Carlos Williams: A New World Naked.* New York: McGraw Hill, 1981.

Whitaker, Charles. *William Carlos Williams.* Boston: Twayne, 1989.

Whittemore, Reed. *William Carlos Williams.* Baltimore: Johns Hopkins University Press, 1975.

Wilson, August (Frederick Kittel) (1945–)
playwright

Born Frederick Kittel in Pittsburgh, Pennsylvania, Wilson was the son of a German baker and Daisy Wilson, an African-American cleaning woman. Wilson rarely saw his father, and later his parents divorced. He then lived in a white suburb and experienced racism firsthand. He dropped out of high school and joined the army. By 1965 he had decided to become a writer and worked at many odd jobs to support himself. Wilson was also active in the Black Power movement even as he helped to found the Black Horizon Theatre Company in Pittsburgh. His first plays were performed in community theaters.

In 1981 Wilson made his professional theater debut with *Black Bar and the Sacred Hills,* a musical satire of the old West. The play was produced in St. Paul, Minnesota, where Wilson had moved in the late 1970s. Wilson's career began to progress when he teamed with director Lloyd Richards at the Yale Repertory Theater in New Haven, Conn. *Ma Rainey's Black Bottom,* a success on Broadway in 1984, had started as a workshop production directed by Richards. The play centers on the singer Ma Rainey and explores the exploitation of black musicians by white record companies in the 1920s. Although critics found fault with the play's structure, they were impressed with its treatment of racism. The play won a New York Drama Critics Circle Award in 1985.

In 1983 Wilson wrote one of his greatest plays, *Fences,* which had successful productions throughout the 1980s at the Yale Repertory Theater, and then on Broadway. The play which won a Pulitzer Prize and other awards, centers on a black family in the 1950s, headed by Troy Maxson, a garbage collector, ex-convict, and former Negro Baseball League player. The family dynamics reminded critics of Arthur MILLER's play *DEATH OF A SALESMAN,* with Maxson as a Willy LOMAN figure.

While *Fences* remained a hit on Broadway, Wilson opened a second play there in 1988. *Joe Turner's Come and Gone,* written in 1984 and produced at Yale in 1986, is set in a Pittsburgh boardinghouse. It explores the consequences of slavery, Reconstruction, and the black migration to northern cities. For this play Wilson won the New York Drama Critics Award.

The Piano Lesson, written in 1986, premiered on Broadway in 1990 and earned Wilson another Pulitzer Prize. Set in the DEPRESSION, it is another family drama, with a piano serving as a metaphor for the family's struggle over its heritage and the meaning of culture.

Two Trains Running, written in 1989 and produced on Broadway in 1992, won American Theatre Critics Association Award. The play is set in Pittsburgh in the 1960s and focuses on a group of characters in a coffee shop who come to terms with the issues of the day.

Wilson's dramas highlight the conflicts in every decade of African-American history. He has avowed a desire not only to tell the story of African Americans but also to develop a self-conscious African-American perspective. Although critics such as Robert Brustein have criticized Wilson's work as propagandistic, the prevailing critical opinion is that Wilson has successfully avoided the pitfalls of didactic art, which forces certain conclusions to the detriment of the work of art itself.

Sources

Bogumil, Mary L. *Understanding August Wilson.* Columbia: University of South Carolina Press, 1999.

Wolfe, Peter. *August Wilson.* New York: Twayne, 1999.

Wilson, Edmund (1895–1972) *critic, novelist, diarist*

One of the central figures of 20th-century American letters, Wilson was born in New Jersey and came from a long line of Puritans who settled the country and pursued learned professions. His father was a lawyer and a politician. Much of Wilson's outlook on American literature and literary figures stems from his rock-solid sense of himself and of tradition. A curious and awesomely intelligent critic, he kept absorbing and writing about world literature, making him also America's most well-read and accomplished critic.

Wilson was educated at Princeton, where he formed a lifelong friendship with F. Scott FITZGERALD. Although Wilson was comfortable in the academy, he spent most of his life outside it, first reporting for the *New York Sun* and then, after service in World War I, for *VANITY FAIR* (1920–1921) and the *NEW REPUBLIC* (1926–1931). In many ways a man of the 1920s, Wilson was a hard-drinking, hard-driving writer.

Especially at *The New Republic* he set a high standard for book reviews and did his utmost to further the careers of outstanding American writers.

Wilson's first important book, *Axel's Castle* (1931), demonstrates his trademark blend of biographical and literary criticism. He wrote in the 19th-century tradition of a man of letters, eschewing critical movements such as the NEW CRITICISM and staying apart from critics grouped around influential journals such as *PARTISAN REVIEW*.

Although Wilson was primarily interested in literature, he also explored political ideology in such magnificent work as *To the Finland Station* (1940), which reflects both his attraction to Marxism and his ultimate rejection of it. *The Wound and the Bow* (1941) is his most extensive foray into the psychological origins of art. *Patriotic Gore* (1962) is a monumental study of the literature of the Civil War. Wilson often engaged in literary polemics—attacking, for example, academic criticism in *The Fruits of the MLA* [Modern Language Association] (1968).

Wilson produced two notable works of fiction: *I Thought of Daisy* (1929), the story of New York bohemians in the 1920s, and *Memoirs of Hecate County* (1946), an account of suburban New York intellectuals. The latter was banned in many communities because of what critics saw as its pornographic content. Wilson's diaries, published in several volumes covering each decade of his life beginning with the 1920s, show ample evidence of his keen delight in sexual experience. While the diaries make frank and informative reading about Wilson's life and times, they are reticent on certain matters, including his contentious marriage to Mary MC-CARTHY.

Among Wilson's other noteworthy collections of criticism are *The Triple Thinkers* (1938), *Classics and Commercials: A Literary Chronicle of the 1940s* (1950), *The Shores of Light: A Literary Chronicle of the Twenties and the Thirties* (1952), and *The Bit Between My Teeth: A Literary Chronicle of 1950–1965* (1965).

Wilson helped sustain and enhance the reputation of F. Scott Fitzgerald, editing Fitzgerald's last unfinished novel, *The Last Tycoon* (1941) and *The Crack-up: With Other Uncollected Pieces*.

Sources

Meyers, Jeffrey. *Edmund Wilson: A Biography*. Boston: Houghton Mifflin, 1995.

Wain, John, ed. *Edmund Wilson: The Man and His Work*. New York: New York University Press, 1978.

Wilson, Harry Leon (1867–1939) *humorist, novelist*

Harry Wilson created two memorable characters in *Ruggles of Red Gap* (1915), the story of a British valet working in a western cattle town, and *Merton of the Movies* (1922), about a store clerk so smitten with movies that he becomes a suc-

cess by effortlessly imitating the roles he has obsessively watched on screen. *Merton* (1922), a play based on this character and written by the comic masters Marc CONNELLY and George S. KAUFMAN had a notable success.

Sources

Kummer, George. *Harry Leon Wilson: Some Account of the Triumphs and Tribulations of an American Writer*. Cleveland, Ohio: Press of Western Reserve University, 1963.

Wilson, Lanford (1937–) *playwright*

Wilson was born in Lebanon, Missouri, and grew up in Springfield and Ozark, Missouri, with his mother and stepfather. Wilson did not get to know his father until he moved to San Diego, and the re-establishment of their relationship seems to have spurred Wilson's playwriting efforts.

Wilson moved across the continent eastward in the late 1950s until he reached New York City, where he became involved in OFF OFF-BROADWAY. He began with experimental one-act plays, including *So Long at the Fair* (1963), *The Madness of Lady Bright* (1964), and *This is Rill Speaking* (1965). His later mature plays are autobiographical and focus on the saga of the *Talley* family. His full-length plays, beginning with *Balm in Gilead* (1965) and *The Hot L Baltimore* (1973), secured his reputation as a major playwright, produced both by the experimental La Mama Theatre and the Circle Repertory Company. *Talley's Folly* (1979) won a Pulitzer Prize.

The settings of Wilson's plays tend to alternate between family homes and seedy hotels, both of which have reminded critics of the dramas of Eugene O'NEILL and William SAROYAN. The sheer theatricality of his work (*Redwood Curtain* [1992] for example) has been compared to Lillian HELLMAN's plays—his characters address the audience directly and engage in intense soliloquys—and his gift for poetic language to Tennessee WILLIAMS's dramas. Wilson also has shown an impressive range of styles from the realistic to the absurd, much like the style of playwrights Sam SHEPARD and David MAMET.

Wilson's work has been collected in *Balm of Gilead and Other Plays* (1985). His later dramas include *Book of Days: Four Short Plays* (1994) and A *Play in Two Acts* (2000).

Sources

Bryer, Jackson R., ed. *Lanford Wilson: A Casebook*. New York: Garland, 1994.

Dean, Anne M. *Discovery and Invention: The Urban Plays of Lanford Wilson*. Rutherford, N.J.: Fairleigh Dickinson University Press, 1994.

Winesburg, Ohio Sherwood Anderson (1919) *short story collection*

This collection of stories greatly influenced Sherwood AN-DERSON's successors, particularly William FAULKNER and

Ernest HEMINGWAY in their collections *In Our Time* (1924), in which Hemingway introduced the character Nick Adams, and *Go Down, Moses* (1942), which introduced Faulkner's character Ike McCaslin.

George Willard is the central character of the closely integrated short stories that make up *Winesburg, Ohio*. The people of Winesburg tell George their stories, which often deal with their solitariness, their dreams, and their failures. George is a cub reporter for the *Winesburg Eagle*, and the stories he hears are part of his own maturation as a writer and as an adult.

George's mother is one of Winesburg's solitaries. She stays in bed, unhappy about her unsatisfactory life with her husband, Tom. She was once a beautiful, intrepid woman, but marriage stifled her dreams. George's father is just the opposite: Practical-minded, he urges his son not to dream but to "wake up."

"Hands" is the most evocative story of *Winesburg*. Wing Biddlebaum breaks his silence to tell George about how his dreams have been destroyed. He is, in fact, the quintessential dreamer. But when his fluttering hands with their long, expressive fingers touch George's shoulders, Wing abruptly leaves. The homoerotic resonance of the scene explains why Wing feels he has had to keep to himself.

Like Wing, Louise Trunnion is attracted to George. "I'm yours if you want me," she tells him. But George is put off by her assertiveness. Another woman, Kate Swift, is also attracted to him and suggests that one day he may write the story of his town. George responds more fully to Belle Carpenter but is shocked when Belle's lover, Ed Handby, thrusts him aside without a word.

George becomes the repository of many other stories of secret desires and disappointed hopes. The expectation is that one day he will be able to tell all these stories, although he does not yet have the wisdom or the skill to do these lives justice.

Sources

Crowley, John W., ed. *New Essays on Winesburg, Ohio.* New York: Cambridge University Press, 1990.

Ferres, John H., ed. *Winesburg, Ohio: Text and Criticism.* Updated edition. New York: Penguin Books, 1996.

Winters, Arthur Yvor (1900–1968) *poet, critic*

Born in Chicago, Yvor Winters had a distinguished teaching career at Stanford University while publishing poetry praised for its classical restraint, exquisite sense of form, and moral discrimination. His *Collected Poems* appeared in 1952 (revised and expanded in 1960 and awarded the Bollingen Prize).

Winters was an astute critic of American literature, especially poetry. His special subject was the ambiguity and obscurity of modern poetry, which he attributed, in part, to the influence of romanticism. His most important critical books are *Primitivism and Decadence* (1937), *Maule's Cure* (1938), *In Defense of Reason* (1947), and the *Function of Criticism: Problems and Exercises* (1957). His *Uncollected Essays* were published in 1973.

Sources

Academy of American Poets. "Poetry Exhibits: Yvor Winters." Academy of American Poets. Available online. URL: http://www.poets.org/poets/poets.cfm?prmID=753. Downloaded October 25, 2001.

Brunner, Edward. "Yvor Winters (1900–1968)." Modern American Poetry. Available online. URL: http://www.english.uiuc.edu/maps/poets/s_z/winters/winters.htm. Downloaded October 25, 2001.

Stanford, Donald E. *Revolution and Convention in Modern Poetry: Studies in Ezra Pound, T. S. Eliot, Wallace Stevens, Edwin Arlington Robinson and Yvor Winters.* Newark: Delaware University Press, 1983.

Woiwode, Larry Alfred (1941–) *short story writer, novelist*

Woiwode was born in Carrington, North Dakota, and spent his childhood nearby, absorbing the austere, beautiful landscape that would contribute to his novels of midwestern life. He attended the University of Illinois but did not earn a degree, and then moved to New York City, working as a freelance writer and publishing in the NEW YORKER. After several writer-in-residence positions at various colleges, he moved his family to North Dakota in 1978 to start an organic farm.

Woiwode's work is striking for its avoidance of the staples of modern American fiction. He is less concerned with alienation or the dehumanization of the individual than he is with personal responsibility and community. Critics have detected what amounts to a religious strain in his writing, a sense of the spiritually demanding life that is found in writers such as Walker PERCY and Flanner O'CONNOR, although he avoids O'Connor's use of the gothic.

Woiwode's first novel, *What I'm Going to Do, I Think* (1969), won the William Faulkner Foundation Award. It is the story of two newlyweds, Chris and Ellen Van Eenanam, who each represent a different way of approaching life. The couple experiences a loss of faith in themselves and in the world, which in turn is defined as a spiritual loss. Although their problems are not resolved, the novel ends with the suggestion that they have recognized the need for a transcendent meaning in their lives.

Beyond the Bedroom Wall (1975), Woiwode's most famous novel, is notable for its expansive and comic mood. It contains 63 characters in what constitutes an episodic novel and a family chronicle. The novel is also notable for its evocations of midwestern speech and its descriptions of the prairie landscape. After the poorly received *Poppa John* (1981)—which deals perhaps too schematically with the story of a soap opera actor who finds God—Woiwode returned to the form of *Beyond the Bedroom Wall* in *Born Brothers* (1988), a novel about two brothers who yearn to reestablish their bond in the context of American society's lapsed faith in communal and family values. *Indian Affairs* (1992) returns to the story of the Van Eenanams, now in the eighth year of their marriage, which is complicated by Chris's exploration of his American Indian roots. The more Indian he feels, the more estranged he is not only from his marriage but also from modern life itself. Ellen, on the other hand, experiments with drugs and seems to come out of her emptiness when she becomes pregnant for the first time. As with *What I'm Going to Do, I Think,* there is no ultimate resolution to the couple's sense of anomie, and this time the possibility that they can overcome the vacuum of values seems more remote.

Woiwode's short fiction is collected in *The Neumiller Stories* (1989) and in *Silent Passengers: Stories* (1993). He has published one book of poetry, *Even Tide* (1977). His nonfiction includes *Acts* (1993) and *What I Think I Did: A Season of Survival in Two Acts* (2000).

Sources

Yancey, Philip, ed. *Reality and Vision: Seventeen Christian Authors Reveal Their Literary Legacy.* Dallas: Word Publishing, 1990.

Wolfe, Nero *character*

One of the great modern detectives in fiction, Wolfe was invented by Rex STOUT. Like Sherlock Holmes, Wolfe has an assistant, Archie, who like Dr. Watson is often employed to do Wolfe's leg work as he sits in his easy chair, drinking beer. Wolfe and Archie's colloquies provide much of the humor and relaxed conversational quality of Stout's work. In the course of this detective series, Stout discloses certain details about Wolfe—he is Montenegran, for example, and he has a passion for growing orchids. Wolfe's sophistication and elegance mark quite a contrast with Dashiell HAMMETT's hard-boiled detectives and with other heroes of American mysteries and crime fiction. Wolfe instead resembles the gentlemen detectives of the British mystery genre.

Sources

Baring-Gould, William Stuart. *Nero Wolfe of West Thirty-Fifth Street: The Life and Times of America's Largest Private Detective.* New York, N.Y.: Penguin, 1982.
Van Dover, Kenneth J. *At Wolfe's Door: The Nero Wolfe Novels of Rex Stout.* San Bernardino, Calif.: Borgo Press, 1991.

Wolfe, Thomas Clayton (1900–1938) *novelist*

Wolfe was born in Asheville, North Carolina. His father was a stonecutter who shaped his son's love of language, and

Wolfe returned his father the compliment by making him a character in his brilliant first novel, *Look Homeward, Angel* (1929).

Early on, Wolfe aspired to be a playwright. After attending the University of North Carolina at Chapel Hill, he enrolled at Harvard to study at George Pierce Baker's famous workshop for dramatists. Baker is transformed into Professor Hatcher in the novel *Of Time and the River* (1935). Wolfe never was able to find the proper dramatic structure for what were both personal and epic feelings. On the broader canvas of the novel, and specifically of the *bildungsroman,* Wolfe could use his own experience to portray the exhilaration and agony of growing up in an America full of promise but also full of pitfalls for those striving as hard as Wolfe was.

In 1925 Wolfe met Aline Bernstein, a stage designer in New York. She became his lover, his mentor, and the inspiration for the character Esther Jack in his novels. Wolfe essentially was writing one huge epic and found it difficult to break it up into parts without the help of editors such as Maxwell PERKINS and later Duncan Aswell. After Wolfe's death, controversy arose about how much his later work—particularly *The Web and the Rock* (1939) and *You Can't Go Home Again* (1940)—owed to the superb editing of Aswell, who carved presentable novels out of chaotic manuscripts.

Perhaps no American writer has ever portrayed the intense feelings of adolescence so poignantly. His extraordinary use of language—ranging from Elizabethan gorgeousness to the extremely colloquial—has appealed to generations of young readers. Scenes in Wolfe's novels, such as his evocation of the sound of trains traveling through the night, inspired generations of restless Americans to explore the continent and the world. In retrospect, mature readers and critics have faulted Wolfe for self-indulgence and for a certain myopia in his heroes, Eugene Gant and Eugene Weber, who become so fixated on themselves that they lose sight of social context even as their author lacked the discipline to structure his work. Yet William FAULKNER ranked Wolfe among the top five writers of his generation, for he admired Wolfe's daring risks with language and his effort to encompass all reality with his words.

Wolfe wrote superb short stories, such as "Only the Dead Know Brooklyn." His short fiction is collected in *The Complete Short Stories of Thomas Wolfe* (1987).

Wolfe wrote about how he came to fiction in *The Story of a Novel* (1936). *The Letters of Thomas Wolfe* appeared in 1956, *The Notebooks of Thomas Wolfe* in 1970, and *My Other Loneliness: Letters of Thomas Wolfe and Aline Bernstein* in 1983.

Sources

Bloom, Harold, ed. *Thomas Wolfe.* New York: Chelsea House, 1987.
Donald, David. *Look Homeward.* Boston: Little, Brown, 1987.

Johnston, Carol Ingalls. *Of Times and the Artist: Thomas Wolfe, His Novels, and the Critics.* Columbia, S.C.: Camden House, 1996.

Klein, Carole. *Aline.* New York: Harper & Row, 1979.

Wolfe, Tom (Thomas Kennerly Wolfe, Jr.) (1931–) *journalist, novelist*

Born and raised in Richmond, Virginia, Wolfe attended Washington and Lee University and went on to Yale to obtain a Ph.D. in American studies. He made his reputation as a witty and often scathing critic of establishment institutions such as the NEW YORKER. He criticized contemporary novelists for turning their backs on social reality and turning inward, thus producing small works that were not commensurate with the size or complexity of American life.

Wolfe sought out subjects that were iconoclastic and countercultural. *The Kandy-Kolored Tangerine-Flake Streamline Baby* (1965) explored the youth culture. *The Electric Kool-Aid Acid Test* (1968) followed the novelist Ken KESEY on a psychedelic tour of the country. Wolfe found his heroes in such figures as the race car driver Junior Johnson. He excoriated the literary establishment for fawning over 1960s radicals and black militants in *Radical Chic and Mau-Mauing the Flak Catchers* (1970). In *The Painted Word* (1975) he dismissed much of modern art, which he found pretentious and too self-involved. He presented a novelized history of the space program in *The Right Stuff* (1979).

In *The New Journalism* (1973) Wolfe argued that the freshest, most engaged, and most imaginative contemporary writing was coming not from novelists but instead from journalists who reported on the social reality of America. He predicted there would come a day when the novel would return to its journalistic roots and once again reflect America in all its diversity. Wolfe makes this argument as well in *Conversations with Tom Wolfe* (1990).

Wolfe himself has attempted to fulfill his prediction in two novels, *Bonfire of the Vanities* (1987) and *A Man in Full* (1998). The first, a riveting story of Sherman McCoy, a Wall Street bond trader and self-described "master of the universe," loses his way returning from the airport in his Mercedes and runs down a black man. The resulting story is a fascinating comment on the nature of race, class, and character in contemporary America. Wolfe's facile style made the novel a best-seller, but some critics said the author relied on stereotypes.

A Man in Full is essentially a study of the new South. Set in Atlanta, the novel follows the story of Charles Croker, ex-football star and real estate magnate. Croker's success is largely veneer in a second bonfire of the vanities, a world still rigidly separated by class and race. This novel features Wolfe's trademark exuberance, cynicism, and remarkable reportorial skills, although some critics still doubt Wolfe's ability to create complex characters with inner lives.

Sources

McKeen, William. *Tom Wolfe.* New York: Twayne, 1995.

Shomette, Doug, ed. *The Critical Response to Tom Wolfe.* Westport, Conn.: Greenwood Press, 1992.

Wolff, Geoffrey Ansell (1937–) *autobiographer, biographer, novelist*

In 1976 Wolff published an unusual biography, *Black Sun: The Brief Transit and Violent Eclipse of Harry Crosby,* a stimulating account of a minor figure from the 1920s that illuminates a decade of American history. Wolff's memoir of his con-man father, *The Duke of Deception* (1979), was highly praised not only for the quality of its writing but also because it raised issues about the way individuals create themselves in modern society. *The Final Club* (1990) is a memoir about Wolff's years at Princeton, and *A Day at the Beach* (1992) is about his wife and sons. Less well known are Wolff's novels: *Bad Debts* (1969), *Providence* (1986), and *The Age of Consent* (1995).

Sources

Rodriguez, Bill. "Life After Providence: A Conversation with Geoffrey Wolff." *The Boston Phoenix.* September 6, 1990. Available on-line. URL: http://www.netsense.net/~billrod/wolff.iv.htm

Wolff, Tobias (1945–) *short story writer, autobiographer*

The brother of Geoffrey WOLFF, Tobias Wolff lived as a child with his mother and an abusive stepfather, a horrifying experience he relates in the well-received memoir *This Boy's Life* (1989). Wolff served in the VIETNAM WAR, took a degree at Oxford University, worked for the *Washington Post,* and began writing stories, collected in *In the Garden of North American Martyrs* (1981) and *Back in the World* (1985). His spare, elegant short fiction has been compared to Raymond CARVER's work. His novel, *The Barracks Thief* (1985), the story of soldiers away from the Vietnam war scene, won the PEN/Faulkner award. *In Pharaoh's Army: Memories of the Lost War* (1994) is Wolff's reckoning with his Vietnam experience. *The Night in Question: Stories* appeared in 1996. He has also edited *The Picador Book of Contemporary American Stories* (1993).

Sources

Hannah, James. *Tobias Wolff: A Study of the Short Fiction.* New York: Twayne, 1996.

Wood, Charles Erskine Scott (1852–1944) *poet*

Born in Pennsylvania, Wood pursued an army career in the West and then became a lawyer in Oregon. He published several volumes of poetry, including *The Poet in the Desert* (1915), which expresses his concern about social justice. His most important work, however, is a series of dialogues, some of which were published in THE MASSES, a radical magazine hospitable to his antiwar views, which became very unpopular during WORLD WAR I. *The Masses* was suppressed before all of Scott's dialogues could be published. They eventually appeared in two volumes, *Heavenly Discourse* (1927) and *Earthly Discourse* (1937). The dialogues, some of which take place in heaven among angels like Thomas Jefferson, Mark Twain, and Thomas Paine, discuss the world's sorry record of intolerance, religious persecution, and other failings.

Sources
Hamburger, Robert. *Two Rooms: The Life of Charles Erskine Scott Wood.* Lincoln: University of Nebraska Press, 1998.

Woodward, Comer Vann (1908–1999) *historian*
Considered by his peers the finest historian of the American South, C. Vann Woodward began his career at Johns Hopkins University and completed it at Yale. His first important work was *Tom Watson: Agrarian Rebel* (1938), the biography of a progressive politician whose career degenerated into race baiting. Watson's fate was the fate of the South, which turned from Reconstruction and efforts to empower African Americans to segregation and the Jim Crow laws, which Woodward wrote about eloquently in *The Strange Career of Jim Crowe* (1955). Woodward's masterpiece in pure historical narrative is *Origins of the New South: 1877–1913* (1951). But his most influential volume—the one that bears comparison with the work of the greatest southern writers such as William FAULKNER and Robert Penn WARREN—is *The Burden of Southern History* (1960), a collection of essays that has reached a broad audience. This work is the most succinct explanation of the South's distinctiveness and is often cited by Woodward's fellow historians as a seminal work. Woodward was also a shrewd commentator on history as a discipline. *Thinking Back: The Perils of Writing History* appeared in 1986. He also edited *Mary Chesnut's Civil War* (1981), which won a Pulitzer Prize. In 1984, he coedited with Elisabeth Muhlenfeld *The Private Mary Chesnut: The Unpublished Civil War Diaries,* by a southern woman who viewed the war from the perspective of a plantation and her marriage to a southern politician.

Sources
Roper, John Herbert, ed. *C. Vann Woodward: A Southern Historian and His Critics.* Athens: University of Georgia Press, 1997.

———. *C. Vann Woodward, Southerner.* Athens: University of Georgia Press, 1987.

Woollcott, Alexander Humphreys (1887–1943)
literary critic
Alexander Woollcott was one of the most famous of the NEW YORKER writers—a wit, a tastemaker, and a public personality. A member of the ALGONQUIN ROUND TABLE, he was a boisterous and cosmopolitan figure whose opinions and influence stretched across the Anglo-American world of entertainment and letters. *The Man Who Came to Dinner* (1939), a play by George S. KAUFMAN and Moss HART, is a good-natured parody of Woollcott as public personality and nuisance. Among Woollcott's books are the essay collections *Shouts and Murmurs* (1922) and *While Rome Burns* (1934), both of which capture his stirring style and robust convictions.

Sources
Chatterton, Wayne. *Alexander Woollcott.* Boston: Twayne, 1978.
Teichmann, Howard. *Smart Aleck: The Wit, World, and Life of Alexander Woollcott.* New York: Morrow, 1976.

Workers' Monthly, The
See MASSES, THE.

World War I (1914–1919)
The war that came to be known as World War I began in August 1914 with Germany and Austria-Hungary (the Central Powers) pitted against Britain, France, and Russia. President Woodrow Wilson soon declared America's neutrality. As a result, both the Germans and the British put restrictions on American trade, and German submarines sank (without warning) U.S. merchant ships. On May 7, 1915, 128 Americans were killed when a German U-boat sank the *Lusitania,* a British ocean liner. The Wilson government protested, but the Germans stepped up the attacks, declaring war on all ships, including those of neutral nations. After several American ships were sunk in February and March 1917, and after the German foreign minister's telegram proposing a German-Mexican alliance was intercepted, the United States entered the war on April 2, 1917.

Wilson had vowed to keep the country out of war, and his change of policy angered and embittered many people, including John DOS PASSOS, who wrote a scathing biographical section on Wilson in *U.S.A.* Wilson appealed to American patriotism and called for American involvement to "make the world safe for democracy." His administration also conducted an intensive propaganda campaign that portrayed the Germans as primitive "Huns" out to destroy the very idea of civilization.

The U.S. Army grew from 200,000 to 4 million, with 2 million troops going overseas in the American Expeditionary Force. The American entry into the war aided the exhausted British and French forces, who had fought the

Germans to a stalemate. Russia, in the grips of its 1917 Revolution, made a separate peace with Germany. All told, 112,432 Americans died in the war, with more than half succumbing not to combat but to disease.

Although the war did not have as great an impact on American society as the Civil War or WORLD WAR II, it nevertheless accelerated changes. African Americans served in the army in larger numbers than ever before, and although they remained in segregated units, they came home with a new feeling of accomplishment and a desire to see their roles in society enhanced. William FAULKNER portrays this changing African-American attitude in *Sartoris* (1929). That novel also features the story of young Bayard Sartoris, whose role in the army air force so disrupts his connection to civil society that he cannot adjust and gives vent to his self-destructive streak. Faulkner dramatized the plight of the alienated veteran in his first novel, *Soldiers' Pay* (1926), and in several short stories. Ernest HEMINGWAY wrote the best fiction about this particular phenomenon in his short story "Soldiers Home" and in his novels *THE SUN ALSO RISES* (1926) and *A FAREWELL TO ARMS* (1929). F. Scott FITZGERALD also portrayed the enthusiasm and disillusionment of American soldiers in his early novels and short stories. In *Three Soldiers* (1921), Dos Passos provided perhaps the most thorough and searching examination of the American forces who fought in the war. E. E. CUMMINGS wrote of the war in his autobiographical novel *The Enormous Room* (1922), which is set in a French military concentration camp near Paris.

Sources

Aichinger, Peter. *The American Soldier in Fiction, 1880–1963: A History of Attitudes Toward Warfare and the Military Establishment.* Ames: Iowa State University, 1975.

Fussell, Paul. *The Great War and Modern Memory* (25th Anniversary Edition). New York: Oxford University Press, 2000.

Tuchman, Barbara. *The Guns of August.* New York: Macmillan, 1962.

World War II (1939–1945)

Although the war began in 1939 with the British and French declaration of war on Germany, which had invaded Poland, the United States did not enter the war until the Japanese attack on Pearl Harbor on December 7, 1941. President Roosevelt, alarmed at the Japanese invasion of Indochina, had frozen Japanese assets in America at the end of July 1941. All American trade with Japan ceased, including the export of oil to Japan. Confronting the loss of its major source of energy, the Japanese saw war with the U.S. as inevitable.

With Germany, an ally of Japan, also declaring war on the United States, the country mobilized rapidly for war, changing its position from pacifist or at least noninterventionist to a belief that the war was necessary to protect vital U.S. interests and to rid the world of a spreading fascist tyranny. James JONES's novel *From Here to Eternity* (1951) presents a vivid account of the U.S. Army in Hawaii just before the Pearl Harbor attack. Jones continued the story of the war years in his novel *The Thin Red Line* (1962), and then explored the postwar lives of the soldiers in *Whistle* (1978). Norman MAILER's THE NAKED AND THE DEAD (1948) vividly dramatized a long patrol on a Japanese-held island. His portrait of General Cummings suggests that the U.S. Army also harbored fascist elements. His novel also emulated the work of John DOS PASSOS in presenting an array of characters from the different regions and ethnic groups that went to war.

Other important novels about World War II include Irwin SHAW's *The Young Lions* (1948) and Gore VIDAL's debut novel, *Williwaw* (1946). Herman WOUK presented a masterly canvas of the United States and of the military in the years leading up to the war in *The Winds of War* (1971). His *War and Remembrance* (1978) contains vivid descriptions of the naval war in the Pacific.

Martha GELLHORN provided a vivid description of the Battle of the Bulge and the liberation of the German concentration camp Dachau in *The Wine of Astonishment* (1948), later reprinted as *Point of No Return*. Ernest HEMINGWAY provided vivid scenes of Europe right after the war in *Across the River and into the Trees* (1950), but the novel is disappointing in its handling of dialogue and character. Joseph HELLER's CATCH-22 (1961) and Kurt VONNEGUT's *Slaughterhouse-Five* (1969) are memorable accounts of the horror and absurdity of war. Other noteworthy works include James Michener's *Tales of the South Pacific* (1944), made into the musical *South Pacific*; John HERSEY's *A Bell for Adano* (1944), a comic story of the American army's occupation of an Italian town; and Thomas Heggen's comic treatment of life in the navy, *Mister Roberts* (1946), which became a popular motion picture starring Jack Lemmon and Henry Fonda.

Arthur MILLER's *Incident at Vichy* (1964) and William STYRON's *In the Clap Shack* (1972) are plays set during World War II. Perhaps the most distinguished poetry about the war was published by Randall JARRELL and James DICKEY.

Sources

Aichinger, Peter. *The American Soldier in Fiction, 1880–1963: A History of Attitudes Toward Warfare and the Military Establishment.* Ames: Iowa State University, 1975.

Fussell, Paul. *Wartime: Understanding and Behavior in the Second World War.* New York: Oxford University Press, 1989.

Higgins, Ian, ed. *The Second World War in Literature: Eight Essays.* Edinburgh: Scottish Academic Press, 1986.

Wouk, Herman (1915–) novelist

Wouk was born in New York City, the son of an immigrant who established a successful laundry business. Wouk studied philosophy and comparative literature and graduated with honors from Columbia University in 1934. He found employment as a gag writer for radio comedians. He joined the navy at the beginning of WORLD WAR II and saw action aboard a minesweeper in the Pacific fleet.

After the war Wouk began to write novels, beginning with *Aurora Dawn* (1947), a satirical attack on the advertising industry. *The City Boy* (1948) tells of Herbie Bookbinder, an urban Tom Sawyer who seeks success but also wishes to be accepted as a "regular guy." *The Caine Mutiny* (1951), which critics consider Wouk's best novel, is a taut drama with memorable characters. Captain Queeg (played with genius by Humphrey Bogart in the movie adaptation) is a weak man whose incompetence is exposed and who reacts like a despot in order to defend himself. Whether the mutineers are in the right is another matter: the novel leaves open the question of whether they could have done better than their captain. The novel derives much of its intensity from its courtroom drama that reveals the fallibility of all the characters involved. Wouk avoids melodrama so that neither the captain nor the mutineers become mere symbols of good and evil.

Wouk's novel *Marjorie Morningstar* (1955) is the story of a Jewish girl (born Morgenstern) whose dream is to be a great movie star. To do so, she must repudiate her Jewish past and fully assimilate herself to the standards set by Hollywood. Although she fails to attain her dream, she achieves a new consciousness of her identity and what it means to be a Jew. *Youngblood Hawke* (1962) is a novel based in part on the life of Thomas WOLFE. It is the story of a great writer whose early success only makes it more difficult for him when critics turn against him and he no longer knows how to use his enormous energies creatively.

Wouk's next two novels— *Don't Stop the Carnival* (1965) and *The Lokokome Papers* (1968)—were decidedly inferior to his previous work, but *The Winds of War* (1971) and *War and Remembrance* (1978), sweeping historical novels based on his own experience in World War II, contain some of the best accounts of naval warfare ever written. Gore VIDAL pointed out Wouk's achievement as a historical novelist, although Vidal also faulted him for creating too many characters whose only purpose is to advance the historical narrative.

Wouk's next three novels—*Inside, Outside* (1985), *The Hope* (1993), and *The Glory* (1994)—explore 20th-century Judaism, politics, and history, including the creation of the state of Israel and the status of U.S. politics from the end of World War II to the 1970s. *Inside, Outside* presents a fascinating account of the Nixon presidency through the eyes of David Goodkind, a special assistant to the president. Indeed, the complex portrait of Nixon juxtaposes the "inside" history of what it was like to work in the White House to the "outside" world of current events.

Sources

Beichman, Arnold. *Herman Wouk: The Novelist as Social Historian.* New Brunswick, N.J.: Transaction Books, 1984.

Mazzeno, Laurence W. *Herman Wouk.* New York: Twayne, 1994.

Wright, Charles (1935–) *poet, translator*

Wright was born in Pickwick Dam, Tennessee. He earned a B.A. degree in history from Davidson College in 1957, then joined army intelligence for three years. He served in Italy, where he read Ezra POUND and formed the ambition to become a poet. After army service Wright studied at the IOWA WRITERS' WORKSHOP under the supervision of Donald JUSTICE, whom Wright credits as a superb mentor.

Heavily influenced by both Emily Dickinson and country music, Wright's poetry has an earthy humor yoked with a philosophical consciousness of the nature of the world. *The Grave of the Right Hand* (1970), generally considered to be his first important work, contains prose poem contemplations of nature set in Italy. *Hard Freight* (1973) is a homage to the influence of such poets as Ezra POUND and Arthur Rimbaud. *Bloodlines* (1975), on the other hand, probes deeply into Wright's southern roots. Although *The Southern Cross* (1981) contains four "self-portraits," the poetry is not CONFESSIONAL and the "I" of the poems seem more like the disembodied I or voice of poetry that Wallace STEVENS developed. *Country Music: Selected Early Poems* (1982) won the American Book Award. A second collection, *The World of the Ten Thousand Things: Poems, 1980–1990* (1990) is of the same high quality.

Wright has also published *Halflife: Improvisations and Interviews 1977–1987* (1988); Quarter *Notes: Improvisations and Interviews* (1995); *Chickamauga* (1995); *Black Zodiac* (1997); *Appalachia* (1998); and *Negative Blue: Selected Later Poems* (2000).

Wright's translations include Eugene Montale's *The Storm and Other Things* (1978) and Dino Campana's *Orphic Songs* (1984).

Sources

Andrews, Tom, ed. *The Point Where All Things Meet: Essays on Charles Wright.* Oberlin, Ohio: Oberlin College Press, 1995.

Wright, James Arlington (1927–1980) *poet*

James Wright was born in Martins Ferry, Ohio, an industrial town on the upper Ohio River. The onset of the GREAT DEPRESSION, along with the contrast between the natural beauty of the Ohio Valley and the blighted urban civilization, inform much of his poetry.

Wright served in Japan during World War II and graduated from Kenyon College in 1952. His first book of poetry, *The Green Wall* (1957), was published in the YALE SERIES OF YOUNGER POETS. His style in these poems ranges from relaxed free verse to more formal blank verse, the latter unusual for a contemporary poet. *The Branch Will*

Not Break (1963) signaled a much more subjective turn in the poet's style—in part the result of the influence of Robert BLY, Wright's colleague at the University of Minnesota. With Bly's encouragement Wright began translating Pablo Neruda and Cesar Valejo, two South American poets who had infused contemporary poetry with a more personal approach that included surreal (see SURREALISM) imagery. *Collected Poems* (1971) shows the evolution and maturation of Wright's work and won a Pulitzer Prize. Wright published one more book, *To a Blossoming Pear Tree* (1977). Just as he was diagnosed with cancer, he completed a final collection of poetry, *This Journey,* published in 1982. *Collected* Prose appeared in 1983 and The *Complete Poems* in 1990.

Wright's translations include Cesar Vallejo's *Twenty Poems* (1962) and *Twenty Poems of Pablo Neruda* (1967).

Sources

Elkins, Andrew. *The Poetry of James Wright.* Tuscaloosa: University of Alabama Press, 1991.

Wright, Richard Nathaniel (1908–1960) *short story writer, novelist, poet*

In *Black Boy* (1945), Richard Wright wrote a searing memoir of his childhood in Mississippi. Brought up by sharecropper parents barely able to take care of him (his mother suffered a stroke), Wright had to work while still a child. He realized that in order to be his own man he would have to leave the segregated South. In the 1930s he moved to Chicago, where he met many writers, joined the Communist-inspired John Reed Club, and became an editor at *The Daily Worker.*

Wright ignited the literary scene in America with the publication of his first novel, NATIVE SON (1940), the terrifying account of Bigger Thomas, who is overwhelmed by his first intimate contact with white people. Cut off from his own family, Thomas panics and murders the daughter of his white employer. This brutal crime is situated in the context of an America where a man like Bigger Thomas has literally no outlet for his feelings. The white girl's attention to him is a torment because there is no way he can respond as a human being: His place is to serve her, yet she affects to treat him as an equal, and her informality confuses and then frightens him.

Wright wrote *Native Son* in the naturalistic mode. The novel has often been compared to Theodore DREISER'S *AN AMERICAN TRAGEDY* because like Dreiser, Wright is keenly aware of how much individuals are shaped by society. What looks like an individual's choice is, from the naturalist's point of view, an action already determined by a society that strictly limits the ways a person can act. To understand why Bigger Thomas murders, one has to understand in depth the environment that triggers his behavior.

Except for *Black Boy,* no other work of Wright's achieved the power of *Native Son.* Wright himself became increasingly disenchanted with American society. Both his leftist politics and his race were held against him, and he immigrated to France in 1946. Later novels, such as *The Outsider* (1953), present an even bleaker picture of life for African Americans.

The second part of Wright's autobiography (the sequel to *Black Boy*) was not published until 1977. Titled *American Hunger,* the book recounts Wright's experiences in Chicago, his attraction to the Communist Party and his break with it in 1944, and his continuing assault on the American institutions that he felt had oppressed African Americans.

Wright's short fiction is collected in *Uncle Tom's Children* (1938) and *Eight Men* (1961). With the playwright Paul GREEN he published a play, *Native Son: The Biography of a Young American* (1941). His nonfiction includes *Twelve Million Black Voices* (1941), *Black Power* (1954), *The Color Curtain* (1956), *Pagan Spain* (1957), and *White Man, Listen!* (1957).

In 1998, *Haiku: This Other World,* a selection of Wright's poetry, was published. In the last 18 months of his life Wright wrote 4,000 haiku and selected 817 as his best. Death and nature dominate these exquisitely written works that took Wright into another realm of expression, although the editors of his haiku note their connections to stories such as "Big Boy Leaves Home" and to *Black Boy.*

Sources

Hakutani, Yoshinobu. *Richard Wright and Racial Discourse.* Columbia: University of Missouri Press, 1996.

Kinnamon, Keneth, ed. *Critical Essays on Richard Wright's "Native Son."* New York: Twayne, 1997.

Walker, Margaret. *Richard Wright: Daemonic Genius.* New York: Warner Books, 1988.

Wylie, Elinor Hoyt (1885–1928) *poet, novelist*

Born in New Jersey, Elinor Wylie had a collection of poetry published in England in 1912, but her debut in the United States came with *Nets to Catch the Wind* (1921). At once elegant and metaphysical, the poems made Wylie an instant literary star. She solidified her success with a similar volume, *Black Armour* (1923). Wylie commanded the heights of the literary world with her marriage to William Rose Benet, one of the most influential authors of the 1920s. *One Person* (1928) is an intensely passionate sonnet sequence. Her *Collected Poems* appeared in 1932, *Collected Prose* in 1933, and *Last Poems* in 1943.

Wylie also wrote novels: *Jennifer Lorn* (1923), *The Venetian Glass Nephew* (1925), *The Orphan Angel* (1926), and *Mr. Hodge & Mr. Hazard* (1928). Her fiction tended to focus on literary figures such as Byron and Shelley and on 18th- and 19th-century England.

Sources

Farr, Judith. *The Life and Art of Elinor Wylie.* Baton Rouge: Louisiana State University Press, 1983.

Gray, Thomas Alexander. *Elinor Wylie.* New York: Twayne, 1969.

Olson, Stanley. *Elinor Wylie: A Life Apart.* New York: Dial Press, 1979.

Yaddo

An artist's retreat in Saratoga Springs, New York, Yaddo has hosted many important writers such as Katherine Anne PORTER and James T. FARRELL. It was founded by Mrs. Katrina Nichols Trask Peabody as a refuge for creative artists. Residence generally is restricted to a month or two, with only a token charge for room and board. About 20 artists and writers can be accommodated at one time. Writers of fiction and nonfiction have applied successfully for stays at Yaddo.

Sources

Toll, Barbara, ed. *Friendships in Arcadia: Writers and Artists at Yaddo in the '90s.* Saratoga Springs, N.Y.: Corporation of Yaddo, 2000.
Waite, Marjorie Peabody. *Yaddo, Yesterday and Today.* Saratoga Springs, N.Y., 1933.

Yale critics

This term is usually applied to Harold Bloom, Paul de Man, Geoffrey Hartman, and J. Hillis Miller, who rejected the NEW CRITICISM and brought into American critical theory many of the ideas promoted in France and the rest of Europe in the 1970s. Deconstruction, a term associated with this group, attacked the idea of literature as the product of a single author whose work could be controlled through the unique use of language. On the contrary, language itself was viewed as a subversive element in literature that destabilized meaning.

The Yale critics were part of a larger movement in literary studies in the 1970s and 1980s, a movement that turned away from conventional analyses of literary works and historical studies of authors' lives and publications in favor of an ex-

ploration of what was generally called "theory." Literary works were subjected to a painstaking "unpacking" of their style and form in order to show how the work of art contained internal contradictions that put into question their ultimate meaning.

Although writing "theory" remains an important part of academic literary studies, emphasis shifted in the 1990s to broader considerations of history, gender, and culture—signaled by a new term, cultural studies.

Sources

Arac, Jonathan. *The Yale Critics: Deconstruction in America.* Minneapolis: University of Minnesota Press, 1987.

Yale Series of Younger Poets

Begun in 1918 to encourage writers under age 40 who had not yet published a volume of verse and run by Yale University Press, this series has published the first books of John ASHBERY, Adrienne RICH, Muriel RUKEYSER, and many other distinguished poets. Stephen Vincent BENET edited the series from 1918 to 1941. W. H. AUDEN and Archibald MACLEISH also served as consultants.

Yerby, Frank Garvin (1916–1991) *novelist*

The African-American Yerby was born in Georgia and graduated with an M.A. degree from Fisk University in 1938. He found his niche by writing historical romances, beginning with *The Foxes of Harrow* (1946), set in the South just before the Civil War. He set his fiction in different periods of the past, sometimes dealing with the history of African

Americans and sometimes with the ancient world. His notable novels include *A Woman Called Fancy* (1951), *Goat Song: A Novel of Ancient Greece* (1967), and *Western: A Saga of the Great Plains* (1982). *McKenzie's Hundred* (1985) returns to the pre–Civil War South.

Sources

Breit, Harvey. *The Writer Observed.* Cleveland: World Publishing, 1956.

Sanders, Arlene. "Frank Yerby: African American Plus Iconoclast in World of Literature." Available on-line. URL: http://www.midsouthtribune.com/page105.html. Downloaded June 17, 2001.

Yezierska, Anzia (c. 1881–1970) *novelist, short story writer*

Yezierska grew up on New York's LOWER EAST SIDE, the daughter of Russian- and Polish-Jewish parents. She drew on her own family experience in her novel *Bread Givers* (1925), which focuses on a daughter's rebellion against the patriarchal values of her community.

Yezierska was a popular novelist in the 1920s. She sold her first two books, *Hungry Hearts* (1923) and *Salome of the Tenements* (1923), to Hollywood. Because she dealt with the sweatshop conditions of her early youth, she was publicized as the "sweatshop Cinderella."

Yezierska maintained an active literary career, publishing short stories and reviewing books for newspapers and periodicals, including the *New York Times.* Interest was renewed in her fiction in the 1970s when publishers were looking for titles in ethnic studies.

Yezierska's romantic relationship with the American philosopher John Dewey appeared in disguised form in her novels *All I Could Never Be* (1932) and *Red Ribbon on a White Horse* (1950).

Sources

Henriksen, Louise Levitas, with the assistance of Jo Ann Boydston. *Anzia Yezierska: A Writer's Life.* New Brunswick: Rutgers University Press, 1988.

Schoen, Carol B. *Anzia Yezierska.* Boston: Twayne, 1982.

Yossarian, John *character*

The hero of Joseph HELLER's black comedy CATCH-22, Yossarian is a bombardier captain in the Fighting 256th Squadron on the Italian island of Pianosa, eight miles south of Elba, in the final years of WORLD WAR II. He is paranoid and accuses everyone—Americans and Germans alike—of trying to kill him. His main goal is to stay alive. His superior, Captain Cathcart, continues to send him out on more missions, and Yossarian continues to find ways to avoid his duty, including pretending to be ill and then insane. Meanwhile, he watches his friends die and observes the callous attitudes of those who send these men to their fate. Inspired by a friend who turns up alive after being shot down over the Mediterranean and presumed dead, Yossarian grabs a raft and plots his own escape. Like Randle Patrick MCMURPHY in Ken KESEY's *ONE FLEW OVER THE CUCKOO'S NEST* (1962), Yossarian is the contrarian, the alienated man confronting American institutions that regiment individual behavior and demand conformity. Like Holden CAULFIELD, he is the odd man out, attempting to find his separate way. He plots his escape from the war just like Huckleberry Finn, who escapes "civilization" by setting out for the "Territory." In sum, Yossarian represents the anarchic impulse in the American character, which inevitably clashes with society's demand for order and capitulation to the status quo.

Sources

Bloom, Harold, ed. *Joseph Heller's Catch-22.* Philadelphia: Chelsea House, 2001.

Nagel, James, ed. *Critical Essays on Catch-22.* Encino, Calif: Dickenson, 1974.

Young, Albert James (1939–) *novelist, poet*

Albert Young, a Mississippi native, has been a resident of California since graduating from the University of California, Berkeley, in 1969. *Snakes* (1970), his first novel, is about a jazz musician. *Who is Angelina* (1975) is about a young African-American woman in quest of her identity. Other novels—*Sitting Pretty* (1976), *Ask Me Now* (1980), and *Seduction by Light* (1988)—range in subjects from the fictional autobiography of an African-American man as told to a retired professional basketball player to an African-American Mississippi woman who finds it difficult to adjust to a new life in Hollywood.

Young's poetry has been compared to Walt Whitman's for its expansive and exuberant use of everyday language. His major collections include *Dancing* (1969), *The Song Turning into Itself* (1971), *Geography of the Near Past* (1976), and *The Blues Don't Change* (1982). This poetry reflects both the African-American experience and the idioms of African Americans, which have been heavily influenced by jazz.

Young has published two memoirs: *Kinds of Blue* (1984) and *Things Ain't What They Used To Be* (1987).

Sources

Bruck, Peter and Wolfgant Karrer, ed. *The Afro-American Novel Since 1960.* Amsterdam: Grüner, 1982.

Lee, Don. "About Al Young." *Ploughshares* 19 (Spring 1993): 219–224.

Young, Stark (1881–1963) *critic, novelist*

A southerner and graduate of the University of Mississippi, Young first established his reputation as a theater critic for the NEW REPUBLIC. He collected his essays and reviews in *The Flower in Drama* (1923), *The Theater* (1927), and *Immortal Shadows* (1948).

Young had a second career as a novelist, publishing *Heaven Trees* (1926), *The Torches Flare* (1928), *River House* (1929), and his best-known work, *So Red the Rose* (1934), a rather florid but evocative work set in Civil War–era Mississippi.

The Street of the Islands (1930) and *Feliciana* (1935) collect Young's short stories. *The Pavilion* (1951) is a memoir. *Stark Young: A Life in the Arts: Letters, 1900–1962* appeared in 1975.

Sources

Pilkington, John. *Stark Young.* Boston: Twayne, 1985.

Zindel, Paul (1936–) *playwright, novelist*

Zindel was born in Staten Island, New York. He grew up with an interest in science, and he began writing plays and acting at a young age. He graduated from Wagner College on Staten Island with B.S. and M.S. degrees granted in 1958 and 1959, then taught high school chemistry from 1960 to 1969 before becoming a full-time writer in 1972. His work is particularly attuned to the development of adolescents who feel alienated from their families and society. He won a Pulitzer Prize for his play *The Effect of Gamma Rays on Man-in-the-Moon Marigolds* (1971), the story of an unhappy girl's relationship with her mother and sister, which was filmed the next year. His other plays include *And Miss Reardon Drinks a Little* (1971), *The Secret Affairs of Mildred Wild* (1973), and *Amulets Against the Dragon Forces* (1989).

Zindel has written several popular and highly praised novels for young adults, including *The Pigman* (1968), *My Darling, My Hamburger* (1969), *Harry and Hortense at Hormone High* (1984), *A Begonia for Miss Applebaum* (1989), and *David & Della* (1993).

Zindel has also published a horror trilogy: *Loch* (1994), *The Doom Stone* (1995), and *Reef of Death* (1998).

He has worked on television movies and the screenplays for the films *Up the Sandbox* (1972) and *Runaway Train* (1985).

Sources

Forman, Jack Jacob. *Presenting Paul Zindel.* Boston: Twayne, 1988.

Zugsmith, Leane (1903–1969) *novelist*

Born in Kentucky, Zugsmith made her name as a novelist of PROLETARIAN LITERATURE. *All Victories Are Alike* (1929) examines a newspaper editor's disillusionment with liberal values. *Goodbye and Tomorrow* (1931) explores the life of an older woman who sponsors artists. *Never Enough* (1932) is a full-scale treatment of the 1920s. *The Reckoning* (1934) is about the life of a slum boy. *A Time to Remember* (1936) portrays the unionization of a department store. *The Summer Soldier* (1938) is an excoriating attack on racism. Zugsmith published two collections of short stories: *Home Is Where You Hang Your Childhood* (1937) and *Hard Times with Easy Payments* (1941).

Sources

Ravitz, Abe. *Leane Zugsmith: Thunder on the Left.* New York: International Publishers, 1992.

Zukofsky, Louis (1904–1978) *poet*

Born on the Lower East Side of Manhattan, Zukofsky was the child of Jewish immigrants. He did well in school, enrolling at Columbia University when he was age 15. By age 20 he had earned an M.A. degree. By the late 1920s he had attracted the attention of Ezra POUND, who introduced Zukofsky to William Carlos WILLIAMS in 1928. Both poets believed in the objectivist approach to poetry, although Zukofsky favored a musical line quite different from Williams's: short, often monosyllabic, tersely worded lines. That same year Zukofsky embarked on his lifelong devotion to "A," a poem in 24 movements that explores the culture and economy of his times as well as his own sensibility.

In 1932 Zukofsky edited an issue of Harriet MONROE's PO-ETRY magazine, which featured the work of Williams, Carl Rakosi, Charles REZNIKOFF, and George OPPEN, which Zukofsky then published as a book, *An "Objectivists" Anthology.* Zukofsky emphasized in his introduction that poetry is the craft of putting words together. The poem is a kind of object, not a mystical, romantic expression of feelings.

Zukofsky, never one to seek recognition, became more reclusive in the 1930s. His poetry had only a small audience, mostly fellow poets. "A" was finally published in 1978. It and much of Zukofsky's other work has yet to find a large following, although critics have predicted that in time his work will prevail.

Zukofsky published *All the Collected Short Poems, 1923–1958* and *All the Collected Short Poems, 1956–1964* in 1965. His *Complete Short Poetry* was published in 1991. His *Collected Fiction* was published in 1990 and *The Collected Critical Essays of Louis Zukofsky* in 1981.

Sources

Scroggins, Mark, ed. *Upper Limit Music: The Writing of Louis Zukofsky.* Tuscaloosa: University of Alabama Press, 1997.

SELECTED BIBLIOGRAPHY

Bercovitch, Sacvan, ed. *The Cambridge History of American Literature.* Vols. 7 and 8. New York: Cambridge University Press, 1996–1999.

Curti, Merle. *The Growth of American Thought.* New York: Harper & Row, 1964.

Drake, William. *The First Wave: Women Poets in America, 1915–1945.* New York: Macmillan, 1987.

Elliot, Emory, ed. *Columbia Literary History of the United States.* New York: Columbia University Press, 1988.

Gray, Richard. *The Literature of Memory: Modern Writers of the American South.* Baltimore: Johns Hopkins University Press, 1977.

Groden, Michael and Martin Kreiswirth. *The Johns Hopkins Guide to Literary Theory and Criticism.* Baltimore: Johns Hopkins University Press, 1994. Updated edition available on-line. URL: http://www.press.jhu.edu/books/hopkins_guide_to_literary_theory/special.html. Downloaded October 25, 2001.

Hart, Stephen M. *A Companion to Spanish-American Literature.* New York: Tamesis Books, 2001.

King, Loverlerie. *A Student's Guide to the Study of African American Literature.* New York: Peter Lang, 2001.

Millgate, Michael. *American Social Fiction.* Edinburgh: Oliver & Boyd, 1964.

Parini, Jay, ed. *The Columbia History of American Poetry.* New York: Columbia University Press, 1993.

Pearce, Roy Harvey. *The Continuity of American Poetry.* Princeton, N.J.: Princeton University Press, 1961.

Rosenblatt, Roger. *Black Fiction.* Cambridge, Mass.: Harvard University Press, 1974.

Summers, Claude J., ed. *The Gay and Lesbian Literary Heritage: A Reader's Companion to the Writers and their Works, from Antiquity to the Present.* New York: Henry Holt, 1995.

Taubmann, Howard. *The Making of the American Theatre.* New York: Coward McCann, 1965.

Wade, Stephen. *Jewish American Literature Since 1945.* Edinburgh: Edinburgh University Press, 2001.

Wilmeth, Don B., and Tice Miller, eds. *Cambridge Guide to American Theatre.* New York: Cambridge University Press, 1993.

Wood, James. *Magazines in the United States.* 3rd ed. New York: Ronald Press, 1971.

INDEX

LIST OF ENTRIES

Andrews, Stephen Pearl **II**
Angelou, Maya **III**
Angstrom, Harry "Rabbit" (character) **III**
Anthony, Susan B. **II**
Anti-Rent War **II**
Appleseed, Johnny. *See* Chapman, John
Appleton's Journal (periodical) **II**
The Arean (periodical) **II**
Arendt, Hannah **III**
Armory Show **II**
Arnold, George **II**
Arnow, Harriet **III**
Arp, Bill. *See* Smith, Charles Henry
Arthur, Timothy Shay **II**
Articles of Confederation **I**
Ashbery, John Lawrence **III**
Ashbridge, Elizabeth Sampson **I**
Asian-American literature **III**
As I Lay Dying (Faulkner) **III**
Asimov, Isaac **III**
Atherton, Gertrude Franklin **II, III**
The Atlantic Monthly (periodical) **II, III**
Auchincloss, Louis Stanton **III**
Auden, Wynstan Hugh **III**
Audubon, John James **II**
Aurora (periodical) **I**
Auster, Paul **III**
Austin, Mary Hunter **II**
Austin, William **I**
Authors League of America **II, III**
The Autobiography of an Ex-Colored Man (Johnson) **III**
The Autobiography of Malcolm X (Haley and Malcolm X) **III**
The Autocrat of the Breakfast Table (Holmes) **II**
The Awakening (Chopin) **II**

B

Babbitt, Irving **III**
Babbitt (Lewis) **III**
Bache, Benjamin Frankin **I**
Bacheller, Irving Addison **II**
Backus, Isaac **I**
Bagby, George William **II**
Bailey, James Montgomery **II**
Baldwin, James **III**
    Go Tell It on the Mountain **III**
    Notes of a Native Son **III**
Ballard, Martha Moore **I**
Ballou, Adin **II**
Ballou, Maturin Murray **II**
Baltimore Sun (periodical) **II**
Bambara, Toni Cade **III**
Bancroft, George **II**
Bancroft, Hubert Howe **II**
Bandelier, Adolph Francis Alphonse **II**

Bangs, John Kendrick **II**
Banks, Russell **III**
Banneker, Benjamin **I**
Bannister, Nathaniel Harrington **II**
Baraka, Amiri **III**
Barkley, Catherine (character) **III**
Barlow, Joel **I**
Barnard, John **I**
Barnes, Charlotte Mary Sanford **II**
Barnes, Djuna **III**
Barnum, Phineas Taylor **II**
Barr, Amelia Edith Huddleston **II**
Barth, John Simmons **III**
Barthelme, Donald **III**
"Bartleby, the Scrivener" (Melville) **II**
Bartlett, John **II**
Bartram, John **I**
Bartram, William **I**
Bassett, John Spencer **II**
Baum, Lyman Frank **II**
The Bay Psalm Book **I**
Beach, Sylvia **III**
Beadle, Erastus **II**
Beats, the **III**
Beattie, Ann **III**
Beauchamp case. *See* Kentucky Tragedy
Beecher, Catharine Esther **II**
Beecher, Henry Ward **II**
Beecher, Lyman **II**
Beer, Thomas **II**
Belasco, David **II**
Belknap, Jeremy **I**
Bell, Robert **I**
Bellamy, Edward **II**
Bellow, Saul **III**
Beloved (Morrison) **III**
Benét, Stephen Vincent **III**
Benezet, Anthony **I**
"Benito Cereno" (Melville) **II**
Benjamin, Park **II**
Benton, Thomas Hart **II**
Berenson, Bernard (Bernhard) **II**
Berger, Thomas **III**
Bernard, William Bayle **II**
Berry, Wendell **III**
Berryman, John **III**
best-sellers **II**
Beverley, Robert **I**
Biblical Repertory (periodical) **II**
Bibliographical Society of America **II**
Biddle, Nicholas **I**
Bidwell, John **II**
Bierce, Ambrose Gwinnett **II**
"The Big Bear of Arkansas" (Thorpe) **II**
Bigelow, John **II**
Billings, Josh. *See* Shaw, Henry Wheeler
Bill of Rights, U.S. **I**

Billy Budd (Melville) **II**
Billy the Kid. *See* Bonney, William H.
Bird, Robert Montgomery **II**
Bishop, Elizabeth **III**
black aesthetic **III**
Black Arts movement **III**
Black Boy (Wright) **III**
Black Hawk **II**
Black Mountain ppoets **III**
Blackmur, Richard Palmer **III**
Blair, James **I**
Bland, Richard **I**
Blavatsky, Helena Petrovna Hahn **II**
Bleeker, Margaretta V. **I**
The Blockheads; or, the Affrighted Officers (Anon.) **I**
Blood, Benjamin Paul **II**
Bloomer, Amelia Jenks **II**
Bly, Nellie. *See* Seaman, Elizabeth Cochran
Bly, Robert Elwood **III**
Bogan, Louise **III**
Boker, George Henry **II**
Bonney, William H. **II**
Bontemps, Arna Wendell **III**
book clubs **III**
The Bookman (periodical) **II, III**
booksellers and bookstores **I**
    City Lights bookstore **III**
Boone, Daniel **II**
Boothe, Clare **III**
Borden, Lizzie Andrew **II**
Boston, Massachusetts **II, III**
Boston Athenaeum **I**
Boston Daily Advertiser (periodical) **II**
Boston Daily Evening Transcript (periodical) **II**
Boston Gazette (periodical) **I**
Boston News-Letter (periodical) **I**
The Boston Quarterly Review (periodical) **II**
Boucher, Jonathan **I**
Boucicault, Dion **II**
Bourjaily, Vance Nye **III**
Bowers, Bathsheba **I**
Bowery, the **II**
Bowery Theatre **II**
Bowles, Jane Auer **III**
Bowles, Paul **III**
Boyesen, Hjalmar Hjorth **II**
Boyle, Kay **III**
Boyle, Thomas Coraghessan **III**
Brackenridge, Hugh Henry **I**
Bradbury, Ray Douglas **III**
Bradford, Andrew **I**
Bradford, Cornelia Smith **I**
Bradford, John **I**
Bradford, William **I**
Bradstreet, Anne **I**
Brady, Mathew B. **II**